THE TIMES
THE SUNDAY TIMES

Good University Guide 2016

John O'Leary

IN ASSOCIATION WITH
milkround

Published in 2015 by Times Books

An imprint of HarperCollins Publishers
Westerhill Road
Bishopbriggs
Glasgow G64 2QT
www.harpercollins.co.uk
times.books@harpercollins.co.uk

First published in 1993. Twenty-second edition 2015

ISBN 978-0-00-815128-7

Patrick Kennedy was the lead consultant with Paul Ruddock for UoE Consulting Limited, which has compiled the main university league table and the individual subject tables for this *Guide* on behalf of *The Times*, *The Sunday Times* and HarperCollins Publishers.

Please see chapters 4 and 5 for a full explanation of the sources of data used in the ranking tables. The data providers do not necessarily agree with the data aggregations or manipulations appearing in this book and are also not responsible for any inference or conclusions thereby derived.

Project editor: Christopher Riches
Design, editorial and additional research: Edenside Computing Services Ltd

A catalogue record for this book is available from the British Library.

Printed and bound in Great Britain by Clays Ltd, St Ives plc.

FSC www.fsc.org
MIX
Paper from responsible sources
FSC™ C007454

FSC™ is a non-profit international organisation established to promote the responsible management of the world's forests. Products carrying the FSC label are independently certified to assure consumers that they come from forests that are managed to meet the social, economic and ecological needs of present and future generations, and other controlled sources.

Find out more about HarperCollins and the environment at
www.harpercollins.co.uk/green

Contents

About the Author

John O'Leary is a freelance journalist and education consultant. He was the Editor of *The Times Higher Education Supplement* from 2002 to 2007 and was previously Education Editor of *The Times*, having joined the paper in 1990 as Higher Education Correspondent. He has been writing on higher education for more than 30 years and is a member of the executive board of the QS World University Rankings. He is the author of *Higher Education in England*, published in 2009 by the Higher Education Funding Council for England. He has a degree in politics from the University of Sheffield.

Acknowledgements

We would like to thank the many individuals who have helped with this edition of *The Times and Sunday Times and Sunday Times Good University Guide*, particularly Greg Hurst, Education Editor of *The Times*, Alastair McCall, *Editor of The Sunday Times University Guide*, and Patrick Kennedy, the lead consultant with Paul Ruddock, for UoE Consulting Limited, which has compiled the main university league table and the individual subject tables for this *Guide* on behalf of *The Times*, *The Sunday Times* and HarperCollins Publishers.

To the members of *The Times and Sunday Times Good University Guide* Advisory Group for their time and expertise: Patrick Kennedy, Consultant, Collective Intelligence Limited; Christine Couper, Head of Planning and Statistics, University of Greenwich; James Galbraith, Senior Strategic Planner, University of Edinburgh; Alison Hartrey, Head of Planning, SOAS London; Mark Langer-Crame, Senior Planning Officer, Cardiff University; Aaron Morrison, Principal Planning Officer, De Montfort University; Komal Patel, Strategic Planning Officer, Imperial College, London; Russell Pottle, Head of Planning, Risk, Intelligence, Management Information and Enhancement, Bournemouth University; Dr Sarah Taylor, Head of Strategy Development, Aberystwyth University; Jenny Walker, Planning Officer, Loughborough University; to James McLaren, Denise Jones and Pip Day of HESA for their technical advice; to Alice Hancock, Greta Keenan and Sue O'Leary for their contributions to the book.

We also wish to thank the publishers of the QS World University Rankings, the Academic Ranking of World Universities and *Times Higher Education* for permission to reproduce some of their main league tables, and all the university staff who assisted in providing information for this edition.

How to Use This Book

The Times and Sunday Times Good University Guide 2016 will help you to select the subject and university of your choice and to guide you through the whole process of getting to university. The answers to the questions below will help you to get the most out of the information we offer.

How do I choose a course?

» The first half of chapter 1 provides advice on what you should consider when choosing a subject area and relevant courses within that subject.
» The tables near the beginning of chapter 2 give details of the employment prospects for all major subjects.
» Chapter 5 provides details for 66 different subject areas (as listed on page 68).
» For each subject there is a league table that provides our assessment of the ranking of universities offering courses in the particular subject area.
» For each subject we also provide some background information and details of employment prospects.
» Specific advice for international students is given in chapter 12.

How do I choose a university?

» The second half of chapter 1 provides advice on choosing a university.
» If you are considering studying abroad, chapter 3 provides guidance and practical information.
» Central is the main *Times and Sunday Times* league table on pages 60–64. This ranks the universities by assessing their quality not just according to teaching quality and the student experience (drawn from the National Student Survey) but also through seven other factors, including research quality, the spending on services and facilities, and graduate employment prospects. This table gives an indication of the overall performance of each university.
» The second half of the book contains two pages on each university, giving a general overview of the institution as well as data on student numbers, how to contact the university, the accommodation provided by the university, and the fees and financial support for 2016–17, wherever possible. Note that details for support for 2016–17 had not been released for some institutions when this book was prepared in August 2015.
» In addition, chapter 10 provides information on sport and sporting facilities across all the universities.
» For those considering Oxford or Cambridge, details of admission processes and of all the colleges can be found in chapter 13.
» Specific advice for international students is given in chapter 12.

How do I apply?

» Chapter 6 outlines the application procedure for university entry.
» It starts by advising you on how to complete the UCAS application, and then takes you through the process that we hope will lead to your university place for autumn 2016.
» Specific information about applying to Oxford and Cambridge is given in chapter 13.

Can I afford it?

» Chapters 7 and 8 outline the costs of studying at university (including the payment of fees) as well as sources of funds (including student loans, grants and bursaries).
» Chapter 9 provides advice on where to live while you are there.
» Accommodation charges for 2015–16 for each university are given in the university profiles in chapter 14. Figures for 2016–17 were not available when this book was printed.

How will university enhance my career?

» The employment prospects and average starting salaries for the main subject groups are given in chapter 2.
» Universities are now doing more to increase the employability of their graduates. Some examples are given in chapter 2 – and check whether your chosen universities provide similar services.

How do I find out more?

» In each university profile (chapter 14) contact details are given (including email addresses and websites), so you can obtain more information on any university you are interested in.
» At the end of each chapter, a selection of useful websites is given.
» A further listing at the back of the book provides contact details for higher education institutions that are not covered elsewhere within the book.
» *The Times and Sunday Times Good University Guide* website at **www.thetimes.co.uk/tto/education/gooduniversityguide** or **www.thesundaytimes.co.uk/sto/newsreview/education/university** will keep you up to date with developments throughout the year and contains further information and online tables

Introduction

This *Guide* has always put a premium on consistency in the way that it assesses universities' performance and presents the results. This year, however, there are subtle but important changes in the tables that are at its heart. The basic framework remains the same, but there is a sharper focus on the teaching that undergraduates receive and new assessments of research to interpret. As a result, there is more movement than usual in universities' positions, although not on the scale seen in some rankings.

The main change gives extra weight to students' satisfaction with teaching, feedback and academic support, compared with other aspects of their course. Overall, the results of the National Student Survey, which is completed by more than 70 per cent of final-year undergraduates, carry the same weight as before. But the two categories are now shown separately, with the teaching sections accounting for two thirds of the points from the survey.

This new presentation, perhaps more than the relatively minor influence on the table, gives prospective students an insight into the key elements of a degree. The scores reveal considerable differences in levels of satisfaction with teaching and feedback compared with the broader student experience at many universities. Some famous names are among the lowest scorers on the teaching sections.

The new approach chimes with the Government's renewed focus on teaching in higher education and its plans for a Teaching Excellence Framework (Tef). Several elements of our table seem likely to be replicated in the official exercise, which will place universities into bands rather than producing an overall order. The first discussions on the framework, before the election, envisaged one comparison taking account of both teaching and research. This remains our approach, to look at a broad range of factors that will impact on undergraduates.

Research quality has always been a key element in our tables because the results of official assessments have considerable implications for the funding of universities and the academics that they can attract. These tables include scores from the first Research Excellence Framework, which take account of the proportion of eligible academics entered for assessment as well as the grades they achieved.

While some elements of the tables may have changed, their role in the process of choosing a university and a course has not. There will be many considerations in coming to a final decision, but this *Guide* may help to narrow down the options and give reassurance. For once, there are no major changes in the conditions facing applicants, except for those who would have been eligible for a Government grant. Those whose household income qualified them for a grant will now be faced with adding to the loans they will need for a degree. Many will never be required to repay the additional loans since repayments start only if and when the cost of tuition has been cleared, but it will be no surprise if the change acts as a disincentive to participation by those from low-income families.

The majority of applicants for the 2016 academic year have been spared the big changes that may be on the horizon, however, and should find that, like the current crop of entrants, they are in a buyer's market. Universities need the income that £9,000 fees bring, and will do what they can to expand. That does not mean there will be a free-for-all, particularly at the leading universities, but the prospects for those with the right qualifications remain bright.

An era of change

Although £9,000 fees have hardly been popular and are back on the political agenda for a Jeremy Corbyn-led Labour Party, they have not led to the protracted slump in the demand for higher education that many critics predicted. Part-time enrolments have been hit hard, but the numbers applying for (and starting) full-time degrees are now growing once more – by about 3 per cent in 2015. More surprisingly, so are the numbers coming from low-income families and areas of low participation in higher education.

What has changed with higher fees, however, is the pattern of applications and enrolments. Students are plainly opting in larger numbers for subjects that they think will lead to well-paid jobs. While there has been a recovery in some arts and social science subjects in 2014 and 2015, the trend towards the sciences and some vocational degrees is unmistakeable. Languages have suffered particularly – perhaps partly because they tend to be four-year degrees – and so have courses associated with parts of the economy that were hardest hit in the recession. Building is one example, where numbers are down even though the subject is in the top ten for employment prospects, with three-quarters of graduates going straight into a professional job.

The vast majority of students take a degree primarily to improve their career prospects, so some second-guessing of the employment market is inevitable. But most graduate jobs are not subject-specific and the best brains in the country are hard-pressed to predict employment hotspots four or five years ahead, when today's applicants will be looking for jobs. Computer science is a good example of the pitfalls. Demand for the subject plummeted when the "dotcom bubble" burst and courses closed. Now parts of the IT industry are booming again and there is a skills shortage. Applications for the subject have shot up, but no one can be certain of market conditions in such a fast-moving industry so far ahead.

Just as it may be unwise to second-guess employment prospects, the same goes for the competition for places in different subjects. Universities may close or reduce the intake to courses that have low numbers of applicants while some of the more selective institutions may make more places available, especially to candidates who achieve good grades at A level. Bristol, Birmingham, Exeter and University College London have all taken hundreds more students than usual since the restrictions were relaxed for high-grade candidates. Now universities such as Sussex and Essex have announced that they intend to grow substantially, while the University of St Mark and St John plans to double in size to achieve economies of scale and become more secure.

Even before the increase in £9,000 fees promised in 2017, it seems that universities of all types see the expansion of undergraduate provision as a sensible strategy. But even those that are expanding may do so only in areas where they are strong and extra students can be taught at reasonable cost. In the absence of clear announcements, applicants are still best advised to go for the courses and universities that meet their requirements, rather than trying to play the system.

Certainly, fee levels are unlikely to play a significant part in applicants' choices of university in 2016 – other than in Scotland and Northern Ireland, where there are big financial incentives to study at a home university. The continuing absence of fees north of the border has been particularly influential in dissuading Scottish students from studying elsewhere, although the cap on recruitment there led to more coming south in 2015. Most candidates were not swayed by differences of a few hundred pounds in the fees charged by universities in England. Even those differences have now practically disappeared: only a handful will charge less than the maximum for any Honours degrees in 2016–17.

Using this *Guide*

The merger of *The Times* and *Sunday Times* university guides two years ago began a new chapter in the ranking of higher education institutions in the UK. The two guides had 35 editions between them and, in their new form, provide the most comprehensive and authoritative assessments of undergraduate education at UK universities. The publication of this book follows several days of coverage in the two newspapers and online.

Three more institutions are included in the main table this year following a change in our approach to specialist universities. Norwich University of the Arts, the Royal Agricultural University and St George's, University of London were all excluded from the main table last year because it was felt that they were too narrowly focused to be compared usefully with more mainstream universities. However, the review group of academic planners who meet after every edition of the *Guide* recommended that they should be added to the table because there were only marginal differences between them and other largely specialist universities that met the previous criteria for inclusion. All three are well-known in their fields and have full university status, and their omission was confusing to many readers.

Although relatively few readers will be choosing between the three newcomers and the generalist universities that make up the bulk of the main table, our practice wherever possible of taking account of the numbers taking different subjects makes for fair comparisons between different types of institution. All three were already included in the relevant subject tables and now make debuts well up the main ranking.

The additions mean that only three public universities with a focus on full-time undergraduate education are absent this year. For different reasons, University College Birmingham, Trinity Saint David and Wolverhampton have all instructed the Higher Education Statistics Agency not to release data on their performance and are missing from the institutional and subject tables. In addition, new private universities such as the University of Law, Regent's University and BPP University, do not currently have the necessary data to be included.

Some famous names in UK higher education have never been ranked because they do not fit the parameters of a system that is intended mainly to guide full-time undergraduates. The Open University, for example, operates entirely through distance learning, while the London Business School has no undergraduates. Birkbeck, University of London, focuses predominantly on part-time education, although growth in the number of full-time students may bring it into the main table before long. Other specialist institutions, including a number of university colleges, appear in relevant subject tables.

There are now 66 subject tables, since the addition of Animal Sciences and Creative Writing last year. Other subject tables will be added in due course because there is growing demand for information at this level. A survey of international students by Hobsons, the education software and services company, found that international students were more influenced by subject rankings than those for whole institutions, and there is no reason to believe that domestic applicants think differently.

With the exception of the separation of National Student Survey scores, outlined above, there has been no change in the basic methodology behind the tables, however. The eight elements of the main table are the same, with the approach to scores in the 2014 Research Excellence Framework mirroring as closely as possible those for previous assessments. In order to reflect the likelihood of undergraduates coming into contact with outstanding researchers, the proportion of eligible academics entered for assessment is part of the calculation, as well as the average grades achieved.

This year's tables

This year's results were bound to show more movement than usual because new research scores could be calculated for the first time since the final Research Assessment Exercise took place in 2008. The division of National Student Survey scores has also had some effect because the three sections of the survey categorised as 'Teaching quality' are given more weight than the remaining four.

By no means all the changes in universities' positions can be attributed to methodology, however. The graduate labour market had begun to improve in 2014 – the year in which the latest available employment survey took place – and some universities had shared in the recovery more than others. Entry standards at some universities were affected by the moves to recruit more undergraduates paying £9,000 fees and there was more variation than usual in the amounts spent on student facilities.

It seems, however, that nothing can shake the dominance of Cambridge and Oxford at the head of the main table – and the majority of the subject tables. After a dead heat in last year's *Guide*, Cambridge has opened up a clear lead over its ancient rival, but there is then a gap of almost 90 points to Imperial College London, in third place. Cambridge also tops 35 of the subject tables and Oxford another eight. Throughout all the years of the *Guide*, the two universities have seldom been challenged, especially in terms of the undergraduate education they offer.

St Andrews remains easily Scotland's top university in the table, despite losing third place overall, while Cardiff is the clear leader in Wales and Queen's, Belfast the same in Northern Ireland. Other movements in the upper reaches of the table have seen Surrey move into the top ten for the first time and Leeds make a significant rise for the second year in a row. Both Sussex and

2016 *Guide* Award Winners

University of the Year	**Surrey**
Runner-up	**Leeds**
Shortlisted	**Durham**
	Imperial College
	Kent
Scottish University of the Year	**Dundee**
Welsh University of the Year	**Cardiff**
Modern University of the Year	**Coventry**
Sports University of the Year	**Exeter**
University of the Year for	
Teaching Quality	**Buckingham**
Student Experience	**Surrey**
Graduate Employment	**Birmingham**
Student Retention	**Royal Agricultural University**

Kent have also made impressive progress. Surrey is our University of the Year, after its rise into the top ten, and is also winner of the award for the best student experience. Leeds, which has gone up 15 places in two years, is the runner-up for the second year in succession, and Kent was shortlisted.

Further down the table, Harper Adams has jumped 14 places and into the top 50, while Ulster, Bath Spa and the University of the Creative Arts have all moved up more than ten places. Coventry is the highest-placed post-1992 university for the third year in a row, but has slipped five places since last year's peak. A number of modern universities continue to feature above some older foundations. The first edition of *The Times Good University Guide* predicted the development of a new pecking order in an era of growing competition between universities, many of which had just acquired that title. It has taken longer than many expected and the top third of the table is still monopolised by old universities, but the previous binary division is breaking down.

Another feature of this year's table is the continuing poor performance of many Scottish universities. Despite the advantages in student recruitment conferred by the absence of fees for Scottish students and a generous conversion rate for Scottish qualifications in the UCAS points tariff, only six of the 15 universities north of the border have gone up in the latest ranking, one more than last year. Only St Andrews appears in the top 20 and there are just five Scottish universities in the top 40. The decline may still be arrested, but it may call into question both national and some institutional strategies.

Making the right choices

Anyone hoping to embark on a degree in 2016 will be well advised to tread carefully and muster as much comparative information as possible before making their choices. This *Guide* is intended as a starting point, a tool to help navigate the statistical minefield that will face applicants, as universities present their performance in the best possible light. There is a chapter on the impact of the fee changes, as well as one focusing on all-important employment issues along with the usual ranking of universities and 66 subject tables.

Whatever their appetite for expansion, most of the leading universities will remain highly selective, particularly in popular subjects. Even when the demand for places dropped in 2012, there were between five and six applications (not applicants) to the place across the whole higher education system. The figure was almost double that at the most popular universities. The demand for places is far from uniform, however; even within the same university the level of competition will vary between subjects. The entry scores quoted in the subject tables in chapter 5 offer a reliable guide to the relative levels of selectivity, but the figures are for entrants' actual qualifications. The standard offers made by departments will invariably be lower.

Making the right choice in 2016 will require a mixture of realism and ambition. Most sixth-formers and college students have a fair idea of the grades they are capable of attaining, within a certain margin for error. Even with five choices of course to make, there is no point in applying to a course where the standard offer is so far from your predicted grades that rejection is virtually certain. If your results do turn out to be much better than predicted, there will be an opportunity through the Adjustment system, or simply through Clearing, to trade up to an alternative university.

With the relaxation of recruitment restrictions, universities that once took pride in their absence from Clearing are now continuing to recruit after A-level results day. As a result, the use of insurance choices – the inclusion of at least one university with lower entrance standards than your main targets – is likely to decline further. It is still a dangerous strategy, but there is now more chance of picking up a place at a leading university if you aimed too high with all your first-round choices. Oxford and Cambridge will not be appearing in the Clearing lists and you are most unlikely to find courses in medicine there, but there will be a wider range of universities to choose from than ever before. Some may even come to you if you sign up for the new arrangements introduced by UCAS this year, which allow universities to approach unplaced candidates on Results Day if their grades are similar to other entrants'.

The Adjustment Period that runs for five days after results have been published is reserved for those with better grades than the offer they have accepted to approach other universities. Although only 1,200 students found places this way in 2014, the numbers may rise as the system becomes better known, especially in the new de-regulated era. Universities at the very top of the table may be full, but there should be more opportunities elsewhere.

The long view

School-leavers who enter higher education in 2016 were not born when our first league table was published and most will never have heard of polytechnics, even if they attend a university that once carried that title. But it was the award of university status to the 34 polytechnics, 23 years ago, that was the inspiration for the first edition of *The Times Good University Guide*. The original poly, the Polytechnic of Central London, had become the University of Westminster, Bristol Polytechnic was now the University of the West of England and – most mysteriously of all – Leicester Polytechnic had morphed into De Montfort University. The new *Guide* charted the lineage of the new universities and offered the first-ever comparison of institutional performance in UK higher education.

The university establishment did not welcome the initiative. The vice-chancellors described the table as "wrong in principle, flawed in execution and constructed upon data which are not uniform, are ill-defined and in places demonstrably false." The league table has changed considerably since then, although even then Oxford and Cambridge reigned supreme. While consistency has been a priority for the *Guide* throughout its 22 years, only six of the original 14 measures have survived. Some of the current components – notably the National Student Survey – did not exist in 1992, while others have been modified or dropped at the behest of the expert group of planning officers from different types of universities that meets annually to review the methodology and make recommendations for the future.

While ranking is hardly popular with academics, the relationship with universities has changed radically, and this *Guide* is quoted on numerous university websites. As Sir David Eastwood, now vice-chancellor of the University of Birmingham and head of the Russell Group, said in launching an official report on university league tables that he commissioned as Chief Executive of the Higher Education Funding Council for England: "We deplore league tables one day and deploy them the next."

Most universities have had their ups and downs over the years, although Oxford and Cambridge have tended to pull away from the rest. Both benefited from the introduction of student satisfaction ratings and from the extra credit given to the top research grades – the two measures that carry an extra weighting in our table. They also have famously high entry standards, much the largest proportions of first and upper-second class degrees and consistently good scores on every other measure. Several other famous names have been among the chasing pack throughout. The London School of Economics, Imperial College and University College London have seldom been out of the top five, while Warwick and, in recent years, Durham and St Andrews have all been fixtures in the top ten.

There have been spectacular rises, however. Exeter, for example, was 36th in the inaugural table and only one place better off in the 2003 *Guide*, but is now enjoying its fifth year in the top ten. Surrey was 45th ten years ago, but enters the top ten in this edition. Perhaps even more impressively, Coventry was only 12 places off the bottom a decade ago and is now inside the top 50, having reached the highest position ever for a modern university last year.

Higher education has changed enormously since this book was first published. The number of universities has increased by another third and the full-time student population has rocketed. Individual institutions are almost unrecognisable from their 1993 forms. Nottingham, for example, had less than 10,000 students then, compared with more than 30,000 now. Manchester Metropolitan, the largest of the former polys, has experienced similar growth. Yet there are universities now which would have been too small and too specialist to qualify for the title in 1992. The diversity of UK higher education is celebrated as one of its greatest strengths, and the modern universities are neither encouraged nor anxious to compete with the older foundations on some of the measures in our table.

The coming years, let along the next 20, may see another transformation in the higher education landscape, with the private sector competing strongly with established universities in some fields and distance learning becoming more popular as there is greater investment in Massive Open Online Courses (MOOCs) and the cost of full-time degrees rises. There may, indeed, be university closures and mergers, although they have been predicted before and seldom come about. Universities are among the most enduring of the UK's institutions, and will take some shifting.

Why university?

Particularly if the UK economy continues its recovery, more young people will be tempted to write off higher education, once the cost of living has been added to the growing fees burden and the attractions of university life balanced against loss of potential earnings. There are plenty of self-made millionaires who still swear by the University of Life as the only training ground for success, and commentators who believe that the expansion of higher education has gone too far. Yet even by narrow financial criteria, it would be rash to dismiss an opportunity to go to university. With so many more competing for jobs, a degree will never again be an automatic passport to a fast-track career. But graduates' financial prospects remain much brighter than school leavers', as are their prospects in other important areas, such as health.

Even for those who cannot or do not wish to afford the costs associated with three or more years of full-time education when they leave school, university remains a possibility. The modular courses adopted by most universities enable students to work through a degree at their own pace, dropping out for a time if necessary, or switching to part-time attendance. Distance learning is another option, and advances in information technology now mean that some nominally full-time courses are delivered mainly online.

For many – perhaps most – students, the university experience is not what it was in their parents' day. There is more assessment, more crowding, more pressure to get the best possible degree while also finding gainful employment for at least part of the year. The proportion of students achieving first-class degrees has risen significantly, while an upper second (rather than the previously ubiquitous 2:2) has become the norm. Research shows that the classification has a real impact in the labour market.

Most graduates do not regret their decision to go to university, however. Students from all over the world flock to British universities, and they offer a valuable resource for those on their doorstep. No league table can determine which is the right university for any candidate, but this *Guide* should provide some of the information necessary to draw up a shortlist for further investigation.

1 What and Where to Study

To read the comments of many politicians and media pundits, it would appear that there is only one reason to go to university: to earn as much as possible when you graduate. That is a big part of the motivation for many students, but there should be more to it than that when you come to choose a university and a course. It is a potentially life-changing decision. Many graduates end up living and working near their university; they often make their closest friends in their student days and may even meet their future partner there. And then there is the little matter of the three or four years you will spend as an undergraduate, which should develop your intellect and shape you as a person.

Of course, in the era of £9,000 fees, no one is suggesting that you should ignore career prospects – although it is dangerous to read too much into employment statistics that are collected only six months after graduation. Whatever else they want out of a degree course, students all over the world are seeking an advantage in the labour market more than anything. This chapter will suggest some of the signs to take into account in selecting the course that is right for you, if indeed you are certain that your immediate future should be in higher education at all.

Most young people with the necessary qualifications to go to university do decide that it is right for them. But applications and enrolments since the introduction of £9,000 fees are beginning to show clear patterns that favour particular subjects and universities – and may make life increasingly difficult for others. It is not surprising that growing numbers should decide to play it safe, as they see it, in choosing what and where to study. Although most graduate jobs continue to be open to students of any discipline, some arts subjects may now seem more of a gamble, and there may be pressure at home to go for a science or business subject if you have the right qualifications.

Your choices must be realistic, however. The course must not only be within your capabilities, but will have to maintain your interest for at least three years – possibly much longer than that if it is then going to determine your field of employment. Ideally, higher education should broaden your options in later life, not narrow them. Most of today's graduates will work in several different fields during their careers. In any case, no one can be sure which skills will be required in four or more years' time, when today's applicants enter the graduate labour market.

Some subjects and universities will be more marketable than others, but which ones? This

Guide may give some pointers – medicine is unlikely to go into decline, for example – but times do change. Computer science, for instance, went through years of falling numbers after the dotcom bubble burst, before recovering strongly in the last two years. Applications for the group of subjects that includes architecture and building remain 20 per cent behind the totals reached before the recession.

Why applicants have reached some of the conclusions they have remains a mystery. Languages, for example, have been hardest hit in terms of applications and enrolments. Yet business leaders are constantly stressing the need for linguists. In this case, decisions made on entry to the sixth-form may be the biggest factor behind falling applications – the numbers taking languages at A level have been dropping for a number of years, perhaps because they are seen as more difficult than other arts subjects.

There will be a number of different factors influencing your choice of university and course, ranging from the limitations imposed by your qualifications to favoured geographical locations. You may want to stay within reach of home – or to get as far away as possible. You may have heard good things about a particular course from friends, or a teacher. This *Guide* – and the tables it contains – offers a reality check to supplement such opinions, and the opportunity to narrow down your options.

Key reasons for going to university

» To improve job opportunities	**76%**
» To improve knowledge in an area of interest	**63%**
» To improve salary prospects	**61%**
» To specialise in a certain subject/area	**59%**
» To obtain an additional qualification	**58%**
» To become more independent	**48%**
» Essential for my chosen profession	**48%**
» Meet new people	**44%**
» It's the obvious next step – just what you do	**40%**
» To experience a different way of life	**38%**
» My parents expected me to	**27%**
» To have a good social life	**26%**
» I didn't want to get a job straight away	**24%**
» I didn't know what else I wanted to do	**20%**
» Can live at home and still go to university	**13%**
» All my friends were going	**12%**

Sodexo University Lifestyle Survey 2014

Is higher education for you?

Before you start, there is one important question to ask yourself: what do you want out of higher education? The answer will make it easier to choose where (and if) to be a student. With three in ten school-leavers going on to university, it is easy to drift that way without much thought, opting for the subject in which you expect the best A-level grades, and looking for a university with a reasonable reputation and a good social life. Your career will look after itself – you hope.

With graduate debt soaring, however, and job prospects varying widely between subjects, now is the time to look at your own motivation. Fewer young people than predicted have opted out of higher education since higher fees were introduced, but apprenticeships and big firms' training schemes are now offering attractive alternatives. Many of those who do choose higher education appear to be rethinking their choice of course to give themselves the best possible chance of a satisfying and lucrative career.

Love of a subject is an excellent reason for taking a degree, and one that allows you to focus almost exclusively on the search for a course that corresponds with your passions. If, however, higher education is a means to an end, you need to think about career ambitions and look carefully at employment rates for any courses you might consider. These are examined in more detail in chapter 2.

Many graduates look back on their student days as the best years of their lives, and there is nothing wrong with wanting to have a good time. Remember, though, that you will be paying for it later (literally) and there will be more studying than partying. If you have not enjoyed sixth-form or college courses, you may be better off in a job and possibly becoming one of the hundreds of thousands each year who return to education later in life.

Setting your priorities

Even in the world of £9,000 fees, there are good reasons to believe that the right degree will still be a good investment. Research by London Economics for the million+ group of universities suggested that, on average, a degree would add £115,000 to lifetime earnings. A recent Labour Force Survey showed working-age graduates earning 50 per cent more on average than non-graduates – a bigger premium than graduates enjoy in most countries.

The majority of graduate jobs are not subject-specific; employers value the transferable skills that higher education confers. Rightly or wrongly, however, most employers are influenced by which university a graduate attended, so the choice of institution remains as important as ever.

Those who want to add value to their degree in the jobs market will find that growing numbers of universities are offering employment-related schemes that are considered in more detail in chapter 2. In many cases, this will involve work experience or extra activities organised by the careers service. Some universities, such as Leicester, now run certificated employability programmes, while others, such as Liverpool John Moores, have built such skills into degree programmes. Such programmes are also highlighted in chapter 2 and in the university profiles in chapter 14.

Narrowing down the field

Once you have decided that higher education is for you, the good news is that, as long as you start early enough, finding the right university can be relatively straightforward. Media attention focuses on the scramble for places on a relatively small proportion of courses where competition is intense, but there are plenty of places at good universities for candidates with the basic qualifications – it's just a matter of finding the one that suits you best. For older applicants, relevant work experience and demonstrable interest in a subject may be enough to win a place.

If anything, the problem is that of too much choice, although universities have reduced the number of degree combinations in anticipation of tougher financial conditions. Students prepared to move away from home will still have more than 100 universities and numerous specialist colleges to consider, most with hundreds – even thousands – of course combinations on offer. Institutions come in all shapes and sizes, so there is work to do at the outset narrowing down your options.

Deciding what you want to study may reduce the field considerably – there are only eight institutions offering veterinary medicine for example, although the total is around 100 in subjects such as law and English. By the time you have factored in personal preferences about the type or location of your ideal university, the list of possibilities may already be reduced to manageable proportions.

After that, you can take a closer look at what the courses contain and what life is really like for students. Prospectuses and university websites will give you an accurate account of course combinations, and important facts like the accommodation available to new students, but it is their job to sell the university. To get a true picture, you need more – preferably a

The UCAS tariff

Tariffs for selected qualifications are given below. The full range of acceptable qualifications and their tariff values are given at **www.ucas.com/ucas/undergraduate/getting-started/entry-requirements/tariff/tariff-tables**

GCE/VCE Qualifications					Points	Scottish Qualifications	
GCE AS/AS VCE	GCE AS Double Award	GCE A level/A VCE	A level with additional AS (9 units)	GCE/AVCE Double Award		Advanced Higher	Higher
				A*A*	**280**		
				A*A	**260**		
				AA	**240**		
				AB	**220**		
			A*A	BB	**200**		
			AA	BC	**180**		
			AB		**170**		
				CC	**160**		
			BB		**150**		
		A*	BC	CD	**140**		
					130	A	
	AA	A	CC	DD	**120**		
	AB		CD		**110**	B	
	BB	B		DE	**100**		
	BC		DD		**90**	C	
	CC	C	DE	EE	**80**		A
					72	D	
	CD				**70**		
					65		B
A	DD	D	EE		**60**		
B	DE				**50**		C
C	EE	E			**40**		
					36		D
D					**30**		
E					**20**		

UCAS tariff for the International Baccalaureate

Points for the International Baccalaureate (IB) are awarded to candidates who achieve the IB Diploma.

IB Dip.	Points	IB Dip.	Points	IB Dip.	Points	IB Dip.	Points	IB Dip.	Points
45	720	40	611	35	501	30	392	25	282
44	698	39	589	34	479	29	370	24	260
43	676	38	567	33	457	28	348		
42	654	37	545	32	435	27	326		
41	632	36	523	31	413	26	304		

visit not just to the university, but to the department where you would be studying. If that is not possible, there are plenty of other sources of objective information, such as the National Student Survey (which is available online, with a range of additional data about the main courses at each institution, at **www.unistats.com**).

Some students' unions publish alternative prospectuses, giving a "warts and all" view of the university, and those that do not provide this service may be able to arrange a brief discussion with a current student, either by phone or email. Your school or college may put you in contact with someone who went to a university that you are considering. Guides and collections of statistics may give you valuable information about a course or a university, but there is no substitute for personal experience.

What to study?

Most people seeking a place in higher education start by choosing a subject and a course, rather than a university. If you take a degree, you are going to spend at least three years immersed in your subject. It has to be one you will enjoy and can master – not to mention one that you are qualified to study. Many economics degrees require maths A level, for example, while most medical schools demand chemistry or biology. The UCAS website **(www.ucas.com)** contains course profiles, including entrance requirements, which is a good starting point, while universities' own sites contain more detailed information. In chapter 5, we describe 66 subject areas and provide league tables for each of them.

Your school subjects and the UCAS tariff

The official yardstick by which your results will be judged is the UCAS tariff, which gives a score for each grade of most UK qualifications considered relevant for university entrance, as well as for the International Baccalaureate (IB). This tariff has become controversial as more subjects and types of qualifications have been included in it. Top scores in the IB, for

---

"Traditional academic" and "non-preferred" subjects

The London School of Economics expects applicants to offer at least two of the traditional subjects listed below, while any of the non-preferred subjects listed should only be offered with two traditional subjects.

Traditional subjects

- Ancient history
- Biology
- Classical civilisation
- Chemistry
- Computing
- Economics
- English
- Further mathematics
- Geography
- Government and politics
- History
- Modern or classical languages
- Mathematics
- Music
- Philosophy
- Physics
- Psychology
- Religious studies
- Sociology

Non-preferred subjects

- Any Applied A level
- Accounting
- Art and design
- Business studies
- Citizenship studies
- Communication and culture
- Creative writing
- Design and technology
- Drama/theatre studies
- Film studies
- Health and social care
- Home economics
- Information and communication technology
- Law
- Leisure studies
- Media studies
- Music technology
- Physical education/Sports studies
- Travel and tourism

General studies, critical thinking, thinking skills, knowledge and enquiry and project work A levels will only be considered as fourth A-level subjects and will not therefore be accepted as part of a conditional offer.

example, earn considerably more points than the maximum for four, let alone three, A levels.

While the majority of universities use the tariff to make offers of places, many of the leading institutions prefer to stipulate the grades that they require. This allows them to specify the subjects in which particular grades must be achieved, as well as to determine which vocational qualifications are relevant to different degrees. In certain universities, some departments, but not others, will use the tariff to set offers. Course profiles on the UCAS website and/or universities' own sites should show whether offers are framed in terms of grades or tariff points. It is important to find out which, especially if you are relying on points from qualifications other than A level or Scottish Highers.

"Soft" subjects

There is a related issue for many of the most selective universities about the subjects studied in the sixth-form or at college. Not only are growing numbers of students applying with vocational (usually BTEC) qualifications, but the variety of A-level courses now available includes many subjects that top universities usually will not consider on a par with traditional academic subjects. For many years a minority of universities have refused to accept General Studies as a full A level for entrance purposes (although even some leading universities

---

Admissions tests

Some of the most competitive courses now have additional entrance tests. The most significant tests are listed below. Note that registration for many of the tests is before 15 October and you will need to register for them as early as possible. All the tests have their own websites.

Some universities also administer their own tests; details are given at: **www.ucas.com/ucas/undergraduate/getting-started/entry-requirements/admissions-tests**

Law

Law National Admissions Test (LNAT): for entry to law courses at Birmingham, Bristol, Durham, Glasgow, King's College London, Nottingham, Oxford, SOAS, University College London.

Mathematics

Mathematics Admissions Test (MAT): for entry to mathematics at Imperial College, London and mathematics and computer science at Oxford.

Sixth Term Examination Papers (STEP): for entry to mathematics at Cambridge and Warwick (also encouraged by Bath, Bristol, East Anglia, Imperial College London and Oxford).

Medical subjects

BioMedical Admissions Test (BMAT):for entry to medicine, veterinary medicine and biomedical sciences at Brighton and Sussex Medical School, Cambridge, Imperial College London, Lancaster, Leeds, Oxford, Royal Veterinary College, University College London.

Graduate Medical School Admissions Test (GAMSAT): for graduate entry to medicine and dentistry at Cardiff, Exeter, Liverpool, Nottingham, Plymouth, St George's, University of London, Swansea.

Health Professions Admissions Test (HPAT-Ulster): for certain health profession courses at Ulster.

UK Clinical Aptitude Test (UKCAT): for entry to medical and dental schools at Aberdeen, Birmingham, Cardiff, Dundee, Durham, East Anglia, Edinburgh, Exeter, Glasgow, Hull York Medical School, Keele, King's College London, Leicester, Liverpool, Manchester, Newcastle, Nottingham, Plymouth, Queen Mary, University of London, Queen's University Belfast, Sheffield, Southampton, St Andrews, St George's, University of London, Warwick.

do). The growth of supposedly "soft" subjects, such as media studies and photography, has prompted a few universities to produce lists of subjects that will only be accepted alongside at least two traditional academic subjects.

The Russell Group of 24 leading universities published an extremely useful report, called *Informed Choices*, on the post-16 qualifications preferred by its members for a wide range of degrees. Although it names media studies, art and design, photography and business studies among the vocational subjects that would normally be given this label, it does not subscribe to the notion of a single list of "soft" subjects. The report suggests you choose at most a single vocational course and primarily select from a list of "facilitating subjects", which are required for many degrees and welcomed generally at Russell Group universities. The list comprises: maths and further maths, English, physics, biology, chemistry, geography, languages (classical and modern) and history. In addition their guide indicates the "essential" and "useful" A-level subjects for 60 different subject areas studied at Russell Group universities.

For most courses at most universities, there are no such restrictions, as long as your main subjects or qualifications are relevant to the degree you hope to take. Nevertheless, when choosing A levels it would be wise to bear the Russell Group lists in mind if you are likely to apply to one or more of the leading universities. At the very least, it is an indication of the subjects that admissions tutors may take less seriously than the rest. Although only the London School of Economics identifies "non-preferred" subjects publicly (see page 19), others may adopt less formal weightings.

Cambridge University

Cambridge Law Test: for entry to law, taken at Cambridge during interview process.

MML Test: for entry to modern and medieval languages at Cambridge, taken at Cambridge during interview process.

Thinking Skills Assessment (TSA) Cambridge: mainly for computer science, economics, engineering, history, human, social and political sciences, land economy, natural sciences, psychological and behavioural sciences at most Cambridge colleges, taken at Cambridge during interview process.

See also STEP and BMAT above.

Oxford University

Specific registration is required for the following subject tests. Tests taken on 4 November 2015, usually at candidate's educational institution.

Classics Admissions Test: classics.

Thinking Skills Assessment (TSA) Oxford: economics and management, experimental psychology, geography, human sciences, philosophy, politics and economics (PPE), psychology.

Physics Aptitude Test: engineering, materials science, physics.

English Literature Admissions Test: English.

History Aptitude Test: history.

Modern Languages Admissions Tests: modern languages and linguistics.

Oriental Languages Aptitude Test: oriental studies.

See also LNAT, MAT and BMAT above.

For fine art, music and philosophy, there will be a test at interview in December 2015.

Full details at **www.ox.ac.uk/admissions/undergraduate/applying-to-oxford/tests**

University College London

Thinking Skills Assessment (TSA) UCL: for entry to European social and political studies; the test is arranged in the interview process.

Vocational qualifications

The Education Department has downgraded many vocational qualifications in school league tables from 2014. This will only add to the confusion surrounding the value placed on diplomas and other qualifications by universities. The engineering diploma has won near-universal approval from universities (for admission to engineering courses and possibly some science degrees), but some of the other diplomas are in fields that are not on the curriculum of the most selective universities. Regardless of the points awarded under the tariff, it is essential to contact universities direct to ensure that a diploma or another vocational qualification will be an acceptable qualification for your chosen degree.

Admission tests

The growing numbers of applicants with high grades at A level have encouraged the introduction of separate admission tests for some of the most oversubscribed courses. There are national tests in medicine and law that are used by some of the leading universities, while Oxford and Cambridge have their own tests in a number of subjects. The details are listed on pages 20–21. In all cases, the tests are used as an extra selection tool, not as a replacement for A level or other general qualifications.

Making a choice

Your A levels or Scottish Highers may have chosen themselves, but the range of subjects across the whole university system is vast. Even subjects that you have studied at school may be quite different at degree level – some academic economists actually prefer their undergraduates not to have taken A-level economics because they approach the subject so differently. Other students are disappointed because they appear to be going over old ground when they continue with a subject that they enjoyed at school. Universities now publish quite detailed syllabuses, and it is a matter of going through the fine print.

The greater difficulty comes in judging your suitability for the many subjects that are not on the school or college curriculum. Philosophy and psychology sound fascinating (and are), but you may have no idea what degrees in either subject entail – for example, the level of statistics that may be required. Forensic science may look exciting on television – more glamorous than plain chemistry – but it opens fewer doors, as the type of work portrayed in *Silent Witness* or *Raising the Dead* is very hard to find.

The ten most popular subject areas for applications, 2015

1	Subjects allied to medicine	395,660
2	Business and admin. studies	347,080
3	Creative arts and design	278,490
4	Biological sciences	275,710
5	Social studies	248,760
6	Engineering	171,600
7	Law	128,580
8	Computer sciences	123,900
9	Physical sciences	112,600
10	Education	94,030

UCAS, applications by 30 June 2015

The ten most popular subject areas for acceptances, 2014

1	Business and admin. studies	63,660
2	Creative arts and design	53,330
3	Subjects allied to medicine	52,405
4	Biological sciences	48,815
5	Social studies	43,325
6	Engineering	29,110
7	Law	23,695
8	Computer sciences	23,585
9	Physical sciences	19,920
10	Education	18,440

UCAS, end of 2014 cycle

Academic or vocational?

There is frequent and often misleading debate about the differences between academic and vocational higher education. It is usually about the relative value of taking a degree, as opposed to a directly work-related qualification. But it also extends to higher education itself, with jibes about so-called "Mickey Mouse" degrees in areas that were not part of the higher education curriculum when most of the critics were students.

Such attitudes ignore the fact that medicine and law are both vocational subjects, as are architecture, engineering and education. They are not seen as any less academic than geography or sociology, but for some reason social work or nursing, let alone media studies and sports science, are often looked down upon. The test of a degree should be whether it is challenging and a good preparation for working life. Both general academic and vocational degrees can do this.

Nevertheless, it is clear that the prospect of much higher graduate debt is encouraging more students into job-related subjects. This is understandable and, if you are sure of your future career path, possibly also sensible. But much depends on what that career is – and whether you are ready to make such a long-term commitment. Some of the programmes that have attracted public ridicule, such as surf science or golf course management, may narrow graduates' options to a worrying extent, but often boast strong employment records.

Number of first degree enrolments by subject area, 2013/14 and percentage change over seven years

Business and administrative studies	**78,240**	**24%**
Biological sciences	**58,870**	**30%**
Subjects allied to medicine	**54,360**	**39%**
Social studies	**50,965**	**14%**
Creative arts and design	**48,880**	**5%**
Engineering and technology	**34,725**	**15%**
Languages	**26,590**	**–6%**
Computer science	**25,290**	**19%**
Law	**23,710**	**7%**
Physical sciences	**22,730**	**16%**
Education	**21,290**	**12%**
History and philosophy	**21,110**	**0%**
Mass communication	**14,050**	**5%**
Mathematical sciences	**11,275**	**24%**
Architecture, building and planning	**9,900**	**–21%**
Medicine and dentistry	**9,375**	**–3%**
Agriculture and related subjects	**3,230**	**19%**
Veterinary science	**1,055**	**9%**
Total for all subjects	**521,990**	**13%**

HESA 2015

As you would expect, many vocational courses are tailored to particular professions. If you choose one of these, make sure that the degree is recognised by the relevant professional body (such as the Engineering Council or one of the institutes) or you may not be able to use the skills that you acquire. Most universities are only too keen to make such recognition clear in their prospectus; if no such guarantee is published, contact the university department running the course and seek assurances.

Even where a course has professional recognition, bear in mind that a further qualification may be required to practise. Both law and medicine, for example, demand additional training to become a fully qualified solicitor, barrister or doctor. Nor is either degree an automatic passport to a job: only about half of all law graduates go into the profession. Both law and medicine also provide a route into the profession for graduates who have taken other subjects. Law conversion courses, though not cheap, are increasingly popular, and there are a growing number of graduate-entry medical degrees, for example at Warwick.

One way to ensure that a degree is job-related is to take a "sandwich" course, which involves up to a year in business or industry. Students often end up working for the organisation which provided the placement, while others gain valuable insights into a field of employment – even if only to discount it. The drawback with such courses is that, like the year abroad that is part of most language degrees, the period away from university inevitably disrupts living arrangements and friendship groups. But most of those who take this route find that the career benefits make this a worthwhile sacrifice.

Employers' organisations calculate that more than half of all graduate jobs are open to applicants from any subject, and recruiters for the most competitive graduate training schemes often prefer traditional academic subjects to apparently relevant vocational degrees. Newspapers, for example, often prefer a history graduate to one with a media studies degree; computing firms are said to take a disproportionate number of classicists. A good degree classification and the right work experience are more important than the subject for most non-technical jobs. But it is hard to achieve a good result on a course that you do not enjoy, so scour prospectuses, and email or phone university departments to ensure that you know what you are letting yourself in for. Their reaction to your approach will also give you an idea of how responsive they are to their students.

Studying more than one subject

You may find that more than one subject appeals, in which case you could consider Joint Honours – degrees that combine two subjects – or even Combined Honours, which will cover several related subjects. Such courses obviously allow you to extend the scope of your studies, but they should be approached with caution. Even if the number of credits suggests a similar workload to Single Honours, covering more than one subject inevitably involves extra reading and often more essays or project work.

The numbers taking such degrees is falling, but there are advantages to them. Many students choose a "dual" to add a vocational element to make themselves more employable – business studies with languages or engineering, for example, or media studies with English. Others want to take their studies in a particular direction, perhaps by combining history with politics, or statistics with maths. Some simply want to add a completely unrelated interest to their main subject, such as environmental science and music, or archaeology and event management – both combinations that are available at UK universities.

At most universities, however, it is not necessary to take a degree in more than one subject in order to broaden your studies. The spread of modular programmes ensures that you can take courses in related subjects without changing the basic structure of your degree. You may not be able to take an event management module in a single-honours archaeology degree, but it should be possible to study some history or a language. The number and scope of the combinations offered at many of the larger universities is extraordinary. Indeed, it has been criticised by academics who believe that "mix-and-match" degrees can leave a graduate without a rounded view of a subject. But for those who seek breadth and variety, close scrutiny of university prospectuses is a vital part of the selection process.

What type of course?

Once you have a subject, you must decide on the level and type of course. Most readers of this *Guide* will be looking for full-time degree courses, but higher education is much broader than that. You may not be able to afford the time or the money needed for a full-time commitment of three or four years at this point in your life.

Part-time courses

Tens of thousands of people each year opt for a part-time course – usually while holding down a job – to continue learning and to improve their career prospects. The numbers studying this way have dropped considerably, but that may change as the new funding arrangements, which give most part-time students access to loans for the first time, become better known and accepted.

Under these arrangements, loans are available for students whose courses occupy between a quarter and three-quarters of the time expected on a full-time course. Repayments are on the same conditions as those for full-time courses, except that repayments will begin after three years of study even if the course has not been completed by then. The downside is that many universities have increased their fees in the knowledge that part-time students will be able to take out student loans to cover fees and employers are now less inclined to fund their employees on such courses. At Birkbeck, University of London, for example, a compromise has been found with full-time courses taught in the evening. For courses classified as part-time, students pay fees in proportion to the number of credits they take.

Part-time study can be exhausting unless your employer gives you time off, but if you have the stamina for a course that will usually take twice as long as the full-time equivalent, this route should still make a degree more affordable. Part-time students tend to be highly committed to their subject, and many claim that the quality of the social life associated with their course makes up for the quantity of leisure time enjoyed by full-timers.

Distance learning

If you are confident that you can manage without regular face-to-face contact with teachers and fellow students, distance learning is an option. Courses are delivered mainly or entirely online or through correspondence, although some programmes offer a certain amount of local tuition. The process might sound daunting and impersonal, but students of the Open University (OU), all of whom are educated in this way, are among the most satisfied in the country, according to the results of the annual National Student Survey. Attending lectures or oversized seminars at a conventional university can be less personal than regular contact with your tutor at a distance.

Of course, not all universities are as good at communicating with their distance-learning students as the OU, or offer such high-quality course materials, but this mode of study does give students ultimate flexibility to determine when and where they study. Distance learning is becoming increasingly popular for the delivery of professional courses, which are often needed to supplement degrees. The OU now takes students of all ages, including a growing number of school-leavers, not just mature students.

In addition, there is now the option of Massive Open Online Courses (MOOCs) provided by some of the leading UK and American universities, usually free of charge. As yet, such courses are the equivalent of a module in a degree course, rather than the entire qualification. Some are assessed formally but none is likely to be seen by employers as the equal of a conventional degree, no matter how prestigious the university offering the course. That may change – some commentators see in MOOCs the beginning of the end of the traditional, residential university – but their main value at the moment is as a means of dipping a toe in the water of higher education. For those who are uncertain about committing to a degree, or who simply want to learn more about a subject without needing a high-status qualification, they are ideal.

A growing number of UK universities are beginning to offer MOOCs through the

Futurelearn platform, run by the Open University (**www.futurelearn.com**). But the beauty of MOOCs is that they can come from all over the world. Perhaps the best-known providers are Coursera (**www.coursera.org**), which originated at Stanford University, in California, and now involves a large number of American and international universities including Edinburgh, and edX (**www.edx.org**), which numbers Harvard among its members. MOOCs are also being used increasingly by sixth-formers to extend their subject knowledge and demonstrate their enthusiasm and capability to admissions tutors.

Foundation degrees

Even if you are set on a full-time course, you might not want to commit yourself for three or more years. Two-year vocational Foundation degrees have become a popular route into higher education in recent years. Many other students take longer-established two-year courses, such as Higher National Diplomas or other diplomas tailored to the needs of industry or parts of the health service. Those who do well on such courses usually have the option of converting their qualification into a full degree with further study, although many are satisfied without immediately staying on for the further two or more years that completing a BA or BSc will require.

Other short courses

A number of universities are experimenting with two-year degrees, squeezing more work into an extended academic year. The so-called "third semester" makes use of the summer vacation for extra teaching, so that mature students, in particular, can reduce the length of their career break. Several universities are offering accelerated degrees as part of a pilot project initiated under the last government. But only at the University of Buckingham, the UK's longest-established private university, is this the dominant pattern for degree courses. Other private institutions – notably BPP University – are following suit.

Other short courses, usually lasting a year, are designed for students who do not have the necessary qualifications to start a degree in their chosen subject. Foundation courses in art and design have been common for many years, and are the chosen preparation for a degree at leading departments, even for many students whose A levels would win them a degree place elsewhere. Access courses perform the same function in a wider range of subjects for students without A levels, or for those whose grades are either too low or in the

Subjects with highest ratio of applications to acceptances, 2014

1	Medicine	11.0
2	Dentistry	10.1
3	Nursing	8.8
4	Medical technology	8.4
5	Veterinary medicine	8.3
6	Anatomy, physiology and pathology	8.1
7	Economics	6.4
8	Mechanical engineering	6.3
9	Architecture	6.2
10	Pharmacology, toxicology and pharmacy	6.1

UCAS 2014 (for subjects with over 1,000 acceptances)

Universities with the highest ratio of applications to acceptances, 2014

1	Buckingham	15.8
2	St George's, University of London	11.6
3	City	10.5
4	Brunel London	10.4
5	London School of Economics	10.3
=6	Edinburgh	10.1
=6	London South Bank	10.1
8	Surrey	10.0
9	Queen Mary, University of London	9.9
10	Middlesex	9.7

UCAS 2014

wrong subjects to gain admission to a particular course. Entry requirements are modest, but students have to reach the same standard as regular entrants to progress to a degree.

Yet more choice

No single guide can allow for personal preferences in choosing a course. You may want one of the many degrees that incorporate a year at a partner university abroad, or to try a six-month exchange on the Continent through the European Union's Erasmus Programme. Either might prove a valuable experience and add to your employability. Or you might prefer a January or February start to the traditional autumn start – there are plenty of opportunities for this, mainly at post-1992 universities.

In some subjects – particularly engineering and the sciences – the leading degrees may be Masters courses, taking four years rather than three (in England). In Scotland, most degree courses take four years and some at the older universities will confer a Masters qualification. Those who come with A levels may apply to go straight into the second year. Relatively few students take this option, but it is easy to imagine more doing so in future at universities that charge students from other parts of the UK the full £9,000 for all years of the course.

Non-academic factors considered when choosing a university

Location-related	
Close to transport links	**35%**
Able to live away from parental home but close enough for support	**33%**
Quality of accommodation	**24%**
Cost of accommodation	**22%**
Low cost of living	**19%**
Able to live at parental home	**18%**
Opportunities for part-time jobs	**10%**
University-related	
Good impression from open days	**50%**
Campus university	**38%**
Attractive environment	**38%**
City centre university	**23%**
Active social life / good social facilities	**23%**
IT/Resource/study facilities	**22%**
Financial support available (bursaries; sponsorship, etc)	**19%**
Clubs and societies	**14%**
Good sporting facilities	**8%**
Good catering and retail facilities	**3%**

Sodexo University Lifestyle Survey 2014

Where to study

Once you have decided what to study, there are still several factors that might influence your choice of university or college. Obviously, you need to have a reasonable chance of getting in, you may want reassurance about the university's reputation, and its location will probably also be important to you. On top of that, most applicants have views about the type of institution they are looking for – big or small, old or new, urban or rural, specialist or comprehensive. Campus universities tend to produce the highest levels of student satisfaction, but big city universities continue to attract sixth-formers in the largest numbers. You may surprise yourself by choosing somewhere that does not conform to your initial criteria, but working through your preferences is another way of narrowing down your options.

Entry standards

Unless you are a mature student or have taken a gap year, your passport to your chosen university will probably be a conditional offer based on your predicted grades, previous exam performance, personal statement, and school or college reference. A number of universities this year have followed Birmingham's lead in making unconditional offers to candidates in selected subjects who have a strong academic record and are predicted high grades. But at most institutions, only those who already have their grades receive unconditional offers.

Supply and demand dictate whether you will receive an offer. Beyond the national picture, your chances will be affected both by the university and the subject you choose. A few universities (but not many) at the top of the league tables are heavily oversubscribed in every subject; others will have areas in which they excel, but may make relatively modest demands for entry to other courses. Even in many of the leading universities, the number of applicants for each place in languages or engineering is still not high. Conversely, three As at A level will not guarantee a place on one of the top English or law degrees, but there are enough universities running courses to ensure that three Cs will put you in with a chance somewhere.

University prospectuses and the UCAS website will give you the "standard offer" for each course, but in some cases this is pitched deliberately low in order to leave admissions staff extra flexibility. The standard A-level offer for medicine, for example, may not demand A*s, but nearly all successful applicants will have one or more.

The average entry scores in our subject tables give the actual points obtained by successful applicants – many of which are far above the offer made by the university, but which give an indication of the pecking order at entry. The subject tables (in chapter 5) are, naturally, a better guide than the main table (in chapter 4), where average entry scores are influenced by the range of subjects available at each university.

Location

The most obvious starting point is the country you study in. Most degrees in Scotland take four years, rather than the UK norm of three. It goes without saying that four years cost more than three, especially given the loss of the year's salary you might have been earning after graduation. A later chapter will go into the details of the system, but suffice to say that students from Scotland pay no fees, while those from the rest of the UK do. Nevertheless, Edinburgh and St Andrews remain particularly popular with English students, despite charging them £9,000 a year for the full four years of a degree. The number of English students going to Scottish universities actually increased by almost a quarter in 2012 and increased again in 2013, despite the fact that there would be no savings on fees, perhaps

Most popular universities by applications, 2014

1	Manchester	61,285
2	Manchester Metropolitan	57,880
3	Edinburgh	55,060
4	Leeds	53,560
5	Nottingham	48,260
6	Birmingham	45,900
7	King's College London	41,270
8	Bristol	40,425
9	Sheffield Hallam	40,085
10	University College London	38,330

UCAS 2014

Most satisfied with students' union

1	Sheffield	95%
2	Leeds	92%
3	Loughborough	91%
4	Dundee	88%
5	Cardiff	87%
6	Keele	86%
7	Reading	85%
8	Teesside	84%
=9	Bath	83%
=9	Nottingham Trent	83%
=9	Winchester	83%

National Student Survey 2015

because the institutions tried harder to attract them. Fees – or the lack of them – are by no means the only influence on cross-border mobility: the number of Scots going to English universities has risen sharply in 2015, in spite of the cost, probably because the number of places is capped in Scotland, but not any longer in England.

Close to home

Far from crossing national boundaries, however, growing numbers of students choose to study near home, whether or not they continue to live with their family. This is understandable for Scots, who will save themselves tens of thousands of pounds by studying at their own fees-free universities. But there is also a gradual increase in the numbers choosing to study close to home either to cut living costs or for personal reasons, such as family circumstances, a girlfriend or boyfriend, continuing employment or religion. Some simply want to stick with what they know.

The trend for full-time students who do go away to study, is to choose a university within about two hours' travelling time. The assumption is that this is far enough to discourage parents from making unannounced visits, but close enough to allow for occasional trips home to get the washing done, have a decent meal and see friends. The leading universities recruit from all over the world, but most still have a regional core.

University or college?

This *Guide* is primarily concerned with universities, the destination of choice for the vast majority of higher education students. But there are other options – and not just for those searching for lower fees. A number of specialist higher education colleges offer a similar, or sometimes superior, quality of course in their particular fields. The subject tables in chapter 5 chart the successes of various colleges in art, agriculture, music and teacher training in particular. Some colleges of higher education are not so different from the newer universities and may acquire that status themselves in future years, as ten did in 2012–13 and one more in the following year.

Further education colleges

The second group of colleges offering degrees are further education (FE) colleges. These are often large institutions with a wide range of courses, from A levels to vocational subjects at different levels, up to degrees in some cases. Although their numbers of higher education students have been falling in recent years, the new fee structure presents them with a fresh opportunity because they tend not to bear all the costs of a university campus. For that reason, too, they may not offer a broad student experience of the type that universities pride themselves on, but the best colleges respond well to the local labour market and offer small teaching groups and effective personal support.

FE colleges are a local resource and tend to attract mature students who cannot or do not want to travel to university. Many of their higher education students apply nowhere else. But, as competition for university places has increased, they also have become more of an option for school-leavers to continue their studies, as they always have done in Scotland. Ministers hope that they will now also become more attractive by virtue of price.

Their predominantly local, mature student populations do FE colleges no favours in statistical comparisons with universities. But it should be noted that the proportion of college graduates unemployed six months after graduation is invariably higher than at universities, as are average graduate salaries.

Both further and higher education colleges are audited by the Quality Assurance Agency and appear in the National Student Survey, where their results usually show wide variation. Some demonstrate higher levels of satisfaction among their students than most universities, while others are at the bottom of the scale

Private universities and colleges

The final group of colleges that present an alternative to university was insignificant in terms of size until recently, but may also prosper under the current fee regime. This is the private sector, seen mainly in business and law, but also in some other specialist fields. By far the longest established – and the only one to meet the criteria for inclusion in our main table – is the University of Buckingham. The best-known "newcomer" currently is BPP University, which became a full university in 2013 and offers degrees, as well as shorter courses, in both law and business subjects. Like Buckingham, BPP offers two-year degrees with short vacations to maximise teaching time – a model that other private providers are likely to follow. Fees are £9,000 a year for a two-year degree in 2015 and £6,000 a year for the three-year equivalent.

At the other end of the cost spectrum, the New College of the Humanities graduated its first students in 2015. Offering economics, English, history, law and philosophy, the college is charging £17,992 a year in 2015–16 for guaranteed small-group teaching and some big-name visiting lecturers. Up to 30 per cent of students are offered bursaries for University of London external degree courses and, from this year, 22 Combined Honours degrees validated by Southampton Solent.

Two other private institutions have been awarded university status in the last three years. Regent's University, attractively positioned in London's Regent's Park, caters particularly for the international market with courses in business, arts and social science subjects priced at £15,350 a year for courses starting in autumn 2015. However, about half of the students at the not-for-profit university, which offers British and American degrees, are from the UK or other parts of Europe. The University of Law, as its name suggests, is more specialised. It has been operating as a college for more than 100 years and claims to be the world's leading professional law school. Law degrees, as well as professional courses, are available in London and Manchester, with fees totalling £18,000 for a full-time course for a UK student, whether taken over two or three years.

The top universities for quality of teaching, feedback and support in the 2016 *Times and Sunday Times* table

1	Buckingham	88%
2	Coventry	87.6%
3	Keele	87%
4	Surrey	86.9%
5	Liverpool Hope	86.8%
=6	Bangor	85.8%
=6	Bath Spa	85.8%
8	Loughborough	84.5%
=9	Dundee	84.4%
=9	Derby	84.4%

The top universities for student experience in the 2016 *Times and Sunday Times* table

1	Surrey	90.3%
2	Keele	90.2%
=3	Loughborough	89.3%
=3	Coventry	89.3%
=3	Harper Adams	89.3%
6	East Anglia	88.8%
=7	Newcastle	88.4%
=7	Buckingham	88.4%
=9	Leeds	88%
=9	Essex	88%

There are also growing numbers of specialist colleges offering degrees, especially in the business sector. Greenwich School of Management (GSM), with more than 3,500 students on two London campuses, is probably the largest in terms of full-time students, but there are others that have forged partnerships with universities or are going it alone. The ifs School of Finance, for example, also dates back more than 100 years and now has university college status (as ifs University College) for its courses in finance and banking. Some others that rely on international students have been hit by tougher visa regulations, but the government is keen to encourage the development of a private sector to compete with the established universities. GSM is charging £6,000 a year for a three-year degree and £8,000 a year for an accelerated, two-year version.

City universities

The most popular universities, in terms of total applications, are nearly all in big cities with other major centres of population within a two-hour travelling window. For those looking for the best nightclubs, top sporting events, high-quality shopping or a varied cultural life – in other words, most young people, and especially those who live in cities already – city universities are a magnet. The big universities also, by definition, offer the widest range of subjects, although that does not mean that they necessarily have the particular course that is right for you. Nor does it mean that you will actually use the array of nightlife and shopping that looks so alluring in the prospectus, either because you cannot afford to, because student life is focused on the university, or even because you are too busy working.

Campus universities

City universities are the right choice for many young people, but it is worth bearing in mind that the National Student Survey shows that the highest satisfaction levels tend to be at smaller universities, often those with their own self-contained campuses. It seems that students identify more closely with institutions where there is a close-knit community and the social life is based around the students' union rather than the local nightclubs. Few UK universities are in genuinely rural locations, but some – particularly among the more recently promoted – are in relatively small towns. Several longer-established institutions in Scotland and Wales also share this type of setting, where the university dominates the town.

Importance of Open Days

The only way to be certain if this, or any other type of university, is for you is to visit. Schools often restrict the number of open days that sixth-formers can attend in term-time, but some universities offer a weekend alternative. The full calendar of events is available at **www.opendays.com** and on universities' own websites. Bear in mind, if you only attend one or two, that the event has to be badly mismanaged for a university not to seem an exciting place to someone who spends his or her days at school, or even college. Try to get a flavour of several institutions before you make your choice.

How many universities to pick?

When that time comes, of course, you will not be making one choice but five; four if you are applying for medicine, dentistry or veterinary science. (Full details of the application process are given in chapter 6.) Tens of thousands of students each year eventually go to a university that did not start out as their first choice, either because they did not get the right offer or because they changed their mind along the way. UCAS rules are such that applicants do not list universities in order of preference anyway – indeed, universities are not allowed to know where else you have applied. So do not pin all your hopes on one course; take just as much care choosing the other universities on your list.

The value of an "insurance" choice

Until recently, nearly all applicants included at least one "insurance" choice on that list – a university or college where entry grades were significantly lower than at their preferred institutions. This practice has been in decline, presumably because candidates expecting high grades think they can pick up a lower offer either in Clearing or through UCAS Extra, the service that allows applicants rejected by their original choices to apply to courses that still have vacancies after the first round of offers. However, it is easy to miscalculate and leave yourself without a place that you want. You may not like the look of the options in Clearing, leaving yourself with an unwelcome and potentially expensive year off at a time when jobs are thin on the ground.

The lifting of recruitment restrictions in 2015 has increased competition between universities and seen even more of the leading institutions taking part in Clearing. For those with good grades, this makes it less of a risk to apply only to highly selective universities. However, if you are at all uncertain about your grades, including an insurance choice remains a sensible course of action – especially since entry requirements have risen in recent years in response to increased demand for places. Even if you are sure that you will match the standard offers of your chosen universities, there is no guarantee that they will make you an offer. Particularly for degrees demanding three As or more at A level, there may simply be too many highly qualified applicants to offer places to all of them. The main proviso for insurance choices, as with all others, is that you must be prepared to take up that place. If not, you might as well go for broke with courses with higher standard offers and take your chances in Clearing, or even retake exams if you drop grades. Thousands of applicants each year end up rejecting their only offer when they could have had a second, insurance, choice.

Reputation

The reputation of a university is something intangible, usually built up over a long period and sometimes outlasting reality. Before universities were subject to external assessment and the publication of copious statistics, reputation was rooted in the past. League tables are partly responsible for changing that, although employers are often still influenced by what they remember as the university pecking order when they were students.

The fragmentation of the British university system into groups of institutions is another factor: the Russell Group (**www.russellgroup.ac.uk**) represents 24 research-intensive universities, nearly all with medical schools; the million+ group (**www.millionplus.ac.uk**) contains many of the former polytechnics and newer universities; the University Alliance (**www.unialliance.ac.uk**) provides a home for 18 universities, both old and new, that did not fit into the other categories; while GuildHE (**www.guildhe.ac.uk**) represents specialist colleges and the newest universities. The Cathedrals Group (**www.cathedralsgroup.org.uk**) is an affiliation of 16 church-based universities and colleges, some of which are also members of other groups. The university profiles in chapter 14 give the affiliation of each university.

Many of today's applicants will barely have heard of a polytechnic, let alone be able to identify which of today's universities had that heritage, but most will know which of two universities in the same city has the higher status. While that should matter far less than the quality of a course, it would be naïve to ignore institutional reputation entirely if that is going to carry weight with a future employer. Some big firms restrict their recruitment efforts to a small group of universities (see chapter 2), and, however short sighted that might be, it is something to bear in mind if a career in the City or a big law firm is your ambition.

Cost

Quite apart from the level of fees, the cost of studying in different parts of the UK inevitably varies. Some cities – notably London – are notoriously expensive for students and non-students alike. But even these comparisons can be complicated by the availability of part-time employment – an important factor for a growing number of students today. The 2010 RBS survey rated London as the cheapest place in the UK to study once earning opportunities are taken into account, although no other surveys have reached this conclusion, and by the 2015 RBS survey it had dropped to 10th place. If you intend to take part-time employment while studying, check that your chosen university has a "job shop", or some other organisation to help you find reasonably paid work.

Accommodation costs listed alongside the university profiles in this *Guide* are probably the nearest proxy for a cost-of-living indicator. The *Guide* also includes a summary of the bursaries available at each university. The size of bursaries varies, as do the rules governing eligibility. Scholarships are awarded for other achievements, regardless of family income.

Facilities

A 2015 survey commissioned by university directors of estates found that the quality of campus facilities was an important factor in choosing a university for two thirds of applicants. Only the course and the university's location had a higher priority. Accommodation is the main selling point for those living away from home, but sports facilities, libraries and computing equipment also play an important part. Even campus nightclubs have become part of the facilities race that has followed the introduction of top-up fees.

Many universities guarantee first-year students accommodation in halls of residence or university-owned flats. But it is as well to know what happens after that. Are there enough places for second- or third-year students who want them, and if not, what is the private market like? Rents for student houses vary quite widely across the country and there have been tensions with local residents in some cities. All universities offer specialist accommodation for disabled students – and are better at providing other facilities than most

---

Checklist

Choosing a subject and a place to study is a major decision. Make sure you can answer these questions:

Choosing a course

» What do I want out of higher education?
» Which subjects do I enjoy studying at school?
» Which subject or subjects do I want to study?
» Do I have the right qualifications?
» What are my career plans and does the subject and course fit these?
» Do I want to study full-time or part-time?
» Do I want to study at a university or a college?

Choosing a university

» What type of university do I wish to go to: campus, city or smaller town?
» How far is the university from home?
» Is it large or small?
» Is it specialist or general?
» Does it offer the right course?
» How much will it cost?
» Have I arranged to visit the university?

public institutions. Their websites give basic information on what is provided, as well as contact points for more detailed inquiries.

Special-interest clubs and recreational facilities, as well as political activity, tend to be based in the students' union – sometimes knows as the guild of students. In some universities, the union is the focal point of social activity, while in others the attractions of the city seem to overshadow the union to the point where facilities are underused. Students' union websites are included with the information found in the university profiles (chapter 14).

Sources of information

With more than 120 universities to choose from, the Unistats and UCAS websites, as well as guides such as this one, are the obvious places to start your search for the right course. Unistats now includes figures for average salaries at course level, as well as student satisfaction ratings and some information on contact hours, although this does not distinguish between lectures and seminars. The site does not make multiple comparisons easy to carry out, but it does contain a wealth of information for those who persevere. Once you have narrowed down the list of candidates, you will want to go through undergraduate prospectuses. Most are available online, where you can select the relevant sections rather than waiting for an account of every course to arrive in the post. Beware of generalised claims about the standing of the university, the quality of courses, friendly atmosphere and legendary social life. Stick, if you can, to the factual information.

If the material that the universities publish about their own qualities is less than objective, much of what you will find on the internet is equally unreliable, for different reasons. A simple search on the name of a university will turn up spurious comparisons of everything from the standard of lecturing to the attractiveness of the students. These can be seriously misleading and are usually based on anecdotal evidence, at best. Make sure that any information you may take into account comes from a reputable source and, if it conflicts with your impression, try to cross-check it with this *Guide* and the institution's own material.

Useful websites

The best starting point is the UCAS website (**www.ucas.com**). On the site there's lots of information on courses, universities and the whole process of applying to university. UCAS has an official presence on Facebook (**www.facebook.com/ucasonline**) and Twitter (**@ UCAS_online**) and now also has a series of video guides (**www.ucas.tv**) on the process of applying, UCAS resources and comments from other students.

For statistical information which allows limited comparison between universities (and for full details of the National Student Survey), visit: **www.unistats.com**.

On appropriate A-level subject choice, visit: **www.russellgroup.ac.uk/informed-choices**.
Narrowing down course choices: **www.ukcoursefinder.com**.
For a full calendar of university and college open days: **www.opendays.com**.
Students with disabilities:
Disability Rights UK: **www.disabilityrightsuk.org/how-can-we-help**

2 Graduate Employment Prospects

Graduate employment levels in this edition of the *Guide* have risen significantly – and have continued to improve since those statistics were collected. The latest surveys are showing healthy increases in vacancies for those graduating in 2015. Across the working population, graduate unemployment was only 2 per cent at the end of 2014, compared with 5 per cent for non-graduates. The unemployment rate for students graduating over the last five years was 7 per cent, compared with 11 per cent for non-graduates in their 20s. It would be premature to assume that the graduate labour market has returned to normal, however, because salary levels have not taken off in the same way, and there is a growing debate about underemployment – the proportion of graduates in jobs that do not require a degree.

Of course, what readers of this book would like to know is how the market will look in four or five years' time, when this year's applicants graduate. Although no one knows that, there would have to be seismic changes in the economy for graduates not to be in a much better position than those without a degree. That has been the case for several decades and all the projections suggest that a growing proportion of the jobs created in the coming years will require a degree. This does not mean, however, that every degree will be a passport to a well-paid job and worth the debts that graduates are going to accrue in the era of £9,000 fees.

Graduate employment and underemployment

Ever since the move to mass higher education, critics have been predicting that the graduate employment market would become saturated and the financial benefits of having a degree would begin to diminish. In overall terms, this has not happened yet: the average graduate earns at least £100,000 more than non-graduates over a working lifetime, and the returns do not seem to be falling. Employment rates for graduates are higher than they have been since 2007 and the "young graduate high-skilled employment rate", which more closely resembles the measure used in our league tables, is also back to pre-recession levels. Certainly, competition for graduate jobs remains stiff – there are now 12 million graduates in the UK, and in Inner London they represent 60 per cent of the working-age population. Today's graduates may take longer than their predecessors to find the right opening and may experiment with internships before committing themselves. Almost 30 per cent of 2014 graduates, compared with 26 per cent in 2013, were in "non-professional" jobs six months after completing a degree.

Aside from anecdotal reporting of the difficulties young graduates face in the labour market, this is why underemployment has come to the fore. It is an important debate, but one with little precision and where the practice of collecting employment data only six months after graduation can be extremely misleading. This *Guide* uses the definition from Higher Education Statistics Agency (HESA) of a graduate job in order to address this issue (see below), but employers' idea of which jobs require a degree – or at least, the jobs for which they prefer graduates – changes over time. Nurses now require a degree partly because the job has changed and requires skills that were not needed 20 years ago. The same is true of many occupations, while in others it may be possible to do the job without a degree, but having one makes it much easier to be employed in the first place.

Nevertheless, Accenture found that 60 per cent of 2013 and 2014 graduates considered themselves underemployed or working in a job that did not require a degree. Eight out of ten said they had considered the availability of jobs in their intended field before selecting their degree course, but only 55 per cent were working in their chosen field. Almost 60 per cent said they would trade salary for a more fulfilling job.

The graduate labour market

Government reports take a longer-term view of the whole labour market, which continue to support the case for taking a degree if you have the opportunity. In the first quarter of 2015, the employment rate for graduates of 87.5 per cent and the unemployment rate of 3.9 per cent were the best since 2007. It was also reported that the salary premium enjoyed by postgraduates had widened over the previous year. The median salary of graduates, however, had dropped by £500 to £31,000, but they still enjoyed a significant premium over non-graduates. Graduates still had not re-established the full earnings premium they enjoyed over non-graduates before the 2008 crash, but they were earning 45 per cent more than non-graduates, compared with around 55 per cent in 2006 – one of the biggest differentials in the western world.

Inevitably, national surveys average out the experiences of millions of people. This chapter will begin to tease out the often contrasting prospects of graduates in different subjects and from different types of institution. The Office for National Statistics (ONS), for example, in its last full survey of Graduates in the Labour Market, found that 67 per cent of

Average annual pay for graduates by the subject of their degree

	Annual pay		Annual pay
Medicine	£45,604	Agricultural sciences	£28,600
Engineering	£42,016	Biological sciences	£27,976
Physical/environmental subjects	£35,984	Humanities	£27,976
Architecture	£34,996	Medical related subjects	£27,508
Maths or computer science	£34,008	Technology	£27,508
Languages	£30,420	Linguistics, English and classics	£26,416
Social sciences and law	£30,004	Arts	£21,944
Business and finance	£30,004	Media and information studies	£21,008
Education	£30,004		

Results based on a survey of male graduates aged between 21 and 64, and female graduates aged between 21 and 59.
Labour Force Survey, as quoted in Graduates in the UK Labour Market 2013, Office for National Statistics

graduates from Russell Group universities were in high-skilled jobs, earning £18.60 an hour, compared with 53 per cent of those from other universities, who earned £14.97 an hour. As the ONS acknowledged, part of the discrepancy was due to the larger proportion of Russell Group graduates who had taken subjects such as medicine, which lead naturally to high-earning jobs. The report did not try to gauge whether there was still a gap in other subjects.

Similarly, a 2014 report for the Million Jobs Campaign, which promotes apprenticeships, found that 46 per cent of graduates from post-1992 universities were earning less than the average young person with a higher apprenticeship. This rose to more than 60 per cent in the humanities and business subjects. But, as with the ONS report, only a close examination of individual universities' employment rates in your subject – possibly supplemented by the salary figures on the Unistats website (**www.unistats.com**) – will tell you whether national trends apply to your chosen course.

The good news is that it is not just Government reports that suggest the worst may be over. The Association of Graduate Recruiters has predicted growth of almost 12 per cent in graduate vacancies in 2015–16, with two-thirds of its members reporting unfilled posts. *The Times* Top 100 employers, surveyed by High Fliers for the 2015 Graduate Market report, expected 8 per cent more vacancies than in 2014, the most for a decade.

However, the High Fliers survey covers only the upper end of the market. For the boom years of graduate employment to return, there will have to be stronger recruitment by small- and medium-sized companies. Increasingly, there will also be a greater proportion of self-employed graduates – and not simply because they cannot find the jobs they want. Many universities report growing demand for the services they provide to help those who want to set up their own companies.

Subject choice and career opportunities

For those thinking of embarking on higher education in 2016, the signs are still positive, but in any year some universities and some subjects produce better returns than others. At the end of 2014, the unemployment rate for those who had graduated six months earlier was 9 per cent, two percentage points better than in the previous year and four better than in 2012. Average starting salaries in graduate jobs had also risen by less than 1 per cent.

The tables later in this chapter give a more detailed picture of the differences between subjects, while the rankings in chapters 4 and 5 include figures for each university and subject area. There are a few striking changes, but mainly among subjects with relatively small and fluctuating numbers of graduates. Celtic studies, for example, has one of the lowest unemployment rates, whereas last year it had one of the highest.

This is the third year of a new classification developed by HESA to distinguish between "graduate-level" work and jobs that do not normally require a degree. In the employment table, subjects are ranked on "positive destinations", which include professional jobs and further study, whether or not combined with a job. Some similar tables do not make a distinction between different types of job. These tend to give the misleading impression that all universities and subjects offer uniformly rosy employment prospects.

It should also be noted that the definition of a graduate job is a controversial one. The statistics include internships and temporary jobs, for example, which may or may not lead to permanent employment. New universities in particular often claim that the whole concept of a graduate job immediately after graduation fails to reflect the employment reality for their alumni, especially in subjects such as media studies or art. In any case, a degree is about enhancing your whole career and your view of the world, not just your first job out of college.

What graduates are doing six months after graduation by subject studied

	Subject	Professional job	Professional job and studying	Studying	Non-professional job and studying	Non-professional job	Unemployed	Positive destinations
1	Medicine	93%	1%	5%	0%	0%	1%	99.3%
2	Dentistry	93%	5%	1%	0%	0%	1%	98.9%
3	Nursing	93%	2%	1%	0%	1%	2%	96.3%
4	Radiography	92%	2%	1%	0%	2%	3%	95.2%
5	Veterinary medicine	92%	1%	2%	0%	1%	4%	95.1%
6	Physiotherapy	88%	2%	2%	0%	3%	5%	92.4%
7	Pharmacology and pharmacy	78%	6%	7%	1%	5%	4%	91.3%
8	Land and property management	75%	3%	4%	0%	8%	10%	82.6%
9	Building	74%	5%	3%	0%	9%	9%	82.2%
10	Civil engineering	68%	4%	10%	1%	8%	10%	81.9%
11	General engineering	66%	3%	12%	1%	8%	11%	80.8%
12	Town and country planning and landscape	61%	6%	11%	1%	11%	9%	79.5%
13	Mechanical engineering	65%	3%	11%	0%	10%	11%	79.0%
14	Architecture	66%	5%	7%	1%	12%	10%	78.8%
15	Chemical engineering	57%	3%	17%	1%	10%	13%	77.9%
16	Physics and astronomy	35%	5%	36%	1%	10%	13%	77.1%
17	Other subjects allied to medicine	58%	3%	13%	2%	15%	8%	76.9%
18	Chemistry	40%	3%	32%	1%	12%	11%	76.5%
19	Electrical and electronic engineering	59%	3%	12%	1%	13%	12%	74.4%
20	Economics	52%	7%	14%	1%	14%	12%	73.9%
21	Mathematics	42%	7%	23%	1%	15%	12%	73.8%
22	Aeronautical and manufacturing engineering	57%	2%	14%	1%	14%	13%	73.4%
23	Anatomy and physiology	37%	3%	31%	2%	16%	11%	73.2%
24	Education	55%	2%	12%	2%	23%	6%	71.2%
25	Computer science	62%	2%	7%	1%	15%	14%	71.0%
25	Law	33%	6%	27%	5%	20%	9%	71.0%
27	German	46%	4%	17%	3%	22%	8%	69.9%
28	Celtic studies	24%	6%	38%	2%	25%	5%	69.8%
29	Social work	57%	3%	7%	1%	21%	11%	68.8%
30	Geology	37%	2%	28%	2%	19%	12%	68.4%
31	Librarianship and information management	56%	4%	7%	2%	25%	7%	68.3%
31	French	44%	4%	18%	3%	21%	11%	68.3%
33	Middle Eastern and African studies	42%	2%	21%	3%	15%	18%	67.9%
34	Classics and ancient history	35%	3%	26%	4%	20%	12%	67.8%
35	Materials technology	45%	2%	19%	2%	20%	12%	67.7%
36	Theology and religious studies	33%	5%	24%	3%	23%	10%	66.3%
37	Food science	53%	2%	9%	2%	23%	11%	66.1%

	Subject	Professional job	Professional job and studying	Studying	Non-professional job and studying	Non-professional job	Unemployed	Positive destinations
38	Iberian languages	46%	3%	14%	2%	20%	14%	66.0%
39	Politics	41%	4%	18%	3%	22%	12%	65.6%
40	Accounting and finance	44%	11%	7%	2%	24%	12%	64.5%
41	Philosophy	35%	4%	22%	4%	22%	13%	64.2%
42	Italian	41%	4%	18%	1%	25%	11%	64.0%
43	Music	41%	5%	15%	2%	28%	9%	63.4%
44	Biological sciences	31%	3%	27%	3%	24%	13%	63.2%
45	Geography	38%	3%	19%	3%	25%	13%	62.5%
46	Russian	44%	2%	15%	2%	23%	15%	62.3%
47	American studies	38%	4%	16%	4%	28%	10%	62.0%
48	Business studies	51%	3%	6%	1%	26%	13%	61.5%
49	Sports science	39%	4%	14%	3%	31%	8%	60.7%
50	Linguistics	36%	3%	18%	3%	29%	11%	60.5%
51	English	33%	3%	19%	4%	30%	11%	59.1%
51	History	31%	3%	21%	4%	29%	12%	59.1%
53	History of art, architecture and design	34%	3%	18%	4%	29%	13%	58.7%
54	Art and design	50%	1%	5%	1%	30%	12%	58.0%
55	Archaeology	34%	2%	16%	4%	32%	12%	56.4%
56	Agriculture and forestry	41%	5%	7%	2%	30%	14%	55.8%
57	Anthropology	35%	2%	15%	3%	32%	13%	55.0%
58	Psychology	30%	4%	17%	5%	34%	11%	54.9%
59	East and South Asian studies	37%	3%	13%	1%	28%	18%	53.9%
60	Communication and media studies	45%	1%	5%	1%	35%	13%	52.3%
61	Drama, dance and cinematics	42%	2%	6%	2%	37%	11%	51.5%
62	Social policy	31%	2%	15%	3%	36%	13%	51.1%
63	Hospitality, leisure, recreation and tourism	42%	1%	4%	2%	40%	12%	48.7%
64	Sociology	31%	2%	12%	3%	39%	12%	48.3%
65	Creative writing	29%	2%	10%	4%	39%	16%	45.4%
66	Animal science	20%	2%	13%	4%	51%	11%	38.9%
	Total	**49%**	**3%**	**13%**	**2%**	**23%**	**10%**	**67%**

NOTE: Table is ranked on the total of positive destinations (the sum of the first four columns), rounded to one decimal place. HESA 2013/2014 return.

The tables on pages 38–41 will help you assess whether your course will pay off in career terms, at least to start with. They show both the amount you might expect to earn with a degree in a specific subject, and the odds of being in work. They reflect the experiences six months after graduation of those who competed their degrees in 2014, and the picture may have improved by the time you leave university. But there is no reason to believe that the pattern of success rates for specific subjects and institutions will have changed radically.

What graduates earn six months after graduation by subject studied

	Subject	Professional employment	Non-professional employment
1	Dentistry	£30,348	..
2	Medicine	£28,683	..
3	Chemical engineering	£28,641	£16,111
4	General engineering	£27,493	£15,348
5	Economics	£26,630	£17,295
6	Mechanical engineering	£26,366	£17,025
7	Veterinary medicine	£26,071	..
8	Electrical and electronic engineering	£25,191	£16,331
9	Physics and astronomy	£24,976	£14,802
10	Aeronautical and manufacturing engineering	£24,969	£17,495
11	Civil engineering	£24,776	£18,303
12	Mathematics	£24,119	£16,161
13	Social work	£24,007	£14,910
14	Computer science	£23,766	£15,382
15	Land and property management	£23,733	£17,800
16	Building	£23,707	£15,402
17	Geology	£23,029	£14,676
18	Nursing	£22,928	£15,828
19	Materials technology	£22,581	£16,769
20	Business studies	£22,449	£16,572
21	Accounting and finance	£22,357	£17,415
22	Radiography	£22,238	..
23	Chemistry	£22,232	£15,705
24	Physiotherapy	£22,014	£13,333
25	Town and country planning and landscape	£21,960	£15,741
26	Politics	£21,940	£16,376
27	Classics and ancient history	£21,635	£14,674
28	Russian	£21,518	£15,437
29	Philosophy	£21,372	£15,347
30	Education	£21,369	£14,302
31	German	£21,232	£14,844
32	Anatomy and physiology	£21,225	£14,684
33	Geography	£21,210	£15,384
34	Food science	£20,901	£15,867
35	Other subjects allied to medicine	£20,760	£14,706
36	French	£20,492	£15,969
37	Theology and religious studies	£20,476	£14,763
38	History	£20,456	£15,063
39	Social policy	£20,304	£16,041
40	Agriculture and forestry	£20,285	£16,438
41	Librarianship and information management	£20,177	..
42	Iberian languages	£20,171	£16,267

	Subject	Professional employment	Non-professional employment
43	Biological sciences	£20,097	£15,036
44	Anthropology	£19,990	£15,851
45	Law	£19,699	£16,035
46	Sociology	£19,651	£15,370
47	Italian	£19,632	£16,103
48	Pharmacology and pharmacy	£19,597	£15,023
49	Archaeology	£19,517	£14,959
50	Middle Eastern and African studies	£19,441	£16,968
51	American studies	£19,410	£15,280
52	Hospitality, leisure, recreation and tourism	£19,369	£15,923
53	History of art, architecture and design	£19,274	£15,228
54	East and South Asian studies	£19,075	£16,272
55	Psychology	£18,973	£14,982
56	Linguistics	£18,949	£15,731
57	Architecture	£18,936	£15,122
58	English	£18,863	£14,908
59	Sports science	£18,753	£14,677
60	Celtic studies	£18,497	£16,484
61	Animal science	£18,327	£14,686
62	Art and design	£18,233	£14,548
63	Communication and media studies	£18,179	£15,139
64	Music	£17,497	£15,002
65	Creative writing	£17,268	£14,856
66	Drama, dance and cinematics	£16,963	£14,381
	Average	**£22,064**	**£15,385**

NOTE: .. indicates a suppressed mean salary based on 7 or fewer graduates
HESA 2013/14 DLHE return

The table of employment statistics does reveal some unexpected results. For example, only 71 per cent of computer science graduates are working in graduate jobs or doing further study. More traditional engineering subjects fare a little better. Indeed, the figures do not support the theory that young people avoid engineering because salaries are low: all five branches of engineering are in the top ten subjects for graduate earnings.

The employment table also shows that graduates in some subjects, especially sciences such as physics, chemistry and geology, are more likely to undertake further study than in others, such as art and design or hospitality. In both physics and Celtic studies, more than 40 per cent of graduates continued to study. Those going into art and design appreciate that it, too, has its own career peculiarities. Periods of freelance or casual work may be an occupational hazard at the start of their career, and perhaps later on as well. Less surprisingly, doctors and dentists are virtually guaranteed a job if they complete a degree, as are nurses. HESA found that only one medic in 100 was unemployed six months after graduating.

The second table, on pages 40–41, gives average earnings of those who graduated in 2014, six months after leaving college. It contains interesting – and in some cases surprising – information about early career pay levels. Few would have placed social work or nursing in the top 20 fields for graduate pay, while business studies and accounting appear in 20th and 21st place respectively. Those positions underline the differences between starting salaries and long-term prospects in different jobs. Over time the accountants may well end up with big rewards. Incidentally, the top non-City pay for a graduate is thought to be with the supermarket group Aldi. Despite its budget image, Aldi pays graduate area manager trainees £42,000 in their first year and adds an Audi A4.

HESA also reported good news in August 2014 on the longer-term outlook for students, based on questioning those who had graduated in 2011. It is an exercise the agency carries out periodically, which invariably shows a more positive (and realistic) picture than the survey six months after graduation. Of the UK graduates surveyed for the latest report, 88 per cent were in employment, 6 per cent were studying full-time and 2.6 per cent were unemployed, compared with 8 per cent when the same cohort was surveyed six months after graduation. The median salary of the 2009 graduates had risen from £22,000 to £26,000 over the same three and a half year period. Almost 6 per cent had seen their incomes rise by over £20,000 and most were at least £5,000 better off than in the initial survey.

Enhancing your employability

Universities are well aware of the difficulties in the graduate employment market and have been introducing all manner of schemes to try to give their graduates an advantage in the labour market. Many have incorporated specially designed employability modules into degree courses; some are certificating extra-curricular activities to improve their graduates' CVs; others are stepping up their efforts to provide work experience to complement degrees.

Opinion is divided on the value of such schemes. Some of the biggest employers restrict their recruitment activities to a small number of universities, believing that these institutions attract the brightest minds and that trawling more widely is not cost-effective (see table below). These companies, often big payers from the City of London and including some of the top law firms, are not likely to change their ways at a time when they are more anxious than ever to control costs. Widening the pool of universities from which they set out to recruit is costly, and unnecessary in a buyers' market like the one we see today. As before,

Universities targeted by the largest number of top employers in 2014–15

1	(2)	Manchester	**11**	(6)	Bath
2	(1)	Nottingham	**12**	(16)	London School of Economics
3	(7)	Warwick	**13**	(11)	Birmingham
4	(3)	Cambridge	**14**	(15)	Edinburgh
5	(4)	Oxford	**15**	(14)	Loughborough
6	(12)	Durham	**16**	(13)	Sheffield
7	(5)	Bristol	**17**	(19)	Southampton
8	(10)	University College London	**18**	(18)	Exeter
9	(9)	Imperial College	**19**	(17)	Newcastle
10	(8)	Leeds	**20**	(22)	King's College London

Last year's position in brackets. Source: Graduate Employment Market in 2015, High Fliers

they will expect outstanding candidates who went to other universities to come to them, either on graduation or later in their careers.

The best advice for those looking to maximise their employment opportunities (and who isn't?) must be to go for the best university you can. But most graduates do not work in the City and most students do not go to universities at the top of the league tables.

University schemes

If a university offers extra help towards employment, it is worth considering whether its scheme is likely to work for you. Some are too new to show results in the labour market, but they may have been endorsed by big employers or introduced at an institution whose graduates already have a record of success in the jobs market. In time, these extras may turn into mandatory parts of degree study, complete with course credits.

At Liverpool John Moores University, for example, the World of Work (WoW) programme was devised with the help of the CBI, Shell, Sony, and Marks and Spencer. Originally an option, it is now taken by students in all subjects, including postgraduates, and offers classes in CV writing, interview skills, finance, entrepreneurship and negotiation skills, among many other topics. There are guest lectures and demonstrations, and employers carry out mock interviews to assess students' strengths and weaknesses.

Hertfordshire is another institution which has demonstrated a sustained focus on its students' job prospects. Employer groups are consulted on the curriculum and often supply guest lecturers on degree courses. Like some other universities, such as Derby, it offers career development support to graduates throughout their working life. Other universities, such as Exeter, have taken a different tack and are helping students make the most of their voluntary, sporting and extra-curricular activities by certificating them. It believes that the Exeter Award will encourage employers to take more notice such participation. The well-established York Award offers its students a framework to gain recognition for voluntary and leisure activities that are not formally recognised through the degree programme.

The value of work experience

The majority of graduate jobs are open to applicants from any discipline. For these general positions, employers tend to be more impressed by a good degree from what they consider a prestigious university than by an apparently relevant qualification. Here numeracy, literacy and communications – the arts needed to function effectively in any organisation – are of vital importance. Specialist jobs – for example in engineering or design – are a different matter. Employers may be much more knowledgeable about the quality of individual courses, and less influenced by a university's overall position in league tables, when the job relies directly on knowledge and skills acquired as a student. That goes for medicine and architecture as well as computer games design or environmental management.

In either case, however, work experience has become increasingly important. The High Fliers survey showed that employers in *The Times* 100 expected to fill more than 30 per cent of their vacancies with graduates who had already worked for them, whether in holiday jobs, internships or placements. Sandwich degrees, extended programmes that include up to a year at work, have always boosted employment prospects. Graduates often end up working where they undertook their placement. And while a sandwich year will make your course longer, it will not be subject to a full year's fees.

Many conventional degrees now include shorter work placements that should offer some advantages in the labour market. Not all are arranged by the university so, unless you have an opening that you would like to pursue, that is something to establish and weigh in the balance when choosing a course. The majority of big graduate employers offer some provision of this nature, although access to it can be competitive.

If your chosen course does not include a work placement, you may want to consider arranging your own part-time or temporary employment. The majority of supposedly full-time students now take jobs during term time, as well as in vacations, to make ends meet. But such jobs can boost your CV as well as your wallet. Even working in a bar or a shop shows some experience of dealing with the public and coping with the disciplines of the workplace. Inevitably, the more prosperous cities are likely to offer more employment opportunities than rural areas or conurbations that have been hard hit in the recession.

The ultimate work-related degree is one sponsored by an employer or even taken in the workplace. Middlesex University provides tailored programmes for Asda and Halifax Bank, among other organisations, and has many students taking courses run by its Institute of Work Based Learning. Most such courses are for people already employed by the companies concerned, rather than as a route into the company. But they may become an alternative to entering full-time higher education straight from school or college.

Consider part-time degrees

Another option, also favoured by ministers, is part-time study. Although enrolments have fallen sharply both leading up to and since the 2012 increases in fees, there are now loans available for most part-time courses. Employers may be willing to share the cost of taking a degree or another relevant qualification, and the chance to earn a wage while studying has obvious attractions. Bear in mind, however, that most part-time courses take twice as long to complete as the full-time equivalent. If your earning power is linked to the qualification, it will take that much longer for you to enjoy the benefits.

Plan early for your career

Whatever type of course you choose, it is sensible to start thinking about your future career early in your time at university. There has been a growing tendency in recent years for students to convince themselves that there would be plenty of time to apply for jobs after graduation, and that they were better off focusing entirely on their degree while at university. In the current employment market, all but the most obviously brilliant graduates need to offer more than just a degree, whether it be work experience, leadership qualities demonstrated through clubs and societies, or commitment to voluntary activities. Many students finish a degree without knowing what they want to do, but a blank CV will not impress a prospective employer.

Half of the leading employers told High Fliers that they are not interested in graduates without previous work experience and that any such applicants would have "little or no chance" for a place on their graduate programmes. He may be overstating the case, but Martin Burchall, High Fliers' Managing Director, claimed that work placements and internships were now "just as important as getting a 2:1 or first-class degree".

Useful websites

Prospects, the UK's official graduate careers website: **www.prospects.ac.uk**
For career advice, internships and student and graduate jobs: **www.milkround.com**
High Fliers: **www.highfliers.co.uk**

3 Going Abroad to University

British students have been notoriously reluctant to go abroad even for part of their degree, let alone an entire course. Poor linguistic skills and good universities at home have encouraged them to stay in their own country, while students elsewhere in the world are travelling in unprecedented numbers. France has three times as many studying abroad, Germany more than four times as many, according to UNESCO. Nepal, with half the UK's population, has roughly the same number of students overseas. This may be about to change, however, at least for those including a period of study at a foreign university in their UK degree. The Government and universities themselves have been encouraging students to take advantage of overseas opportunities to strengthen their employment prospects – and finally there appears to be a response. The numbers going abroad as part of a UK degree jumped from 20,000 to almost 29,000 last year.

There has been speculation since £9,000 fees were introduced that more students would apply to universities on the Continent, where the equivalent charges are low or even non-existent. More sixth-formers – particularly at independent schools – do appear to be considering it, but the predicted surge has yet to materialise. There has been an increase in the numbers going to universities in the USA, where the fees gap has narrowed, at least with state universities, but it is still very much a minority pursuit. There were 10,000 UK students at US universities last year, but many were postgraduates and/or the children of Britons working on the other side of the Atlantic.

Research by the British Council has shown that one student in three is interested in some form of overseas study. And, good though UK universities are by international standards, other studies suggest that they are right to do so. Research by QS, publishers of the World University Rankings, found that 60 per cent of employers worldwide – and 42 per cent of those in the UK – gave extra weight to an international student experience when recruiting graduates. Of course, everything will depend on what and where that experience was. Harvard is going to carry more weight than the University of Lapland, which has tried to attract British students. But leaving the UK to study, even for a short period, can confer advantages in the employment market.

Some of the obstacles that have held British students back are now being removed. The maximum fee for a year abroad while studying at a UK university remains at £1,350, for example, and many universities are charging less than that. But there is still one important disincentive to taking a full degree overseas: although support from the Student Loans Company continues for a year abroad during a UK degree course, it is not available for degrees from non-UK institutions. There has been some campaigning to reverse this in the light of the Government's enthusiasm for international mobility, but it is unlikely that the regulations will change in time for entry in 2016.

Universities in some countries – notably the Netherlands and the USA – now mount frequent recruitment campaigns in the UK. Numbers of British students have been rising sharply at Dutch universities, where fees in 2015/16 are €1,951 for most courses, but they still account for only about 1,000 of the 2.5-million UK student population. Leading independent schools report serious interest in American universities and attendance at the Fulbright Commission's recruitment fairs continues to rise, but the numbers enrolling remain modest, despite attractive incentives in the form of scholarships, bursaries and campus employment opportunities.

Nevertheless, it would be surprising if high fees at home and an increasingly international graduate labour market did not encourage continuing growth in overseas study. Most students who go abroad are motivated by a desire to study at a "world-class" institution, according to a study for the Department of Business, Innovation and Skills. Often the trigger is failure to win a place at a leading UK university and being unwilling to settle for second best. Other motivations include a desire for adventure and a belief that overseas study might lead to an international career. The question is how to judge a university that may be thousands of miles from home against more familiar names in the UK. This chapter will make some suggestions, including the use of the growing number of global rankings that are available online or in print.

It is possible to have your academic cake and eat it by going on an international exchange or work placement organised by a UK university, or even to attend a British university in another country. Nottingham University has campuses in China and Malaysia; Middlesex can offer Dubai or Mauritius, where students registered in the UK can take part or all of their degree. Other universities, such as Liverpool, also have joint ventures with overseas institutions which offer an international experience (in China, in Liverpool's case) and degrees from both universities.

In most cases, however, an overseas study experience means a foreign university – through a partnership with a UK institution. Until recently, this was usually for a postgraduate degree – and there are still strong arguments for spending your undergraduate years in the UK before going abroad for more advanced study. Older students taking more specialised programmes may get more out of an extended period overseas than those who go at 18 and, since first degrees in the UK are shorter than elsewhere, it may also be the more cost-effective option.

If cost is the main consideration, however, even the generally longer courses at Continental universities can work out cheaper than a degree in the UK. The main obstacle, apart from British students' traditional reluctance to take degrees anywhere else, concerns the language barrier. Although there are now thousands of postgraduate courses taught in English at Continental universities, first-degree programmes are still much thinner on the ground. A few universities, like Maastricht and others in the Netherlands, are offering a wide range of subjects in English. But most European universities teach undergraduates in the host language – and, up to now, that has always deterred UK students.

The obvious alternative lies in American, Australian and Canadian universities, all of which are keen to attract more international students. Here, cost and distance are the main obstacles. Four-year courses add considerably to the cost of affordable-looking fees, while the state of the pound has been another serious disadvantage. Add in the natural reluctance of most 18-year-olds to commit to life on the other side of the world (or even just the Atlantic), and the prospect of a dramatic increase in student emigration lessens considerably.

Where do students go to?

There is remarkably little official monitoring of how many students leave the UK, let alone where they go. But it seems that for all the economic advantages of studying in Continental Europe, the USA remains by far the most popular student destination. Most surveys put Canada, France and Germany (in that order) as the biggest attractions outside the USA. Australia also features prominently in some surveys.

A few British students find their way to unexpected locations, like South Korea or Slovakia, but usually for family reasons or to study the language. The figures suggest that British students are more attracted to countries that are familiar or close at hand, and where they can speak English. Many are doubtless planning to stay in their adopted country after they graduate, although visa regulations may make this difficult.

Studying in Europe

More than 10,000 UK students now attend Continental European universities and colleges, according to UNESCO. But international statistics pick up those whose parents emigrated or are working abroad, as well as those who actually leave the UK to take a degree. A minority are undergraduates, if only because the availability of courses taught in English is so much greater at postgraduate level.

The increased interest in Continental universities arises both from the generally low fees they charge and from the growth in the number of courses offered in English. Some countries charge no fees at all, even to international students, and public universities in the European Union are obliged to charge UK students the same as local residents. In the EU, you will also be able get a job while studying. Farther afield, your student visa might not allow you to take on paid work.

Undergraduates can study at a French university for less than £150 a year but, not surprisingly, nearly all first degrees are taught in French. Only 68 of the 1,135 programmes taught in English and listed on the Campus France website (**www.campusfrance.org/en**) are at the Licence (Bachelors equivalent) level – and 21 of them have some teaching in French. Germany is much the same, despite attracting large numbers of international students. The DAAD website (**www.daad.de/en**) lists 131 undergraduate programmes taught wholly or mainly in English – 18 fewer than last year – but many are at private universities like Jacobs University in Bremen, which charges up to €10,000 a semester. There are cheaper alternatives in the public sector, where tuition fees have been abolished, but they remain relatively scarce.

Any potential saving has to be considered with care. Despite the Bologna process – an intergovernmental agreement which means that degrees across Europe are becoming more similar in content and duration – most Continental courses are longer than their UK equivalents, adding to the cost and to your lost earnings from attending university. And, of course, you will have higher travel costs. It is harder to generalise about the cost of living. It can be lower than the UK in southern Europe, but frighteningly high in Scandinavia.

Obviously, the cost of an international experience and the commitment involved is much reduced if you opt for an exchange scheme or other scheme arranged by a UK university, many of which have partners all over the world. There are opportunities for everything from a summer school of less than a month to a full year abroad, and a number of universities now have targets to increase the numbers taking advantage of such schemes.

The most common offering is the EU's Erasmus scheme, which funds exchanges of between three months and a year, the work counting towards your degree. More than 2 million students throughout Europe have used the scheme, and there are 2,000 universities to choose from in 30 countries. Over 15,000 UK students used the scheme in 2013–14 – a healthy increase on the previous year and one that is expected to continue. Applications are made through universities' international offices, and must be approved by the UK university as well as by the Erasmus administrators. Erasmus students do not pay any extra fees and they are eligible for grants to cover the extra expense of travelling and living in another country. During 2015–16 academic year, this will amount to €250–€300 a month for studying abroad, and €350–€400 a month for doing a traineeship abroad, depending on the country you choose to go to.

Studying in America

American universities remain the first choice of British students going abroad to take a degree, just as the UK is the first choice for Americans. Regardless of any special relationship, this is not surprising since international rankings consistently show US and UK universities to be the best in the world (as well as teaching in English).

Around half of the British students taking courses in the USA are undergraduates. Already by far the most popular student destination, the attractions of an American degree have multiplied since fees trebled in England. The Fulbright Commission, which promotes American higher education, has seen a 30 per cent increase in the number of Britons taking US university entrance exams. Even before the latest rise in UK fees, the top American universities had seen demand rise sharply, and this is spreading to universities further down the rankings.

The sheer depth of the US university system means that if you are thinking of studying abroad, the USA is almost bound to be on the list of possibilities. Tuition fees at Ivy League institutions are notoriously high – Harvard's are $45,278 in 2015–16 and the university put the full cost of attendance at $60,259 a year – but generous student aid programmes ensure that most pay far less than the "sticker price". Outside the Ivy League, the fee gap for UK students has been narrowing, but fees at many state universities have shot up in the last three

Top ten countries, as destinations for UK students, 2012

1	United States of America	9,060
2	Ireland	2,062
3	France	2,013
4	Australia	1,678
5	Germany	1,499
6	Canada	1,056
7	Netherlands	888
8	United Arab Emirates	809
9	Denmark	653
10	Austria	610

UNESCO Institute for Statistics, 2015

Top ten student cities in the world, 2015

1	Paris	France
2	Melbourne	Australia
3	London	United Kingdom
4	Sydney	Australia
5	Hong Kong	Hong Kong
6	Boston	United States of America
7	Tokyo	Japan
8	Montreal	Canada
9	Toronto	Canada
10	Seoul	South Korea

QS Best Student Cities in the World, 2015

years as politicians have tried to balance the books. At Texas A&M University, for example, ranked in the top 200 in the world, international students now pay $28,000 a year for tuition, and the university put undergraduates' total costs at $43,000. Fees are below $20,000 at the State University of New York, although the university puts the total cost for those living on campus at $40,000. Only at much lower-ranked state universities do the costs compare with those in the UK – at South Dakota State University, for example, the yearly cost is put at $18,400 (£11,732 at the time of writing).

The individual systems of state universities and private universities mean that there is a great variation in the financial support given to international students. Fulbright advises students considering a US degree to assess and negotiate a funding package at the same time as pursuing their application. Otherwise, they may end up with a place they cannot afford, losing valuable time in the quest for a more suitable one.

Which countries are best?

Anyone going abroad to study will be in search of a memorable and valuable all-round experience, not just a good course. Most international students are motivated by location – both the country and the city in which a university is based – as well as by the reputation of the institution. QS publishes an annual ranking of student cities, based on quality of life indicators as well as the number of places at world-ranked universities. Paris topped the ranking in 2015, with Melbourne second, London third and Sydney fourth.

Many Asian countries are looking to recruit more foreign students, both as part of a broader internationalisation agenda and to compensate for falling numbers of potential students at home. Japan is a case in point. The high cost of living may put off many potential students, as may the unfamiliarity of its language, but more support is being offered to attract foreign students and more courses are being taught in English. However, as with any non-English speaking country, the language of instruction is only part of the story. You will need to know enough of the local language to manage the shops and the transport system, and, of course, to make friends and get the most out of being there.

Another option of growing interest is China. The country has already grown massively in importance. Its university system is growing in quality, especially at the C9 group of international institutions, which have become known as the Chinese Ivy League. Familiarity with China is unlikely to be a career disadvantage for anyone in the 21st century. Some see Hong Kong, which has several world-ranked universities and a familiar feel for Britons, as the perfect alternative to mainland Chinese universities.

Will my degree be recognised?

Even in the era of globalisation, you need to bear in mind that not all degrees are equal. At one extreme is the MBA, which has an international system for accrediting courses, and a global admissions standard. But with many professional courses, study abroad is a potential hazard. To work as a doctor, engineer or lawyer in the UK, you need a qualification which the relevant professional body will recognise. It is understandable that to practise law in England, you need to have studied the English legal system. For other subjects, the issues are more to do with the quality and content of courses outside UK control.

There are ways of researching this issue in advance. One is to contact NARIC, the National Recognition Centre for the UK (**www.ecctis.co.uk/naric**). NARIC exists to examine the compatibility and acceptability of qualifications from around the world. The other approach is to ask the UK professional body in question – maybe an engineering institution, the relevant law society or the general teaching, medical or dental councils – about the qualification you propose to study for.

Which are the best universities?

Going abroad to study is a big and expensive decision, and you want to get it right. Whether your ultimate aim is to become an internationally mobile high-flyer, or simply to broaden your experience, you will want to know that the university you are going to is taken seriously around the world.

At the moment there are three main systems for ranking universities on a world scale. One is run by QS (Quacquarelli Symonds), an educational research company based in London (**www.topuniversities.com**). Another is by Shanghai Ranking Consultancy, a company set up by Shanghai Jiao Tong University, in China, and is called the Academic Ranking of World Universities (ARWU) (**www.shanghairanking.com**). These two have been joined by *Times Higher Education* (**www.timeshighereducation.co.uk**), a weekly magazine with no connection to *The Times*, which produced its own ranking for the first time in 2010, having previously published the QS version.

There are several more international ranking systems that an online search might throw up, but most are either specialist – like the Webometrics ranking of universities' web activity – or limited in their readership and influence. Some are still developing: the European Commission's U-Multirank (**www.umultirank.org**), for example, is still limited in the subjects it covers, but may become a more widely used source of information in time.

The QS system uses a number of measures including academic opinion, employer opinion, international orientation, research impact and staff/student ratio to create its listing, while the ARWU uses measures such as Nobel Prizes and highly cited papers, which are more related to excellence in scientific research. The *Times Higher Education* has added a number of measures to the QS model, including research income and a controversial global survey of teaching quality. Despite these different approaches, many universities appear in all three rankings. If you go to a university that features strongly in any of the tables, you will be at a place that is well-regarded around the world. After all, even the 200th university on any of these rankings is an elite institution in a world with more than 4,000 universities. The top 50 universities in all three rankings are listed on the following pages.

These systems tend to favour universities which are good at science and medicine. Places that specialise in the humanities and the social sciences, such as the London School of Economics, can appear in deceptively modest positions. In addition, the rankings tend to look at universities in the round, and contain only limited information on specific subjects. QS published the first 26 global subject rankings in 2011 and has since increased this to 36. One advantage of the QS ranking system is that 10 per cent of a university's possible score comes from a global survey of recruiters. So you can look at this column of the table for an idea about where the major employers like to hire. Note that the author of this *Guide* has a role in developing the QS Rankings.

Other options for overseas studies

For the growing numbers who want to study abroad without committing themselves to a complete degree, a number of options are available. A language degree will typically involve a year abroad, and a look at the UCAS website will show many options for studying another subject alongside your language of choice. UK universities offer degrees in information technology, science, business and even journalism with a major language such as Chinese.

Many universities offer a year abroad, either studying or in a work placement, even to those who are not taking a language. At Aston University, for example, 70 per cent of students do a year's work placement and a growing number do so abroad. China and Chile have been among recent destinations. Other universities offer the opportunity to take shorter credit-bearing courses with partner institutions overseas. American universities are again the most popular choice. The best approach is to decide what you want to study and then see if there is a UK university that offers it as a joint degree or with a placement abroad. Make sure that all the universities involved are well-regarded, for example by looking at their rankings on one or other of the websites mentioned at the end of the table on the following pages.

Useful websites

Prospects: studying abroad: **www.prospects.ac.uk/studying_abroad.htm**
Association of Commonwealth Universities: **www.acu.ac.uk**
Campus France: **www.campusfrance.org/en**
College Board (USA): **www.collegeboard.org**
DAAD (for Germany): **www.daad.de/en/**
Study in Holland: **www.studyinholland.co.uk**
Education Ireland: **www.educationinireland.com/en**
Erasmus Programme (EU): **www.erasmusplus.org.uk**
Finaid (USA): **www.finaid.org**
Fulbright Commission: **www.fulbright.org.uk**
Study in Australia: **www.studyinaustralia.gov.au**
Study in Canada: **www.studyincanada.com**

For information on the recognition in the UK of international degrees, visit the National Recognition Centre for the UK (NARIC): **www.naric.org.uk**

The top 50 universities in the world in 2015 according to QS World University Ranking (QS), the Academic Ranking of World Universities (ARWU) and *Times Higher Education* (*THE*)

QS Rank	Institution	Country	ARWU Rank	Institution	Country	THE Rank	Institution	Country
1	Massachusetts Institute of Technology	USA	1	Harvard University	USA	1	California Institute of Technology	USA
2	Harvard University	USA	2	Stanford University	USA	2	Harvard University	USA
=3	University of Cambridge	UK	3	Massachusetts Institute of Technology	USA	3	University of Oxford	UK
=3	Stanford University	USA	4	University of California, Berkeley	USA	4	Stanford University	USA
5	California Institute of Technology	USA	5	University of Cambridge	UK	5	University of Cambridge	UK
6	University of Oxford	UK	6	Princeton University	USA	6	Massachusetts Institute of Technology	USA
7	University College London	UK	7	California Institute of Technology	USA	7	Princeton University	USA
8	Imperial College London	UK	8	Columbia University	USA	8	University of California, Berkeley	USA
9	ETH Zurich (Swiss Federal Institute of Technology)	Switz.	9	University of Chicago	USA	=9	Imperial College London	UK
10	University of Chicago	USA	10	University of Oxford	UK	=9	Yale University	USA
11	Princeton University	USA	11	Yale University	USA	11	University of Chicago	USA
12	National University of Singapore	S'pore	12	University of California, Los Angeles	USA	12	University of California, Los Angeles	USA
13	Nanyang Technological University	S'pore	13	Cornell University	USA	13	ETH Zurich (Swiss Federal Institute of Technology)	Switz.
14	École Polytechnique Fédérale de Lausanne	Switz.	14	University of California, San Diego	USA	14	Columbia University	USA
15	Yale University	USA	15	University of Washington	USA	15	Johns Hopkins University	USA
16	Johns Hopkins University	USA	16	Johns Hopkins University	USA	16	University of Pennsylvania	USA
17	Cornell University	USA	17	University of Pennsylvania	USA	17	University of Michigan	USA
18	University of Pennsylvania	USA	=18	University College London	UK	18	Duke University	USA

=19	Australian National University	Australia	**=18**	University of California, San Francisco	USA	**19**	Cornell University	USA
=19	King's College London	UK	**20**	ETH Zurich (Swiss Federal Institute of Technology)	Switz.	**20**	University of Toronto	Canada
21	University of Edinburgh	UK	**21**	University of Tokyo	Japan	**21**	Northwestern University	USA
22	Columbia University	USA	**22**	University of Michigan	USA	**22**	University College London	UK
23	École Normale Supérieure, Paris	France	**23**	Imperial College London	UK	**23**	University of Tokyo	Japan
24	McGill University	Canada	**24**	University of Wisconsin, Madison	USA	**24**	Carnegie Mellon University	USA
25	Tsinghua University	China	**25**	University of Toronto	Canada	**25**	National University of Singapore	S'pore
26	University of California, Berkeley	USA	**26**	Kyoto University	Japan	**26**	University of Washington	USA
27	University of California, Los Angeles	USA	**27**	New York University	USA	**27**	Georgia Institute of Technology	USA
28	Hong Kong University of Science and Technology	Hong Kong	**28**	Northwestern University	USA	**28**	University of Texas at Austin	USA
29	Duke University	USA	**29**	University of Illinois, Urbana-Champaign	USA	**=29**	University of Illinois, Urbana-Champaign	USA
=30	University of Michigan	USA	**30**	University of Minnesota, Twin Cities	USA	**=29**	Ludwig Maximilian University of Munich	Germany
=30	University of Hong Kong	Hong Kong	**31**	Duke University	USA	**=29**	University of Wisconsin, Madison	USA
32	Northwestern University	USA	**32**	Washington University in St Louis	USA	**32**	University of British Columbia	Canada
33	University of Manchester	UK	**33**	Rockefeller University	USA	**33**	University of Melbourne	Australia
34	University of Toronto	Canada	**34**	University of Colorado at Boulder	USA	**=34**	École Polytechnique Fédérale de Lausanne	Switz
35	London School of Economics	UK	**35**	University of Copenhagen	Denmark	**=34**	London School of Economics	UK
36	Seoul National University	S. Korea	**36**	Pierre and Marie Curie University, Paris 6	France	**36**	University of Edinburgh	UK
37	University of Bristol	UK	**37**	University of Texas at Austin	USA	**37**	University of California, Santa Barbara	USA
38	Kyoto University	Japan	**38**	University of California, Santa Barbara	USA	**38**	New York University	USA
39	University of Tokyo	Japan	**39**	University of North Carolina at Chapel Hill	USA	**39**	McGill University	Canada

The top 50 universities in the world in 2015 according to QS World University Ranking (QS), the Academic Ranking of World Universities (ARWU) and *Times Higher Education* (*THE*)

QS Rank	Institution	Country	ARWU Rank	Institution	Country	THE Rank	Institution	Country
40	École Polytechnique Paris Tech	France	**40**	University of British Columbia	Canada	**40**	King's College London	UK
41	Peking University	China	**41**	University of Manchester	UK	**41**	University of California, San Diego	USA
42	University of Melbourne	Australia	**42**	University of Paris Sud, Paris 11	France	**42**	Washington University in St Louis	USA
43	Korea Advanced Institute of Science and Technology	S. Korea	**43**	University of Maryland, College Park	USA	**43**	University of Hong Kong	Hong Kong
44	University of California, San Diego	USA	**=44**	University of Melbourne	Australia	**44**	Karolinska Institute	Sweden
45	University of Sydney	Australia	**=44**	University of Texas Southwestern Medical Center at Dallas	USA	**45**	Australian National University	Australia
=46	University of New South Wales	Australia	**46**	Heidelberg University	Germany	**=46**	University of Minnesota	USA
=46	University of Queensland	Australia	**47**	University of Edinburgh	UK	**=46**	University of North Carolina at Chapel Hill	USA
48	University of Warwick	UK	**48**	Karolinska Institute	Sweden	**48**	Peking University	China
49	Brown University	USA	**49**	University of Southern California	USA	**49**	Tsinghua University	China
50	University of British Columbia	Canada	**50**	University of California, Irvine	USA	**50**	Seoul National University	S. Korea

We gratefully acknowledge permission to reproduce these three rankings. The full QS World University Rankings 2015–16 can be consulted at **www.topuniversities.com**, the full Academic Ranking of World Universities 2015 at **www.arwu.org** and the full T*imes Higher Education* 2014–15 rankings at **www.timeshighereducation.co.uk**.

4 The Top Universities

Universities publish reams of statistics about themselves – more than ever now that the Government insists on greater transparency. But even some of the official attempts to provide prospective students with better information can leave the reader more confused, rather than less. Our main table has been developed over 22 years to focus on the fundamentals of undergraduate education and make meaningful comparisons in an accessible way.

What distinguishes a top university? And who is to say that one course is better than another – especially when the university system is so reluctant to make any such comparison? Critics of league tables insist that this is because every university has different priorities, and every course has a different ways of approaching a subject. Students must choose the one that suits them best. So they must. Not everyone would find the top universities to their taste, even if they were able to secure a place. But that does not mean that there are not important differences in the quality of universities and the courses they offer. These, in turn, can have a crucial bearing on future employment prospects.

The table in this chapter offers applicants and others with an interest in higher education a means to assess the standing of UK universities with undergraduate education in mind. The institutions will have their own ideas about what should go into comparisons of this type, but ours has stood the test of time because it uses the statistics that universities themselves employ to measure their own performance and combines them in a way that generations of students have found revealing.

Every element of the table in this chapter has been chosen for the light it shines on the undergraduate experience and a student's future prospects. The selection of these measures and the way in which they are combined give a particular view of universities' overall strengths, and it is one that has stood the test of time. Unlike some others, *The Times and Sunday Times Good University Guide* has placed a premium on consistency, confident that the measures are the best available for the task. Some changes have been forced upon us. Universities stopped assessing teaching quality by subject, when this was the most heavily weighted measure in the table, for example. However, the arrival of the National Student Survey (NSS) ten years ago has enabled the student experience to be reflected in the table. The NSS is an initiative of the Funding Councils for England, Northern Ireland and Wales. Scottish universities are not automatically included in the survey, although all 15 opted to take part in the latest survey. It is designed, as an element of the quality assurance for higher education, to inform prospective students and their advisers in choosing what and where to study. It gives the views of final-year students on the quality of their courses.

This year we have split the student satisfaction measure in two while keeping the overall contribution of the NSS to the table ranking unchanged. The new "teaching quality" indicator reflects the average scores of the teaching, assessment and feedback, and academic support sections of the NSS, while the "student experience" indicator is drawn from the average of organisation and management, learning resources, and personal development sections and the overall satisfaction question in the survey. We favour teaching quality over student experience and so it accounts for 67 per cent of the overall student satisfaction score, with student experience making up the remaining 33 per cent.

The basic information that applicants need, however, in order to judge universities and their courses does not change. A university's entry standards, staffing levels, completion rates, degree classifications and graduate employment rates are all vital pieces of intelligence for anyone deciding where to study. Research grades, while not directly involving undergraduates, bring with them considerable funds and enable a university to attract top academics.

Any of these measures can be discounted by an individual, but the package has struck a chord with readers. The ranking is the most-quoted of its type both in Britain and overseas, and has built a reputation as the most authoritative arbiter of changing fortunes in higher education. The measures used are kept under review by a group of university administrators and statisticians, which meets annually. The raw data that go into the table in this chapter and the 66 subject tables in chapter 5 are all in the public domain and are sent to universities for checking before any scores are calculated.

Indeed, while the various official bodies concerned with higher education do not publish league tables, several produce system-wide statistics in a format that invites comparisons. The Higher Education Funding Councils' Research Assessment Exercise (now the Research Excellence Framework) was one early example of this. The Higher Education Statistics Agency (HESA), which supplies most of the figures used in our tables, also publishes annual "performance indicators" on everything from completion rates to research output at each university.

Any scrutiny of league table positions is best carried out in conjunction with an examination of the relevant subject table – it is the course, after all, that will dominate your undergraduate years and influence your subsequent career.

How *The Times and Sunday Times* league table works

The table is presented in a format that displays the raw data, wherever possible. In building the table, scores for student satisfaction (combining the teaching quality, student experience scores) and research quality were weighted by 1.5; all other measures were weighted by 1.

For entry standards, student–staff ratio, good honours and graduate prospects, the score was adjusted for subject mix. For example, it is accepted that engineering, law and medicine graduates will tend to have better graduate prospects than their peers from English, psychology and sociology courses. Comparing results in the main subject groupings helps to iron out differences attributable simply to the range of degrees on offer. This subject-mix adjustment means that it is not possible to replicate the scores in the table from the published indicators because the calculation requires access to the entire dataset.

The indicators were combined using a common statistical technique known as Z-scores, to ensure that no indicator has a disproportionate effect on the overall total for each university, and the totals were transformed to a scale with 1,000 for the top score. The Z-score technique makes it impossible to compare universities' total scores from one year to the next, although their relative positions in the table are comparable. Individual scores are dependent on the top performer: a university might drop from 60 per cent of the top score to 58 per cent but still have improved, depending on the relative performance of other universities.

Only where data are not available from HESA are figures sourced directly from universities. Where this is not possible scores are generated according to a university's average performance on other indicators.

The organisations providing the raw data for the tables are not involved in the process of aggregation, so are not responsible for any inferences or conclusions we have made. Every care has been taken to ensure the accuracy of the tables and accompanying information, but no responsibility can be taken for errors or omissions.

The Times and Sunday Times league table uses nine important indicators of university activity, based on the most recent data available at the time of compilation:

- Teaching quality
- Student experience
- Research quality
- Entry standards
- Student–staff ratio
- Services and facilities spend
- Completion
- Good honours
- Graduate prospects

Teaching quality and student experience

This year the student satisfaction measure has been split into two components which give the students' views of the quality of their courses. The National Student Survey (NSS) was the source of this data. Data from the survey published in 2015 were used.

- The National Student Survey covers six aspects of a course, with an additional question gauging overall satisfaction. Students answer on a scale from 1 (bottom) to 5 (top) and the score in the table is the percentage of positive responses (4 and 5) in each section The teaching quality indicator reflects the average scores of the teaching, assessment and feedback, and academic support sections. The student experience indicator is drawn from the average scores of the organisation and management, learning resources, and personal development sections and the additional question on overall satisfaction.
- Teaching quality is favoured over student experience and accounts for 67 per cent of the overall score covering student satisfaction score, with student experience making up the remaining 33 per cent.
- The survey is based on the opinion of final-year students rather than directly assessing teaching quality. Most undergraduates have no experience of other universities, or different courses, to inform their judgements. Although all the questions relate to courses, rather than the broader student experience, some types of university – notably medium-sized campus universities – tend to do better than others.

Research quality

This is a measure of the quality of the research undertaken in each university. The information was sourced from the 2014 Research Excellence Framework (REF), a peer-review exercise used to evaluate the quality of research in UK higher education institutions undertaken by the UK Higher Education funding bodies. Additionally, academic staffing data for 2013–14 from the Higher Education Statistics Agency have been used.

» A research quality profile was given to every university department that took part. This profile used the following categories: 4* world-leading; 3* internationally excellent; 2* internationally recognised; 1* nationally recognised; and unclassified. The Funding Bodies have directed more funds to the very best research by applying weightings, and for the 2015 *Guide* we used the weightings adopted by HEFCE (the funding council for England) for funding in 2013–14: 4* is weighted by a factor of 3 and 3* is weighted by a factor of 1. Outputs of 2* and 1* carry zero weight. This means a maximum score of 3. In the interests of consistency, and to ensure that changes in research scores from RAE to REF are not influenced by changes in weighting, the above weightings continue to be applied this year.
» The scores in the table are presented as a percentage of the maximum score. To achieve the maximum score all staff would need to be at 4* world-leading level.
» Universities could choose which staff to include in the REF, so, to factor in the depth of the research quality, each quality profile score has been multiplied by the number of staff returned in the REF as a proportion of all eligible staff.

Entry standards

This is the average score, using the UCAS tariff (see page 18), of new students under the age of 21 who took A and AS Levels, Scottish Highers and Advanced Highers and other equivalent qualifications (eg, International Baccalaureate). It measures what new students actually achieved rather than the entry requirements suggested by the universities. The data comes from HESA for 2013–14. The original sources of data for this measure are data returns made by the universities themselves to HESA.

» Using the UCAS tariff, each student's examination results were converted to a numerical score. HESA then calculated an average for all students at the university. The results have then been adjusted to take account of the subject mix at the university.
» A score of 360 represents three As at A level. Although all but six of the top 50 universities in the table have entry standards of at least 360, it does not mean that everyone achieved such results – let alone that this was the standard offer. Courses will not demand more than three subjects at A level and offers are pitched accordingly. You will need to reach the entry requirements set by the university, rather than these scores.

Student–staff ratio

This is a measure of the average number of students to each member of the academic staff, apart from those purely engaged in research. In this measure a low value is better than a high value. The data comes from HESA for 2013–14. The original sources of data for this measure are data returns made by the universities themselves to HESA.

» A low value means that there are a small number of students for each academic member of staff, but this does not, of course, ensure good teaching quality or contact time with academics.
» Student–staff ratios vary by subject, for example the ratio is usually low for medicine. In building the table, the score is adjusted for the subject mix taught by each university.

Services and facilities spend

The expenditure per student on staff and student facilities, including library and computing facilities. The data comes from HESA for 2012–13 and 2013–14. The original data sources for this measure are data returns made by the universities to HESA.

- This is a measure calculated by taking the expenditure on student facilities (sports, grants to student societies, careers services, health services, counselling, etc.) and library and computing facilities (books, journals, staff, central computers and computer networks, but not buildings) and dividing this by the number of full-time-equivalent students. Expenditure is averaged over two years to even out the figures (for example, a computer upgrade undertaken in a single year).

Completion

This measure gives the percentage of students expected to complete their studies (or transfer to another institution) for each university. The data comes from the HESA performance indicators, based on data for 2013–14 and earlier years.

- This measure is a projection, liable to statistical fluctuations.

Good honours

This measure is the percentage of graduates achieving a first or upper second class degree. The results have been adjusted to take account of the subject mix at the university. The data comes from HESA for 2013–14. The original sources of data for this measure are data returns made by the universities themselves to HESA.

- Four-year first degrees, such as an MChem, are treated as equivalent to a first or upper second.
- Scottish Ordinary degrees (awarded after three years of study) are excluded.
- Universities control degree classification, with some oversight from external examiners. There have been suggestions that since universities have increased the numbers of good honours degrees they award, this measure may not be as objective as it should be. However, it remains the key measure of a student's success and employability.

Graduate prospects

This measure is the percentage of the total number of graduates undertaking further study or in a professional job. The results have been adjusted for subject mix. The data come from HESA for 2014 graduates.

- HESA surveys graduates six months after graduation to find out what they are doing and the data are based on this survey.

2016 Rank	2015 Rank		Teaching quality (%)	Student experience (%)	Research quality (%)	Entry standards	Student–staff ratio	Services and facilities spend per student (£)	Completion (%)	Good honours (%)	Graduate prospects (%)	Total
1	=1	Cambridge	83.8	86.3	57.3	602	11.3	3,432	98.4	89.3	89.3	1,000
2	=1	Oxford	83.1	86.8	53.1	573	10.6	3,229	96.3	92.1	87.1	974
3	4	Imperial College	79.8	87.8	56.2	568	11.3	2,974	96.5	87.3	91.1	886
4	3	St Andrews	83.2	86.8	40.4	517	11.4	2,572	95.3	89.6	83.3	876
5	6	Durham	81.9	86.7	39.0	523	14.9	2,648	96.6	87.4	84.4	860
6	8	Warwick	79.6	85.0	44.6	482	12.6	2,505	96.7	82.3	79.8	813
7	7	Exeter	82.6	87.7	38.0	463	15.6	2,559	95.7	84.1	79.8	810
8	11	Surrey	86.9	90.3	29.7	424	13.7	2,487	92.2	78.9	78.8	805
9	5	London School of Economics	72.1	78.4	52.8	533	11.4	2,584	94.8	82.1	78.5	802
10	9	University College London	74.2	81.3	51.0	502	10.3	2,608	94.6	87.9	83.1	800
11	12	Lancaster	82.3	85.4	39.1	436	13.7	2,566	93.5	76.9	82.5	799
12	10	Bath	82.7	87.0	37.3	479	16.2	2,023	96.1	84.1	85.2	792
13	13	Loughborough	84.5	89.3	36.3	397	14.7	2,339	93.2	79.8	83.7	791
14	17	Leeds	83.7	88.0	36.8	431	13.6	2,418	93.5	82.2	78.4	779
15	16	York	81.7	86.6	38.3	437	14.7	2,163	94.3	81.6	76.0	756
16	18	Southampton	79.3	86.5	44.9	411	12.0	2,221	92.5	80.4	78.1	755
17	15	Birmingham	80.8	84.2	37.1	426	15.5	2,461	94.8	84.4	86.7	751
18	14	East Anglia	83.2	88.8	35.8	408	13.7	2,378	91.9	78.8	70.3	743
19	25	Sussex	78.6	85.0	31.8	386	15.5	2,618	92.9	78.6	84.1	738
20	19	Bristol	75.5	81.5	47.3	487	13.7	1,976	96.6	86.3	79.6	720
21	21	Sheffield	81.3	87.2	37.6	428	14.9	2,031	94.4	80.4	75.7	718
22	=22	Edinburgh	74.5	82.4	43.8	484	12.2	2,052	91.3	83.0	78.6	716
=23	30	Kent	81.5	85.4	35.2	363	12.9	1,513	90.7	80.0	76.7	713

=23	=22	Newcastle	82.0	88.4	37.7	424	15.6	1,807	95.1	79.2	79.1	713
25	=22	Nottingham	79.5	83.9	37.8	428	14.0	2,055	93.2	79.3	81.3	710
26	26	Glasgow	80.0	86.9	39.9	470	14.7	2,142	88.4	77.8	79.3	704
27	29	King's College London	73.9	79.7	44.0	455	11.3	2,198	92.8	83.2	85.7	699
=28	20	Leicester	77.5	84.4	31.8	386	12.2	2,600	92.5	78.3	72.1	695
=28	28	Manchester	79.0	84.7	39.8	435	13.2	1,926	92.9	75.7	78.5	695
30	=34	Aston	83.3	87.9	25.8	369	15.5	1,997	90.9	75.1	78.8	693
31	38	Queen's, Belfast	81.6	87.3	39.7	385	14.9	1,996	91.0	75.8	78.7	688
32	33	Reading	80.5	85.8	36.5	373	14.1	1,900	92.3	76.2	70.3	687
33	27	Cardiff	80.7	86.0	35.0	426	14.2	1,638	93.4	77.8	80.1	685
34	37	Queen Mary, London	80.5	83.3	37.9	411	12.2	2,347	91.2	75.3	73.3	681
35	32	Essex	83.7	88.0	37.2	313	15.1	2,574	85.6	68.9	64.1	674
36	=34	Royal Holloway	82.6	84.1	36.3	398	15.3	1,665	92.3	75.9	62.7	673
37	45	Dundee	84.4	87.1	31.2	410	13.9	1,545	86.0	76.1	80.0	669
=38	48	Buckingham	88.0	88.4		304	10.5	1,972	86.3	50.7	83.4	663
=38	41	Heriot-Watt	80.8	84.2	36.7	413	16.9	2,120	87.4	72.0	78.1	663
=38	36	Liverpool	77.9	83.4	31.5	404	11.8	2,217	91.3	75.4	76.1	663
=41	46	City	82.7	85.6	21.4	379	16.1	2,368	86.0	73.8	78.9	661
=41	43	Swansea	82.6	86.5	33.7	326	15.3	1,787	89.7	74.4	81.4	661
43	40	Keele	87.0	90.2	22.1	358	13.9	1,273	90.8	68.4	76.1	653
44	31	SOAS, London	75.2	80.8	27.9	407	10.9	2,135	80.7	82.9	68.3	648
45	44	Aberdeen	77.4	83.7	29.9	446	13.4	2,107	84.1	77.1	76.2	640
46	39	Strathclyde	76.2	85.6	37.7	476	19.3	1,872	87.6	77.9	72.0	637
47	42	Coventry	87.6	89.3	3.8	310	14.6	1,732	85.8	67.4	74.2	622
48	n/a	St George's, London	78.7	81.6	22.2	418	12.9	4,034	92.7	70.4	93.4	620
49	63	Harper Adams	82.6	89.3	5.7	331	17.9	2,077	90.6	58.3	73.3	607
50	53	Stirling	78.7	82.3	30.5	375	15.0	1,665	85.7	67.9	73.3	596
51	n/a	Royal Agricultural University	79.3	85.6	1.1	307	20.9	2,887	96.3	62.6	69.7	592
52	50	Bangor	85.8	87.8	27.2	321	16.5	1,387	81.8	64.1	67.7	589

2016 Rank	2015 Rank		Teaching quality (%)	Student experience (%)	Research quality (%)	Entry standards	Student–staff ratio	Services and facilities spend per student (£)	Completion (%)	Good honours (%)	Graduate prospects (%)	Total
53	54	De Montfort	82.4	84.6	8.9	307	18.7	1,924	86.5	70.9	76.9	584
54	52	Nottingham Trent	83.6	85.8	6.5	310	17.0	1,812	89.6	69.2	67.6	582
55	49	Oxford Brookes	83.2	85.7	11.4	348	17.6	1,429	89.4	71.1	69.2	576
56	51	Falmouth	83.7	83.5	4.6	309	21.5	1,755	85.4	72.0	74.5	573
57	69	Ulster	82.9	87.0	31.8	306	16.2	1,710	82.3	66.5	63.6	572
58	70	Bath Spa	85.8	85.8	7.9	318	19.0	1,517	89.9	74.5	55.1	571
59	57	Portsmouth	83.4	85.9	8.6	310	16.5	1,617	87.6	72.7	66.9	569
60	47	Brunel	78.2	83.8	25.4	352	16.4	1,904	87.7	68.8	63.4	568
61	n/a	Norwich University of the Arts	83.8	83.5	5.6	357	17.8	1,236	88.7	70.5	63.4	564
=62	74	University for the Creative Arts	82.7	81.5	3.4	332	11.7	2,122	85.8	60.4	52.0	563
=62	60	Lincoln	81.1	84.6	10.3	335	18.0	1,665	87.6	65.0	70.7	563
=64	66	Northumbria	82.9	85.1	9.0	363	17.8	1,484	87.6	67.6	66.3	556
=64	61	Winchester	84.2	85.0	5.8	307	16.9	1,226	85.2	75.5	60.7	556
66	55	Goldsmiths, London	76.6	76.3	33.4	360	14.8	1,319	82.4	81.4	56.0	550
67	58	Hull	80.0	83.8	16.7	332	17.3	1,698	86.0	71.2	66.7	542
68	72	Edge Hill	83.2	83.5	4.9	319	15.7	1,809	86.2	65.8	63.8	539
=69	65	Chichester	84.0	85.3	6.4	310	17.4	1,194	89.9	69.3	57.5	534
=69	=77	Huddersfield	82.2	84.0	9.4	333	17.8	1,551	83.0	64.1	74.1	534
=69	64	Robert Gordon	80.6	83.5	4.0	385	19.4	1,335	83.4	67.0	83.1	534
72	62	Sheffield Hallam	80.9	83.9	5.4	319	17.1	1,932	86.9	65.7	64.7	529
73	68	West of England	80.0	82.5	8.8	324	19.5	1,931	84.9	71.4	70.8	527
74	71	Liverpool John Moores	81.6	85.0	8.9	344	18.4	1,332	84.2	74.9	63.3	525
75	76	Bradford	78.8	84.4	9.2	314	17.8	1,731	83.8	74.0	75.2	523

76	79	Hertfordshire	78.6	82.8	5.6	318	17.7	1,964	86.0	67.0	75.3	522
77	89	Manchester Metropolitan	81.0	82.2	7.5	347	17.7	1,516	84.4	69.8	63.0	520
78	73	Roehampton	78.0	79.9	24.5	286	16.8	2,207	81.7	67.2	60.9	519
=79	93	Aberystwyth	78.4	80.4	28.1	312	17.8	1,386	89.3	65.1	62.5	517
=79	n/a	Liverpool Hope	86.8	86.4	9.2	304	19.4	1,667	82.8	63.4	53.9	517
81	59	Arts University Bournemouth	81.4	80.0	2.4	322	15.3	684	92.3	66.2	61.4	514
=82	88	Bournemouth	75.2	78.8	9.0	329	17.4	1,831	86.0	75.5	66.4	513
=82	56	Northampton	82.3	84.1	3.2	283	20.3	2,387	85.0	64.5	60.7	513
84	81	Derby	84.4	85.3	2.5	290	15.4	1,540	83.7	62.7	60.0	512
=85	75	Middlesex	78.7	81.8	9.7	270	18.5	2,967	77.8	61.3	64.9	500
=85	80	Plymouth	82.3	84.1	15.9	312	17.5	1,424	84.8	67.0	60.2	500
87	67	Chester	82.7	83.7	4.1	299	16.4	1,714	80.5	63.4	63.6	497
88	83	Gloucestershire	79.8	82.6	3.8	317	19.7	1,720	86.3	72.4	55.7	496
89	87	York St John	82.4	83.0	4.1	292	20.6	1,284	90.4	65.4	65.3	494
90	82	Brighton	78.6	80.9	7.9	321	17.1	1,357	86.9	68.2	66.9	491
91	=91	Leeds Trinity	83.5	82.3	2.0	284	21.7	1,470	81.7	68.9	65.8	487
92	=77	Central Lancashire	80.4	83.5	5.6	315	17.1	2,052	81.6	60.0	62.4	481
93	97	Edinburgh Napier	80.2	83.7	4.6	347	20.3	1,155	81.2	71.4	69.1	478
94	84	Glasgow Caledonian	77.0	82.5	7.0	372	21.2	1,545	83.2	70.1	70.2	477
95	101	Staffordshire	81.8	82.8	16.5	274	16.8	1,620	78.4	63.2	58.4	475
96	86	Queen Margaret, Edinburgh	78.9	82.3	6.6	341	19.1	1,336	82.4	74.2	59.6	474
97	106	Abertay	80.0	83.1	5.1	338	21.4	1,563	75.5	70.4	65.6	466
98	105	Salford	80.1	80.9	8.3	334	17.0	1,646	79.5	65.2	59.5	465
99	85	University of the Arts London	75.9	74.5	8.0	320	15.1	1,711	85.5	61.8	59.2	464
=100	100	St Mary's, Twickenham	80.5	84.8	4.0	289	20.6	1,069	83.7	63.8	66.7	463
=100	107	Worcester	81.4	84.5	4.3	301	19.0	1,062	85.8	61.9	63.9	463
102	94	Teesside	82.9	84.3	3.6	306	17.7	1,676	80.8	59.3	59.8	456
103	90	Cardiff Metropolitan	79.1	81.8	3.9	317	19.0	1,712	82.2	60.6	59.8	454
104	99	Sunderland	82.5	84.2	5.8	294	19.6	1,484	81.4	49.5	62.3	446

2016 Rank	2015 Rank		Teaching quality (%)	Student experience (%)	Research quality (%)	Entry standards	Student–staff ratio	Services and facilities spend per student (£)	Completion (%)	Good honours (%)	Graduate prospects (%)	Total
105	=91	Birmingham City	78.0	79.3	4.3	300	20.4	1,693	84.4	67.3	64.8	444
106	98	Greenwich	79.2	82.4	4.9	315	19.6	1,479	84.7	62.9	58.2	443
107	96	Canterbury Christ Church	80.7	81.9	4.5	279	18.4	1,212	82.3	66.5	57.8	438
108	110	Anglia Ruskin	82.5	83.9	5.4	254	19.0	1,419	79.3	58.4	65.0	428
109	116	Buckinghamshire New	81.5	81.1	1.5	257	21.8	1,997	82.5	57.0	57.6	421
110	108	Bedfordshire	80.4	82.7	7.0	229	18.3	1,721	80.1	56.6	58.3	419
111	117	Kingston	76.1	79.9	5.1	299	19.3	1,637	82.2	67.4	60.7	418
=112	=102	Bishop Grosseteste	80.9	80.6	2.1	284	28.6	743	90.0	60.4	69.1	412
=112	114	South Wales	77.5	78.3	4.0	322	19.6	1,425	81.7	63.6	59.0	412
114	111	Leeds Beckett	78.5	82.7	4.1	288	20.7	1,341	78.8	61.8	58.5	408
=115	104	Newman	83.1	84.6	2.8	293	18.9	1,458	73.3	56.0	54.6	401
=115	115	Southampton Solent	79.5	82.1	0.5	276	18.3	1,480	76.8	60.2	54.6	401
=115	112	Westminster	72.9	80.6	9.8	311	19.9	1,491	80.4	68.8	55.1	401
118	118	West of Scotland	81.8	81.8	4.3	305	21.1	1,291	70.0	63.2	65.7	395
119	95	Cumbria	76.9	77.6	1.2	299	22.3	1,093	85.7	64.7	64.9	392
120	122	London South Bank	77.0	81.3	9.0	248	17.2	1,523	74.6	61.0	67.9	386
121	109	West London	76.9	77.5	1.6	259	17.3	2,214	73.9	58.8	60.5	385
122	113	Glyndŵr	80.5	79.3	2.3	257	23.3	1,757	75.8	53.6	66.3	374
=123	120	Bolton	81.6	80.8	2.9	287	17.9	959	71.2	54.9	60.1	370
=123	=102	St Mark and St John	76.3	77.3		319	21.2	1,250	82.6	58.8	60.4	370
125	123	London Metropolitan	76.0	78.6	3.5	239	19.6	1,000	75.3	55.1	47.7	287
126	121	Highlands and Islands	78.8	76.5		272		558	68.6	57.9	56.0	276
127	119	East London	75.0	78.5	7.2	281	23.6	1,636	67.5	53.9	45.6	269

Notes on the Table

Institutions new to the main table this year are Norwich University of the Arts, Royal Agricultural University and St George's, London.

Liverpool Hope reappear this year after previously requesting their data to be suppressed from the table.

University College Birmingham, Trinity Saint David, University of Wales, and Wolverhampton have refused the release of data, so do not appear in this year's league table.

The following universities provided corrected data as follows:
Central Lancashire, Exeter, Northumbria, Royal Veterinary College and Manchester Metropolitan provided replacement services and facilities spend per student data;
Central Lancashire, Exeter and St George's, London provided replacement student–staff ratio data;
Durham and University of South Wales provided replacement graduate prospects data;
Durham, Leeds Beckett, Queen's, Belfast and University of West of England provided replacement entry standards data.

5 The Top Universities by Subject

The rankings of whole institutions capture all the headlines when university guides appear, but recent surveys suggest that subject tables are becoming increasingly influential. Knowing where a university stands in the pecking order of higher education is a vital piece of information for any prospective student, but the quality of the course is what matters most – particularly in the short term. Your chosen course, rather than the character of the whole university, will determine what you get out of taking a degree and may have a big bearing on your employment prospects. As the 2014 Research Excellence Framework confirmed, the most modest institution may have a centre of specialist excellence, and even famous universities have mediocre departments. This chapter offers some pointers to the leading universities in a wide range of subjects. With a number of universities reviewing the courses they will offer in the future, it is possible that not all institutions listed in a particular subject area will be running courses in 2016.

The subject tables in this *Guide* include scores from the National Student Survey (NSS). These distil the views of final-year undergraduates on various aspects of their course, and this year the results are presented in two columns. The teaching quality indicator reflects the average scores of the teaching, assessment and feedback, and academic support sections of the survey. The student experience indicator is drawn from the average of the organisation and management, learning resources, and personal development sections and the overall satisfaction question. The three other measures used are research quality, students' entry qualifications and graduate employment prospects. None of the measures is weighted. A full explanation of the measures is given on the next page.

Many subjects, such as dentistry or sociology, have their own table, but others are grouped together in broader categories, such as "other subjects allied to medicine". The specialisms of animal science and creative writing are now in separate subject tables. Scores are not published where the number of students is too small for the outcome to be statistically reliable. In the NSS, a 50 per cent response rate is required from a minimum of 10 students. If there is no student satisfaction score, then to qualify for inclusion in the table a university has to have data for at least two of the other measures.

Cambridge is again the most successful university. It tops 35 of the 66 tables. Oxford has the next highest number of top places with 8, followed by Birmingham and Glasgow with 3, while 18 other universities also gain top spots. The subject rankings demonstrate that there are "horses for courses" in higher education. For a summary of top universities by subject, see page 200.

Research quality

This is a measure of the quality of the research undertaken in the subject area. The information was sourced from the 2014 Research Excellence Framework (REF), a peer-review exercise used to evaluate the quality of research in UK higher education institutions, undertaken by the UK Higher Education Funding Bodies. The approach mirrors that in the main table, with the REF results weighted and then multiplied by the percentage of eligible staff entered for assessment.

For each subject, a research quality profile was given to those university departments that took part, showing how much of their research was in various quality categories. These categories were: 4* world-leading; 3* internationally excellent; 2* internationally recognised; 1* nationally recognised; and unclassified. The Funding Bodies have directed more funds to the very best research by applying weightings, and for the 2015 *Guide* we used the weightings adopted by HEFCE (the funding council for England) for funding in 2013–14: 4* is weighted by a factor of 3 and 3* is weighted by a factor of 1. Outputs of 2* and 1* carry zero weight. This results in a maximum score of 3. In the interests of consistency and to ensure that changes in research scores from RAE to REF are not influenced by changes in weighting, the above weightings continue to be applied this year.

The scores in the table are presented as a percentage of the maximum score. To achieve the maximum score all staff would need to be at 4* world-leading level.

Universities could choose which staff to include in the REF, so, to factor in the depth of the research quality, each quality profile score has been multiplied by the number of staff returned in the REF as a proportion of all eligible staff.

Entry standards

This is the average UCAS tariff score for new students under the age of 21, based on A and AS Levels and Scottish Highers and Advanced Highers and other equivalent qualifications (including the International Baccalaureate), taken from HESA data for 2013–14. Each student's examination grades were converted to a numerical score using the UCAS tariff (see page 18 for details) and added up to give a total score. HESA then calculated an average score for each university.

Teaching quality and student experience

This year we have split the student satisfaction measure into two components which give the students' views of the quality of their courses. These indicators are taken from the National Student Survey (NSS) results published in 2014 and 2015. A single year's figures are used when that is all that is available, but an average of the two years' results is used in all other cases. The NSS covers six aspects of a course, with an additional question gauging overall satisfaction. Students answer on a scale from 1 (bottom) to 5 (top) and the scores in the table is calculated from the percentage of positive responses (4 and 5) in each section. The teaching quality indicator reflects the average scores of the teaching, assessment and feedback, and academic support sections. The student experience indicator is drawn from the average scores of the organisation and management, learning resources, and personal development sections and the additional question on overall satisfaction. Teaching quality is favoured over student experience and accounts for 67 per cent of the overall student satisfaction score, with student experience making up the remaining 33 per cent.

Graduate prospects

This is the percentage of graduates undertaking further study or in a professional job ("positive destinations"), in the annual survey by HESA six months after graduation. Two years of data (2013 and 2014 graduates) are aggregated to make the data more reliable. A low score on this measure does not necessarily indicate unemployment – some graduates may have taken jobs that are not categorised as professional work. The averages for each subject are given close by the relevant subject table in this chapter and in two tables in chapter 2 (see pages 38–41).

The Education table uses a fifth measure: Ofsted, a measure of the quality of teaching based on the outcomes of Ofsted inspections of teacher training courses.

Note that in the tables that follow, when a figure is followed by *, it refers to data taken from the 2015 *Guide* as no data were available for this year.

The subjects listed below are covered in the tables in this chapter:

Accounting and Finance
Aeronautical and Manufacturing Engineering
Agriculture and Forestry
American Studies
Anatomy and Physiology
Animal Science
Anthropology
Archaeology
Architecture
Art and Design
Biological Sciences
Building
Business Studies
Celtic Studies
Chemical Engineering
Chemistry
Civil Engineering
Classics and Ancient History
Communication and Media Studies
Computer Science
Creative Writing
Dentistry
Drama, Dance and Cinematics
East and South Asian Studies
Economics
Education
Electrical and Electronic Engineering
English
Food Science
French
General Engineering
Geography and Environmental Sciences
Geology
German
History
History of Art, Architecture and Design
Hospitality, Leisure, Recreation and Tourism
Iberian Languages
Italian
Land and Property Management
Law
Librarianship and Information Management
Linguistics
Materials Technology
Mathematics
Mechanical Engineering
Medicine
Middle Eastern and African Studies
Music
Nursing
Other Subjects Allied to Medicine (see page 168 for included subjects)
Pharmacology and Pharmacy
Philosophy
Physics and Astronomy
Physiotherapy
Politics
Psychology
Radiography
Russian and East European Languages
Social Policy
Social Work
Sociology
Sports Science
Theology and Religious Studies
Town and Country Planning and Landscape
Veterinary Medicine

Accounting and Finance

Employment rates in accounting and finance have improved since the last *Guide*, but the subjects still come a surprisingly long way down that table – just in the top 40 subjects. Those who do find graduate jobs are relatively well paid, however. At an average of almost £22,357 in 2014, they were close to the top 20. Finance degrees have been faring better than the larger accounting group in terms of both applications and acceptances: there was 10 per cent growth in the demand for finance in 2014, when the number of places grew accordingly.

Leeds has shot to the top of the table for the first time, improving all its scores to move up from tenth place. Surrey recorded the best score in the new teaching quality category, taken from the National Student Survey (NSS), a fraction of a point ahead of equal 38th-placed Edinburgh Napier, who did manage the best score on the student experience questions in the NSS. The highest employment score is at Bristol, in 16th place, while the London School of Economics (LSE), although surprisingly not in the top ten overall, was the unquestioned leader in the research quality.

Strathclyde retains second place, thanks partly to the highest entry score in the table. The generous points awarded to Scottish qualifications in the UCAS tariff keep it ahead of the LSE on this measure. Robert Gordon was the top performing post-1992 university, and the only one in the top 20, although it has fallen four places over last year. The new table shows growing variation in graduates' employment prospects. While four universities, rather than last year's one, registered positive destinations (graduate-level jobs or further study) for more than 90 per cent of graduates, seven universities, compared with four last year, slipped below 40 per cent on this measure. One student in five takes a further qualification, but relatively few (7 per cent) do so full-time.

Some of the leading universities demand maths A level and all welcome it, but with 97 universities qualifying for the table, six more than last year, there is considerable variation in entry standards. More than 140 institutions expect to offer accounting, either alone or in combination, in 2016.

Accounting and Finance	Research quality %	Entry standards	Teaching quality %	Student experience %	Graduate prospects %	Overall score
1 Leeds	39.3	464	89.6	92.6	81.5	100.0
2 Strathclyde	44.3	516	80.0	89.3	82.7	99.7
3 Queen's, Belfast	32.7	415	88.0	94.5	90.6	98.8
4 Lancaster	42.6	419	88.2	90.3	82.5	98.7
5 Bath	41.8	490	79.5	89.4	82.0	98.3
6 Warwick	40.4	493	74.7	87.9	84.3	97.2
7 Loughborough	32.6	407	83.5	91.5	90.3	97.0
8 Queen Mary, London	31.3	403	87.0	89.0	80.5	95.7
9 Reading	29.3	394	86.7	90.8	82.5	95.6
=10 Exeter	24.4	469	80.6	87.5	85.9	95.5
=10 Glasgow	22.1	507	80.4	87.8	80.9	95.5
12 London School of Economics	52.3	513	67.1	76.9	75.0	95.0
=13 Surrey	15.8	416	92.3	93.3	71.1	94.1
=13 City	27.8	443	82.8	88.5	72.8	94.1

Accounting and Finance cont

	Research quality %	Entry standards	Teaching quality %	Student experience %	Graduate prospects %	Overall score
15 Ulster	40.4	318	87.9	91.8	70.3	94.0
16 Bristol	32.1	459	69.9	80.9	91.6	93.9
17 Newcastle	20.7	433	80.9	87.4	82.3	93.5
18 Robert Gordon	2.6	405	88.1	90.6	90.2	93.1
19 Nottingham	32.6	393	80.6	87.4	73.7	92.9
=20 Aston	19.7	401	83.3	87.1	77.1	92.2
=20 Cardiff	32.0	410	78.4	84.7	72.3	92.2
=22 Swansea	22.0	302	86.0	91.8	82.9	91.9
=22 Manchester	33.3	427	77.3	86.4	65.5	91.9
24 Sheffield	26.8	368	81.2	86.8	75.4	91.7
=25 Durham	23.1	426	78.0	83.9	75.3	91.5
=25 Birmingham	29.1	400	75.2	84.3	78.0	91.5
=25 Kent	24.8	372	79.7	85.2	80.0	91.5
=28 Edinburgh	25.8	455	69.9	81.8	80.6	91.3
=28 East Anglia	28.1	379	82.8	89.0	64.8	91.3
=30 Dundee	12.1	394	85.3	86.8	77.1	91.2
=30 Aberdeen	24.9	416	74.3	85.4	78.2	91.2
32 Heriot-Watt	18.8	403	78.3	85.8	79.1	91.0
33 Southampton	24.0	384	77.0	86.7	76.8	90.8
34 Liverpool	20.1	393	83.7	85.8	65.5	90.3
35 De Montfort	10.7	295	90.7	91.3	75.9	90.0
36 Stirling	25.2	410	74.1	79.7	75.8	89.9
37 Essex	25.1	317	83.5	88.5	66.7	89.4
=38 Sussex	23.7	384	70.2	79.8	82.4	89.0
=38 Edinburgh Napier	2.3	346	92.1	94.9	62.9	89.0
40 Bangor	23.4	278	87.6	90.0	63.0	88.7
41 Liverpool John Moores		321	88.2	92.4	74.3	88.3
42 Leicester	24.3	390	78.8	76.8		88.1
43 Lincoln	4.8	297	88.5	90.1	73.2	88.0
44 Huddersfield	4.1	316	83.9	90.0	73.2	87.3
45 Portsmouth	9.5	306	81.0	86.7	76.3	87.2
46 Plymouth	13.1	275	89.9	89.9	55.6	86.5
47 Chester	0.5	277	88.0	90.3	71.2	86.4
=48 Hull	10.2	334	83.1	86.3	61.0	86.3
=48 Brunel	23.0	329	75.1	84.6	62.2	86.3
=48 Northumbria	4.0	356	83.0	85.8	64.3	86.3
51 Salford	5.9	288	91.1	93.5	50.4	85.7
52 Central Lancashire	4.4	308	90.0	92.6	50.1	85.6
=53 Oxford Brookes	5.1	326	81.8	89.3	61.5	85.5
=53 Glasgow Caledonian	1.8	365	80.9	88.4	59.8	85.5
55 Middlesex	10.5	249	86.5	90.1	59.8	85.2
56 West of Scotland	2.9	331	86.5	88.8	53.5	85.1
57 South Wales	0.2	302	81.0	83.9	74.1	84.9

=58 Gloucestershire		306	85.1	84.8	63.1	84.5
=58 Bradford	11.8	324	79.9	85.4	54.5	84.5
=60 Coventry	1.6	293	81.6	86.7	67.0	84.4
=60 Nottingham Trent	4.6	301	80.6	84.9	66.0	84.4
=62 West of England	5.5	302	80.6	82.7	65.8	84.3
=62 Manchester Metropolitan	4.7	316	84.6	87.7	53.0	84.3
=62 Buckingham		290	82.8	85.0	68.4	84.3
65 Keele	10.2	323	77.3	85.3	57.6	84.0
66 Greenwich	3.3	316	85.0	89.4	47.3	83.6
67 Sunderland	0.4	282	84.8	87.2	59.1	83.5
68 Edge Hill		234	90.7	89.3	56.4	83.4
=69 Bolton		241*	90.3	93.1	50.0	83.2
=69 York St John	0.8	242*	75.8	82.4	83.3	83.2
71 Aberystwyth	14.5	293	78.1	79.5	55.6	82.9
72 Worcester	0.9	265	81.8	85.8	62.5	82.7
73 Hertfordshire	0.9	308	75.5	84.6	64.8	82.6
74 Kingston	9.2	299	80.8	87.8	44.7	82.5
75 Cardiff Metropolitan		287	86.7	87.3	47.4	82.4
=76 Derby	0.9	274	84.7	86.4	52.7	82.3
=76 Sheffield Hallam	0.6	307	79.0	87.7	54.3	82.3
78 Staffordshire	2.6	234	90.0	90.6	43.5	82.0
79 Winchester		283	82.8	82.4	55.0	81.8
80 Bournemouth	8.8	318	71.4	78.7	59.8	81.6
81 Canterbury Christ Church		241	84.6	91.7	48.4	81.4
82 London South Bank	2.1	230	88.8	92.4	36.7	80.8
83 Birmingham City	1.3	249	81.3	87.1	48.8	80.4
=84 Leeds Beckett	0.8	240	80.4	87.0	48.9	79.9
=84 Brighton	6.5	298	72.8	79.8	51.0	79.9
=86 Northampton	1.0	236	77.0	85.6	52.7	79.4
=86 Glyndŵr		264	74.1	74.7	64.3	79.4
88 Westminster	2.4	326	66.5	80.5	55.1	79.3
89 Anglia Ruskin	3.4	229	76.8	80.7	48.8	78.2
90 Chichester		228	75.6	81.3	52.9	78.1
91 East London	0.8	236	84.8	87.1	28.5	77.9
92 London Metropolitan	0.6	209	79.3	85.5	37.3	76.8
93 West London		218	71.2	78.5	43.4	75.0
94 Bedfordshire	3.1	215	68.8	80.3	39.4	74.5
95 Buckinghamshire New	1.8	225	69.7	75.8	39.4	74.1
96 Southampton Solent		229	69.2	75.1	37.9	73.5
97 Liverpool Hope		284	73.7	64.4	24.0	72.5

Employed in professional job:	44%	Employed in non-professional job and studying:	2%
Employed in professional job and studying:	11%	Employed in non-professional job:	24%
Studying:	7%	Unemployed:	12%
Average starting professional salary:	£22,357	Average starting non-professional salary:	£17,415

Aeronautical and Manufacturing Engineering

More so than in many subjects, apprenticeships at leading firms like Rolls-Royce provide an attractive alternative to a degree in aeronautical or manufacturing engineering, but both applications and enrolments were up in 2014. Prospective applicants will see a £370 decrease in graduate-level salaries over 2013, but the subject still maintains its place in the top ten of the 66 subject groups. Even those who had to settle for non-graduate jobs earned almost £17,500, one of the highest salaries in any subject. However, the subjects remain outside the top 20 for the proportion of engineers going straight into graduate-level jobs or further study, and unemployment is still above average, at 13 per cent.

Most of the courses in this ranking focus on aeronautical or manufacturing engineering, but it includes some with a mechanical title. To add to the confusion, manufacturing degrees often go under the rubric of production engineering. Cambridge has maintained a comfortable lead, registering by far the best scores for research, entry standards and graduate prospects. Leeds, in sixth place, again has the most satisfied students, achieving the best scores both for teaching quality and student experience. Imperial remains in second place, while Swansea has made the most progress, moving up 11 places to enter the top ten.

Many universities demand maths and physics at A Level, and give extra credit for further maths, computing and/or design technology. Entry grades are high at the leading universities, with Cambridge averaging more than 640 points and Imperial College, Bristol and Bath more than 520. Only one university averages less than 250 points. Two post-1992 universities, Teesside and Coventry, feature in this year's top 20.

Almost 60 per cent of the 2014 graduates went straight into high-level work, and there was less variation between institutions than in many subjects. Although Cambridge saw almost 97 per cent of its graduates go straight into graduate jobs or further study and Plymouth only 48 per cent, good scores were distributed throughout the table, with over four-fifths of the universities in the table seeing over 60 per cent of graduates go into professional jobs or take up further study.

Aeronautical and Manufacturing Engineering	Research quality %	Entry standards	Teaching quality %	Student experience %	Graduate prospects %	Overall score
1 Cambridge	67.0	642	86.0	91.3	96.6	100.0
2 Imperial College	59.6	581	81.2	90.7	87.7	94.7
3 Bath	37.4	521	90.8	95.1	90.4	93.4
4 Bristol	52.3	540	79.8	88.8	92.2	93.1
5 Southampton	52.3	489	76.6	86.8	92.1	90.9
6 Leeds	40.9	422	91.8	96.3	78.8	89.6
7 Swansea	45.5	368	80.8	87.8	90.7	87.7
8 Surrey	30.8	465	83.1	89.9	80.9	87.1
9 Loughborough	41.8	407	75.8	89.2	89.0	86.9
10 Nottingham	40.8	427	78.1	85.9	84.7	86.6
11 Queen's, Belfast	36.7	386	85.2	91.4	66.7	83.8
12 Glasgow	47.2	484	63.9	74.8	80.5	83.7
13 Strathclyde	37.2	469	70.3	83.0	71.4	82.7
14 Sheffield	36.0	417	66.3	75.8	86.8	82.4

15 Liverpool	32.1	394	76.6	81.8	74.1	81.8
16 Ulster		331	87.1	92.4	80.0	80.6
=17 Manchester	35.1	445	69.8	76.3	69.5	80.5
=17 Teesside	5.8	342	84.1	91.3		80.5
19 Queen Mary, London	46.7	365	72.1	79.4	64.8	80.1
20 Coventry	10.3	310	84.6	85.3	75.0	79.2
21 Brunel	23.7	372	75.4	84.2	65.7	78.6
22 Aston	20.6	338	68.3	77.6	83.3	78.4
23 City	20.2	309	84.0	90.6	60.6	78.2
24 West of Scotland	9.0	299	85.1	90.0	66.7	77.8
25 Sussex		368	73.9	77.8	78.3	76.7
=26 Manchester Metropolitan	16.3	323	82.2	85.3	52.8	75.6
=26 Staffordshire	5.7	251	81.0	80.4	74.1	75.6
28 Portsmouth	9.1	284	78.9	83.7	66.7	75.4
29 West of England	10.6	326	69.7	77.8	73.3	75.2
30 Hertfordshire	16.5	299	67.9	74.8	74.3	74.8
31 Salford	4.4	307	68.0	81.0	77.3	74.7
32 Sheffield Hallam		281	80.6	84.6	61.2	73.6
33 South Wales		286	76.1	68.3	68.1	72.1
34 Plymouth		253	86.2	88.0	48.0	72.0
35 Brighton	7.4	344	66.7	82.8	52.2	71.2
36 Buckinghamshire New		224	74.4	72.8	58.8	69.0
37 Kingston	2.9	305	68.7	73.0	51.0	68.7

Employed in professional job:	57%	Employed in non-professional job and studying:	1%
Employed in professional job and studying:	2%	Employed in non-professional job:	14%
Studying:	14%	Unemployed:	13%
Average starting professional salary:	£24,969	Average starting non-professional salary:	£17,495

Agriculture and Forestry

The separation of animal sciences from agriculture and forestry produced some big changes in last year's agriculture table and the new methods of calculating research and student satisfaction scores have done the same in this edition. Newcastle has dropped from first to fifth, partly because its scores for satisfaction with teaching and feedback were among the lowest in the table. Reading has taken over at the top after registering the best of an extremely variable set of employment scores. Its positive destinations of more than 80 per cent contrasted with success rates of less than 30 per cent at the bottom of the table.

Both applications and enrolments reached record levels in 2014, when there was a 10 per cent increase in the demand for places to study agriculture. But with fewer than four applicants to the place (and less than that in forestry and arboriculture), entry standards remain low. This is the only table in the *Guide* in which no university averages more than 400 points at A level, although only three universities average less than 300 points.

Satisfaction rates are high, with only Lincoln dropping below 70 per cent for teaching quality or student experience. Nottingham Trent registered the best teaching score and would have finished higher than 11th if it had entered the Research Excellence Framework in

Agriculture and Forestry cont

this subject. The top research score was at Queen's, Belfast, which also topped the table for the student experience. Two of the 17 institutions in the table are specialist universities: the Royal Agricultural University and Harper Adams, which is the highest-placed of seven post-1992 universities in the ranking.

Glasgow is Scotland's only representative, but Scotland's Rural College, one of several institutions with too little data to qualify for this table, is now the only place to take a full degree in agriculture north of the border. Aberdeen offers forestry and plant and soil science, while Highlands and Islands provides a number of forestry courses, including sustainable forest management. Overall, the subjects are not in the top 50 for employment, but they do rather better in the salary table, taking 40th place out of 66 subject groupings. The unemployment rate of 14 per cent was one of the highest, but those who found graduate jobs were paid an average of £20,285.

Agriculture and Forestry	Research quality %	Entry standards	Teaching quality %	Student experience %	Graduate prospects %	Overall score
1 Reading	50.7	379	83.6	91.3	81.4	100.0
2 Queen's, Belfast	56.3	365	75.9	93.8	72.7	97.3
3 Nottingham	36.4	385	83.1	85.7	62.5	95.0
4 Glasgow	42.3	347	88.4	79.1		93.7
5 Newcastle	28.4	363	74.6	81.9	80.5	92.5
6 Aberystwyth	38.2	343	87.7	89.3	47.0	91.5
7 Bangor	29.7	297	92.7	90.6	57.3	89.6
=8 Kent		391	79.4	87.2	64.3	89.4
=8 Harper Adams	5.7	331	83.9	91.5	77.9	89.4
10 Lincoln	31.1		63.7	63.0	76.7	84.5
11 Nottingham Trent		294	94.8	92.0	50.0	84.4
12 Royal Agricultural University	2.1	311	76.8	84.8	56.4	82.2
13 Greenwich	19.5	323			36.7	82.1
14 Plymouth	17.4		82.3	85.5	28.6	82.0
15 Cumbria		284	80.1	80.3	29.1	76.5

Employed in professional job:	41%	Employed in non-professional job and studying:	2%
Employed in professional job and studying:	5%	Employed in non-professional job:	30%
Studying:	7%	Unemployed:	14%
Average starting professional salary:	£20,285	Average starting non-professional salary:	£16,438

American Studies

American Studies had been a fixture in the bottom ten of the employment and salary tables for as long as they have been published – but not this year. A £1,400 rise in average salaries has taken the subject to the verge of the top 50 for graduate earnings and it is nearly out of the bottom 20 for employment levels. With only 420 students starting degrees in American studies in 2014, numbers are sufficiently small to be more volatile than in most other subjects, but the progress is still welcome. The good news is yet to reach most applicants, however: the demand for places dropped for the third year in a row in 2014.

The most striking feature of the new table is the decline of Warwick, which topped the ranking for almost a decade but has dropped from second last year to 12th this year. It achieved the best results in the Research Excellence Framework, but satisfaction levels for teaching quality and the broader student experience are among the lowest in the table. Sussex has taken over at the top after registering the best employment score. Birmingham is only a fraction of a point behind, while last year's leader, Manchester, has slipped to fifth place despite having the highest entry standards.

Entry scores remain modest overall: Manchester is the only university to average more than 400 points, while five of the 17 universities with enough students to compile reliable scores average less than 300 points. But student satisfaction is generally high: Hull, with the most satisfied students last year, has the best record on the teaching quality indicators, while Dundee scored an impressive 97 per cent on the other measures in the National Student Survey.

More than 50 universities and colleges expect to offer American studies in some form in 2016. Some focus on Latin America, whereas most concentrate on the culture and politics of the USA and Canada. A growing number of courses offer the opportunity of a year at an American or Canadian university as part of a four-year degree. The leading universities are likely to expect English or history at A level or the equivalent.

American Studies	Research quality %	Entry standards	Teaching quality %	Student experience %	Graduate prospects %	Overall score
1 Sussex	45.6	394	83.1	84.2	75.2	100.0
2 Birmingham	48.8	380	83.6	85.9	72.5	99.7
3 Nottingham	39.9	378	86.3	87.1	66.6	97.2
4 Kent	47.3	344	83.1	82.5	69.0	96.5
5 Manchester	49.1	411	73.1	82.8	57.3	94.7
6 East Anglia	33.1	394	80.8	90.2	59.4	93.8
7 Leicester	34.3	354	84.5	84.8	56.0	91.9
8 Keele	29.8	341	88.5	88.8	56.1	91.8
9 Goldsmiths, London	34.9	332	88.6	85.8	52.3	91.3
10 Hull	26.1	319	91.0	90.7	57.3	91.1
11 Portsmouth	32.2	280	85.6	83.8	65.5	90.5
12 Warwick	51.7		69.8	65.8	69.4	90.4
13 Dundee	30.4		88.4	97.3	48.5	90.3
14 Swansea	18.5	315	76.8	83.0	72.7	88.6
15 Essex		303	88.1	85.6	58.8	84.1
16 Liverpool	33.4		68.9	59.1	63.3	83.3
17 York St John		259	85.9	78.9	66.7	82.7
18 Canterbury Christ Church	16.3	243	89.9	82.9	43.0	81.3
19 Derby	13.5	251	84.4	86.4	39.7	79.3
20 Winchester		278	86.6	88.2	42.9	79.2

American Studies cont

Employed in professional job:	38%	Employed in non-professional job and studying:	4%
Employed in professional job and studying:	4%	Employed in non-professional job:	28%
Studying:	16%	Unemployed:	10%
Average starting professional salary:	£19,410	Average starting non-professional salary:	£15,280

Anatomy and Physiology

This table covers a broad range of courses, including the biomedical science degrees that have been growing in popularity over recent years. Very few actually have the title of anatomy or physiology, but they include degrees in cell biology, neurosciences and pathology. The subjects are a popular choice, with eight applications for every place. The 34,000 applications in 2014 represented the sixth successive increase and there was a 6 per cent increase in the number of new enrolments. In some cases, the courses are used as a fall-back for candidates whose real target was medical school, so average entry qualifications at some of the leading universities are extremely high – nearly 650 points in Cambridge's case. Partly because of the range of courses included in the category, entry grades also vary widely, however, with four universities averaging less than 300 points.

Cambridge remains at the head of the table, with much the highest entry standards, but the top scores on the other measures are spread around the table. Dundee, in 18th place, shares the best results in the Research Excellence Framework with 4th-placed University College London, while the best graduate prospects are at Huddersfield, the leading post-1992 university in a creditable eighth place. St Andrews has entered the table in third place, just behind Oxford, with the second highest scores on teaching and feedback in the National Student Survey, losing out to Brighton for the top score. Although only eight places off the bottom of the table, Coventry has the most satisfied students in other areas of the survey.

Universities often demand at least two science subjects – usually biology and chemistry – although some new universities will accept just one science. Student satisfaction is generally high and there is much less variation in employment levels this year. Although the subjects do not do as well for employment as some in the health sphere, they are still close to the top 20 with more than a third of graduates going on to further study. They are rather lower in the earnings table, with average salaries of £21,225 for those starting in professional jobs. Salaries have been rising steadily over the past two years.

Anatomy and Physiology	Research quality %	Entry standards	Teaching quality %	Student experience %	Graduate prospects %	Overall score
1 Cambridge	52.5	648	86.0	86.3	87.4	100.0
2 Oxford	50.9	571	85.1	86.7	85.5	97.1
3 St Andrews	37.6	479	96.1	92.9		96.5
4 University College London	55.4	512	76.8	87.8	76.7	92.7
5 Newcastle	47.8	446*	89.7	86.7	70.0	90.9
6 Leeds	40.9	420	85.8	94.8	73.7	90.1
7 Aberdeen	34.7	441	90.5	92.2	70.2	89.8
8 Huddersfield	7.8	387	89.6	89.6	97.3	89.5

9	Sussex	46.8	401	76.7	83.5	84.1	89.3
=10	Queen's, Belfast	33.3	408	84.1	91.2	79.2	89.1
=10	Glasgow Caledonian	8.1	410	87.5	90.8	93.8	89.1
12	Glasgow	33.4	468	76.8	86.2	80.4	88.9
13	Salford	12.7	361	91.1	87.9	87.4	87.5
=14	Manchester	38.3	438	82.4	85.9	68.0	87.4
=14	Brighton	4.8	313	96.2	95.4	89.6	87.4
16	Loughborough	52.1	365	84.8	92.0	61.8	87.2
17	Leicester	36.5	405	85.5	93.8	62.6	86.7
18	Dundee	55.4		77.6	75.3	75.9	86.6
19	Liverpool	31.7	402	91.7	93.0	58.0	86.2
20	King's College London	38.0	435	74.7	83.5	71.8	86.1
21	Nottingham	26.5	415	85.8	87.8	66.1	85.6
22	Manchester Metropolitan	12.0	320	88.3	89.8	84.0	85.2
23	Bristol	43.7	454	74.3	77.3	63.3	85.0
24	Edinburgh	52.8		76.6	89.9	61.9	84.3
25	Cardiff Metropolitan		337	82.4	84.1	92.6	83.9
26	Keele	16.5	384	89.6	92.1	59.3	83.2
27	St George's, London	20.0	354	70.7	67.6	94.1	83.1
28	Reading	26.6	367	73.1	82.1	75.0	82.7
29	Ulster		344	80.6	87.9	80.8	81.8
30	Northampton		259*	81.0	80.6	94.3	81.3
31	Sheffield Hallam	10.4	334	86.6	86.3	61.8	80.2
=32	Coventry	4.5	271	93.2	95.6	60.0	79.7
=32	Central Lancashire	8.3	350	83.1	85.7	62.5	79.7
34	Oxford Brookes	21.3	317	73.6	83.7	66.7	79.2
35	Portsmouth	8.1	309	83.2	77.6	67.4	78.5
36	Plymouth		313	80.4	83.3	71.4	78.4
37	East London		303	77.3	88.4	64.3	76.7
38	Westminster	21.2	255	72.1	82.6	62.4	76.2
39	Queen Margaret, Edinburgh		292	60.0	66.4	83.3	74.0

Employed in professional job:	37%	Employed in non-professional job and studying:	2%
Employed in professional job and studying:	3%	Employed in non-professional job:	16%
Studying:	31%	Unemployed:	11%
Average starting professional salary:	£21,225	Average starting non-professional salary:	£14,684

Animal Science

Animal Science was one of two new tables in *The Times and Sunday Times Good University Guide* last year, a reflection of growing interest in the group of subjects under this heading. Extracted from the agriculture category, degree courses range from animal behaviour to equine science and veterinary nursing. Together they recorded among the biggest increases in both applications and enrolments in 2013. Although they could not repeat this performance in 2014, applications grew by another 6 per cent, but enrolments were almost static having risen by more than 20 per cent in the previous year.

Animal Science cont

Already there have been big changes in the table, with only three universities occupying the same places as last year. Surrey has taken over the leadership from Nottingham, despite not entering the Research Excellence Framework in this field. It has by far the highest entry standards and its 83 per cent score for graduate prospects is almost 20 percentage points better than its nearest challenger. Many of the other employment scores are worryingly low: below 30 per cent at half of the universities in the table and only 3 per cent at Edinburgh Napier. The subject is again bottom of the employment table, with more than half of those completing courses in 2014 going into non-graduate work. Animal science has at least moved out of the bottom five for salaries in graduate jobs, with nearly a £500 increase taking the average to £18,327.

Despite its problems in the employment market, Edinburgh Napier has the best score for student satisfaction in the three teaching sections of the National Student Survey, but the figures had to be taken from the 2013 survey because there were not enough final-year undergraduates to compile a reliable score this year. The best of this year's scores on this measure were at Nottingham Trent, while the most satisfied students in relation to the student experience were at the Royal Veterinary College. Second-placed Reading achieved the best results in the Research Excellence Framework, but only 11 of the 18 universities in the table entered.

Animal Science	Research quality %	Entry standards	Teaching quality %	Student experience %	Graduate prospects %	Overall score
1 Surrey		502	84.2	91.1	83.3	100.0
2 Reading	50.7	387	83.3	78.2	50.0	96.7
3 Nottingham	36.4	394	77.1	89.0	55.4	94.9
4 Liverpool	32.9	396	67.8	75.2	63.5	91.6
5 Aberystwyth	38.2	333	89.8	84.8	21.3	89.6
6 Bristol	33.2	416	73.6	74.0	22.2	88.3
7 Royal Veterinary College		380	80.6	93.0	50.6	87.9
8 Glasgow	42.3		67.9	80.4	38.5	86.9
9 Anglia Ruskin	24.6	308	87.3	91.1	28.0	86.7
10 Nottingham Trent	4.1	334	91.1	91.3	36.4	86.4
11 Lincoln		376	74.0	70.8	64.3	85.4
12 Harper Adams	5.7	365	82.5	86.3	24.3	84.1
13 Plymouth		352	82.3	85.5	25.0	82.2
14 Canterbury Christ Church		269	87.0	89.7	36.0	80.7
15 Greenwich	19.5	304			26.7	80.5
16 Edinburgh Napier		327	91.2*	85.3*	3.0	79.8
17 Chester	7.9	332	66.5	79.3	18.3	77.0
18 Middlesex		341	84.7	61.5	6.9	76.9

Employed in professional job:	20%	Employed in non-professional job and studying:	4%
Employed in professional job and studying:	2%	Employed in non-professional job:	51%
Studying:	13%	Unemployed:	11%
Average starting professional salary:	£18,327	Average starting non-professional salary:	£14,686

Anthropology

Anthropology has been going from strength to strength since £9,000 fees were introduced. Instead of prompting a decline, as its own association predicted, higher charges have coincided with an extraordinary increase in the demand for places which now sees applications running at twice the level they reached before 2010. Last year brought the biggest increases yet – more than 30 per cent – in both applications and enrolments. More than 1,500 students started anthropology degrees, compared with 695 in the year before the fees went up. Some attribute the subject's rise in popularity to television series, but there has been no firm explanation. Much of the growth has come in joint Honours degrees, pairing the subject with everything from accountancy to linguistics or law. The number of universities in the table has jumped from 20 to 29 in two years, and 48 have courses advertised for 2016 on the UCAS website.

There are no subject-specific requirements for most degree courses, although some Russell Group universities favour candidates with biology or another science at AS level. The subject has tended to be the preserve of old universities, but there are ten post-1992 institutions in the latest table.

Cambridge maintains its accustomed leadership, but Birmingham, a new entry to the table, has taken second place from Oxford after achieving the best results in the Research Excellence Framework. Cambridge has the highest entry standards and the best graduate prospects. For the third year in a row, Brunel, in 11th place, boasts much the most satisfied students in all areas of the National Student Survey. Chester, at equal 18th, is the highest-placed post-1992 university.

Employment prospects will be the main concern of those considering a degree in anthropology. Success rates fluctuated while smaller numbers were taking the subject, but it is now in the bottom ten for the proportion of graduates going into "professional" jobs or further study. This is reflected in the table, with 13 of the 29 universities reporting positive destinations for fewer than half of their graduates. Nationally, more than a third of graduates started out in "non-professional" jobs, although the picture was brighter in salary terms. Anthropology is outside the bottom 20 of the 66 subject groups for those who do secure graduate-level jobs, with average salaries of almost £20,000.

Anthropology	Research quality %	Entry standards	Teaching quality %	Student experience %	Graduate prospects %	Overall score
1 Cambridge	40.4	551	83.7	84.0	78.3	100.0
2 Birmingham	50.9	384	90.9	84.5	77.5	98.7
3 Oxford	38.8	538	78.3	87.8	73.6	97.8
4 University College London	49.3	481	76.9	85.5	74.6	97.6
5 London School of Economics	41.3	484	81.8	81.2	74.0	96.7
6 Sussex	34.4	412	86.0	87.8	72.6	95.0
7 Durham	29.1	463	81.6	84.8	74.1	94.3
8 Edinburgh	42.2	444	77.1	81.2	68.0	93.6
9 Queen's, Belfast	49.0	360	90.0	86.3	48.5	92.8
10 Manchester	36.7	402	81.4	89.7	62.4	92.6
11 Brunel	29.3	337	96.4	94.7	51.7	91.8

Anthropology cont	Research quality %	Entry standards	Teaching quality %	Student experience %	Graduate prospects %	Overall score
12 East Anglia	38.6		79.3	94.2	54.5	91.5
13 St Andrews	25.0	479	77.4	79.3	66.7	91.0
14 Leeds		426	84.9	87.1	68.9	88.2
15 Aberdeen	31.8	384*	83.0	86.3	43.9	88.0
16 SOAS, London	31.1	440	73.7	79.5	48.9	87.2
17 Kent	20.5	326	80.8	87.5	62.5	87.0
=18 Goldsmiths, London	34.5	354	80.6	76.6	48.2	86.5
=18 Chester	6.4	307*	92.1	84.6	64.6	86.5
20 Roehampton	27.7	292	83.7	82.0	50.0	85.2
21 Liverpool John Moores	15.1	362	81.1	87.8	48.5	84.9
22 Oxford Brookes	17.3	321	87.2	85.2	42.8	84.2
23 Bournemouth	19.9	303	83.3	81.9	33.8	81.3
24 Stirling		395	78.5	77.7	45.8	80.6
25 Sheffield Hallam		307	81.2	80.1	40.8	78.2
26 Southampton Solent		253	81.9	91.5	38.5	77.9
27 South Wales		318	73.6	79.6	36.4	75.9
28 East London	13.7	238	64.6	69.8	47.4	74.4
29 Birmingham City	3.8	314	67.0	71.4	36.8	73.9

Employed in professional job:	35%	Employed in non-professional job and studying:	3%
Employed in professional job and studying:	2%	Employed in non-professional job:	32%
Studying:	15%	Unemployed:	13%
Average starting professional salary:	£19,990	Average starting non-professional salary:	£15,851

Archaeology

Three more universities have joined the archaeology table this year despite the fact that the numbers starting courses have dropped for four years in a row. Only 415 students embarked on degrees in 2014, as applications failed to maintain the previous year's recovery. Nevertheless, 54 universities and colleges plan to offer archaeology courses in 2016. Many of those attracted onto courses are mature students – often retired – who are studying the subject out of interest and not for career progression. Employment prospects improved somewhat in 2014, but archaeology is still outside the top 50 of 66 subject groupings. Those who find graduate jobs fare a little better in the latest table, with average salaries rising by nearly 4 per cent since the last edition.

Cambridge has taken over from Durham at the top of the table, leapfrogging Oxford in the process. Cambridge has the highest entry standards, while Dundee achieved the best results in the Research Excellence Framework and has shot up 19 places to fourth. Glasgow, in sixth place, registered the best graduate prospects and also posted the highest score in the three sections on teaching in the National Student Survey. Newcastle, in twelfth place, was the leader in the sections devoted to the broader student experience. Satisfaction levels were high throughout most of the institutions in the table, with only two universities failing to reach 70 per cent overall. Robert Gordon was again the only post-1992 university in the top 20.

There are no specific subject requirements for a degree in archaeology, although geography, history and science subjects are all considered relevant. The increase in the number of universities offering the subject has had the effect of spreading out entry scores, which now range from little more than 200 points to over 550. Only 11 of the 56 universities in the ranking averaged more than 400 points in 2014. More than one student in five stays on for a postgraduate qualification, either full or part-time, but almost one in three starts work in a "non-professional" job.

Archaeology	Research quality %	Entry standards	Teaching quality %	Student experience %	Graduate prospects %	Overall score
1 Cambridge	47.2	551	83.3	83.2	78.3	100.0
2 Durham	41.2	475	91.0	90.3	76.8	98.7
3 Oxford	42.9	541	81.5	87.3	75.4	98.5
4 Dundee	55.4	488	94.7	95.0	50.0	98.0
5 University College London	51.4	482	89.5	90.9	62.7	97.9
6 Glasgow	16.4	441	96.4	94.8	79.3	95.5
7 Exeter	33.6	413	88.8	93.2	72.6	94.4
8 York	35.1	403	93.1	92.4	67.7	94.3
9 Reading	44.7	351	93.8	89.8	64.0	93.4
10 Southampton	43.5	385	83.7	87.2	62.6	91.5
11 Sheffield	31.6	402	86.4	88.9	64.0	91.1
12 Newcastle	25.8	366	95.3	95.6	60.5	91.0
13 Leicester	37.2	374	86.8	85.3	64.5	90.9
14 Swansea	39.4	316	90.6	86.8	66.7	90.7
15 Liverpool	33.5	381	86.5	80.8	67.0	90.3
=16 Manchester	24.7	329	93.8	91.1	68.2	90.1
=16 Robert Gordon	8.8	368	90.3	93.6	78.0	90.1
18 Aberdeen	29.4	410*	82.2	90.8	61.6	89.9
=19 Birmingham	40.3	437	72.3	66.3	71.1	89.2
=19 Edinburgh	20.9	476	77.4	83.3	64.7	89.2
21 Kent	33.1	357	83.6	84.4	65.0	88.9
22 Bristol	11.2	385	86.2	84.2	71.5	87.8
=23 Cardiff	31.1	321	83.8	84.8	60.8	86.6
=23 Middlesex	21.1		89.2	85.9	55.0	86.6
=23 Bradford	23.6	272	91.2	91.7	63.1	86.6
26 Nottingham	23.7	370	82.5	81.8	56.3	85.5
27 Queen's, Belfast	36.9	335	82.2	86.0	47.3	85.4
28 De Montfort		308	85.5	91.7	78.3	85.3
29 Keele		366	84.4	86.2	65.5	84.0
=30 Plymouth	25.8		87.2	84.1	46.2	83.9
=30 Hull	31.7	318	84.4	89.4	42.3	83.9
32 Huddersfield		334	80.4	86.0	71.3	83.1
33 Coventry		305	91.1	92.1	55.9	82.3

Archaeology cont	Research quality %	Entry standards	Teaching quality %	Student experience %	Graduate prospects %	Overall score
34 Liverpool John Moores		336	87.8	90.2	51.3	81.6
=35 Glasgow Caledonian	4.7	336	84.6	85.2	53.5	81.5
=35 Lincoln		342	81.5	85.7	60.2	81.5
37 Winchester	7.5	266	90.2	84.5	57.0	81.4
38 Nottingham Trent	4.1	318	81.2	90.9	56.6	81.3
39 Staffordshire		302	90.0	92.0	50.3	81.0
40 West London		284	84.1	81.7	64.1	80.3
41 Bournemouth	19.9	303	80.8	83.3	43.8	80.1
42 Derby		298	84.7	90.1	52.6	79.9
=43 Central Lancashire	9.8	318	79.9	80.3	48.0	79.1
=43 Worcester	8.1	265	87.6	85.2	47.1	79.1
45 Chester	15.4	280	82.2	73.3	49.4	78.7
46 Canterbury Christ Church	16.3	283	80.0	83.8	42.6	78.5
47 Teesside		342	76.4	79.4	49.7	77.7
=48 West of England		344	71.4	82.4	52.4	77.5
=48 Kingston	6.9		85.5	89.3	33.3	77.5
50 Anglia Ruskin	24.6	204	81.7	79.3	41.5	76.9
51 Cumbria	1.5		88.7	89.5	28.6	76.3
52 West of Scotland		319	68.3	79.8	54.3	76.0
53 South Wales		334	76.0	82.8	37.2	75.4
54 Birmingham City		353	58.2	63.3	62.2	74.3
55 Greenwich		294	64.7	77.3	41.1	71.6
56 London South Bank		215	75.1	73.4	19.0	66.7

Employed in professional job:	34%	Employed in non-professional job and studying:	4%
Employed in professional job and studying:	2%	Employed in non-professional job:	32%
Studying:	16%	Unemployed:	12%
Average starting professional salary:	£19,517	Average starting non-professional salary:	£14,959

Architecture

Three years into their careers, architects are among the least likely of all graduates to say that they wished they had taken a different degree or chosen a different profession. Initial employment prospects are good: architecture is just inside the top 15 of the 66 subject groups for the proportion of graduates finding high-level work or continuing to study. Over 70 per cent of those completing courses in 2014 went straight into a professional role and the unemployment rate fell from 12 per cent to 10 per cent. Starting salaries are low – just outside the bottom ten, at a little below £19,000 – but later career prospects are much brighter.

Yet architecture seems not to have recovered from the recession in the minds of degree applicants. The demand for places stabilised in 2014 after two years of decline, but both applications and enrolments remain well behind the levels seen before higher fees were introduced. The length of courses may be one reason that architecture is yet to share fully in the recovery taking place in other subjects. Qualification usually takes seven years, in which the first degree is but a step on the way. With fees of £9,000 a year, that is a considerable commitment, especially when course materials can add another £1,000 to the burden. Nevertheless, there were still close to six applications per place in 2014 and satisfaction rates are higher after graduation than during the course itself.

Cambridge and Bath have taken it in turns to lead the table since 2009, so it is no surprise to see Cambridge jump from fourth to first place this year, due partly to its customary high entry standards. The top universities on the other measures are less predictable: East London, for example, has the highest level of satisfaction (almost 95 per cent) on the teaching sections of the National Student Survey. West of England has the best scores in the rest of the survey and, at 12th, is the highest-placed post-1992 institution. Dundee posts a rare 100 per cent graduate employment record, while University College London has the top research score.

Some universities ask for art at A level, while others look for a mix of art and science subjects. Candidates may be asked to produce a portfolio of work if they have not taken an art or design-based A level. Entry standards have slipped slightly since the last edition of the *Guide*: only three universities, compared with five last year, average more than 500 points on the UCAS tariff and five, rather than only one, now average less than 250 points. The table contains one name that may be unfamiliar: Manchester School of Architecture is a joint enterprise between Manchester and Manchester Metropolitan universities.

Architecture	Research quality %	Entry standards	Teaching quality %	Student experience %	Graduate prospects %	Overall score
1 Cambridge	49.0	578	90.3	86.8	93.3	100.0
2 Bath	52.9	538	89.5	89.9	93.7	99.7
3 Cardiff	40.7	466	91.8	87.9	94.4	95.8
4 Sheffield	36.6	479	86.6	87.0	93.1	94.1
5 University College London	54.1	494	75.7	73.8	88.9	93.0
6 Kent	33.3	406	87.8	89.6	91.1	91.4
7 Edinburgh	35.1	503	73.0	81.7	90.7	90.9
8 Liverpool	43.5	422	76.1	78.4	87.5	89.3
9 Newcastle	43.7	435	75.2	84.5	83.1	89.2
10 Strathclyde	23.0	465	75.4	73.8	94.0	88.1
11 Queen's, Belfast	35.2	384	89.8	92.9	72.8	87.7
12 West of England	10.6	335	94.5	96.3	91.5	87.5
13 Northumbria	5.9	403	92.1	90.9	87.0	86.8
14 Dundee	8.7	422	78.9	76.3	100.0	86.6
15 Nottingham	14.8	459	77.1	77.4	90.7	86.5
16 Robert Gordon	8.3	390	88.9	83.9	88.6	85.8
17 Oxford Brookes	17.6	417	85.2	84.0	80.2	85.5
18 Brighton	13.1	360	90.5	90.8	82.7	85.4
=19 Coventry	10.3	310	93.5	94.8	85.4	85.0
=19 Manchester School of Architecture	12.6	423	81.0	84.0	84.1	85.0
21 De Montfort	35.9	291	79.1	80.2	86.0	84.5

Architecture cont	Research quality %	Entry standards	Teaching quality %	Student experience %	Graduate prospects %	Overall score
22 University for the Creative Arts	3.4	340	92.1	92.1	82.6	83.6
=23 Huddersfield		328	92.2	92.3	86.2	83.5
=23 Sheffield Hallam	13.4	340	83.2	88.1	84.5	83.5
25 Arts University Bournemouth	2.4	306	87.6	89.8	85.0	81.7
26 Nottingham Trent	3.4	315	84.9	88.9	84.2	81.4
27 Salford	19.6	310	89.9	94.6	65.5	81.3
28 University of the Arts London		370	86.9	84.3	78.8	81.2
29 Plymouth	13.2	313	85.5	89.5	74.6	81.0
30 Leeds Beckett	5.6	297	85.4	89.4	81.0	80.7
=31 Liverpool John Moores	4.9	338	87.2	86.4	75.2	80.5
=31 Westminster	10.7	370	84.3	83.8	70.1	80.5
=33 Kingston	10.1	319	84.6	87.2	71.4	79.5
=33 Ulster	28.6	298	72.5	78.3	75.2	79.5
=35 Greenwich	2.0	353	88.8	80.8	70.5	79.1
=35 Portsmouth		314	84.1	87.1	78.2	79.1
37 Edinburgh Napier	5.7	387	71.6	73.0	80.6	78.9
38 East London	8.1	272	94.8	91.5	60.6	77.7
=39 Lincoln	3.2	356	64.3	73.5	79.3	75.9
=39 Cardiff Metropolitan		286	75.9	70.8	82.7	75.9
41 London South Bank	19.6	247	80.8	78.8	62.7	75.3
=42 Middlesex	13.3	232	84.9	87.3	60.3	74.9
=42 Birmingham City	9.6	320	71.7	77.4	67.0	74.9
44 Derby	6.7	282	78.9	79.4	66.6	74.8
45 Central Lancashire	3.0	312	68.6	71.6	76.6	74.5
46 London Metropolitan	7.2	270	75.8	72.3	70.0	73.9
47 Southampton Solent		225	88.8	88.7	61.9	73.8
48 Anglia Ruskin	5.2	227	77.4	77.8	67.9	72.7
49 Northampton		244	79.4	69.8	68.0	71.8
50 Bolton	2.5		52.9	62.8	74.1	66.8
51 Glasgow Caledonian	9.1		63.1	71.2	42.9	61.6

Employed in professional job:	66%	Employed in non-professional job and studying:	1%
Employed in professional job and studying:	5%	Employed in non-professional job:	12%
Studying:	7%	Unemployed:	10%
Average starting professional salary:	£18,936	Average starting non-professional salary:	£15,122

Art and Design

Both fine art and design are back within striking distance of the level of enrolments seen before £9,000 fees were introduced, but they are fishing in a smaller pool of applicants. Even after a 6,000 increase in applications in 2014, design courses were still 11,000 short of the total in 2011. Nevertheless, only nursing attracts more applications than art and design, despite the fact that the subjects always feature in the lower reaches of the tables for employment and earnings. This year they have escaped the bottom ten for the numbers going into graduate-level jobs or further study, but are still in the bottom five for starting salaries. However, artists and designers have always accepted that they are likely to have a period of lowly paid self-employment early in their career while they find a way to pursue their vocation.

Most courses in art and design are at post-1992 institutions – including three more specialist arts universities, created in the last three years – but older foundations fill the top 16 places. Oxford, the oldest of them all, where fine art is taught at the Ruskin School of Drawing, retains top place. Not surprisingly, it has by far the highest entry standards. Only 12 of the 80 universities average more than 400 points, but most artists would argue that entry grades are of less significance than in other subjects. Selection in art and design rests primarily on the quality of candidates' portfolios and many undergraduates enter through a one-year Art Foundation course.

University College London, where students attend the Slade School of Fine Art, shares second place with Loughborough in the new table. Ulster surprised some observers by producing the best scores in the Research Excellence Framework and has shot up 38 places and into the top 20 as a result. It is the most dramatic of a number of big moves: Heriot-Watt, Essex and Bangor have also arrived in the top 20 after rises of at least 20 places. Essex has the best score for the student experience sections of the National Student Survey, while Winchester, which is up 28 places to 23rd, is the leader on the teaching sections. Bangor has the best graduate prospects, overtaking Glasgow, which has dropped overall from second to sixth after a dip in student satisfaction scores. Northumbria is the best placed post-1992 university at 17th, while Falmouth has fallen from 12th last year to 20th.

Art and Design	Research quality %	Entry standards	Teaching quality %	Student experience %	Graduate prospects %	Overall score
1 Oxford	39.7	541	87.7	89.4	81.5	100.0
=2 University College London	44.7	398	95.6	93.6	57.4	92.7
=2 Loughborough	35.3	461	83.0	83.9	72.0	92.7
4 Newcastle	37.3	445	93.6	92.3	56.7	92.6
5 Brunel	32.8	383	85.0	87.7	81.8	92.3
6 Glasgow	37.2	505	62.7	78.3	83.6	91.8
7 Lancaster	48.0	447	81.4	85.3	60.3	91.5
8 Heriot-Watt	31.1	390	85.9	85.0	70.0	89.8
9 Leeds	33.6	440	77.7	80.0	67.0	89.0
10 Goldsmiths, London	25.9	451	83.6	83.5	61.2	88.8
11 Southampton	35.4	366	85.4	85.4	63.2	88.1
12 Dundee	39.9	420	82.8	83.8	51.0	87.6
13 Edinburgh	27.9	462	75.0	73.5	66.0	87.5
=14 Essex	46.9	273	93.4	94.0	52.4	86.9
=14 Bangor		305	89.8	89.3	88.4	86.9
16 Ulster	57.2	323	83.9	84.5	50.6	86.8
17 Northumbria	13.3	412	86.7	89.0	60.3	86.6
=18 Kingston	10.1	416	84.3	84.7	66.1	86.4

Art and Design cont	Research quality %	Entry standards	Teaching quality %	Student experience %	Graduate prospects %	Overall score
=18 Reading	38.9	354	72.1	77.2	73.8	86.4
20 Falmouth	3.0	347	85.9	86.8	78.9	85.9
21 Oxford Brookes	10.4	377	95.5	91.2	52.3	85.4
22 Kent	44.3	342	74.0	73.4	66.5	85.3
23 Winchester		288	95.8	92.3	73.7	85.0
24 Manchester Metropolitan	9.7	449	80.3	79.9	60.3	84.9
25 Robert Gordon	11.5	375	83.6	80.8	67.1	84.6
26 De Montfort	10.2	346	83.6	83.9	71.0	84.5
27 Lincoln	7.1	373	83.0	85.0	65.3	83.9
28 Nottingham Trent	4.7	345	83.3	84.4	71.7	83.8
29 Coventry	18.1	362	79.6	79.7	64.8	83.7
30 Norwich University of the Arts	5.6	368	86.0	85.9	61.5	83.5
31 Huddersfield	4.8	357	86.3	85.6	63.8	83.4
32 Edinburgh Napier		385	84.9	83.9	62.3	82.9
33 Brighton	13.1	352	85.0	81.6	54.9	82.0
34 Chichester		355	90.1	92.3	52.2	81.8
35 Westminster	22.5	399	75.2	76.3	51.8	81.7
=36 West of England	15.0	342	81.7	77.7	59.0	81.5
=36 Sheffield Hallam	15.5	327	85.4	85.1	52.9	81.5
38 Bath Spa	9.6	357	83.4	81.0	55.5	81.3
39 Arts University Bournemouth	2.4	320	85.0	81.5	64.5	81.0
=40 Anglia Ruskin	8.5	322	88.7	85.1	52.9	80.9
=40 Teesside	2.9	336	87.8	88.9	53.1	80.9
42 Hertfordshire	5.8	319	82.6	84.1	61.6	80.7
43 Middlesex	13.3	305	82.9	83.9	57.9	80.6
44 Cumbria	6.1	348	87.8	86.9	47.5	80.5
45 Derby	5.1	313	89.2	89.8	51.1	80.4
46 University for the Creative Arts	3.4	352	84.8	82.7	51.8	79.9
=47 Bournemouth	15.0	328	69.5	73.3	69.2	79.8
=47 York St John		357	86.1	83.2	51.2	79.8
49 Worcester	11.1	306	84.8	86.6	50.3	79.5
=50 Plymouth	14.7	322	88.5	86.2	40.5	79.4
=50 Northampton	2.9	343	82.1	81.7	54.6	79.4
52 Buckinghamshire New	6.1	328	80.6	75.6	59.6	79.3
53 Aberystwyth	21.6	357	80.0	73.0	43.2	79.0
54 Liverpool Hope		313	91.3	85.6	47.1	78.8
55 Portsmouth		319	89.7	84.3	47.6	78.6
56 Cardiff Metropolitan	7.9	299	79.9	80.5	57.9	78.5
57 University of the Arts London	8.0	339	75.4	74.0	58.5	78.4
=58 Liverpool John Moores	7.2	367	79.9	81.4	44.3	78.3
=58 Glasgow Caledonian	1.8	380	73.2	84.6	51.5	78.3
=60 Salford	8.0	336	82.6	82.0	45.5	78.2
=60 Abertay		362	72.9	74.6	61.4	78.2

62 Staffordshire	2.3	284	85.2	88.7	51.4	77.9
63 Central Lancashire	3.9	306	78.9	79.8	57.5	77.8
64 Leeds Beckett	1.2	311	85.7	86.9	46.3	77.6
65 Birmingham City	9.6	336	77.0	73.0	50.2	77.1
66 Glyndŵr	7.8	263	80.7	76.6	58.3	76.9
=67 Chester	6.2	300	77.5	77.3	54.9	76.8
=67 Sunderland	9.8	299	85.3	83.4	40.6	76.8
69 Southampton Solent	1.6	288	87.3	83.9	44.9	76.5
70 Bolton		289	85.1	78.0	50.6	76.3
=71 Greenwich	3.5	346	72.6	64.3	56.3	75.8
=71 South Wales	3.3	313	72.7	73.7	57.0	75.8
73 Canterbury Christ Church	7.3	252	81.7	82.3	50.6	75.7
74 Gloucestershire		316	76.5	78.5	50.6	75.5
75 East London	9.8	298	80.0	79.7	38.9	74.8
76 London Metropolitan	4.7	302	76.1	73.3	46.2	74.1
77 West London	4.5	277	72.8	60.3	56.0	72.9
78 Hull	11.2		67.7	68.8	52.4	72.8
79 London South Bank	12.8	232	73.4	66.8	40.6	70.2
80 Bedfordshire		248	77.4	74.8	34.8	69.5

Employed in professional job:	50%	Employed in non-professional job and studying:	1%
Employed in professional job and studying:	1%	Employed in non-professional job:	30%
Studying:	5%	Unemployed:	12%
Average starting professional salary:	£18,233	Average starting non-professional salary:	£14,548

Biological Sciences

Biology and the various more specialist degrees in the same area are the most popular sciences among degree applicants, as they are at A level. The same cannot be said for graduates, however: three years after graduation one in three biologists wish they had chosen a different subject – one of the biggest proportions in the arts or sciences. Nevertheless, the biological sciences have seen big increases in applications and enrolments every year since £9,000 fees were introduced. Enrolments were up 10 per cent in 2014, following an even bigger increase in the previous year. Microbiology provides the stiffest competition, with more than six applications to the place in 2014, but the leading universities' requirements can be tough across the whole area. Many will demand two sciences at A level, or the equivalent – usually biology and chemistry – for any of the biological sciences.

Cambridge and Oxford (in that order) make it 11 years in a row at the head of the table. But there is considerable change in the rest of the table, not least in third position, which is occupied by Edinburgh after a rise of 13 places. Sussex had an even bigger rise of 23 places to seventh. Cambridge's Natural Sciences degree boasts some of the highest entry grades in any subject, averaging 648 points, as well as providing the best graduate prospects. However, in the Research Excellence Framework, both of the ancient universities were eclipsed by Edinburgh (and, to a lesser extent, Imperial College London); it was 10 percentage points ahead of Cambridge and 12 per cent ahead of Oxford.

The most satisfied students are to be found at universities rather lower down the table.

Biological Sciences cont

Gloucestershire, which has had the top scores in the National Student Survey for the last two years, does it again for the questions on teaching, feedback and academic support. It shares 71st place overall, while Kent, the leader on the student experience questions, is 22nd. Oxford Brookes and Nottingham Trent are the only modern universities in the top 40.

Employment scores and graduate salaries are surprisingly modest. Only four universities saw 80 per cent or more of those finishing courses go straight into graduate-level employment or go on to postgraduate study in 2014. The biological sciences are outside the top 40 in the tables for graduate destinations and starting salaries. The average salary in a graduate-level job remained just above £20,000 in 2014. A third of students stay on for a postgraduate qualification, either full or part-time, but the 13 per cent unemployment rate is above average for all subjects.

Biological Sciences	Research quality %	Entry standards	Teaching quality %	Student experience %	Graduate prospects %	Overall score
1 Cambridge	52.5	648	86.0	86.3	87.5	100.0
2 Oxford	50.9	565	83.4	87.4	83.8	96.5
3 Edinburgh	62.9	502	80.8	90.9	66.8	93.1
=4 University College London	55.4	493	75.8	86.0	79.5	92.6
=4 Sheffield	57.4	457	83.6	89.0	72.4	92.6
6 Imperial College	61.6	522	69.3	81.5	78.9	92.1
7 Sussex	46.8	394	83.6	90.4	83.4	91.7
8 Surrey	37.5	422	85.7	91.6	80.0	91.2
=9 Bath	31.5	462	86.8	91.8	77.2	91.1
=9 York	41.9	466	84.1	91.7	72.2	91.1
11 Birmingham	38.1	417	87.0	87.1	79.6	90.8
12 Exeter	39.7	447	86.2	91.3	72.2	90.7
13 St Andrews	37.6	525	82.0	90.2	67.5	90.6
14 Lancaster	46.5	447	84.4	85.7	71.1	90.3
15 Bristol	46.8	475	78.9	86.7	71.7	90.2
16 Durham	32.9	536	75.6	83.1	77.8	89.9
17 Manchester	38.3	453	82.4	89.6	72.3	89.7
18 Warwick	37.1	420	86.6	87.5	72.5	89.3
19 Leeds	40.9	421	82.4	89.3	71.5	89.0
20 Glasgow	33.4	466	81.7	87.7	70.6	88.6
21 Queen's, Belfast	47.3	369	80.8	86.8	74.4	88.3
=22 Kent	39.1	365	87.3	93.4	66.9	87.9
=22 East Anglia	38.8	405	83.7	91.1	66.8	87.9
24 Southampton	34.2	397	81.5	90.7	71.5	87.4
25 Swansea	38.6	339	85.8	89.2	72.0	87.3
=26 Dundee	55.4	415	78.8	80.9	61.4	87.0
=26 King's College London	38.0	433	75.9	85.1	71.6	87.0
28 Aston	39.1	370	86.5	85.6	66.9	86.9
29 Leicester	36.5	399	78.3	89.2	68.2	86.3
30 Nottingham	26.5	414	81.9	87.4	70.0	86.2

31 Strathclyde	52.2	438	68.4	79.3	68.4	86.1
32 Cardiff	33.3	431	76.7	86.8	65.7	85.6
33 Newcastle	28.4	394	83.7	89.0	64.4	85.4
34 Aberdeen	34.7	408	79.4	86.0	63.1	85.1
35 Heriot-Watt	26.3	398	80.5	78.5	73.3	84.9
36 Liverpool	33.9	410	78.5	85.8	59.0	84.1
37 Brunel	18.2	352	85.4	91.1	65.5	83.8
38 Keele	16.5	376	85.5	88.5	64.6	83.7
=39 Oxford Brookes	21.3	342	82.2	83.4	70.9	83.3
=39 Nottingham Trent	24.1	305	85.3	90.4	65.8	83.3
=41 Central Lancashire	8.3	326	87.5	89.8	70.8	83.1
=41 St George's, London	20.0	413	74.5	80.8	70.9	83.1
43 Edge Hill	6.2	304	90.5	84.9	73.1	82.6
44 Queen Mary, London	26.1	412	72.8	80.0	66.1	82.5
45 Portsmouth	24.3	322	81.7	85.5	64.6	82.2
46 Bangor	31.5	349	81.6	86.7	54.5	82.1
=47 Abertay	4.3	351	87.9	91.3	63.0	82.0
=47 Stirling	49.0	400	66.9	82.7	53.4	82.0
49 Bath Spa		296	92.6	83.8	72.6	81.8
50 Robert Gordon	4.9	357	77.8	78.9	77.5	81.3
51 Reading	26.6	365	75.9	84.9	56.9	80.9
=52 Essex	17.8	305	79.5	86.7	66.1	80.8
=52 Royal Holloway, London	25.7	361	76.7	81.0	59.7	80.8
=54 Worcester	10.9	287	86.5	87.5	64.5	80.7
=54 Aberystwyth	38.2	302	79.4	83.0	54.0	80.7
=56 Edinburgh Napier	8.9	364	78.6	82.2	67.0	80.6
=56 West of Scotland	29.0	324	83.3	89.4	48.2	80.6
58 Hull	31.7	343	74.0	81.1	58.5	80.4
59 Lincoln		322	86.9	91.3	61.9	80.2
60 Northumbria	14.0	346	75.1	86.8	63.9	80.1
=61 Sheffield Hallam	10.4	324	83.2	86.1	58.7	79.6
=61 Bradford	9.5	299	76.8	84.4	70.6	79.6
63 Huddersfield	7.8	305	76.6	81.9	72.1	79.4
64 Glasgow Caledonian	8.1	385	74.1	84.2	60.3	79.1
65 Hertfordshire	10.9	314	70.6	78.3	75.0	78.9
66 Coventry	4.5	245	79.2	83.3	73.7	78.4
67 West of England	8.2	294	84.6	89.0	53.8	78.2
68 St Mary's, Twickenham		301*	84.4	88.9	57.5	78.0
=69 Manchester Metropolitan	12.0	335	79.6	81.2	54.4	77.9
=69 Bedfordshire	25.1	207	82.7	87.7	55.1	77.9
=71 Kingston	2.6	275	86.3	86.9	57.8	77.8
=71 Gloucestershire	14.5	306	92.8	90.9	35.0	77.8
73 Brighton	4.8	326	73.8	76.8	64.7	76.9
74 Bolton		289	76.7	78.8	65.8	76.3
75 Canterbury Christ Church	11.9	258	78.4	77.0	59.0	76.0
76 Sunderland	7.5	240	77.1	81.7	62.2	75.8
77 South Wales		361	71.0	79.0	58.3	75.6

Biological Sciences cont	Research quality %	Entry standards	Teaching quality %	Student experience %	Graduate prospects %	Overall score
78 Salford	12.7	325	81.3	81.8	40.3	75.5
=79 Plymouth		343	79.9	83.1	46.9	75.4
=79 Liverpool John Moores	15.1	339	78.2	82.0	39.6	75.4
=79 Chester	12.0	285	77.5	87.6	46.0	75.4
=82 Staffordshire		274	83.2	84.2	51.5	75.3
=82 Greenwich	7.4	318	73.9	82.5	51.4	75.3
84 Ulster		267	68.2	87.3	66.7	75.2
85 Leeds Beckett	3.5	282	78.4	81.9	53.8	75.1
86 Liverpool Hope		301	75.6	69.3	63.0	74.7
87 Queen Margaret, Edinburgh		329	79.4	87.1	38.5	73.8
88 Middlesex	10.0	220	73.3	82.2	55.6	73.6
89 Anglia Ruskin	2.2	229	83.4	87.4	44.6	73.5
=90 Westminster	21.2	283	63.5	80.1	49.2	73.3
=90 Cardiff Metropolitan		307	60.9	66.7	72.7	73.3
=90 Roehampton	20.6	273	69.8	77.4	45.9	73.3
93 Northampton		273	86.2	91.5	32.7	73.2
94 Derby	1.6	249	79.1	80.2	42.8	71.8
95 Bournemouth	4.7	279	71.0	72.2	45.3	70.7
96 London South Bank	35.0	186	57.8	71.5	50.0	70.4
97 Teesside		306	66.7	67.4	50.0	70.2
98 London Metropolitan		223	71.7	82.2	42.6	69.6
99 East London		266	52.7	64.0	47.0	65.2

Employed in professional job:	31%	Employed in non-professional job and studying:	3%
Employed in professional job and studying:	3%	Employed in non-professional job:	24%
Studying:	27%	Unemployed:	13%
Average starting professional salary:	£20,097	Average starting non-professional salary:	£15,036

Building

Building is among the top ten subjects for employment prospects and in the top 20 for starting salaries in graduate-level jobs, averaging £23,700 in 2014. Nearly 80 per cent of those finishing degrees went straight into graduate-level jobs. This encouraging message is yet to filter through to sixth-forms and colleges, however. The numbers of applications and enrolments for building stabilised in 2014 but they have almost halved since the recession began in 2008. Applicants and careers advisers can be forgiven for not realising the scale of the improvement in the labour market: only three years ago, building was 40th in the employment table and starting salaries still have not regained their 2008 level. But, with fewer than four applications to the place and entry qualifications among the lowest in the *Guide*, the subject is surely a good bet once more.

The top three in the table remain unchanged, with University College London (UCL) recording the highest entry grades and the best graduate prospects. UCL's Project Management for Construction degree is again the only one in the table to register average entry grades of more than 400 points. Elsewhere, there is less variation in entry grades than in most subjects: half of the universities average between 300 and 400 points and only two dropped below 250 in 2014. Satisfaction rates are similarly bunched. South Wales produced the best scores for teaching in the National Student Survey, while Southampton Solent did the same for the student experience, satisfying almost 98 per cent of final-year undergraduates. Only four universities slipped below 70 per cent satisfaction overall.

Courses in this category include surveying and building services engineering, as well as construction. The table is dominated by post-1992 universities, although older foundations take the top four places. The best grades in the Research Excellence Framework came at second-placed Loughborough. Robert Gordon is the highest-placed modern university, with Oxford Brookes, Glasgow Caledonian and South Wales also making the top ten. No fewer than 85 institutions are planning to offer courses in this area in 2016. A significant proportion are colleges, many of which focus on part-time degrees and Higher National Diplomas.

Employed in professional job:	74%	Employed in non-professional job and studying:	0%
Employed in professional job and studying:	5%	Employed in non-professional job:	9%
Studying:	3%	Unemployed:	9%
Average starting professional salary:	£23,707	Average starting non-professional salary:	£15,402

Building	Research quality %	Entry standards	Teaching quality %	Student experience %	Graduate prospects %	Overall score
1 University College London	54.1	439	80.9	89.4	96.4	100.0
2 Loughborough	58.3	339	81.7	92.5	95.2	96.3
3 Reading	40.0	364	83.4	86.0	95.6	94.6
4 Heriot-Watt	38.1	388*	85.4	87.4	88.8	94.2
5 Robert Gordon	8.3	339	88.4	89.8	94.2	90.1
6 Oxford Brookes	17.6	315	82.8	91.0	91.1	88.6
7 Ulster	28.6	316	84.8	91.0	81.2	87.9
8 Nottingham	14.8	369*	80.8	81.1	84.6	87.6
9 Glasgow Caledonian	9.1	355	75.5	82.0	92.6	87.4
10 South Wales		325*	92.8	95.1	82.6	86.7
=11 Portsmouth		307	80.5	87.7	92.9	85.6
=11 West of England	10.6	297	82.5	86.3	88.2	85.6
13 Sheffield Hallam	13.4	311	77.5	84.3	86.1	84.9
=14 Nottingham Trent	3.4	274	84.8	86.3	90.6	84.6
=14 Coventry	10.3	296	80.6	84.1	87.0	84.6
16 Liverpool John Moores	4.9	332	86.0	89.1	77.1	84.4
17 Edinburgh Napier	5.7	293	91.5	91.0	78.2	84.2
18 Northumbria	5.9	337	78.6	81.3	82.7	84.1
19 Aston	20.6	351	63.3	75.8	85.2	84.0
20 Southampton Solent		210	92.4	97.8	88.9	83.4
21 Westminster	10.7	287	75.3	80.9	87.1	83.0
22 Anglia Ruskin	5.2	291	79.1	83.6	84.4	82.7
23 Salford	19.6	331	71.3	74.7	78.2	82.5
24 Leeds Beckett	5.6	255	83.9	86.0	83.7	82.1

Building cont	Research quality %	Entry standards	Teaching quality %	Student experience %	Graduate prospects %	Overall score
25 Plymouth	13.2	252	90.4	91.3	71.9	81.6
26 Brighton		287	73.5	78.6	83.7	80.1
27 Central Lancashire	3.0	313	77.0	82.6	71.7	79.5
28 Kingston		291	70.0	68.0	84.6	78.8
29 Greenwich	2.0	316	66.2	68.9	76.7	77.5
30 Birmingham City	2.7	259	72.4	82.3	71.3	76.1
31 London South Bank	19.6	255	64.2	73.6	70.8	75.8
32 Bolton	2.5	229	82.4	87.5	65.5	75.6

Business Studies

The various branches of business and management are the largest recruiters of undergraduates in the UK, with 63,000 students starting courses in 2014. That represented a 5 per cent increase on the previous year and was a response to nearly 330,000 applications, 13,000 more than in 2013. Numbers have now passed the levels reached before £9,000 fees were introduced. Management is the more competitive field, attracting nearly six applications for every place, one more than for business studies. The subjects are the mainstay of many new universities, but some of the most famous business schools are absent from this ranking because they do not offer undergraduate courses. Manchester Business School provides Manchester's undergraduate courses.

With Cambridge dropping out of the table because there were not enough entrants or graduates to compile reliable scores, Bath only had Oxford to overtake to reach the top of the Business Studies ranking. This it did with a good performance across the board without having the top score on any individual measure. Oxford has the highest entry grades and is only a fraction of a point behind Bath and ahead of St Andrews. The London School of Economics (LSE), which shares fifth place with Lancaster, has the highest research score and the best graduate prospects, but is prevented from challenging for the leading positions by one of the lowest levels of student satisfaction for teaching, feedback and academic support.

Falmouth, a specialist arts university, sprung a major surprise by producing the best scores in both the teaching and student experience sections of this year's National Student Survey, achieving 95 per cent satisfaction overall. Student satisfaction is much higher throughout the table in relation to the student experience than on teaching and feedback. Only two universities reached 90 per cent satisfaction on teaching, compared with 12 for the student experience. More than half of the institutions in one of our biggest tables are modern universities, but only seven appear in the top 50. Falmouth is the highest-placed, at 23rd, and might have reached the top 20 if it had entered the Research Excellence Framework.

Employment scores are extremely variable, ranging from 97 per cent at the LSE to less than 40 per cent at two universities. Overall, business and management fare less well than might be expected in the employment table, barely making the top 50. Those who secure graduate-level jobs do better in comparison with those from other subjects, however. The average starting salary of almost £22,500 has reached the top 20 this year, and the £16,572 average for non-professional jobs is in the top seven for graduates for all subjects.

Business Studies	Research quality %	Entry standards	Teaching quality %	Student experience %	Graduate prospects %	Overall score
1 Bath	41.8	490	81.3	91.4	90.7	100.0
2 Oxford	32.0	590	77.1	87.3	90.7	99.7
3 St Andrews	43.8	521	75.9	86.6	91.5	99.3
4 Leeds	39.3	442	85.0	91.9	80.8	97.8
=5 Lancaster	42.6	425	82.0	87.3	87.8	97.5
=5 London School of Economics	52.3	520	63.2	80.6	97.5	97.5
7 Loughborough	32.6	418	82.4	91.1	90.3	96.8
8 Warwick	40.4	475	73.3	85.2	87.9	96.2
9 Durham	23.1	443	81.7	89.9	91.1	95.9
10 Strathclyde	44.3	514	78.0	89.0	63.6	95.8
11 Surrey	15.8	412	90.8	96.0	80.4	95.4
12 Exeter	24.4	471	79.0	88.7	82.8	94.8
13 Nottingham	32.6	398	83.0	89.9	79.9	94.7
14 Cardiff	32.0	399	82.3	90.1	75.6	93.8
15 King's College London	38.2	481	70.3	79.2	83.4	93.7
16 City	27.8	459	78.4	85.2	78.7	93.6
17 University College London	43.9	472	69.1	78.5	80.8	93.5
18 Queen's, Belfast	32.7	377	85.7	88.4	69.0	92.9
19 Kent	24.8	365	82.8	90.1	80.0	92.6
20 Sheffield	26.8	382	79.0	89.4	79.4	92.3
=21 Birmingham	29.1	406	73.6	80.8	87.6	91.9
=21 Manchester	33.3	414	75.1	86.8	73.6	91.9
23 Falmouth		261	94.6	96.3	91.7	91.5
24 East Anglia	28.1	370	83.4	90.0	66.2	91.3
25 Southampton	24.0	387	74.9	85.0	84.7	91.1
26 York	24.0	390	80.8	88.6	69.7	90.9
27 Reading	29.3	388	76.7	85.6	70.8	90.4
28 Aston	19.7	392	77.3	86.1	76.8	90.2
29 Edinburgh	25.8	450	69.4	84.6	72.4	89.9
30 Aberdeen	24.9	432	74.2	81.3	71.4	89.8
31 Heriot-Watt	18.8	398	80.7	83.3	65.7	89.0
32 Newcastle	20.7	415	68.6	81.1	81.2	88.8
=33 Sussex	23.7	383	69.0	81.3	82.3	88.7
=33 Glasgow	22.1	446	71.0	83.2	67.3	88.7
35 Stirling	25.2	389	76.0	81.3	68.1	88.6
=36 Robert Gordon	2.6	406	79.9	85.7	75.5	88.4
=36 Coventry	1.6	304	88.8	90.9	76.0	88.4
=38 Swansea	22.0	316	80.3	82.9	74.2	88.3
=38 De Montfort	10.7	283	84.9	91.0	76.3	88.3
=38 Buckingham		301	86.5	90.8	81.2	88.3
=41 Liverpool	20.1	391	75.0	83.3	69.3	88.2
=41 SOAS, London	25.0	377	73.5	82.5	70.5	88.2
43 Northumbria	4.0	358	81.0	88.2	72.3	87.4

Business Studies cont	Research quality %	Entry standards	Teaching quality %	Student experience %	Graduate prospects %	Overall score
44 Keele	10.2	338	80.3	86.1	71.8	87.3
=45 Dundee	12.1	386	79.5	89.0	57.7	87.0
=45 Bangor	23.4	310	82.0	85.1	60.1	87.0
=45 Essex	25.1	313	79.3	86.3	61.0	87.0
48 Harper Adams		295	86.5	86.7	77.3	86.9
=49 Leicester	24.3	364	70.9	80.4	70.1	86.8
=49 Lincoln	4.8	317	80.4	88.7	75.4	86.8
51 Ulster	40.4	291	80.4	85.5	47.0	86.7
52 Portsmouth	9.5	313	78.4	85.6	76.0	86.6
=53 Oxford Brookes	5.1	340	82.1	88.8	66.0	86.5
=53 Queen Mary, London	23.5	383	75.7	79.7	58.6	86.5
55 Royal Holloway, London	27.0	373	74.1	81.2	56.6	86.2
=56 Nottingham Trent	4.6	327	76.2	83.5	74.5	85.2
=56 Bristol	32.1	406	62.0	81.2		85.2
=58 West of England	5.5	311	78.0	86.1	69.3	84.9
=58 Huddersfield	4.1	328	80.8	85.5	63.5	84.9
=58 Hertfordshire	0.9	326	82.2	88.5	61.7	84.9
61 Hull	10.2	312	77.0	86.0	65.5	84.8
62 Liverpool John Moores		338	83.0	86.8	59.9	84.7
=63 Edinburgh Napier	2.3	353	81.7	87.7	55.0	84.6
=63 Chester	0.5	291	79.5	84.8	75.1	84.6
65 Plymouth	13.1	282	81.7	86.8	55.4	84.2
66 Brunel	23.0	350	72.4	82.8	51.6	84.1
=67 Sheffield Hallam	0.6	313	81.2	88.2	60.9	84.0
=67 Winchester		304	81.8	87.8	62.3	84.0
69 University of the Arts London		394	81.3	80.7	52.9	83.9
70 Manchester Metropolitan	4.7	333	74.1	81.2	68.8	83.7
=71 Brighton	6.5	317	78.6	84.0	59.5	83.6
=71 Central Lancashire	4.4	306	82.2	85.9	56.3	83.6
=71 Bournemouth	8.8	324	74.7	80.9	65.2	83.6
=74 Salford	5.9	310	82.9	86.5	49.2	83.2
=74 Edge Hill		301	87.7	91.2	45.0	83.2
=74 Sunderland	0.4	280	83.6	86.4	59.3	83.2
77 Bath Spa		290	85.0	87.2	53.3	83.0
78 Bradford	11.8	304	72.1	83.2	62.7	82.8
79 Worcester	0.9	304	76.5	85.9	62.8	82.7
80 Anglia Ruskin	3.4	239	84.8	87.7	55.3	82.4
=81 Glasgow Caledonian	1.8	368	73.0	82.3	55.8	82.2
=81 St Mary's, Twickenham		265	84.6	87.5	53.3	82.2
83 West of Scotland	2.9	291	80.9	83.8	54.4	82.1
84 Leeds Trinity		250	76.9	81.8	71.2	81.8
85 Abertay		298	75.4	82.9	62.8	81.7
86 Royal Agricultural University		295	71.9	81.6	69.9	81.6

87 Aberystwyth	14.5	292	72.1	77.3	58.1	81.4
88 Northampton	1.0	267	76.3	84.8	61.5	81.3
89 York St John	0.8	260	75.8	82.4	64.1	81.0
90 Middlesex	10.5	251	81.0	87.3	40.8	80.6
=91 Greenwich	3.3	319	77.3	82.5	43.7	80.3
=91 Buckinghamshire New	1.8	250	81.5	83.6	50.1	80.3
93 Derby	0.9	274	78.4	81.0	53.2	80.2
94 Gloucestershire		302	71.5	77.2	63.3	80.1
95 South Wales	0.2	334	76.2	78.9	47.6	80.0
=96 Birmingham City	1.3	274	79.7	84.2	45.9	79.9
=96 Queen Margaret, Edinburgh		307	75.1	83.1	49.5	79.9
98 Teesside	2.0	267	78.2	82.4	46.9	79.3
99 West London		239	79.4	82.2	47.6	78.6
100 Cardiff Metropolitan		297	71.1	74.8	56.6	78.5
101 Kingston	9.2	283	68.6	79.8	46.6	78.1
102 Chichester		252	71.2	76.2	59.4	77.9
=103 Southampton Solent		261	71.0	77.7	56.0	77.8
=103 Leeds Beckett	0.8	260	68.0	78.4	59.6	77.8
105 Canterbury Christ Church		255	74.4	79.5	48.9	77.7
106 London South Bank	2.1	220	76.1	82.8	45.2	77.4
=107 Bolton		310	70.0	76.3	46.9	77.3
=107 Liverpool Hope		282	73.6	74.0	48.1	77.3
=107 Cumbria	5.6	213	77.6	78.7	44.4	77.3
110 Newman		282	73.3	84.5	38.0	77.2
111 Westminster	2.4	319	63.7	79.7	47.6	77.1
112 Glyndŵr		197	72.9	73.3	59.7	76.4
113 Roehampton	4.5	254	66.1	70.7	56.6	76.2
114 London Metropolitan	0.6	208	73.1	77.7	47.0	75.6
115 Staffordshire	2.6	248	66.9	76.5	47.4	75.4
116 East London	0.8	292	67.3	74.1	41.4	75.2
117 Bedfordshire	3.1	208	72.1	75.4	39.6	74.3

Employed in professional job:	51%	Employed in non-professional job and studying:	1%
Employed in professional job and studying:	3%	Employed in non-professional job:	26%
Studying:	6%	Unemployed:	13%
Average starting professional salary:	£22,449	Average starting non-professional salary:	£16,572

Celtic Studies

Only 145 students started full-time Celtic studies degrees in 2014, making it one of the smallest categories in the *Guide*. Applications rose sharply after a big drop in 2013, but are still nowhere near their peak before the switch to higher fees, while the wider languages group is still struggling to attract students. The number of universities in our table remains at ten this year, however, and 17 plan to run degree courses in 2016, either in Celtic studies or one of the Celtic languages.

Celtic Studies cont

The ranking is split between four universities from Wales, which naturally major in Welsh, and the remaining six, which focus on Irish or Gaelic studies. Ironically, it is the only one from England that tops the table for the fourth year in a row. Cambridge's average entry grades are more than 100 points ahead of its nearest rival and it posted the best scores in the teaching sections of the National Student Survey (NSS), as well as achieving the best results in the 2014 Research Excellent Framework (REF). Queen's, Belfast ran Cambridge close in the REF and moved up four places to fourth overall.

Second-placed Bangor had the best scores in the sections of the NSS devoted to the student experience, while Aberystwyth saw the highest proportion find graduate-level jobs or continue their studies. The Welsh universities all registered good scores for graduate prospects, reflecting a strong labour market for speakers of the language and active recruitment to postgraduate courses. This has helped Celtic studies to a place in the top 30 in the employment table, with 46 per cent of graduates – the largest proportion for any subject – moving on to a postgraduate course. The small numbers make for extremely volatile results from year to year, especially for graduate prospects. In the 2015 *Guide*, 15 per cent of graduates were unemployed, for example, whereas this year's figure is only 5 per cent. The story is not as positive where graduate salaries are concerned: the £18,497 average in graduate-level jobs was in the bottom ten of the 66 subject groupings. Students seem to enjoy their courses, however: all ten universities satisfied at least 85 per cent of their final-year undergraduates both on teaching and the broader student experience. The results were the best for any subject.

Celtic Studies	Research quality %	Entry standards	Teaching quality %	Student experience %	Graduate prospects %	Overall score
1 Cambridge	54.0	568	98.7	96.9	65.5	100.0
2 Bangor	39.6	382	96.3	98.0	83.6	96.3
3 Cardiff	32.5	451	93.4	88.5	78.4	93.9
4 Queen's, Belfast	53.6	355	91.1	95.0	57.6	93.6
5 Glasgow	41.1		93.1	90.8	65.4	93.0
6 Aberystwyth	23.7	398	86.8	88.5	86.7	91.0
7 Liverpool	38.9		92.2	94.3	45.0	90.3
8 Swansea	19.4	303	90.0	89.1	81.1	89.2
9 Ulster	35.7	259	90.6	93.1	35.1	87.2
10 Highlands and Islands		351*	85.0	95.1	64.3	85.5

Employed in professional job:	24%	Employed in non-professional job and studying:	2%
Employed in professional job and studying:	6%	Employed in non-professional job:	25%
Studying:	38%	Unemployed:	5%
Average starting professional salary:	£18,497	Average starting non-professional salary:	£16,484

Chemical Engineering

Chemical engineering is booming: the numbers starting degrees rose by 25 per cent in 2014, following the sixth successive rise in the demand for places. Applications have increased by almost 50 per cent in two years and are running at twice the numbers seen five years before that. Although not yet as popular as some other branches of engineering, it is closing the gap rapidly. High graduate salaries may have something to do with it: although the average salary in graduate-level jobs fell by more than £1,000 between 2013 and 2014, the figure of £28,641 was bettered only by dentistry and medicine. The subject has dropped out of the top ten for employment this year after rises in unemployment and the numbers starting out in "non-professional" jobs, but it is still in the top 15.

Cambridge tops the table for the 14th year in a row and its three nearest challengers are also unchanged since the 2015 *Guide*. Cambridge has much the highest entry standards, the best employment record and the top research score. Both Cambridge and second-placed Imperial were ranked by QS among the top six universities in the world for chemical engineering in 2015. The most satisfied students were at third-placed Bath, while the West of Scotland was the highest-placed of four post-1992 universities in the table. Four more universities than last year appear in the new table and 39 institutions are planning to offer chemical engineering in 2016. They include specialist options such as renewable energy engineering at Ulster and chemistry with green nanotechnology at Glyndŵr.

Degree courses normally demand chemistry and maths A levels or their equivalent and often physics as well. Four out of five chemical engineers come with A levels or equivalent qualifications, and average entry grades are the highest for any engineering subject – all but eight of the 26 universities in the table average more than 400 points at entry. This helps produce engineering's largest proportion of Firsts and 2:1s. Most courses offer industrial placements in the final year and lead to Chartered Engineer status.

Chemical Engineering	Research quality %	Entry standards	Teaching quality %	Student experience %	Graduate prospects %	Overall score
1 Cambridge	62.0	650	86.0	91.3	96.4	100.0
2 Imperial College	59.6	617	80.9	89.9	90.8	96.7
3 Bath	37.4	505	89.7	95.0	90.4	93.0
4 Birmingham	47.0	467	87.1	91.3	92.7	92.9
5 Heriot-Watt	47.8	449	79.5	86.7	85.9	89.3
6 Newcastle	30.2	450	83.1	90.7	88.2	88.4
7 Leeds	30.7	453	83.9	93.1	81.9	87.9
=8 Lancaster	41.6	413	82.9	86.8		87.6
=8 Edinburgh	50.3	500	65.5	75.4	91.4	87.6
10 Loughborough	41.8	439	76.5	85.5	86.3	87.5
11 Manchester	48.4	489	69.8	80.2	84.1	87.3
12 Nottingham	40.8	430	76.2	85.5	84.9	86.8
13 Sheffield	36.8	412	80.9	91.6	79.7	86.6
14 Queen's, Belfast	36.7	404	80.4	88.2	83.3	86.5
15 Swansea	45.5	339	79.0	91.6	83.3	86.4
16 Strathclyde	37.2	518	63.2	80.0	87.6	85.6

Chemical Engineering cont	Research quality %	Entry standards	Teaching quality %	Student experience %	Graduate prospects %	Overall score
17 Surrey	30.8	428	78.0	83.4	80.6	84.6
18 University College London	44.6	479	64.2	76.8	72.0	82.8
19 Aberdeen	28.4	468	66.1	70.2	86.4	82.2
20 Bradford	7.7	315	86.3	88.7	78.6	80.5
21 Hull	16.5	291	79.6	85.3		78.2
22 West of Scotland	9.0	352	74.2	84.3	66.7	76.5
23 Teesside	5.8	307	82.9	92.7	58.6	76.4
24 Aston	20.6	348	68.3	77.6	61.3	75.2
25 Portsmouth	9.1	291	82.6	83.3	42.9	72.5
26 London South Bank	19.6	219	66.2	81.3	50.0	70.1

Employed in professional job:	57%	Employed in non-professional job and studying:	1%
Employed in professional job and studying:	3%	Employed in non-professional job:	10%
Studying:	17%	Unemployed:	13%
Average starting professional salary:	£28,641	Average starting non-professional salary:	£16,111

Chemistry

Chemistry's recovery from the period in which it was considered an endangered subject is continuing apace. Applications rose by 10 per cent in 2014, as they had the previous year, and for the first time more than 5,000 students started undergraduate courses. In 2016, 100 universities and colleges – five more than in the current year – plan to offer the subject, as student demand continues to rise.

For many, chemistry remains the classic science and forensic science has become an attractive alternative. Some courses demand maths as well as chemistry, and most successful candidates for the leading universities take more than one science at A level. Forensic science covers aspects of biology, physics, mathematics and statistics, as well as chemistry. The skills acquired on degree courses are much in demand: chemistry is firmly established in the top 20 in the employment table, with more than a third of all graduates going on to further study. The average salary of £22,232 in graduate-level jobs is also close to the top 20.

Cambridge has maintained its substantial lead at the top of the table with the highest entry standards and the best research grades – 97 per cent of the work submitted for the Research Excellence Framework was considered world-leading or internationally excellent. Both Cambridge and Oxford, which has retaken second place from Durham, are among the top six universities in the world for chemistry, according to QS. Loughborough, in 16th place, has the most satisfied students for its teaching quality, while Nottingham Trent, in 31st place has the highest student experience score. East Anglia, at equal 19th, has the best employment rate.

Chemistry is mainly old university territory, with no post-1992 institutions in the top 30, although Nottingham Trent is only one place outside it. There are now 15 modern universities in the table as a whole, however, with the West of Scotland, South Wales and Sheffield Hallam all in the top 40. The contrast between the top and bottom of the table in terms of entry grades is starker than ever. While Cambridge entrants average almost 650 points and those at five other universities top 500 points, ten universities in the new table, compared with only four last year, average less than 300 points on the UCAS tariff. Nearly nine out of ten undergraduates have A levels or their equivalent.

Chemistry	Research quality %	Entry standards	Teaching quality %	Student experience %	Graduate prospects %	Overall score
1 Cambridge	70.3	648	86.0	86.3	87.4	100.0
2 Oxford	63.1	585	80.6	85.3	89.1	96.7
=3 Edinburgh	48.4	502	82.0	86.2	88.1	93.2
=3 Durham	49.1	594	84.7	90.8	73.6	93.2
5 York	44.6	482	86.0	90.8	85.2	93.0
6 St Andrews	50.3	502	79.1	89.9	86.0	92.8
7 Warwick	50.8	431	88.7	89.9	82.2	92.5
8 Sussex	25.8	408	92.7	92.8	91.1	92.0
9 Bristol	56.6	494	84.0	87.2	76.0	91.9
10 Bath	43.0	444	87.5	87.6	84.4	91.8
11 Nottingham	48.5	440	83.6	89.7	84.1	91.7
12 Imperial College	54.6	540	71.9	77.3	85.4	91.0
=13 Sheffield	38.9	428	86.9	92.3	80.6	90.4
=13 Cardiff	30.9	404	85.2	91.3	89.7	90.4
=13 Glasgow	41.1	484	83.9	88.3	78.8	90.4
16 Loughborough	23.9	347	94.8	96.3	86.3	90.2
17 Southampton	50.7	408	81.3	90.5	80.9	90.1
18 Birmingham	37.3	423	83.8	88.0	83.3	89.5
=19 Heriot-Watt	34.2	417	91.3	92.2	75.5	89.4
=19 Surrey	30.8	377	86.1	91.8	86.8	89.4
=19 East Anglia	39.2	367	79.6	84.8	93.0	89.4
22 Manchester	46.0	444	79.6	88.8	78.9	89.3
23 Liverpool	55.6	384	78.7	83.9	82.3	89.2
=24 Leeds	35.9	429	82.8	86.0	80.6	88.4
=24 University College London	56.0	498	68.8	79.7	79.1	88.4
26 Strathclyde	40.1	446	75.2	84.9	82.3	88.0
27 Keele	41.1	368	86.9	93.2	72.0	87.5
28 Lancaster	37.5	397	83.2	83.5		87.1
29 Queen's, Belfast	34.7	411	74.2	81.3	87.2	87.0
30 Leicester	32.8	377	86.8	89.1	70.2	85.8
31 Nottingham Trent	24.1	290	90.6	96.8	75.0	85.5
32 Bradford	9.5	261	92.4	93.9	84.9	85.3
33 West of Scotland	29.0	290	84.6	83.9	83.3	85.2
34 Newcastle	28.5	405	80.4	88.8	72.6	85.0
35 Kent	27.5	352	81.4	82.8	72.2	83.1
36 Bangor	19.1	314	76.3	87.2	82.6	82.9
37 Reading	27.3	326	82.6	82.8	69.5	82.2
38 South Wales		305	84.4	87.8	80.7	81.7

Chemistry cont	Research quality %	Entry standards	Teaching quality %	Student experience %	Graduate prospects %	Overall score
39 Aberdeen	31.6	420	76.1	73.3	65.9	81.5
40 Sheffield Hallam		296	88.9	88.7	73.7	81.0
41 Hull	24.2	316	74.4	87.3	72.6	80.9
42 Aston	20.6	320	84.0	76.8	68.3	80.5
43 Huddersfield	11.0	296	78.5	83.6	75.8	80.0
=44 Queen Mary, London	37.0	361	72.2	72.9	65.2	79.8
=44 Liverpool John Moores	6.0	342	79.7	79.8	73.6	79.8
46 Northumbria	14.0	336	84.2	84.8	62.2	79.6
47 Manchester Metropolitan	16.3	326	77.8	83.8	67.5	79.4
48 Brighton	4.8	328	73.7	82.8	70.8	77.7
49 Central Lancashire	11.7	307	72.2	72.3	71.9	76.8
50 Kingston	2.6	265	73.8	73.1	75.8	76.1
51 Plymouth		291	82.5	83.3	56.4	75.0
52 Greenwich	7.4	287	75.7	83.5	58.3	74.8
53 London Metropolitan		233	86.6	86.6	53.8	74.4
54 University of the Arts London		291	67.7	70.3	69.2	73.2

Employed in professional job:	40%	Employed in non-professional job and studying:	1%
Employed in professional job and studying:	3%	Employed in non-professional job:	12%
Studying:	32%	Unemployed:	11%
Average starting professional salary:	£22,232	Average starting non-professional salary:	£15,705

Civil Engineering

Civil engineering managed a small increase in applications in 2014, but still suffered its fourth successive drop in enrolments at a time when other branches of engineering are flourishing. The decline set in before the introduction of £9,000 fees and may have more to do with applicants' concerns about the state of the construction industry. If so, they are not borne out by the latest employment figures: civil engineering is in the top ten subjects for graduate jobs and only just outside it for starting salaries. Even the 9 per cent of graduates who start out in "non-professional" jobs earn more than in any other subject, averaging £18,300 in 2014. This is reflected in this table, where a third of the 53 universities saw at least nine out of ten leavers go straight into graduate-level jobs or on to postgraduate study. The rate was 100 per cent at Northumbria, in 18th place, and Derby, which is 33rd.

The top four in the table are unchanged since the 2015 *Guide*. Cambridge, the perennial leader, has by far the highest entry standards and, like second-placed Imperial College London, is rated among the top five universities in the world by QS. Undergraduates at the West of Scotland, in 29th place overall, were the most satisfied with their teaching, feedback and academic support. Imperial had the best scores in the rest of the National Student Survey. Only four universities failed to satisfy at least three-quarters of final-year undergraduates, taking all sections of the survey into account.

Some of the top degrees in civil engineering are four-year courses leading to an MEng; others are sandwich courses incorporating a period at work. The leading departments will expect physics and maths A levels, or their equivalent. Fewer than half of all civil engineering undergraduates are admitted with A levels, however, reflecting the popularity of BTEC. Almost half of the universities in the table are post-1992 institutions. Northumbria, a new entrant this year, is the only one to reach the top 20. It is joined in the top 30 by Abertay, after a leap of 24 places fuelled mainly by high satisfaction ratings, Coventry, West of Scotland and Liverpool John Moores.

Civil Engineering	Research quality %	Entry standards	Teaching quality %	Student experience %	Graduate prospects %	Overall score
1 Cambridge	67.0	642	86.0	91.3	96.6	100.0
2 Imperial College	61.5	563	86.5	94.3	93.3	97.4
3 Bath	52.9	507	86.4	92.3	95.6	95.3
4 Southampton	52.3	468	89.2	93.8	90.5	94.1
5 Sheffield	43.1	463	84.8	88.6	94.2	92.1
=6 Edinburgh	50.3	473	77.2	90.1	93.2	91.8
=6 Dundee	46.2	431	87.4	92.2	89.6	91.8
8 Glasgow	47.2	480	77.3	86.2	92.2	90.8
9 Bristol	52.3	511	75.8	83.8	87.9	90.6
=10 Leeds	32.0	416	86.9	90.6	88.8	89.3
=10 Swansea	45.5	339	82.1	85.3	97.3	89.3
12 Newcastle	40.9	385	81.8	89.8	90.8	89.0
13 Cardiff	35.0	432	75.2	89.1	94.8	88.8
=14 Nottingham	40.8	417	79.7	86.3	89.2	88.6
=14 Heriot-Watt	47.8	417	77.9	85.4	87.6	88.6
16 Loughborough	26.9	391	84.5	90.3	92.6	88.4
17 Birmingham	21.9	420	85.6	91.1	90.1	88.3
18 Northumbria	30.7	343	85.6	79.4	100.0	88.1
19 Manchester	36.4	414	79.0	84.3	87.7	87.3
20 Surrey	30.8	421	80.0	90.5	84.3	87.1
21 Strathclyde	35.7	429	77.5	86.1	84.8	86.9
22 Aberdeen	28.4	402	77.1	78.4	96.4	86.7
23 Exeter	36.4	432	70.8	79.3	92.4	86.4
24 Queen's, Belfast	31.3	368	75.0	90.3	88.5	85.8
25 Liverpool	32.1	381	74.4	82.5	88.5	85.1
26 Abertay	16.3	320	90.0	93.4	79.2	84.3
=27 Ulster		280	87.3	92.6	94.0	83.9
=27 Coventry	10.3	292	88.9	93.8	84.7	83.9
29 West of Scotland	9.0	260	93.6	92.3	82.7	83.4
=30 Bradford	17.8	298	80.1	87.2	83.9	82.3
=30 Liverpool John Moores		345	79.2	86.0	90.7	82.3
=30 Brunel	23.7	340	77.9	89.0	76.7	82.3
33 Derby	6.7	236	79.5	80.0	100.0	81.8
34 University College London	23.1	494	55.3	72.7	88.2	81.6

Civil Engineering cont	Research quality %	Entry standards	Teaching quality %	Student experience %	Graduate prospects %	Overall score
=35 Nottingham Trent		281	81.2	88.1	87.9	80.9
=35 City	20.2	342	76.2	78.3	80.2	80.9
37 West of England	10.6	276	86.4	86.9	76.2	80.5
38 Salford	19.6	284	81.3	83.6	75.8	80.3
39 Brighton	5.1	303	80.6	85.6	81.1	80.2
40 Plymouth		284	86.2	88.0	79.1	80.1
=41 South Wales		284	79.3	82.9	88.0	80.0
=41 Teesside	5.8	320	85.2	90.3	70.5	80.0
=43 Greenwich	5.5	304	87.8	92.2	67.6	79.8
=43 Portsmouth	9.1	297	76.3	84.2	82.4	79.8
45 Anglia Ruskin	5.2	260	79.2	81.8	85.7	79.4
46 Glasgow Caledonian	9.1	370	62.5	74.4	85.7	78.3
47 East London	2.3	274*	81.2	86.4	73.0	77.8
48 Edinburgh Napier	7.7	327	66.0	82.9	75.3	76.8
49 London South Bank	19.6	274	77.9	83.7	60.9	76.4
50 Kingston	2.9	285	75.4	84.2	62.0	74.5
51 Leeds Beckett	5.6	212	60.7	72.8	88.5	74.3
52 Bolton		220*	70.7	82.7	66.7	72.6
53 West London		224	80.0	88.4	50.0	71.8

Employed in professional job:	68%	Employed in non-professional job and studying:	1%
Employed in professional job and studying:	4%	Employed in non-professional job:	8%
Studying:	10%	Unemployed:	10%
Average starting professional salary:	£24,776	Average starting non-professional salary:	£18,303

Classics and Ancient History

The demand for places in classics recovered dramatically in 2014 after two years of decline since the introduction of £9,000 fees. Applications rose by almost 20 per cent to their highest level since 2007 and universities responded with a record number of places. Ancient history was already sharing in the increases enjoyed by other history departments. Independent schools dominate provision of Latin and Greek at A level, producing some of the highest average grades of any subjects. However, most universities offering classics teach the subject from scratch, as well as to more practised students.

Cambridge has topped the table with Oxford in second place for the last ten years, but the lead has never been as big. Cambridge has the highest scores in the table for research and entry grades, as well as for the sections of the National Student Survey devoted to the student experience. Royal Holloway, although only seven places off the bottom of the table, posted the highest level of satisfaction on teaching, feedback and academic support. Satisfaction rates are universally high: only two universities failed (narrowly) to win the approval of three-quarters of final-year undergraduates.

However, classics does not quite live up to its reputation as a magnet for IT companies and management consultants, who value the logic and precision demanded of classicists. Although starting salaries in graduate-level jobs are in the top 30, average earnings have dropped slightly since the 2015 *Guide*. The proportion going straight into professional jobs or on to further study is just outside the top half of the table of 66 subject groupings. About a third of graduates opt for postgraduate courses, but only marginally more go straight into graduate jobs.

More than 30 universities plan to offer classics courses in 2016. They are mainly older institutions – Roehampton is the only post-1992 university in our ranking. Several universities teach the subjects as part of a modular degree scheme, but not as a degree in its own right, while most providers now broaden their offering with degrees in classical studies or classical civilisation that range beyond language.

Classics and Ancient History	Research quality %	Entry standards	Teaching quality %	Student experience %	Graduate prospects %	Overall score
1 Cambridge	65.0	591	91.0	93.2	85.7	100.0
2 Oxford	58.3	568	82.3	87.5	80.2	94.7
3 Durham	54.3	526	87.7	85.6	79.7	94.0
4 St Andrews	43.2	478	86.9	84.3	86.0	91.6
5 Exeter	45.0	465	86.3	83.8	81.6	90.6
6 Warwick	45.0	433	86.0	90.1	76.6	89.7
7 Newcastle	44.7	382	86.2	87.2	77.9	88.3
8 King's College London	43.6	455	86.9	85.2	65.4	87.8
9 Nottingham	52.0	384	84.0	84.8	67.7	87.2
10 University College London	42.7	500	77.8	70.8	69.0	85.6
11 Glasgow	32.7	391	92.1	91.3	58.0	85.0
12 Birmingham	40.3	402	75.0	73.8	76.3	83.7
13 Bristol	42.2	459	69.8	71.9	71.8	83.3
=14 Manchester	31.0	370	86.1	85.2	64.5	83.2
=14 Reading	45.2	367	82.5	87.1	53.3	83.2
16 Royal Holloway, London	20.4	373	93.9	87.0	62.1	83.1
17 Liverpool	28.9	409	87.7	83.7	58.2	83.0
18 Kent	33.1	340	88.5	88.6	58.1	82.8
19 Edinburgh	34.9	497	79.6	81.0	50.0	82.7
20 Swansea	25.0	305	89.5	85.6	69.7	82.3
21 Leeds	29.1	398	79.3	84.6	65.6	82.1
22 Roehampton		270	86.7	83.3	40.2	71.4

Employed in professional job:	35%	Employed in non-professional job and studying:	4%
Employed in professional job and studying:	3%	Employed in non-professional job:	20%
Studying:	26%	Unemployed:	12%
Average starting professional salary:	£21,635	Average starting non-professional salary:	£14,674

Communication and Media Studies

Courses in communication and media studies seem to have confounded the sceptics who believed that a combination of £9,000 fees and poor employment prospects would bring about a decline in recruitment long predicted in the media itself. An 18 per cent increase in applications for media studies in 2014, following a rise of similar proportions in 2013, has produced record levels of enrolment. The increases in journalism and associated degrees such as publicity studies have been more modest, but the demand for the subject group as a whole is back to the level seen before the fees went up.

Communication and media studies used to be the preserve of the new universities, but older universities have been moving in and now monopolise the top 20. Lancaster has taken over top place from Warwick without registering the top score on any individual measure. Second-placed Loughborough, which is only a fraction behind Lancaster and the same distance ahead of Newcastle, has the best research score, while the highest entry standards are at Strathclyde. Like last year, Southampton has the most satisfied students in all areas of the National Student Survey. Robert Gordon, at 22nd place, is the highest post-1992 university.

The division of jobs into professional and non-graduate fields of employment hits communication and media studies harder than most other subjects. Academics in the field argue that it is normal for students completing media courses to take "entry level" work that is not classified as a graduate job. The subjects have escaped from the bottom five of the employment league this year, but are still well inside the bottom ten. Starting salaries for those who do find graduate-level work are in the bottom four, with a lower average than last year.

The effect on the table is obvious. Kent is well ahead of the field with nine out of ten graduates going straight into professional jobs or staying on for a postgraduate course. Of the remaining 90 institutions, only Sheffield, Lancaster, Loughborough and Newcastle managed positive destinations for three-quarters of its graduates and the rate was below 40 per cent at a dozen universities. Entry scores remain modest: although no institution averages less than 210 points, almost half registered averages below 300 points in 2014.

Communication and Media Studies	Research quality %	Entry standards	Teaching quality %	Student experience %	Graduate prospects %	Overall score
1 Lancaster	51.4	406	85.3	82.1	81.8	100.0
2 Loughborough	62.3	370	82.1	86.9	81.0	99.8
3 Newcastle	37.8	408	92.3	92.8	75.8	99.6
4 Cardiff	55.4	407	89.7	88.1	67.4	99.3
5 Warwick	61.7	423	93.0	92.5	49.6	98.4
6 King's College London	55.8	454	89.2	84.6	52.8	97.8
7 Leeds	54.5	411	83.7	90.9	64.6	97.7
8 Sheffield	37.9	419	75.9	88.1	82.4	97.3
9 Southampton	42.7	391	93.8	94.5	54.5	95.6
10 Surrey	30.2	396	90.2	85.8	63.2	93.9
11 Leicester	46.1	364	79.8	82.3	65.4	92.7
12 Liverpool	27.5	390	83.9	88.9	63.1	92.1

13 City	30.1	412	74.7	79.0	70.8	91.9
14 Queen Mary, London	35.1	414	86.1	83.3	50.5	91.5
15 Sussex	43.6	372	69.9	77.2	72.3	91.3
16 Queen's, Belfast	38.3	347	86.4	89.9	51.4	90.1
17 East Anglia	43.8	376	80.5	83.0	50.1	89.8
=18 Strathclyde	39.4	459	69.5	75.0	50.0	89.4
=18 Stirling	36.0	389	80.7	83.4	50.5	89.4
20 Goldsmiths, London	60.0	386	68.2	75.0	50.8	89.2
21 Keele	25.0	316	84.2	89.8	64.4	89.0
22 Robert Gordon	7.5	372	83.3	82.9	69.9	88.9
23 Royal Holloway, London	38.1	386	77.9	76.1	53.4	88.7
24 Bangor	24.7	305	92.9	90.7	51.0	87.7
25 Swansea	18.5	312	92.7	93.8	52.3	87.6
26 De Montfort	31.2	281	82.7	83.3	64.8	87.4
27 Exeter		455	82.7	83.0	47.7	86.5
28 Coventry	18.1	300	88.7	89.4	55.9	86.4
29 Westminster	28.3	353	75.2	79.3	55.4	85.9
30 Glasgow Caledonian	15.2	410	74.1	77.9	53.8	85.7
31 Northumbria	22.2	342	84.3	85.3	47.3	85.5
=32 Edinburgh Napier	9.5	390	80.0	84.3	49.8	85.2
=32 Bournemouth	15.1	353	77.1	78.9	59.6	85.2
=34 Nottingham Trent	10.0	299	83.2	85.8	61.7	84.7
=34 Lincoln	4.0	339	77.7	84.3	64.4	84.7
=36 Kent		387	55.5	62.1	90.9	84.2
=36 Oxford Brookes	25.3	339	79.3	77.5	48.7	84.2
38 Roehampton	26.4	255	79.3	81.0	62.4	84.0
39 Portsmouth	12.8	286	86.7	84.8	52.9	83.3
=40 Ulster	34.0	283	80.0	83.6	44.2	83.0
=40 Bradford		296	79.9	84.1	65.9	83.0
=40 Salford	36.9	343	74.4	76.3	39.6	83.0
43 Brunel	23.0	337	77.5	81.2	44.4	82.9
44 Leeds Trinity	3.9	269	86.5	85.8	57.4	82.3
=45 Winchester	15.8	296	84.2	85.1	45.8	82.2
=45 York St John	4.4	280	89.8	85.3	51.2	82.2
=47 Leeds Beckett	11.0	270	86.0	83.2	53.2	82.1
=47 Gloucestershire	9.3	308	87.1	83.0	45.6	82.1
49 St Mary's, Twickenham	9.1	256	86.7	88.1	53.6	82.0
50 Falmouth		279	83.1	77.8	63.8	81.7
51 Central Lancashire	7.9	320	71.6	79.6	60.1	81.6
52 Liverpool John Moores	6.2	327	75.1	80.9	54.1	81.4
53 Manchester Metropolitan	29.0	331	71.3	74.3	44.0	81.3
54 Anglia Ruskin	26.4	233	84.9	87.1	44.4	81.2
55 Birmingham City	6.0	315	73.2	74.8	59.9	80.9
56 West of England	18.6	297	78.0	71.9	50.9	80.8
57 Chester	4.3	273	84.6	85.1	51.1	80.7
=58 Huddersfield		285	77.5	82.5	60.4	80.6
=58 Bath Spa	13.9	306	80.8	80.2	44.0	80.6

Communication and Media Studies cont	Research quality %	Entry standards	Teaching quality %	Student experience %	Graduate prospects %	Overall score
=58 Queen Margaret, Edinburgh	14.0	342	81.1	78.5	37.1	80.6
61 Sunderland	13.0	293	78.8	81.5	47.7	80.5
62 Sheffield Hallam	14.4	289	76.4	78.4	49.5	79.9
63 West of Scotland	11.3	302	77.0	82.5	45.3	79.8
64 Southampton Solent	0.8	279	80.1	83.0	52.3	79.4
=65 Hull	11.2	312	81.3	68.4	42.2	78.8
=65 University for the Creative Arts	3.4	264	79.4	79.5	53.3	78.8
=67 University of the Arts London		266	75.1	76.7	58.1	78.1
=67 Glyndŵr	7.8	275	71.8	74.6	55.6	78.1
69 Middlesex	11.0	270	74.4	73.4	51.5	78.0
70 Chichester		257	93.6	85.6	34.3	77.8
71 Buckinghamshire New		243	84.0	81.9	48.2	77.6
72 Worcester	8.2	286	73.7	77.9	46.4	77.5
73 Canterbury Christ Church	7.3	280	73.2	76.2	49.1	77.4
74 Staffordshire	6.7	265	73.4	75.6	51.9	77.2
=75 Brighton	16.2	297	71.7	72.1	41.8	77.1
=75 Edge Hill	10.2	309	78.5	75.4	34.3	77.1
77 Kingston	15.7	279	67.3	71.9	48.7	76.8
78 Derby	13.5	260	80.2	81.6	34.6	76.6
79 Teesside	2.9	275	75.0	79.0	43.0	76.0
80 East London	13.9	265	73.6	78.3	38.8	75.9
81 Liverpool Hope		297	78.1	82.3	34.3	75.7
82 London Metropolitan	5.9	259	71.4	75.5	46.6	75.3
83 Bedfordshire	8.2	210	82.1	78.9	40.8	75.1
=84 Aberystwyth	9.2	291	68.8	73.3	38.3	74.6
=84 Northampton		250	76.5	74.5	44.6	74.6
86 St Mark and St John		279	77.9	74.2	30.3	73.0
87 West London	4.5	256	62.4	59.4	53.9	72.5
88 Cumbria		282	66.9	64.4	41.5	71.9
89 South Wales		317	66.6	60.1	36.6	71.8
90 Greenwich	3.5	299	63.7	70.7	34.3	71.7
91 London South Bank	12.8	245	67.3	77.8	30.1	71.6

Employed in professional job:	45%	Employed in non-professional job and studying:	1%
Employed in professional job and studying:	1%	Employed in non-professional job:	35%
Studying:	5%	Unemployed:	13%
Average starting professional salary:	£18,179	Average starting non-professional salary:	£15,139

Computer Science

Computer science is the ultimate example of students reacting to their perception of the jobs market when they choose courses. Applications declined for a decade after the dot.com bubble burst but, with the exception of single year when £9,000 fees were introduced, have risen strongly throughout this decade. There was another 13 per cent increase in 2014 and enrolments were the highest ever. It seems that the various courses in the computing field are once again seen as a natural route into a rewarding career. Although unemployment is still high, at 14 per cent, the latest survey showed nearly two-thirds of graduates going straight into professional roles and the subject was 14th in the salary league, averaging £23,766 in graduate-level jobs.

The top four in the table remain the same as last year, when Oxford took over the leadership from Cambridge. Oxford is rated as third in the world for computer science by QS, but does not lead in any of the measures in our new table. Cambridge has the highest entry standards, while third-placed Imperial College produced the best grades in the Research Excellence Framework. St Andrews, in fourth place, posted some of the highest grades in any subject in the National Student Survey, exceeding 96 per cent satisfaction for teaching as well as the student experience. Lancaster, which shares 23rd place with three other universities, had the best record in the jobs market. Lincoln is the highest-placed modern university, just outside the top 40.

Entry standards vary more widely than in most subjects, with average scores on the UCAS tariff ranging from more than 550 points at the top three universities to barely 200 points at four of the lowest-ranked institutions. Some of the leading universities demand maths at A level, or the equivalent, while others want computing or computer science. The most competitive area is the small field of artificial intelligence, where there were less than 100 places in 2014, while the strongest growth has been in computer games courses, where the number of applications doubled in a year after a big increase in 2013. A total of 214 institutions, including a large number of further education colleges, are offering courses at undergraduate level in 2016.

Computer Science	Research quality %	Entry standards	Teaching quality %	Student experience %	Graduate prospects %	Overall score
1 Oxford	60.6	584	89.5*	92.4*	94.7	100.0
2 Cambridge	57.1	618	85.3	82.4	96.7	98.6
3 Imperial College	64.1	564	83.7	89.2	95.1	98.2
4 St Andrews	33.4	499	96.7	98.5	97.3	97.2
5 Warwick	54.8	477	80.3	85.5	88.3	92.4
6 Bristol	49.2	516	74.2	81.2	96.0	92.2
7 Swansea	47.5	323	90.7	93.3	95.0	91.7
8 Durham	38.8	466	80.5	85.3	96.7	91.6
=9 Southampton	48.2	479	73.3	85.5	94.8	91.2
=9 Manchester	50.7	451	79.9	89.9	85.2	91.2
=11 Exeter	40.7	423	85.3	89.4		91.0
=11 York	46.9	469	79.1	84.3	89.4	91.0
13 Sheffield	51.1	408	78.8	85.1	95.2	90.8
14 Edinburgh	54.3	499	76.1	85.9	79.5	90.6
15 Bath	33.3	465	83.8	85.1	86.3	89.8
16 Birmingham	46.4	424	79.5	83.8	89.3	89.7
17 Glasgow	50.3	443	78.0	83.3	85.1	89.6
18 Leeds	41.6	402	84.3	87.7	85.6	89.5

Computer Science cont	Research quality %	Entry standards	Teaching quality %	Student experience %	Graduate prospects %	Overall score
19 Dundee	29.4	374	90.7	94.9	82.7	89.1
20 University College London	62.7	502	61.2	75.3	91.2	89.0
21 Surrey	25.3	410	82.2	87.2	94.1	88.6
22 Newcastle	49.7	408	76.0	84.7	85.8	88.4
=23 Lancaster	44.8	417	68.1	81.6	97.4	87.9
=23 Strathclyde	21.1	475	78.2	86.1	88.2	87.9
=23 Royal Holloway, London	35.1	376	85.9	85.5	84.8	87.9
=23 Heriot-Watt	39.5	414	80.2	87.5	81.3	87.9
27 Nottingham	45.4	401	76.4	83.7	86.4	87.8
=28 Liverpool	40.5	400	79.5	84.5	84.8	87.7
=28 Aston	21.7	362	86.4	89.4	92.1	87.7
=30 Loughborough	18.7	366	87.5	89.7	89.4	87.3
=30 Aberdeen	37.4	414	78.3	80.0	87.8	87.3
32 Kent	37.8	363	75.7	84.3	92.5	86.7
33 East Anglia	35.9	354	79.4	89.0	81.8	85.9
34 Cardiff	25.0	396	74.2	83.9	92.1	85.7
35 Queen's, Belfast	29.5	361	77.1	86.3	88.7	85.6
36 Sussex	21.6	364	77.2	83.8	90.8	84.8
37 Essex	34.3	309	82.9	87.2	78.6	84.5
38 Aberystwyth	38.4	297	77.7	80.6	89.2	84.4
=39 King's College London	47.6	422	64.7	72.6	83.6	84.2
=39 Hull	22.2	324	83.0	84.3	84.9	84.2
41 Keele	10.8	361	85.9	91.8	75.9	83.9
42 City	19.2	369	84.1	84.5	75.7	83.8
43 Lincoln	13.6	334	82.6	87.5	80.3	83.0
44 Oxford Brookes	13.0	434	78.6	83.2	70.5	82.5
=45 Queen Mary, London	37.4	374	67.3	76.3	82.2	82.4
=45 Bangor	17.6	277	84.1	81.4	86.4	82.4
47 Leicester	30.2	390	68.8	71.1	85.9	82.3
=48 Brunel	25.2	351	74.7	81.3	75.7	81.5
=48 Reading	16.3	356	68.8	80.5	89.7	81.5
50 Coventry	3.3	302	88.8	90.9	71.9	81.2
51 West of England	5.9	326	80.4	80.8	83.7	81.0
=52 Edge Hill	0.3	305	89.6	90.7	70.1	80.8
=52 Northampton		285	88.1	88.7	77.2	80.8
54 Abertay	3.4	377	82.5	83.6	69.9	80.7
55 Goldsmiths, London	29.2	337	77.2	78.2	66.2	80.2
56 Plymouth	21.8	313	76.9	79.0	74.6	80.1
57 Central Lancashire		332	81.6	86.2	75.0	80.0
58 Ulster	16.6	300	77.8	82.7	73.5	79.6
59 Huddersfield	7.4	348	81.2	78.7	69.9	79.4
60 De Montfort	13.4	306	71.5	78.8	82.7	79.0
=61 Stirling	14.0	354	65.9	73.7	85.4	78.9

=61	Derby	5.0	305	80.9	80.1	75.0	78.9
63	Bournemouth	8.5	328	72.6	75.6	81.8	78.7
64	Liverpool John Moores	3.2	340	79.4	81.8	67.9	78.4
65	Buckinghamshire New		235	94.6	90.6	60.4	78.3
=66	Nottingham Trent	5.2	297	75.0	82.4	77.1	78.1
=66	Salford	15.3	347	77.8	76.6	62.6	78.1
68	Northumbria	4.0	351	75.9	76.4	70.4	77.7
69	Manchester Metropolitan	5.6	344	77.9	78.8	65.0	77.6
70	Sheffield Hallam		303	80.1	80.9	68.8	77.2
=71	Robert Gordon	4.3	363	68.1	72.4	78.1	77.1
=71	Liverpool Hope	8.8	291	82.0	81.7	60.7	77.1
73	Portsmouth	7.2	300	77.1	82.7	65.4	77.0
74	Leeds Beckett	0.2	263	84.9	84.7	64.2	76.9
75	Chester	1.3	298	76.9	75.8	74.9	76.8
=76	Glasgow Caledonian	4.0	337	77.8	79.3	61.6	76.7
=76	South Wales	3.6	325	74.3	76.8	70.8	76.7
=76	Hertfordshire	7.8	308	72.4	80.8	70.1	76.7
79	Worcester		274	80.0	85.4	66.7	76.6
80	Staffordshire	0.4	295	81.0	81.8	62.4	76.3
81	Southampton Solent		262	82.7	82.2	65.4	76.2
=82	Edinburgh Napier	5.2	315	74.5	78.1	65.1	75.9
=82	Gloucestershire		281	80.3	77.3	67.4	75.9
84	Teesside	3.4	332	78.9	78.7	54.5	75.5
85	Greenwich	7.3	313	77.6	82.6	53.3	75.4
86	Middlesex	14.2	239	76.5	81.5	59.6	74.9
87	Bradford		290	73.8	80.7	65.5	74.8
88	Anglia Ruskin		202	87.6	85.9	56.8	74.7
89	Brighton	6.4	294	65.8	73.8	74.8	74.6
90	Cardiff Metropolitan		293	72.3	76.7	67.2	74.4
91	Sunderland	1.8	303	70.5	75.5	64.1	73.8
92	Glyndŵr	3.9	293	77.5	75.0	54.0	73.6
93	London South Bank	19.6	231	72.4	83.0	52.6	73.5
94	West of Scotland	3.2	316	74.1	76.5	52.0	73.3
95	Bolton		318	75.0	61.9	61.1	72.8
96	Kingston	5.3	269	71.3	75.5	57.3	72.4
97	Birmingham City	4.9	294	63.1	69.4	66.6	71.9
98	Canterbury Christ Church		245	64.8	71.1	73.2	71.7
99	West London	1.2	206	83.8	86.7	38.9	71.2
100	London Metropolitan	0.7	204	75.6	78.1	53.8	70.7
101	Bedfordshire	9.1	200	69.7	74.1	57.6	70.4
102	Westminster	2.9	269	65.3	77.3	48.4	69.5
103	East London	2.3	245	71.5	74.8	44.8	69.2

Employed in professional job:	62%	Employed in non-professional job and studying:	1%
Employed in professional job and studying:	2%	Employed in non-professional job:	15%
Studying:	7%	Unemployed:	14%
Average starting professional salary:	£23,766	Average starting non-professional salary:	£15,382

Creative Writing

Our table for creative writing appeared for the first time last year and already seven more universities have joined the ranking. Imaginative writing, as it is known by UCAS, has been a significant, but little-noticed area of growth in higher education over recent years. No fewer than 86 universities and colleges plan to offer full-time undergraduate courses in the subject starting in 2016. Many are still too small to qualify for the table or are part of a joint honours programme. Creative writing is paired with subjects as diverse as ceramics, business and biology, but more normally with English. Nearly 3,500 applications were received in 2014, however – a 13 per cent increase on the previous year. More than 850 students took up places.

Warwick has extended its lead in the subject after topping the inaugural table. It has the highest entry grades and the best research scores, and is second for graduate prospects. Birmingham remains the leader on that measure, while Staffordshire, in 36th place, posted the best scores for teaching, feedback and academic support in the National Student Survey. Students at Westminster, the top modern university, in 11th place, were the most satisfied with other elements of the student experience.

Employment is, perhaps not surprisingly, the Achilles heel of creative writing when compared with other subjects. It is just one place off the bottom of the employment table, with only 31 per cent of graduates starting out in professional jobs and an unemployment rate of 16 per cent. Average salaries for those who did find a professional job in 2014 were also the second-lowest in any subject, at £17,268. Most of the universities with enough graduates to compile an employment score saw less than half of their graduates go into professional employment or further study.

With fewer than four applications to the place, entry standards are generally low – only five of the 48 universities averaged more than 400 points on the UCAS tariff. The table is largely composed of post-1992 universities, although the top ten are all older foundations.

Creative Writing	Research quality %	Entry standards	Teaching quality %	Student experience %	Graduate prospects %	Overall score
1 Warwick	59.8	497	75.9	81.5	75.0	100.0
2 Queen's, Belfast	53.1	371	88.6	90.8	72.7	96.8
3 Birmingham	37.0	430	89.7	81.5	77.9	96.6
4 Lancaster	47.0	450	76.7	76.8	73.3	95.0
5 Newcastle	54.3	391	84.9	88.7		94.1
6 Nottingham	56.6	398	79.5	76.5	63.4	93.1
7 Surrey	39.1		82.4	82.8	73.7	92.5
=8 Bangor	46.3	323	93.9	91.8	56.4	91.6
=8 Royal Holloway, London	49.9	434	77.8	75.9	56.4	91.6
10 East Anglia	36.2	442	77.7	85.9	55.7	90.5
11 Westminster	28.9	283	93.5	96.0	52.1	86.3
12 Bath Spa	23.5	332	91.0	82.5	50.9	85.1
13 Birmingham City	30.9	279	89.2	87.4	54.2	84.9
14 Northampton	15.3	277	89.1	87.3	65.1	84.2
15 Hull	22.7	384	77.8	73.2	54.9	84.0

=16 Coventry	18.1	276	92.7	94.6		83.8
=16 De Montfort	24.1	295	82.9	79.9	62.3	83.8
18 Brunel	30.9	343	82.9	86.3	34.1	82.2
19 Aberystwyth	31.2	311	74.6	77.4	52.9	81.8
20 Manchester Metropolitan	29.0	295	77.7	68.3	54.9	80.8
21 West of England	35.4		81.8	76.6	40.0	80.7
22 Portsmouth	17.1	279	81.8	80.6	56.0	80.5
23 Plymouth	30.5	268	84.1	79.5	44.2	80.4
24 Liverpool John Moores	17.9	343	83.0	79.3	36.9	79.7
=25 Winchester		321	91.1	91.9	40.3	79.4
=25 Bolton	14.4	291	84.8	78.6	48.4	79.4
27 Chester	10.7	309	81.6	86.3	45.4	79.1
28 South Wales	12.8	303	85.3	76.8	44.2	78.7
29 Chichester	16.3	292	90.7	85.3	32.1	78.6
30 Gloucestershire	9.3	301	85.3	84.6	42.3	78.5
31 Canterbury Christ Church	8.0	297	82.7	85.0		78.4
32 Central Lancashire	9.9	279	82.5	81.2	49.7	78.2
33 St Mary's, Twickenham	14.6	258	87.5	90.3	38.0	77.9
34 Derby	13.5	288	84.3	82.0	38.0	77.3
35 Sheffield Hallam	14.6	297	87.2	80.9	29.6	76.8
36 Staffordshire		228	96.1	92.5	38.9	76.3
37 Kingston	15.7	307	71.1	68.7	46.6	75.9
38 Middlesex	11.0	255	83.2	84.7	37.9	75.5
39 Worcester	8.2	278	90.1	82.5	25.7	74.9
40 Edge Hill	12.1	324	76.6	77.3	29.9	74.8
41 Bournemouth	15.1	346	58.4	63.2	50.0	74.7
42 Southampton Solent		292	80.5	78.5	39.8	74.2
43 Salford	7.8	354	64.3	65.1	40.7	73.4
44 London South Bank	12.8	247	82.0	78.8	31.0	73.2
45 Bedfordshire	45.8	241	66.0	65.8	26.7	73.1
46 St Mark and St John		199*	91.5	87.5	32.6	72.3
47 Greenwich	14.4	303	60.6	58.4	40.3	70.7
48 Cumbria		212*	82.8	85.3	26.9	69.5

Employed in professional job:	29%	Employed in non-professional job and studying:	4%
Employed in professional job and studying:	2%	Employed in non-professional job:	39%
Studying:	10%	Unemployed:	16%
Average starting professional salary:	£17,268	Average starting non-professional salary:	£14,856

Dentistry

For the third year in a row, dentistry is the only subject whose graduates were paid more than £30,000 in "professional" jobs six months after leaving university. There is no figure for less skilled work because virtually every graduate goes on to become a dentist, so the subject is very close to medicine at the top of the employment table. None of the 15 undergraduate dental schools saw less than 97 per cent of graduates going into professional jobs or further

Dentistry cont

study. This measure is not used to determine positions so as not to exaggerate the impact of tiny numbers delaying their entry into the profession. Even so, for the fourth year in a row, there was a small drop in applications in 2014.

Most degrees last five years, although several universities offer a six-year option for those without the necessary scientific qualifications. The number of places has been increased in recent years to tackle shortages, but there are still nearly ten applications to the place – more than in any subject except medicine. Entry standards are correspondingly high: none of the schools averages less than 460 points, although only three, compared with six last year, are over 500. Most demand chemistry and biology, and some also demand maths or physics.

Scores in the subject are so close that the ranking changes frequently. Cardiff has jumped eight places – more than half the ranking – to take the lead this year. It has the highest entry standards and good scores on the other indicators. Second-placed Queen's, Belfast has also enjoyed a big rise – five places – after recording the best score for teaching quality in the National Student Survey, while Liverpool managed the best score for student experience. Last year's leader, Glasgow, is third in this edition, while fifth-placed Manchester produced the best results in the Research Excellence Framework, as it did in the 2008 assessments.

Last year, Plymouth became the first post-1992 university to enter the ranking in its own right, having previously partnered Exeter in the Peninsula Medical and Dental School. The two universities went their own ways in 2013 and Plymouth alone now offers dentistry. It has been joined this year by Central Lancashire, which opened a purpose-built dental school in 2007 and now has sufficient data to be ranked.

Dentistry	Research quality %	Entry standards	Teaching quality %	Student experience %	Graduate prospects %	Overall score
1 Cardiff	36.8	551	88.0	92.6	99.1	100.0
2 Queen's, Belfast	50.7	474	98.3	98.3	98.8	99.1
3 Glasgow	29.3	533	91.5	94.5	99.4	98.5
4 Newcastle	43.6	498	93.2	94.8	97.7	98.1
5 Manchester	57.1	495	89.3	90.0	98.5	98.0
6 Queen Mary, London	48.3	492	93.1	91.4	98.6	97.7
7 Liverpool	31.7	477	97.9	98.7	99.2	96.3
8 Dundee	22.1	509	90.3	95.2	100.0	94.8
=9 Birmingham	19.2	497	93.9	94.3	100.0	94.2
=9 King's College London	40.9	478	88.3	94.5	99.1	94.2
11 Leeds	31.7	483	86.8	91.5	97.7	92.2
12 Sheffield	28.5	463	91.2	94.5	99.1	91.7
13 Plymouth	9.5	479	95.8	95.3	100.0	91.6
14 Bristol	47.1	461	79.3	86.8	99.0	89.4
15 Central Lancashire	8.3		83.7	79.5	100.0	82.0

Employed in professional job:	93%	Employed in non-professional job and studying:	0%
Employed in professional job and studying:	5%	Employed in non-professional job:	0%
Studying:	1%	Unemployed:	1%
Average starting professional salary:	£30,348	Average starting non-professional salary:	

Drama, Dance and Cinematics

Drama has become one of the most popular subjects in UK higher education, with cinematics and photography not far behind. As a group, the three main subjects in this table attracted more than 90,000 applications between them in 2014, an improvement on the previous year, but still nowhere near the numbers seen before fees reached £9,000 a year. Universities have been rebalancing their intakes to reflect changes within the group, which have seen drama recover more strongly than the other subjects. In 2014, more places were filled in drama than before the fees went up, while dance and cinematics were close to those levels.

There are now more than six applications to the place in drama, although the ratio is nearer 5:1 in dance and cinematics and photography. The subjects' popularity has never been reflected in high entry grades. Although 14 of the 95 universities and colleges in the table average more than 400 points at entry, none reaches 500 and 16 universities have averages of less than 300 points. Bristol has the highest entry standards, but it is Sheffield and Birmingham which tie for the leadership of the table, taking over from Warwick. Sheffield had the most satisfied students where the student experience was concerned, but the best scores on other indicators came from outside the top four. Queen Mary, University of London, has the top research grades and Sussex the best graduate prospects. Northampton, in equal 33rd place, satisfied the most students in relation to teaching. The majority of institutions offering drama, dance or cinematics are post-1992 universities, but only Edinburgh Napier and Robert Gordon made the top 20.

The subjects are in the bottom six for employment and have the lowest average salaries for those in graduate-level jobs six months after completing a course. Almost 40 per cent of graduates start out in low-level jobs and those who find "professional" work were paid less than £17,000 on average in 2014 – nearly £400 less than in the previous year. As in other performing arts, freelancing and periods of temporary employment are common for new graduates. Standards of performance may be influential in the selection process for dance and drama, but drama courses at leading universities are likely to require English literature A level.

Drama, Dance and Cinematics	Research quality %	Entry standards	Teaching quality %	Student experience %	Graduate prospects %	Overall score
=1 Sheffield	60.0	443	93.0	94.3	57.4	100.0
=1 Birmingham	36.9	413	91.2	93.2	82.0	100.0
3 Warwick	61.7	441	79.0	81.4	68.5	98.1
4 Exeter	46.3	452	90.0	93.0	57.5	97.8
5 Bristol	48.7	481	82.7	77.0	62.1	97.3
6 Glasgow	53.9	447	84.0	85.0	59.9	96.9
7 Queen Mary, London	68.4	421	86.8	87.3	51.7	96.7
8 Surrey	27.2	419	89.9	88.0	71.1	95.8
9 Manchester	58.6	393	88.7	88.3	50.6	94.2
10 Lancaster	48.0	399	70.9	77.0	78.3	93.9
11 Essex	37.7	324	93.3	94.2	68.6	93.2
12 East Anglia	43.8	464	77.3	90.3	48.2	93.0
13 Sussex	45.6	385	65.4	72.3	86.2	92.8

Drama, Dance and Cinematics cont	Research quality %	Entry standards	Teaching quality %	Student experience %	Graduate prospects %	Overall score
14 Leeds	28.0	403	85.1	86.7	65.4	92.7
15 Reading	34.8	391	87.5	88.6	58.9	92.3
16 Kent	44.3	365	81.4	85.0	64.9	91.9
17 Royal Holloway, London	50.6	418	75.7	75.2	56.7	91.4
18 Edinburgh Napier	37.9	422	79.7	73.4	60.4	91.3
19 York	26.0	428	81.0	78.8	60.4	90.8
20 Robert Gordon	11.5		83.8	81.4	72.4	90.5
21 Edinburgh	48.0	412	70.9	66.5	61.8	89.8
22 Coventry	18.1	341	90.8	92.4	62.9	89.4
23 Central School of Speech and Drama	47.7	355	74.3	75.5	64.3	89.1
24 Roehampton	46.6	326	82.2	80.8	57.1	88.3
25 Oxford Brookes	27.8	358	93.6	79.9	47.9	87.7
26 Royal Conservatoire of Scotland	11.3	348	79.0	82.0	74.5	87.6
27 Loughborough	32.4	371	76.7	78.0	57.5	87.1
28 Huddersfield	28.0	335	82.0	81.0	59.2	86.6
29 De Montfort	14.5	332	83.8	82.9	64.0	86.1
30 Nottingham	45.8	326	82.0	77.8	48.7	85.9
31 Chichester	9.7	349	89.3	91.6	51.0	85.7
32 Middlesex	16.1	307	83.0	86.2	62.3	84.9
=33 Lincoln	6.5	335	83.6	78.4	64.9	84.8
=33 Northampton		329	95.3	92.8	51.2	84.8
35 Cardiff Metropolitan		327	93.5	91.7	51.3	84.2
=36 Brunel	32.6	349	83.0	85.2	38.3	84.1
=36 Bath Spa	10.7	345	87.1	84.2	50.0	84.1
38 Liverpool John Moores		357	88.4	88.4	48.8	83.7
39 Falmouth	6.2	309	74.7	77.7	74.5	83.6
40 Bangor	24.7	277*	85.9	80.7	56.6	83.3
41 Ulster	40.0	289	88.5	87.4	36.4	83.0
=42 Queen's, Belfast	38.3	342	78.6	83.4	36.1	82.9
=42 Birmingham City	11.6	331	80.6	78.7	56.5	82.9
44 Aberdeen	29.3		83.2	89.7	36.6	82.6
45 Queen Margaret, Edinburgh	14.0	383	82.9	75.5	40.0	82.5
46 Hull	11.2	331	81.2	82.2	51.9	82.4
47 Norwich University of the Arts		335	79.1	77.5	60.4	81.9
48 Arts University Bournemouth	2.4	329	78.1	78.4	60.4	81.8
49 Northumbria	13.3	358	79.9	81.3	42.7	81.7
50 Gloucestershire		332	85.1	84.9	48.9	81.4
51 Central Lancashire	3.9	323	81.6	80.6	52.7	81.0
52 Nottingham Trent		336	81.0	78.8	52.6	80.8
53 St Mary's, Twickenham		322	80.5	85.9	51.5	80.5
=54 Manchester Metropolitan	7.5	368	76.2	72.6	46.0	80.4
=54 Winchester	11.2	333	84.3	83.4	38.7	80.4
56 Portsmouth		316	82.2	81.7	52.1	80.3

=57	Chester	4.3	300	82.1	85.0	49.6	79.8
=57	Sunderland	4.2	300	86.5	85.9	44.5	79.8
=59	West of England		330	81.5	75.1	50.3	79.7
=59	Teesside	2.9	284	88.7	82.8	48.1	79.7
61	Aberystwyth	30.3	308	74.8	77.1	40.6	79.5
=62	Plymouth	20.2	289	85.2	82.4	34.9	78.7
=62	Leeds Beckett	1.7	310	85.8	81.8	41.9	78.7
64	Derby	5.1	309	76.0	73.1	52.5	78.4
65	West of Scotland		323	79.6	74.0	48.1	78.3
66	East London	11.2	325	69.8	70.7	50.8	78.1
=67	Glyndŵr		284	76.9	79.1	55.5	77.9
=67	Kingston	15.7	318	72.0	71.1	46.2	77.9
69	Sheffield Hallam		324	80.1	78.4	42.2	77.7
70	Goldsmiths, London	28.3	338	60.1	64.8	47.0	77.6
=71	Hertfordshire	5.3	326	66.0	67.6	57.1	77.5
=71	University for the Creative Arts	3.4	320	75.4	77.1	45.1	77.5
=73	Bournemouth	15.1	386	54.4	62.2	50.5	77.4
=73	Bolton		288	85.1	79.6	43.7	77.4
75	Westminster		314	78.3	78.8	44.2	77.3
=76	Canterbury Christ Church	15.2	292	81.3	79.3	36.0	77.2
=76	University of the Arts London		325	72.5	68.6	51.9	77.2
78	Newman	9.6	305	88.6	91.5	22.3	77.1
79	Anglia Ruskin	16.9	278	82.5	83.2	34.1	77.0
80	West London	2.3	308	71.2	65.4	55.3	76.7
=81	Edge Hill	3.8	332	76.1	73.9	38.4	76.5
=81	Liverpool Hope	3.0	311	75.2	76.7	43.6	76.5
=81	South Wales	6.4	324	72.5	69.0	44.9	76.5
=81	Bedfordshire	5.6	262	87.6	85.1	36.8	76.5
85	Staffordshire		271	83.4	82.6	43.3	76.4
86	York St John	10.5	297	69.8	72.2	45.9	75.7
87	London South Bank		265	83.9	81.5	40.8	75.6
88	Southampton Solent		267	81.5	79.8	41.8	75.2
89	Cumbria		313	77.8	80.9	32.7	74.9
90	Brighton	13.1	331	63.3	60.7	44.6	74.8
91	Salford	7.2	341	63.9	62.8	42.6	74.5
=92	Buckinghamshire New		262	80.9	77.3	41.0	74.3
=92	Greenwich	3.5	332	68.9	68.1	38.6	74.3
94	Worcester	3.5	282	80.5	82.1	30.5	74.1
95	Bishop Grosseteste		276	60.6	63.0	41.2	69.1

Employed in professional job:	42%	Employed in non-professional job and studying:	2%
Employed in professional job and studying:	2%	Employed in non-professional job:	37%
Studying:	6%	Unemployed:	11%
Average starting professional salary:	£16,963	Average starting non-professional salary:	£14,381

East and South Asian Studies

The apparent surge in interest in China, including the promotion of Mandarin in some sixth forms, is yet to have an impact in higher education. The numbers taking Chinese studies dropped in 2014 and only 400 students started undergraduate courses in East and South Asian studies as a whole. Japanese attracted the largest numbers, overtaking Chinese, but still saw a small decline and enrolments have dropped by a third since 2010. The subjects share the recruitment problems that have afflicted all modern language programmes since higher fees arrived in 2012. Most undergraduates learn their chosen language from scratch, although universities expect to see evidence of potential in other modern language qualifications.

Degrees in these subjects are afforded extra protection by the Government because of their small size and their economic and cultural importance, but the low numbers can make for exaggerated swings in the ranking. This year's table is relatively stable, although Cambridge has moved up four places to take over the leadership and Manchester is up five places to third. Cambridge just beats second-placed Oxford to the highest entry grades, while Oxford graduates had the best record in the employment market. Manchester achieved the best research score, while Sheffield had the highest levels of satisfaction for teaching and Leeds posted the best scores in the rest of the National Student Survey.

One additional university – fourth-placed Durham – entered the table this year, but still only 12 have enough students taking any of the subjects to qualify. A total of 39 institutions are offering Chinese studies and 23 Japanese in 2016. Others include modules in modern languages or area studies degrees, while the School of Oriental and African Studies, in London, offers a range of languages, including Burmese, Indonesian, Thai, Tibetan and Vietnamese. South Asian Studies is available at only four universities, which saw just 70 students begin courses in 2014. Even this was almost twice the number of starters in the

East and South Asian Studies	Research quality %	Entry standards	Teaching quality %	Student experience %	Graduate prospects %	Overall score
1 Cambridge	45.0	571	75.7	75.3	75.8	100.0
2 Oxford	36.2	568	70.5	63.8	80.0	96.2
3 Manchester	48.9	408	79.3	83.8	57.0	94.3
4 Durham	34.6	432	80.2	83.9		94.2
5 Leeds	30.6	420	80.7	88.1	65.1	93.5
6 Edinburgh	30.1	507	80.8	83.8	55.4	93.2
7 Nottingham	27.3	366	76.8	80.3	76.1	91.7
8 SOAS, London	26.3	422	79.4	78.9	61.0	90.4
9 Sheffield	16.7	406	85.0	85.6	56.8	89.4
10 Westminster	11.3	305*	74.5	72.2	59.1	81.5
11 Central Lancashire		289	79.3	76.3	47.3	78.1
12 Oxford Brookes		381	65.7	65.3	49.2	75.6

Employed in professional job:	37%	Employed in non-professional job and studying:	1%
Employed in professional job and studying:	3%	Employed in non-professional job:	28%
Studying:	13%	Unemployed:	18%
Average starting professional salary:	£19,075	Average starting non-professional salary:	£16,272

previous year. The small numbers also make for exaggerated swings in the employment table. As a group, East and South Asian studies have dropped into the bottom ten this year, with the highest unemployment rate in our table, 18 per cent, shared with Middle Eastern and African Studies.

Economics

Economics remains in the top five for graduate starting salaries, reflecting the value that employers place on a subject that they see combining the skills of the sciences and the arts. Although it is lower for overall employment rates, the subject is still in the top 20. Its reputation as a highly marketable degree has helped economics to withstand the impact of higher fees. Almost 8,000 students started undergraduate courses in 2014, a record number despite a small decline in applications. Competition for places remains stiff, with approaching seven applications for every degree place.

Many of those considering a degree in economics underestimate the mathematical skills required. Most of the leading universities demand maths at A level or its equivalent as part of offers that are consistently high. Entry standards in this year's table reflect this, with the top five universities all averaging over 540 points – the equivalent of four As at A level and another at AS level. The range of entry scores has been widening, however, as more universities have joined the table. The bottom eight all have averages of less than 270 points.

First place in economics has changed for the fourth year in a row. Oxford is back on top, replacing Warwick, although it does not lead on any of the individual measures. Cambridge has the highest entry grades and the best graduate prospects, despite dropping to fourth place, while the London School of Economics took the laurels in the Research Excellence Framework. For the third successive year, the most satisfied students are at Coventry, which would have been higher than equal 36th place had it not been for an unusually low research score. De Montfort is a fraction of a point ahead as the leading post-1992 university.

Nearly 60 per cent of economists go straight into jobs categorised as professional, while 22 per cent continue studying, either full or part-time. The leading universities invariably produce some of the highest graduate salaries of the year. While the average for 2014 in "professional" jobs was £26,630, graduates of Cambridge's economics BSc earned an average of £40,000.

Economics	Research quality %	Entry standards	Teaching quality %	Student experience %	Graduate prospects %	Overall score
1 Oxford	58.0	598	78.4	86.6	87.1	100.0
2 University College London	70.2	543	73.0	78.7	86.4	98.1
3 Warwick	49.6	548	77.7	88.8	88.7	97.9
4 Cambridge	45.0	622	74.6	77.8	93.7	97.8
5 London School of Economics	70.7	561	69.5	78.2	83.9	97.4
6 Leeds	39.3	447	83.5	90.8	83.3	94.3
7 Durham	23.1	559	77.2	85.1	90.5	93.8
8 Lancaster	42.6	428	80.6	86.8	83.1	93.1
9 Nottingham	31.7	482	76.0	88.1	87.3	92.7

Economics cont	Research quality %	Entry standards	Teaching quality %	Student experience %	Graduate prospects %	Overall score
10 Loughborough	32.6	408	83.3	92.3	83.4	92.5
=11 Exeter	26.9	482	78.0	85.4	85.8	91.8
=11 Bristol	43.6	522	69.6	81.4	79.4	91.8
=11 Surrey	33.0	439	83.4	87.5	78.5	91.8
14 Queen Mary, London	31.3	422	86.1	88.4	74.0	90.9
15 St Andrews	23.6	524	68.1	78.8	92.2	90.5
=16 Queen's, Belfast	32.7	364	88.6	91.9	71.9	90.3
=16 Strathclyde	44.3	504	78.7	88.5	57.6	90.3
18 Essex	43.6	308	88.5	91.7	69.6	90.1
19 Birmingham	26.6	415	77.4	85.3	85.6	89.9
=20 East Anglia	25.7	377	84.5	92.5	77.6	89.8
=20 Kent	14.6	393	84.2	88.3	88.1	89.8
=22 Edinburgh	30.2	467	71.5	82.6	83.6	89.7
=22 Bath	41.8	497	60.1	68.6	93.6	89.7
24 York	22.6	441	77.7	85.1	84.0	89.6
25 Heriot-Watt	18.8	391	83.0	85.4	82.8	88.8
26 Sussex	25.1	368	73.6	85.8	87.3	88.0
27 Reading	29.3	360	78.3	84.5	79.5	87.8
28 Sheffield	16.6	419	77.9	83.6	81.9	87.6
29 Royal Holloway, London	31.3	389	82.9	87.8	64.2	87.5
30 Newcastle	20.7	421	79.3	87.3	72.7	87.4
31 Glasgow	26.4	428	66.8	81.6	84.7	87.2
32 Aston	19.7	420	74.5	86.4	76.7	86.8
33 Stirling	25.2	375	71.7	74.6	88.2	86.4
34 Southampton	23.4	421	74.2	82.2	74.1	86.3
35 De Montfort	10.7	264	89.7	95.2	78.1	86.2
=36 Coventry	1.6	301	95.5	96.2	72.5	86.1
=36 Buckingham		320	93.8	85.8	80.6	86.1
=38 Salford	5.9	314	88.6	91.7		86.0
=38 Liverpool	20.1	383	75.5	80.4	80.4	86.0
40 Cardiff	32.0	407	66.7	77.6	78.7	85.9
41 Manchester	26.8	427	70.4	81.3	73.2	85.8
42 SOAS, London	22.9	414	69.3	79.2	77.7	85.2
43 Swansea	22.0	294	79.9	81.8	79.9	85.1
=44 Dundee	12.1	433	83.9	90.2	58.2	85.0
=44 City	15.1	371	80.2	84.6	72.3	85.0
46 Aberdeen	16.0	402	68.9	84.4	80.3	84.9
47 Manchester Metropolitan	4.7	326	87.2	88.0	67.3	83.3
48 Hertfordshire	0.9	290	87.5	91.6	69.6	82.8
=49 Central Lancashire	4.4	295	93.8	93.5	55.8	82.5
=49 Portsmouth	9.5	298	78.9	86.3	73.6	82.5
51 Hull	10.2	318	75.0	84.4	75.9	82.4
52 Leicester	21.4	349	67.4	76.4	73.2	81.7

=53 Nottingham Trent		300	82.8	83.6	71.6	81.2
=53 Greenwich	3.3	305	89.5	92.6	53.6	81.2
55 Bangor	23.4	300	80.3	84.3	52.2	80.7
=56 Ulster		296	77.8	83.7	72.9	80.3
=56 Bradford	12.7	254	81.7	84.7	63.0	80.3
58 West of England	5.5	305	80.1	82.3	64.3	80.1
59 Brunel	9.9	319	72.8	81.6	64.6	79.4
60 Sheffield Hallam		311	77.7	84.5	63.2	78.9
61 Plymouth		285	82.0	86.1	58.7	78.6
62 Oxford Brookes	5.1	313	75.9	81.3	55.1	77.4
63 Leeds Beckett	0.8	237	77.0	84.3	57.4	75.9
64 Aberystwyth	14.5	285	66.1	73.8	59.2	75.8
65 Keele	10.2	317	59.4	70.2	65.3	75.1
66 Kingston	9.2	246	78.7	80.5	43.4	74.7
67 Birmingham City	1.3	242	72.1	79.2	55.3	73.9
68 Northampton		229	79.4	82.4	45.2	73.6
69 Anglia Ruskin	3.4	203	78.8	80.8	47.2	73.4
70 London Metropolitan		217	73.7	79.8	51.6	72.9
71 Middlesex	10.5	239	70.4	76.3	45.5	72.7
72 East London	0.8	252	70.0	65.3	58.5	72.4
73 Cardiff Metropolitan		264	70.5	67.1	47.8	70.9

Employed in professional job:	52%	Employed in non-professional job and studying:	1%
Employed in professional job and studying:	7%	Employed in non-professional job:	14%
Studying:	14%	Unemployed:	12%
Average starting professional salary:	£26,630	Average starting non-professional salary:	£17,295

Education

Morale is often said to be low in the teaching profession, but the official survey of graduates three years into their careers shows that those who studied education are among the least likely to wish they had taken a different subject. Only those who took medicine or dentistry are more satisfied. Applications for teacher training courses have declined for the last three years as the Government has promoted other routes into the profession, but courses classified as Academic Studies in Education have been recruiting more strongly. Entry to the BEd courses that train teachers at undergraduate level is still competitive, with nearly six applications to the place, but the chances of winning a place on the other education courses – which include early years qualifications, as well as those for youth work and outdoor education – is more than twice as good. The BEd remains the most common route into primary teaching, whereas alternatives such as the Postgraduate Certificate in Education, Teach First and the Government's Schools Direct programme have limited the demand for undergraduate training at secondary level.

Education is the only ranking that contains inspection scores – because teacher training assessments are carried out by Ofsted at English universities. Sixteen universities, including seven from outside the top 30, tie for the best of these scores. Glasgow has taken over from Cambridge at the top of the table, thanks partly to an exceptionally high employment

Education	Research quality %	Ofsted	Entry standards	Teaching quality %	Student experience %	Graduate prospects %	Overall score
1 Glasgow	32.5		417	89.2	91.9	98.2	100.0
2 Cambridge	36.6	4.0	535	81.6	81.0	87.5	99.7
3 Durham	38.9	4.0	453	86.7	86.2	90.2	99.3
4 Birmingham	40.9	4.0	414	79.2	85.8	84.5	96.0
5 Strathclyde	19.8		456	80.2	85.9	87.1	95.0
6 Dundee	11.7		392	88.4	88.5	91.2	94.5
7 West of Scotland	7.5		371	91.0	90.8	92.5	94.3
8 Edinburgh	23.1		422	72.4	79.3	97.1	92.7
9 Stirling	29.2		422	72.3	73.3	94.9	92.2
=10 Bangor	39.6		331	85.9	88.5	73.6	91.7
=10 Southampton	41.1	3.0	421	81.6	80.6	82.9	91.7
12 Northumbria		4.0	343	89.4	92.9	84.6	91.5
13 Royal Conservatoire of Scotland			499	68.5	70.5	97.6	91.0
=14 York	43.3	3.0	378	85.4	83.1	77.7	90.9
=14 Brunel	20.4	3.5	361	90.4	89.1	74.2	90.9
=16 Reading	25.8	3.5	349	84.7	84.7	79.7	90.3
=16 Canterbury Christ Church	2.8	4.0	336	82.8	84.3	90.9	90.3
=16 Manchester	46.0	4.0	387	73.7	71.2	61.7	90.3
=19 Huddersfield	5.9	3.5	332	92.0	91.6	80.5	89.6
=19 Brighton	1.6	4.0	338	82.5	84.6	86.5	89.6
21 Manchester Metropolitan	5.8	4.0	352	84.8	81.6	76.4	89.4
=22 Cardiff	35.3		364	77.7	87.1	68.3	89.3
=22 Keele	25.0	3.5	338	86.8	92.9	65.2	89.3
24 West of England	5.3	3.8	336	84.8	83.6	81.4	88.8
25 Chichester		4.0	308	83.9	87.0	84.9	88.7
=26 Sunderland	3.8	3.5	351	83.3	85.3	87.4	88.5
=26 Oxford Brookes	3.3	3.5	387	86.2	88.7	71.8	88.5
=26 Warwick	43.6	3.8	379	76.3	76.2	50.6	88.5
=29 Sheffield	32.9	3.0	354	85.0	86.8	65.2	87.6
=29 East Anglia	27.2	3.0	401	80.7	83.3	68.0	87.6
=31 St Mary's, Twickenham	1.8	4.0	298	76.8	83.4	89.4	87.4
=31 Staffordshire	7.6	4.0	266	84.8	87.4		87.4
33 Derby	1.1	4.0	304	88.7	90.1	62.7	87.2
34 Gloucestershire		3.8	319	85.1	90.6	70.0	86.9
=35 Leeds	31.6	3.0	361	87.2	83.8	57.5	86.8
=35 Coventry	18.1			84.0	87.3	66.7	86.8
37 Birmingham City	1.8	4.0	287	81.6	84.9	76.7	86.6
38 Worcester	2.5	4.0	313	81.3	85.4	69.2	86.5
39 Edge Hill	1.4	4.0	329	75.5	77.0	80.9	86.4
=40 Bath Spa	3.2	4.0	295	82.0	85.4	69.9	86.3
=40 Winchester	2.2	3.5	327	83.7	85.3	77.0	86.3
42 Sheffield Hallam	2.0	3.3	324	83.6	88.4	76.2	85.4
43 Liverpool John Moores	3.0	3.5	349	81.2	83.6	68.1	85.2

44 Ulster	27.5		295	88.3	89.8	46.7	84.9
=45 Liverpool Hope	7.3	3.0	321	90.6	91.8	62.6	84.7
=45 Aberdeen	7.6		388	62.0	68.4	94.5	84.7
47 Hertfordshire		3.0	327	82.6	85.5	83.7	84.5
48 Middlesex	14.9	3.0	264	81.2	82.9	88.2	84.3
49 De Montfort	11.2		310	84.1	85.0	60.3	84.1
50 Glyndŵr			308	89.0	83.8	61.3	84.0
51 Chester	1.4	3.8	303	75.4	80.7	71.7	83.9
=52 Aberystwyth			295	89.7	85.2	60.5	83.6
=52 York St John	1.5	3.3	305	78.0	80.1	82.5	83.6
=52 Hull	5.0	3.0	313	82.9	86.7	74.1	83.6
55 Bishop Grosseteste	1.4	3.5	290	81.8	80.8	71.5	83.4
56 Portsmouth		3.5	294	83.9	86.3	60.6	83.0
57 Roehampton	20.2	3.0	303	79.6	80.1	66.1	82.8
=58 Leeds Trinity		3.0	306	80.6	79.3	81.4	82.5
=58 Plymouth	9.4	3.5	305	76.1	77.3	64.3	82.5
60 Kingston		3.5	271	84.0	84.0	64.0	82.4
=61 St Mark and St John			299	74.7	75.1	82.6	82.2
=61 Northampton	1.8	3.0	295	83.6	85.2	71.0	82.2
63 Bedfordshire	3.1	3.0	252	85.1	88.4	72.9	81.9
64 Newman	2.2	3.0	307	80.2	82.0	66.1	81.1
65 Nottingham Trent	2.6	3.0	304	82.6	85.3	59.1	80.9
66 South Wales			315	77.5	77.8	63.3	80.8
67 Greenwich	0.8	3.3	310	75.8	78.4	63.0	80.6
68 Central Lancashire			289	83.4	83.4	54.4	80.4
69 Cardiff Metropolitan			303	82.0	85.8	48.4	80.0
70 Teesside	15.0		290	81.1	85.0	42.4	79.9
71 Leeds Beckett	2.3		284	71.3	74.6	72.7	79.2
72 Goldsmiths, London	17.4		288	79.0	79.4	44.0	79.0
73 University College London	40.2		224	74.1	75.0	52.2	78.6
74 London Metropolitan	3.3	3.0	262	82.8	82.3	50.2	78.3
75 Cumbria	0.4	3.0	313	64.6	68.3	76.2	77.8
76 Anglia Ruskin	0.8	3.0	303	66.6	69.6	65.3	76.7
77 East London	2.8	3.0	290	75.8	78.5	37.8	75.7

Employed in professional job:	55%	Employed in non-professional job and studying:	2%
Employed in professional job and studying:	2%	Employed in non-professional job:	23%
Studying:	12%	Unemployed:	6%
Average starting professional salary:	£21,369	Average starting non-professional salary:	£14,302

score. Cambridge has entry standards that are more than 35 points ahead of its nearest challenger, but Manchester now has the best research grade. The Cambridge course is an example of those that do not offer Qualified Teacher Status, but combines the academic study of education with other subjects. Huddersfield posted the best scores in the sections of the National Student Survey covering teaching, feedback and academic support, while Northumbria and Keele share the highest levels of satisfaction for the rest of the survey.

Education cont

Employment scores at different universities reflect to some extent the variations in demand for new staff between primary and secondary schools, as well as between different parts of the UK. Universities that specialise in primary training are at an advantage at the moment in terms of employment. Some of the best-known education departments are absent from the table because they offer only postgraduate courses. University College London's Institute of Education, which is ranked top in the world in this field by QS, and Oxford, which achieved the top grades in the 2014 Research Excellence Framework, are two examples.

Electrical and Electronic Engineering

The demand for places in electrical and electronic engineering is taking longer to recover from the introduction of £9,000 fees than was the case in other branches of the discipline. There was a 5 per cent increase in applications in 2014, but the numbers enrolling were still lower than in 2010, the last year unaffected by higher charges. Some natural applicants have been diverted into courses such as computer games design and, at around five applications to the place, selection is less competitive than in most other branches of engineering. Nevertheless, only mechanical courses attract more students. The subject is in the top 20 for employment prospects and the top ten for salaries in graduate-level jobs.

Cambridge maintained its lead in electrical and electronic engineering this year, with the best research grades and a lead of almost 80 points over second-placed Imperial College on entry standards. The scores are close together for much of the top 20: Surrey, for example, has dropped from second place to 13th with a total that is not even two points lower than last year's. Aberdeen narrowly failed to repeat last year's 100 per cent employment score, but continues to lead on this measure. Coventry has become the highest-placed post-1992 institution, just outside the top 30, in a subject where old universities predominate. The teaching and feedback at Anglia Ruskin, in equal 52nd place, satisfied more students than at any other university, while Kent was the leader in other sections of the National Student Survey. Northumbria, in 32nd position, is the highest-placed post-1992 university.

Most of the top courses demand maths and physics at A level, or the equivalent, but the table displays a big divide in entry standards. Cambridge and Imperial College average more than 550 points on the UCAS tariff, but there are 20 universities with averages of less than 300 points. There are also considerable variations in employment rates and the gap in earnings between those in professional jobs and lower-level employment is among the widest of any subject, at almost £9,000. Nearly three-quarters of graduates go straight into professional jobs or continue their studies, but the 12 per cent unemployment rate is above the average for all subjects.

Employed in professional job:	59%	Employed in non-professional job and studying:	1%
Employed in professional job and studying:	3%	Employed in non-professional job:	13%
Studying:	12%	Unemployed:	12%
Average starting professional salary:	£25,191	Average starting non-professional salary:	£16,331

Electrical and Electronic Engineering	Research quality %	Entry standards	Teaching quality %	Student experience %	Graduate prospects %	Overall score
1 Cambridge	67.0	642	75.0	86.7	96.6	100.0
2 Imperial College	65.0	564	81.6	88.8	90.5	97.8
3 Southampton	53.3	489	81.4	88.6	95.6	94.7
4 Strathclyde	41.7	470	84.5	87.1	88.7	91.6
5 Glasgow	47.2	491	75.7	86.8	89.0	91.2
6 University College London	59.0	484	68.2	82.3	90.9	91.0
=7 Leeds	41.8	429	86.9	91.5	85.3	90.7
=7 Queen's, Belfast	47.3	415	82.7	89.9	88.7	90.7
=9 Bristol	52.3	468	71.9	86.5	90.0	90.5
=9 Sheffield	42.6	389	84.0	91.6	93.3	90.5
11 Manchester	37.0	425	88.0	91.3	85.1	90.1
12 Bath	28.6	444	87.1	88.1	90.0	89.7
=13 Surrey	36.3	427	80.6	87.5	93.9	89.6
=13 Birmingham	32.1	410	86.1	89.5	92.6	89.6
15 Dundee	34.1		84.2	87.8	90.0	89.3
16 Edinburgh	50.3	485	73.6	85.7	80.2	89.2
17 Lancaster	41.6	416	80.7	84.3		88.0
18 Aberdeen	28.4	458*	73.9	82.5	96.9	87.9
19 Swansea	45.5	346	80.9	85.3	86.1	86.9
=20 Nottingham	40.8	390	79.2	86.7	81.8	86.5
=20 Exeter	36.4	432	70.8	79.3	92.4	86.5
22 Newcastle	39.4	389	77.2	87.2	83.5	86.2
23 Loughborough	23.8	368	81.7	89.4	90.9	85.8
24 Kent	27.3	309	88.1	94.5	85.5	85.5
25 Essex	34.3	302	81.5	82.8	95*	85.4
26 Heriot-Watt	47.8	416	68.8	73.2	85.6	85.3
27 York	21.4	393	85.1	88.8	81.2	85.1
28 Brunel	26.4	353	86.6	88.3	78.3	84.4
29 Liverpool	30.4	378	80.0	84.1	79.7	84.1
30 Queen Mary, London	41.9	409	74.5	79.3	72.5	83.7
31 Reading	16.3	376	79.4	82.8	85.7	82.8
32 Northumbria	30.7	347	86.8	88.2	65.8	82.5
33 Aston	25.8	324	73.4	77.3	94.9	82.4
34 Bangor	31.9	269	85.6	90.9	74.6	82.0
35 Derby	6.7	306	85.1	87.8	90.9	81.9
36 Portsmouth	7.2	318	83.5	84.2	88.8	81.3
=37 Cardiff	30.2	400	62.5	73.8	84.4	80.7
=37 West of England	10.6	308	76.3	81.0	95.3	80.7
39 Robert Gordon	8.8	387	72.2	82.5	86.4	80.5
40 Manchester Metropolitan	16.3	338	80.7	84.5	76.5	80.3
41 Ulster	22.8	301	69.6	81.9	86.0	79.3
42 Hull	16.5	309	81.6	81.4	73.7	78.8
43 City	20.2	362	85.0	88.3	52.4	78.6

Electrical and Electronic Engineering cont	Research quality %	Entry standards	Teaching quality %	Student experience %	Graduate prospects %	Overall score
44 Liverpool John Moores	8.7	344	77.1	81.0	75.0	78.0
45 Sussex	24.0	320	68.0	71.9	82.1	77.9
=46 Hertfordshire	16.5	282	76.3	88.2	74.1	77.7
=46 Huddersfield	10.2	328	77.6	82.0	74.1	77.7
48 Sheffield Hallam	17.8	298	76.2	83.6	72.4	77.5
49 Aberystwyth		329	76.2	72.1	87.9	77.4
50 Brighton	7.4		77.6	86.8	66.7	76.5
51 Central Lancashire	11.7	313	79.5	84.2	64.5	76.4
=52 Plymouth	13.3	311	73.9	84.3	68.2	76.0
=52 Anglia Ruskin	9.1	237	90.6	91.5	60.0	76.0
54 Coventry	10.3	280	76.2	82.4	72.1	75.7
55 Bolton		293*	90.5	85.8	59.4	75.6
56 Salford	4.4	326	80.0	81.0	60.0	74.6
57 De Montfort	12.5	295	68.9	76.9	73.1	74.4
58 Teesside	5.8	304	85.2	83.0	51.6	73.9
59 Staffordshire	5.7	285*	77.4	80.3	64.4	73.7
60 Kingston		241*	81.8	85.1	66.7	73.4
61 Bradford		316	71.8	81.8	67.5*	73.3
62 Birmingham City		301	77.4	78.0	62.2	72.7
63 Southampton Solent		239	77.3	80.6	70.2	72.6
64 Glasgow Caledonian	4.7	331	64.5	71.1	68.6	72.0
=65 Greenwich	7.5	271	74.7	82.3	56.5	71.7
=65 London South Bank	19.6	268	76.0	85.0	44.1	71.7
=67 Westminster	2.9	299	69.5	77.5	62.5	71.3
=67 South Wales		279	71.1	78.7	65.5	71.3
69 Bedfordshire	9.1	200*	79.7	85.5	56.5	71.2
70 Glyndŵr	20.1		57.4	49.1	70.0	66.6
71 East London	2.3	260	46.8	48.8	44.4	58.6

English

Degrees in English are a perennial favourite of university applicants, despite the fact that they never feature among the top 50 subjects for employment prospects or starting salaries in professional jobs. Applications and enrolments dropped slightly in 2014, but English remained among the top ten choices for a degree. The table is one of the largest in the *Guide* and entry standards are high at the leading institutions. Five of them average more than 500 points on the UCAS tariff, as does Bristol, in 45th place.

Durham has deposed Cambridge at the top of the table this year without registering the top score in any of the individual measures. However, it is a single point behind Oxford (and ahead of Cambridge) on entry grades and second only to Cambridge on graduate prospects. Queen Mary, London, in 18th place, produced the best results in the Research Excellence Framework, with University College London its nearest challenger.

Less predictable names dominated the 2015 National Student Survey: Bolton, in 41st place overall, satisfied 97 per cent of final-year undergraduates on teaching, feedback and academic support, while Southampton Solent, which shares 79th place, had the best scores on the questions relating to the student experience. Only Oxford Brookes, of the modern universities, made the top 40.

Just over a quarter of English graduates continue their studies, while a third go into graduate-level jobs. Unemployment is only slightly above average for all subjects, but more than a third of all graduates start out in lower-level jobs. Employment rates have improved since the last edition of the *Guide*, but only Cambridge, Durham and Birmingham saw eight out of ten graduates go straight into graduate-level work or further study. English has produced consistently good levels of student satisfaction, however. In the results published this year, every one of the 106 universities in the table satisfied at least three-quarters of the final-year undergraduates. Their graduates may have been less satisfied with their starting salaries, however: the average of £18,863 was in the bottom ten for all subjects in 2014.

English		Research quality %	Entry standards	Teaching quality %	Student experience %	Graduate prospects %	Overall score
1	Durham	57.9	555	86.0	87.3	81.7	100.0
2	Cambridge	50.0	547	88.2	87.6	83.8	99.9
3	St Andrews	60.4	506	89.0	89.6	77.3	99.7
4	University College London	61.7	515	92.8	88.6	67.0	99.4
5	Oxford	50.7	556	86.9	83.4	77.8	98.4
=6	Nottingham	56.6	448	86.4	87.2	78.0	97.1
=6	Exeter	46.2	487	89.1	90.3	71.8	97.1
8	York	61.5	485	80.6	86.5	72.5	96.0
9	Birmingham	37.0	419	90.3	85.6	81.2	95.7
10	Newcastle	54.3	435	87.7	89.3	63.6	95.1
=11	Sheffield	42.2	424	90.2	90.5	66.4	94.8
=11	Warwick	59.8	473	82.5	81.2	68.7	94.8
13	Lancaster	47.0	445	83.8	83.1	76.0	94.5
14	Sussex	45.6	400	84.2	88.3	77.4	94.4
15	Loughborough	32.4	390	90.1	88.8	75.7	94.1
16	Royal Holloway, London	49.9	420	85.9	84.4	64.7	93.3
17	Leeds	38.6	453	83.0	85.3	71.3	93.1
18	Queen Mary, London	64.0	415	82.7	81.2	61.0	92.9
=19	Southampton	38.4	402	84.9	88.8	69.8	92.8
=19	Queen's, Belfast	53.1	378	87.7	90.6	55.9	92.8
=19	Swansea	43.6	326	86.2	86.8	76.5	92.8
22	Kent	47.3	368	84.1	86.3	71.1	92.7
=23	Surrey	39.1	440	83.5	82.7	69.2	92.4
=23	Dundee	32.8	402	90.7	90.8	58.8	92.4
25	Bangor	46.3	306	91.0	90.8	61.6	92.3
26	Glasgow	52.0	441	80.5	84.8	61.8	92.2
27	King's College London	47.6	457	79.4	77.1	71.2	92.1
28	Leicester	45.4	378	84.1	82.9	68.2	91.8

English cont		Research quality %	Entry standards	Teaching quality %	Student experience %	Graduate prospects %	Overall score
29	Reading	36.3	381	87.1	90.0	60.8	91.5
=30	Edinburgh	43.6	471	79.4	83.1	62.5	91.4
=30	East Anglia	36.2	437	82.8	90.2	60.1	91.4
32	Cardiff	35.1	420	85.2	85.8	61.7	91.3
33	Manchester	49.1	419	79.8	81.8	63.3	91.0
34	Aberdeen	46.3	437	84.2	84.6	51.4	90.9
35	Liverpool	47.8	403	81.5	84.5	59.2	90.7
36	Keele	29.8	357	87.5	88.1	63.4	90.5
37	Strathclyde	39.4	463	80.0	84.3	55.4	90.1
38	Stirling	29.8	399	84.4	84.6	59.3	89.5
39	Essex	37.7	321	86.2	85.8	59.0	89.3
40	Oxford Brookes	27.8	326	89.7	90.5	54.2	89.2
41	Bolton	14.4	208	97.3	92.4	64.8	89.1
42	Edinburgh Napier	37.9	390	88.1	83.3	44.4	88.8
=43	Brunel	30.9	360	89.2	88.5	45.3	88.6
=43	West of England	35.4	328	85.6	85.8	56.2	88.6
45	Bristol	30.0	505	74.5	70.3	68.2	88.5
46	Coventry	18.1	284	88.9	85.4	68.2	88.4
=47	Manchester Metropolitan	29.0	333	88.9	87.0	49.8	88.2
=47	Huddersfield	29.9	344	85.2	80.8	60.6	88.2
=47	Buckingham		283	92.4	91.8	67.8	88.2
=47	Liverpool Hope	26.9	298	87.6	87.4	58.6	88.2
51	Lincoln	16.2	321	86.9	88.8	63.0	88.1
52	Bath Spa	23.5	309	89.2	91.3	51.6	88.0
53	Portsmouth	17.1	294	89.2	88.4	58.5	87.6
54	Teesside	15.6	265	91.5	91.1	55.1	87.3
55	Nottingham Trent	30.0	280	88.1	87.3	49.4	86.9
56	Plymouth	30.5	312	87.9	82.3	48.6	86.8
57	Falmouth		276	94.2	90.5	57.0	86.7
=58	De Montfort	24.1	268	83.1	82.6	67.3	86.6
=58	Roehampton	20.8	294	86.1	83.8	58.6	86.6
60	Aston	23.4	331	77.4	83.3	66.9	86.4
=61	Liverpool John Moores	17.9	327	87.8	87.0	46.5	86.0
=61	Goldsmiths, London	34.9	345	80.1	74.2	57.3	86.0
63	Chester	10.7	308	87.1	88.1	53.8	85.9
64	Cumbria		228	95.3	91.1	54.6	85.8
65	Bedfordshire	45.8	209	88.2	88.4	37.7	85.6
66	Northumbria	27.2	341	81.5	83.5	49.0	85.5
67	York St John	9.7	281	88.0	87.5	54.5	85.4
=68	Birmingham City	30.9	282	81.7	85.8	50.0	85.2
=68	Newman	9.6	288	87.5	89.7	51.2	85.2
=70	Hull	22.7	339	84.1	81.9	46.1	85.1
=70	Aberystwyth	31.2	319	76.9	79.3	58.7	85.1

=70	Chichester	16.3	275	94.5	92.2	31.6	85.1
=70	St Mary's, Twickenham	14.6	265	87.2	89.5	50.3	85.1
=74	Ulster	35.1	283	87.9	87.3	32.3	85.0
=74	Edge Hill	12.1	317	87.1	88.4	45.6	85.0
76	Bournemouth	15.1	357	84.6	81.6	47.1	84.8
77	Bishop Grosseteste	6.7	262	87.1	83.6	59.9	84.7
78	Bradford		296*	88.1	88.4	52.8	84.6
=79	Kingston	15.7	287	85.5	86.2	48.0	84.4
=79	Southampton Solent		237	91.8	94.6	47.4	84.4
=79	Westminster	28.9	277	83.4	85.8	43.8	84.4
82	East London	13.7	263	91.1	89.4	38.3	84.2
83	South Wales	12.8	305	88.4	85.3	40.7	84.1
84	Northampton	15.3	263	86.1	88.5	45.4	84.0
85	Hertfordshire	7.8	321	77.6	83.0	60.7	83.6
86	Derby	13.5	273	87.1	88.9	39.2	83.4
87	Gloucestershire	9.3	298	85.1	84.9	44.8	83.2
=88	Cardiff Metropolitan		276	87.6	82.8	50.8	83.0
=88	Sunderland	15.3	279	83.0	79.4	50.6	83.0
=90	Brighton	16.2	310	80.1	82.0	48.1	82.9
=90	Leeds Trinity	6.2	265	83.4	80.2	57.4	82.9
92	Winchester		311	83.8	84.7	49.9	82.8
93	Staffordshire		221	84.1	88.8	56.3	82.5
94	London South Bank	12.8	233	89.0	86.9	34.5	82.0
=95	Glyndŵr		271*	83.4	81.2	52.0	81.7
=95	Worcester	8.2	271	81.6	82.8	47.8	81.7
=97	Anglia Ruskin	16.3	250	81.9	79.6	45.7	81.5
=97	Leeds Beckett	11.0	266	81.1	82.3	46.3	81.5
=97	Canterbury Christ Church	8.0	254	83.4	83.3	45.3	81.5
=100	Salford	7.8	314	82.7	83.3	37.2	81.4
=100	London Metropolitan		265	88.5	87.8	35.0	81.4
102	Sheffield Hallam	14.6	324	74.8	79.3	47.5	81.2
103	Central Lancashire	9.9	310	78.0	76.4	49.6	81.1
104	Greenwich	14.4	309	82.2	77.8	36.6	81.0
105	Middlesex	11.0	228	76.8	75.4	60.0	80.6
106	St Mark and St John		241	84.4	74.6	33.6	77.8

Employed in professional job:	33%	Employed in non-professional job and studying:	4%
Employed in professional job and studying:	3%	Employed in non-professional job:	30%
Studying:	19%	Unemployed:	11%
Average starting professional salary:	£18,863	Average starting non-professional salary:	£14,908

Food Science

The courses classified by UCAS as Food and Beverage Studies have not reaped the benefits of television's obsession with cookery to the same extent as forensic science or, arguably, anthropology. Applications have risen for six of the last seven years, but still

Food Science	Research quality %	Entry standards	Teaching quality %	Student experience %	Graduate prospects %	Overall score
1 Surrey	37.5	473	83.7	88.9	92.8	100.0
2 Queen's, Belfast	56.3	358	89.3	94.7	89.5	98.1
3 Leeds	36.8	425	87.8	92.7	81.1	96.4
4 Glasgow Caledonian	8.1	437*	95.4	100.0	78.8	94.4
5 King's College London	46.8	453	66.1	77.7	85.4	94.3
6 Nottingham	36.4	391	76.7	81.6	91.2	93.1
7 Reading	50.7	368	74.7	82.2	76.2	91.1
8 Coventry		380	90.7	89.7	92.5	90.5
9 Ulster	42.5	318	91.1	92.0	69.8	90.3
10 Robert Gordon	4.9	443	87.6	92.3	61.5	88.7
11 Hertfordshire	14.8	319	84.7	82.1	93.1	87.8
12 Newcastle	28.4	372	69.2	67.0	83.3	86.3
13 Lincoln	31.1		76.2	78.4	75.0	86.1
14 Plymouth	17.4	348	86.3	90.3	56.9	84.4
15 Leeds Beckett		347	87.9	91.1	69.8	84.3
16 Harper Adams	5.7	309	75.0	85.7	92.1	84.1
17 Bournemouth	4.7	317	81.1	88.1	80.0	83.6
18 Liverpool John Moores	6.0	352	87.6	91.2	58.8	83.4
19 Chester	12.0	326	70.0	79.5	82.4	82.6
20 Sheffield Hallam		312	88.0	90.0	70.7	82.5
21 Kingston	2.6	313*	98.5	98.9	50.0	82.3
22 Northumbria	14.0	335	87.9	91.0	47.6	81.9
=23 Bath Spa		314	90.3	93.2	55.2	80.6
=23 Central Lancashire	8.3	336	85.4	88.2	50.0	80.6
25 Roehampton	20.6	279	70.8	77.6	77.3	80.5
26 Queen Margaret, Edinburgh		336	78.6	80.8	66.1	80.1
27 Liverpool Hope		330	83.6	86.3	55.6	79.4
28 Leeds Trinity		315	84.4	78.2	60.2	78.7
29 Cardiff Metropolitan		295	82.5	81.0	64.0	78.4
30 Edge Hill		313	74.8	73.6	69.2	77.9
31 London Metropolitan		300	73.6	82.8	67.2	77.6
32 Oxford Brookes	3.0	364	64.0	69.5	63.3	77.4
33 Greenwich	19.5		75.0	79.6	50.0	77.2
34 Westminster		276	79.5	86.7	55.6	75.8
35 Abertay		297*	69.5	72.9	66.7	75.4
36 Huddersfield		270	79.4	78.2	55.6	74.5
37 Manchester Metropolitan	12.0	315*	60.0	65.3	60.0	74.4
38 St Mary's, Twickenham		307	76.6	79.4	38.4	73

Employed in professional job:	53%	Employed in non-professional job and studying:	2%
Employed in professional job and studying:	2%	Employed in non-professional job:	23%
Studying:	9%	Unemployed:	11%
Average starting professional salary:	£20,901	Average starting non-professional salary:	£15,867

only 575 students started courses in 2014. Degrees range from professional cookery to food manufacturing and nutrition. The subject is just below half way in the employment and salaries tables this year, with 55 per cent of graduates finding "professional" jobs within six months of completing a course. The unemployment rate had risen since the previous survey, but is still close to the average for all subjects.

Surrey has retaken the lead in food science from King's College London, which has dropped to fifth after leading on three of the four measures last year. Surrey now has the highest entry standards, while second-placed Queen's, Belfast produced the best results in the 2014 Research Excellence Framework. Kingston, in 21st place, achieved unusually high levels of satisfaction in the National Student Survey and had the best scores in the teaching sections, but could not match Glasgow Caledonian's rare 100 per cent satisfaction rate in the sections on the student experience, which took the university to fourth place overall. It remains the leading modern university.

Entry standards have been rising – none of the universities in this year's ranking averages less than 270 points – but there were still less than four applications per place in 2014. Almost a third of entrants to food science courses arrive with alternative qualifications to A levels, usually BTECs. Average salaries in graduate-level jobs have been declining in relation to other subjects and fell slightly in cash terms in 2014, dipping a little further below £21,000.

French

Languages have suffered a well-publicised decline in recent years – enrolments were dropping before the introduction of £9,000 fees and the process has accelerated since. Some universities are now closing their language departments, but 74 of them (surprisingly, no colleges) are offering full-time undergraduate courses in or including French for 2016. Only 520 started degrees in French in 2014, but another 2,500 opted for broader modern language courses. French remains the most popular language at degree level, attracting nearly 3,000 applications in 2014, but a continuing decline at A level suggests more tough times ahead.

Nevertheless, entry standards remain relatively high. In spite of the falling numbers, there were almost six applications to the place in 2014 and many of the candidates came from high-achieving independent schools. Over half of the 50 universities in the table averaged more than 400 points on the UCAS tariff and only six were below 300. Perhaps not surprisingly, nine out of ten undergraduates enter with A levels or their equivalents, although many universities will teach the language from scratch, especially as part of joint degrees.

Cambridge remains at the top of the table, with the best research grades and the highest entry standards, while Queen's, Belfast has moved up ten places to second. Queen's was just behind Cambridge in the Research Excellence Framework. Oxford Brookes, in 43rd place without entering the REF in modern languages, had the highest NSS score for teaching, while Nottingham Trent, in 40th place, did best on the other sections of the survey. Manchester Metropolitan, three places higher, is the leading modern university this year.

Lancaster was the only university to see nine out of ten graduates go straight into "professional" jobs or continue their studies. French is just outside the top 30 subjects for employment, with almost a quarter of graduates starting out in lower-level jobs in 2014. But it has regained the ground it lost last year in relation to salaries in graduate-level employment. An increase of over £800 brought the average close to £20,500.

French		Research quality %	Entry standards	Teaching quality %	Student experience %	Graduate prospects %	Overall score
1	Cambridge	54.0	566	89.9	89.8	83.9	100.0
2	Queen's, Belfast	53.6	402	93.8	95.8	75.4	96.0
3	Oxford	41.3	553	83.0	86.5	81.6	95.2
4	Durham	34.6	537	80.3	83.8	86.4	93.5
5	Southampton	42.7	417	86.4	94.8	77.8	93.1
6	Lancaster	47.0	436	81.0	74.0	90.2	92.6
7	Newcastle	36.3	412	88.1	91.5	81.1	92.5
8	Birmingham	33.7	403	90.1	88.5	82.8	92.3
9	Exeter	35.1	470	85.7	89.4	76.8	92.2
10	York	37.3	409	85.4	90.3	80.4	91.7
=11	Sheffield	41.2	420	83.7	89.1	75.7	91.3
=11	Warwick	45.2	455	83.4	80.7	73.5	91.3
13	Nottingham	39.4	420	84.4	91.3	74.1	91.1
14	Manchester	48.9	428	80.8	83.5	73.2	90.9
15	St Andrews	26.4	505	83.4	84.1	78.5	90.8
16	University College London	43.7	490	79.1	83.4	69.6	90.6
17	Bath	27.4	441	82.0	89.0	82.0	90.2
18	Leeds	30.6	425	85.2	89.1	75.8	90.0
19	King's College London	42.1	442	77.7	76.1	81.3	89.9
20	Liverpool	33.4	387	88.1	92.8	69.6	89.6
21	Royal Holloway, London	48.3	388	86.2	89.2	58.0	89.2
22	Stirling	29.8	423	81.4	87.4	78.0	89.1
23	Glasgow	26.3	490	82.8	85.0	65.3	88.2
24	Bristol	36.0	476	77.9	81.6	67.3	88.1
=25	Queen Mary, London	35.1	338	92.2	88.5	61.0	87.7
=25	Aston	23.4	346	91.9	92.0	69.1	87.7
27	Kent	41.9	341	78.9	88.1	72.5	87.5
28	Leicester	16.9	381	89.2	93.3	71.3	87.4
29	Cardiff	32.5	399	77.0	81.1	78.3	87.1
30	Reading	41.7	391	81.2	81.0	60.5	86.5
=31	Edinburgh	30.3	476	73.4	76.1	70.4	86.0
=31	Heriot-Watt	26.3	450	77.3	81.5	68.6	86.0
33	Aberdeen	29.3	456	80.2	85.0	56.6	85.7
34	Swansea	22.8	321	81.7	87.8	78.1	85.5
35	Sussex		392	81.9	90.0	79.9	84.2
36	Hull	22.7	317	85.4	87.6	64.8	84.0
37	Manchester Metropolitan	29.0	321	88.7	87.3	52.9	83.9
38	Strathclyde	42.0	489	72.6	81.1	41.5	83.7
39	Central Lancashire	15.2		83.1	83.3	65.7	83.4
40	Nottingham Trent	7.6	289	91.7	97.6	60.5	82.8
41	Ulster	22.4	276	88.2	88.4	56.6	82.3
42	Aberystwyth	16.6	338	73.2	80.0	79.5	82.2
43	Oxford Brookes		315	94.5	92.9	55.8	81.6

44 Coventry		257*	91.5	95.7	66.7	81.5
45 Bangor	39.6	280	79.6	83.1	49.6	81.3
46 Portsmouth	32.2	318*	84.7	93.2	33.3	80.8
47 Edinburgh Napier		347	81.9	89.1	65.8	80.6
48 Chester	17.3	271	76.5	78.0	72.4	80.0
49 Salford	4.8		82.8	77.0	58.7	78.7
50 Westminster	2.0	297	77.2	81.1	54.8	75.7

Employed in professional job:	44%	Employed in non-professional job and studying:	3%
Employed in professional job and studying:	4%	Employed in non-professional job:	21%
Studying:	18%	Unemployed:	11%
Average starting professional salary:	£20,492	Average starting non-professional salary:	£15,969

General Engineering

Applications for general engineering courses shot up by almost a quarter in 2014, as the numbers starting undergraduate courses grew significantly for the third year in a row. Although they do not yet attract as many applications as the established specialist branches of engineering, the general courses are attracting students who are looking for maximum career flexibility. Another reason for its success may be that general engineering has become a fixture in the top four of the graduate salaries table, with those in professional jobs averaging almost £27,500 a year – £1,100 more than in the last *Guide*. The subject has also moved one place closer to the top ten in the overall employment table, with nearly 70 per cent of graduates going straight into "professional" jobs.

Cambridge has stayed at the top of the table but its lead over Imperial College is down to a fraction of a point. Cambridge still has the highest entry grades, but Imperial has benefited from a big rise in student satisfaction. The most satisfied students of all were at the University of the West of England, which achieved the best scores in all sections of the National Student Survey. Third-placed Oxford produced the best grades in the Research Excellence Framework, while both Cardiff, in eighth place, and Coventry (15th) saw all their 2014 graduates go straight into high-level work or continue studying. Lincoln, three places higher, at 12th, has taken over as the leading modern university in the subject.

The growth in applications has brought rising entry grades, particularly in the lower half of the table. Only Coventry averages less than 250 points and most universities are comfortably over 300. Most of the leading universities will require both maths and physics at A level, with further maths, design technology and/or computing welcome additions. About one student in seven goes on to a postgraduate course, either full or part-time.

Employed in professional job:	66%	Employed in non-professional job and studying:	1%
Employed in professional job and studying:	3%	Employed in non-professional job:	8%
Studying:	12%	Unemployed:	11%
Average starting professional salary:	£27,493	Average starting non-professional salary:	£15,348

General Engineering	Research quality %	Entry standards	Teaching quality %	Student experience %	Graduate prospects %	Overall score
1 Cambridge	67.0	642	72.6	85.4	96.6	100.0
2 Imperial College	60.1	546	92.9	93.1	88.2	99.7
3 Oxford	68.7	593	74.3	79.3	88.7	96.8
4 Durham	39.4	549	84.2	88.9	88.9	94.7
5 Glasgow	47.2	525	77.3	86.2		93.1
6 Nottingham	40.8	494	88.5	92.4	77.8	92.3
7 Warwick	47.2	429	76.1	84.2	88.0	90.4
8 Cardiff	30.2	427	70.5	79.1	100.0	88.9
9 Heriot-Watt	47.8	390	78.8	86.3		88.5
=10 Exeter	36.4	432	70.8	79.3	92.4	88.3
=10 Swansea	45.5	336*	80.9	87.7	84.2	88.3
12 Lincoln	12.4	346	84.5	84.4	94.7	86.6
13 West of Scotland	9.0		94.5	96.5	70.0	86.5
14 West of England	10.6	317	96.2	97.0	80.7	86.3
15 Coventry	10.3	199	88.9	93.8	100.0	85.7
16 Liverpool	32.1	445	79.1	84.8	68.4	85.0
17 Queen Mary, London	46.7	395*	73.4	80.8	70.3	84.5
18 Aberdeen	28.4	452	71.8	74.7		84.0
19 Ulster		314	85.6	94.8	78.7	81.9
20 London South Bank	19.6	256	86.0	87.7	75.0	81.5
21 Leicester	34.4	344	61.8	72.5	82.9	81.0
22 City	20.2	339	76.2	78.3	70.8	79.7
23 Liverpool John Moores	14.2	344	79.8	85.5	64.2	79.1
24 Central Lancashire	7.1	308	81.8	84.7	70.4	78.9
25 De Montfort	12.5		79.8	81.8	64.3	78.0
26 Edinburgh Napier		347	73.7	79.0	76.3	77.9
27 Glasgow Caledonian	4.7	336	73.4	76.0	75.0	77.6
=28 Aston	20.6	292	68.3	77.6		76.2
=28 Sheffield Hallam		289	70.1	78.8	78.4	76.2
30 Bradford	7.7	298	82.6	88.3	56.1	76.1
31 Northampton		336	69.3	71.2	75.0	75.5
32 Greenwich	5.5		77.9	84.1	53.8	73.3
33 Bournemouth	8.5	302	54.4	63.6	80.0	73.1

Geography and Environmental Sciences

Geography and environmental sciences continue to benefit from strong interest in "green" issues among young people. Applications and enrolments for physical geography and what UCAS describes as the "science of terrestrial and aquatic environments" have been broadly steady since before £9,000 fees arrived, while human and social geography courses have seen two years of growth. The subjects' attractions do not seem to be related to career prospects since geography and environmental science are not in the top 40 in the employment table. They fare better in the comparison of earnings, where an average starting salary of £21,210 in professional jobs places them half way up that table.

There were big changes in the table last year, with Cambridge dropping from first to fifth place and Durham taking over at the top. This year Cambridge is back up to second place, registering the highest entry grades, while Oxford assumes the leadership and Durham is third. Bristol, in fourth place, did best in the Research Excellence Framework, when more than half of its submission was rated as world-leading, while the London School of Economic had the best employment rate. Students at Coventry were most satisfied with the teaching quality, but a low research score restricted the university to 34th place, while students at Derby rated the student experience most highly, Winchester was the best-placed post-1992 institution and the only one to feature in the top 30.

Physical geography courses may give preference to candidates with a science or maths A level in addition to geography, while for environmental science, most of the leading universities will ask for two from biology, chemistry, maths, physics and geography at A level or the equivalent. Average entry scores range from around 550 points at Oxford and Cambridge to only 200 at the foot of the table. Satisfaction ratings are generally good in both branches of geography, but employment scores in the latest table are mediocre. No university saw nine out of ten graduates go straight into professional jobs or onto postgraduate courses, and the proportion dropped below half at 14 of the 74 universities.

Geography and Environmental Sciences	Research quality %	Entry standards	Teaching quality %	Student experience %	Graduate prospects %	Overall score
1 Oxford	41.1	549	88.4	94.0	84.4	100.0
2 Cambridge	57.3	567	81.5	87.3	80.1	99.6
3 Durham	55.0	521	83.3	91.3	79.7	98.8
4 Bristol	61.3	475	78.0	85.2	83.3	96.9
5 London School of Economics	46.9	486	79.9	85.1	88.6	96.6
6 Exeter	43.7	448	84.1	88.2	77.9	94.5
7 Cardiff	36.8	383	86.2	92.8	85.5	94.1
8 Newcastle	43.1	409	86.8	92.0	74.9	93.9
=9 Lancaster	46.5	421	83.4	86.0	78.6	93.8
=9 Royal Holloway, London	45.8	387	93.5	91.6	67.1	93.8
11 Leeds	42.3	424	81.0	89.7	74.9	92.6
12 Southampton	45.8	400	82.7	89.3	73.4	92.4
13 St Andrews	44.2	498	77.0	73.9	76.4	92.3
14 Edinburgh	38.2	474	81.9	89.2	66.4	92.1
15 Glasgow	42.4	438	80.1	80.8	76.2	91.9
=16 Queen Mary, London	45.1	369	86.5	89.2	69.8	91.7
=16 Manchester	36.6	412	87.7	90.3	66.9	91.7
=18 Birmingham	42.0	405	79.0	78.3	80.8	91.1
=18 East Anglia	47.4	403	82.2	89.9	64.4	91.1
20 Nottingham	39.6	424	80.5	86.0	69.8	90.7
21 Aberdeen	38.2	449	78.2	85.0	70.2	90.6
22 Loughborough	24.3	373	86.0	90.1	78.8	90.4

Geography and Environmental Sciences cont	Research quality %	Entry standards	Teaching quality %	Student experience %	Graduate prospects %	Overall score
=23 Liverpool	26.3	392	84.4	90.5	68.9	89.2
=23 University College London	52.3	487	60.3	64.3	82.9	89.2
=25 Dundee	28.3	423	83.8	92.2	61.0	89.0
=25 Winchester	7.5		81.9	83.8	87.0	89.0
=27 Sheffield	31.1	419	78.7	83.8	69.5	88.6
=27 Sussex	35.8	387	77.2	83.4	73.2	88.6
29 Stirling	30.3	401	78.9	85.5	68.6	88.1
30 Swansea	39.4	329	82.1	86.2	66.0	87.6
31 York	23.9	380	82.1	81.9	71.2	87.3
32 Queen's, Belfast	36.9	340	83.2	88.3	60.9	87.2
33 Aberystwyth	38.6	315	82.5	87.1	64.7	87.1
34 Coventry	2.0	318	96.6	96.2	68.0	87.0
=35 King's College London	40.0	410	69.2	74.9	73.1	86.9
=35 Oxford Brookes	17.3	309	88.6	90.8	70.9	86.9
37 Keele	16.4	322	90.2	93.0	63.5	86.5
38 Hull	31.7	323	86.1	89.9	58.2	86.4
39 Bangor	31.5	302	86.2	90.1	60.5	86.2
=40 Leicester	29.7	366	80.4	86.0	59.7	85.8
=40 Reading	35.0	361	76.0	82.2	65.1	85.8
42 Salford	16.7	296	91.5	91.8	55.6	84.5
43 Portsmouth	14.9	304	88.0	88.3	59.1	83.9
44 Edge Hill	6.2	281	92.5	95.3	56.6	83.5
45 Northumbria	15.4	334	84.0	82.8	59.6	83.3
46 Hertfordshire		280	90.1	92.8	64.0	83.0
47 Gloucestershire	14.5	306	90.3	92.7	47.4	82.9
48 Plymouth	25.8	299	82.3	84.8	53.8	82.5
49 Derby	3.6	251	94.0	97.6	52.8	82.2
=50 West of England	6.4	303	85.0	87.9	60.5	82.1
=50 Strathclyde	31.9		91.0	88.3	32.5	82.1
52 Liverpool Hope	1.6	287	82.5	84.3	71.6	81.9
53 Chester	6.4	298	83.9	81.9	62.8	81.4
54 Bradford	23.6		71.6	73.8	68.2	80.8
=55 Northampton	7.7	264	89.4	91.4	48.3	80.5
=55 Manchester Metropolitan	14.9	306	85.0	85.3	45.7	80.5
57 Staffordshire		269	84.8	87.4	62.1	80.4
58 Ulster		287	87.9	92.1	50.2	80.1
59 Greenwich	7.4	312	84.5	90.6	43.8	79.8
60 Central Lancashire	9.8	264	86.5	85.6	49.6	79.6
61 Brighton	5.1	292	79.1	85.1	55.9	79.1
62 Nottingham Trent	4.1	275	89.2	85.3	44.8	78.9
=63 Liverpool John Moores		315	85.9	81.1	46.2	78.4
=63 Worcester	8.1	279	83.1	87.1	45.4	78.4
65 Canterbury Christ Church		246	84.9	87.3	53.9	78.3

66 Kingston	6.9	263	81.7	79.3	52.9	77.9
67 Leeds Beckett	5.6	266	84.7	83.5	42.6	77.2
=68 Bath Spa		275	86.7	84.8	40.4	76.9
=68 South Wales		330	71.1	81.8	54.4	76.9
70 St Mary's, Twickenham		240	81.6	79.3	54.7	76.5
71 Sheffield Hallam		311	76.1	80.7	48.4	76.3
72 Cumbria	1.5	276	79.5	80.4	38.6	74.5
73 Bournemouth	19.9	291	59.3	64.0	50.7	72.9
74 Southampton Solent		200	71.7	70.4	35.4	68.5

Employed in professional job:	38%	Employed in non-professional job and studying:	3%
Employed in professional job and studying:	3%	Employed in non-professional job:	25%
Studying:	19%	Unemployed:	13%
Average starting professional salary:	£21,210	Average starting non-professional salary:	£15,384

Geology

There has been a surge in interest in geology since £9,000 fees were introduced and more students have opted for what they see as marketable degrees. Applications have increased by more than a quarter in three years, culminating in another 8 per cent rise in 2014. There have been gradual increases in enrolments every year since 2008, but there are still more than five applications to the place and entry standards are high. Cambridge recorded its normal astronomical entry grades (648 points in 2014) and another three of the 31 universities in the table topped 500 points. Some of the leading universities expect candidates to have two scientific or mathematical subjects at A level, or the equivalent.

Graduate salaries and the prospect of an international career no doubt contribute to the subject's growing popularity. Geology is in the top 20 in the salary table, although average earnings were still £700 lower in 2014 than they had been in 2012. The subject is lower in the overall employment table, but still in the top 30. Less than 40 per cent of graduates went straight into professional jobs in 2014, but there is always a high take-up for postgraduate degrees. Almost a third took this route in 2014.

Imperial College has taken over from Cambridge at the top of the table, with the top research grades and exceptional scores in the National Student Survey for the third year in a row. Over 99 per cent of final-year undergraduates were satisfied with their course in the latest survey. Cambridge still has by far the highest entry standards, while third-placed St Andrews again has much the best employment record. Imperial was the only other university to see more than 90 per cent of graduates gain a professional job or go on to further study. No post-1992 university reaches the top 20, but Plymouth is again only one place outside it.

Employed in professional job:	37%	Employed in non-professional job and studying:	2%
Employed in professional job and studying:	2%	Employed in non-professional job:	19%
Studying:	28%	Unemployed:	12%
Average starting professional salary:	£23,029	Average starting non-professional salary:	£14,676

Geology	Research quality %	Entry standards	Teaching quality %	Student experience %	Graduate prospects %	Overall score
1 Imperial College	59.6	553	99.9	99.2	90.8	100.0
2 Cambridge	58.0	648	86.0	86.3	87.4	96.8
3 St Andrews	44.2	514	79.3	89.2	93.5	91.7
4 Oxford	52.1	582	70.9	88.4	85.1	90.9
5 Bristol	55.8	464	84.9	90.3	71.3	89.4
6 Durham	42.2	489	82.9	90.8	77.2	88.7
7 University College London	47.9	447	84.2	86.1	78.1	88.5
8 Leeds	41.9	430	81.4	87.3	82.5	87.6
9 East Anglia	47.4	377	83.9	88.9	80.0	87.5
=10 Exeter	45.7	392	78.9	87.3	82.8	86.8
=10 Southampton	58.3	391	75.4	87.6	77.1	86.8
12 Leicester	37.2	393	91.2	93.1	71.3	86.7
13 Glasgow	38.5	470	77.9	89.3	76.5	86.3
14 Edinburgh	38.2	464	80.8	80.7	78.6	86.2
15 Liverpool	30.3	393	84.0	85.3	80.1	85.0
16 Manchester	44.5	427	79.6	84.1	70.5	84.9
17 Royal Holloway, London	43.4	364	78.0	87.2	76.8	84.5
18 Birmingham	38.6	390	78.5	72.9	76.7	82.9
19 Aberdeen	38.2	415	66.6	75.3	79.6	81.6
20 Cardiff	21.3	368	80.0	87.1	69.9	80.4
21 Plymouth	25.3	301	86.2	94.0	62.6	80.2
22 Hull	31.7	296	78.6	89.0		79.3
23 Bangor	31.5	285	87.1	86.8	56.3	78.9
24 Keele	12.2	337	91.8	93.2	55.2	78.8
25 Aberystwyth	34.9	269	85.3	82.9	54.8	78.0
26 Derby	3.6	272	92.8	92.7	54.9	76.2
27 Portsmouth	19.8	299	80.5	80.2	58.6	75.8
28 Brighton	5.1	272	80.5	80.9	65.9	74.5
29 Edge Hill		275	92.4	92.4	48.5	74.4
30 Kingston	6.9	274	72.7	67.3	68.3	72.1
31 South Wales		256	74.0	73.0	55.3	69.1

German

For the second year in a row, only 210 students started degrees in German in 2014, although many others are learning the language through broader modern languages degrees. German has suffered more than other European languages from the decline in the numbers taking courses in the sixth-form, or even earlier. The introduction of £9,000 fees undoubtedly contributed to falling numbers, but there has been a worldwide decline in the language that has been worrying the German government, as well as academic linguists. Courses in the language will be available at 57 universities in 2016, but only about half are offering single Honours in the language.

Cambridge makes it ten years in a row at the top of the table for German and has extended its lead in the new *Guide*, with the highest entry standards and the best score from the Research Excellence Framework (REF). Bristol has moved up 13 places to second after an improvement of more than 10 percentage points in student satisfaction. However, even an average of more than 93 per cent satisfaction in the National Student Survey (NSS) could not compare with scores of more than 95 per cent in the teaching and student experience sections of the survey at the University of East Anglia. The university still finishes in the bottom three because it has almost the lowest graduate employment rate in the table and did not enter the REF in modern languages. Most universities scored well in the NSS; only two failed to satisfy at least 75 per cent of final-year undergraduates. Portsmouth, though dropping six places, remains the highest-placed of just five post-1992 universities in the ranking.

Most universities in the table offer German from scratch as well as catering for those who took the subject at A level. Employment prospects are better than in other modern languages, although the small numbers mean that the differences can be slight. German is in the top 30 for the proportion of graduates going into professional jobs or onto postgraduate courses, and only ten subjects have a lower unemployment rate. St Andrews, which shares eighth place with Oxford, has the best employment score, but no university recorded 90 per cent positive destinations in 2014. An increase of £1,800 in average starting salaries in graduate-level jobs put an end to two years of declining earnings and has taken German 17 places up the salaries table to the verge of the top 30.

German	Research quality %	Entry standards	Teaching quality %	Student experience %	Graduate prospects %	Overall score
1 Cambridge	54.0	566	89.9	89.8	83.9	100.0
2 Bristol	36.0	468	94.3	93.0	78.0	94.2
3 Southampton	42.7	452	85.4	92.2	83.3	94.1
4 Warwick	45.2	444	85.4	87.6	81.3	93.5
5 Durham	34.6	537	80.3	83.8	86.4	93.1
6 Newcastle	36.3	427	87.1	91.1	83.1	92.4
7 Glasgow	26.3	451	90.5	89.3	85.3	92.0
=8 St Andrews	26.4	511	81.8	86.8	87.4	91.8
=8 Oxford	41.3	546	77.2	83.8	75.2	91.8
10 Exeter	35.1	470	85.7	89.4	76.8	91.5
11 Leeds	30.6	452	91.1	92.7	75.0	91.3
12 Sheffield	41.2	431	90.7	92.6	64.9	90.8
=13 Manchester	48.9	418	81.7	85.7	67.9	89.8
=13 Birmingham	33.7	430	87.7	82.3	76.3	89.8
15 York	37.3	394	88.1	87.9		89.4
16 Nottingham	39.4	391	86.4	86.4	71.7	89.2
17 Lancaster	47.0	439	75.4	81.0	71.4*	88.8
18 Reading	41.7	356	91.3	91.6	61.5	88.4
19 Royal Holloway, London	48.3	382*	85.6	83.4	59.0	87.6
20 Bath	27.4	437	76.3	79.4	82.5	87.1
21 Kent	41.9	359	86.4	79.5	61.1	86.0

German cont	Research quality %	Entry standards	Teaching quality %	Student experience %	Graduate prospects %	Overall score
=22 University College London	43.7	493	78.3	75.2	51.6	85.5
=22 Aston	23.4	356	87.3	90.8	70.1	85.5
=24 Hull	22.7	331	92.1	90.3	68.0	85.3
=24 Heriot-Watt	26.3	450	77.3	81.5	70.7	85.3
26 King's College London	42.1	428	75.8	71.4	63.7	85.0
27 Cardiff	32.5	380	73.9	75.9	77.1	84.7
=28 Edinburgh	30.3	523	74.3	79.9	58.3	84.6
=28 Liverpool	33.4	397	76.8	76.6	70.0	84.6
30 Swansea	22.8	287	93.2	92.5	65.7	84.3
31 Portsmouth	32.2	268	84.1	88.8	67.4	83.6
32 Queen Mary, London	35.1	354	80.8	77.8		83.4
33 Bangor	39.6	243	83.6	88.1	57.7	82.3
=34 Chester	17.3	305	86.1	81.3	71.2	81.9
=34 Manchester Metropolitan	29.0	302	87.1	84.9	57.1	81.9
36 East Anglia		413	95.6	95.3	54.2	81.4
37 Central Lancashire	15.2		83.1	83.3	61.6	80.6
38 Nottingham Trent	7.6	287	91.5	90.7	60.2	79.6

Employed in professional job:	46%	Employed in non-professional job and studying:	3%
Employed in professional job and studying:	4%	Employed in non-professional job:	22%
Studying:	17%	Unemployed:	8%
Average starting professional salary:	£21,232	Average starting non-professional salary:	£14,844

History

History has registered healthy increases in applications and enrolments for the last two years and by 2014 had more of both than there were before the arrival of £9,000 fees. Yet the subject is in the bottom 15 for employment, with the same number of graduates starting out in low-level jobs as in those categorised as professional occupations. There was a £400 rise in average starting salaries in the professional jobs taken by historians in 2014, but the subject remained in the bottom half of the table. Surveys suggest that they often rise to the top later in their careers, however.

Durham and Cambridge had taken it in turns to lead the history table for the last six years, but Oxford have separated them in this edition. Cambridge continues to lead with the highest entry standards and the top score from the 2014 Research Excellence Framework (REF), as well as the best graduate prospects. Glyndŵr has the most satisfied students in terms of teaching, feedback and academic support, but did not enter the REF in history and is restricted to 64th place as a result. East Anglia, in 16th place, has the best scores in the remaining sections of the National Student Survey. Satisfaction levels are high throughout the ranking: only Bristol and bottom-placed East London failed to satisfy at least 70 per cent of final-year undergraduates.

The older institutions continue to dominate the table: only Huddersfield, Oxford Brookes and Hertfordshire, of the modern universities, appear in the top 40. Average entry scores have dropped slightly at the leading universities since last year. Five universities, compared with seven last year, top 500 points – the equivalent of more than four As at A level – but another five in the lower reaches of the ranking average less than 250 points. Employment scores are disappointing at many of the 93 universities in the table. Thirty-five institutions saw less than half of those graduating in 2014 go into professional jobs or start postgraduate courses by the end of the year, and the figure was below 40 per cent at 14 of them.

History	Research quality %	Entry standards	Teaching quality %	Student experience %	Graduate prospects %	Overall score
1 Cambridge	56.3	563	88.0	88.7	83.9	100.0
2 Oxford	56.1	544	82.3	87.4	81.3	97.5
3 Durham	41.4	552	86.8	86.9	82.2	96.7
=4 St Andrews	46.7	521	86.9	86.8	71.1	95.1
=4 Exeter	45.6	474	87.0	88.4	78.7	95.1
6 London School of Economics	46.8	486	86.0	86.1	77.3	94.9
7 University College London	51.9	503	82.3	83.3	75.5	94.5
8 Warwick	51.7	480	82.7	81.8	78.8	94.3
=9 Sheffield	53.7	438	87.6	89.6	66.9	94.0
=9 York	43.3	488	85.6	87.9	73.6	94.0
11 Birmingham	48.8	400	85.6	85.0	81.2	93.3
12 King's College London	45.3	470	84.1	83.6	74.6	93.0
=13 Southampton	50.6	391	87.7	89.8	68.8	92.7
=13 Lancaster	37.0	456	87.2	87.0	74.8	92.7
15 Leeds	43.6	450	84.6	84.3	73.1	92.3
16 East Anglia	47.4	410	88.8	92.5	61.0	92.2
17 Glasgow	47.7	439	83.9	85.8	65.0	91.4
=18 Newcastle	29.0	428	88.7	90.4	69.9	90.9
=18 Sussex	41.3	379	83.2	87.3	78.3	90.9
20 Queen Mary, London	43.7	390	89.2	85.0	62.4	90.5
21 Nottingham	36.9	420	83.7	84.3	73.0	90.3
22 Kent	41.3	386	84.9	85.9	69.8	90.1
23 Royal Holloway, London	40.6	408	88.5	84.3	60.3	89.9
24 Manchester	39.8	412	83.7	85.7	65.2	89.6
25 Edinburgh	46.9	488	74.3	81.7	64.4	89.5
26 Queen's, Belfast	46.3	371	85.6	90.1	55.4	89.1
27 Loughborough	22.5	351	85.9	89.9	79.8	88.7
28 Liverpool	38.9	402	85.2	85.5	57.4	88.4
29 Keele	32.8	345	89.6	89.0	62.4	88.3
30 Cardiff	31.4	402	88.2	84.3	59.6	88.2
31 Strathclyde	42.0	463	82.9	84.9	45.1	87.9
32 Huddersfield	22.3	339	91.8	84.9	67.9	87.5
33 Reading	35.4	373	84.2	85.3	60.3	87.3
34 Oxford Brookes	35.0	323	91.6	88.8	52.2	87.1
=35 Leicester	34.3	384	82.3	85.5	60.2	86.9
=35 Essex	34.8	314	87.3	89.4	59.3	86.9

History cont	Research quality %	Entry standards	Teaching quality %	Student experience %	Graduate prospects %	Overall score
37 Hertfordshire	46.7	321	82.1	81.0	60.5	86.6
=38 Hull	26.1	324	89.4	88.9	60.9	86.5
=38 Swansea	25.0	315	87.9	88.8	66.1	86.5
40 Aberdeen	36.1	409	79.6	80.3	59.7	86.4
41 Dundee	30.4	379	90.0	91.5	41.3	86.2
42 Bristol	40.6	486	68.3	65.3	70.6	85.9
43 Lincoln	25.9	328	89.0	86.3	57.0	85.6
44 Liverpool Hope	15.7	287	95.7	88.0	59.8	85.4
45 Stirling	28.5	384	84.2	84.0	53.2	85.3
46 Brunel	32.4	335	91.1	85.8	43.1	85.2
47 Northumbria	30.7	348	86.7	83.8	51.2	85.1
48 SOAS, London	20.8	369	80.2	82.4	68.6	84.8
49 Bangor	24.3	309	91.7	89.8	48.4	84.7
=50 West of England	28.9	334	88.9	82.1	48.8	84.5
=50 De Montfort	23.4	280	89.1	81.8	64.1	84.5
=52 Portsmouth	32.2	293	84.2	84.0	55.5	83.9
=52 Coventry	5.6	286	91.8	87.7	67.2	83.9
54 Teesside	27.9	266	89.0	87.8	51.4	83.7
=55 Manchester Metropolitan	18.0	312	87.7	84.7	50.9	82.6
=55 Winchester	19.1	301	87.6	84.9	51.5	82.6
57 Goldsmiths, London	34.5	300	79.3	72.5	57.5	82.1
=58 Chester	9.1	310	88.6	85.0	53.1	81.8
=58 Sheffield Hallam	38.3	300	81.5	84.8	37.4	81.8
60 Edge Hill	23.6	292	88.6	84.3	40.2	81.6
=61 Northampton	21.5	264	87.4	84.8	46.5	81.2
=61 Newman	12.0	282	94.0	87.6	39.3	81.2
63 Aberystwyth	19.5	315	82.2	80.3	52.1	81.1
64 Glyndŵr		282	97.1	85.3	46.4	81.0
65 South Wales	15.8	307	90.1	89.5	33.9	80.9
=66 Plymouth	22.6	287	87.2	84.1	37.1	80.5
=66 Liverpool John Moores	15.9	330	83.5	83.5	43.5	80.5
=66 Bath Spa	8.3	291	88.7	90.3	43.5	80.5
=69 Derby	13.5	268	93.4	87.8	35.3	80.4
=69 Chichester	15.8	266	89.1	88.7	40.1	80.4
71 Canterbury Christ Church	16.3	273	89.9	81.8	40.3	80.0
=72 Nottingham Trent	17.5	275	82.4	83.8	47.8	79.7
=72 St Mary's, Twickenham	11.0	270	88.8	91.8	37.5	79.7
74 Bradford	12.7	317*	74.2	78.2	63.8	79.6
75 Salford		308	87.8	81.8	47.9	79.1
76 Brighton	13.1	274	83.3	74.7	54.1	79.0
77 Sunderland	7.7	290	81.8	84.8	48.2	78.7
=78 York St John		279	87.6	84.7	47.3	78.6
=78 Bishop Grosseteste	7.0	262	77.6	78.6	66.4	78.6

=80 Ulster	24.0	266	81.8	84.3	32.8	78.2
=80 Leeds Beckett	11.0	243	90.5	86.0	33.6	78.2
82 Central Lancashire	12.0	278	84.3	76.2	41.8	77.6
83 Roehampton	21.4	283	72.0	71.3	56.1	77.5
84 Greenwich	8.6	290	85.3	81.5	32.5	77.0
85 Leeds Trinity	10.3	235	88.9	79.4	35.5	76.9
86 Kingston		261	83.1	82.0	43.8	76.1
87 Gloucestershire	11.2	303	78.0	79.9	33.3	75.8
88 Anglia Ruskin	15.3	225	83.5	78.4	31.5	75.3
89 Westminster	11.8	267	76.9	80.9	34.8	75.0
90 Worcester	19.5	251	71.1	70.6	48.1	74.9
91 Highlands and Islands		292	75.5	74.5	42.1	73.8
92 Staffordshire		245	81.7	70.9	38.1	73.1
93 East London	13.9	245*	66.5	60.8	44.6	71.0

Employed in professional job:	31%	Employed in non-professional job and studying:	4%
Employed in professional job and studying:	3%	Employed in non-professional job:	29%
Studying:	21%	Unemployed:	12%
Average starting professional salary:	£20,456	Average starting non-professional salary:	£15,063

History of Art, Architecture and Design

There are big changes this year in the table for the history of art, architecture and design. The Courtauld Institute, an independent college of the University of London based in Somerset House, and previously the only specialist institution to top any of our league tables, has dropped three places despite producing the best results in the Research Excellence Framework. Ninety-five per cent of the Courtauld's submission was rated as world-leading or internationally excellent, but its entry standards and student satisfaction rate had declined in 2014. The new leader is Cambridge, which was only sixth in last year's *Guide*. It has the highest entry grades and good levels of student satisfaction.

However, even Cambridge did not see three-quarters of graduates go straight into "professional" jobs or onto a postgraduate course. Just four of the 29 universities did, and only Leicester exceeded 80 per cent positive destinations. The subjects are outside the top 50 in the employment and graduate earnings tables, with the average starting salary in professional jobs reaching £19,274 in 2014. One graduate in three starts out in low-level employment, while a quarter go on to postgraduate study.

Exeter has entered the table in second place with Oxford, the leader two years ago, remains third. Satisfaction levels are high throughout the table. Oxford Brookes, the leading modern university in 21st place, has the best rating for teaching, feedback and academic support, while seventh-placed East Anglia is the leader for the student experience.

The numbers starting courses in the history of art, architecture and design has been falling, but 44 universities are offering degrees in the subjects – often in combination with other disciplines – for 2016. Entry standards are high: only four universities in the table average less than 350 points and the top three all average more than 500 points.

History of Art, Architecture and Design	Research quality %	Entry standards	Teaching quality %	Student experience %	Graduate prospects %	Overall score
1 Cambridge	49.0	560	87.2	88.3	73.8	100.0
2 Exeter	45.6	510	87.4	88.8		98.7
3 Oxford	39.7	539	82.3	87.5	76.2	97.1
4 Courtauld Institute	66.0	445	80.1	87.3	72.5	96.9
5 York	53.2	433	87.0	88.5	62.1	95.6
6 St Andrews	42.1	477	87.2	86.9	65.2	95.5
7 East Anglia	36.9	428	88.8	92.5	69.6	95.4
8 University College London	44.7	497	82.3	82.9	69.4	95.1
9 Warwick	53.0	459	83.2	81.8	67.0	95.0
10 Leicester	42.0	396*	82.9	84.9	84.8	94.9
11 Essex	46.9		86.5	88.3	61.9	94.7
12 Birmingham	43.7	384	85.0	84.1	74.3	93.7
13 Manchester	54.0	370	84.6	86.3	63.3	93.3
14 Glasgow	37.2	416	84.3	86.0	66.9	92.6
15 Kent	44.3	326	85.3	85.9	73.4	92.5
16 Sussex	25.2	392	83.2	87.3	77.8	91.9
17 Edinburgh	27.9	480	74.8	81.8	75.9	91.1
18 SOAS, London	40.9	415	80.2	82.4	62.5	90.8
19 Leeds	30.0	396	84.8	84.6	57.2	89.7
20 Nottingham	30.9	374	83.9	84.1	58.0	89.1
21 Oxford Brookes	35.0	325	91.6	88.8	39.0	88.4
22 Bristol	28.3	453	70.0	67.6	67.9	86.1
23 Aberdeen	36.1		79.7	80.3	47.7	85.8
24 Goldsmiths, London	25.9	409	79.3	72.5	51.9	85.7
25 Aberystwyth	21.6		82.2	80.3	46.7	84.7
26 Plymouth	14.7	274	87.2	84.1	52.9	84.6
27 Manchester Metropolitan	9.7	359*	87.7	84.7	33.3	83.5
28 Liverpool John Moores	7.2		83.5	83.5	42.9	83.1
29 Brighton	13.1	271	84.0	75.1	48.7	81.7

Employed in professional job:	34%	Employed in non-professional job and studying:	4%
Employed in professional job and studying:	3%	Employed in non-professional job:	29%
Studying:	18%	Unemployed:	13%
Average starting professional salary:	£19,274	Average starting non-professional salary:	£15,228

Hospitality, Leisure, Recreation and Tourism

This group of subjects covers a variety of courses directed towards management in the leisure and tourism industries, mainly delivered at modern universities. It remains in the top 20 for applications, which have increased for the last two years, but does surprisingly poorly in the graduate employment market, given the size of the sectors it serves. The group remains in the bottom four in the employment table because over 40 per cent of graduates are in low-level work six months after completing a course. The subjects do better in the earnings table, finishing just outside the top 50 with an average salary of £19,369 in "professional" jobs. The numbers starting courses in 2014 rose for the second year in a row, but are not yet back at the level seen in 2010, the last year unaffected by the move to £9,000 fees. Entry standards are low overall, but have been rising at some of the leading universities. The top three in the new table all average more than 400 points on the UCAS tariff, but only seven others have averages of more than 350 points.

Only nine institutions in the table are pre-1992 universities, but they include the top four. Birmingham has taken over from Surrey at the top of the table, moving up from fifth place last year. It had by far the best results in the Research Excellence Framework, when 90 per cent of its submission was considered world-leading or internationally excellent, and also has the best employment score. Only Birmingham and second-placed Exeter saw three-quarters of graduates go straight into professional jobs or continue their studies. Coventry had the most satisfied students with all aspects of their course.

More than 100 universities and colleges are offering courses in one or more of the hospitality, leisure, recreation and tourism subjects in 2016. Satisfaction rates are invariably high: only three universities failed to achieve at least 70 per cent approval. Liverpool John Moores has jumped no fewer than 44 places to become the leading modern university, in fifth position. It is joined in the top ten by Oxford Brookes, Coventry, Robert Gordon and Hertfordshire.

Hospitality, Leisure, Recreation and Tourism	*Research quality %*	*Entry standards*	*Teaching quality %*	*Student experience %*	*Graduate prospects %*	*Overall score*
1 Birmingham	63.7	419	68.7	84.9	84.8	100.0
2 Exeter	24.4	471	79.1	88.6	82.8	97.8
3 Surrey	33.6	409	88.4	91.4	60.2	94.9
4 Strathclyde	44.3		84.3	87.5	68.3	93.9
5 Liverpool John Moores	45.3	342	91.7	90.9	36.1	90.2
6 Edinburgh	26.1	385	73.0	87.7		88.4
7 Oxford Brookes	5.1	374	87.5	85.6	68.0	88.3
8 Coventry	1.6	317	95.3	94.9	71.1	88.1
9 Robert Gordon	2.6	381	83.9	87.2	60.3	86.4
10 Hertfordshire	0.9	325	91.8	94.5	55.1	84.9
11 Ulster	31.0	286	92.1	92.4	34.8	84.8
12 De Montfort		298	87.7	87.3	68.4	83.9
13 Lincoln	11.4	318	83.1	77.9	61.5	83.7
=14 Sheffield Hallam	8.5	325	83.0	87.2	53.1	83.2
=14 Edinburgh Napier	2.3	353	87.2	89.3	43.8	83.2
16 Manchester		380	67.5	77.7	69.6	82.8
17 Cumbria	3.2	258	94.1	91.8	58.4	82.6
18 Chester	6.6	304	84.5	84.5	55.9	82.3
19 Winchester		291	90.1	91.5	53.4	82.0
20 Salford	5.9	368	80.5	80.8	40.9	81.6
21 Huddersfield		291	82.6	83.8	65.0	81.5
22 Bournemouth	9.0	314	75.4	82.6	57.6	81.4

Hospitality, Leisure, Recreation and Tourism cont	Research quality %	Entry standards	Teaching quality %	Student experience %	Graduate prospects %	Overall score
23 Central Lancashire	5.1	295	85.6	87.9	50.7	81.3
24 Falmouth		255	88.1	87.3	64.7	81.1
=25 Manchester Metropolitan	4.7	324	77.8	79.9	55.8	81.0
=25 Brighton	10.9	297	81.1	81.6	51.9	81.0
=27 Plymouth		303	87.1	90.2	46.0	80.6
=27 Leeds Beckett	12.6	297	75.3	81.6	55.4	80.6
=27 Arts University Bournemouth		278	80.5	84.6	66.0	80.6
30 University of the Arts London		358	79.6	78.7	46.3	80.5
31 Greenwich	3.3	329	76.6	82.3	51.7	80.4
32 Middlesex	10.5	290	84.1	88.1	42.0	80.3
33 Sunderland	2.4	311	87.2	87.8	38.8	80.0
34 Cardiff Metropolitan	7.7	292	77.7	82.3	53.3	79.7
35 Derby	0.9	305	83.3	84.9	46.0	79.5
36 Gloucestershire	6.0	309	69.8	76.0	61.9	79.3
37 London South Bank	35.0	242	78.3	85.1	32.8	79.2
=38 Northampton		274	83.4	83.6	50.6	78.4
=38 Southampton Solent	0.6	292	73.7	82.3	57.6	78.4
40 Portsmouth	8.1	268	74.2	83.6	52.5	77.9
41 St Mary's, Twickenham	4.8	250	92.6	87.4	34.8	77.8
42 South Wales	10.8	297	70.8	75.2	48.6	77.5
43 Chichester		273	80.2	78.3	52.5	77.3
=44 West of Scotland	9.1	296	77.6	80.1	34.4	76.8
=44 Queen Margaret, Edinburgh		315	72.4	81.3	43.8	76.8
46 Aberystwyth	14.5	310	78.5	84.8	17.4	76.4
47 East London	0.8	283*	72.2	72.7	55.0	76.0
48 Canterbury Christ Church	19.0	270	68.7	71.8	42.5	75.7
49 Glasgow Caledonian	15.2		72.0	73.0	41.8	75.6
50 Hull	10.2		79.3	85.8	26.3	75.4
51 Staffordshire	19.1	260	70.5	78.5	33.3	74.9
52 Buckinghamshire New	0.9	248	79.4	81.1	39.1	74.2
53 Highlands and Islands		268	65.9	66.3	61.5	74.1
54 Bedfordshire	6.7	200	82.8	86.3	38.4	74.0
=55 Liverpool Hope	10.9	279	75.0	63.0	36.0	73.9
=55 Anglia Ruskin	3.4	277	84.8	88.9	13.6	73.9
57 Westminster	10.7	320	71.3	79.1	12.3	73.2
58 West London		246	75.1	78.3	34.7	71.9
59 West of England		315	57.7	65.8	40.4	71.2
60 London Metropolitan		235	69.6	74.6	39.6	70.6

Employed in professional job:	42%	Employed in non-professional job and studying:	2%
Employed in professional job and studying:	1%	Employed in non-professional job:	40%
Studying:	4%	Unemployed:	12%
Average starting professional salary:	£19,369	Average starting non-professional salary:	£15,923

Iberian Languages

Spanish was gaining on French as the most popular language at degree level, following its rise at school level. But the numbers are small and a decline in 2014 suggests that progress has stalled: only 315 students started undergraduate courses after a 2 per cent decline in applications, although the statistics do not capture those who learn the language as part of a broader modern languages programme. The table also includes Portuguese, but not a single student embarked on a degree in the language in 2013 or 2014. Just five had done so the previous year, but Portuguese will still be available – either alone or as part of a modern languages degree – at 24 universities in 2016. It can even be combined with Czech at Bristol.

Cambridge has maintained a clear lead at the top of the table, but Oxford is now the nearest challenger after overtaking Durham. Cambridge is just three points ahead of Oxford on entry grades and has an equally slender lead over Queen's, Belfast on research. Surrey, in 11th place, has the students most satisfied with teaching quality while Queen's, Belfast topped the ranking for student experience, and has moved up seven places to fifth in the table overall. Lancaster, one place lower, is the only university to see nine out of ten graduates go straight into professional jobs or start postgraduate degrees. The languages have dropped 12 places in the employment table after a sharp rise (in percentage terms) in unemployment.

There are six additional universities in this year's table, Warwick entering in fourth place. Ten of the 52 institutions are post-1992 universities, three more than last year. Roehampton, one of the new entrants, is the only modern university in the top 30. Rising entry standards have come to at least a temporary halt, but four universities still average more than 500 points at A level or the equivalent. Average starting salaries in professional jobs had fallen by almost £500 in 2014, dropping Iberian languages out of the top 40.

Iberian Languages	Research quality %	Entry standards	Teaching quality %	Student experience %	Graduate prospects %	Overall score
1 Cambridge	54.0	566	89.9	89.8	83.9	100.0
2 Oxford	41.3	563	84.2	89.3	82.2	95.9
3 Durham	34.6	537	80.3	83.8	86.4	93.5
4 Warwick	45.2	470	85.5	85.3		92.4
5 Queen's, Belfast	53.6	382	94.7	97.5	63.8	91.6
6 Lancaster	47.0	422	75.2	75.3	90.2	91.4
7 Newcastle	36.3	412	85.4	89.2	84.5	91.3
8 Exeter	35.1	470	85.7	89.4	76.8	91.1
9 Bath	27.4	463	83.5	90.1	84.3	90.8
10 Southampton	42.7	415	79.5	92.4	79.3	90.5
11 Surrey	39.1		96.1	97.2	61.5	90.1
12 University College London	43.7	481	74.8	80.3	76.8	89.8
13 St Andrews	26.4	504	77.5	80.4	82.8	89.2
14 York	37.3	393	86.1	91.6		88.7
15 East Anglia	33.1	413	93.6	95.3	64.8	88.5
16 Leeds	30.6	437	84.6	91.2	73.1	88.4
17 Nottingham	39.4	398	78.4	87.2	77.4	88.2

Iberian Languages cont	Research quality %	Entry standards	Teaching quality %	Student experience %	Graduate prospects %	Overall score
18 Sheffield	41.2	428	82.9	84.0	68.4	87.9
=19 Edinburgh	30.3	491	75.5	83.6	73.9	87.4
=19 Manchester	48.9	402	79.7	80.8	67.6	87.4
21 Royal Holloway, London	48.3	364	83.1	82.3	64.0	86.2
22 Bristol	36.0	445	74.0	77.3	73.2	86.0
=23 Glasgow	26.3	463	82.0	88.8	65.2	85.7
=23 King's College London	42.1	434	76.7	74.1	67.4	85.7
25 Birmingham	33.7	394	69.9	69.1	87.0	85.6
26 Roehampton	21.8		89.3	93.4	65.0	85.3
27 Leicester	16.9	372	89.0	94.6	73.5	85.2
28 Kent	41.9	335	79.4	85.6	68.7	84.8
29 Queen Mary, London	35.1	346	84.7	76.0	71.8	84.7
30 Liverpool	33.4	385	80.6	83.6	67.9	84.5
31 Strathclyde	42.0	469	77.3	84.9	48.8	83.7
32 Aston	23.4	338	86.6	89.1	70.0	83.6
33 Heriot-Watt	26.3	450	77.3	81.5	64.4	83.4
34 Cardiff	32.5	370	71.8	78.3	74.2	83.1
35 Coventry	18.1	329	88.8	94.6	68.2	82.9
36 Swansea	22.8	296	85.0	84.3	73.6	82.2
37 Chester	17.3	296	88.5	89.7	71.8	82.1
38 Aberdeen	29.3	420	69.9	73.7	67.7	81.6
39 Manchester Metropolitan	29.0	335	90.7	89.1	53.5	81.5
40 Hull	22.7	304	80.4	90.1	69.5	81.2
41 Portsmouth	32.2	268	78.4	86.0	68.3	80.8
42 Northumbria		352	86.5	92.6	73.1	80.6
43 Aberystwyth	16.6	339	75.4	74.4	75.0	79.7
44 Sussex		394	84.3	86.3	67.8	79.5
45 Stirling	29.8	397	56.4	70.4	72.4	78.9
46 Ulster	22.4	290	90.2	87.2	51.3	78.2
47 Nottingham Trent	7.6	284	91.5	90.7	60.5	78.0
48 Bangor	39.6	288	72.3	78.9	51.6	76.9
49 Central Lancashire	15.2	291	83.1	83.3	56.5	76.2
50 Leeds Beckett		261	81.1	82.3	65.0	73.9
51 Westminster	2.0	305	81.5	86.1	54.1	73.5
52 Salford	4.8		72.6	66.2	58.7	70.6

Employed in professional job:	46%	Employed in non-professional job and studying:	2%
Employed in professional job and studying:	3%	Employed in non-professional job:	20%
Studying:	14%	Unemployed:	14%
Average starting professional salary:	£20,171	Average starting non-professional salary:	£16,267

Italian

Applications for degrees in Italian had recovered to some extent in 2014 from a big drop in the previous year, but are still only half the level they reached at their peak. Numbers were never large, but only 40 students started undergraduate courses in 2014, compared with 80 five years earlier. Many more students will have included Italian in broader language degrees or as one or more modules in another subject, and 40 universities are continuing to offer the language in 2016. Most students have no previous knowledge of Italian, although they are likely to have taken another language at A level.

The small numbers make for exaggerated swings in the graduate employment statistics. Average starting salaries in professional jobs have dropped by over £700, for example, after rising by £1,600 in last year's *Guide*. The gap between professional and lower-level jobs is only £3,500 as a result – one of the smallest differentials in any subject. More than a quarter of graduates start out in jobs that are categorised as non-professional.

Cambridge remains well clear at the top of the table, but Oxford has dropped five places from second place last year due to a sharp decline in student satisfaction, coming last on both measures. Cambridge registered the top grades in the 2014 Research Excellence Framework and has the highest entry standards. Durham, which has moved up to second place, again has the best employment record. The students most satisfied with their teaching are at Manchester Metropolitan, only five places off the bottom of the table but still the highest-placed modern university, while Leeds, in 12th place, has the best scores in the remainder of the National Student Survey.

Entry standards remain surprisingly high, given the small numbers of applicants. Four of the 22 universities in the ranking average more than 530 points at entry and only two drop below 300 points. There is a high response rate and scores have generally been good in the National Student Survey. No university failed to satisfy at least seven out of ten final-year undergraduates taking Italian.

Italian	Research quality %	Entry standards	Teaching quality %	Student experience %	Graduate prospects %	Overall score
1 Cambridge	54.0	566	89.9	89.8	83.9	100.0
2 Durham	34.6	537	80.3	83.8	86.4	93.3
3 Exeter	35.1	470	85.7	89.4	76.8	91.9
4 Warwick	45.2	456	89.9	86.1	63.5	91.3
5 Bath	27.4	437	92.0	89.7	76.0	90.9
6 Bristol	36.0	485	83.6	83.4	73.3	90.5
=7 Oxford	41.3	531	71.4	71.0	83.3	90.4
=7 University College London	43.7	496	79.3	82.5	69.2	90.4
9 Edinburgh	30.3	458	81.5	86.7	77.6	89.6
10 Reading	41.7	354	89.6	90.7	64.6*	89.1
11 St Andrews	26.4	552	74.5	78.8	78.2*	88.7
12 Leeds	30.6	425	88.8	94.8	61.7	88.3
13 Glasgow	26.3	462	82.3	88.5		88.1
14 Manchester	48.9	384	77.2	78.8	67.2	87.5
15 Birmingham	33.7		81.6	81.0	68.3	86.5

Italian cont	Research quality %	Entry standards	Teaching quality %	Student experience %	Graduate prospects %	Overall score
=16 Royal Holloway, London	48.3	388	82.9	81.8	46.2	84.9
=16 Kent	41.9	314	83.8	79.9		84.9
18 Manchester Metropolitan	29.0	302	96.8	89.6	54.1	84.8
19 Portsmouth	32.2	268	84.1	88.8	67.8	84.5
20 Cardiff	32.5	366	73.9	78.4	61.4	82.1
21 Central Lancashire	15.2		83.1	83.3	60.0	81.4
22 Nottingham Trent	7.6	294	91.5	90.7	60.2	80.8

Employed in professional job:	41%	Employed in non-professional job and studying:	1%
Employed in professional job and studying:	4%	Employed in non-professional job:	25%
Studying:	18%	Unemployed:	11%
Average starting professional salary:	£19,632	Average starting non-professional salary:	£16,103

Land and Property Management

The property market is definitely recovering if the salaries of graduates in land and property management are anything to go by. Those who found professional jobs in 2013 enjoyed the biggest increase in average salaries of any subject, and there was another £1,000 rise in 2014, taking the subjects into the top 15 in the earnings table. They are even higher in the new employment table, into the top ten after a rise of 15 places; three-quarters of graduates go straight into professional jobs. In the main, the subject table reflects those high employment rates: almost 96 per cent of graduates at second-placed Reading found high-level work or continued to study, although at Plymouth the rate was below 17 per cent.

The table is still less than half the size of a decade ago, with no representation from Scotland or Wales, but here, too, there are signs of recovery. Only one university, compared with three last year, had too few entrants to compile a reliable score, and 27 universities and colleges are offering courses in this area in 2016. They include degrees in woodland ecology and conservation, property investment and management, and even a Foundation degree in sports turf, as well as the real estate degrees that are the largest recruiters. Cambridge has a predictably big lead, with the best research score, the most satisfied students and entry grades that are 170 points ahead of the nearest challenger. Fourth-placed Sheffield Hallam is the leading post-1992 institution.

The subjects have acquired a reputation for recruiting disproportionate numbers from independent schools, but property firms have donated more than £500,000 to support a "Pathways to Property" scheme to try to widen participation. Those who take the courses appear to enjoy the experience: only one university in the table recorded less than 75 per cent satisfaction in the teaching or student experience sections in the National Student Survey.

Employed in professional job:	75%	Employed in non-professional job and studying:	0%
Employed in professional job and studying:	3%	Employed in non-professional job:	8%
Studying:	4%	Unemployed:	10%
Average starting professional salary:	£23,733	Average starting non-professional salary:	£17,800

Land and Property Management	Research quality %	Entry standards	Teaching quality %	Student experience %	Graduate prospects %	Overall score
1 Cambridge	49.0	561	82.9	90.7	90.2	100.0
2 Reading	40.0	390	75.4	86.1	95.8	93.5
3 Ulster	28.6	271	78.5	84.0	93.5	90.0
4 Sheffield Hallam	13.4	312	80.8	88.0	87.8	89.9
5 Nottingham Trent	3.4	283	75.4	83.3	91.9	86.5
6 Birmingham City	2.7	260	77.8	83.3	83.3	85.8
=7 Plymouth	13.2		81.7	87.3	16.7	83.7
=7 Greenwich	2.0	308	76.2	81.5	52.4	83.7
9 Westminster	10.7	295	63.4	79.8	68.0	82.4

Law

Having reached the milestone of 100,000 applications in the previous year, the demand for places to study law remained broadly steady in 2014 and enrolments grew for the fourth year in succession. It remains one of the most popular subjects, unaffected by the move to higher fees. Entry standards reflect this: only in medicine do so many universities make such testing demands. Nine of the 101 universities in the table average more than 500 points and more than a third have average entry scores of over 400 points. However, so many universities now offer law that it was still possible to find one (Bedfordshire) where the average was below 200 points in 2014.

Cambridge has held on to the top place it regained from Oxford two years ago. It has the highest entry grades and was the only university to see more than nine out of ten graduates go straight into professional jobs or continue their studies. Although most of the scores for graduate prospects are good, the proportion enjoying "positive destinations" was below half at seven universities. Law is just in the top 25 subjects in the employment table and is 45th for early career earnings. Only about half of all law graduates go on to practice, and training contracts for those who do keep the average in graduate-level jobs below £20,000.

The London School of Economics achieved the best results in the 2014 Research Excellence Framework. Once again, the most satisfied students are not at one of the leading universities in the table. Abertay, the only post-1992 university in the top 20 and in equal 13th place, has that distinction, with an almost unprecedented 99.3 per cent of final-year undergraduates declaring themselves satisfied with the teaching, feedback and academic support. They were also the most satisfied with the student experience.

Aspiring solicitors in England go on to take the Legal Practice Course, while those aiming to be barristers take the Bar Vocational Course, so it is no surprise that almost 40 per cent of all law graduates are engaged in postgraduate study six months after completing a degree. Note that in Scotland, most law courses are based on the distinctive Scottish legal system, which also has different professional qualifications.

Employed in professional job:	33%	Employed in non-professional job and studying:	5%
Employed in professional job and studying:	6%	Employed in non-professional job:	20%
Studying:	27%	Unemployed:	9%
Average starting professional salary:	£19,699	Average starting non-professional salary:	£16,035

Law	Research quality %	Entry standards	Teaching quality %	Student experience %	Graduate prospects %	Overall score
1 Cambridge	58.7	577	85.9	89.6	92.6	100.0
2 Oxford	51.8	561	86.1	90.9	83.9	97.7
3 London School of Economics	64.5	563	80.1	83.8	84.3	97.0
4 University College London	57.7	537	78.0	85.9	87.4	96.0
5 Nottingham	45.2	494	83.5	91.5	77.8	94.1
6 Durham	32.8	564	81.3	87.1	83.2	93.8
7 King's College London	39.2	544	79.0	86.0	81.0	93.1
8 Glasgow	33.8	532	73.8	89.5	86.9	92.6
9 Edinburgh	40.8	500	74.6	87.5	85.0	92.3
10 Bristol	50.5	485	73.9	82.6	84.4	92.2
11 Leeds	40.1	438	81.5	87.8	81.3	91.8
12 Queen's, Belfast	40.3	412	83.6	89.8	77.6	91.5
=13 Warwick	41.9	481	75.3	82.3	83.3	91.1
=13 Kent	43.9	372	81.9	87.7	82.4	91.1
=13 Abertay	1.2	369	99.3	96.0	83.3	91.1
16 Aberdeen	20.9	480	80.8	89.8	84.1	91.0
=17 Birmingham	33.6	430	81.3	83.8	83.8	90.6
=17 East Anglia	26.5	412	86.3	93.5	75.4	90.6
19 Newcastle	25.4	460	78.7	89.5	82.8	90.4
=20 York	30.3	476	76.4	90.4	78.2	90.3
=20 Heriot-Watt	18.8	410	89.3	89.0	79.8	90.3
22 Robert Gordon	3.9	411	89.3	91.4	87.2	90.1
23 Lancaster	38.9	430	78.6	84.3	78.8	90.0
24 Strathclyde	29.4	515	74.5	84.8	79.1	89.9
25 Dundee	16.3	463	84.7	91.5	74.5	89.7
=26 Queen Mary, London	23.7	483	84.5	86.2	69.9	89.4
=26 Swansea	20.4	325	89.1	91.1	82.4	89.4
28 Sussex	23.3	382	83.6	87.8	81.2	89.1
29 Aston	19.7	375	90.3	87.3	75.9	89.0
30 Reading	31.2	412	79.3	86.8	76.0	88.7
31 Exeter	21.4	475	75.9	84.6	80.7	88.6
32 Portsmouth	32.2	324	82.6	88.8	78.4	88.4
33 Cardiff	27.2	413	79.4	86.8	75.5	88.2
34 Sheffield	31.9	421	73.8	85.7	78.1	88.0
35 Manchester	27.2	438	76.0	82.7	78.3	87.9
36 Keele	30.5	342	77.0	85.8	82.9	87.7
=37 Salford	5.9	308	94.5	93.0	68.3	86.5
=37 Buckingham		325	86.2	87.8	86.5	86.5
39 Stirling	19.4	402	81.2	83.6	72.1	86.4
40 Southampton	18.2	431	76.9	82.8	74.6	86.3
41 Leicester	26.4	388	71.9	81.5	81.8	86.2
42 Ulster	48.5	321	83.6	86.0	53.1	86.1
=43 Surrey	8.5	401	82.8	86.2	72.3	85.9

=43 Liverpool	19.6	400	74.4	82.8	78.7	85.9
=43 Bangor	12.0	329	87.5	88.8	70.8	85.9
=43 SOAS, London	26.7	417	69.6	83.8	76.5	85.9
=47 Edinburgh Napier		371	87.1	89.0	73.2	85.7
=47 Essex	31.6	331	76.3	86.1	72.0	85.7
49 Oxford Brookes	5.1	371	83.8	86.0	75.0	85.5
50 De Montfort	5.2	284	85.8	90.3	79.2	85.3
51 Brunel	20.3	362	80.0	85.5	67.3	85.0
52 City	9.1	346	81.4	85.1	74.0	84.6
53 Chester		308	89.5	88.8	67.4	83.9
54 Derby	2.4	305	81.7	90.5	74.2	83.8
55 Manchester Metropolitan	14.9	335	76.5	82.6	73.7	83.6
=56 Nottingham Trent	2.3	305	82.1	85.5	75.8	83.4
=56 Greenwich	2.1	334	87.6	92.0	58.8	83.4
=56 West of England	3.5	327	79.1	89.3	72.4	83.4
59 Northumbria	2.5	366	80.8	88.7	65.7	83.3
=60 Hull	12.6	329	79.7	85.2	67.0	83.2
=60 Lincoln	5.0	322	77.0	87.4	75.1	83.2
62 Coventry	5.6	290	79.7	82.9	78.2	83.0
63 Central Lancashire	5.3	318	82.7	85.8	66.9	82.8
64 Huddersfield		340	78.9	79.4	77.7	82.6
65 Aberystwyth	14.3	327	75.9	77.6	74.2	82.5
66 Teesside	15.0	269	89.6	88.4	51.3	82.3
=67 Bournemouth	8.8	332	79.4	81.9	66.4	82.2
=67 Edge Hill	12.1	282	90.3	91.0	47.4	82.2
=67 Bradford	11.8	310	78.2	84.0	67.3	82.2
70 Hertfordshire		313	79.3	84.6	70.9	81.8
71 Gloucestershire		302	85.4	83.4	63.9	81.6
72 Cumbria		267	90.7	86.6	58.0	81.5
=73 Liverpool John Moores	2.7	341	77.0	84.4	65.2	81.3
=73 Middlesex	21.4	245	76.4	85.2	64.6	81.3
=73 London South Bank	20.1	210	84.9	90.9	53.0	81.3
76 Anglia Ruskin	5.2	242	88.5	90.4	54.8	81.2
=77 Sheffield Hallam		323	82.7	87.6	57.7	81.1
=77 Westminster	7.5	313	75.2	83.1	67.7	81.1
=77 Bolton		247	81.9	91.3	65.9	81.1
80 St Mary's, Twickenham		237	84.1	86.7	66.1	80.7
81 Buckinghamshire New		247	83.9	85.3	64.6	80.5
=82 Brighton	6.5	317	72.2	72.3	76.9	80.3
=82 Northampton		254	85.1	87.4	58.6	80.3
84 Glasgow Caledonian	1.8	418	70.9	83.8	55.4	79.8
=85 Plymouth		305	82.3	86.0	51.9	79.4
=85 West of Scotland		282	87.4	86.6	47.6	79.4
87 Liverpool Hope		272	87.9	83.0	46.2	78.6
=88 Winchester		294	80.2	88.2	48.3	78.5
=88 London Metropolitan	0.3	226	81.5	85.5	58.0	78.5
90 Sunderland	0.7	247	86.5	90.8	42.5	78.4

Law cont	Research quality %	Entry standards	Teaching quality %	Student experience %	Graduate prospects %	Overall score
91 South Wales		305	76.2	81.8	56.1	78.2
92 Staffordshire		256	76.7	81.4	62.0	78.1
93 Kingston		299	68.6	79.7	66.5	77.8
94 Bedfordshire	3.6	196	80.6	79.8	56.4	77.0
95 Birmingham City	2.8	267	69.1	76.5	65.1	76.8
96 Leeds Beckett		262	71.9	81.7	58.6	76.7
=97 Roehampton		269	78.8	83.8	43.9	76.3
=97 Canterbury Christ Church	3.2	278	80.8	79.8	41.4	76.3
99 West London		264	73.9	71.9	54.2	75.0
100 East London	8.6	239	71.3	74.7	49.4	74.6
101 Southampton Solent		264	64.6	77.2	53.1	73.6

Librarianship and Information Management

Average starting salaries for graduates in librarianship and information management have dropped by more than £2,700 since the last *Guide*, making a £3,800 decline in two years. Traditionally one of the top 20 subjects for graduate salaries, it is now out of the top 40. Only five universities are left in the table – half the number of a decade ago – and none of them has a degree with librarianship in the title. Most of the courses in this category concern broader information services, but only 145 students started undergraduate courses in 2014 – and even this was an increase on the previous year.

Loughborough has maintained its lead over Sheffield, with the highest employment rate and the best of four low entry scores. It was the only university to average more than 350 points on the UCAS tariff. Leeds, which has entered the table this year in third place, produced the best score in the Research Excellence Framework and has the highest satisfaction levels in relation to the student experience. Sheffield posted the best scores in the teaching sections of the National Student Survey, while Manchester Metropolitan is the higher-placed of the two post-1992 universities remaining in the table.

There is less variation on graduate prospects than these subjects have displayed in recent years. Although only the top two saw more than 80 per cent of graduates go straight into professional jobs or started postgraduate courses in 2014, none of the five institutions dipped below 55 per cent. Overall, library and information management are back in the top half of

Librarianship and Information Management	Research quality %	Entry standards	Teaching quality %	Student experience %	Graduate prospects %	Overall score
1 Loughborough	45.1	357	83.0	86.1	82.1	100.0
2 Sheffield	37.9	337*	86.1	93.3	81.7	97.9
3 Leeds	54.5		85.0	94.9	56.5	96.7
4 Manchester Metropolitan	4.7	342	80.3	86.9	62.4	92.8
5 Northumbria	21.0	335	73.6	79.6	66.0	91.7

the employment league. A respectable 60 per cent find professional work, but only 13 per cent take a postgraduate qualification, full or part-time.

Employed in professional job:	56%	Employed in non-professional job and studying:	2%
Employed in professional job and studying:	4%	Employed in non-professional job:	25%
Studying:	7%	Unemployed:	7%
Average starting professional salary:	£20,177	Average starting non-professional salary:	

Linguistics

Linguistics has fared much better than might have been expected since the introduction of £9,000 fees. Applications have risen for the past two years and, although there was a small dip in enrolments in 2014, numbers are still higher than in the years before the fees went up. While only 625 students began undergraduate courses, 66 universities and colleges are offering the subject in 2016, some of them as the language component of a degree in English. In its pure form, linguistics examines how language works, and can lead to work in speech therapy or the growing field of teaching English as a foreign language. Almost three-quarters of the students are female.

There are now about five applications for each place and entry standards are comparatively high. Only three of the 29 universities in the table average less than 300 points, while the norm at top-placed Cambridge and Oxford, the nearest challenger, is more than 550 points. Oxford has the best employment score and the highest entry standards in the table, but Cambridge's lead over its ancient rival in research is decisive. Edinburgh, which has dropped from second place to sixth, actually produced the best results of all in the Research Excellence Framework. Bangor's students are the most satisfied with the teaching and feedback they receive, while Queen's, Belfast, a new entrant to the table in third place, has the best scores in the other elements of the National Student Survey. Manchester Metropolitan is the highest-placed modern university and is joined in the top 20 by the University of the West of England.

Linguistics has improved its standing in this year's employment, but is still only just in the top 50. Nearly a third of graduates start off in low-level jobs and only Oxford saw eight out of ten of those completing a linguistics degree go straight into professional work or onto a postgraduate course. The subject is only just outside the bottom ten for graduate salaries, with an average of less than £19,000 in professional jobs at the end of 2014.

Linguistics	Research quality %	Entry standards	Teaching quality %	Student experience %	Graduate prospects %	Overall score
1 Cambridge	54.0	551	81.9	80.0	76.7	100.0
2 Oxford	41.3	552	81.3	84.8	80.1	99.3
3 Queen's, Belfast	53.1		85.2	92.4	72.1	97.7
4 Lancaster	47.0	453	90.2	87.8	68.7	96.3
5 Sheffield	42.2	425	87.7	87.8	74.4	95.5
6 Edinburgh	57.7	484	76.5	85.8	63.2	94.5
7 University College London	43.7	451	72.2	79.3	76.3	92.8
8 Newcastle	36.3	404	81.9	82.9	76.4	92.6

Linguistics cont	Research quality %	Entry standards	Teaching quality %	Student experience %	Graduate prospects %	Overall score
9 Leeds	30.6	413	87.3	91.3	62.6	90.7
10 Aberdeen	46.3	429*	85.0	81.3	55.8	90.3
11 York	37.3	428	79.8	84.3	61.8	89.7
12 Bangor	39.6	301	94.5	90.1	58.3	88.7
13 King's College London	42.1	427	65.6	81.3	66.2	88.1
=14 Kent	41.9	374	79.0	76.2	62.7	87.7
=14 Manchester	48.9	399	74.3	79.3	57.7	87.7
16 Cardiff	35.1	420*	81.5	81.4	54.7	87.3
17 SOAS, London	26.0	374	80.9	85.7	63.6	86.9
18 Manchester Metropolitan	29.0	297	90.4	89.0	60.9	86.6
19 Queen Mary, London	50.3	385	67.1	66.5	63.3	85.9
20 West of England	9.5	328	89.8	91.3	52.7	82.7
21 Ulster	22.4	301	85.5	86.6	51.5	82.0
22 Essex	36.0	306	71.8	74.8	50.0	79.6
23 Nottingham Trent	10.0	284	82.2	84.8		79.5
24 Salford	4.8	313*	89.5	88.6	44.3	78.9
25 Brighton	16.2	318	72.5	76.1	56.0	78.8
26 York St John	9.7	280	83.9	83.4	50.5	78.4
27 Westminster	2.0	312	78.6	83.0	50.9	77.1
28 Hertfordshire		333	81.9	84.7	43.7	76.7
29 Greenwich	8.2		60.4	57.5	46.4	67.2

Employed in professional job:	36%	Employed in non-professional job and studying:	3%
Employed in professional job and studying:	3%	Employed in non-professional job:	29%
Studying:	18%	Unemployed:	11%
Average starting professional salary:	£18,949	Average starting non-professional salary:	£15,731

Materials Technology

Courses in this table cover four distinct areas: materials science, mining engineering, textiles technology and printing, and marine technology. The various subjects are highly specialised and attract relatively small numbers – 400 started courses in 2014 – but recruitment has begun to pick up after a dip when £9,000 fees were introduced. More than 300 students started courses in materials technology itself in 2014, a 13 per cent increase to follow a 20 per cent rise in the previous year. Although there are only 14 universities in the table – three less than last year – 48 institutions are planning to run courses in this area in 2016. The leading universities demand chemistry and sometimes also physics, maths or design technology at A level or its equivalent.

Cambridge enjoys a big lead over Imperial College in the table, although the gap has narrowed slightly this year. Cambridge has much the highest scores for entry standards and research: only 3 per cent of the university's submission to the Research Excellence Framework was considered less than world-leading or internationally excellent. Imperial College has the best graduate prospects, as the only university where nine out of ten graduates went straight into professional jobs or onto a postgraduate course. The most satisfied students as far as teaching is concerned are at Huddersfield, which is only four places off the foot of the table but still the highest-placed modern university. Swansea, in fifth place, posted the best scores in the other sections of the National Student Survey.

Materials technology is in the top 20 subject groups for salaries in graduate-level jobs, although the average of £22,581 is £1,700 lower than in last year's *Guide*. The subjects are less than half way up the table based on graduate destinations. Almost a quarter of graduates continue their studies, either full or part-time, and approaching half are in professional jobs six months after graduation.

Materials Technology	Research quality %	Entry standards	Teaching quality %	Student experience %	Graduate prospects %	Overall score
1 Cambridge	78.3	648	86.0	86.3	87.4	100.0
2 Imperial College	62.3	538	81.2	89.3	91.5	94.8
3 Oxford	70.8	587	73.2	73.9	87.6	93.1
4 Birmingham	49.3	433	80.3	90.2	85.5	89.1
5 Swansea	45.5	294	91.6	92.3	89.7	88.6
6 Loughborough	41.8	342	86.2	88.1	84.4	86.7
7 Sheffield	41.0	420	83.8	87.8	73.9	86.0
8 Exeter	36.4	385	74.6	76.4	89.7	84.0
9 Manchester	36.4	407	79.5	82.9	69.6	82.7
10 Queen Mary, London	40.0	365	76.5	82.3	71.6	81.7
11 Huddersfield	10.2	368	93.5	90.0	46.7	77.9
12 Sheffield Hallam	17.8	277	78.7	82.8	60.0	74.8
13 De Montfort	12.5	337	62.6	57.9	70.7	71.2
14 Buckinghamshire New		328	77.8	72.4	47.7	70.1

Employed in professional job:	45%	Employed in non-professional job and studying:	2%
Employed in professional job and studying:	2%	Employed in non-professional job:	20%
Studying:	19%	Unemployed:	12%
Average starting professional salary:	£22,581	Average starting non-professional salary:	£16,769

Mathematics

Maths has been remarkably consistent in the numbers it attracts: applications in 2014 were within 90 of the previous year's total and exactly the same number (7,770) began undergraduate courses. With record numbers taking A level in 2015 and universities in England receiving funding for new teaching facilities in maths, engineering and the sciences, increases must be likely in future years. Entry standards are already high: the top three in this year's table average more than 600 points and the next five are all over 500. The scores are boosted by the fact that most successful candidates for the leading universities have taken two A levels in the subject, as well as two or three others. But the table also covers a wide spread of entry scores: 11 universities average less than 300 points.

There was a brief decline in applications and enrolments when £9,000 fees were introduced in 2012, but maths remains one of the most popular subjects among those

Mathematics cont

considering higher education. It is often cited as one of the subjects most likely to lead to a lucrative career, and the earnings table seems to bear this out. The average of £24,119 in graduate-level jobs was close to the top ten subjects in 2014. Maths is also close to the top 20 for the proportion of graduates going straight into professional jobs or becoming postgraduate students, as almost one in three does. Employment scores in the table reflect this, with around half of the 69 universities, including all the top 20, recording positive destinations for at least 75 per cent of their graduates.

Oxford and Cambridge share the lead this year in a rare joint first place. Cambridge has the highest entry grades and the best graduate prospects, while Oxford produced the best results in the Research Excellence Framework. Almost 60 per cent of its research was considered world-leading. Much the highest scores in the teaching sections of the National Student Survey were at Bolton, in 45th place, where 97 per cent of final-year undergraduates were satisfied. Coventry and Liverpool Hope, the highest-placed modern university, in 32nd place, did best in the sections relating to the student experience.

Mathematics	Research quality %	Entry standards	Teaching quality %	Student experience %	Graduate prospects %	Overall score
=1 Cambridge	60.7	642	87.5	86.3	93.1	100.0
=1 Oxford	67.5	628	89.4	88.8	86.5	100.0
3 Imperial College	59.7	616	81.3	88.0	88.5	97.4
4 St Andrews	44.2	546	88.0	90.0	87.8	95.6
5 Warwick	55.8	565	81.4	85.6	83.5	94.6
6 Durham	44.0	589	83.1	86.5	84.2	94.2
7 Bath	35.7	523	86.1	84.8	87.3	92.9
8 Bristol	57.3	523	76.2	81.7	81.6	92.0
9 Lancaster	45.8	446	83.5	85.9	84.8	91.8
10 Dundee	48.2	453	87.4	85.5	77.6	91.5
11 Edinburgh	43.7	512	77.2	85.6	81.1	90.7
12 Nottingham	44.8	488	81.2	85.6	78.0	90.6
13 Newcastle	32.0	427	90.0	90.5	79.1	90.5
14 Glasgow	41.4	467	80.2	83.5	81.7	90.0
15 Leeds	42.0	460	79.6	85.1	79.3	89.6
=16 Surrey	31.5	438	85.9	86.6	80.0	89.4
=16 Loughborough	31.0	419	85.8	89.2	80.5	89.4
18 Exeter	37.9	474	77.0	82.8	82.7	89.2
=19 Queen's, Belfast	25.0	418	88.1	91.2	78.4	89.0
=19 Heriot-Watt	42.3	418	85.0	83.7	75.8	89.0
21 Birmingham	34.1	421	83.3	84.1	81.7	88.9
22 University College London	42.0	542	75.0	82.1	74.5	88.8
23 Sussex	28.5	366	82.1	87.5	88.1	88.7
24 Cardiff	31.6	440	81.9	84.6	78.1	88.0
25 Keele	19.5	366	92.0	92.5	75.9	87.8
26 Strathclyde	34.6	463	77.2	88.8	74.2	87.7
=27 East Anglia	33.7	381	84.8	87.7	74.3	87.4

=27 York	27.0	438	81.9	82.8	79.2	87.4
29 Manchester	44.3	464	76.5	82.3	71.7	87.3
30 London School of Economics	28.7	553	68.5	76.0	82.0	86.8
31 Reading	35.3	351	83.5	84.6	74.2	86.3
32 Liverpool Hope	8.8	301	90.2	94.0	81.5	86.2
=33 Sheffield	34.0	427	78.5	84.9	70.8	85.9
=33 Southampton	41.9	431	68.7	79.3	79.0	85.9
=35 King's College London	37.1	468	76.3	78.8	69.9	85.7
=35 Kent	28.2	337	79.6	85.4	80.1	85.7
37 Coventry	9.4	309	91.3	94.0	76.6	85.6
38 Leicester	25.0	378	74.5	84.2	83.4	85.5
39 Swansea	20.7	326	83.2	84.6	81.5	85.4
=40 South Wales	10.1	354	90.8	86.8	71.2	84.4
=40 Northumbria	16.7	361	85.7	90.3	69.2	84.4
42 Hertfordshire	20.2	282	84.7	81.3	80.0	84.0
43 West of England	10.6	296	89.4	89.4	73.7	83.9
44 Royal Holloway, London	35.5	406	76.0	79.3	66.4	83.6
45 Nottingham Trent	18.4	298	91.3	89.7	64.1	83.4
=46 Plymouth	9.3	336	92.6	88.6	63.5	83.0
=46 Liverpool John Moores	3.2	327	86.2	87.5	75.6	83.0
=46 Aberdeen	32.0	414	72.7	78.6	69.0	83.0
49 Liverpool	29.8	394	73.9	80.3	68.8	82.8
50 Sheffield Hallam		303	88.1	91.6	73.6	82.7
51 Aberystwyth	19.4	347	82.8	81.3	69.0	82.6
52 Central Lancashire	19.8	313	90.5	83.8	59.5	81.9
53 Brunel	25.8	333	78.9	82.8	64.2	81.5
54 Bolton		280	97.1	90.6	61.0	81.4
=55 Portsmouth	11.2	285	83.6	84.8	70.4	81.3
=55 City	30.2	358	84.0	83.0	52.6	81.3
57 Stirling	14.0	366	77.5	76.3	72.4	81.2
58 Greenwich	5.1	277	91.9	93.5	59.4	81.0
59 Aston	21.7	350	74.0	78.0	70.1	80.9
=60 Chester	7.1	303	78.7	78.1	77.4	80.6
=60 Queen Mary, London	30.3	374	73.7	76.0	62.7	80.6
62 Brighton	6.4	292	80.6	84.0	72.2	80.5
63 Derby	5.0	281	79.1	83.4	74.0	80.1
64 Staffordshire		205	84.0	85.8	77.4	80.0
65 Manchester Metropolitan	5.6	337	84.3	83.6	61.9	79.8
66 Essex	34.3	358	69.4	74.5	62.7	79.7
67 Oxford Brookes	13.9	341	86.4	80.9	54.3	79.4
68 Kingston		268	72.5	73.0	65.9	74.8
69 London Metropolitan	13.5	215	82.7	82.8	42.3	74.0

Employed in professional job:	42%	Employed in non-professional job and studying:	1%
Employed in professional job and studying:	7%	Employed in non-professional job:	15%
Studying:	23%	Unemployed:	12%
Average starting professional salary:	£24,119	Average starting non-professional salary:	£16,161

Mechanical Engineering

Mechanical engineering is by far the biggest branch of engineering, attracting twice as many applicants as any of the other subjects. Indeed, it is comfortably inside the top 20 for all degree choices. The introduction of higher fees has only increased the subject's popularity: the 10 per cent rise in applications in 2014 was the sixth in succession. Enrolments have not quite kept pace but have also seen annual increases since 2009.

It is not hard to see why. Throughout the economic downturn, mechanical engineering was among the top ten subjects for early career prospects and for starting salaries in graduate-level employment. It is now sixth in the earnings table, with average salaries of more than £26,000 in professional jobs. The subject is a little lower this year (13th) in the employment table, but two-thirds of graduates go straight into such jobs and only one in ten has to settle for a lower-level role.

Cambridge remains the leader in mechanical engineering, but Imperial College London has narrowed the gap considerably since the last *Guide*. The two universities are both ranked in the top six in the world for the subject by QS. Cambridge has by far the highest entry standards and the best research grades. But Lancaster, in seventh place, has the best graduate prospects, an impressive 98 per cent of graduates finding professional work or beginning a postgraduate course by six months after graduation. Once again, the most satisfied students are at a university in the bottom half of the table: Anglia Ruskin had the best scores in the National Student Survey for teaching and the student experience. Coventry is the highest-placed modern university, at equal 23rd.

Four universities have dropped out of the table since last year, but no fewer than 125 universities and colleges plan to offer mechanical engineering in 2016. Most of the leading universities demand maths – preferably with a strong component of mechanics – and another science subject (usually physics) at A level or its equivalent. With almost seven applications to the place overall, entry standards are high at the leading universities, five of which averaged more than 500 points in 2014. Only one institution averaged less than 250 points.

Employed in professional job:	65%	Employed in non-professional job and studying:	0%
Employed in professional job and studying:	3%	Employed in non-professional job:	10%
Studying:	11%	Unemployed:	11%
Average starting professional salary:	£26,366	Average starting non-professional salary:	£17,025

Mechanical Engineering	Research quality %	Entry standards	Teaching quality %	Student experience %	Graduate prospects %	Overall score
1 Cambridge	67.0	642	76.3	84.5	96.6	100.0
2 Imperial College	59.6	590	88.1	93.5	88.9	99.4
3 Bristol	52.3	527	82.8	94.0	84.4	94.9
4 Bath	37.4	502	85.3	91.4	89.0	93.4
5 Leeds	40.9	461	84.3	90.1	93.1	93.3
6 Loughborough	41.8	419	85.9	92.3	93.6	93.1
7 Lancaster	41.6	410	83.0	87.8	98.0	92.6
8 Heriot-Watt	47.8	431	85.1	91.4	85.1	92.1

9	Birmingham	37.7	438	82.8	85.5	94.1	91.7
10	Southampton	52.3	464	70.2	83.6	93.0	91.3
11	Strathclyde	37.2	508	74.5	88.2	86.6	90.5
12	Sheffield	36.0	475	79.1	87.3	87.7	90.4
=13	Nottingham	40.8	436	81.5	89.1	85.4	90.3
=13	Surrey	30.8	429	82.2	91.3	90.3	90.3
15	Cardiff	30.2	440	78.5	87.3	92.9	89.8
16	Swansea	45.5	340	81.8	88.1	89.2	89.2
17	Glasgow	47.2	469	65.5	80.8	87.9	88.4
18	Edinburgh	50.3	491	63.1	77.4	86.9	88.3
19	Aberdeen	28.4	458	72.9	79.4	93.6	88.1
20	Exeter	36.4	432	70.8	79.3	92.4	87.8
=21	Manchester	35.1	462	70.4	81.3	86.8	87.4
=21	University College London	44.6	496	65.8	79.3	82.1	87.4
=23	Dundee	34.1	431	77.6	81.2	80.0	86.4
=23	Coventry	10.3	341	87.9	90.7	90.8	86.4
25	Liverpool	32.1	377	73.1	84.4	89.3	86.2
26	Newcastle	30.2	404	69.2	83.8	90.1	86.0
27	Queen's, Belfast	36.7	389	71.3	81.0	85.9	85.7
28	Brunel	23.7	387	76.9	83.5	83.2	84.7
=29	Robert Gordon	8.8	427	74.4	79.2	91.5	84.4
=29	Sussex	24.0	351	75.3	79.1	90.1	84.4
31	Queen Mary, London	46.7	374	72.2	81.4	73.6	84.2
32	De Montfort	12.5	275	90.5	91.6	83.0	83.9
33	Derby	6.7	274	90.4	88.3	87.3	83.6
=34	Hull	16.5	319	78.9	86.3	86.4	83.4
=34	Teesside	5.8	326	79.3	85.9	92.5	83.4
=34	Sunderland	8.8	260	86.9	85.1	91.9	83.4
37	Aston	20.6	337	71.3	80.8	87.5	82.5
38	Bradford	7.7	301	82.9	90.7	82.9	82.3
=39	Salford	4.4	300	75.4	86.3	90.9	81.5
=39	Portsmouth	9.1	299	82.9	85.0	81.7	81.5
=41	Liverpool John Moores	4.7	348	80.3	84.4	80.8	81.4
=41	Anglia Ruskin	9.1	250	93.7	94.5	72.2	81.4
43	City	20.2	306	85.9	80.3	72.2	81.1
44	Oxford Brookes	13.9	366	81.8	87.5	67.9	81.0
45	Northumbria	30.7	348	70.5	72.8	77.6	80.8
46	Ulster		315	74.9	84.5	86.8	80.1
47	Manchester Metropolitan	16.3	327	83.1	85.3	64.7	79.5
48	Plymouth		313	75.7	83.3	82.9	79.2
49	Huddersfield	10.2	308	69.2	81.5	83.5	79.1
50	Greenwich	29.5	285	77.2	86.0	62.3	78.7
51	Harper Adams		292	71.3	85.4	84.0	78.3
52	Hertfordshire	16.5	315	64.9	69.6	76.3	76.3
53	Central Lancashire	7.1	301	70.9	77.4	71.4	75.8
=54	West of England	10.6	318	66.6	73.0	73.1	75.6
=54	Glasgow Caledonian	4.7	351	64.8	70.8	75.8	75.6

Mechanical Engineering cont	Research quality %	Entry standards	Teaching quality %	Student experience %	Graduate prospects %	Overall score
=54 West of Scotland	9.0	307	80.1	84.7	56.3	75.6
=57 Sheffield Hallam		298	70.1	78.1	75.4	75.5
=57 Staffordshire	5.7	258	75.7	74.8	73.5	75.5
59 Brighton	7.4	320	62.7	78.8	64.6	73.3
60 London South Bank	19.6	277	68.0	78.4	52.5	72.3
61 Birmingham City		239	62.6	68.3	72.7	70.7
62 Kingston	2.9	279	67.8	73.7	54.5	69.9

Medicine

There are more than 11 applications for every place in medicine – easily the highest ratio in any subject and all the more remarkable since candidates can only apply to four medical schools. Entry standards are correspondingly fearsome: although six of the 33 schools, compared with two last year, averaged less than 500 points, four of them were within nine points of this mark. In spite of this, medicine is in the top five subjects for the volume of applications, which increased yet again in 2014. Nearly all schools demand chemistry and most biology. Physics or maths is required by some, either as an alternative or addition to biology. Universities will want to see evidence of commitment to the subject through work experience or voluntary work. Almost all schools interview candidates, and several use one of the two specialist aptitude tests (*see* chapter 1).

The subject carries unique prestige and is the perennial leader in the employment table – just ahead of dentistry this year. Employment scores for individual schools are no longer used in the ranking (although they are still shown for guidance) to avoid small differences distorting positions in a subject where virtually all graduates become junior doctors or researchers. A dozen schools reported full employment in 2014, and only two dropped below 99 per cent. The average starting salary of £28,683 for junior doctors is second only to dentists' remuneration.

There are two new medical schools in this year's table – Lancaster and Swansea – which have not had enough data to be included until now. The top two have been the same for the last six years, but there is plenty of movement elsewhere in the table. Keele, for example, has gone up eight places to finish sixth; Cardiff, one place lower, has jumped 14 places. Oxford has the most satisfied students, while Cambridge has the highest entry standards. There was little to separate the leading universities in the Research Excellence Framework, but Lancaster came out on top.

Undergraduates have to be prepared to work long hours, particularly towards the end of the course, which will usually be five years long. Many students are now opting for the postgraduate route into the medical profession instead, although this is even longer. Levels of satisfaction on the undergraduate courses are generally high, but at seven schools the approval rate dropped below 70 per cent on the three sections covering teaching, feedback and academic support.

Medicine	Research quality %	Entry standards	Teaching quality %	Student experience %	Graduate prospects %	Overall score
1 Oxford	48.9	612	93.8	96.8	93.4	100.0
2 Cambridge	52.0	628	80.1	84.6	99.0	97.2
3 Imperial College	54.6	564	76.6	90.4	99.4	92.4
4 Queen Mary, London	40.2	560	89.3	93.9	99.6	91.4
5 University College London	53.3	570	73.9	84.4	99.3	90.9
6 Keele	50.0	506	92.5	93.7	100.0	90.3
7 Cardiff	34.5	606	77.0	86.6	99.8	89.7
8 Newcastle	44.8	540	83.1	92.3	100.0	89.3
9 Lancaster	55.2	494	88.2	90.0		89.2
10 Glasgow	42.3	559	77.6	86.3	99.8	88.0
11 Edinburgh	49.8	571	65.3	78.7	100.0	87.1
12 Swansea	44.7		74.9	88.3	100.0	86.9
13 Exeter	41.6	515	83.9	92.1	99.7	86.4
14 Hull-York Medical School	36.2	521	85.2	92.8	99.6	85.8
=15 Birmingham	31.5	552	79.2	90.3	100.0	85.2
=15 Sheffield	36.5	494	91.2	94.8	100.0	85.2
17 Aberdeen	20.2	561	86.6	92.5	99.7	84.9
18 Bristol	47.9	523	68.9	87.4	100.0	84.6
19 Leeds	32.1	518	84.4	93.9	99.3	84.3
20 St Andrews	19.8	550	85.5	95.5	98.3	84.1
21 Dundee	25.1	554	82.5	87.8	99.2	84.0
22 Southampton	35.6	491	83.1	90.7	100.0	82.1
23 Manchester	34.6	516	77.3	85.3	99.9	81.8
24 Queen's, Belfast	34.6	498	78.8	90.6	99.2	81.5
25 East Anglia	31.8	520	77.0	84.8	100.0	81.2
26 Plymouth	23.1	505	83.9	92.1	99.7	80.2
27 Leicester	33.3	528	64.4	84.6	100.0	79.4
28 King's College London	48.3	506	60.1	73.8	99.5	79.0
29 Brighton and Sussex Medical School	8.6	510	91.2	96.3	99.6	78.8
30 Nottingham	36.8	525	60.2	69.0	99.5	76.6
31 St George's, London	22.4	483	79.7	83.7	100.0	75.7
32 Warwick	26.2		68.1	75.2	100.0	73.2
33 Liverpool	31.7	469	60.5	76.5	99.8	71.5

Employed in professional job:	93%	Employed in non-professional job and studying:	0%
Employed in professional job and studying:	1%	Employed in non-professional job:	0%
Studying:	5%	Unemployed:	1%
Average starting professional salary:	£28,683	Average starting non-professional salary:	n/a

Middle Eastern and African Studies

This is one of the smallest categories in the *Guide* in terms of student numbers at degree level. Only 115 students started courses in Arabic or Middle Eastern Studies in 2014, and the total for African Studies was a mere 15. The subjects enjoy some official protection because they are classed as "vulnerable" and of national importance. It is just as well because non-European languages have suffered the biggest decline of any subject area since the introduction of £9,000 fees. There were only 55 applications for African studies, less than half the numbers applying before the fees went up. Demand has held up rather better in the Middle Eastern courses, but worldwide interest in the region has not produced the predicted increase in applications.

Birmingham has taken over from Cambridge at the top of the table after producing the best scores in the Research Excellence Framework. It has not had enough entrants in the last two years to compile a reliable score for entry standards, so one is generated from its performance on other indicators. Cambridge has the highest entry standards, while Exeter, in sixth place, has the best employment score. The most satisfied students are at Leeds, one place higher in the table. There are no universities in the ranking from outside England and only one (Westminster) from the post-1992 sector.

The small numbers inevitably make for big swings even in the national statistics. Middle Eastern and African Studies shares the highest unemployment rate of all the 66 subject groupings, at 18 per cent, but has moved up eight places in the employment table. The subjects are somewhat lower for starting salaries in professional jobs, but still in the top 50. Applicants for courses in Arabic or African languages are not expected to have previous knowledge of the language, although they would normally be expected to demonstrate an aptitude for learning other languages.

Middle Eastern and African Studies	Research quality %	Entry standards	Teaching quality %	Student experience %	Graduate prospects %	Overall score
1 Birmingham	50.9		91.4	89.8	73.2	100.0
2 Cambridge	45.0	568	84.1	83.1	65.5	96.5
3 Durham	34.6	529	80.2	83.9	81.5	96.4
4 Oxford	36.2	534	63.2	73.7	81.8	92.8
5 Leeds	30.6	416	91.7	91.8	70.6	92.3
6 Exeter	36.0	422	62.6	73.6	92.5	92.0
7 Edinburgh	30.1	457	69.3	78.3	81.8	90.7
8 Manchester	48.9	388	72.4	74.8	60.9	87.8
9 SOAS, London	26.3	398	72.3	77.0	65.8	84.3
10 Westminster	11.3	270	81.7	91.2	59.9	78.9

Employed in professional job:	42%	Employed in non-professional job and studying:	3%
Employed in professional job and studying:	2%	Employed in non-professional job:	15%
Studying:	21%	Unemployed:	18%
Average starting professional salary:	£19,441	Average starting non-professional salary:	£16,968

Music

Big rises in applications – 15 per cent in 2014 and 20 per cent in the previous year – have confirmed that music is no longer suffering from the impact of introducing £9,000 fees. But the pace of expansion in the supply of places has dropped after a remarkable 46 per cent increase in enrolments in 2013. The latest rise was less than 3 per cent, although the 8,550 students starting courses were still far more than before the fees went up.

One effect has been that the number of applications per place has dropped from more than five to a little over four. Entry grades are relatively low at most universities – 17 average less than 300 UCAS points – although music grades and the quality of auditions carry more weight in selecting students. Nine out of ten degree applicants come with A levels and most university departments expect music to be among them, although they may accept a distinction or merit in Grade 8 music exams. The character of courses varies considerably, from the practical and vocational programmes in conservatoires to the more theoretical degrees in some of the older universities, and everything from creative sound design and new media to sonic arts elsewhere. No fewer than 194 universities, colleges and other providers are offering undergraduate courses in 2015.

Oxford remains ahead of Manchester at the top of the table, while Durham has moved up nine places to third with the highest entry grades. Southampton had the best performance in the 2014 Research Excellence Framework and also moved up nine places to sixth. Students at Northampton, in 55th place, are the most satisfied with the teaching, feedback and academic support they received on their course, while Manchester has the best scores for the sections of the National Student Survey covering the student experience. Huddersfield remains the leading post-1992 university, despite dropping eight places to 30th.

The Royal College of Music again has the best employment score, with an impressive 98.8 per cent of graduates going straight into professional work or postgraduate study. The specialist institutions do far better than most university departments on this measure – only Oxford and King's College London could match any of the four royal institutions in 2014. Music does better than the other performing arts in the employment table, although it is still not in the top 40. The 9 per cent unemployment rate is no worse than the average for all subjects, but 30 per cent of leavers were in non-graduate occupations six months after graduation. The subject is in the bottom three for the average salaries of those who do find professional work.

Music	Research quality %	Entry standards	Teaching quality %	Student experience %	Graduate prospects %	Overall score
1 Oxford	66.3	500	88.2	89.5	93.1	100.0
2 Manchester	56.3	521	91.9	95.9	76.9	98.0
3 Durham	64.9	573	76.7	77.8	81.8	96.4
4 Royal Holloway, London	55.0	489	89.2	87.8	72.7	94.5
5 Cambridge	48.0	534	81.3	79.7	82.6	94.1
6 Southampton	70.7	404	88.6	86.0	74.2	93.7
7 Glasgow	46.0	510	84.6	92.6	67.1	92.4
=8 Nottingham	55.4	423	87.5	87.5	75.3	92.3
=8 Surrey	27.2	480	93.0	94.3	74.9	92.3

Music cont	Research quality %	Entry standards	Teaching quality %	Student experience %	Graduate prospects %	Overall score
10 Bristol	48.0	496	78.1	78.8	78.9	91.3
11 King's College London	43.5	498	79.4	67.9	86.1	91.1
12 Sheffield	60.0	404	86.8	84.9	70.1	91.0
13 Cardiff	47.0	426	87.1	87.8	70.9	90.4
14 Bangor	24.7	411	92.4	93.1	76.9	89.7
15 York	37.1	412	85.3	87.8	79.0	89.6
16 City	34.0	432	92.4	86.8	66.1	89.1
17 Sussex	30.2	377	89.4	88.6	81.8	89.0
18 Leeds	44.2	474	79.1	84.3	67.0	88.8
19 SOAS, London	60.0	372	85.3	82.3	66.7	88.6
20 Edinburgh	48.0	464	73.6	75.0	76.7	88.4
21 Keele	41.7	379	88.2	86.4	70.1	88.0
22 Birmingham	50.7	448	64.9	74.1	85.1	87.6
=23 Goldsmiths, London	51.1	383	77.2	77.9	72.6	86.5
=23 Royal College of Music	10.9	336	85.7	84.3	98.8	86.5
=25 Newcastle	40.8	385	78.4	86.2	68.8	85.6
=25 Queen's, Belfast	38.3	371	84.5	87.1	64.9	85.6
27 Royal Academy of Music	23.9	342	78.1	78.7	93.9	85.3
28 Royal Northern College of Music	12.3	322	87.6	86.6	87.8	85.0
29 Royal Conservatoire of Scotland	11.3	418	76.7	79.0	85.5	84.4
30 Huddersfield	28.0	325	84.0	84.5	75.7	84.1
31 Birmingham City	11.6	339	88.1	84.5	79.2	83.9
32 Aberdeen	32.0	416	80.3	83.4	56.8	83.5
33 Ulster	40.0	289	90.9	92.9	51.9	82.9
34 Liverpool Hope	15.5	314	94.6	91.6	57.0	81.9
35 Bath Spa	10.7	313	86.0	89.7	73.0	81.8
36 Liverpool	31.4	409	77.6	84.7	50.3	81.5
37 Oxford Brookes	30.2	313	84.4	84.1	56.6	80.7
38 Middlesex	16.1	267	84.1	81.1	77.4	80.4
39 Leeds Beckett	1.7	285	92.1	92.9		80.2
40 Hull	11.2	370	83.5	81.9	57.3	79.7
41 Edinburgh Napier		408	81.2	84.8	56.9	79.2
42 Lancaster		364*	83.3	69.9	71.6	79.1
43 Kent	44.3	332	70.7	63.3	62.9	79.0
44 Brunel	32.6	323	83.4	83.8	41.5	78.5
45 Falmouth	6.2	274	86.4	87.5	64.2	78.2
46 Sunderland	4.2	287	90.2	89.5	55.3	77.9
47 Essex		257	93.5	94.3	55.7	77.6
48 Hertfordshire	5.3	323	81.5	79.8	60.7	77.1
49 Liverpool John Moores		311*	94.4	90.9	42.6	77.0
50 South Wales	6.4	324	80.4	75.8	62.3	76.9
=51 Salford	7.2	352	84.5	82.2	46.3	76.8
=51 West of Scotland	11.3	366	83.5	82.9	41.3	76.8

=53 Westminster	22.5	310	68.7	72.5	67.6	76.6
=53 Manchester Metropolitan	7.5	325	86.2	83.3	47.1	76.6
55 Northampton		289	94.7	85.5	46.0	76.3
56 Brighton	13.1	338	77.6	76.6	51.1	75.8
57 Derby		302	86.3	84.5	50.7	75.6
58 Chester	4.3	311	75.1	70.8	65.9	75.0
59 Central Lancashire	3.9	311	77.1	76.8	58.9	74.9
60 East London	11.2	288	82.1	76.4	48.8	74.5
61 Southampton Solent		279	89.7	88.8	39.8	74.2
62 De Montfort	14.5	283	80.7	77.1	45.8	74.0
63 York St John	10.5	265	79.2	83.5	50.0	73.9
64 Bournemouth	15.0	315	76.7	66.3	50.0	73.8
65 University of the Arts London		239*	79.8	74.0	66.7	73.6
66 Chichester	9.7	332	71.4	74.9	50.7	73.5
67 West London	2.3	291	71.3	66.7	68.5	73.2
68 Gloucestershire		308	83.9	81.7	40.5	73.1
69 Kingston		306	78.1	75.7	50.2	72.8
70 Plymouth	20.2	269	74.7	72.2	44.6	72.2
71 Canterbury Christ Church	15.2	281	75.9	76.6	40.5	71.9
72 London South Bank	12.8	273	75.0	68.7	47.8	71.5
73 Winchester	11.2	329	77.0	74.9	27.9	70.9
74 Buckinghamshire New		261	78.3	73.1	43.9	69.9
75 Coventry	18.1	309	62.2	58.2	50.0	69.7
76 Anglia Ruskin	16.9	247	62.0	66.8	55.6	69.3
77 Cumbria		330	60.4	67.3	51.6	68.8

Employed in professional job:	41%	Employed in non-professional job and studying:	2%
Employed in professional job and studying:	5%	Employed in non-professional job:	28%
Studying:	15%	Unemployed:	9%
Average starting professional salary:	£17,497	Average starting non-professional salary:	£15,002

Nursing

Nursing continues to attract more than twice as many applications as any other subject, the numbers rising by another 13,000 in 2014. There has been phenomenal growth since the move towards an all-graduate profession, with the number of applications passing 100,000 for the first time in 2008 and now heading towards 250,000. Universities accepted another 2,200 student nurses in 2014, but there were still almost nine applications to every place. Even so, entry requirements are low. Although just two universities averaged less than 250 points, only four have averages of more than 400 points.

Glasgow remains at the top of the table, thanks partly to the highest entry standards, but Surrey has become its nearest challenger after moving up 12 places after a big improvement in its research score. Southampton, in 12th place, produced much the best results of all in the Research Excellence Framework, when 94 per cent of its work was rated as world-leading or internationally excellent. Portsmouth, in fifth place, has the most satisfied students for teaching, feedback and academic support in the National Student Survey, while Liverpool

Nursing cont

has the most satisfied with the student experience. Portsmouth is joined by Manchester Metropolitan as the two post-1992 universities in the top ten.

Five universities, compared with 11 three years ago, achieved full employment in 2014, and all but one saw more than 90 per cent go straight into professional jobs. The perfect scores were at Bolton, Brunel, De Montfort, Keele and Manchester Metropolitan. The subject remains in the top three for employment prospects, with only 2 per cent unemployed and 1 per cent in lower-level jobs. It is only just in the top 20 in the earnings league, however, with average starting salaries now close to £23,000.

Almost two-thirds of the students arrive without A levels, many of them upgrading other health-related qualifications. A quarter of those who join pre-registration programmes drop out, but the rate is nearer 10 per cent thereafter.

Nursing	Research quality %	Entry standards	Teaching quality %	Student experience %	Graduate prospects %	Overall score
1 Glasgow	42.3	472	92.1	90.5	96.0	100.0
2 Surrey	37.5	405	89.4	92.3	99.4	99.4
3 Liverpool	35.3	379	95.9	97.8	96.9	98.4
4 Portsmouth	24.3	380*	96.5	96.0	97.2	97.7
5 Keele	20.9	341	94.4	94.3	100.0	97.5
6 Manchester	57.1	383	80.2	78.3	96.9	96.9
7 Leeds	31.7	394	78.2	80.2	99.6	96.7
8 Birmingham	37.0	405	76.5	83.4	98.0	96.5
9 Edinburgh	53.4	452	84.7	83.9	90.9	96.3
10 Manchester Metropolitan	12.0	353	88.2	86.1	100.0	95.8
11 East Anglia	24.9	386	79.5	79.3	98.9	95.6
12 Southampton	65.7	356	66.1	72.5	98.0	95.4
=13 Bangor	34.7	341	80.5	78.0	98.9	95.2
=13 Huddersfield	13.2	368	83.6	83.5	99.2	95.2
15 Cardiff	36.8	364	77.7	80.3	97.5	95.0
16 Brunel	18.2		77.0	83.1	100.0	94.8
=17 King's College London	34.6	386	65.4	75.8	99.0	94.5
=17 Queen Margaret, Edinburgh	1.5	357	86.0	88.9	98.9	94.5
=19 York	40.2	377	68.8	79.4	97.3	94.4
=19 Northumbria	14.0	359	86.2	81.4	97.8	94.4
21 South Wales	2.2	371	86.4	85.1	97.9	94.2
22 Coventry	4.5	341	93.0	94.5	96.0	94.0
23 Birmingham City	1.5	360	85.1	82.8	98.6	93.9
=24 Swansea	14.5	355	82.3	86.8	97.0	93.8
=24 Bradford	9.5	363	80.3	80.0	98.6	93.8
26 Nottingham	31.4	352	71.5	67.6	99.3	93.7
=27 Oxford Brookes	3.0	354	86.6	85.3	97.6	93.6
=27 De Montfort	13.0	342	77.4	75.2	100.0	93.6
29 Staffordshire		327	86.3	83.3	99.4	93.5
=30 West of England	8.2	351	76.9	78.7	99.5	93.4

=30 Chester	12.0	316	84.6	81.3	98.8	93.4
32 Edge Hill	2.0	350	91.4	92.4	95.3	93.3
33 Teesside	2.4	333	87.2	88.4	97.1	93.1
=34 Liverpool John Moores	6.0	356	78.1	86.5	97.6	93.0
=34 Ulster	27.7	334	79.9	81.8	95.9	93.0
=36 Stirling	34.1	263	82.3	86.7	97.2	92.9
=36 Bournemouth	4.7	353	81.3	78.8	97.9	92.9
=36 Bedfordshire	25.1	287	81.1	84.1	97.8	92.9
=39 Sheffield Hallam	3.7	345	80.1	81.6	98.3	92.8
=39 Glasgow Caledonian	8.1	317	84.6	87.8	97.3	92.8
=41 City	19.2	324	80.9	80.1	96.9	92.7
=41 Worcester	2.6	304	87.0	86.7	98.0	92.7
43 Central Lancashire	8.3	339	83.4	88.9	95.6	92.5
=44 Plymouth	9.5	297	84.7	83.8	97.7	92.3
=44 Bolton		288	81.7	84.6	100.0	92.3
=44 Anglia Ruskin	3.1	299	83.5	86.6	98.4	92.3
47 Brighton	4.8	367	73.3	73.1	98.4	92.2
48 Cumbria	0.7	319	82.6	80.3	98.0	92.0
49 Leeds Beckett	3.5	306	84.8	86.7	96.3	91.6
50 Derby		318	75.3	80.8	98.8	91.5
51 Salford	3.8	372	76.3	78.3	95.6	91.4
=52 Lincoln	22.6	321	69.9	74.4	97.0	91.2
=52 Kingston/St George's, London	2.6	286	77.5	80.3	99.2	91.2
=54 Dundee	22.1	246	82.1	83.6	96.7	91.1
=54 West London	2.5	282	81.8	81.8	98.0	91.1
=56 Canterbury Christ Church	2.2	309	79.6	82.5	96.9	91.0
=56 Northampton	1.6	297	78.5	77.9	98.4	91.0
58 Hertfordshire	4.0	308	75.9	80.0	97.5	90.8
59 Greenwich	2.2	313	84.3	86.1	94.6	90.7
=60 Queen's, Belfast	34.7	332	69.2	70.9	94.0	90.5
=60 London South Bank	13.7	307	71.5	77.8	96.8	90.5
62 Essex		224	86.1	88.1	97.5	90.0
63 Edinburgh Napier	5.3	279	75.9	80.8	96.2	89.5
64 Buckinghamshire New	1.0	287	82.2	85.8	94.3	89.4
65 Hull	16.7	361	78.5	75.7	89.5	89.0
66 Middlesex	10.0	284	72.4	74.9	95.4	88.8
67 West of Scotland	29.0	266	80.8	79.8	90.4	88.3
68 Robert Gordon	4.9	319	70.7	74.8	93.7	88.2
69 Abertay		304	81.1	81.8	91.2	87.8

Employed in professional job:	93%	Employed in non-professional job and studying:	0%
Employed in professional job and studying:	2%	Employed in non-professional job:	1%
Studying:	1%	Unemployed:	2%
Average starting professional salary:	£22,928	Average starting non-professional salary:	£15,828

Other Subjects Allied to Medicine

This table was shorn of two of the most popular subjects in the group when physiotherapy and radiography were given rankings of their own. But taken together, the remaining subjects still recruit more students than the totals for most other tables. Those subjects include audiology, complementary therapies, counselling, health services management, health sciences, nutrition, occupational therapy, optometry, ophthalmology, orthoptics, osteopathy, podiatry and speech therapy. Only ophthalmics managed increased enrolments when £9,000 fees arrived, but both applications and enrolments for the group as a whole improved in 2013 and again this year.

Most of the universities in the table are post-1992 institutions, but Kingston, at equal eighth is the only new university in the top ten. Aston, which is famously strong in ophthalmics, remains the leader and is the only university in the top 20 to occupy the same position as last year. But Surrey, which has one of three 100 per cent graduate employment records, has moved up from third place and is close behind. The other universities to have seen full employment in 2014 are Brighton and St Mark and St John, in Plymouth.

Cambridge has the highest entry standards by more than 150 points, but did not enter the Research Excellence Framework (REF) in this category and is restricted to sixth place as a result. Southampton, in tenth place overall, produced the best performance in the REF. Worcester, in 18th place, has the highest levels of satisfaction for the teaching sections of the National Student Survey, while 12th-placed Robert Gordon does best on questions relating to the student experience.

The choice of specialism naturally affects graduate employment rates, which range from better than 90 per cent positive destinations at 16 universities to less than 60 per cent at nine others. Overall, the subjects are in the top 20 for employment prospects, with only 8 per cent unemployed six months after graduating. Average salaries in professional jobs had fallen over £500 to £20,760 in 2014, however, taking the subjects out of the top 30.

Other Subjects Allied to Medicine	Research quality %	Entry standards	Teaching quality %	Student experience %	Graduate prospects %	Overall score
1 Aston	39.1	419	95.3	95.5	97.3	100.0
2 Surrey	37.5	487*	85.6	90.3	100.0	99.7
3 University College London	48.4	484	84.3	91.4	87.7	98.8
4 Manchester	57.1	426	82.4	85.4	91.8	97.6
5 Cambridge		648	86.0	86.3	87.4	97.4
6 Cardiff	36.8	425	87.6	88.0	97.4	97.2
7 Reading	42.3	488	80.0	89.3	85.7	96.6
=8 Lancaster	55.2	421	88.4	91.8	73.0	96.0
=8 Kingston	2.6		96.2	96.7	90.9	96.0
10 Southampton	65.7	398	74.4	76.9	94.0	95.3
11 City	19.2	376	93.3	94.9	92.5	94.6
12 Robert Gordon	4.9	403	96.3	97.0	92.0	94.3
13 Newcastle	47.8	452	81.3	87.3	73.7	94.1
=14 Leeds	31.7	409	74.5	93.0	94.4	93.3
=14 Kent	42.3	369	85.7	90.7	81.2	93.3

16	East Anglia	24.9	434	85.4	89.3	83.0	93.2
17	Strathclyde	52.2	449	71.1	82.0	76.4	92.1
18	Worcester	2.6	316	98.3	96.0		90.8
=19	Swansea	44.7	345	73.8	73.9	96.6	90.7
=19	Glasgow Caledonian	8.1	435	80.0	85.7	91.3	90.7
21	Brighton	4.8	333*	87.9	87.1	100.0	90.3
22	Oxford Brookes	3.0	344	91.8	92.0	89.7	90.1
23	Dundee	31.3	496	71.4	76.3	75.0	90.0
24	Liverpool	35.3	373	80.8	77.9	82.1	89.9
=25	Birmingham	31.5	429	74.0	82.4	77.6	89.6
=25	Exeter		480	87.0	77.4	80.0	89.6
27	Sunderland	7.5		80.6	84.0	92.3	89.5
28	Sheffield	38.3	423	72.1	84.5	72.3	89.3
=29	Ulster	27.7	351	87.2	91.6	66.4	88.6
=29	Bradford	9.5	375	81.2	88.4	85.7	88.6
=29	Warwick	25.3	413	84.6	84.3	64.8	88.6
=32	Portsmouth	24.3		90.4	87.2	65.0	88.5
=32	Plymouth	9.5	347	84.7	84.0	89.7	88.5
34	Bournemouth	4.7	342	84.0	88.3	91.1	88.3
35	Anglia Ruskin	3.1	287	88.2	90.3	94.9	88.2
=36	Northampton	1.6	328	87.3	87.3	83.8	86.8
=36	St Mark and St John		334	76.8	83.8	100.0	86.8
=38	Manchester Metropolitan	12.0	370	84.8	80.1	74.5	86.5
=38	Cumbria	0.7	393	82.3	84.4	79.0	86.5
40	Canterbury Christ Church	2.2	308	86.3	88.3	85.6	86.4
41	Bedfordshire	25.1	273	81.1	84.1	81.3	86.0
=42	De Montfort	13.0	307	82.4	84.9	80.8	85.8
=42	Hull	16.7		78.5	75.9	82.1	85.8
44	Salford	3.8	359	86.1	85.6	71.7	85.6
=45	Nottingham	31.4	351*	82.4	85.9	55.4	85.5
=45	Essex		298	87.5	87.7	82.5	85.5
47	Liverpool John Moores	6.0	340	86.0	90.7	68.5	85.3
=48	Sheffield Hallam	3.7	337	85.5	87.3	73.1	85.1
=48	Westminster	21.2	324	79.2	81.8	73.8	85.1
50	Coventry	4.5	311	84.7	87.2	77.4	85.0
51	Glyndŵr	3.6	394*	88.4	87.5	56.7	84.9
52	Lincoln	22.6	315	79.1	83.0	71.4	84.7
=53	Queen Margaret, Edinburgh	6.7	386	80.8	83.0	67.4	84.6
=53	Derby		316	88.7	88.4	71.9	84.6
55	Edinburgh Napier	5.3		75.9	80.8	82.4	84.5
=56	Birmingham City	1.5	381	79.3	83.2	72.5	84.3
=56	York St John	1.9	315	80.8	82.0	83.4	84.3
=58	Hertfordshire	4.0	330	74.2	80.0	87.2	84.0
=58	Cardiff Metropolitan	3.6	333	81.0	81.8	76.9	84.0
60	South Wales	2.2	352	71.1	76.8	87.8	83.5
=61	Brunel	18.2	384	63.6	74.7	79.6	83.4
=61	London South Bank	13.7		75.5	70.9	81.8	83.4

Other Subjects Allied to Medicine cont	Research quality %	Entry standards	Teaching quality %	Student experience %	Graduate prospects %	Overall score
=63 Huddersfield	13.2	313	79.5	78.1	71.3	82.8
=63 Northumbria	14.0	378	76.7	75.4	63.8	82.8
65 West of England	8.2	332	77.3	81.3	71.1	82.7
66 Greenwich	2.2	312	80.3	83.3	73.3	82.5
=67 Teesside	2.4	311	85.0	87.8	62.7	82.3
=67 West of Scotland	29.0	271	79.3	86.3	57.8	82.3
69 Chester	12.0	285	79.7	86.4	65.3	81.8
70 St Mary's, Twickenham		333	70.3	79.7	77.8	81.0
=71 Central Lancashire	8.3	318	80.9	82.2	57.5	80.8
=71 Middlesex	10.0	284	71.1	82.1	75.1	80.8
73 Leeds Beckett	3.5	303	78.0	81.1	66.8	80.5
74 Newman		272	84.1	87.8	50.0	78.3
75 Bolton		251*	81.7	84.6	54.8	77.5
76 Abertay		301	69.5	72.9	63.2	76.4
77 East London	7.6	258	71.5	78.4	53.2	75.5
78 Edge Hill	2.0		76.0	74.8	42.9	72.7
79 London Metropolitan	5.2		64.4	78.9	47.9	71.5

Employed in professional job:	58%	Employed in non-professional job and studying:	2%
Employed in professional job and studying:	3%	Employed in non-professional job:	15%
Studying:	13%	Unemployed:	8%
Average starting professional salary:	£20,760	Average starting non-professional salary:	£14,706

Pharmacology and Pharmacy

The Coalition Government decided not to reduce the number of places in pharmacy after a funding council inquiry, but was anxious for applicants to know that a degree in the subject was no guarantee of employment as a pharmacist. The message seems to be getting through because applications were down by nearly 10 per cent in 2014, the third decline in succession. Not that the employment table suggests cause for concern in the graduate labour market: the subjects were seventh out of 66 groups, with 84 per cent of graduates going straight into professional jobs and only 4 per cent unemployed. Pharmacology was not part of the inquiry, which focused on the growth in the numbers taking the MPharm course, the only direct route to professional registration as a pharmacist. The qualification is now offered at 30 institutions, while another dozen are running a BSc in the subject.

There was a 5 per cent decline in enrolments in 2014, but that still left more than six applications for every place. Departments in England are evenly split between those specialising in pharmacy and pharmacology. Only four cover both. While the MPharm degree takes four years, pharmacology is available either as a three-year BSc or as an extended course. Most degrees require chemistry and another science or maths at A level or the equivalent. Partly because of the training structure for pharmacists, the subjects are not in the top 40 in the earnings league: averaging little more than £19,500 in professional-level jobs.

Cambridge remains top of the table, where the university's normal high entry standards make the difference: they are 140 points ahead of the rest. Keele has a rare 100 per cent employment rate, with half of the 44 universities in the table registering over 90 per cent. Students give the subjects high satisfaction ratings. Ulster, which has moved up 16 places to fourth, has the highest overall, with 94 per cent approving of the teaching, feedback and academic support, while it shares the top spot with Keele for the student experience. Queen's, Belfast, which remains second in the table, produced the best results in the 2014 Research Excellence Framework.

Employed in professional job:	78%	Employed in non-professional job and studying:	1%
Employed in professional job and studying:	6%	Employed in non-professional job:	5%
Studying:	7%	Unemployed:	4%
Average starting professional salary:	£19,597	Average starting non-professional salary:	£15,023

Pharmacology and Pharmacy	Research quality %	Entry standards	Teaching quality %	Student experience %	Graduate prospects %	Overall score
1 Cambridge	52.5	648	86.0	86.3	87.4	100.0
2 Queen's, Belfast	60.0	411	88.2	94.9	99.5	97.8
3 Cardiff	36.8	501	89.8	94.3	97.3	97.6
4 Ulster	42.5	375	94.0	97.4	97.1	96.3
5 Aston	39.1	405	91.4	93.7	99.0	95.9
6 Manchester	57.1	440	84.2	89.1	93.4	95.7
7 Nottingham	51.2	455	81.4	87.8	96.7	95.1
8 Keele	20.9	391	92.2	97.4	100.0	94.3
9 East Anglia	38.1	413	85.7	91.7	96.8	94.1
10 Bath	56.2	438	77.6	79.7	96.4	93.2
11 King's College London	46.8	415	80.8	90.8	89.8	92.9
12 Newcastle	47.8	457	82.0	89.9	77.3	92.6
=13 Kent	42.3	332	85.7	90.7	99.1	92.5
=13 Strathclyde	52.2	508	69.2	80.1	94.8	92.5
=13 Bristol	43.7	438	89.5	91.5	68.8	92.5
16 University College London	51.3	460	73.7	80.4	95.8	92.4
=17 Reading	34.2	371	82.1	92.7	99.0	92.1
=17 Leeds	40.9	406	80.6	91.8	89.5	92.1
19 Aberdeen	34.7	412	83.4	93.0	84.1	91.7
20 Portsmouth	24.3	347	90.5	94.8	89.5	91.4
21 Glasgow	33.4	477	71.4	83.8	91.3	90.2
22 Liverpool	31.7	420	83.7	91.5	74.2	90.1
23 Huddersfield	13.2	383	82.2	86.8	98.1	89.2
24 Robert Gordon	4.9	450	78.8	84.2	99.3	89.1
25 Dundee	55.4	497	69.4	74.1	72.7	88.9
26 Brighton	4.8	395	83.5	87.3	96.9	88.8
27 Liverpool John Moores	6.0	366	82.9	89.6	99.1	88.7

Pharmacology and Pharmacy cont	Research quality %	Entry standards	Teaching quality %	Student experience %	Graduate prospects %	Overall score
28 Hertfordshire	10.9	333	86.2	86.8	91.1	87.6
29 Birmingham	19.2	407	77.5	87.3		87.5
30 Bradford	9.5	359	80.4	87.9	93.6	87.3
31 Sunderland	7.5	335	79.3	83.3	96.9	86.0
32 Central Lancashire	8.3	383	69.0	86.2	99.2	85.7
33 Leicester		418	79.9	93.1	69.8	85.3
34 De Montfort	13.0	323	73.2	81.3	95.6	84.5
35 Edinburgh	49.8		75.0	85.6	59.2	84.0
36 Greenwich	2.7	330	81.1	91.3	73.2	83.8
37 Hull	16.7		74.2	88.4	69.7	82.7
38 Kingston	2.6	297	79.1	84.8	79.6	82.3
39 Queen Margaret, Edinburgh	1.5	327	79.9	81.8	71.4	81.7
40 Glasgow Caledonian	8.1	350	78.8	85.8	52.9	80.9
41 Coventry	4.5	258	82.8	93.4	52.0	79.9
42 Westminster	21.2	259	73.0	82.7		79.4
43 London Metropolitan	5.2	210	82.9	87.5	45.3	77.0
44 East London	7.6	234	73.3	84.4	43.7	75.1

Philosophy

The demand for places in philosophy rose by 6 per cent in 2014, but applications are still nearly 1,000 lower than before £9,000 fees were introduced. The numbers starting courses – 1,600 in 2014 – are closer to previous levels and sufficient for 73 universities to be offering the subject in 2016. Philosophy is no longer among the most selective subjects in the arts and social sciences, although six universities average more than 500 points at entry. Nineteen institutions had an average of 400 points or above in 2014, compared with 25 in last year's table. Relatively few philosophy undergraduates studied the subject at A level – indeed, Bristol warns that even an A in the subject is "not necessarily evidence of aptitude for philosophy at university". Degrees can require more mathematical skills than many candidates expect, especially when there is an emphasis on logic in the syllabus.

Cambridge has taken the lead this year, but Oxford is only a fraction of a point behind. Oxford still has the highest entry standards in the table and produced the best grades in the 2014 Research Excellence Framework, but Cambridge's higher scores for student satisfaction and graduate prospects proved decisive. The most satisfied were at Anglia Ruskin, only eight places off the bottom of the table. Philosophers are generally satisfied with their courses: only five universities had an approval rating below 75 per cent in the teaching or student experience sections of the National Student Survey.

Graduate employment has been more of a problem, but there were improvements in 2014. Five universities, rather than just Cambridge in 2013, saw 80 per cent of philosophers go straight into professional jobs or onto postgraduate courses in 2014, and the number where the rate dropped below half was down from 15 to 12. The best performance was at Birmingham, where there were positive destinations for 87 per cent of the graduates.

Philosophy has moved up six places in the employment table and is now close to the top 40, but has gone in the opposite direction in the comparison of average salaries in professional-level jobs, which have dropped by £500 since the last *Guide*. A high proportion – three in ten – stay on as postgraduates, whether full or part-time.

Philosophy	Research quality %	Entry standards	Teaching quality %	Student experience %	Graduate prospects %	Overall score
1 Cambridge	51.6	575	87.1	87.9	84.4	100.0
2 Oxford	61.3	586	81.6	86.1	82.2	99.8
3 St Andrews	52.7	515	87.5	88.3	75.8	97.6
4 London School of Economics	48.6	541	82.0	86.0	82.4	97.0
5 Birmingham	52.8	397	88.0	81.1	87.3	95.4
6 Exeter	41.0	464	83.9	88.0	77.7	94.0
7 Lancaster	53.0	416	78.0	81.2	83.3	93.1
8 Newcastle	54.3	394	80.8	89.5	70.3	92.6
9 University College London	55.6	505	68.2	76.9	77.5	92.0
10 Sussex	34.2	400	85.9	86.5	78.5	91.8
11 King's College London	53.9	459	74.1	75.5	76.4	91.6
12 Bristol	40.9	496	76.8	82.7	71.4	91.5
13 Warwick	47.7	477	73.9	80.1	73.9	91.4
=14 Sheffield	48.3	414	85.4	80.6	65.3	91.3
=14 Durham	30.1	541	78.7	84.0	69.1	91.3
16 Edinburgh	49.7	473	76.3	81.2	66.2	91.1
17 Leeds	39.5	396	83.5	85.3	71.1	90.7
18 Essex	44.0	338	85.9	86.8	66.6	90.0
19 Liverpool	28.4	391	89.3	90.5	61.5	89.6
20 Keele	23.7	343	91.4	87.9	70.0	89.1
=21 East Anglia	28.6	381	88.3	91.2	57.5	88.7
=21 Southampton	31.7	403	82.1	85.8	65.6	88.7
=23 Queen's, Belfast	40.3	368	83.6	89.1	55.3	88.3
=23 Dundee	27.7	403	92.6	89.1	47.7	88.3
=23 Hertfordshire	32.9	308	83.0	87.3	75.0	88.3
26 Royal Holloway, London	30.5	391	85.4	82.6	63.4*	88.2
27 York	30.7	429	77.2	82.8	67.7	87.9
28 Nottingham	28.2	380	83.1	81.8	69.2	87.8
29 Kent	31.0	336	87.1	87.3	61.3	87.6
30 Aberdeen	39.1	398	80.8	82.7	55.9	87.4
31 Cardiff	36.3	386	78.5	77.0	68.5	87.3
32 Manchester	31.9	413	77.6	79.1	67.1	87.2
33 Reading	28.6	362	83.3	83.3	63.2	86.8
34 West of England	18.6	313	92.4	94.1	56.3	86.7
35 Glasgow	18.9	456	84.7	86.5	46.7	86.0
36 Stirling	22.7	365	84.2	77.9	53.1	83.9
37 Oxford Brookes	8.4	321	91.3	89.8	50.6	83.7
38 Central Lancashire	8.3	268	90.2	87.8	53.3	82.3

Philosophy cont	Research quality %	Entry standards	Teaching quality %	Student experience %	Graduate prospects %	Overall score
39 Manchester Metropolitan	12.5	323	88.8	85.7	41.5	81.9
40 Liverpool Hope		271	96.2	91.7	44.2	81.7
41 Nottingham Trent	10.0	284	87.1	80.7		81.2
42 Anglia Ruskin		241	97.7	94.9	37.2	80.7
=43 Brighton	13.1	278	87.8	80.3	40.0	79.6
=43 Staffordshire		258*	93.2	84.8	43.2	79.6
=43 Bath Spa		302	91.9	85.5	37.5	79.6
46 St Mary's, Twickenham	7.0	231	91.7	91.3	35.2	79.3
47 Hull	10.5	308	71.2	79.0	54.1	78.1
48 Heythrop College		314	83.1	80.4	39.3	77.4
49 Roehampton		275	79.6	85.8	44.4	77.2
50 Greenwich		283	74.9	68.7	36.0	72.7

Employed in professional job:	35%	Employed in non-professional job and studying:	4%
Employed in professional job and studying:	4%	Employed in non-professional job:	22%
Studying:	22%	Unemployed:	13%
Average starting professional salary:	£21,372	Average starting non-professional salary:	£15,347

Physics and Astronomy

The long decline in the numbers taking physics in the sixth-form and university was being reversed before higher fees arrived. The numbers starting physics degrees have increased for seven years in a row and went up again in 2014 to almost 5,000. The "Brian Cox effect" has been credited with the recent boom in popularity, in recognition of the engaging Manchester University professor's many television appearances. There are now more applications for physics than for chemistry – almost six for every place. Astronomy and astrophysics degrees are even more selective and are being offered by over 30 universities in 2016.

Entry scores are correspondingly high. No fewer than 11 universities average more than 500 points at entry and four top 600. Cambridge, which leads the table and is in the top three universities in the world according to QS, has the highest entry standards and also produced the best grades in the 2014 Research Excellence Framework. The students most satisfied with teaching, feedback and academic support on their course are at Nottingham Trent, which is in the bottom ten universities overall. Surrey, in equal eighth place, has a marginally higher satisfaction rate in the sections of the National Student Survey relating to other elements of the student experience.

For the third year in a row, Surrey also has the best graduate prospects. It was the only university in 2014 where more than 90 per cent of those completing courses were in professional jobs or continuing their studies six months after graduation. Physics and astronomy have moved into the top 10 for starting salaries in this edition of the *Guide*, averaging just under £25,000 in professional jobs. The subjects are only a little lower in the overall comparison of graduate prospects, with 42 per cent taking postgraduate courses, either full or part-time.

Most universities demand physics and maths at A level for both physics and astronomy, as well as good grades overall. Only six of the 46 universities in the table are post-1992 institutions: Northumbria is the highest-placed, just outside the top 30. Just one undergraduate in five is female and a similarly small proportion arrives without A levels or their equivalent. About 5 per cent transfer to other courses or drop out, usually at the end of the first year, but well over half of those who remain get firsts or 2:1s.

Physics and Astronomy	Research quality %	Entry standards	Teaching quality %	Student experience %	Graduate prospects %	Overall score
1 Cambridge	55.7	648	86.0	86.3	87.4	100.0
2 St Andrews	51.0	529	90.8	91.6	83.8	97.3
3 Oxford	52.1	614	79.8	81.0	87.1	96.7
4 Warwick	46.1	517	87.2	91.2	84.2	95.4
5 Imperial College	49.6	601	75.2	82.3	87.9	95.3
6 Birmingham	33.8	529	90.6	90.8	89.5	95.2
7 Manchester	44.9	553	82.2	90.5	83.6	94.8
=8 Exeter	42.4	478	85.8	92.0	88.6	94.7
=8 Surrey	39.6	426	89.7	93.7	92.3	94.7
10 Durham	46.2	601	75.1	84.9	84.9	94.4
11 Southampton	44.1	438	89.4	92.6	83.3	93.7
12 Lancaster	37.6	498	86.4	85.7	88.0	93.5
13 Bath	40.0	511	83.8	87.8	81.7	92.6
=14 Bristol	43.7	496	78.7	87.0	84.4	92.4
=14 Glasgow	42.0	491	77.3	87.8	87.3	92.4
16 Leicester	40.8	409	87.1	90.2	84.4	91.9
17 Nottingham	48.3	473	83.6	89.6	74.3	91.8
=18 Leeds	41.8	451	80.7	86.3	84.0	91.3
=18 Strathclyde	45.3	430	88.5	91.5	73.4	91.3
20 Edinburgh	48.7	527	68.9	77.4	84.3	90.9
21 Queen's, Belfast	44.4	399	84.3	86.0	80.4	90.5
22 Aberdeen	32.0	398	88.3	85.1	87.0	90.3
23 University College London	45.1	537	71.2	79.8	79.0	90.1
24 Cardiff	34.9	414	82.7	90.8	81.4	89.6
25 York	35.8	432	82.1	89.4	74.4	88.4
26 Sheffield	36.8	421	79.1	85.6	77.5	87.9
=27 Sussex	24.7	398	81.7	88.1	85.7	87.8
=27 King's College London	35.8	449	81.1	84.7	73.6	87.8
=29 Loughborough	19.0	372	89.2	91.2	83.2	87.5
=29 Heriot-Watt	44.1	418	83.2	83.7	67.0	87.5
31 Northumbria	30.7	371	84.2	84.8		86.3
32 Keele	31.8	356	88.3	87.8	71.0	86.2
33 Liverpool	31.5	401	74.2	79.5	83.5	86.1
34 Dundee	34.1	381	89.7	92.0	61.2	85.9
35 Hertfordshire	20.2	319	84.2	91.6	84.4	85.8
36 Portsmouth	21.8	277	91.5	93.4	77.8	85.4

Physics and Astronomy cont	Research quality %	Entry standards	Teaching quality %	Student experience %	Graduate prospects %	Overall score
37 Central Lancashire	19.8	336	82.8	81.0	85.0	84.7
38 Nottingham Trent	20.1	308	94.2	93.5	68.3	84.3
39 Royal Holloway, London	31.5	410	83.5	88.4	59.7	84.1
40 Hull	24.2	323	89.0	92.8	65.7	83.7
41 Swansea	33.0	353	73.8	80.3	74.4	83.3
42 Queen Mary, London	27.6	373	82.2	84.0	62.1	82.3
43 Aberystwyth	12.4	306	81.0	84.2	82.4	82.1
44 Kent	30.7	334	62.6	73.8	77.5	80.1
45 Salford	4.4	312	84.2	92.1	45.2	74.5
46 West of Scotland	19.1	333	63.3	66.3		73.3

Employed in professional job:	35%	Employed in non-professional job and studying:	1%
Employed in professional job and studying:	5%	Employed in non-professional job:	10%
Studying:	36%	Unemployed:	13%
Average starting professional salary:	£24,976	Average starting non-professional salary:	£14,802

Physiotherapy

Nine out of ten physiotherapy graduates go straight into a professional job – a far cry from the days, not long ago, when unemployment among newly graduated physiotherapists had become a cause for concern because opportunities in the labour market had not kept pace with growth in higher education courses. Despite consistent increases in enrolments, the subject is now in the top six for graduate prospects. Applications are well above the level before £9,000 fees arrived and the numbers starting courses rose again in 2014. Most of the leading courses demand biology A level or equivalent, but some may also want another science or maths. The Chartered Society of Physiotherapy accredits all degrees in the subject in the UK.

The ranking is in its third year, the subject having appeared previously as part of the table for "other subjects allied to medicine". Until this edition of the *Guide*, Cardiff had topped the table, but Southampton has jumped 31 places to take over the leadership. Southampton produced the best results in the Research Excellence Framework (REF) and was one of two universities where every leaver was in professional work or still studying within six months of graduation in 2014. The other was Keele, which has dropped five places to seventh with a relatively low REF score. Keele's replacement in second place is Birmingham, which has also enjoyed a big rise (15 places) this year. Cardiff, now third, still has the highest entry grades, while Bradford is close to 100 per cent student satisfaction with teaching, feedback and academic support, and East Anglia had highest satisfaction rate in the sections of the National Student Survey relating to other elements of the student experience.

Entry standards have been rising and vary less than in most subjects. Although every university in the table has an average of less than 500 points, nearly half are over 400 and only one university averages less than 350. Two-thirds of the universities in the table are post-1992 institutions, but they have lost ground against their older counterparts this year,

Physiotherapy	Research quality %	Entry standards	Teaching quality %	Student experience %	Graduate prospects %	Overall score
1 Southampton	65.7	441	92.0	90.3	100.0	100.0
2 Birmingham	63.7	456	77.3	87.2	98.9	97.9
3 Cardiff	36.8	486	84.4	87.9	97.0	96.9
4 East Anglia	24.9	459	92.7	98.8	96.9	96.4
=5 Liverpool	35.3	405	91.7	93.0	96.8	94.6
=5 Robert Gordon	4.9	481	92.3	92.1	96.2	94.6
7 Keele	20.9	408	89.6	92.1	100.0	94.2
8 Bradford	9.5	424	99.5	98.5	95.0	93.7
9 Nottingham	40.6	428	85.8	87.8	92.0	93.1
10 Bournemouth	4.7	391	96.3	98.5	94.6	91.2
11 Northumbria	14.0	396	94.9	91.9	93.2	91.1
=12 Sheffield Hallam	3.7	403	86.6	86.3	98.1	90.8
=12 Glasgow Caledonian	8.1	441	87.5	90.8	91.4	90.8
14 Huddersfield	13.2	408	89.6	89.6	92.7	90.5
15 Coventry	4.5	380	93.2	95.6	95.1	90.4
=16 King's College London	34.6	445	74.7	83.5	88.8	90.3
=16 Hertfordshire	4.0	395	95.3	92.3	93.5	90.3
18 Manchester Metropolitan	12.0	389	88.3	89.8	94.0	90.0
19 Brighton	4.8	377	96.2	95.4	93.3	89.9
=20 Brunel	18.2	382	89.5	92.0	89.5	88.9
=20 Oxford Brookes	3.0	427	73.6	83.7	95.6	88.9
22 West of England	8.2	391	79.7	89.4	94.2	88.6
=23 York St John	1.9	385	92.7	93.6	90.7	88.4
=23 Queen Margaret, Edinburgh	1.5	472*	60.0	66.4	97.6	88.4
25 Ulster	27.7	386	80.6	87.9	88.9	88.3
26 Teesside	2.4	383	81.5	84.4	95.1	87.9
27 East London	7.6	355	77.3	88.4	95.4	87.1
28 Leeds Beckett	3.5	393	81.2	84.1	91.4	87.0
29 Kingston/St George's, London	2.6	411	70.7	68.0	93.1	85.8
30 Cumbria	0.7	376	88.3	95.1	85.4	85.5
31 Plymouth	9.5	354	80.4	83.3	90.6	85.4
32 Worcester	2.6	329	87.6	87.4		84.5
33 Salford	3.8	370	91.1	87.9	82.9	84.4
34 Central Lancashire	8.3	350	83.1	85.7	82.8	82.8

taking only two of the top ten places, compared with six last year. Robert Gordon, in a share of fifth place, is the highest-placed of them. It is joined in the top ten by Bournemouth. Satisfaction levels are high, with a dozen universities topping 90 per cent overall. Employment scores are equally impressive: over three-quarters of the universities in the table saw at least nine out ten leavers find professional jobs or start postgraduate courses within six months of graduation. The average starting salary in professional roles was just over £22,000.

Physiotherapy cont

Employed in professional job:	88%	Employed in non-professional job and studying:	0%
Employed in professional job and studying:	2%	Employed in non-professional job:	3%
Studying:	2%	Unemployed:	5%
Average starting professional salary:	£22,014	Average starting non-professional salary:	£13,333

Politics

The number of students starting politics degrees in 2014 rose by almost 10 per cent despite a small decline in applications. The growth in capacity gave applicants some respite from rising entry grades, with fewer of the leading universities averaging more than 500 points and more of the lower-ranked institutions below 300. Politics had been enjoying a boom before the introduction of £9,000 fees and, although there was a slump in enrolments in 2012, this has been followed by successive increases which have added nearly 1,000 to the annual entry. Even so, there were around eight applications for every place in 2014. Consequently, 109 universities and colleges are offering courses at undergraduate level in 2016.

The top two remain unchanged, with Oxford followed a little more closely by Cambridge this year. Oxford, which is rated by QS as third in the world for politics, has the highest entry grades in the UK. Essex, in eighth place, was well ahead of the field in the Research Excellence Framework, with 87 per cent of its work considered world-leading or internationally excellent. Final-year undergraduates at Liverpool Hope, in 54th place, were the most satisfied with the teaching, feedback and academic support they had received, while Surrey did best in other sections of the National Student Survey. Middlesex was the highest-placed modern university overall and the only one in the top 30.

Politics students are generally satisfied with their courses: only one university, the London School of Economics, dropped below 70 per cent on both aspects of this measure. But employment scores are less impressive: politics is in the bottom half of the employment table, with a quarter of all politics graduates going on to take postgraduate courses, but the same proportion starting their careers in low-level employment. Early-career salaries in professional jobs are only just outside the top 25 of the 66 subject groupings, however, average earnings almost reaching £22,000 in 2014. Exeter, in seventh place, had the best employment record in 2014, but only seven other universities registered more than 80 per cent positive destinations and 12 were below 50 per cent. Nationally, unemployment is above average at 12 per cent, but still lower than in 2013.

Politics	Research quality %	Entry standards	Teaching quality %	Student experience %	Graduate prospects %	Overall score
1 Oxford	61.1	593	79.8	85.4	84.4	100.0
2 Cambridge	38.2	551	86.2	86.8	82.8	96.9
3 Warwick	52.7	487	84.3	89.3	79.5	96.8
4 St Andrews	38.4	535	83.6	83.7	81.9	95.4
5 Sheffield	48.3	438	84.8	86.3	78.3	94.4
6 Lancaster	53.0	432	81.3	81.3	82.6	94.2
7 Exeter	29.8	460	84.8	87.1	86.1	93.6

8 Essex	69.6	332	82.3	88.4	68.6	92.9
9 York	36.9	434	85.4	88.7	77.0	92.8
10 University College London	57.0	510	70.4	78.2	74.3	92.4
11 Durham	27.0	504	80.2	82.0	83.2	92.1
12 London School of Economics	54.6	527	67.0	69.1	76.4	90.9
=13 Sussex	33.6	385	82.4	87.5	75.8	90.0
=13 Aston	38.6	329	88.0	87.8	71.7	90.0
=15 Loughborough	22.5	356	87.1	90.5	79.8	89.8
=15 SOAS, London	30.5	445	80.7	82.6	74.2	89.8
=17 Nottingham	30.8	419	77.4	80.8	82.7	89.6
=17 Glasgow	30.5	444	82.8	86.8	67.5	89.6
19 Reading	37.0	359	83.4	90.0	69.8	89.4
20 Kent	27.8	344	84.3	88.1	79.6	89.3
21 Southampton	37.0	375	82.7	85.3	70.6	89.2
22 Surrey	12.5	412	91.6	95.7	65.3	89.0
23 Leeds	25.1	398	81.1	85.1	75.5	88.4
24 East Anglia	35.5	394	80.2	89.6	63.3	88.2
25 Queen Mary, London	28.1	400	84.2	85.3	66.3	88.1
26 Edinburgh	44.5	480	65.4	80.0	69.3	88.0
27 Newcastle	22.0	404	84.9	86.2	68.5	87.9
28 Cardiff	30.4	399	79.1	83.6	70.9	87.8
=29 Strathclyde	41.6	463	82.1	87.4	43.5	87.6
=29 Middlesex	14.9		89.0	89.3	63.6	87.6
=31 Birmingham	31.1	391	73.3	73.6	84.1	87.3
=31 Royal Holloway, London	30.5	374	80.0	81.3	72.3	87.3
=33 King's College London	29.0	469	74.3	73.7	72.8	87.2
=33 Bristol	30.4	456	72.0	70.3	78.9	87.2
=33 City	24.6	359	81.9	82.8	75.3	87.2
36 Queen's, Belfast	35.0	374	82.7	87.7	57.6	86.9
37 Manchester	28.4	422	75.3	81.8	68.5	86.6
38 Bath	27.4	454	67.8	77.4	77.6	86.4
39 Stirling	33.8	387	79.3	81.3	62.3	86.3
40 Keele	24.0	334	87.7	89.3	60.5	86.2
=41 Huddersfield	9.5	329	92.0	84.7	67.8	85.5
=41 Dundee	10.8	424	88.0	91.6	52.3	85.5
43 De Montfort	10.7	293	89.2	87.7	72.5	85.3
44 Coventry	5.6	283	90.7	91.9	72.6	85.2
45 Portsmouth	32.2	287	88.9	86.3	54.4	85.0
46 Aberystwyth	40.2	318	79.5	77.8	58.5	84.4
47 West of England	13.8	311	88.4	90.8	58.2	84.0
48 Leicester	20.0	347	78.9	83.2	63.8	83.6
49 Brunel	32.4	314	81.8	77.9	57.3	83.5
50 Hull	10.8	334	79.9	84.9	68.3	83.1
51 Aberdeen	18.4	439	68.6	78.3	66.3	83.0
52 Oxford Brookes	17.8	312	86.0	85.8	52.7	82.5
53 Lincoln	7.7	295	83.2	88.3	65.7	82.4
54 Liverpool Hope	7.0	267	93.2	88.0	56.4	82.3

Politics cont	Research quality %	Entry standards	Teaching quality %	Student experience %	Graduate prospects %	Overall score
55 Liverpool	12.0	392	73.8	80.8	64.8	82.2
56 Swansea	18.5	278	72.6	80.8	75.0	81.7
57 Manchester Metropolitan	18.0	331	85.2	79.4	50.6	81.6
58 Northumbria	12.7	342	80.4	75.6	57.6	80.7
59 Bradford	12.7	266	76.3	78.9	69.2	80.2
=60 Bournemouth	15.1	329	76.8	76.5		79.7
=60 Winchester		282	89.4	85.7	51.8	79.7
62 Greenwich	8.6	301	86.5	82.3	47.0	79.5
63 Ulster	20.9	278	87.9	80.3	38.0	79.3
64 Nottingham Trent		272	87.6	85.7	52.9	79.2
65 East London	13.7	166	84.5	88.2	58.3	79.1
66 Westminster	14.3	267	81.7	83.0	47.7	78.6
67 Brighton	13.1	294	74.9	87.5	50.0	78.5
68 Goldsmiths, London	16.8	312	79.2	72.5	49.4	78.4
=69 Sheffield Hallam		274	90.0	89.4	37.6	77.7
=69 Canterbury Christ Church	3.2	232	85.8	83.5	51.6	77.7
71 Salford	4.8	285	81.9	79.7	46.6	77.0
=72 Leeds Beckett		234	86.2	87.8	43.8	76.6
=72 Central Lancashire	12.0		84.2	76.7	38.7	76.6
74 Plymouth		280	80.3	83.2	47.8	76.5
75 Kingston		253	75.3	78.4	51.1	74.6
76 London Metropolitan	1.2	236	76.1	75.0	52.5	74.3
77 Chester		229	78.4	70.5	47.3	73.0
78 Northampton		261	65.4	72.8	42.9	70.3

Employed in professional job:	41%	Employed in non-professional job and studying:	3%
Employed in professional job and studying:	4%	Employed in non-professional job:	22%
Studying:	18%	Unemployed:	12%
Average starting professional salary:	£21,940	Average starting non-professional salary:	£16,376

Psychology

Psychology was one of only three subjects to attract more than 100,000 applications in 2014, even overtaking law in popularity. It has the biggest table in the *Guide*, with two more universities joining this year, reflecting another 9 per cent rise in enrolments. Almost 20,000 students started undergraduate courses – easily a record for the subject. Its popularity endures in spite of poor performances in the graduate employment market: it has dropped into the bottom ten for the proportion of graduates with "positive destinations", and occupies a similar position for average starting salaries in professional-level jobs. Almost 40 per cent of graduates begin their careers in low-level jobs.

Most undergraduate programmes are accredited by the British Psychological Society, which ensures that key topics are covered, but the clinical and biological content of courses still varies considerably. Some universities require maths and/or biology A levels among three high-grade passes, but others are much less demanding. The contrast is obvious in the ranking, with 29 universities averaging more than 400 points at entry but with 12 below 270 points. Surprisingly, Cambridge's average is 80 points lower than in the last *Guide*, but it is still the highest in the table and the university also has the best graduate prospects and remains the leader overall. Like last year, Bath has narrowed the gap at the top after registering almost the highest score in the National Student Survey, just beaten by Lincoln on the teaching quality measure and equalling Lincoln on student experience. Loughborough, in equal 16th place, achieved the best results in the Research Excellence Framework, while Lincoln is the highest-placed modern university for the third year in a row and the only one in the top 30.

St Andrews has made the most progress at the top of the table, moving up seven places to fourth. New to the table, Buckingham, though only sharing 32nd place, might have been much higher if it was not barred, as a private university, from taking part in the Research Excellence Framework. It was one of only three universities where four out of five graduates went straight into professional work or continued studying. The others were Cambridge and Birmingham. At seven universities, the proportion of graduates with positive destinations was below 40 per cent.

Psychology		Research quality %	Entry standards	Teaching quality %	Student experience %	Graduate prospects %	Overall score
1	Cambridge	57.5	584	85.5	87.9	82.8	100.0
2	Bath	56.2	531	92.0	95.3	76.3	99.6
3	Oxford	58.6	561	85.1	90.2	76.0	98.5
4	St Andrews	45.4	503	86.7	90.5	74.8	95.4
5	University College London	57.0	508	75.8	83.3	76.7	94.0
6	Glasgow	52.9	452	80.6	90.8	75.5	93.8
7	Cardiff	55.7	456	82.2	90.7	70.2	93.6
8	Birmingham	55.8	419	78.8	84.5	82.2	93.2
9	Durham	37.1	491	80.4	85.7	76.9	92.4
=10	York	46.7	457	85.1	90.4	61.6	91.6
=10	Newcastle	50.0	411	85.4	93.7	63.7	91.6
12	Southampton	47.8	414	80.3	88.3	73.1	91.2
13	Exeter	43.3	457	79.3	82.6	72.7	90.9
14	Royal Holloway, London	37.8	442	90.1	88.9	60.8	90.8
15	Bristol	48.2	485	74.0	85.3	67.2	90.5
=16	Loughborough	62.3	375	81.5	84.0	66.2	90.4
=16	Surrey	22.0	440	86.8	89.9	72.8	90.4
18	Sussex	42.3	398	79.6	87.5	74.1	90.1
19	Kent	38.8	412	78.5	83.1	77.8	89.9
20	Leeds	33.0	435	84.2	90.7	64.8	89.7
21	Nottingham	36.4	425	79.3	85.3	70.9	89.2
22	Manchester	44.9	441	82.2	85.5	58.8	89.1
23	Warwick	43.1	428	78.1	86.7	62.7	88.5
24	Dundee	22.7	420	87.6	90.3	62.6	88.4

Psychology cont	Research quality %	Entry standards	Teaching quality %	Student experience %	Graduate prospects %	Overall score
=25 Aston	39.1	391	83.2	87.8	61.8	88.1
=25 East Anglia	33.2	401	86.9	92.3	56.2	88.1
27 Strathclyde	23.5	464	84.8	89.3	57.3	88.0
28 Lancaster	38.5	406	75.9	82.0	71.3	87.8
29 Aberdeen	38.7	443	78.5	86.1	57.2	87.4
30 Lincoln	7.9	348	93.5	95.5	66.9	87.3
31 Edinburgh	52.8	494	62.9	75.0	64.6	87.0
=32 Essex	41.0	344	83.5	90.9	58.4	86.9
=32 Buckingham		331	90.9	87.9	81.5	86.9
34 Bangor	32.0	322	84.3	88.5	67.6	86.7
35 Swansea	44.7	348	72.5	82.7	73.4	86.6
36 Leicester	29.6	366	82.3	88.7	61.9	86.2
37 Stirling	40.1	390	80.9	84.1	54.8	85.9
38 Queen's, Belfast	40.2	372	78.6	89.0	56.0	85.8
39 Portsmouth	21.0	337	87.7	88.4	56.2	84.4
40 City	23.5	356	82.3	85.6	58.6	84.1
41 Reading	42.3	378	76.6	83.8	50.2	84.0
42 De Montfort	11.2	304	87.2	91.7	62.5	83.8
=43 Sheffield	38.8	422	64.9	78.1	61.2	83.6
=43 York St John	11.0	291	87.5	88.4	66.0	83.6
45 Nottingham Trent	19.3	324	87.6	89.5	53.6	83.5
46 Keele	17.7	360	80.6	87.1	58.0	83.3
47 Abertay	15.1	332	84.2	87.0	59.0	83.1
48 Coventry	7.8	289	86.6	87.5	65.7	82.8
49 Oxford Brookes	18.1	338	80.0	87.5	57.4	82.5
50 Manchester Metropolitan	12.0	341	88.1	87.8	47.9	82.0
51 Plymouth	33.8	334	78.9	84.4	46.0	81.6
=52 Northumbria	18.7	361	78.5	84.8	51.3	81.5
=52 Heriot-Watt	26.9	402	66.1	74.6	62.2	81.5
54 Edinburgh Napier	5.3	363	82.7	84.2	52.8	81.0
=55 West of England	8.2	353	80.1	87.9	50.4	80.6
=55 Liverpool	34.6	389	67.6	75.9	51.5	80.6
57 Bradford	9.5	274	79.1	84.5	65.5	80.5
=58 Bath Spa		322	81.7	86.0	59.4	80.4
=58 Chichester	10.3	303	90.7	87.8	42.9	80.4
60 Queen Margaret, Edinburgh	8.6	331	80.9	90.7	48.4	80.2
61 Goldsmiths, London	40.4	345	68.2	74.8	51.3	80.1
=62 Edge Hill	18.8	311	85.8	85.9	40.8	79.9
=62 Leeds Trinity		290	88.5	80.1	57.7	79.9
64 Huddersfield	9.5	325	77.8	79.1	59.1	79.8
=65 Brunel	26.6	343	73.4	82.4	47.2	79.7
=65 Roehampton	26.4	286	77.6	81.3	52.0	79.7
67 Ulster	23.2	305	84.9	89.3	35.6	79.6

=68	Liverpool Hope	5.5	311	86.8	89.0	43.9	79.5
=68	Salford	3.8	342	81.3	81.7	52.2	79.5
=68	Cumbria		239	89.6	90.8	54.2	79.5
71	Chester	7.9	299	87.4	88.1	43.2	79.3
72	Staffordshire	8.2	261	86.1	88.0	49.7	79.2
73	Hertfordshire	6.0	313	78.8	82.8	55.2	79.1
74	Hull	26.8	327	68.6	76.5	55.2	78.9
75	Teesside	15.0	282	80.5	85.6	47.9	78.7
=76	Middlesex	7.6	291	74.2	79.7	62.6	78.6
=76	Winchester	6.5	322	78.6	87.3	47.5	78.6
78	Glyndŵr	3.6	238	84.8	81.8	58.3	78.4
79	Central Lancashire	12.2	315	74.9	82.8	50.8	78.2
=80	Queen Mary, London	26.1	390	67.4	70.2	47.5	78.1
=80	Liverpool John Moores	7.8	341	75.9	85.6	45.7	78.1
=82	West of Scotland	9.4	318	77.3	80.8	49.1	77.9
=82	Derby	8.4	280	83.8	86.9	43.3	77.9
=82	West London	7.6	251	81.1	83.4	53.8	77.9
85	Sunderland	7.5	272	79.3	78.6	55.6	77.7
86	Bolton	3.6	266	80.7	78.0	54.9	77.2
=87	Greenwich	6.7	312	79.7	85.6	40.5	77.1
=87	Anglia Ruskin	12.6	253	80.7	84.5	45.3	77.1
89	Aberystwyth		314	75.8	82.3	50.3	76.8
=90	East London	8.3	276	77.6	84.2	46.0	76.6
=90	Leeds Beckett	6.5	303	79.7	84.4	40.5	76.6
92	Buckinghamshire New		242	86.3	85.8	44.4	76.4
93	Birmingham City		264	73.7	80.2	58.6	76.1
=94	Glasgow Caledonian	8.1	384	77.1	77.9	31.4	76.0
=94	South Wales	0.9	322	79.0	80.5	41.8	76.0
96	Bedfordshire	25.1	217	75.8	80.5	45.1	75.9
=97	Westminster	9.3	317	68.8	81.0	46.4	75.6
=97	St Mary's, Twickenham		279	81.5	86.5	39.1	75.6
99	Worcester	7.1	289	72.3	81.9	46.5	75.5
=100	Sheffield Hallam		326	72.8	79.7	44.4	75.1
=100	Newman	0.8	264	75.3	86.6	45.6	75.1
102	Northampton	0.4	276	77.6	83.2	43.4	75.0
103	Kingston	6.5	279	72.6	78.5	47.9	74.9
104	Canterbury Christ Church	2.2	294	77.9	78.4	38.4	74.3
105	Southampton Solent		261	76.4	83.6	41.1	73.9
106	Brighton	12.4	331	64.2	71.9	44.3	73.8
107	Cardiff Metropolitan		309	74.1	78.9	37.0	73.4
108	Bournemouth	13.0	308	62.7	69.8	47.6	73.2
109	London South Bank	8.6	274	71.5	78.5	38.5	73.1
110	Gloucestershire		315	70.5	72.7	37.6	72.1
111	London Metropolitan		253	72.6	74.8	42.3	71.9

Psychology cont

Employed in professional job:	30%	Employed in non-professional job and studying:	5%
Employed in professional job and studying:	4%	Employed in non-professional job:	34%
Studying:	17%	Unemployed:	11%
Average starting professional salary:	£18,973	Average starting non-professional salary:	£14,982

Radiography

Radiography moved into the top four subjects for employment in 2014. Indeed, only dentistry and nursing had a higher proportion going straight into professional jobs than the 94 per cent of radiographers. The subject was still outside the top 20 in the earnings table, however, with average salaries of £22,238. Courses are divided into diagnostic and therapeutic specialisms. Diagnostic courses usually involve two years of studying anatomy, physiology and physics followed by further training in sociology, management and ethics, and the practice and science of imaging. The therapeutic branch covers much of the same scientific content in the first year, but follows this with training in oncology, psycho-social studies and other modules. Degrees require at least one science subject, usually biology, among three A levels or the equivalent.

The table is in its third year, radiography having been listed previously among "other subjects allied to medicine" in the *Guide*. A total of 25 universities expect to offer the subject in 2016, two more than the number in this edition of the table, which is headed for the first time by Bangor. The Welsh university has moved up 11 places, partly because it was one of three institutions to record 100 per cent employment among its radiographers in 2014. Liverpool, in fifth place, and Cardiff, in seventh, were the other two. Exeter, which is only a fraction of a point behind in second place, was the clear leader in the Research Excellence Framework (REF), while third-placed Robert Gordon had the highest entry grades. Derby, which might have been higher than eighth if it had entered the REF, had the most satisfied students in the teaching sections of the National Student Survey, while Robert Gordon and City did best on the student experience.

Employment scores reflect the subject's elevated position in the employment table: all but three universities saw more than nine out of ten graduates go straight into professional jobs or further study. Entry grades have been rising: although there were still only three universities averaging more than 400 points in 2014, the remaining scores are tightly bunched. Two universities averaged less than 320 points in 2013, but there was none in this position 12 months later.

Radiography	Research quality %	Entry standards	Teaching quality %	Student experience %	Graduate prospects %	Overall score
1 Bangor	34.7	403*	88.3	81.3	100.0	100.0
2 Exeter	42.4	376	86.1	87.8	98.6	99.4
3 Robert Gordon	4.9	433	96.4	96.3	93.3	99.3
4 Leeds	31.7	421	83.0	85.9	96.2	99.1
5 Liverpool	35.3	365	81.5	87.8	100.0	97.8
6 Portsmouth	24.3	385	90.4	87.2	94.2	97.3

7 Cardiff	36.8	398	70.0	80.6	100.0	97.1
8 Derby		359	97.7	94.0	98.1	96.5
9 Sheffield Hallam	3.7	366	88.6	90.5	99.2	95.8
10 City	19.2	333	94.2	96.3	92.4	95.3
11 Glasgow Caledonian	8.1	399	81.2	80.9	96.4	94.9
12 Cumbria	0.7	341	90.3	90.6	98.9	94.5
13 Bradford	9.5	372	85.0	87.0	93.2	94.0
=14 Teesside	2.4	368	81.4	85.3	97.7	93.7
=14 Canterbury Christ Church	2.2	333	92.0	88.8	96.8	93.7
16 Salford	3.8	396	82.0	80.8	93.8	93.6
17 Birmingham City	1.5	369	81.9	84.5	97.1	93.5
18 Ulster	27.7	364	84.3	90.1	84.2	93.1
19 Hertfordshire	4.0	348	86.6	88.6	92.5	92.5
20 Kingston/St George's, London	2.6	333	88.6	92.0	90.3	91.6
21 West of England	8.2	322	77.3	84.8	98.0	91.5
22 London South Bank	13.7	330	87.7	84.5	83.9	89.8
23 Queen Margaret, Edinburgh	1.5	348	79.3	84.1	85.0	88.4

Employed in professional job:	92%	Employed in non-professional job and studying:	0%
Employed in professional job and studying:	2%	Employed in non-professional job:	2%
Studying:	1%	Unemployed:	3%
Average starting professional salary:	£22,238	Average starting non-professional salary:	n/a

Russian and Eastern European Languages

Three universities have joined the table for Russian and Eastern European languages this year, beginning to reverse a decline that still leaves it with 50 per cent fewer universities than there were a decade ago. The recovery may be temporary, however, since only 19 universities plan to offer any of the languages in 2016. Only 55 students started degrees in Russian in 2014, although many more joined modern languages programmes in which it was a component. The small numbers inevitably make for exaggerated swings in statistics. Russian has dropped more than 20 places in the employment table, having done the same in last year's comparison of graduate starting salaries. The 15 per cent unemployment rate is among the highest in any subject, although still a big improvement on two years ago, when it reached 22 per cent.

The top three in the table are unchanged, with Cambridge extending its lead over Oxford. Cambridge has the highest entry standards and the best research score, as well as most satisfied students where teaching is concerned. Sheffield, in seventh place, did better on the sections of the National Student Survey relating to the student experience, while Durham had the best graduate prospects. Portsmouth is the sole representative of the post-1992 universities and there are no institutions from Wales or Northern Ireland.

Most undergraduates learn the language from scratch. Despite the small numbers, entry standards remain high throughout the table: the top three all average well over 500 points and only four universities are below 400 points on the UCAS tariff. Satisfaction levels are also high. Nearly every university in the table satisfied at least three-quarters of its final-year undergraduates.

Russian and Eastern European Languages	Research quality %	Entry standards	Teaching quality %	Student experience %	Graduate prospects %	Overall score
1 Cambridge	54.0	566	89.7	89.8	83.9	100.0
2 Oxford	41.3	561	88.2	84.8	83.3	95.8
3 Durham	34.6	537	82.4	86.2	86.4	92.9
4 Birmingham	33.7		84.4	85.7	82.4	91.6
5 Exeter	35.1	470	85.7	89.4	76.8	91.4
6 Bristol	36.0	435	83.2	80.5	83.1	89.9
7 Sheffield	41.2	429*	87.6	92.4	50.5	89.3
8 St Andrews	26.4	490	84.8	85.3		89.0
9 University College London	43.7	472	76.8	79.5	66.2	88.8
10 Bath	27.4	425	87.4	86.4		88.1
11 Manchester	48.9	370	75.9	81.1	62.5	87.2
12 Nottingham	39.4	349	80.0	82.9	73.6	87.1
13 Edinburgh	30.3	477	73.7	80.9		84.8
=14 Portsmouth	32.2	268	84.1	88.8	67.8	84.4
=14 Queen Mary, London	35.1	407	87.9	82.3	37.5*	84.4
16 Leeds	30.6	389	79.7	74.4	64.1	83.5
17 Glasgow	26.3	490	72.9	76.5	62.3	83.3

Employed in professional job:	44%	Employed in non-professional job and studying:	2%
Employed in professional job and studying:	2%	Employed in non-professional job:	23%
Studying:	15%	Unemployed:	15%
Average starting professional salary:	£21,518	Average starting non-professional salary:	£15,437

Social Policy

Unlike most of the social sciences, social policy suffered a drop in applications in 2014. There was already less competition for places than in any of the 66 subject groupings featured in this chapter. In 2014, there were barely three applications for every place. Yet there are still 34 universities in the table – one more than last year – and 90 universities and colleges plan to offer courses in this area in 2016. Nor are entry standards especially low: while only five universities average more than 400 points on the UCAS tariff, just three dropped below 250 points. More than 1,400 students started courses in 2014, but this was 10 per cent down on the previous year.

Last year, the London School of Economics (LSE) lost the lead in social policy for the first time in more than 15 years that the table had been published, dropping to fourth place with the lowest student satisfaction in the ranking. It is back at the top in the new edition, although its scores in the National Student Survey (NSS) are still relatively low. The LSE was a long way ahead of the field in the Research Excellence Framework and has high scores for entry grades and graduate prospects. Edinburgh, in fifth place, has the highest entry standards, while Nottingham was a long way ahead of the rest for the proportion of graduates going straight into professional jobs or joining postgraduate courses. Student satisfaction is highest in Wales: Swansea did best on the teaching sections of the NSS, while

Cardiff posted the best scores in relation to the student experience.

Nationally, the subject has dropped into the bottom five for employment, with almost 40 per cent of graduates starting out in low-level jobs. This is reflected in the table for social policy, where less than half of the graduates at eight of the 34 universities found professional work or continued studying. The picture is more positive in the comparison of starting salaries in graduate-level jobs, where an average of £20,300 in 2014 took it into the top 40 subjects.

Social Policy	Research quality %	Entry standards	Teaching quality %	Student experience %	Graduate prospects %	Overall score
1 London School of Economics	74.9	441	77.9	83.8	70.6	100.0
2 Bangor	39.6		92.4	89.9	70.5	98.5
3 Leeds	47.6	398	85.4	86.5	71.4	97.2
4 Bristol	47.9	416	82.2	85.7	68.3	96.5
5 Edinburgh	53.4	455	77.1	81.1	63.1	95.9
6 Kent	59.0	320	81.8	89.3	72.5	95.5
7 Swansea	22.7	364	93.6	91.9	69.7	95.1
8 Glasgow	41.8	406	85.1	83.0	61.4	94.5
9 York	47.5	336	83.8	90.9	65.9	94.1
10 Stirling	33.8	399	86.8	89.2	51.7	92.6
11 Nottingham	43.5	351*	69.6	69.8	90.0	92.4
12 Aston	38.6	329	81.2	87.2	69.5	92.2
=13 Birmingham	40.1	362	79.4	78.2	68.4	91.8
=13 Bath	43.4	408	79.5	77.8	56.2	91.8
15 Loughborough	40.6	350	79.3	79.9	64.7	91.0
16 Cardiff	30.8	331	85.8	94.5	55.2	90.8
17 Bolton	1.0		92.6	87.0	61.6	90.7
18 Queen's, Belfast	26.2	338	89.1	94.3	51.4	90.5
19 Sheffield	26.8	375	77.3	86.3	58.3	89.4
20 Keele	25.0	335	82.4	84.4	59.3	88.8
21 Salford	27.7	322	88.9	91.7	44.2	88.5
22 Sheffield Hallam		396	85.6	87.3	52.3	87.8
23 West of Scotland	9.4		86.3	80.6	55.9	86.7
=24 Lincoln	5.8	300	87.2	93.5	43.5	84.6
=24 Liverpool Hope	8.6	285	88.4	87.5	47.4	84.6
26 Northampton		270	82.6	87.3	50.8	82.1
=27 Ulster	39.2	277	76.8	83.2	29.6	81.6
=27 Middlesex	14.9	294	76.5	77.5		81.6
29 Birmingham City	3.8	262	68.6	75.8	66.7	80.3
30 Brighton	12.4	306	71.3	76.7	43.1	79.6
31 Anglia Ruskin	5.4	216	83.8	80.3	43.5	78.9
32 London Metropolitan	8.8	240	77.9	86.8	36.4	78.4
33 Canterbury Christ Church	3.2	260	65.7	76.0	55.6	77.5
34 Plymouth	16.0	212	79.7	79.7	30.8	76.7

Social Policy cont

Employed in professional job:	31%	Employed in non-professional job and studying:	3%
Employed in professional job and studying:	2%	Employed in non-professional job:	36%
Studying:	15%	Unemployed:	13%
Average starting professional salary:	£20,304	Average starting non-professional salary:	£16,041

Social Work

Social work degrees have begun to recover after three years of decline in which the number of applications dropped from 80,000 to 60,000. The demand for places is still well below that seen before the transition to higher undergraduate fees, but applications and enrolments both increased in 2014. More than 13,000 students started courses, and 133 universities and colleges – 10 more than this year – plan to offer courses in 2016. A combination of falling demand and increasing provision has seen the number of applications per place drop from more than seven in 2010 to less than five. Only two universities, compared with five last year, average (just) more than 400 points, and almost a third of the 80 universities in the table average less than 300.

Like last year, there are big changes in the table, and only one of the top 40 occupies the same position. Glasgow has climbed ten places to take over the leadership, despite not having the top score on any individual indicator. It had too few entrants in 2014 to calculate a reliable score for entry standards, so the score for this measure is derived from its performance on other indicators. East Anglia, in ninth place, has the highest entry standards, while Kent, four places lower, produced the top grades in the Research Excellence Framework. The best graduate prospects were at Swansea, one of eight universities where at least 90 per cent of graduates found professional jobs or continued their studies. The most satisfied students were at Middlesex, in twelfth place, where almost 97 per cent of final-year undergraduates gave a positive verdict on the teaching quality of their course. Students at Bournemouth were most satisfied by the overall student experience. Middlesex, in 12th place, is the highest-placed post-1992 university, and is joined in the top 20 by Robert Gordon, West of England and Glasgow Caledonian.

A new attempt has been launched to attract graduates of other subjects into social work through the Frontline programme, modelled on the Teach First. For the moment, however, social work degrees remain the main route into the profession. Sixty per cent of graduates become social workers or find other professional work, and their average starting salaries, which topped £24,000 in 2014, are well established in the top 15 of the 66 subject groupings.

Social Work	Research quality %	Entry standards	Teaching quality %	Student experience %	Graduate prospects %	Overall score
1 Glasgow	41.8		93.5	86.8	93.3	100.0
2 Lancaster	51.4	405	83.3	85.1	90.0	99.5
3 Edinburgh	53.4	396	87.7	86.3	76.9	97.8
4 Bath	43.4	398	85.9	86.8	83.5	97.3
5 Dundee	31.1	393	86.8	93.8	81.0	95.7
6 Queen's, Belfast	39.3	387	74.0	81.6	87.5	93.8
=7 Leeds	47.6	381	84.3	86.6	67.9	93.6

=7	Birmingham	40.1	384	70.7	80.8	90.3	93.6
9	East Anglia	45.8	409	83.7	80.1	64.3	93.4
10	Swansea	22.7		78.6	86.2	96.9	93.3
11	Stirling	33.8	373	78.8	90.6	81.5	93.1
12	Middlesex	14.9	301	96.9	93.6	91.8	92.6
13	Kent	59.0	309	76.7	81.7	82.2	92.1
14	Sheffield	26.8		81.4	85.6	87.5	92.0
=15	Robert Gordon	18.0	352	83.9	85.5	90.4	91.9
=15	West of England	10.9	353	83.7	83.8	96.8	91.9
17	Manchester	57.1		81.8	92.5	64.7	91.0
18	Strathclyde	31.9	380	80.2	89.5	66.7	90.5
=19	Glasgow Caledonian	8.1		84.0	92.1	84.0	90.0
=19	Sussex	27.9	378	72.9	70.2	86.2	90.0
21	Bolton	1.0		90.5	87.9	81.3	89.6
22	Ulster	39.2	309	84.4	89.8	70.2	89.3
23	Keele	25.0	326	77.4	80.8	88.5	89.2
=24	Liverpool Hope	8.6	335	81.3	88.2	89.5	89.1
=24	Portsmouth	12.1	334	83.2	80.3	89.4	89.1
26	Bedfordshire	16.3		80.1	80.8	84.7	88.4
27	Salford	27.7	355	78.5	76.8	74.1	88.2
28	Bournemouth	4.7	330	92.6	94.3	71.2	87.8
=29	York	47.5	344	67.6	55.6	81.8	87.5
=29	Huddersfield	9.5	345	81.2	84.5	80.2	87.5
31	Nottingham	43.5	362	61.6	56.4	85.2	87.3
32	West of Scotland	9.4	339	86.1	77.9	78.4	87.2
33	Teesside	15.0	288	84.3	84.5	84.5	86.8
34	Oxford Brookes		387	65.8	77.2	92.5	86.7
35	Winchester		322	88.7	89.5	76.8	86.4
36	Kingston/St George's, London		317	81.9	81.7	89.3	86.3
37	Hull	14.3	342	75.6	76.7	80.2	86.1
38	Manchester Metropolitan	6.9	356	83.3	81.7	70.2	86.0
39	Lincoln	5.8	336	79.1	78.5	82.6	85.9
40	De Montfort	11.2	316	78.5	85.1	79.7	85.6
41	Coventry	5.6	300	85.4	89.8	76.6	85.3
42	London South Bank	20.1		83.6	83.3	66.7	85.2
43	Northumbria	12.7	352	77.2	82.7	60.3	83.5
44	Goldsmiths, London	13.5		71.1	77.0	80.0	83.1
45	Chester	0.3	291	80.3	83.3	79.3	82.8
46	West London		257	86.2	85.2	80.0	82.5
47	Central Lancashire	11.8	318	78.0	82.3	64.0	82.4
48	Nottingham Trent	5.1	304	87.9	84.0	59.5	82.0
49	Anglia Ruskin	5.4	273	77.9	77.5	79.6	81.5
50	Hertfordshire	4.0	323	66.2	71.5	82.6	81.4
51	Sunderland	1.9	311	83.1	84.9	61.0	81.3
52	Staffordshire		271	75.8	81.0	83.1	81.2
53	Birmingham City	3.8	289	78.5	81.1	71.3	81.0
54	Brunel	28.5	356	55.6	53.5	73.2	80.9

Social Work cont	Research quality %	Entry standards	Teaching quality %	Student experience %	Graduate prospects %	Overall score
=55 Sheffield Hallam		311	70.4	70.7	81.5	80.8
=55 Leeds Beckett	6.4	288	81.2	85.3	63.6	80.8
=57 Derby		275	84.7	83.0	67.9	80.6
=57 Southampton Solent		296	65.9	75.9	86.9	80.6
59 Essex		256*	84.7	89.5	68.0	80.2
=60 Northampton		300	75.8	78.8	70.1	80.0
=60 South Wales	15.4	302	72.5	76.8	62.6	80.0
62 Brighton	12.4	268	82.9	82.3	59.0	79.8
=63 Bangor		261	89.5	87.8	58.3	79.5
=63 Liverpool John Moores	5.8	344	73.1	75.5	55.6	79.5
65 Cardiff Metropolitan		313	69.8	73.4	72.7	79.4
66 Chichester		292	79.0	79.0	65.0	79.3
67 East London	10.6	279	74.3	75.7	66.2	79.0
68 Buckinghamshire New		281	68.6	74.8	78.6	78.7
69 Edge Hill	5.7	299	85.7	84.5	44.8	78.6
70 Greenwich	2.2	253*	80.2	83.9	66.1	78.5
71 Bradford	10.6	302	66.8	74.6	65.0	78.3
72 Plymouth	16.0	279	68.3	66.0	68.6	78.0
73 Gloucestershire		286	62.6	76.6	76.6	77.4
74 Cumbria		280	80.0	77.1	57.9	77.3
75 Glyndŵr		238	78.7	78.1	70.0	77.2
76 Newman	2.2	268	81.8	84.3	44.8	75.5
=77 London Metropolitan	8.8	273	72.0	77.3	50.6	75.1
=77 Worcester		197	78.6	90.5	64.4	75.1
79 St Mark and St John		259	81.9	84.5	46.3	75.0
80 Canterbury Christ Church	2.2	273	77.8	80.8	46.5	74.9

Employed in professional job:	57%	Employed in non-professional job and studying:	1%
Employed in professional job and studying:	3%	Employed in non-professional job:	21%
Studying:	7%	Unemployed:	11%
Average starting professional salary:	£24,007	Average starting non-professional salary:	£14,910

Sociology

Sociology is enjoying a spectacular renaissance after seeing demand drop when £9,000 fees were introduced. Applications increased by 20 per cent in 2014 to almost 30,000, the second successive year of growth. The numbers actually taking up places did not quite keep pace, but a 7 per cent increase was enough to persuade 11 more universities and colleges to offer the subject in 2016, bringing the total to 129. Labour market signals are not responsible in this case: sociology is in the bottom three for the proportion of graduates finding professional work or continuing their studies. More than half of those graduating in 2014 were in low-level jobs or unemployed at the end of the year. Those who did find professional work did rather better, but their average salary of £19,651 was still close to the bottom 20.

Cambridge has extended its lead over Bath at the top of the table, with big leads on entry standards and graduate prospects. It was the only university where more than 80 per cent of sociologists went straight into professional jobs or began postgraduate courses. The best performance in the Research Excellence Framework was at Kent, which shared tenth place overall. As in the 2008 assessments, the sociology panel was no respecter of reputations: neither Cambridge nor the London School of Economics is among the top eight universities on this measure, and the LSE has dropped out of the top 40 overall with much the lowest rate of student satisfaction in the table. The most satisfied students for teaching, feedback and academic support were at Northampton, while Lincoln had the best scores for the broader student experience. Robert Gordon, sharing 25th place, is the highest-placed post-1992 university, and is joined in the top 30 by Oxford Brookes and Portsmouth.

Courses for 2016 will include subjects such as criminology, urban studies, women's studies and some communication studies, as well as sociology itself, and a large number of institutions teach the subject as part of a combined studies or modular programme. Entry standards are moderate: around 40 per cent of the 93 universities in the table average less than 300 points on the UCAS tariff.

Sociology	Research quality %	Entry standards	Teaching quality %	Student experience %	Graduate prospects %	Overall score
1 Cambridge	39.2	551	86.2	86.8	82.8	100.0
2 Bath	43.4	385	84.7	83.8	78.8	93.1
3 Exeter	41.0	419	87.5	90.3	64.9	92.7
4 Glasgow	41.8	469	83.2	85.1	61.7	92.4
5 Lancaster	51.4	410	83.5	85.9	63.9	92.3
6 Edinburgh	48.8	477	75.3	82.3	63.5	92.0
7 Leeds	47.6	399	85.1	87.0	63.5	91.8
8 Durham	28.7	444	78.8	82.9	76.9	91.1
9 Surrey	30.2	414	90.8	88.2	62.6	90.9
=10 Kent	59.0	312	82.2	87.8	65.2	90.1
=10 York	45.1	373	86.9	87.8	59.2	90.1
12 Loughborough	40.6	343	86.1	89.3	68.3	90.0
13 Aberdeen	31.0	412	79.1	83.4	71.7	89.4
14 Sussex	29.7	356	79.6	86.2	79.0	89.0
15 Warwick	31.7	421	81.0	82.1	64.3	88.7
16 Sheffield	26.8	379	82.9	88.5	64.1	87.5
17 Nottingham	43.5	336	76.9	80.7	67.4	87.0
18 Southampton	52.8	376	76.1	88.1	46.8	86.5
19 Leicester	18.4	369	86.5	89.2	61.5	86.3
20 Manchester	50.4	381	74.2	78.8	53.5	86.2
21 Bangor	39.6	290	88.8	86.9	54.4	85.6
=22 Keele	25.0	331	85.6	86.4	61.3	85.3
=22 Essex	44.3	325	79.7	86.3	53.6	85.3
=22 Cardiff	30.8	375	79.3	86.1	55.8	85.3
=25 Stirling	33.8	394	76.6	75.8	57.9	85.1
=25 Robert Gordon	4.9	355	82.4	92.3	72.3	85.1

Sociology cont	Research quality %	Entry standards	Teaching quality %	Student experience %	Graduate prospects %	Overall score
=25 Aston	38.6	323	83.3	86.9	53.0	85.1
28 Newcastle	30.3	346	79.0	85.3	60.4	84.9
29 Oxford Brookes	17.8	312	88.4	85.8	63.0	84.4
=30 Queen's, Belfast	26.2	334	83.8	88.8	52.3	83.8
=30 Portsmouth	32.2	310	85.6	87.9	50.3	83.8
32 Birmingham	31.1	371	65.7	62.5	77.6	83.6
33 Goldsmiths, London	33.4	320	84.9	82.8	47.5	83.0
=34 East Anglia	45.8	446*	71.5	75.8	33.0	82.9
=34 Edinburgh Napier	5.3	376	90.0	89.2	49.1	82.9
36 Bristol	46.7	420	56.7	52.3	65.5	82.3
37 Lincoln		313	88.1	93.4	61.3	82.1
=38 Huddersfield	9.5	252*	90.7	92.1	61.9	81.9
=38 Royal Holloway, London		387	86.2	82.8	54.3	81.9
40 Strathclyde	31.9		83.8	88.9	40.5	81.7
41 City	19.2	347	81.8	82.8	49.0	81.4
42 London School of Economics	45.2	443	52.4	49.2	64.4	81.3
43 Coventry	5.6	291	89.1	89.2	54.4	80.6
44 Liverpool	24.5	374	72.0	75.2	51.3	80.5
45 Anglia Ruskin	26.4	245	90.6	89.0	40.9	79.9
46 Glasgow Caledonian	12.7	403	80.0	79.6	39.9	79.8
47 Bath Spa	13.9	309	83.5	82.2	47.7	79.2
48 Manchester Metropolitan	14.9	331	82.3	84.3	41.4	78.9
49 Abertay	5.0	319	79.7	77.1	57.8	78.7
50 Northampton		248	92.9	84.7	54.5	78.6
51 Northumbria	12.7	344	80.5	79.8	41.9	78.2
52 Nottingham Trent		291	87.4	86.5	49.7	78.1
53 Chester	6.4	283	92.1	84.6	39.8	77.8
=54 Hull	14.3	310	78.2	84.9	43.8	77.7
=54 Roehampton	24.9	251	79.8	86.5	43.8	77.7
56 Gloucestershire	14.5	309	82.0	87.2	36.4	77.3
=57 Salford	27.7	308	76.7	74.3	38.9	77.2
=57 West of Scotland	9.4	300	86.3	80.6	40.0	77.2
=57 De Montfort	11.2	284	79.9	80.0	49.9	77.2
60 Bradford	10.6	285	73.5	81.1	54.5	76.7
61 Sunderland	1.9	296	88.5	86.3	37.9	76.6
62 Bedfordshire	16.3	215	85.6	87.5	44.0	76.5
=63 Central Lancashire	11.8	295	81.3	81.3	40.6	76.4
=63 Queen Margaret, Edinburgh		286	82.6	89.3	45.7	76.4
=63 St Mary's, Twickenham		251	78.2	81.8	62.3	76.4
66 Liverpool Hope	8.6	273	88.0	88.8	34.5	76.3
67 Brighton	12.4	293	76.0	79.2	47.0	76.2
68 Edge Hill	5.7	274	80.7	78.6	50.7	76.1
69 Derby	13.5	261	82.8	79.5	42.3	75.9

70 Winchester	4.4	289	79.4	75.6	50.2	75.8
=71 Ulster		269	91.2	92.0	32.9	75.6
=71 Staffordshire		261	87.3	86.1	42.3	75.6
=73 Teesside	15.0	268	81.5	85.7	35.0	75.3
=73 Canterbury Christ Church		261	83.2	83.4	47.4	75.3
=75 Birmingham City	3.8	290	77.9	77.8	48.2	75.2
=75 Brunel	26.0	301	72.7	74.3	36.3	75.2
77 Middlesex	14.9	238	77.7	81.4	46.7	75.1
78 Greenwich		295	84.6	82.5	36.8	74.7
=79 West of England	10.9	326	69.5	72.7	45.0	74.5
=79 East London	13.7	257	79.7	83.3	37.2	74.5
81 Buckinghamshire New		252	82.7	79.4	45.9	74.1
82 South Wales		321	81.1	84.7	31.2	74.0
83 Westminster		259	84.2	83.8	37.7	73.6
84 Sheffield Hallam		301	79.7	80.2	36.8	73.5
85 Plymouth		265	81.0	80.0	40.2	73.1
86 Leeds Beckett	6.4	253	79.9	79.6	37.5	72.9
87 London South Bank	20.1	207	74.9	77.2	39.7	72.3
88 London Metropolitan		258	76.8	83.4	37.6	71.8
=89 Liverpool John Moores	5.8	322	65.9	77.0	37.1	71.7
=89 Kingston		279	75.6	77.5	38.4	71.7
91 Bournemouth	4.7	288	77.3	74.8	31.6	71.6
=92 Worcester		265	72.7	75.3	44.4	71.5
=92 Highlands and Islands		234	75.6	69.7	50.0	71.5

Employed in professional job:	31%	Employed in non-professional job and studying:	3%
Employed in professional job and studying:	2%	Employed in non-professional job:	39%
Studying:	12%	Unemployed:	12%
Average starting professional salary:	£19,651	Average starting non-professional salary:	£15,370

Sports Science

Sports science has been one of the big growth areas of UK higher education over the past decade: nearly 160 universities and colleges – seven more than this year – plan to offer the subject in 2016. Although there was a substantial drop in applications with the introduction of higher fees in 2012, both applications and enrolments recovered strongly in the following year and there was further growth in 2014. Sports science remains on the verge of the top ten subjects at degree level. The subject covers more than 40 specialisms, from sports therapy to equestrian sport studies and marine sport technology. Many courses contain more science and less physical activity than candidates may expect. Essex, for example, requires maths or one of the sciences at A level. Many universities now offer sports scholarships for elite performers, but most are not tied to a particular course and, officially at least, do not mean that the normal entry requirements are waived.

All the universities at the top of the table have excellent sports facilities and successful teams, but it is their performance in research and sports degree courses that counts here. Exeter has moved up four places to take over from Birmingham at the top of the table.

Sports Science cont

Loughborough, the most famous name in university sport, is now second, but neither of the top two lead on any individual measure. Although third, Birmingham still has the top research score, while Edinburgh has the best graduate prospects and Glasgow has the highest entry standards. Kingston, which is only just in the top 50, has the most satisfied students for teaching, feedback and academic support, while Portsmouth, in ninth place, had the best scores for the broader student experience and is again the highest-placed post-1992 university. It is joined in the top ten by Liverpool John Moores.

Sports science is in the bottom ten for starting salaries in professional jobs, but just makes it to the top 50 subjects for graduate prospects. Only 8 per cent of 2014 graduates were unemployed at the end of the year, a rate bettered by just ten subjects. More than a third of graduates start out in low-level work, but one in five stays on in higher education.

Sports Science	Research quality %	Entry standards	Teaching quality %	Student experience %	Graduate prospects %	Overall score
1 Exeter	50.8	427	90.4	95.6	74.7	100.0
2 Loughborough	52.1	418	85.3	91.5	80.1	99.4
3 Birmingham	63.7	383	83.4	89.5	81.5	99.0
4 Durham	28.7	430	94.2	93.9	73.3	97.7
5 Glasgow	42.3	470	76.4	87.8	75.0	96.8
6 Bath	54.0	409	79.3	86.7	76.0	96.5
7 Leeds	50.5	400	92.0	96.2	61.0	96.4
8 Edinburgh	26.1	412	83.0	87.7	86.6	96.2
9 Portsmouth	8.1	372	92.4	96.2	73.5	92.6
10 Liverpool John Moores	45.3	372	82.4	86.3	59.6	91.0
11 Swansea	38.8	348	73.3	83.7	76.6	90.5
=12 East Anglia	27.2	398	84.1	85.8	60.9	90.3
=12 Brunel	46.4	371	77.6	83.5	62.3	90.3
14 Robert Gordon	4.9	358	93.7	91.3	66.7	89.8
15 Stirling	33.6	372	80.7	89.7	60.3	89.7
16 Huddersfield		342	84.8	83.1	84.8	89.5
17 Bangor	30.6	336	83.1	90.3	64.9	89.4
18 Kent	21.0	365	77.8	80.5	74.7	89.1
19 Ulster	31.0	362	83.8	87.9	58.3	89.0
20 Aberdeen	34.7	403*	79.2	85.9	51.3	88.4
21 Coventry	4.5	322	89.2	88.8	70.3	87.8
22 Brighton	10.9	357	81.9	85.4	67.9	87.5
23 Oxford Brookes	3.0	378	84.8	93.3	59.5	87.2
24 Cardiff Metropolitan	7.7	360	82.5	88.5	64.8	87.1
=25 Nottingham Trent	7.3	331	87.6	88.9	63.9	86.8
=25 Salford	3.8	344	82.8	86.6	69.6	86.8
27 Chester	6.6	299	86.1	88.2	72.1	86.7
28 Hull	14.2	346	86.2	87.6	57.8	86.6
=29 Manchester Metropolitan	12.0	332	87.2	87.2	60.8	86.5
=29 Chichester	15.2	327	84.7	88.0	61.9	86.5

=31 Middlesex	10.0	299	78.0	78.0	81.2	86.1
=31 Southampton Solent	0.6	326	90.3	91.4	61.6	86.1
33 Hertfordshire	0.9	337	77.2	82.2	76.8	85.9
=34 Northumbria	4.4	376	84.6	88.5	55.1	85.7
=34 Worcester	4.9	334	80.8	87.6	67.0	85.7
=34 Glyndŵr	3.6	248	94.5	93.0	68.1	85.7
37 Leeds Beckett	12.6	328	80.7	87.8	61.7	85.3
38 Staffordshire	19.1	285	88.4	88.0	57.0	85.0
=39 Lincoln	11.4	353	77.1	79.3	64.2	84.9
=39 Bradford	9.5	354	77.4	84.0		84.9
=39 York St John	5.5	309	81.6	80.0	71.6	84.9
=42 Central Lancashire	5.1	334	85.7	90.2	55.8	84.6
=42 St Mary's, Twickenham	4.8	305	81.4	84.0	69.0	84.6
=42 Newman	2.8	327	90.5	88.7	54.0	84.6
45 Bedfordshire	6.7	260	86.7	88.6	68.4	84.5
46 Kingston	2.6	278	95.4	95.9	53.9	84.4
=47 Essex	25.8	323	72.8	82.4	61.1	84.2
=47 Sheffield Hallam	8.5	353	80.5	84.5	56.6	84.2
49 Bournemouth	9.0	337	74.8	81.4	65.8	84.0
50 Cumbria	3.2	265	87.7	85.1	67.8	83.9
51 Canterbury Christ Church	19.0	291	86.7	88.4	51.6	83.8
52 Bolton		309	81.8	71.3	71.0	83.1
53 Greenwich	7.4	338	79.9	82.0	55.9	82.9
54 Leeds Trinity	0.8	292	86.8	88.4	56.5	82.6
55 Edinburgh Napier	5.3	369	76.2	82.3	52.7	82.5
=56 Gloucestershire	6.0	349	78.3	83.2	53.0	82.4
=56 Liverpool Hope	10.9	291	91.6	93.2	42.2	82.4
58 St Mark and St John		353	75.6	77.8	61.2	82.3
=59 Abertay	8.9	311	72.4	85.2	62.1	82.1
=59 London South Bank	35.0	202	85.1	85.0	55.0	82.1
=61 Roehampton	20.6	297	69.5	69.7	68.9	81.9
=61 Bishop Grosseteste		269	80.5	81.1	69.2	81.9
=63 Sunderland	2.4	309	84.0	86.3	51.8	81.6
=63 Derby	1.7	291	85.4	85.3	54.6	81.6
65 South Wales	10.8	326	75.4	85.0	52.5	81.5
66 Winchester		270	80.7	81.9	65.4	81.3
67 Teesside	2.4	310	82.3	83.7	52.7	81.1
=68 Edge Hill	7.7	344	79.8	82.3	45.4	81.0
=68 Aberystwyth	23.5	295	79.8	81.5	45.7	81.0
70 West of Scotland	9.1	290	80.8	78.6	54.6	80.7
71 Northampton		279	76.6	81.5	61.3	79.9
72 Plymouth		302*	86.2	85.3	42.5	79.4
73 Anglia Ruskin		262	75.9	80.8	60.0	78.7
74 West of England		307*	68.4	67.1	64.7	78.3
75 East London	7.6	313	66.0	73.7	56.1	77.9
76 Buckinghamshire New	0.9	222	78.9	81.7	51.8	76.1
77 London Metropolitan		257	70.9	72.3	54.3	75.2

Sports Science cont

Employed in professional job:	39%	Employed in non-professional job and studying:	3%
Employed in professional job and studying:	4%	Employed in non-professional job:	31%
Studying:	14%	Unemployed:	8%
Average starting professional salary:	£18,753	Average starting non-professional salary:	£14,677

Theology and Religious Studies

The table for theology and religious studies shows its sixth change of leadership in as many years. Cambridge has taken over from Durham again, although there is only half a point between them. Cambridge has the highest entry standards and the best graduate prospects, while Durham achieved the best results in the Research Excellence Framework, as it did in the previous assessments, in 2008. Exeter again has the most satisfied students. This is one of the few subjects in which final-year undergraduates are more satisfied with the teaching, feedback and academic support that they had received than with the broader student experience. Theology and religious studies produce high levels of satisfaction in general, with Exeter's rating of almost 99 per cent in the teaching sections among the highest in any subject. Competition is particularly keen in Scotland, which has four of the top 10 universities, led by St Andrews, in third place.

By no means all graduates go into the church, but the vocation has helped to maintain relatively healthy employment records up to now. The two subjects remain in the top 40 in both the employment and earnings tables. Nearly a third of those completing courses take postgraduate degrees, either full or part-time.

Some 1,100 students began degrees in theology or religious studies in 2014 – slightly more than in the previous year, but still well short of the totals before higher fees were introduced. Applications have dropped by more than a quarter in that time and there are now little more than four to the place. Nevertheless, 55 universities and colleges – three more than this year – plan to offer courses in the subjects in 2016. Of the 38 institutions in the current table, 15 are post-1992 universities, but Chester is the only one to reach the top half of the ranking.

Theology and Religious Studies	Research quality %	Entry standards	Teaching quality %	Student experience %	Graduate prospects %	Overall score
1 Cambridge	44.6	515	87.1	87.9	84.7	100.0
2 Durham	56.6	475	84.9	89.8	80.1	99.5
3 St Andrews	28.9	502	92.4	93.3	83.2	98.8
=4 Exeter	38.9	430	98.6	97.6	74.3	98.4
=4 Oxford	46.7	499	82.6	88.3	82.3	98.4
6 Edinburgh	43.2	424	87.3	89.0	84.0	97.1
7 Nottingham	43.9	400	85.5	84.3	83.1	95.3
8 Aberdeen	39.9	418	83.6	94.1	72.0	93.9
9 Birmingham	36.2	364	89.0	91.0	73.0	92.7
10 Glasgow	21.4	464	89.6	89.1	66.7	92.2
11 Sheffield	25.3	434	81.2	79.4	81.1	91.5
12 Lancaster	53.0	422	72.5	75.3	73.1	91.4
13 Leeds	44.4	370	87.3	89.0	60.9	91.2

14	King's College London	37.1	412	84.7	80.3	66.2	90.7
15	Bristol	36.0	402	77.0	74.6	77.0	89.8
16	Manchester	37.2	397	82.7	82.7	62.2	89.4
17	Cardiff	33.5	370	81.8	75.2	72.5	88.8
18	Kent	44.1	341	84.8	84.0	58.1	88.6
19	Chester	11.1	287	96.9	90.5	72.3	88.1
20	Liverpool Hope	17.7	324	92.3	87.6	64.9	87.4
21	Oxford Brookes		311	91.5	80.8	73.1	84.9
22	Heythrop College	14.0	287	86.8	86.8	63.7	84.2
23	SOAS, London	34.1	357	76.0	77.3	55.2	84.1
24	Gloucestershire	6.9	296	90.6	91.8	57.7	83.7
=25	Stirling	29.8		83.8	81.5	50.7	83.2
=25	Cumbria		256	88.7	89.5	70.5	83.2
=27	Canterbury Christ Church	16.3	281	85.7	80.5	61.5	82.9
=27	Roehampton	24.3	290	81.5	77.5	60.4	82.9
29	Bath Spa	8.3	309	98.4	88.2	43.1	82.8
30	Newman	3.5	261	90.8	84.8	61.1	81.9
31	Winchester	18.0	301	78.5	72.2	63.7	81.5
32	Chichester		273	95.2	92.8	48.9	81.4
33	York St John	4.8	274	89.0	86.7	52.5	80.7
34	St Mary's, Twickenham	9.4	259	82.8	81.0	57.3	79.8
35	Queen's, Belfast		343	75.0	73.2	58.7	78.3
36	Hull	14.3		74.5	85.8	42.0	75.9
37	South Wales		280*	76.2	78.5	50.0	75.7
38	Leeds Trinity	9.9	275	73.4	81.5	40.7	75.1

Employed in professional job:	33%	Employed in non-professional job and studying:	3%
Employed in professional job and studying:	5%	Employed in non-professional job:	23%
Studying:	24%	Unemployed:	10%
Average starting professional salary:	£20,476	Average starting non-professional salary:	£14,763

Town and Country Planning and Landscape

Two-thirds of graduates in the planning and landscape groups go straight into professional jobs, placing the subjects in the top 15 in the employment table. But enrolments have fallen for six years in a row. The demand for places began to decline after the 2008 recession, but there were signs of a recovery before the introduction of £9,000 fees. Numbers have held up better in landscape and garden design than in the planning courses, but less than 200 students started landscape courses in 2014. Cambridge continues to have a big lead over Cardiff at the top of the table, with the highest entry standards and good scores on the other indicators. Cardiff has the best employment score, fractionally ahead of Gloucestershire, which has the most satisfied students and remains the top post-1992 institution, in fifth place. Loughborough, which has moved up seven places to third in the table, achieved the best results in the Research Excellence Framework.

Over 40 universities and colleges are offering courses in landscape or garden design in 2016, some of them as an element of a broader degree in geography or architecture. About 70 are expecting to run courses in various areas of planning, including disaster management and

Town and Country Planning and Landscape cont

emergency planning, rural enterprise and land management, and coastal safety management.

Starting salaries vary by course as well as by university, but the average in professional jobs has risen by more nearly £1,700 over the last two years. Four universities in 2014 – Cambridge, Cardiff, Gloucestershire and the Royal Agricultural University – saw more than nine out of ten graduates go straight into professional jobs or continue studying, compared with two last year, but the proportion at bottom two universities is below 60 per cent.

Town and Country Planning and Landscape	Research quality %	Entry standards	Teaching quality %	Student experience %	Graduate prospects %	Overall score
1 Cambridge	49.0	561	82.9	90.7	90.2	100.0
2 Cardiff	36.8	398	85.3	90.6	91.4	93.1
3 Loughborough	58.3	365	81.4	83.9	87.9	92.8
4 Sheffield	36.6	405	88.6	89.6	84.5	92.2
5 Gloucestershire	20.6	309	98.9	96.6	91.3	90.8
=6 Queen's, Belfast	35.2	314	95.4	95.6	84.3	90.7
=6 Newcastle	43.7	347	84.7	84.7	87.9	90.7
8 Reading	40.0	393	83.4	86.0		90.6
9 University College London	54.1	493	67.2	76.0	74.2	89.9
10 Birmingham	42.0	385	75.5	74.5	89.1	89.2
11 Liverpool	26.3		86.0	88.6	79.4	87.9
12 Manchester	36.5	355	87.1	88.3	74.7	87.7
13 Heriot-Watt	38.1	376	79.1	83.2	78.0	87.4
14 Royal Agricultural University		336*	88.8	89.5	90.5	85.9
15 Dundee	8.7		77.6	84.6	89.2	85.7
16 Oxford Brookes	17.6	335	79.1	83.7	86.7	85.0
17 West of England	10.6	323	81.4	85.0	84.8	83.7
18 Edinburgh	35.1	426	64.5	63.6	76.9	83.6
19 Northumbria	5.9	334*	81.6	83.6	82.4	82.7
20 Ulster	28.6	260	91.7	92.5	64.5	82.1
21 Nottingham Trent	3.4	298	77.5	80.3	82.5	79.9
=22 Manchester Metropolitan	9.7	334	75.8	80.0	73.3	79.7
=22 Glasgow Caledonian	9.1	322	80.0	87.9	68.8	79.7
24 Leeds Beckett	5.6	271	87.2	88.2	70.4	79.2
25 Aberdeen	40.6		63.2	74.8	73.3	79.0
26 Sheffield Hallam	13.4	298	78.2	85.5	67.6	78.6
27 Birmingham City	2.7	247	84.3	76.1	70.0	75.9
28 Westminster	10.7	312	64.7	77.6	52.7	71.8
29 Greenwich	2.0		71.4	67.3	54.5	67.9

Employed in professional job:	61%	Employed in non-professional job and studying:	1%
Employed in professional job and studying:	6%	Employed in non-professional job:	11%
Studying:	11%	Unemployed:	9%
Average starting professional salary:	£21,960	Average starting non-professional salary:	£15,741

Veterinary Medicine

Only medicine itself has higher entry standards than veterinary medicine, where successful candidates had an average of 518 points in 2014 and there were more than eight applications for every place. An eighth veterinary school opened in 2013 at the University of Surrey, but it will be several years before there are enough data to include it in this table. Nottingham was the last newcomer, opening in 2006, and it has already enjoyed the last three years at the top of the table, before dropping to fourth this year. Nottingham still has the most satisfied students, but Cambridge has taken over the leadership, partly because it has much the highest entry grades. Edinburgh, in second place, achieved the best results in the Research Excellence Framework, as it did in the 2008 assessments.

Veterinary medicine is another of the rankings in which employment scores have been removed from the calculations that determine universities' positions. The scores are still shown in the table, but the review group of academic planners consulted on the *Guide* agreed that employment rates in the subject were so tightly bunched that small differences could distort the overall ranking. Veterinary medicine is back in the top five in the employment table this year, but is still only seventh for earnings in professional jobs, despite average salaries of more than £26,000 in 2014.

Applications were down a little in 2014, but the number of places is centrally controlled. Most courses demand high grades in chemistry and biology, with some accepting physics or maths as one alternative subject. Cambridge and the Royal Veterinary College also set applicants a specialist aptitude test that is used by a number of medical schools. Few candidates win places without evidence of practical commitment to the subject through work experience, either in veterinary practices or laboratories. The norm for veterinary science degrees is five years, but the Cambridge course takes six years and both Bristol and Nottingham offer a "pre-veterinary" year. Both Edinburgh and the Royal Veterinary College run four-year courses for graduates. There are no degrees in the subject in Wales or Northern Ireland, or in the post-1992 universities, although a number of them and several colleges offer veterinary nursing.

Veterinary Medicine	Research quality %	Entry standards	Teaching quality %	Student experience %	Graduate prospects %	Overall score
1 Cambridge	43.1	611	79.9	84.9	97.3	100.0
2 Edinburgh	46.8	529	80.1	81.4	96.8	97.1
3 Glasgow	42.3	541	81.4	84.8	94.3	96.7
4 Nottingham	36.4	466	89.9	94.9	94.6	95.5
5 Royal Veterinary College	40.8	499	79.0	86.6	93.4	93.2
6 Bristol	33.2	519	81.1	87.3	89.0	91.6
7 Liverpool	32.9	463	76.9	80.5	98.2	85.8

Employed in professional job:	92%	Employed in non-professional job and studying:	0%
Employed in professional job and studying:	1%	Employed in non-professional job:	1%
Studying:	2%	Unemployed:	4%
Average starting professional salary:	£26,071	Average starting non-professional salary:	n/a

The top university for each subject covered in *The Times and Sunday Times Guide*

Cambridge	Aeronautical and Manufacturing Engineering
	Anatomy and Physiology
	Anthropology
	Archaeology
	Architecture
	Biological Sciences
	Celtic Studies
	Chemical Engineering
	Chemistry
	Civil Engineering
	Classics and Ancient History
	East and South Asian Studies
	Electrical and Electronic Engineering
	French
	General Engineering
	German
	History
	History of Art, Architecture and Design
	Iberian Languages
	Italian
	Land and Property Management
	Law
	Linguistics
	Materials Technology
	Mathematics
	Mechanical Engineering
	Pharmacology and Pharmacy
	Philosophy
	Physics and Astronomy
	Psychology
	Russian and East European Languages
	Sociology
	Theology and Religious Studies
	Town and Country Planning and Landscape
	Veterinary Medicine
Oxford	Art and Design
	Computer Science
	Economics
	Geography and Environmental Sciences
	Mathematics
	Medicine
	Music
	Politics
Birmingham	Drama, Dance and Cinematics
	Hospitality, Leisure, Recreation and Tourism
	Middle Eastern and African Studies
Glasgow	Education
	Nursing
	Social Work
Surrey	Animal Science
	Food Science
Aston	Other Subjects Allied to Medicine
Bangor	Radiography
Bath	Business Studies
Cardiff	Dentistry
Durham	English
Exeter	Sports Science
Imperial College	Geology
Lancaster	Communication and Media Studies
Leeds	Accounting and Finance
London School of Economics	Social Policy
Loughborough	Librarianship and Information Management
Reading	Agriculture and Forestry
Sheffield	Drama, Dance and Cinematics
Southampton	Physiotherapy
Sussex	American Studies
University College London	Building
Warwick	Creative Writing

6 Making Your Application

There will be nothing you can do about your grades once you have taken your exams, but making your application is firmly under your own control – and much more important than many students realise. The art of conveying knowledge of, and enthusiasm for, your chosen subject – preferably with supporting evidence from your school or college – can make all the difference.

Too many people take their eye off the ball when actually applying for a higher education place. Surprising numbers of applicants each year spell their own name wrongly, or enter an inaccurate date of birth, or the wrong course code. And that is to say nothing of the damage that can be done in the personal statement and teachers' references. While UCAS will decode misspelt names, other errors in grammar or spelling present admissions officers with an easy starting point in cutting applications down to a more manageable number.

There is renewed support for a change of system to one in which applications are made after students have their results, but for the moment decisions have to be made well before that point. You will be able to make up to five choices, although you do not have to use all five if you do not want to. Some people make only a single application, perhaps because they do not want to leave home or they have very particular requirements – but you will give yourself the best chance of success if you go for the maximum.

A number of relatively minor changes were made to UCAS procedures for entry in 2014, but no more are planned for 2016. Perhaps the most important recent change allowed candidates to submit a new personal statement if their initial applications are unsuccessful and they use the UCAS Extra process. This and other changes are outlined below.

The application process

Most applications for full-time higher education courses go through UCAS, although there is still a different process for the music conservatoires. The trend is towards the UCAS model even among specialist providers, however: recruitment to nursing and midwifery diploma and degree courses in Scotland switched to the UCAS system in 2010, and the art and design courses that used to recruit using the separate "Route B" scheme have also moved to the main system.

Some universities that have not filled all their places, even during Clearing, will accept direct applications up to and sometimes after the start of the academic year, but UCAS is both the official route and the only way into the most popular courses.

All UCAS applications are made online. The Apply electronic system is accessed via the UCAS website and is straightforward to use. For those who do not have the internet at home and prefer not to use school or college computers, the UCAS website lists libraries all over the UK where you can make your application. Apply is available 24 hours a day, and, when the time comes, information on the progress of your application may arrive at any time.

Registering with Apply

The first step in the process is to register. If you are at a school or college, you will need to obtain a "buzzword" from your tutor or careers adviser – it is used when you log on to register. It links your application to the school or college so that the application can be sent electronically to your referee (usually one of your teachers) for your reference to be attached. If you are no longer at a school or college, you do not need a "buzzword", but you will need details of your referee. More information is given on the UCAS website.

To register, go to the UCAS website and click on "Apply". The system will guide you through the business of providing your personal details and generating a username and password, as well as reminding you of basic points, such as amending your details in case of a change of address. You can register separate term-time and holiday addresses – a useful option for boarders, who could find offers and, particularly, the confirmation of a place, going to their school when they are miles away at home. Remember to keep a note of your username and password in a safe place.

Throughout the process, you will be in sole control of communications with UCAS and your chosen universities. Only if you nominate a representative and give them your unique nine-digit application number (sent automatically by UCAS when your application is submitted), can a parent or anyone else give or receive information on your behalf, perhaps because you are ill or out of the country.

Improved video guides on the application process are available on the UCAS website. Once you are registered, you can start to complete the Apply screens. The sections that follow cover the main screens.

Personal details

This information is taken from your initial registration, and you will be asked for additional information, for example, on ethnic origin and national identity, to monitor equal opportunities in the application process. UK students will also be asked to complete a student finance section designed to speed up any loan application you might make.

The main screens to be completed in UCAS Apply

- » Personal and contact details and some additional non-educational details for UK applicants.
- » Student finance, a section for UK-resident applicants.
- » Your course choices.
- » Details of your education so far, including examination results and examinations still to be taken.
- » Details of any jobs you have done.
- » Your personal statement.
- » A reference from one of your teachers.
- » Payment details (applications cost £23, or £12 to apply to just one course).
- » A declaration that you confirm that the information is correct and that you will be bound by the UCAS rules.

Choices

In most subjects, you will be able to apply to a maximum of five universities and/or colleges. The exceptions are medicine, dentistry and veterinary science, where the maximum is four, but you can use your fifth choice as a back-up to apply for a different subject.

The other important restriction concerns Oxford or Cambridge, because you can only apply to one or the other; you cannot apply to both Oxford and Cambridge in the same year, nor can you apply for more than one course. For both universities you may need to take a written test (see pages 20–21) and submit examples of your work, depending on the course selected. In addition, for Cambridge, you will be asked to complete an online Supplementary Application Questionnaire once the university has received your application from UCAS. The deadline for Oxbridge applications – and for all medicine, dentistry and veterinary science courses – is 15 October. For all other applications the deadline is 15 January (or 24 March for some specified art and design courses). The other exceptions to this rule are the small but growing number of courses that start in January or February. If you are considering one of these, contact the university concerned for application deadlines.

Most applicants use all five choices. But if you do choose fewer than five courses, you can still add another to your form up to 30 June, as long as you have not accepted or declined any offers. Nor do you have to choose five different universities if more than one course at the same institution attracts you – perhaps because the institution itself is the real draw and one course has lower entrance requirements than the other. Universities are not allowed to see where else you have applied, or whether you have chosen the same subject elsewhere. But they will be aware of multiple applications within their own institution. Remember that it is more difficult to write a convincing personal statement if it has to cover two subjects.

For each course you select, you will need to put the UCAS code on the form – and you should check carefully that you have the correct code and understand any special requirements that may be detailed on the UCAS description of the course. It does not matter what order you enter in your choices as all your choices are treated equally. You will also need to indicate whether you are applying for a deferred entry (for example, if you are taking a gap year – see page 211).

Education

In this section you will need to give details of the schools and colleges you have attended, and the qualifications you have obtained or are preparing for. The UCAS website gives plenty of advice on the ways in which you should enter this information, to ensure that all your relevant qualifications are included with their grades. While UCAS does not need to see qualification certificates, it can double-check results with the examination boards to ensure that no one is tempted to modify their results.

In the Employment section that follows, add details of any paid jobs you have had (unpaid or voluntary work should be mentioned in your personal statement).

Personal statement

As the competition for places on popular courses has become more intense, so the value attached to the personal statement has increased. Admissions officers look for a sign of potential beyond the high grades that growing numbers of applicants offer. Many academics responsible for admissions value success in extracurricular activities such as drama, sport or the Duke of Edinburgh's Award scheme. But your first priority should be to demonstrate an enthusiasm for and understanding of your subject beyond the confines of the exam syllabus.

This is not easy in a relatively short statement that can readily sound trite or pretentious. You should resist any temptation to exaggerate, let alone lie, particularly if there is any chance of an interview. A claim to have been inspired by a book that you have not read will backfire instantly under questioning and, even without an interview, experienced academics are likely to see through grandiose statements that appear at odds with a teacher's reference.

Genuine experiences of after-hours clubs, lectures or visits, work experience or actual reading around the syllabus are much more likely to strike the right note. If you are applying for medicine, for example, any practical work experience or volunteering in medical or caring settings should be included. Take advice from teachers and, if there is still time before you make your application, look for some subject-related activities that will help fill out your statement.

Admissions officers are also looking for evidence of character that will make you a productive member of their university and, eventually, a successful graduate. Taking responsibility in any area of school or college life suggests this – leading activities outside your place of learning even more so. Evidence of initiative and self-discipline is also valuable, since higher education involves much more independent study than sixth-formers are used to.

UCAS top ten personal statement tips

1. Express interest in the subject and show real passion.
2. Go for a strong opening line to grab the reader's attention.
3. Relate outside interests to the course.
4. Think beyond university.
5. Get the basics right.
6. Don't try to sound too clever.
7. Take time and make it your best work.
8. Don't leave it until the last minute – remember the 15 January deadline!
9. Get a second opinion.
10. Honesty is the best policy

Your overall aim in writing your personal statement is to persuade the admissions officer to pick yours out from the piles of applications. That means trying to stand out from an often rather dull and uniform set of statements based around the curriculum and the more predictable sixth-form activities. Everyone is going to say they love reading, for example; narrow your interest down to an area of (real) interest. Don't be afraid to include the unusual, but bear in mind that an academic's sense of humour may not be the same as yours.

Give particular thought to why you want to study your chosen subject – especially if it is not one you have taken at school or college. You need to show that your interests and skills are well suited to the course and, if it is a vocational degree, that you know how you envisage using the qualification. Admissions officers want to feel that you will be committed to their subject for the length of the course, which could be three, four or even five years, and capable of achieving good results. If your five choices cover more than one subject, be careful not to focus too much on one; try to make more general comments on your academic strengths and enthusiasms. And, since the same statement goes to all your chosen departments, avoid expressing any preference for an individual institution.

Your school or college should be the best source of advice, since they see personal statements every year, but there are others. The UCAS website has a useful checklist of themes that you may wish to address, while sites such as **www.studential.com** also provide tips. But do not fall into the trap of cutting and pasting from the model statements included on such sites – both UCAS and individual universities have software that will spot plagiarism immediately. In one year, no fewer than one in 20 applicants came to grief in this way. Plagiarists of this type are unlikely to be disqualified, but they destroy the credibility of their application.

Try not to cram in more than the limited space will allow – admissions officers will have many statements to go through, and judicious editing may be rewarded. As long as you write clearly – preferably in paragraphs and possibly with sub-headings – it will be up to you what to include. It is a *personal* statement. But consider the points listed below and make sure that you can answer all the questions raised. Once you have completed your statement show it to others you trust. It is really important to have others read your statement before submitting it – sometimes things that are clear to you may not be to fresh eyes.

The Apply system allows 4,000 characters (including spaces) or 47 lines for your statement. While there is no requirement to fill all the space, it should not look embarrassingly short. Indeed, from 2014, your statement has had to be at least 1,000 characters long. It is hard to believe that many candidates could not rustle up 200 words to support their application, but presumably significant numbers were not doing so. UCAS recommends using a word-processing package to compile the statement before pasting it into the application system. This is because Apply will time-out after 35 minutes of inactivity, so there is a danger of losing valuable material. Working offline also has the advantage of leaving you with a copy and making it easier to show it to others.

References

Hand in hand with your personal statement goes the reference from your school, college or, in the case of mature students, someone who knows you well, but is not a friend or family member. Since 2014, even referees who are not your teachers have been encouraged to predict your grades, although they are allowed to opt out of this process. Whatever the source, the reference has to be independent – you are specifically forbidden to change any part of it if you send off your own application – but that does not mean you should not try to influence what it contains.

Most schools and colleges conduct informal interviews before compiling a reference, but it does no harm to draw up a list of the achievements that you would like to see included, and ensure your referee knows what subject you are applying for. Referees cannot know every detail of a candidate's interests and most welcome an aide-memoire.

The UCAS guidelines skirt around the candidate's right to see his or her reference, but it does exist. Schools' practices vary, but most now show the applicant the completed reference. Where this is not the case, the candidate can pay UCAS £10 for a copy, although at this stage it is obviously too late to influence the contents. Better, if you can, to see it before it goes off, in case there are factual inaccuracies that can be corrected.

Key points to consider in writing your personal statement

- What attracts you to this subject (or subjects, in the case of dual or combined honours)?
- Have you undertaken relevant work experience or voluntary activities, either through school or elsewhere?
- Have you taken part in other extra-curricular activities that demonstrate character – perhaps as a prefect, on the sports field or in the arts?
- Have you been involved in other academic pursuits, such as Gifted and Talented programmes, widening participation schemes, or courses in other subjects?
- Which aspects of your current courses have you found particularly stimulating?
- Are you planning a gap year? If so, explain what you intend to do and how it will affect your studies. Some subjects – notably maths – actively discourage a break in studies.
- What other outside interests might you include that show that you are well-rounded?

Timetable for applications for university admission in 2016

2015	
May onwards	Find out about courses and universities. Attend open days.
early July	Registration starts for UCAS Apply.
mid September	UCAS starts receiving applications.
15 October	Final day for applications to Oxford and Cambridge, and for most courses in medicine, dentistry and veterinary science.
2016	
15 January	Final day for all other applications from UK and EU students including all art and design courses except those which have a 24 March deadline (specified in UCAS Course Search).
16 January–30 June	New applications continue to be accepted by UCAS, but only considered by universities if the relevant courses have vacancies.
25 February	Start of applications through UCAS Extra.
24 March	Final day for applications to art and design courses that specify this date.
31 March	Universities should have sent decisions on all applications received by 15 January.
4 May	Final day by which applicants have to decide on their choices if all decisions received by 31 March (exact date for each applicant will be confirmed by UCAS). **If you do not reply to UCAS, they will decline your offers.**
5 May	UCAS must have received all decisions from universities if you applied by 15 January.
8 June	Final day by which applicants have to decide on their choices if all decisions received by 5 May .
23 June	Final day by which applicants have to decide on their choices if all decisions received by 8 June.
1 July	Any new application received from this date held until Clearing starts.
4 July	Final day for applications through UCAS Extra.
5 July	International Baccalaureate results published.
14 July	Universities must give decisions on all applications submitted by 30 June. You must make a decision on these offers by 22 July.
9 August	SQA results published. Scottish Clearing starts.
18 August	A level results published. Full Clearing and Adjustment starts.
31 August	Adjustment closes. Last date for you to meet any offer conditions, after which university might not accept you.
20 September	Last day UCAS will accept applications for courses about to start.
30 September	Clearing vacancy search closes. You can still use Track, but contact universities first to find vacancies.
20 October	Last date for adding Clearing choices and last date on which a university can accept you through Clearing.

Timing

The general deadline for applications through UCAS is 15 January, but even those received up to 30 June will be considered if the relevant courses still have vacancies. After that, you will be limited to Clearing, or an application for the following year. In theory – and usually in practice – all applications submitted by the January deadline are given equal consideration. But the best advice is to get your application in early: before Christmas, or earlier if possible. Applications are accepted from mid-September onwards, so the autumn half-term is a sensible target date for completing the process. Although no formal offers are made before the deadline, many admissions officers look through applications as they come in and may make a mental note of promising candidates. If your form arrives with the deadline looming, you may appear less organised than those who submitted in good time; and your application may be one of a large batch that receives a more cursory first reading than the early arrivals. Under UCAS rules, last-minute applicants should not be at a disadvantage, but why take the risk?

Next steps

Once your application has been processed by UCAS, you will receive an email confirming that your application has been sent to your university choices and summarising what will happen next. The email will also confirm your Personal ID, which you can use to access "Track", the online system that allows you to follow the progress of your application. Check all the details carefully: you have 14 days to contact UCAS to correct any errors. Universities can make direct contact with you through Track, including arranging interviews.

After that, it is just a matter of waiting for universities to make their decisions, which can take days, weeks or even months, depending on the university and the course. Some obviously see an advantage in being the first to make an offer – it is a memorable moment to be reassured that at least one of your chosen institutions wants you – and may send their response almost immediately. Others take much longer, perhaps because they have so many good applications to consider, or maybe because they are waiting to see which of their applicants withdraw when Oxford and Cambridge make their offers. Universities are asked to make all their decisions by the end of March, and most have done so long before that.

Interviews

Unless you are applying for a course in health or education that brings you into direct contact with the public, the chances are you will not have a selection interview. For prospective medics, vets, dentists or teachers, a face-to-face assessment of your suitability will be crucial to your chances of success. Likewise in the performing arts, the interview may be as important as your exam grades. Oxford and Cambridge still interview applicants in all subjects, and a few of the top universities see a significant proportion. But the expansion of higher education has made it impractical to interview everyone, and many admissions experts are sceptical about interviews.

What has become more common, however, is the "sales" interview, where the university is really selling itself to the candidate. There may still be testing questions, but the admissions staff have already made their minds up and are actually trying to persuade you to accept an offer. Indeed, you will probably be given a clear indication at the end of the interview that an offer is on its way. The technique seems to work, perhaps because you have invested time and nervous energy in a sometimes lengthy trip, as well as acquiring a more detailed impression of both the department and the university.

The difficulty can come in spotting which type of interview is which. The "real" ones require lengthy preparation, revisiting your personal statement and reading beyond the exam syllabus. Impressions count for a lot, so dress smartly and make sure that you are on time. Have a question of your own ready, as well as being prepared to give answers.

While you would not want to appear ignorant at a "sales" interview, lengthy preparation might be a waste of valuable time during a period of revision. Naturally, you should err on the side of caution, but if your predicted grades are well above the standard offer and the subject is not one that normally requires an interview, it is likely that the invitation is a sales pitch. It is still worth going, unless you have changed your mind about the application.

Offers

When your chosen universities respond to your application, there will be one of three answers:

- Unconditional Offer (U): This used to be a possibility only if you applied after satisfying the entrance requirements – usually if you are applying as a mature student, while on a gap year, after resitting exams or, in Scotland, after completing Highers. However, a growing number of universities competing for bright students have begun to make unconditional offers to those who are predicted high grades – just how high will depend on the university. If you are fortunate (and able) enough to receive one, do not assume that grades are no longer important because they may be taken into consideration when you apply for jobs as a graduate.
- Conditional Offer (C): The vast majority of students will still receive conditional offers, where each university offers a place subject to you achieving set grades or points on the UCAS tariff.
- Rejection (R): You do not have the right qualifications, or have lost out to stronger competition.

If you have chosen wisely, you should have more than one offer to choose from, so you will be required to pick your favourite as your firm acceptance – known as UF if it was an unconditional offer and CF if it was conditional. Candidates with conditional offers can also accept a second offer, with lower grades, as an Insurance choice (CI). You must then decline any other offers that you have.

You do not have to make an Insurance choice – indeed, you may decline all your offers if you have changed your mind about your career path or regret your course decisions. But most people prefer the security of a back-up route into higher education if their grades fall short. You must be sure that your firm acceptance is definitely your first choice because you will be allocated a place automatically if you meet the university's conditions. It is no good at this stage deciding that you prefer your Insurance choice because UCAS rules will not allow a switch.

The only way round those rules, unless your results are better than your highest offer (see Adjustment, below), is through direct contact with the universities concerned. Your firm acceptance institution has to be prepared to release you so that your new choice can award you a place in Clearing. Neither is under any obligation to do so but, in practice, it is rare for a university to insist that a student joins against his or her wishes. Admissions staff will do all they can to persuade you that your original choice was the right one – as it may well have been, if your research was thorough – but it will almost certainly be your decision in the end.

UCAS Extra

If things do go wrong and you receive five rejections, that need not be the end of your higher education ambitions. From the end of February until the end of June, you have another chance through UCAS Extra, a listing of courses that still have vacancies after the initial round of offers. Extra is sometimes dismissed (wrongly) as a repository of second-rate courses. In fact, even in the boom years for applications, most Russell Group universities still have courses listed in a wide variety of subjects.

You will be notified if you are eligible for Extra and can then select courses marked as available on the UCAS website. In order to assist students who choose different subjects after a full set of rejections in their original application, you will be able to submit a new personal statement for Extra. Applications are made, one at a time, through UCAS Track. If you do not receive an offer, or you choose to decline one, you can continue applying for other courses until you are successful. About half of those applying through Extra normally find a place. Some 7,600 were successful this way in 2014.

Results Day

Rule Number One on results day is to be at home, or at least in easy communication – you cannot afford to be on some remote beach if there are complications. The day is bound to be stressful, unless you are absolutely confident that you achieved the required grades – more of a possibility in an era of modular courses with marks along the way. But for thousands of students, Track has removed the agony of opening the envelope or scanning a results noticeboard. On the morning of A-level results day, the system informs those who have already won a place on their chosen course. You will not learn your grades until later, but at least your immediate future is clear.

If you get the grades stipulated in your conditional offer, the process should work smoothly and you can begin celebrating. Track will let you know as soon as your place is confirmed and the paperwork will arrive in a day or two. You can phone the university to make quite sure, but it should not be necessary and you will be joining a long queue of people doing the same thing.

If the results are not what you hoped – and particularly if you just miss your grades – you need to be on the phone and taking advice from your school or college. In a year when results are better than expected, some universities will stick to the letter of their offers, perhaps refusing to accept your AAC grades when they had demanded ABB. Others will forgive a dropped grade to take a candidate who is regarded as promising, rather than go into Clearing to recruit an unknown quantity. Admissions staff may be persuadable – particularly if there are extenuating personal circumstances, or the dropped grade is in a subject that is not relevant to your chosen course. Try to get a teacher to support your case, and be persistent if there is any prospect of flexibility.

If your results are lower than predicted, one option is to ask for papers to be re-marked, as growing numbers do each year. The school may ask for a whole batch to be re-marked, and you should ensure that your chosen universities know this if it may make the difference to whether or not you satisfy your offer. If your grades improve as a result, the university will review its decision, but if by then it has filled all its places, you may have to wait until next year to start.

If you took Scottish Highers, you will have had your results for more than a week by the time the A-level grades are published. If you missed your grades, there is no need to wait for A levels before you begin approaching universities. Admissions staff at English universities may not wish to commit themselves before they see results from south of the border, but Scottish universities will be filling places immediately and all should be prepared to give you an idea of your prospects.

Adjustment

If your grades are better than those demanded by your first-choice university, there is now an opportunity to "trade up". Introduced in 2009, the Adjustment Period runs from when you receive your results until 31 August, and you can only use it for five 24-hour periods during that period, so there is no time to waste. First, go into the Track system and click on "Register for Adjustment" and then contact your preferred institutions to find another place. If none is available, or you decide not to move, your initial offer will remain open. The number of students switching universities in this way slipped back slightly in 2014, but there were still 1,160 successful candidates. The process has become as established part of the system and, without the previous restrictions on the number of students they could recruit, many leading universities see it as a good source of talented undergraduates. UCAS does not publish a breakdown of which universities take part – some, such as Oxford and Cambridge, simply do not have places available – but it is known that many students successfully go back to institutions that had rejected them at the initial application stage. Even if you are eligible for Adjustment, you may decide to stick with the offer you have, but it is worth at least exploring your options.

Clearing

If you do not have a place on Results Day, there will still be plenty of options through the UCAS Clearing scheme. More than 60,000 people – about one successful applicant in nine – found a place through this route in 2014 and the numbers rose again in 2015. With recruitment restrictions lifted, universities that used to regard their absence from Clearing as a point of pride are appearing in the vacancy lists. It is likely that this trend will continue in 2016, as more universities seek to expand, particularly in arts, social science and business subjects.

Although the most popular courses may still fill up quickly, many remain open up to and beyond the start of the academic year. And, at least at the start of the process, the range of courses with vacancies is much wider than in Extra. Most universities will list some courses, and most subjects will be available somewhere.

Clearing runs from A-level Results Day until the end of September, matching students without places to full-time courses with vacancies. As long as you are not holding any offers and you have not withdrawn your application, you are eligible automatically. You will be sent a Clearing number via Track to quote to universities.

There are now two ways of entering Clearing: the traditional method of ringing universities that still have vacancies, or by using the system introduced this year which allows universities to approach candidates with suitable grades for one of their courses. You will be given the option of signing up for this service in an email from UCAS and issued with a code word to be used by universities contacting you on Results Day or subsequently. You will be approached by a maximum of five universities or colleges. UCAS advises students to approach universities themselves in any case, but the new system does add an extra string to their bow and may take some of the anxiety out of Clearing.

Assuming you are making your own approaches, the first step is to trawl through the lists on the UCAS website, and elsewhere, before ringing the university offering the course that appeals most, and where you have a realistic chance of a place – do not waste time on courses where the standard offer is far above your grades. Universities run Clearing hotlines and have become adept at dealing with a large number of calls in a short period, but you can still spend a long time on the phone at a time when the most desirable places are beginning to disappear. If you can't get through send an email setting out your grades and the course that interests you.

The best advice is to plan ahead and not to wait for Results Day to draw up a list of possible Clearing targets. Many universities publish lists of courses that are likely to be in Clearing on their websites from the start of August. Think again about some of the courses that you considered when making your original application, or others at your chosen universities that had lower entrance requirements. But beware of switching to another subject simply because you have the right grades – you still have to sustain your interest and be capable of succeeding over three or more years. Many of the students who drop out of degrees are those who chose the wrong course in a rush during Clearing.

In short, you should start your search straight away if you do find yourself in Clearing, and act decisively, but do not panic. You can make as many approaches as you like, until you are accepted on the course of your choice. Remember that if you changed your personal statement for applications in Extra, this will be the one that goes to any universities that you approach in Clearing, so it may be difficult to return to the subjects in your original application.

Most of the available vacancies will appear in Clearing lists, but some of the universities towards the top of the league tables may have a limited number of openings that they choose not to advertise – either for reasons of status or because they do not want the administrative burden of fielding large numbers of calls to fill a handful of places. If there is a course that you find particularly attractive – especially if you have good grades and are applying late – it may be worth making a speculative call. Sometimes a number of candidates holding offers drop grades and you may be on the spot at the right moment.

What are the alternatives?

If your results are lower than expected and there is nothing you want in Clearing, there are several things you can do. The first is to resit one or more subjects. The modular nature of most courses means that you will have a clear idea of what you need to do to get better grades. You can go back to school or college, or try a "crammer". Although some colleges have a good success rate with re-takes, you have to be highly focused and realistic about the likely improvements. Some of the most competitive courses, such as medicine, may demand higher grades for a second application, so be sure you know the details before you commit yourself.

Other options are to get a job and study part-time, or to take a break from studying and return later in your career. The part-time route can be arduous – many young people find a job enough to handle without the extra burden of academic work. But others find it just the combination they need for a fulfilling life. It all depends on your job, your social life and your commitment to the subject you will study. It may be that a relatively short break is all that you need to rekindle your enthusiasm for studying. Many universities now have a majority of mature students, so you need not be out of place if this is your chosen route.

Taking a gap year

The other popular option is to take a gap year. In most years, about 7 per cent of applicants defer their entry until the following year while they travel, or do voluntary or paid work. A whole industry has grown up around tailor-made activities, many of them in Asia, Africa or Latin America. Some have been criticised for doing more for the organisers than the underprivileged communities that they purport to assist, but there are programmes that are useful and character-building, as well as safe. Most of the overseas programmes are not cheap, but raising the money can be part of the experience.

Various organisations can help you find voluntary work. Some examples include vInspired (**www.vinspired.com**), Lattitude Global Volunteering (**www.lattitude.org.uk**) and Volunteer Africa (**www.volunteerafrica.org**). Voluntary Service Overseas (**www.vsointernational.org.uk**) works mainly with older volunteers but has an offshoot, run with five other volunteering organisations, International Citizen Service (**www.volunteerics.org**), that places 18–25-year-olds around the world.

The alternative is to stay closer to home and make your contribution through organisations like Volunteering Matters (**http://volunteeringmatters.org.uk**) or to take a job that will make higher education more affordable when the time comes. Work placements can be casual or structured, such as the Year in Industry Scheme (**www.etrust.org.uk**). Sponsorship is also available, mainly to those wishing to study science, engineering or business. Buyer beware: we cannot vouch for any of these and you need to be clear whether the aim is to make money or to plump up your CV. If it is the second, you may end up spending money, not saving it.

Many admissions staff are happy to facilitate gap years because they think it makes for more mature, rounded students than those who come straight from school. The longer-term benefits may also be an advantage in the graduate employment market. Both university admissions officers and employers look for evidence that candidates have more about them than academic ability. The experience you gain on a gap year can help you develop many of the attributes they are looking for, such as interpersonal, organisational and teamwork skills, leadership, creativity, experience of new cultures or work environments, and enterprise.

There are subjects – maths in particular – that discourage a break because it takes too long to pick up study skills where you left off. From the student's point of view, you should also bear in mind that a gap year postpones the moment at which you embark on a career. This may be important if your course is a long one, such as medicine or architecture.

If you are considering a gap year, it makes sense to apply for a deferred place, rather than waiting for your results before applying. The application form has a section for deferments. That allows you to sort out your immediate future before you start travelling or working, and leaves you the option of changing your mind if circumstances change.

Useful websites

The essential website for making an application is, of course, that of UCAS:
www.ucas.com/ucas/undergraduate/apply-and-track
For applications to music conservatoires: **www.ucas.com/ucas/conservatoires**
For advice on your personal statement:
www.ucas.com/ucas/after-gcses/apply/writing-personal-statement

Gap years

To help you consider options and start planning: **www.gapadvice.org**
For links to volunteering opportunities in the UK: **www.do-it.org.uk**
For links to many gap year organisations: **www.yearoutgroup.org**
Also see above.

7 University Tuition Fees

The introduction of a maximum fee of £9,000 never produced as much variation as ministers expected, but any there was will have practically disappeared when students start courses in 2016. None of the English or Welsh institutions in our table will charge less than £9,000 for Honours degree courses, although bursaries and fee waivers will bring the actual cost down for those from low-income families. University College Birmingham is the only university to have set a lower maximum fee, settling for £8,830, but leaving itself less scope for reductions for poor students as a result. After 2016, fees will rise for the first time since 2012 – something to bear in mind when considering whether to defer a place by a year – but the increase will be no more than inflation.

Bursaries, scholarships and fee waivers mean that the average fees charged in England, let alone other parts of the UK, will vary much more widely than media reporting might suggest. But this only matters to those who qualify for one of the awards, usually by virtue of family income or their academic performance; most students will pay the maximum. For the record, the average fee for UK and European Union undergraduates at higher education institutions, when all forms of financial support are taken into account, will be £8,487. It will range from £7,767 at Sunderland to £8,984 at Middlesex. Some further education colleges will still be offering average fees of less than £6,000 after accounting for financial support.

This *Guide* quotes the higher headline fees, but even these will vary according to whether you are from inside or outside the EU, studying full-time or part-time, and whether you are taking a Foundation degree or an Honours programme. Non-European medical students may pay as much as £35,000 a year, Britons taking part-time Foundation degrees as little as £3,500. But all the attention has been focused on full-time Honours degrees for British and other EU undergraduates because those are the courses for which the maximum fees shot up to £9,000 in 2012.

Fees and loans

Student numbers dropped in the first year of higher fees, but prospective students long since appear to have resigned themselves to the new charges. Both applications and enrolments rose in 2014 and are up by another 3 per cent this year. There is little sign that applicants are basing their choices on the marginal differences in fee levels at different universities, and numbers from the poorest socio-economic groups are at record levels – albeit still severely under-represented compared with more affluent groups. Concern remains, however, over the impact on part-time courses and, in years to come, on the numbers prepared to continue to postgraduate study.

Most readers of *The Times and Sunday Times Good University Guide* will be choosing full-time undergraduate or Foundation degree courses. The fees for 2016–17 are listed alongside each university's profile in chapter 14, and access agreements for universities in England, including details of bursaries and scholarships, are on the website of the Office for Fair Access (OFFA). Institutions in Scotland, Wales and Northern Ireland will continue to have lower charges for their own residents, but will charge varying amounts to students from other parts of the UK. Only those living in Scotland and studying at Scottish universities will escape all fees, although there will be reduced fees for those living in Wales and Northern Ireland.

The number of bursaries and scholarships offered to reduce the burden on new students has been falling since OFFA has suggested that such initiatives do little to attract students from low-income households. Most of the evidence pre-dates £9,000 fees so may no longer be correct, but universities have acted on its advice and the Government has switched its National Scholarship Programme from an undergraduate to a postgraduate scheme. It is also turning the grants paid to the poorest students into loans from 2016–17. While this decision may not affect many of those qualifying for the new loans because repayment will only begin if and when they have paid off the loans for their tuition fees, it remains to be seen whether the fear of yet more debt will be the final straw that puts some off higher education.

Variations among universities

The lowest full-time fee at an English university in 2016–17 will be £3,500 a year, charged for the small number of Foundation degrees in education and theology at York St John University. But even there, Honours degree students will pay £9,000. At 47 university-level institutions, every course will cost £9,000 and at several others the only exceptions will be during work placements or years abroad, when fees cannot exceed £1,800 for work placements and £1,350 for a year abroad, and are often less.

Many universities will continue to devote a substantial proportion of the income they receive from higher fees to access initiatives, whether in the form of bursaries or outreach activities. In the case of the London School of Economics, half of all of its fee income above £6,000 will be spent in this way. The lowest proportion will be 10 per cent at Wolverhampton. These measures appear to be having some success in attracting students from disadvantaged backgrounds. There was a 10 per cent increase in enrolments by students from disadvantaged groups in 2014, as the gap between rich and poor began to close to some extent.

Fees for students from other EU countries are the same as for those from the UK, but charges will be higher for those from other countries.

Even if it is closer to business as usual than many universities dared hope in the run-up to such a dramatic fees hike, that does not mean that financial considerations will be irrelevant to the decision-making process. In the current economic circumstances, students will want to keep their debts to a minimum and are bound to take the cost of living into account. They will also want the best possible career prospects and may choose their subject accordingly.

Alternative options

Some further education colleges will offer substantial savings on the cost of a degree, or Foundation degree, but they tend to have very local appeal, generally in a limited range of vocational subjects. Similarly, the private sector may be expected to compete more vigorously in future, following the success of two-year degrees at the University of Buckingham and BPP University in particular. Most will continue to undercut the traditional universities, although Regent's University, one of the latest to be awarded that title, has been charging more than £15,000, and the New College of the Humanities, also in London, charges £17,992. Like other private institutions, both are yet to set fees for 2016–17.

Impact on subject and university choice

Fee levels have had little impact on students' choices of university, but that is not the case for choices of subject. Predictions that old universities and/or vocational subjects would prosper at the expense of the rest have been shown to be too simplistic. Some, but not all, arts subjects have suffered, while in general science courses have prospered. For many young people, the options have not changed. If you want to be a doctor, a teacher or a social worker, there is no alternative to higher education. And, while there are now more options for studying post A level, it remains to be seen whether they offer the same promotion prospects as a degree.

Most subjects (surprisingly not including medicine and dentistry, or other health subjects) did attract increased applications in 2015. Combined subject degrees in all areas declined in popularity, but there were big increases in applications for biological sciences, business and management, computing, engineering, social studies and education. It should be noted, however, that even some of these subjects are yet to return to the level of applications seen before the fees went up.

It is enrolments that matter in the end, however, and here the pattern is slightly different. In 2014, only languages and combined subject degrees failed to recruit as many students as in 2013, and there were significant increases for health subjects, biological sciences, computing, social studies, business and management, and art and design. Computer science is up by 17 per cent since 2011 and engineering is up significantly over the same period.

It will take time to be certain whether the new fees regime brings about more fundamental changes in subject choice, starting at A level or the equivalent, if not before that. Sixth formers studying English, history and French cannot suddenly switch to a chemistry degree, but those entering university in 2016 will have made choices after GCSE knowing what a university education would cost. Not all of the trends in undergraduate education are shaped by fee levels: there were signs in schools, well before the fees went up, of a renaissance in the sciences and a decline in languages.

There is little doubt, however, that applicants are looking more carefully at future career prospects when choosing a degree, and they have decided (rightly or wrongly) that some careers are more secure, or more lucrative, than others. Applications for law remain buoyant and medicine is holding its own, despite a long and now much more expensive training. Enrolments in architecture and building were down again in 2014 and are considerably lower than they were before £9,000 fees were introduced, but the state of the construction industry may be main factor behind this decline.

With no real pattern yet established, those hoping to start courses in 2016 would be unwise to jump to conclusions about levels of competition in different subjects, or between whole universities. A drop in applications may mean less competition for places, or it may lead universities to close courses and possibly even intensify the race for entry. The only reliable forecast is that competition for places on the most popular courses will remain stiff, just as it has been since before students paid any fees.

Getting the best deal

There will still be a certain amount of variation in student support packages in 2016–17, so it will be possible to shop around, particularly if your family income is low. But remember that the best deal, even in purely financial terms, is one that leads to a rewarding career. By all means compare the full packages offered by individual universities, but consider whether marginal differences in headline fees really matter as much as the quality of the course and the likely advantages it will confer in the employment market. Higher career earnings will soon account for more than £3,000 in extra fees to be repaid over 30 years. It is all a matter of judgement – Scottish students can save themselves £27,000 by opting to study north of the border. That is a very different matter to the much smaller saving that is available to students in England, particularly if the Scottish university is of comparable quality to the alternatives elsewhere.

Those who are eligible for means-tested bursaries may not be able to afford to ignore the financial assistance they offer. No one has to pay tuition fees while they are a student, but you still have to find thousands of pounds in living costs to take a full-time degree. In some cases, bursaries may make the difference between being able to afford higher education and having to pass up a potentially life-changing opportunity. Some are worth up to £3,000 a year, although most are less generous than this, often because large numbers of students qualify for an award.

Some scholarships are even more valuable, and are awarded for sporting and musical prowess, as well as academic achievement. Most scholarships are not means-tested, but a few are open only to students who are both high performers academically and from low-income families.

How the £9,000 fee system works

What follows is a summary of the position for British students in summer 2015. While there are substantial differences between the four countries of the UK, there is one important piece of common ground. Up-front payment of fees is not compulsory, as students can take out a fee loan from the Student Loans Company to cover them (see chapter 8). This is repayable in instalments after graduation, when earnings reach £21,000 for English students, a threshold set by the Government.

With undergraduate fees remaining at a maximum of £9,000, the most you can borrow to pay fees will also stay at £9,000, with lower sums set for private colleges and part-time study. There are different levels of fees and support for UK students who are not from England. Students from other EU countries will pay the same rate as home students in the UK nation in which they study. Those from outside the EU are not affected by the changes, and may well have to pay quite a lot more than home and European students. The latest information on individual universities' fees at the time of going to press is listed at the end of this chapter and alongside their profiles in chapter 14.

With changes, large or small, becoming almost an annual occurrence, it is essential to consult the latest information provided on the websites of the relevant Government agencies.

Fees in England

In England, the maximum tuition fee for full-time undergraduates from the UK or anywhere in the European Union will be £9,000 a year in 2016–17. Most courses will demand fees of £9,000, or close to it, in order to recoup the money removed from their Government grants and leave room for further investment and student support.

In many public universities, the lowest fees will be for Foundation degrees and Higher National Diplomas. Although some universities have chosen to charge the same for all courses, in many universities and further education colleges, these two-year courses will remain a cost-effective stepping stone to a full degree or a qualification in their own right. Those universities that offer extended work placements or a year abroad, as part of a degree course, will charge much less than the normal fee for the "year out". The maximum fees for a placement year is 20 per cent of the full tuition fee (£1,800) and for a year abroad, 15 per cent (£1,350).

Fees in Scotland

At Scottish universities and colleges, students from Scotland and those from other EU countries outside the UK pay no fees directly. The universities' vice-chancellors and principals have appealed for charges to be introduced at some level to save their institutions from falling behind their English rivals in financial terms, but Alex Salmond, when he was Scotland's First Minister, famously declared that the "rocks will melt with the sun" before this happens.

Students whose home is in Scotland and are who studying at a Scottish university apply to the Student Awards Agency for Scotland (SAAS) to have their fees paid for them. Note, too, that three-year degrees are rare in Scotland, so most students can expect to pay four years of living costs.

Students from England, Wales and Northern Ireland studying in Scotland will pay fees at something like the level that applies in England and will have access to finance at similar levels to those available for study in England. Several Scottish universities are offering a "free" fourth year to bring their total fees into line with English universities, but Edinburgh and St Andrews are charging £9,000 in all four years of their degree courses.

Fees in Wales

Welsh universities have, in previous years, applied a range of fees up to £9,000, but for 2016–17 all have opted for £9,000. Students who live in Wales will be able to apply for a Tuition Fee Loan as well as a Tuition Fee Grant, wherever they study. The grant was intended to pay fees

---

Tuition fees

The figures below show the maximum fees that students can be charged in 2016–17.

Domicile of student	Location of institution			
	England	Scotland	Wales	Northern Ireland
England	£9,000	£9,000[1]	£9,000	£9,000
Scotland	£9,000	No fee	£9,000	£9,000
Wales[2]	£3,810	£3,810[1]	£3,810	£3,810
Northern Ireland	£9,000	£9,000[1]	£9,000	£3,805[3]
European Union	£9,000	No fee	£9,000	£3,805[3]
Other international	Variable	Variable	Variable	Variable

1 Note that Honours degrees in Scotland take four years and some universities charge £9,000 for each year.
2 Welsh-domiciled students are entitled to a tuition fee grant for any fees above £3,810 wherever they study in the UK (2015–16; figure for 2016–17 not announced at time of going to press).
3 Figures for 2015–16; figures for 2016–17 not announced at time of going to press.

beyond £3,810 a year in 2015–16. The 2016–17 arrangements have not been announced at the time of writing.

Fees in Northern Ireland

The two universities of Northern Ireland are charging local students £3,805 a year for 2015–16. Students can receive a fee loan to postpone paying this until their earnings are above £17,335 a year. For students from elsewhere in the UK, the fee is currently £6,000 a year at Ulster – still good value compared to much English provision – and £9,000 at Queen's, Belfast. The arrangements for 2016–17 have not been announced at the time of writing and are more uncertain than usual because of large cuts in the two universities' budgets.

Useful websites

With changes, large or small, becoming almost an annual occurrence, it is essential to consult the latest information provided by Government agencies. It is worth checking the following websites for the latest information:

England: **www.gov.uk/student-finance** and **www.sfengland.slc.co.uk**
Wales: **www.studentfinancewales.co.uk**
Scotland: **www.saas.gov.uk**
Northern Ireland: **www.studentfinanceni.co.uk**

University tuition fees for UK/EU and international students

England

The fees given for UK/EU undergraduates are those for **2016–17**. The fees shown are for full degrees and do not include the sometimes lower fees charged for Foundation degrees or for Foundation years (Year 0). The International student (non-EU) fees are for **2015–16**. Please check university websites for the most recent information.

	Undergraduate fees UK / EU students 2016–17	Undergraduate fees International students 2015–16
Anglia Ruskin	£9,000	£10,300–£12,250
Arts University Bournemouth	£9,000	£13,500
University of the Arts London	£9,000	£15,950
Aston	£9,000	£13,500–£16,500
Bath	£9,000	£14,300–£18,100
Bath Spa	£9,000	£11,300
Bedfordshire	£9,000	£9,750
Birkbeck	£9,000	£13,000
Birmingham	£9,000	£13,195–£17,145; £17,145–£31,000 (medicine)
Birmingham City	£9,000	£11,500–£12,600; £14,900 (Conservatoire and acting)
University College Birmingham	£8,830	£9,300
Bishop Grosseteste	£9,000	£10,000
Bolton	£9,000	£11,250
Bournemouth	£9,000	£9,500–£13,000
Bradford	£9,000	£12,100–£14,410
Brighton	£9,000	£11,780–£13,500; £27,405 (medicine)
Bristol	£9,000	£15,200–£18,300
		£18,300–£33,000 (dentistry, medicine, veterinary medicine)
Brunel	£9,000	£13,500–£16,500
Buckingham	£12,444; £35,525 (medicine)[1]	£17,160[1]; £35,525 (medicine)
Buckinghamshire New	£9,000	£9,500, £13,000
Cambridge	£9,000	£15,063–£22,923; £36,459 (medicine)[2]
Canterbury Christ Church	£9,000	£9,710
Central Lancashire	£9,000; £7,000[3]	£11,450–£12,450
Chester	£9,000	£10,800
Chichester	£9,000	£10,250–£11,700
City	£9,000	£13,000–£16,500
Coventry	£8,581–£9,000	£10,766–£12,871
University for the Creative Arts	£9,000	£11,870
Cumbria	£9,000	£10,500–£15,500
De Montfort	£9,000	£11,750–£12,250
Derby	£9,000	£10,900–£11,725
Durham	£9,000	£14,900–£18,900
East Anglia	£9,000	£14,000–£17,500; £28,000 (medicine)
East London	£9,000	£10,700
Edge Hill	£9,000	£11,150
Essex	£9,000	£12,500–£14,500
Exeter	£9,000	£15,500–£18,000; £27,000 (medicine)

	Undergraduate fees UK / EU students 2016–17	Undergraduate fees International students 2015–16
Falmouth	£9,000	£12,000
Gloucestershire	£9,000	£11,500
Goldsmiths	£9,000	£12,700–£18,850
Greenwich	£9,000	£10,850
Harper Adams	£9,000	£10,200
Hertfordshire	£9,000	£11,000–£11,500
Huddersfield	£9,000	£12,500–£13,500
Hull	£9,000	£12,300–£14,700; £25,930 (medicine)
Imperial	£9,000	£23,500–£26,500; £36,400 (medicine)
Keele	£9,000	£12,500–£15,100; £25,100 (medicine)
Kent	£9,000	£12,890–£15,380
King's College London	£9,000	£15,600–£20,700; £36,050 (medicine and dentistry)
Kingston	£9,000	£11,300–£13,700
Lancaster	£9,000	£13,930–£17,470; £27,500 (medicine)
Leeds	£9,000	£13,500–£17,500; £28,800 (medicine); £30,750 (dentistry)
Leeds Beckett	£9,000	£9,500
Leeds Trinity	£9,000	£10,000–£11,500
Leicester	£9,000	£14,000–£17,270; £17,270–£35,170 (medicine)
Lincoln	£9,000	£12,084–£14,522
Liverpool	£9,000	£13,400–£16,800 £29,950 (medicine, dentistry and veterinary medicine)
Liverpool Hope	£9,000	£10,800
Liverpool John Moores	£9,000	£11,000–£12,000
London Metropolitan	£9,000	£10,500
London School of Economics	£9,000	£17,040
London South Bank	£9,000	£10,500–£11,500
Loughborough	£9,000	£14,300–£17,950
Manchester	£9,000	£14,500–£19,000; £19,000–£33,000 (medicine)
Manchester Metropolitan	£9,000	£11,150–£19,000
Middlesex	£9,000	£11,200
Newcastle	£9,000	£13,315–£15,490; £17,080–£31,610 (medicine and dentistry)[4]
Newman	£9,000	£10,500
Northampton	£9,000	£10,700–£11,700
Northumbria	£9,000	£12,000–£14,000
Norwich University of the Arts	£9,000	£12,500
Nottingham	£9,000	£14,140–£18,210; £18,210–£26,970 (veterinary medicine) £19,180–£33,340 (medicine)
Nottingham Trent	£9,000	£11,800–£12,300
Oxford	£9,000	£14,845–£21,855; £17,040–£30,100 (medicine)[5]
Oxford Brookes	£9,000	£12,640–£14,500[4]
Plymouth	£9,000	£12,250–£12,500; £17,800–£33,000 (medicine)
Portsmouth	£9,000	£12,000–£13,700[4]
Queen Mary, London	£9,000	£13,650–£16,950; £30,000–£30,860 (medicine and dentistry)
Reading	£9,000	£14,350–£17,350
Roehampton	£9,000	£12,000

	Undergraduate fees UK / EU students 2016–17	Undergraduate fees International students 2015–16
Royal Agricultural University	£9,000	£10,000
Royal Holloway, London	£9,000	£13,200–£14,900
St George's, London	£9,000	£14,300–£15,970; £18,630–£32,663 (medicine)
St Mark and St John	£9,000	£10,500–£11,250
St Mary's, Twickenham	£9,000	£10,130
Salford	£9,000	£11,090–£13,050
Sheffield	£9,000	£14,500–£18,750; £18,750–£34,000 (medicine)
Sheffield Hallam	£9,000	£11,500–£12,400
SOAS, London	£9,000	£16,090
Southampton	£9,000	£14,660–£18,010; £18,010–£38,315 (medicine)
Southampton Solent	£9,000	£10,380–£10,930
Staffordshire	£9,000	£10,500
Sunderland	£8,750–£9,000	£10,000
Surrey	£9,000	£13,300–£17,100; £24,500 (veterinary medicine)
Sussex	£9,000	£14,450–£17,850; £27,450 (medicine)
Teesside	£9,000	£10,750
University College London	£9,000	£15,660–£20,700; £30,800 (medicine)
Warwick	£9,000	£15,820–£20,180; £18,480–£32,200 (medicine)
West London	£9,000	£10,650
West of England	£9,000	£11,250
Westminster	£9,000	£12,000
Winchester	£9,000	£11,300
Wolverhampton	£9,000	£11,050
Worcester	£9,000	£10,920
York	£9,000	£15,150–£19,500; £25,930 (medicine)
York St John	£9,000	£10,000–£11,500

1 Courses starting in January 2016. Note that courses only lasts two years (eight terms), except medicine (4.5 years).

2 Plus Cambridge College fees (£5,400–£7,720). UK and EU students who are eligible for tuition fee support not liable for College fees.

3 £7,000 charged for degrees at UClan's Burnley campus.

4 2016–17 figures.

5 Plus Oxford College fees £6,925 (£2,848 for clinical medicine years). UK and EU students who are eligible for tuition fee support not liable for College fees.

Wales

For **2016–17**, universities can to charge up to £9,000, with the Welsh Assembly paying fees above £3,810 (2015–16) for Welsh students.

	Undergraduate fees UK / EU students 2016–17	Undergraduate fees International students 2015–16
Aberystwyth	£9,000	£10,500–£12,000
Bangor	£9,000	£11,500–£15,000
Cardiff	£9,000	£14,000–£26,130; £17,500–£31,000 (medicine and dentistry)
Cardiff Metropolitan	£9,000	£10,200–£11,400
Glyndŵr	£9,000	£10,250
South Wales	£9,000	£11,600
Swansea	£9,000	£12,500–£15,500
Trinity St David (UWTSD)	£9,000	£10,000

Scotland

In **2015–16** there are no fees for Scottish and EU students, but there are fees for students from elsewhere in the UK. As Scottish Honours degrees are four years in length, the cost of some degrees in Scotland for students from the rest of the UK will be higher than in England, although some universities have put a maximum cap on charges to maintain equality with English fees. There is some financial support from the universities specifically for students from the rest of the UK. Please consult university websites for the fees to be charged in **2016–17**, as arrangements have not been announced at time of writing.

	Fees for Scottish students and eligible non-UK EU students 2015–16[1]	Fees for students from elsewhere in the UK 2015–16	Undergraduate fees International students 2015–16
Aberdeen	No fee	£9,000[2]	£13,000–£16,200; £28,600 (medicine)
Abertay	No fee	£7,250	£10,700–£12,700
Dundee	No fee	£9,000[3]	£12,950–£15,950
			£21,000–£31,500 (medicine)
			£28,600–£40,000 (dentistry)
Edinburgh	No fee	£9,000	£15,850–£20,850
			£24,400–£47,200 (medicine)
			£29,000 (veterinary medicine)
Edinburgh Napier	No fee	£9,000[4]	£11,250–£13,060
Glasgow	No fee	£9,000[5]	£14,500–£18,200; £33,000[6]
Glasgow Caledonian	No fee	£7,000[7]	£10,200–£11,000
Heriot Watt	No fee	£9,000	£13,020–£16,420
Highlands and Islands	No fee	£7,920–£9,000[8]	£8,800–£10,560
Queen Margaret	No fee	£7,000	£10,700–£12,400
Robert Gordon	No fee	£5,000–£6,750	£11,000–£14,300
		£8,500 (pharmacy)	
St Andrews	No fee	£9,000	£17,040; £24,500 (pre-clinical medicine)
Stirling	No fee	£6,750	£11,275–£13,425
Strathclyde	No fee	£9,000[4]	£12,200–£17,700
West of Scotland	No fee	£7,000	£11,000

1 For all eligible students, SAAS will pay fees of £1,820 direct to the universities
2 Capped at £27,000 for 4-year courses and £36,000 for 5-year courses; no cap for medicine and dentistry.
3 Capped at £27,000, except for architecture, dentistry and medicine.
4 Capped at £27,000 for 4-year courses and £36,000 for 5-year courses.
5 Capped at £27,000, except for modern languages (£28,820); MSci 5-year degree (£31,500); dentistry, medicine and veterinary medicine (£45,000).
6 Medicine, dentistry, and veterinary medicine.
7 Capped at £25,000 for 4-year courses.
8 Capped at £23,760–£27,000 for 4-year courses.

Northern Ireland

For **2015–16** there are different fees for students resident in Northern Ireland and students coming from other parts of the UK. Please consult university websites for the fees to be charged in **2016–17**, as arrangements had not been announced at the time of writing.

	Fees for Northern Irish students and eligible non-UK EU students 2015–16	Fees for students from elsewhere in the UK 2015–16	Undergraduate fees International students 2015–16
Queen's, Belfast	£3,805	£9,000	£13,280–£17,035
			£17,590–£33,170 (medicine); £26,938 (dentistry)
Ulster	£3,805	£6,000	£12,495

8 The Cost of Studying

The abolition of grants for students from low-income families in England and their replacement by loans has focused attention once more on the cost of higher education. As with the introduction of £9,000 fees, there will be no immediate impact on students because repayments will begin only after graduation when the borrower's salary reaches £21,000, but the prospect of yet more debt may still deter applicants from this already under-represented section of society. That was not the case when the fees went up in 2012, but no one can be sure what will happen this time.

Most new undergraduates, who would not have qualified for grants in any case, will be marginally better off than their predecessors because they will be able to borrow up to £500 more to help with living expenses, although that naturally brings increased debt on graduation. Loans for tuition will remain the same because fee levels are unchanged.

There are different arrangements in other parts of the UK, which are addressed later in this chapter. But wherever you study, there are two quite different timescales to consider: in the short term the calculations are all about affordability, while the long term is more about value for money. Most commentary on the subject conflates the two, focusing on the total debt that the average student will have at graduation. Although an intimidating figure and one that should not be ignored by those contemplating a degree, it has little to do with whether you can afford three or more years as an undergraduate.

Affordability

While the introduction of £9,000 fees added enormously to graduates' debts, it has made no difference to the amount of money you will need as a student. That calculation is about bridging the gap between a maintenance loan, which in England will now be worth up to £8,200 (or £10,702 in London) in 2016–17, and the real cost of living. With hall fees topping £5,000 a year at some universities, there will be a gap for most students, but this was so before the fees went up. Through a combination of parental help, part-time employment and institutional bursaries, most students find a way to make ends meet.

How well you can live on these sums will vary from person to person. But analysis by the National Union of Students suggests that it is not possible to get by on student loans alone. Savings, earnings, and help from family and friends have to be added to the pot. The information provided here will help you understand how big your pot needs to be, and what you can expect to be added and taken away from it. But it takes careful budgeting to avoid adding credit card debt to the income-contingent variety offered by the Government and repaid (or not) over 30 years.

Value for money

Only when you are sure you can cope with the costs of student life should you move on to the longer-term question of whether your chosen degree will be worth repaying £40,000 or more in student loans. Even in purely financial terms, there are too many uncertainties to be sure of the answer. You may never earn enough (£21,000 a year) to be required to repay any of it – although no one goes to university with those expectations and very few will be in that position. Or your degree may help you land such a well-paid job that university was cheap at the price. Most graduates will be somewhere in the middle, and the system is too new for any to have experienced the impact of loan repayments of 9 per cent of salary above £21,000 for such an extended period.

Contrary to some recent alarmist media coverage of graduate employment prospects, most surveys suggest that, on average, a degree is still a worthwhile investment in terms of future salary expectations, even after adding in the amount you might have earned while you were at university. A study by London Economics for the million+ group of post-1992 universities put the average graduate premium at £115,000 over a working lifetime. But averages can be deceiving: more recent research suggested that almost half of the graduates of post-1992 universities were earning less than young people who took higher apprenticeships.

This *Guide* should help to fill in some of the detail on employment rates on different courses at different universities. Salary data by course is available on the Unistats website, but no one can be certain of salary prospects over an entire career, possibly spanning a number of employment fields. Many satisfying jobs are open only to graduates, while in others the vast majority of new entrants have degrees.

Even before higher fees arrived, graduates and current students still on courses owed more than £40 billion between them in England alone, making them a major component of the public finances. Virtually all of this debt was in the form of income-contingent loans. The money was owed by 3.8 million borrowers, of whom 2.5 million were earning enough to make repayments, making the average debt just over £10,000 per person. Those figures are rising rapidly, and a survey of final-year undergraduates by High Flyers in 2015 put the average debt at £30,000.

Planning your finances

This chapter will focus on the costs while at university and the support that is available to get you through your undergraduate years. Like maximum fees, national student support schemes are the responsibility of the devolved UK administrations. There are separate sections for Northern Ireland, Wales and Scotland that follow the advice given for English students below. Where the rates for 2016–17 had not been announced when this book went to press, the figures quoted are for 2015–16.

With changes, large or small, becoming almost an annual occurrence, it is essential to consult the latest information provided by Government agencies. It is worth checking the following websites for the latest information:

» England: **www.gov.uk/student-finance** and **www.sfengland.slc.co.uk**
» Wales: **www.studentfinancewales.co.uk**

» Scotland: **www.saas.gov.uk**

» Northern Ireland: **www.studentfinanceni.co.uk**

Student loans for English students

More than 80 per cent of students take out a student loan, and it is not difficult to see why. The National Union of Students estimates that undergraduates spend £12,000 a year outside London and £13,500 in the capital. While some other estimates are marginally lower, most students find it impossible to cover all their living costs on savings and earnings alone and would require significant family support to cover the difference if they did not take out a loan.

Experts such as Martin Lewis, who writes regularly on student finance, agree that student loans are a good deal compared with other forms of borrowing. In particular, he counsels against using family savings to pay fees upfront, especially since the Government's own estimates suggest that most graduates will not repay the whole amount that they borrow. There are two types of student loan – one to cover the cost of tuition fees and another to help you cover the cost of living.

Tuition fees loan

You can borrow up to the full amount needed to cover the cost of your tuition fees wherever you study in the UK and it is not dependent upon your household income.

Tuition fees loans for part-time students

The most that universities or colleges can charge for part-time courses in 2016–17 is between £4,500 and £6,750 a year. They cannot charge more than 75 per cent of the full-time course fee. New part-time students will be able to apply for a tuition fee loan that is not dependent on household income or on age, which has led to some courses having a surprising number of pensioner students. Eligibility depends on the "intensity" of the course being at least 25 per cent of a full-time course. This measure works by comparing the course to a full-time equivalent. So if a course takes six years to complete and the full-time equivalent takes three, the intensity will be 50 per cent.

Maintenance loan

The second type of student loan, a maintenance loan, is means-tested. The amount you can borrow depends on a number of factors, including your family income, where you intend to study, and whether you expect to be living at home.

Although you are legally an adult, your student finance options depend heavily on your family income, frequently termed "household income", which in practice means your mother's and father's earning power. If your parents are separated, divorced or widowed, then only the income of the parent with whom you normally live will be assessed. However, if that parent has married again, entered into a civil partnership, or has a partner of the opposite sex, then both their incomes will be taken into account.

For 2016 entry, the maximum loan for those living at home is £6,904, but only if the combined household income is less than £25,000. If the combined income is £60,000, the maximum loan is £3,035. For students living away from home outside London, the amount is £8,200, and for those living away from home in London, £10,702, but again these are rates for a household income of less than £25,000. Outside London, loans are available for students whose parents earn up to £65,000, but the maximum is £3,821 at this level.

You can even get up to £9,391 for a year studying abroad as part of a UK course. Final-year students receive less than those in earlier years. Sixty-five per cent of the maintenance loan is available to you regardless of your family circumstances, while the remaining 35 per cent is means-tested. Note, too, that there is extra cash available for future teachers, social workers and healthcare workers, including doctors and dentists.

Students who would have qualified for maintenance grants will be able to borrow up to £8,200, which is £766 more than they would have received in 2015–16. In London the maximum will be £10,702; for those living in the parental home £6,904, and for those studying overseas, £9,361. Those who qualify for benefits and would have received a Special Supplementary Grant will now receive an increased loan of £9,347 (studying away from home), £11,671 (in London) and £8,144 (at home).

Repaying loans

Full-time students will begin accumulating interest during their course and will start repaying in the April after graduation, if they earn over £21,000. They will then pay 9 per cent of their income above £21,000, but repayments will stop during any period in which annual income falls below the threshold. Repayments are normally taken automatically through tax and National Insurance. If the loan has not been paid off after 30 years, no further repayments will be required.

During the repayment period, the amount of interest will vary according to how much you earn. If you earn less than £21,000, interest will be at the rate of inflation as measured by the Retail Price Index; between £21,000 and £41,000 you will be charged inflation plus up to 3 per cent; and if you earn over £41,000, interest will be at inflation plus the full 3 per cent. The Government website set up to guide prospective students through these arrangements includes a repayments calculator based on starting salaries for a range of careers, at **www.gov.uk/student-finance**. At the time of writing, the interest rate was set at 1.5 per cent, so

---

Maintenance loan for a first-year English student 2016–17

The maximum loan for those living at home is £6,904; for those living away from home, but not in London, £8,200; and for those living away from home in London is £10,702. Just under half the loan is on a sliding scale depending on household income and the table below shows the reduction in the loan as household income increases.

Household income	Living at home	Living away from home but not in London	Living away from home in London
£25,000 and below	£6,904	£8,200	£10,702
£30,000	£6,322	£7,612	£10,103
£35,000	£5,740	£7,023	£9,503
£40,000	£5,158	£6,434	£8,904
£42,875	£4,824	£6,095	£8,559
£45,000	£4,576	£5,845	£8,304
£50,000	£3,994	£5,256	£7,705
£55,000	£3,412	£4,667	£7,105
£60,000	£3,039	£4,078	£6,506
£65,000	£3,039	£3,821	£5,906
£70,000 and above	£3,039	£3,821	£5,330

Department for Business, Innovation and Skills

anyone earning £25,000 a year would face monthly repayments of £61 a month. If you are on £50,000, the sum rises to £248 a month, a fair bite even from that healthy paycheque. By the time you graduate, the interest rate will probably have changed and the repayment threshold may have risen, if only by inflation. Currently the threshold is fixed at £21,000 until 2020.

Student loans and grants for Northern Ireland students

Maintenance loans in 2015–16 vary from a maximum of £3,750 for students living at home, £4,840 for those studying away from home, all the way to £6,780 for those studying in London (and only 25 per cent of the loan is means-tested). There are also extra sums for people taking courses longer than 30 weeks a year, worth up to £108 a week if you are in London. Tuition fee loans are available for the full amount of tuition fees, regardless of where you study in the UK. For 2015–16, maintenance grants range from £3,475 for students with household incomes of £19,203 or below, to zero if the figure is £41,066 or above. Your maximum loan is reduced by the size of any grant you receive. Loan repayments of 9 per cent of salary start once your income reaches £16,910 and interest is calculated on the retail price index or 1 per cent above base rate, whichever is lowest. The loan will be cancelled after 25 years.

As in England, there are also special funds for people with disabilities and other special needs, and for those with children or adult dependants. There are modest special bursaries of up to £2,000 for students studying in the Republic of Ireland, who also have their fees paid by their local Education and Library Board. Decisions are yet to be announced on levels for 2016–17.

Student loans and grants for Welsh students

The Welsh Government offers a range of support for students from Wales, regardless of whether or not they remain in the country. For 2015–16, the maximum maintenance loan is £4,162 for students living at home, £5,376 for those living away from home and outside London, £6,202 for a year studying abroad, and £7,532 for those living in London (and only 25 per cent of the loan is means-tested). Tuition fee loans are available to cover the first £3,810 of tuition fees, while the remainder is covered by a non-means-tested grant of up to £5,315. Repayment of loans starts once a graduate's income reaches £21,000. Interest repayments and the length of loan is as for England (see above).

In addition, students in Wales are also able to apply for Welsh Government Learning Grants of up to £5,161. They are scaled according to household income, which in 2015–16 ranges from £18,370 for a full grant to £50,020 for the smallest payment of £50. The loan you can get is reduced by 50p for every £1 of grant you receive up to £2,575. There are also special funds for people with disabilities and other special needs, and for those with children or adult dependants. Again, decisions are yet to be announced on levels for 2016–17.

Student loans and grants for Scottish students

The Scottish Government has a commitment to a minimum income of £7,625 a year for students from poorer backgrounds – not bad in a setting where tuition is also free. Students from a family with an income below £19,000 can get a £1,875 Young Students' Bursary (YSB) as well as a loan of £5,750. This bursary does not have to be repaid. It tapers off to zero for family incomes of £34,000, at which point the maximum loan also falls from £5,750 to £4,750. The loan does not vary in size depending on whether you live at home or where you are studying in the UK. Higher loans but more limited bursaries are available for "independent" students – those who are married, mature or without family support. Note that you must be under 50 when you first apply for a loan. Repayment of the loan starts when your income reaches £17,335 and repayments will continue until the loan is paid off, with any outstanding amount being cancelled after 35 years.

As elsewhere in the UK, there are also special funds for people with disabilities and other special needs, and for those with children or adult dependants. No tuition fee loans are required by Scottish students studying in Scotland, but such loans are available for Scottish students studying elsewhere in the UK.

Living in one country, studying in another

As each of the countries of the UK develops its own distinctive system of student finance, the effects on students leaving home in one UK nation to go and study in another have become knottier. UK students who cross borders to study pay the tuition fees of their chosen university and are eligible for a fee loan, and maybe a partial grant, to cover them. They are also entitled to apply for the scholarships or bursaries on offer from that institution. Any maintenance loan or grant will still come from the awarding body of their home country. If you are in this position, you must check with the authorities in your home country about the funding you are eligible for.

European Union laws stipulate that EU students from outside the UK must be charged the same tuition fees as those paid by nationals of the country where they are studying, rather than the higher fees paid by students from outside the EU. They can also apply for a fee loan and may be considered for some of the scholarships and bursaries offered by individual institutions. Only students who have been living and studying in the UK for at least three years can apply for a maintenance loan or grant. If you haven't, then you will need to apply for such assistance from the authorities in your own country. Tuition fee rules for non-UK European Union students are the same in Scotland as for Scottish students – that is, they do not have to pay tuition fees. There are also no fees to pay for exchange students coming to the UK, including those on the Socrates Programme.

Applying for support

English students should apply for grants and loans through Student Finance England, Welsh students through Student Finance Wales, Scottish students through the Student Awards Agency for Scotland, and those in Northern Ireland through Student Finance NI or their Education and Library Board. You should make your application as soon as you have received an offer of a place at university. Maintenance loans are usually paid in three instalments a year into your bank or building society account. European Union students

Scottish maintenance bursaries and loans 2016–17

Young student (under 25 at start of course)				Independent student			
	Bursary	Loan	Total		Bursary	Loan	Total
£0–£18,999	£1,875	£5,750	£7,625	£0–£18,999	£800	£6,750	£7,625
£19,000–£23,999	£1,125	£5,570	£6,875	£19,000–£23,999	0	£6,750	£6,750
£24,000–£33,999	£500	£5,750	£6,250	£24,000–£33,999	0	£6,250	£6,250
£34,000 and over	0	£4,750	£4,750	£34,000 and over	0	£4,750	£4,750

Repayments start at a salary above £17,335 and are over 35 years from outside the UK will usually be sent an application form for tuition fee loans by the university that has offered them a place.

University scholarships and bursaries

As well as taking out student loans for both tuition and living costs, you can shop around for university bursaries, scholarships and other sponsorship packages, and seek out supplementary support to which you may be entitled. There may be reductions for a range of other groups, including local students, which vary widely from university to university and which are usually detailed on university websites. Some examples are given alongside the university profiles in chapter 14 and the details of the financial support offered by all universities in England are listed in the access agreements published on the website of the Office for Fair Access (**www.offa.org.uk**).

Although English universities have continued to scale back their support for 2016–17, there is still a bewildering variety of bursaries and scholarships on offer at UK universities. Some awards are guaranteed depending on your financial circumstances, while scholarships are available through open competition. In general, bursaries that provide students with the money to make ends meet at university have (rightly) proved more popular than fee waivers giving relief from repayments that may stretch over 30 years. Some universities offer eligible students the choice of accommodation discounts, fee waivers or cash. Most also have hardship funds for those who find themselves in financial difficulties.

Do take note of the application procedures for scholarships and bursaries, as these vary from institution to institution, and even from course to course within individual institutions.

Funding timetable

It is vital that you sort out your funding arrangements before you start university. Each funding agency has its own arrangements, and it is very important that you find out the exact details from them. The dates below give general indications of key dates.

March/April

- Online and paper application forms become available from funding agencies.
- You must contact the appropriate funding agency to make an application.
- Complete application form as soon as possible. At this stage select the university offer that will be your first choice.
- Check details of bursaries and scholarships available from your selected universities.

May/June

- Funding agencies will give you details of the financial support they can offer.
- Last date for making an application to ensure funding is ready for you at the start of term (exact date varies significantly between agencies).

August

- Tell your funding agency if the university or course you have been accepted for is different from that originally given them.

September

- Take letter confirming funding to your university for registration.
- After registration, the first part of funds will be released to you.

There may be a deadline you have to meet to apply for an award. In some cases the university will work out for you whether you are entitled to an award by referring to your funding agency's financial assessment. If your personal circumstances change part-way through a course, your entitlement to a scholarship or bursary may be reviewed.

If you feel you still need more help or advice on scholarships or bursaries, you can usually find it on a university's website or in its prospectus. Some institutions also maintain a helpline. Some questions you will need answered include whether the bursary or scholarship is automatic or conditional and, if the latter, when you will find out whether your application has been successful. For some awards, you won't know whether you have qualified until you get your exam results. Another obvious question is how the scholarship or bursary on offer compares with awards made by another university you might consider applying to. Watch out for institutions that list entitlements that others don't mention, but which you would get anyway.

Students with disabilities

Extra financial help is available to disabled students studying whether full-time or part-time through Disabled Students' Allowances, which are paid in addition to the standard student finance package. They are available for help with education-related conditions such as dyslexia, and for other physical and mental disabilities. They do not depend on income and do not have to be repaid. The cash is available for extra travel costs, equipment and to pay helpers. The maximum for a non-medical helper is £20,725 a year, or £15,543 a year for a part-time student. The Government plans to make universities increasingly responsible for these allowances from 2016–17. At the time of writing, proposals are out for consultation. If you would benefit from this allowance, you must check for the latest information.

Further sources of income

If you are feeling daunted by the potential costs, you can take some comfort from this section, which outlines just some of the ways you can raise additional funds.

Taking a gap year

Gap years (see chapter 6) have become increasingly popular both for travelling and to earn some money to help pay for higher education. Many students will simply want to travel, but others will be more focused on boosting the bank balance in preparation for life as a student. Work opportunities can be structured or casual. An example of the structured variety is the Year in Industry Scheme (**www.etrust.org.uk**).

Further support

There are various types of support available for students in particular circumstances, other than the main loans, grants and bursaries.

» Undergraduates in financial difficulties can apply for help to their university's student hardship fund. These are allocated by universities to provide support for anything from day-to-day study and living costs to unexpected or exceptional expenses. Many universities have committed to increasing the size of their hardship funds in 2016. The university decides which students need help and how much money to award them. These funds are often targeted at older or disadvantaged students, and finalists who are in danger of dropping out. The sums range up to a few thousand pounds, are not repayable and do not count against other income.

- » Students with children can apply for a Childcare Grant, worth £155.24 a week if you have one child and £266.15 a week if you have two or more children under 15, or under 17 with special needs; and a Parents' Learning Allowance, for help with course-related costs, of between £50 and £1,573 a year.
- » Any students with a partner, or another adult family member who is financially dependent on them, can apply for an Adult Dependants' Grant of up to £2,757 a year.

If you do not qualify for any of this kind of financial support you may still be able to apply for a Professional and Career Development Loan available from certain banks, in partnership with the National Careers Service. Students on a wide range of vocational courses can borrow from £300 to £10,000 at a fixed rate of interest to fund up to two years of learning, but the loans cannot be used for first full-time degrees.

Part-time work

The need to hold down a part-time job during term time is now a fact of life for almost half of students. Students from a working-class background are more likely to need to earn while they learn.

If you need to earn during term time, it is important to try to ensure that you do not work so many hours that it starts to affect your studies. A survey by the NUS found that 59 per cent of students who worked felt it had an impact on their studies, with 38 per cent missing lectures and over a fifth failing to submit coursework because of their part-time jobs. You may find that new universities are better geared-up to cope with working students than more traditional institutions.

Student employment agencies, which can now be found on many university campuses, can help you get the balance right. These introduce employers with work to students seeking work, sometimes even offering jobs within the university itself. But they also abide by codes of practice that regulate both minimum wages and the maximum number of hours worked in term time (typically 15 hours a week).

Some firms, such as the big supermarkets, offer continuing part-time employment to their school part-time employees when they go to university. Some students make use of their expertise in areas like web design to earn some extra money, but most take on casual work in retail stores, restaurants, bars and call centres.

Most students, including those who don't work during term time, get a job during vacations. A Government survey found that 86 per cent of students in their second year of study or above worked during their summer vacation. Most of this kind of work is casual, but some is formalised in a scheme like STEP (**www.step.org.uk**) or may be part of a sponsorship programme. Many vacation jobs are fairly mundane, but it is possible to find more interesting work. Some students broaden their experience by working abroad, others work as film extras, do tutoring, or do a variety of jobs at big events such as festivals. It is also a good idea to try to use the summer holidays to get some work experience in a field that has some relevance to your career aspirations. Even if you don't get paid, this can significantly enhance your chances of finding employment after graduation.

What you will need to spend money on

Living costs

Certain costs are unavoidable. You have to have a roof over your head, eat enough, clothe yourself, and probably do a certain amount of travelling. But the cost of even these essential items can be cut down significantly through a mixture of shopping around and careful budgeting. If you set aside a certain amount of money a week for food, you will find it goes much further if you keep takeaways and ready-meals to a minimum, and stick to a shopping list when you go to a supermarket. Some catering outlets at your university or in the students' union may well offer good value meals, but probably the most economical way to eat is to cook and share meals with fellow students with whom you may be living in a shared house. Make sure you make full use of student travel cards and other offers and facilities available locally to help you cut the cost of travel. In certain locations, a bicycle is a very worthwhile investment (as is buying a lock for it).

If you can keep your essential costs down, you will have more money for what you would probably prefer to spend your money on – going out and personal items. Most students spend a proportion of their budget on socialising, and this is certainly an important part of the university experience. You can have plenty of fun and keep your leisure costs down by making the most of your student union's facilities and events.

It is easy to let "other costs" get out of hand to the extent that they start to eat into your budget for day-to-day living. Mobile phone bills are a case in point: the latest edition of an annual survey of student life by RBS put average spending at £6.80 a week, but Sodexo found that many students were spending £20 a week on them. Look at your previous bills, or think carefully about your usage, and then shop around for the best deal to cover what you need. Extras like downloading games or music, or sending pictures, can add significantly to your bill. Most of all, try to avoid getting tied up with an expensive and inflexible contract.

The RBS survey also shows that students spend almost twice as much on groceries (£23 a week) as they do on the next-biggest item, which is eating out. Alcohol comes further down the list, at £10.89 a week on average – perhaps a slightly misleading figure since a growing number of students spend nothing on it. An earlier survey by Sodexo suggested that half of all students have altered their eating and socialising habits for lack of money. It is not just leisure that is being cut back: 65 per cent of students claimed to spend nothing on books in a typical week. Perhaps the most striking item in the RBS survey was the £7-a-week average spent on computer games, more than twice the spending on football.

Studying costs

An NUS survey estimated that the average student spent about £1,000 a year on costs associated with course work and studying, mainly books and equipment. The amount you spend will be determined largely by the nature of your course and what you study. Additional financial support may be available for certain expenditure, but this is unlikely to cover you fully for spending on books, stationery, equipment, fieldwork or electives. A long reading list could prove very expensive if you tried to buy all of the required books brand new. Find out as soon as possible which books are available either in your university library or local libraries. Another approach is to buy books second-hand from students who no longer need them. Your students' union or your university may run second-hand book sales or offer a service helping students to buy and sell books.

Overdrafts and credit cards

Other costs it is best to avoid are the more expensive forms of debt. Many banks offer free overdraft facilities for students, but if you go over that limit without prior arrangement, you can end up paying way over the odds for your borrowing. Credits cards can be useful if managed properly. The best way to manage a credit card is to set up a direct debit to pay off your balance in full every month, which means you will avoid paying any interest. One of the worst ways is just paying the minimum charge each month, which can cost you a small fortune over a long period. If you are the kind of person who spends impulsively and doesn't keep track of your spending, you are probably better off without a credit card. That way, you can't spend money you don't have.

Insurance

One kind of additional spending that can actually end up saving you money is getting insurance cover for your possessions. Most students arrive at university with laptops and other goodies such as digital cameras, mobile phones and iPods, not to mention bikes, that are tempting to petty thieves. It is estimated that around a third of students fall victim to crime at some point during their time at university. If you shop around, you should be able to get a reasonable amount of cover for these kinds of items without it costing you an arm and a leg. It may also be possible to add this cover cheaply to your parents' domestic contents policy.

Planning your budget

University websites, the National Union of Students and many other sites offer guidance on preparing a budget, usually with the basic headings provided for you to complete. First, list all your likely income (bursaries, loans, part-time work, savings, parental support) and then see how this compares with what you will spend. Try to be realistic, and not too optimistic, about both sides of the equation. With care, you will end up either only slightly in the red, or preferably far enough in the black for you to be able to afford things you would really like to spend your money on.

Above all, keep track of your finances so that your university experience isn't ruined by money worries, or finding you can't go to the ball because the cash machine has eaten your card. Spreadsheets make doing this simpler, and it is one skill you can learn at college that you are definitely going to need for the rest of your life.

If all else fails, your campus almost certainly has a student money adviser who is a member of NASMA, the National Association of Student Money Advisers. You can find them via **www.nasma.org.uk.** NASMA reports that some students, especially those with children, are struggling financially. However, the bargains available in student shops can mean that you might not experience the most exorbitant prices on the high street.

More than two-thirds of young people aged 18–24 say they received no financial education at school. This chimes with the experience of NASMA, which finds that many students have low levels of basic financial awareness and planning ability. In addition, advisers have noticed that students are increasingly likely to spend money they cannot afford on TV and online gambling, so make sure to avoid this temptation.

Useful websites

For the basics of fees, loans, grants and other allowances:
www.gov.uk/student-finance
www.gov.uk/browse/education/student-finance

UCAS provides helpful advice: **www.ucas.com/ucas/undergraduate/finance-and-support/managing-money**

For England, visit Student Finance England: **www.sfengland.slc.co.uk**
Office for Fair Access: **www.offa.org.uk**
For Wales, visit Student Finance Wales: **www.studentfinancewales.co.uk**
For Scotland, visit the Student Awards Agency for Scotland: **www.saas.gov.uk**
For arrangements for Scottish students studying in the UK or EU, and for students from the rest of the UK studying in Scotland:
www.gov.scot/Topics/Education/UniversitiesColleges/16640/financial-help
For Northern Ireland, visit Student Finance Northern Ireland: **www.studentfinanceni.co.uk**

All UK student loans are administered by the Student Loans Company: **www.slc.co.uk**

For guidance on the tax position of students, visit HM Revenue and Customs:
www.gov.uk/student-jobs-paying-tax

NHS Student Bursaries for students on pre-registration health professional and social work training courses: **www.nhsbsa.nhs.uk/students**

For finding out about availability of scholarships: **www.scholarship-search.org.uk**

9 Finding Somewhere to Live

Not since the 1990s has student accommodation captured so many headlines. Then, photographs of students sleeping on gym floors adorned newspapers at the start of every academic year. With the lifting of the cap on undergraduate recruitment in England, there has been media speculation that such scenes may return as universities overstretch their stocks of accommodation, at the very least prompting further rises in already exorbitant private sector rents. It remains to be seen whether such fears are well founded: the rise in enrolments in 2015 is not as large as many predicted, so most universities should be able to cope. But no one knows how 2016 will compare, and those expecting to start a course then would be wise to plan ahead.

Students spend almost three times as much on rent as any other area of expenditure, so it is vital to make the right choice of accommodation. It would be a key decision whatever the financial implications because where you live will have an impact on your whole university experience. Particularly in your first year – and especially if it is your first time away from home – you are likely to be happier and more successful academically in accommodation of reasonable quality, preferably in a setting that helps you meet other students. Of course, whatever you choose has to be affordable, but if your budget will stand it, that may mean a hall of residence or university flat.

Three-quarters of applicants hope to live in a hall of residence, but only 60 per cent actually do so, according research by Unite Students. Indeed, the survey shows halls gaining in popularity among second- and third-year undergraduates, with the proportion opting for shared houses in their second year falling to little more than half. With tastes apparently changing and the numbers going to university continuing to rise, the student market has become the biggest growth area in the property market. Rents have been rising at more than 3 per cent a year and billions of pounds have been committed to student housing deals in 2015 alone. Campus Living Villages, for example, bought a portfolio of 4,500 beds from the Opal Student Property Group, with the aid of a £210-million bond, taking its total stock to more than 8,000 beds.

Particularly in the big student cities, but increasingly in other university towns as well, student accommodation now comes in all shapes and sizes – and prices. Despite considerable expansion by universities themselves, property consultants JLL estimate that more than a third of residential places for students are now in private hands. Most of the developments are in big complexes, but there are also niche providers such as Student Cribs, which convert properties and rent them to students providing a rather higher spec than the traditional student landlord. The company now has 135 houses in 11 cities, and rents can be £250 a week in London, or £95 a week sharing a six-bedroom house in Liverpool.

Of the big providers, Unite Students has more than 44,000 beds in 23 towns and cities, some provided in partnership with universities and others in developments that serve more than one institution. UPP manages 30,000 residential places in complexes it has built for nine universities, where rents are negotiated with the university, often in consultation with the students' union.

Term-time type of accommodation of full-time and sandwich students

	2013/14
University maintained property	19.2%
Private-sector halls	6.4%
Parental/guardian home	19.0%
Own residence	15.1%
Other rented accommodation	30.4%
Other	3.5%
Not known	5.0%

HESA 2015 (adapted)

There is even an award for the best private halls of residence – won for the last two years by the Student Housing Company, which has 7,000 beds in nine cities and has plans for many more. The best university halls in 2015 were judged to be at Lancaster, where UPP is the university's partner, with Northumbria and Bournemouth runners-up.

For most students, it will not matter whether the owner of their accommodation is the university, a private landlord or larger organisation if the quality and the price are right. But successive reports by the National Union of Students (NUS) have told a story of increasingly unaffordable rents, often poor facilities and rushed decisions by inexperienced students. While those who can afford it – or think they can – are living in luxury, NUS found others coping with mice, slugs, mould, cold, or all of these. So it is worth putting some effort into basic decisions on this subject.

Living at home

Although student loan repayments start only after graduation, many undergraduates are understandably cautious about the debts they run up, so the option of avoiding big accommodation charges is a tempting one for those who are attracted by a local university. The pattern of recent applications shows that the trend towards studying at home is accelerating, albeit only gradually, and there is no reason to think that this will change in the near future. Indeed it may be a permanent shift, given the rising costs of student housing and the willingness of many young people to live with their parents well into their twenties. The proportion of students living at home was already rising before undergraduate fees went up, according to research by Sodexo. Including mature students, many of whom live at home because of their family circumstances, the proportion is now close to 20 per cent. Among younger students, women are more likely than men to stay at home, and Asian women are particularly likely to take this option. Home study is also four times more common at post-1992 universities than older institutions, again reflecting the larger numbers of mature students at the newer universities and a generally younger and more affluent student population at the older ones.

For those considering studying from home, there are important considerations, of which the relationship with your parents and the availability of quiet space are the most obvious ones. You will still be entitled to a maintenance loan, although it will be a maximum of

£6,904 in England, rather than £8,200 if you were living away from home outside London. There may be advantages in terms of academic work if the alternative involves shopping, cooking and cleaning as well as the other distractions of a student flat. The downside is that you may miss out on a lot of the student experience, especially the social scene and the opportunity to make new friends. There is no evidence that students living at home do any worse academically. You can always move out at a later date if you think you are missing out – many initially home-based students do so in their second year.

Living away from home

Most of those who can afford it still see moving away to study as integral to the rite of passage that student life represents. Some have little option if, in spite of the expansion of higher education, the course they want is not available locally. Others are happy to travel to secure their ideal place and widen their experience.

For the lucky majority, the search for accommodation will be over quickly because the university can offer a place in one of its halls of residence or self-catering flats. The choice may come down to the type of accommodation and whether or not to do your own cooking. But for others, there will be an anxious search for a room in a strange city. Most universities will help with this if they cannot offer accommodation of their own.

Going to university will oblige those who take the "away" route to think for the first time about the practicalities of living independently. This can make the decision about where to live – in terms of location and the type of accommodation – doubly difficult. It may even influence your choice of university, since there are big differences across the sector and the country in the cost and standard of accommodation, and in its availability.

How much will it cost?

A survey by RBS put the average student rent in 2015 at £85.31, although this may include catered halls of residence and Oxbridge colleges. Oxford, Cambridge, Reading, Bristol, London and Exeter all averaged more than £100 a week, according to the survey, while Cardiff, Glasgow and Belfast were all below £70 a week. However accurate such figures may be, they conceal a wide range of actual rents, particularly in London. This was always the case, but has become even more obvious with the rapid growth of a luxury market at the same time as many students are willing to accept sub-standard accommodation to keep costs down.

The latest Unite Students report says that the need for good Wi-Fi has overtaken reasonable rents as students' top priority in choosing accommodation, but obviously you have to be able to afford the rent in the first place. Only 64 per cent of respondents said reasonably priced accommodation was "very important", while 78 per cent felt Wi-Fi was "very important" (cleanliness came third, at 57 per cent). Rents for the cheapest self-catered room in 2015–16 range from £57 a week at Teesside to £143 a week at West London, while the most expensive accommodation will set you back £339 a week at the London School of Economics (their cheapest room is £124 a week, however).

Most universities with a range of accommodation find that their most expensive rooms fill up first, and that students appear to have higher expectations than they used to. Almost half of all the rooms in the last NUS survey had en-suite facilities. The downside of this trend is that there can be fewer university-owned places available at the lowest price band, which is also the one where rents have seen the biggest percentage rises.

It is important to remember that both your living costs and your potential earnings should be factored into your calculations when deciding where to live. While living costs in London are by far the highest, potential part-time earnings are nearly double those in other parts of the country.

The choices you have

The NUS puts accommodation into 16 categories, ranging from luxurious university halls to a bedsit in a shared house. The choices include:

- » University hall of residence, with individual study bedrooms and a full catering service. Many will have en-suite accommodation.
- » University halls, flats or houses where you have to provide your own food.
- » Private, purpose-built student accommodation.
- » Rented houses or flats, shared with fellow students.
- » Living at home.
- » Living as a lodger in a private house.

This chapter will help you decide where you would like to live and whether you can afford it.

Making your choice

Finance is not the only factor you should consider when deciding where to live. It is worth investing time to find the right place, and to avoid the false economy of choosing somewhere cheap, where you may end up feeling depressed and isolated. Most students who drop out of university do so in the first few months, when homesickness and loneliness can be felt most acutely.

Being warm and well fed is likely to have a positive effect on your studies. Perhaps for these reasons, most undergraduates in their first year plump for living in university halls, which offer a convenient, safe and reliable standard of accommodation, along with a supportive community environment. If meals are included, this extra adds further peace of mind both for students and their parents. The NUS survey found that the difference in cost between full board and self-catering is £45–75 a week on average, not unreasonable for two hot meals a day. But nowadays most are self-catering, with groups of students sharing a kitchen. The sheer number of students – especially first years – in halls also makes this form of accommodation an easy way of meeting people from a wide range of courses and making friends.

Wherever you choose to live, there are some general points you will need to consider, such as how safe the neighbourhood seems to be, and how long it might take you to travel to and from the university, especially during rush hour. A survey of travel time between term-time accommodation and the university found that most students in London can expect a commute of at least 30 minutes and often over an hour, while students living in Wales are usually much less than 30 minutes away from their university.

In chapter 14, we provide details of what accommodation each university offers, covering the number of places, the costs, and policy towards first-year students.

What universities offer

You might think that opting to live in university accommodation is the most straightforward choice, especially since first-year students are invariably given priority in the allocation of places in halls of residence, and it is possible to arrange university accommodation in advance and at a distance. Searching for private housing can often be a matter of having to be in the right place at the right time. However, you may still need to select from a range of options, because most universities will have a variety of accommodation on offer. You will need to consider which best suits your pocket and your preferred lifestyle.

New student accommodation

At the top end of the market, private firms usually lead the way, at least in the bigger student cities. Companies such as UPP, Unite Students and Liberty Living offer some of the most luxurious student accommodation the UK sector has ever seen, either in partnerships with universities or in their own right. Rooms in these complexes are nearly always en suite and may include facilities such as your own phone line, satellite TV and internet access. Shared kitchens are top-quality and fitted out with all the latest equipment.

This kind of accommodation naturally comes at a higher price, but offers the advantages of flexibility both in living arrangements and through a range of payment options. An NUS survey found little difference between the rents charged by higher education institutions for their own accommodation and those for rooms managed by private companies under contract, but private providers operating outside institutional links charged over £20 a week more.

Halls of residence

Many new or recently refurbished university-owned halls offer a standard of accommodation that is not far short of the privately built residences. This is partly because rooms in these halls can be offered to conference delegates during vacations. Even though these halls are also at the pricier end of the spectrum, you will probably find that they are in great demand, and you may have to get your name down quickly to secure one of the fancier rooms. That said, you can often get a guarantee of some kind of university accommodation if you give a firm acceptance of an offered place by a certain date in the summer. If you have gained your place through Clearing, this option might have gone, although rooms in private halls might still be on offer at this stage.

While a few halls are single-sex, most are mixed, and often house over 500 students. Indeed, in student villages the numbers are now counted in thousands. They are therefore great places for making friends and becoming part of the social scene. One possible downside is that they can also be noisy places where it can be difficult at times to get down to some work. Indeed, 44 per cent of those responding to the Unite Students survey identified noise as the biggest challenge in student accommodation. Peace and quiet was a higher priority than access to public transport or good nightlife. The more successful students learn, before too many essay deadlines and exams start to loom, to get the balance right between all-night partying and escaping to the library for some undisturbed study time. Remember that some libraries, especially new ones, are now open 24 hours a day.

University self-catering accommodation

An alternative to halls, now offered by most universities, are smaller, self-catering properties fitted out with a shared kitchen and other living areas. Students looking for a more independent and flexible lifestyle often prefer this option. But as well as having to feed yourself, you may also have heating and lighting bills to pay. University properties are often on campus or nearby, so travel costs should not be a problem.

Catering in university accommodation

Many universities have responded to a general increase in demand from students for a more independent lifestyle by providing more flexible catering facilities. A range of eateries, from fast food outlets to more traditional refectories, can usually be found on campus or in student villages. Students in university accommodation may be offered pay-as-you-eat deals as an alternative to full-board packages.

What after the first year?

After your first year of living in university residences you may well wish, and will probably be expected, to move out to other accommodation. The main exceptions are the collegiate universities – particularly Oxford and Cambridge – which may allow you to stay on in college for another year or two, and particularly for your final year. Students from outside the EU are also often guaranteed accommodation. At a growing number of universities, where there is a sufficiently large stock of residential accommodation, it is not uncommon for students to move back in to halls for their final year.

Practical details

Whether or not you have decided to start out in university accommodation, you will probably be expected to sign an agreement to cover your rent. Contract lengths vary. They can be for around 40 weeks, which includes the Christmas and Easter holiday periods, or for just the length of the three university terms. These term-time contracts are common when a university uses its rooms for conferences during vacations, and you will be required to leave your room empty during these weeks. It is therefore advisable to check whether the university has secure storage space for you to leave your belongings. Otherwise you will have to make arrangements to take all your belongings home or to store them privately between terms. International students may be offered special arrangements by which they can stay in halls during the short vacation periods. Organisations like **www.hostuk.org** can arrange for international students to stay in a UK family home at holiday times such as Christmas.

Parental purchases

One option for affluent families is to buy a house or flat and take in student lodgers. This might not be the safe bet it once appeared, but it is still tempting for many parents. Agents Knight Frank have had a student division since 2007, mostly working with new developers to sell specially adapted homes. The Sodexo University Lifestyle Survey for 2014 found that a surprising 7 per cent of students live in houses owned by their own or fellow students' parents. Those who are considering this route tend to do so from their first year of study to maximise the return on the investment.

Being a lodger or staying in a hostel

A small number of students live as a lodger in a family home, an option most frequently taken up by international students. The usual arrangement is for a study bedroom and some meals to be provided, while other facilities such as the washing machine are shared. Students with particular religious affiliations or those from certain countries may wish to consider living in a hostel run by a charity catering for a specific group. Most of these are in London.

Renting from the private sector

Around a third of students live in privately rented flats or houses. Every university city or town is awash with such accommodation, available via agencies or direct from landlords. Indeed, this type of accommodation has grown to the point where so-called "student ghettoes", in which local residents feel outnumbered have become hot political issues in some cities. Into this traditional market in rented flats and houses have come the new private-sector complexes and residences, adding to the options. Some are on university campuses, but others are in city centres and usually open to students of more than one university. Examples can be seen online; some sites are listed at the end of this chapter.

While there are always exceptions, a much more professional attitude and approach to managing rented accommodation has emerged among smaller providers, thanks to a combination of greater regulation and increasing competition. Nevertheless, it is wise to take certain precautions when seeking out private residences.

How to start looking for rented property

Contact your university's accommodation service and ask for its list of approved rented properties. Some have a Student Accommodation Accreditation Scheme, run in collaboration with the local council. To get onto an approved list under such schemes, landlords must show they are adhering to basic standards of safety and security, such as having an up-to-date gas and electric safety certificate. University accommodation officers should also be able to advise you on any hidden charges. For instance, you may be asked to pay a booking or reservation fee to secure a place in a particular property, and fees for references or drawing up a tenancy agreement are sometimes charged. The practice of charging a "joining fee", however, has been outlawed. It would be wise to speak to older students with first-hand experience of renting in the area. Certain companies in the area may be notorious among second and third years and you can try to avoid them. In addition to websites and accommodation services designed for students, you can also use sites such as Gumtree that cater for the population at large.

Making a choice

Once you have made an initial choice of the area you would like to live in and the size of property you are looking for, the next stage is to look at possible places. If you plan to share, it is important that you all have a look at the property. If you will be living by yourself, take a friend with you when you go to view a property, since he or she can help you assess what you see objectively, and avoid any irrational or rushed on-the-spot decisions. Don't let yourself be pushed into signing on the dotted line there and then. Take time to visit and consider a number of options, as well as checking out the local facilities, transport and the general environment at various times of the day and different days of the week.

If you are living in private rented accommodation, it is likely that at least some of your neighbours will not be students. Local people often welcome students, but resentment can build up, particularly in areas of towns and cities that are dominated by student housing. It is important to respect your neighbours' rights, and not to behave in an anti-social manner.

Preparing for sharing

The people you are planning to share a house with may have some habits that you find at least mildly irritating. How well you cope with some of the downsides of sharing will be partly down to the kind of person you are – where you are on the spectrum between laid back and highly strung – but it will help a lot if you are co-habiting with people whose outlook on day-to-day living is not too far out of line with your own. According to the Unite Students report, 31 per cent of female students find sharing more difficult than they had expected, compared with 22 per cent of men.

Some students sign for their second year houses as early as November. While it is good to be ahead of the rush, you may not yet have met your best friends at this stage. If you have not selected your own group of friends, universities and landlords can help by taking personal preferences and lifestyle into account when grouping tenants together.

Potential issues to consider when deciding whether to move into a shared house include whether any of the housemates smoke or own a loud musical instrument. It will also be important to sort out broadband arrangements that will work for everyone in the house, and that you will be able to arrange access to the university system. It is also a good idea to agree a rota for everyone to share in the household cleaning chores from the start. Otherwise it is almost certain that you will live in a state of unhygienic squalor or that one or two individuals will be left to clear up everyone else's mess.

The practical details about renting

It is a good idea to ask whether your house is covered by an accreditation scheme or code of standards. Such codes provide a clear outline of what constitutes good practice as well as the responsibilities of both landlords and tenants. Adhering to schemes like the National Code of Standards for Larger Student Developments compiled by Accreditation Network UK (**www.anuk.org.uk**) may well become a requirement for larger properties, including those managed by universities, now that the Housing Act is in force.

At the very least, make sure that if you are renting from a private landlord, you have his or her telephone number and home address. Some can be remarkably difficult to contact when repairs are needed or deposits are due to be returned.

Multiple occupation

If you are renting a private house it may be subject to the 2004 Housing Act in England and Wales (similar legislation applies in Scotland and Northern Ireland). Licenses are compulsory for all private Houses in Multiple Occupation (HMOs) with three or more storeys and that house five or more unrelated residents. The provisions of the Act also allow local authorities to designate whole areas in which HMOs of all sizes must be licensed. The good news is that these regulations can be applied in sections of university towns and cities where most students live. This means that a house must be licensed, well-managed and must meet various health and safety standards, and its owner subject to various financial regulations. The bad news is that this could lead to a reduction in the number and range of privately rented properties on the market, or an increase in rental prices.

Tenancy agreements

Whatever kind of accommodation you go for, you must be sure to have all the paperwork in order and be clear about what you are signing up to before you move in. If you are taking up residence in a shared house, flat or bedsit, the first document you will have to grapple with is a tenancy agreement or lease offering you an "assured shorthold tenancy". Since this is a binding legal document, you should be prepared to go through every clause with a fine-tooth comb. Remember that it is much more difficult to make changes or overcome problems arising from unfair agreements once you are a tenant than before you become one.

You would be well advised to seek help in the likely event of your not fully understanding some of the clauses. Your university accommodation office or students' union is a good place to start – they should know all the ins and outs, and have model tenancy agreements to refer to. A Citizens Advice Bureau or Law Advice Centre should also be able to offer you free advice. In particular, watch out for clauses that may make you jointly responsible for the actions of others with whom you are sharing the property. If you name a parent as a guarantor to cover any costs not paid by you, they may also be liable for charges levied on all tenants for damage that was not your fault. A rent review clause could allow your landlord to increase the rent at will, whereas without such a clause, they are restricted to one rent rise a year. Make sure you keep a copy of all documents, and get a receipt (and keep it somewhere safe) for anything you have had to pay for that is the landlord's responsibility.

Contracts with private landlords tend to be longer than for university accommodation. They will frequently commit you to paying rent for 52 weeks of the year. Leaving aside the cost, there are probably more advantages than disadvantages to this kind of arrangement. It means you don't have to move out during vacation periods, which you will have to in most university halls. You can store your belongings in your room when you go away (but don't leave anything really valuable behind if you can help it). You may be able to negotiate a rent discount for those periods when you are not staying in the property. The other advantage, particularly important for cash-strapped students, is that you have a base from which to find work and hold down a job during the vacations. Term dates are also not as dictatorial as they might be in halls; if you rent your own house then you can come back when you wish.

Deposits

On top of the agreed rent, you will need to provide a deposit or bond to cover any breakages or damage. This will probably set you back the equivalent of another month's rent. The deposit should be returned, less any deductions, at the end of the contract. However, be warned that disputes over the return of deposits are common, with the question of what constitutes reasonable wear and tear often the subject of disagreements between landlord and tenant. To protect students from unscrupulous landlords who withheld deposits without good reason, the 2004 Housing Act introduced a National Tenancy Deposit Scheme under which deposits are held by an independent body. This is designed to ensure that deposits are fairly returned, and that any disputes are resolved swiftly and cheaply.

Inventories and other paperwork

You should get an inventory and schedule of condition of everything in the property. This is another document that you should check very carefully – and make sure that everything listed is as described. Write on the document anything that is different. The NUS even suggests taking photographs of rooms and equipment when you first move in (setting the correct date on your camera), to provide you with additional proof should any dispute arise

---

Security in rented accommodation

Students in private housing are twice as likely to be burgled as those in university halls. When looking at accommodation, use this NUS security checklist:

- Check that the front and back doors are fitted with five-lever mortise locks in addition to standard catch locks.
- Make sure the door to your room has a lock, and always lock up when you leave it, especially for long periods such as during vacations.
- Check the locks and catches on accessible windows, especially those at ground-floor level.
- Before you move in, try to talk to neighbours about how safe the area is and whether there have been many instances of burglary.
- Ask your landlord to ensure that all previous tenants and holders of keys no longer have copies.
- If you find a property that you like but have some security concerns, discuss these with the letting agency or landlord.

when your contract ends and you want to get your deposit back. If you are not offered an inventory, then make one of your own. You should have someone else witness and sign this, send it to your landlord, and keep your own copy. Keeping in contact with your landlord throughout the year and developing a good relationship with him or her will also do you no harm, and may be to your advantage in the long run.

You should ask your landlord for a recent gas safety certificate issued by a qualified CORGI engineer, a fire safety certificate covering the furnishings, and a record of current gas and electricity meter readings. Take your own readings of meters when you move in to make sure these match up with what you have been given, or make your own records if the landlord doesn't supply this information. This also applies to water meters if you are expected to pay water rates (although this isn't usually the case).

Finally, students are not liable for Council Tax. If you are sharing a house only with other full-time students, then you will not have to pay it. However, you may be liable to pay a proportion of the Council Tax bill if you are sharing with anyone who is not a full-time student. You may need to get a Council Tax exemption certificate from your university as evidence that you do not need to pay Council Tax.

Safety and security

Once you have arrived and settled in, remember to take care of your own safety and the security of your possessions. You are particularly vulnerable as a fresher, when you are still getting used to your new-found independence. This may help explain why so many students are burgled or robbed in the first six weeks of the academic year. Take care with valuable portable items such as mobile phones, tablet computers and laptops, all of which are tempting for criminals. Ensure you don't have them obviously on display when you are out and about and that you have insurance cover. If your mobile phone is stolen, call your network or 08701 123123 to immobilise it. Students' unions, universities and the police will provide plenty of practical guidance when you arrive. Following their advice will reduce the chance of you becoming a victim of crime, and help you to enjoy living in the new surroundings of your chosen university town.

Useful websites

For advice on a range of housing issues, visit: **www.nus.org.uk/en/advice/housing-advice**
The Shelter website has separate sections covering different housing regulations in England, Wales, Scotland and Northern Ireland: **www.shelter.org.uk**

As examples of providers of private hall accommodation, visit:
www.upp-ltd.com
www.unite-students.com
www.libertyliving.co.uk
www.campusliving.com
http://thestudenthousingcompany.com

A number of sites will help you find accommodation and/or potential housemates, including:
www.accommodationforstudents.com
www.sturents.com, **www.studentpad.co.uk**
www.let4students.com
http://student.spareroom.co.uk, **http://uk.easyroommate.com**

10 Sporting Opportunities

Most people will never again have as much opportunity to exercise and play different sports as they do in their undergraduate years. Even those whose timetable dictates long hours in the laboratory will find plenty of activity in the evenings and at weekends. Especially at the big universities – but also at many of the smaller ones – sporting provision is now both diverse and high quality. And it is not going to waste: two-thirds of students take part in sport of some sort while at university and participation levels are still rising. More than half of all students use the facilities at least once a week.

The quality of those facilities will not be the clinching factor in most students' choice of university – and nor should it be – but nearly a third of applicants say it played some part in their decision-making. Universities are well aware of this and have invested on an unprecedented scale to expand and upgrade their provision. Some of the biggest multi-sports developments of recent years have been on university campuses, where facilities nationally are said to be worth an astonishing £20 billion. As a result, half of all universities were chosen as training bases for Great Britain squads in the run-up to the 2012 Games and 30 hosted other nations' teams. Nor has the process ended yet: Nottingham is planning a £40-million sports complex and other universities are building on a smaller scale.

Perhaps partly as a result, standards have been rising in elite student sport. If the students and alumni of UK universities and colleges had been a team at the London Games, they would have finished fifth in the medals table. They repeated their successes in 2014 at the Commonwealth Games and European Championships, and returned from the 2015 World Student Games in South Korea with a record medal haul. Kelly Simm, from Southampton Solent University, won gold in the all-around artistic gymnastics, silver in the vault and bronze in the floor exercises, while Jay Lelliott, of the University of Bath, won gold in the 400m freestyle and silver in the 800m freestyle. The UK's 60-strong team came from 30 different universities and returned from Guangju with three gold medals, four silvers and four bronze. The British Universities and Colleges Sport (BUCS) 2015 Sportsman of the Year, Mohamed Elshorbagy of the University of the West of England, was the current world number one in men's squash, while Aimee Wilmott of the University of East London, the 2015 Sportswoman of the Year, won three medals at the 2014 Commonwealth Games.

Naturally, most students will never aspire to such heights, but may still welcome the chance to use top-grade facilities. Research for BUCS suggests that at least 1.7 million students take part in regular physical activity, from gym sessions to competitive individual or team sports. There are good reasons, beyond fitness, for doing so, according to the BUCS research. In 2013, graduates who had played and/or volunteered in sport were found to be earning between £4,624 and £5,616 more than those who had not, and were 25 per cent less likely to have been unemployed. Nine out of ten employers thought that participation in university sport helped to develop valuable skills in potential employees.

Sporting opportunities

Some specialist facilities may be reserved at times for elite performers, but all universities are conscious of the need for wider access. Surveys show that two-thirds of sessions at university sports facilities are taken by students, roughly a quarter by the local community and the rest by staff. Many institutions still encourage departments not to schedule lectures and seminars on Wednesday afternoons, to give students free time for sport. There are student-run clubs for all the major sports and – particularly at the larger universities – a host of minor ones. In addition, there are high-quality gyms, with staff on hand to devise personalised training regimes and to run popular activities such as Zumba and Pilates. The cost varies widely between universities, and membership fees can represent a large amount to lay out at the start of the year, but most provide good value if you are going to be a regular user.

Sport for all

For most universities, it is in the area of "sport for all" that most attention has been focused. Beginners are welcomed and coaching provided in a range of sports, from Ultimate Frisbee to tai-chi, that would be difficult to match outside the higher education system. Check on university websites to see whether your usual sport is available, but do not be surprised if you come across a new favourite when you have the opportunity to try out something different as a student. Many universities have programmes designed to encourage students to take up a new sport, with expert coaching provided.

All universities are conscious of the need to provide for a spread of ability. Sports scholarships for elite performers are now commonplace, but there will be plenty of opportunities, too, for beginners. University teams demand a hefty commitment in terms of training and practice sessions – often several times a week – and in many sports standards are high. University teams often compete in local and national leagues.

For those who do not aspire to such heights, or whose interests are primarily social, there are thriving internal, or intramural, leagues. These provide opportunities for groups from halls of residence or faculties, or even a group of friends, to form a team and participate on a regular basis. A recent BUCS survey found 41,000 participants in the intramural programmes of 41 institutions. The largest programme was at the University of Brighton, where more than 6,000 students were playing sports ranging from football, rugby and badminton to softball, orienteering and fencing. Nor is university sport a male preserve – student teams were among the pioneers in mixed sport and are still strong in areas such as women's cricket, football and rugby.

Some universities have cut back sports budgets, but representative sport continues to grow. There are plans for a home nations competition at international level and in London, 34 institutions take part in the London Universities Sport League. This now involves more than 400 teams – male, female and mixed – competing at a variety of levels in 14 different sports. A BUCS initiative that started in 2012, the leagues are intended to reach students and include sports that are not in the main national competitions.

First-year sport

Halls of residence and university-owned flats will often have their own sports teams. At some universities, these are part of the intramural network of leagues, while others have separate arrangements for first years. In such cases, a Sports Captain, elected the year previously as part of the Junior Common Room, takes responsibility for organising trials and picking the teams, as well as arranging fixtures for the year. Hall sport is a great way of meeting like-minded people from your accommodation and over the course of the years, friendly rivalries often develop with other halls or flats. Generally there will be teams for football (both five- and 11-a-side), hockey, netball, cricket, tennis, squash, badminton and even golf. If your lodgings are smaller then don't worry, they are often twinned with similar flats to enable as many first-year students as possible to get involved in freshers' sport.

Other opportunities

You may even end up wanting to coach, umpire or referee – and this is another area in which higher education has much to offer. Many university clubs and sports unions provide subsidised courses for students to gain qualifications that may be of use to the individual in later life, as well as benefiting university teams in the short term. Or you might want to try your hand at some sports administration, with an eye to your career. In most universities there is a sports (or athletic) union, with autonomy from the main students' union, which organises matches and looks after the wider interests of those who play. There are plenty of opportunities for those seeking an apprenticeship in the art of running a club, or larger organisation. Southampton Solent University, for example, deploy students on volunteer coaching placements in more than 70 local schools. These placements increase a university's community engagement as well as enhancing student employability with minimal investment.

Universities that excel

A few universities are known particularly for sport. Exeter and Loughborough men's teams have played national Premier League hockey, for example, while Bath, Loughborough and Northumbria have teams in the Netball Super League. The University of London women's volleyball team has won the English Volleyball Championships, and "Team Bath" have tasted success in the FA Cup. Several of this elite group had a head start as former physical education colleges. Loughborough is probably the best-known of them, but Leeds Beckett and Brunel are others with a similar pedigree. Other universities with different traditions, such as Bath and East Anglia, also have a variety of outstanding facilities, while the likes of Stirling and Cardiff Metropolitan have the same in a narrower range of sports.

As in so much else, Oxford and Cambridge are in a category of their own. The Boat Race and the Varsity Match (in rugby union) are the only UK university sporting events with a big popular following – although there are varsity matches in several university cities that have become big occasions for students – and there is a good standard of competition in other sports. But you should not assume that success in school sport will be a passport to an Oxbridge place, for the days of special consideration for sporty undergraduates are long since over.

Representative sport

Competitive standards have been rising in university sport, as have the numbers taking part in it. More than 6,000 students competed in ten sports at the 2015 BUCS Nationals in Sheffield. BUCS (**www.bucs.org.uk**) runs competitions in almost 50 sports, and ranks participating institutions based on the points earned in the competitive programme. Over 4,700 teams compete in BUCS leagues, making the organisation the largest provider of league sport across Europe. More than a third of those teams are female and many others mixed. There is also international competition in a number of sports, and the World Student Games have become one of the biggest occasions in the international sporting calendar.

BUCS is the national organisation for higher education sport in the UK, providing a comprehensive, multi-sport competition structure and managing the development of services and facilities for participative, grass-roots sport and healthy campuses, through to high-performance elite athletes. Its mission is to raise the profile of student sport and drive the university sport agenda by influencing government and key stakeholders in the sector.

University sports facilities

Even the smallest university should provide reasonable indoor and outdoor sports facilities – a sports hall, modern gym equipment and outdoor pitches (usually including an all-weather surface and floodlights). Many will also have a swimming pool and extras such as climbing walls, but some smaller universities make arrangements for students to use local sports centres and clubs when it is not feasible to provide for minority sports. The same goes for the really expensive sports, like golf, which is usually the subject of an arrangement with one or more local clubs that give students a discount. Specialist facilities, like boat houses and climbing huts, obviously depend on location, but the most landlocked university is likely to have a sailing club that organises regular activities away from campus, and a skiing club that runs at least annual trips to the mountains.

Many of the larger universities have spent millions of pounds improving their sports facilities, sometimes in partnership with local authorities or national sporting bodies. University campuses are ideal locations for national coaching centres, and many have been established in recent years. Although elite coaching generally takes place in closed sessions, students may occasionally find themselves rubbing shoulders with star players.

It is estimated that close to £500 million has been spent on new or upgraded sports facilities at UK universities over the past decade, and planned investment will add at least £170 million to this figure. Universities now boast a significant proportion of the UK's 50-metre pools, for example, the latest opening at the University of Surrey. Innovative schemes include Leeds Beckett's development of the Headingley cricket and rugby league grounds, providing teaching space for students during the week and improved facilities for players and spectators on match days.

Beyond scrutinising the prospectus for the extent of university facilities, there are two important questions to ask: how much do they cost and where are they? Neither is easy to track down on the average university website.

How much?

University prospectuses tend to major on the quality of the sports facilities without being as forthcoming about the prices. Students who are used to free (if inferior) facilities at school often get a nasty surprise when they find that they are expected to pay to join the Athletic Union and then pay again to use the gym or play football. Because most university sport is subsidised, the charges are reasonable compared to commercial facilities, but the best deal may require a considerable outlay at the start. Some campus gyms and swimming pools now charge more than £300 a year, for example, which is still considerably cheaper than paying per visit if you intend to use the facilities regularly (and provides an incentive to carry on doing so). Some universities are offering sports facility membership as part of the £9,000 fee, but most offer a variety of peak- and off-peak membership packages – some for the entire length of your course.

Outdoor sports are usually charged by the hour, although clubs will also charge a membership fee. You may be required to pay up to £60 for membership of the Athletic Union (although not all universities require this). Fees for intramural sport are seldom substantial; teams will usually pay a fee for the season, while courts for racket sports tend to be marginally cheaper per session than in other clubs.

How far away?

The other common complaint by students is that the playing fields are too far from the campus – understandable in the case of city-centre universities, but still aggravating if you have to arrange your own transport. This is where campus universities have a clear advantage. For the rest, there has to be some trade-off between the quality of outdoor facilities and the distance you have to travel to use them. But universities are beginning to realise that long journeys depress usage of important (and expensive) facilities, and some have tried to find suitable land closer to lectures and halls of residence. Indoor sports centres should all be within easy reach.

Sport as a degree subject

Sports science and other courses associated with sport had seen consistent increases in applications until the imposition of higher fees. The subject remains very popular, with more than 67,000 applications at degree level in 2014. The demand for places had recovered from a decline in 2012. A separate ranking for the subject is on page 193. If you are hoping to be rewarded with an academic qualification for three years on the sports field, you will be disappointed because there is serious science involved. However, sport is a growing employment field and one that demands qualifications like any other.

Other degrees in the sports area are more closely focused on management, with careers in the leisure industry in mind – golf course management, for example, has proved popular with students despite being a target of those who see anything beyond the traditional academic portfolio as "dumbing down". The question is not whether the courses are up to standard, but whether a less specialised one will offer more career flexibility if a decline in popularity for the particular sport limits future opportunities.

Sports scholarships

The number and range of sports scholarships have expanded just as rapidly as courses in the subject, but the two are usually not connected. Sports scholarships are for elite performers, regardless of what they are studying – indeed, they exist at universities with barely any degrees in the field. Imported from the USA, scholarships now exist in an array of sports. At Birmingham University, for example, there are specialist golf awards (as there are at ten other universities) and a scholarship for triathletes, as well as others open to any sport.

The value of scholarships varies considerably – sometimes according to individual prowess. The Royal and Ancient scholarships for golfers, for example, range from £500 for promising handicap golfers to £10,000 for full internationals, and are available at eleven universities. All of them demand that you meet the normal entrance requirements for your course and maintain the necessary academic standards, as well as progressing in your sport. In practice, most departments will be flexible about attendance and deadlines, as long as you make your requests well in advance.

Many sports scholarships offer benefits in kind, in the form of coaching, equipment or access to facilities. The Government-funded Talented Athlete Scholarship Scheme (TASS), which is restricted to students at English universities who have achieved national recognition at under-18 level and are eligible to represent England in one of 40 different sports, is one such example. Winning Students is a similar scheme in Scotland. Some 200 current or former TASS athletes took part in the London Olympics, 44 of them winning a medal. The scholarships are worth £3,500 a year and can be put towards costs such as competition and training costs, equipment or mentoring. Further details are available at **www.tass.gov.uk**.

Leading performers in many sports still look first to US universities – often unfamiliar ones – for sports scholarships. In some sports, such as American football or basketball, this is the main route into professional sport, while in others it may provide bigger awards – and in some cases better coaching – than are available in the UK. Half of the UK's six-strong tennis team at the World Student Games were from US universities. The gold medal winners in the men's doubles, Darren Walsh and Joe Salisbury, were from the Southern Methodist University in Texas and the University of Memphis respectively – not household names on this side of the Atlantic. For the most promising athletes, US scholarships can cover the full cost of university; for others they may be worth only a few thousand dollars, but may make the difference in gaining admission. Further details are available at **www.fulbright.org.uk/study-in-the-usa/undergraduate-study/funding/sports-scholarships**.

Part-time work

University sports centres are an excellent source of term-time (and out-of-term) employment. You may also be trained in first aid, fire safety, customer care and risk assessment – all useful skills for future employment. The experience will help you secure employment in commercial or local authority facilities – and even for jobs such as stewarding at football grounds and music venues. Most universities also have a sabbatical post in the Athletic Union or similar body, a paid position with responsibility for organising university sport and representing the sporting community within the university.

Comparing facilities

Different students look for different things from their sport while at university and the table that follows gives an initial guide to what's on offer at different institutions and, where appropriate, their various campuses.

The table is based on a detailed survey of university sport undertaken by BUCS in early 2012 and updated in 2013. The information in the table relates only to the facilities and services that universities provide centrally for all their students and does not include any facilities there may be in halls of residence or colleges.

The table contains a mix of factual information and "1–5" rankings, with five dots the best and one dot the worst. If there is no dot there is no facility. All the ratings take account of the number of students at each university, or on each campus, so they provide comparative information. The information in the table includes:

» The university's overall BUCS ranking and number of teams in BUCS competitions. Teams get points for their success in inter-university competitions and BUCS uses them to compile an annual league table. Some multi-site universities (eg, South Wales) have a BUCS ranking for each of their campuses, others (eg, Cumbria) have only one.

- » The type of pool, if any (25m, 50m or other) at each university and the extent of its availability to students. The availability rating takes account of the extent to which the pool may be reserved for outside users, for example by a local swimming club or squad.
- » Ratings for the range and availability of indoor dry sports facilities, such as sports halls, dance studios, squash courts and fitness gyms, derived from the total at-one-time capacity of the facilities and number of students. The more dots in the "Range" column, the more extensive the facilities in relation to the student population. A significant difference in the rating for range and availability indicates that while facilities exist, students may have restricted access to them.
- » The total number of fitness training machines, plus an asterisk if the university's fitness facilities are accredited under the Inclusive Fitness Initiative (IFI) by the English Federation of Disability Sport. However, note that the IFI scheme does not operate in Northern Ireland, Scotland or Wales.
- » Ratings for the range and availability of outdoor grass and artificial pitches and tennis or netball courts.
- » The number of sports with intramural competitions.
- » The availability of taught or instructor-led classes.
- » The number of sports scholarships or bursaries available; they may be any mix of funding and free access to facilities or elite athlete support services.
- » The number of different forms of support for achieving sporting excellence, such as coaching, sports psychology, nutritional advice, access to sports medicine or specialist strength and conditioning training.

University sports websites are given in the university profiles (chapter 14).

University sporting facilities

Name	BUCS Ranking 2014–15	Teams in BUCS Leagues	Swimming pool	Availability of pools	Range of indoor dry sports facilities	Availability of indoor dry sports facilities
Aberdeen	35	72	Other	•	•••••	••••
Abertay	95	23			••	•••
Aberystwyth	65	21	Other	••	••••	•••••
Anglia Ruskin	77	1			•••	•••
Arts University Bournemouth	-	No information available				
Aston	88	25	Other	•	••••	••••
Bangor	67	35			•••	••••
Bath	7	71	50m	•••••	•••	••••
Bath Spa	110	No information available				
Bedfordshire	75	6			•••••	•••••
Birmingham	5	65	25m	•••	••	••
Birmingham City	107	No information available				
University College Birmingham	126	No information available				
Bishop Grosseteste	140	No information available				
Bolton	125	No information available				
Bournemouth	28	32			•	••
Bradford	93	29	25m	•	••••	••••
Brighton (Brighton)	43	40			•••	••
Brighton (Eastbourne)	43	40	25m	••	•••••	•••••
Bristol	15	48			••	•
Brunel	38	No information available				
Buckingham	-	0			•••••	•••••
Buckinghamshire New	80	No information available				
Cambridge	12	37			•••••	••••
Canterbury Christ Church	73	No information available				
Cardiff	16	57			•••••	•••••
Cardiff Metropolitan	13	37			•	•
Central Lancashire	53	31			••	•••
Chester (Chester)	79	No information available				
Chester (Warrington)	144	No information available				
Chichester	57	29			•••••	•••••
City	90	13			•	•
Coventry	40	31			••	•••
Creative Arts	145	No information available				
Cumbria (Ambleside)	133	0			••••	•••••
Cumbria (Carlisle)	133	3			•	•
Cumbria (Lancaster)	133	13			•	••
Cumbria (Penrith)	133	2			•••••	•••••
Cumbria (Preston)	133	0			•	•••
De Montfort	87	30			•	•
Derby	61	27			••	••
Dundee	55	39	25m	•••	•••	••••
Durham	2	61			••••	•••
East Anglia	50	26	50m			
East London	63	0			•	•
Edge Hill	92	30			•••	•••
Edinburgh	3	71	25m	•••	•••••	••••
Edinburgh Napier	86	13			••	•••
Essex	37	64			••••	••••
Exeter	6	58	25m	•••	•••••	•••••

Fitness machines	Number of winter pitches	Availability of winter pitches	Outdoor courts	Availability of outdoor courts	Sports with intramural competitions	Availability of taught classes	Sports scholarships/ bursaries	Forms of elite athlete support
200	•••••	•••••	•	•	1	•••••	29	6
35					1	•	0	10
76	••••	••••	•••••	•••••	1	•••••	30	5
20					3	••••	25	0
103	••••	•••	•	••	0	••	6	2
93	•••	•••	••	••	6	•••	10	0
101*	••••	•••	••••	•••	2	•••	39	10
19	•••	•••	•••	•••	6	•	67	2
90*	••••	••••	•	•	6	•••••	67	10
55					10	•••	55	9
100*	••	•	•••	•••	17	•••	8	0
88	•••	•••	••••	••••	8	•	30	10
47	••••	••••	•••••	•••••	7	••••	30	10
100	••••	•••	••••	•	9	••	26	10
16	••	••			1	•••••	0	0
470					19	••	15	5
90	••	•••	•	••	3	••	60	9
55	•	•	•	•	2	•	28	6
108	••	•	••••	••••	1	••••	12	8
28	•••••	•••••	•••	•••	2	•	16	3
0					5	••	0	0
86	••	••			10	••	65	10
0	•	•			0	••	0	0
21					0	••	10	7
17	•••	•••			0	•	10	7
15	•••••	•••••			5		10	7
0	••	••	••••	•	0	•	0	8
90					6	•	0	0
37	•	•	••	••	0		6	10
125	••	••	•••	•••	8	•••••	12	10
242	•••••	•••••	••••	••••	20	•••	45	10
80							0	0
10					6	•	22	10
56	••••	•••			0	••••	18	10
266	••	••	•	••	11	••••	278	10
57					0	•	4	1
88	•••	••••	•••	•••	20	•••	7	10
125	•••••	•••••	•••••	•••••	16	•••••	60	10

Name	BUCS Ranking 2014–15	Teams in BUCS Leagues	Swimming pool	Availability of pools	Range of indoor dry sports facilities	Availability of indoor dry sports facilities
Falmouth	108	0			•••	••••
Glasgow	27	36	25m	•••••	••	•
Glasgow Caledonian	89	18			•	•
Gloucestershire	39	46			•••••	•••••
Glyndŵr	119	No information available				
Goldsmiths	136	8			••••	•
Greenwich	121	13			•	••
Harper Adams	106	18			•••••	•••••
Heriot-Watt	60	28			•••	•••
Hertfordshire	45	33	25m	••••	•••	•••
Highlands and Islands	113	No information available				
Huddersfield	100	16			•	•
Hull	69	48			•	••
Imperial College	19	48	25m	•••••	•••••	•••••
Keele	72	25			••••	•••••
Kent	62	41			•	•
King's College London	41	57			••	••
Kingston	84	26			•	•
Lancaster	48	41	25m	••••	••••	••••
Leeds	14	70	25m	••••	•••	••
Leeds Beckett	10	66	Other	••	•••	•••
Leeds Trinity	122	15		••••	•••••	
Leicester	47	34			••••	••
Lincoln	70	34			••	••
Liverpool	30	81	25m	••••	••	•••
Liverpool Hope	112	No information available				
Liverpool John Moores	66	No information available				
London Metropolitan	127	No information available				
LSE	63	No information available				
London South Bank	94	No information available				
Loughborough	1	66	50m	•••••	•••••	••••
Manchester	17	77	50 m	•••	••	••
Manchester Metropolitan (MMU)	34	29			••••	•••
MMU (Cheshire)	34	0			••••	••••
Middlesex	76	19			••	••
Newcastle	11	69			••	••••
Newman	135	No information available				
Northampton	81	No information available				
Northumbria	8	68	25m	•	•••••	•••
Nottingham	4	72	25m	•••••	•••	••••
Nottingham Trent	21	44			•••	••
Oxford	9	No information available				
Oxford Brookes	33	35	25m	••	••••	••
Plymouth	44	23			•	•
Portsmouth	46	51			••	•••
Queen Margaret	131	7			•••••	•••••
Queen Mary	64	34			•••	••
Queen's, Belfast	109	No information available				
Reading	51	51			••••	••••
Robert Gordon	78	22	25m		••••	•••
Roehampton	98	23			•••	••••
Royal Holloway	52	46			•••	•••

Fitness machines	Number of winter pitches	Availability of winter pitches	Outdoor courts	Availability of outdoor courts	Sports with intramural competitions	Availability of taught classes	Sports scholarships/ bursaries	Forms of elite athlete support
40			•••	•••	2	••••	6	3
145	•••	•••	••••	••••	4	•••••	38	4
110					0	•••••	18	5
40*	•••••	•••••	•••••	•••••	4	•••••	18	10
113	•	•	••	••	3	••••	0	0
38*	•	•	•••	•••	0		0	3
22	•••••	•••••	•••••	•••••	0	••••	1	1
51	••••	••••	•••	••••	5	•••••	41	6
102*	•••••	•••••	•••	•••	2	•••	20	10
26					3	••	0	0
53*	•••	••	•••	•••	2	•	0	10
242	•••••	•••••	••	•••	7	••••	44	10
57	•••	•••	•	•	1	••••	0	2
110					9		51	9
32	••	•••	••	••	0	•	0	1
40	•	•	••	•	3	•	8	10
90	•••	••••	••	•••	16	•••••	0	0
221*	•	••	••	••	17	•••	35	10
169	•••	••••	•••	••••	4	•	52	10
16	••••	•••••	•••	•••	8	••••	0	3
96	••	••	••••	••••	13	•••	5	4
44*	••••	••••	••	••	5	••	15	7
92	•••	••••	••	••	7	••••	40	10
233	•••••	•••••	•••••	•••••	45	••••	135	10
105	•	•	•	••	12	•••	40	8
178*			•	•	0		0	10
50	•••••	•••••	•••••	•••••	3		0	10
78			•	•	8	••	43	10
108	••	•••	••	••	7	••	32	9
240	•••	•••			0		100	10
184	•••	••••	•••••	•••••	8	•••	35	10
140	••••	••••	••	••	4	•••	50	10
107	•••	•••	•••••	•••••	5	••••	25	8
43					10	••	20	6
96	•	•	••	••	13	•••••	15	6
50					0	•••••	0	0
70	•	•			4	•••	0	2
103	•••	•••	••••	••••	3	•••••	40	7
98*					0	••••	20	9
37*	•	•	••••	••••	0		23	10
48	••	••	•••••	•••••	0		28	4

Name	BUCS Ranking 2014–15	Teams in BUCS Leagues	Swimming pool	Availability of pools	Range of indoor dry sports facilities	Availability of indoor dry sports facilities
St Andrews	25	51			•••	•••
St Mark and St John (Marjon)	71	19	25m	••	•••••	•••••
St Mary's, Twickenham	56	No information available				
Salford	82	22	25m	••	•	•
SOAS	138	No information available				
Sheffield	20	56	25m	••••	••	•
Sheffield Hallam	18	46			•	•
South Wales (Newport)	105	11			•••	••••
South Wales (Pontiprydd)	54	31			••••	••••
Southampton	23	57	25m			
Southampton Solent	74	17			•••••	•••••
Staffordshire	91	38			•••••	•••
Stirling	26	41	50m	•••••	••••	•••••
Strathclyde	42	0	Other	•	••	•
Sunderland	85	20			••	••
Surrey	31	40	50m	•••••	•••••	•••••
Sussex	58	30			•••	••
Swansea	29	No information available				
Teesside	101	26			••	••
Trinity Saint David (Carmarthen)	120	No information available				
Trinity Saint David (Swansea)	128	No information available				
Ulster	114	0			•	•
University College London	24	66			•	•
University of the Arts London	115	No information available				
West of England, Bristol	32	39			••	•
West of England, Hartpury	68	No information available				
Warwick	20	3	25 m	••••	••••	•••
West London	135	No information available				
West of Scotland	104	No information available				
Westminster	99	No information available				
Winchester	97	No information available				
Wolverhampton	96	18			•	•
Wolverhampton (Walsall)	96	18	25 m	•	•••••	•••••
Worcester	59	38			••••	••••
York	36	55	25 m	•••	•••	•••
York St John	83	26			•	••

Fitness machines	Number of winter pitches	Availability of winter pitches	Outdoor courts	Availability of outdoor courts	Sports with intramural competitions	Availability of taught classes	Sports scholarships/ bursaries	Forms of elite athlete support
45	•••••	•••••	•••••	•••••	14	••••	15	8
45	•••••	•••••	•••••	•••••	3	•••••	5	4
46	•	•			0	•	0	6
140	••	••			0		27	5
98	•	•	•	•	5	•••	36	10
35	•	•	•••	••••	3	••••	15	10
134	••••	••••			7	•••	24	9
140					11			
175	••••	••	•	•	20	•••	28	10
68	•••••	•••••	•••••	•••••	2	••	0	10
86	••••	••••	••••	••••	3	•••••	91	8
97	•	••			3	•••	44	5
60					0		10	10
110	•••••	•••••	••••	••••	0		14	10
103	•••	••	•••	•••	5	•••	27	4
50*	••	••			3	••••	12	10
45	••	••			2	•	0	9
75*	•	•	•	•	3	••	26	7
100*	•	•			5	••	19	10
98*	••••	••••	••	•	7	••••	No	9
17					7	••	0	10
38	••••	••••	••••	••••	7	••••	30	10
60	•••••	••••			1	••	27	10
71*	•••	••	•••••	•••••	14	•	13	4
18	••	•••			0		1	9

11 What Parents Should Do

Nearly half of all parents in the UK think university is now poor value for money, according to a survey by HSBC. But a larger proportion also believe that higher education is essential to their children's career prospects and are willing to help them through it. Indeed, nine out of ten expect to make a financial contribution to their children's time at university – and to spend up to eight years paying off the debts they incur in the process. But money is only part of what most parents now provide in the modern higher education system: they are more involved than ever in the selection process and often have their say on the quality of the student experience offered by the university. Of course, throughout the *Guide*, all references to parents apply equally to guardians and step-parents.

The introduction of £9,000 fees was meant to make the student responsible for his or her higher education – including paying for it – but parents' involvement has, if anything, increased under the new system. That is because most parents are paying towards students' living costs, not their tuition. Maintenance loans may be larger than they were, but few students will get by on the £5,740 available to most undergraduates outside London in 2015–16. Those parents who can are often anxious to spare their children yet more debt on top of the cost of tuition. Surprising numbers of students from affluent families are not taking out loans at all, and are relying instead on support from parents or sometimes grandparents. Up to half the students at some leading universities are doing without Government maintenance loans, although throughout England, well over 80 per cent are taking them up.

Operating the "bank of mum and dad" may be the most indispensable role played by parents, but there are plenty of others, from chauffeur on open days to cookery coach in their first experience of living away from home. The scale of parental involvement naturally depends on individual relationships, but the right advice and encouragement before, during and after the selection process can be invaluable. Many parents have been to university themselves and will be more adept than a teenager at reading between the lines of a self-congratulatory prospectus or website. But it is important to remember who is going to be the student and not to allow your own (inevitably dated) preconceptions to muddy the waters. Those who are not graduates are just as capable of doing the necessary research to offer a second opinion on universities and courses.

Laying the ground

The first thing any parent can do to smooth the path to university is to be encouraging about the value of higher education. Ideally, this should have started long before the application process, but it is especially important at this point. Now that student debt and variable graduate employment prospects have become frequent media topics, it is only natural for sixth-formers and others to have second thoughts about higher education.

The lure of a regular wage packet will be tempting, should one be available, and there are plenty of young people who are not suited to full-time higher education. More big companies are choosing to employ promising 18-year-olds, rather than rely entirely on graduate recruitment, and there has been a rapid development of apprenticeships. Even after the years of enormous university expansion, most people still do not go to university. Nevertheless, those who are capable of going generally do not regret the decision. Many people look back on their student days as the best period of their life, as well as the one that shaped their personality and their career. Time as a student should still pay off for the individual in terms of lifetime earnings, as well as personal development. A little reassurance at this stage may make all the difference.

There are important decisions to be made before the sixth-form even begins because the choice of A levels or vocational qualifications – and even GCSEs – can close off avenues at degree level. A core of traditional academic subjects will help to keep options open, but there are specific requirements for some degrees that can easily be overlooked until it is too late. Maths A level will be needed for many economics courses, for example, as well as for most sciences.

Making the choice

Any parent wants to help a son or daughter through the difficult business of choosing where and what to study. How big a role you play will depend on a number of factors, not the least of which is the extent to which your advice is wanted. If the quality of advice available at school or college is good, parental involvement may be marginal. But often that is not the case, and you may have to call on other resources, including your own research. Avoid second-hand opinions gleaned through the media or dinner party gossip. You may think that some subjects are a sure-fire route to lucrative employment, while others are shunned by employers, but are you right? And do you really know the strengths and weaknesses of more than 100 universities? Above all, do not try to rewind your own career decisions through your children. The fact that you enjoyed – or hated – a subject or a university does not mean that they will. You may have always regretted missing out on the chance to go to Oxbridge or to become a brain surgeon, but they have their own lives to lead. Students who switch courses or drop out frequently complain that they were pressured into their original choice by their parents. The tables in chapters 2 and 4 offer a reality check, but even they cannot take account of the differences within institutions. The subject tables in chapter 5 show that the best graduate employment rates are often not at the obvious universities.

Parents are encouraged by many schools and colleges to play an active role in the process of choosing a course. At the most basic (but vital) level, this means keeping an eye on deadlines, but it is also about acting as a sounding board and trying to guide your child towards the right university and course. Check that choices are being made for sensible reasons, not on the basis of questionable gossip or trivial criteria. But beyond that, you should stay in the background unless there is a very good reason to play a more substantive role. Make a point of looking for important aspects of university life that the applicant might miss. Security, for example, usually does not feature near the top of a teenager's list of priorities; likewise other practical issues, such as the proximity of student accommodation to lectures, the library and the students' union.

Many universities now publish guides specifically for parents and put on programmes for them at Open Days. The latter may be a way of separating prospective applicants from their more demanding "minders", but the programmes themselves can be interesting and informative. Do not worry that you will be an embarrassment by attending Open Days – thousands of parents do so, and you may add a critical edge to the proceedings. Like prospectuses, Open Days are part of the sales process, and it is easy for a sixth-former to be carried away by the excitement surrounding a lively university. You are much more likely to spot the defects – even if they are ignored in the final decision. Most of today's sixth-formers and college students seem happy to have their parents' help and advice – even if they do not take it in the end. Research by the Knowledge Partnership consultancy found that more than half of the parents of first-year undergraduates felt they had exerted some influence on their children's choices of university and course, although only about 7 per cent characterised this as "a lot".

UCAS also publishes its own guide for parents, offering useful tips and outlining the deadlines that applicants will have to meet. The school should be on top of the timing and offering the necessary advice, but there is no harm in providing a little back-up, especially on parts of the process that take time and thought, such as writing the personal statement. There is little a parent can do as the offers and/or rejections come rolling in, other than to be supportive. If the worst happens and there are five rejections, you may have to start the advice process all over again for a new round of applications through UCAS Extra. If so, a cool head is even more necessary, but the same principles apply.

Results day

Then, before you know it, results day is upon you. Make sure you are at home, rather than in some isolated holiday retreat. Your son or daughter needs to have access to instant advice at school or college, and to be able to contact universities straight away if Clearing or Adjustment is required. And your moral support will be much more effective face to face, rather than down a telephone line. Whatever happens, try not to transmit the anxiety that you will inevitably be feeling to your son or daughter, especially if the results are not what was wanted. It is easy to make rash decisions about re-sitting exams or rejecting an insurance offer in the heat of the moment. Try to slow the process down and encourage clear and realistic thinking. Make sure you know in advance what might be required, such as where to access Clearing lists, and if Clearing or Adjustment is being used, you will need to be on hand to offer advice and help with visits to possible universities. For most applicants, Clearing or Adjustment is all but over in a week, so the agony should be short-lived.

Before they go

Little more than a month after the tension of results day, everything should be ready for the start of term. Unless your son or daughter chooses to stay at home to study, there will be forms to fill in to secure university accommodation, as well as student loans to sort out and registration to complete. You can perform useful services, like supplying recipe books if the first year is to be spent in self-catering accommodation, but now is the time for independence to become reality. Make sure that important details like insurance are not forgotten, but otherwise stand clear.

Then it is just a matter of agreeing a budget, assuming you are in a position to make a financial contribution. How large that contribution is will depend on family circumstances and your attitude to independent living. Some parents want to ensure that their children leave university debt-free; others could never afford to do that. The important thing is that students and parents know where they stand.

Student finance and parental involvement

After a mortgage, a university degree can be the most significant debt families have to repay, according to HSBC. The debt usually combines student loans for tuition fees and maintenance, and is repayable only when a graduate is paid £21,000 a year and can never amount to more than 9 per cent of his or her salary above that threshold. The immediate priority, however, is budgeting for the cost of living, which the National Union of Students puts at £12,000 a year outside London and £13,500 in the capital. Other estimates are slightly lower – Manchester University puts average costs for its students at £9,000 for a 40-week year – but the final bill is still substantial.

Hundreds of thousands of undergraduates – particularly mature students – pay their own way through university. Many undergraduates of all ages supplement their income with term-time and vacation jobs. But every survey shows that families play an important (and growing) role where students move straight from school to higher education. More than half of all students consider the family contribution crucial to their ability to afford a university education. This may rise with the withdrawal of grants for students from the poorest families in 2016, although there will actually be more cash available through the replacement loan system.

Costs are likely to be higher if the choice is an overseas university, although most American institutions have generous scholarships and employment opportunities. Even so, HSBC found that most parents were prepared to pay more for the experience, although they would prefer that their children stayed closer to home.

A frank discussion on what the family can afford is essential before the student leaves home. It is all too easy for a young person who has never had to budget for themselves to get into financial difficulties in the social whirl that is the first term of a degree course. In the worst cases, this can lead to excessive term-time employment to keep up with spiralling debts and pressures that contribute towards a student dropping out.

After they've left

Any new student is going to be nervous if he or she is leaving home for the first time and having to settle into a strange environment. But in most cases it is not going to last long because everyone is in the same boat and freshers' weeks hardly leave time for homesickness. In any case, they will not want to let their apprehension show. The people who are most likely to be emotional are the parents – especially if they are left with an empty nest for the first time. It can take a while to get used to an orderly, quiet house after all those years of mayhem.

Resist any temptation to decorate their bedroom and turn it into an office – it is more common than you might think, and psychologists say it can do lasting damage to family relationships. Keep in touch by phone, text or email, but try not to pry. You're not going to be told everything anyway – which is probably just as well. They will be back soon enough and, just as you were getting used to having the place to yourself, a weekend visit or the Christmas vacation will remind you of how things used to be. If things are not going smoothly at university, this may be the time for more reassurance – more students drop out at Christmas of their first year than at any other time.

"Helicopter parents"

Growing numbers of parents now want to play their part in ensuring that their children get value for money at university, but there is a fine line between constructive involvement and unwelcome interference. Universities report that anxious mothers and fathers are more inclined than ever to question what their children are getting for their now substantial fees. There have been stories of parents challenging not just the amount and quality of tuition, but even the marking of essays and exams. The phenomenon, first reported in the USA, has given rise to the phrase "helicopter parents" – so called because they hover over their children's education when they should be letting go. No one wants to think of themselves in that category, but it is not surprising – or reprehensible – that parents are taking more of an interest.

One of the reasons that some overstep the mark is that they are shocked that the amount of teaching and size of seminar groups are not what they recall from their own "free" higher education. The new fees are meant to herald improvements in the student experience, including more contact hours, but these have been marginal in most universities so far. It may be that fewer and larger seminars are here to stay in the arts and social sciences, where almost all state support for teaching has been withdrawn, and more learning opportunities will be provided online.

An associated reason for greater parental involvement is that family relationships have changed. Many teenage applicants are glad to accept a lift to an open day to get a second opinion on a university and their prospective course. They are also more likely than previous generations of students to come home at the weekend – or to live there in the first place – and to air any grievances. By all means, give advice, but leave direct contact with university administrators and academics to the student. Universities will cite the Data Protection Act, in any case, to say they can only deal with students, not parents. What they really mean is that students are adults and should look after themselves.

Useful websites

Many universities have sections on their websites for parents of prospective students. UCAS has a Parents section and a guide on its website:
www.ucas.com/sites/default/files/ucas-parent-guide-2016-entry_4.pdf

To find out more about open days, visit: **www.opendays.com**

12 Coming to the UK to Study

UK universities have been a magnet for international students for many years – only the huge higher education system in the USA attracts more. The UK's 12 per cent share of the world's young people who choose to study outside their own country is important to its universities and welcomed by British students. The Government also says it wants more university students to come from other countries, although some of its changes to visa regulations have created the impression that it does not. Overseas polling, particularly on the Indian subcontinent, has suggested that prospective international students feel less welcome than before and are turning their attention to alternative destinations such as Canada.

Nevertheless, the number of undergraduates coming from other EU countries and farther afield rose again in 2014 and this year's applications have continued the trend. Global surveys have shown that UK universities are seen as offering high quality in a relatively safe environment, with the added advantage of allowing students to learn and immerse themselves in English. And, while the UK is seen as an expensive place to study, courses that are relatively short by international standards cut the overall costs and speed progress into the employment market.

More than 4 million people now travel abroad to study, and universities in many parts of the world compete aggressively to attract them. The students concerned may see other countries' universities as better than their own, or they may want to master another language and/or experience another culture, but most also see international study as a boost to their career prospects. Surveys in a number of countries have shown that employers – particularly those engaged in global markets – favour applicants with an international education.

While both EU students (who pay the same fees as their British counterparts) and those from the rest of the world (who pay considerably more) have continued to favour UK universities, the numbers of undergraduates coming from individual countries have varied considerably over recent years. The source of most stability has been China, which sends by far the largest numbers (17 per cent of all international students), but there has been fluctuation elsewhere, often due to economic or political factors. In 2013, the numbers coming from Malaysia, for example, rose by 15 per cent in a year while the numbers from Hong Kong rose by 40 per cent, and were second only to China. In 2014, however, there were big rises from France and other EU countries, but falls from Hong Kong and Nigeria.

Universities in the UK continue to be extremely proactive in the recruitment of international students, participating in international fairs and sometimes opening their own offices in target countries. The fees such students pay is the obvious motivation, but universities also value the cultural richness that a diverse international intake contributes to student life.

Why study in the UK?

Aside from the strong reputation of UK degree courses and the opportunity to be taught and surrounded by English, research shows that most graduates are handsomely rewarded when they return home. A report from the Department for Business, Innovation and Skills (BIS) shows that UK graduates earn much higher salaries than those who studied in their own country. The starting salaries of UK graduates in China and India were more than twice as high as those for graduates educated at home, while even those returning to the USA enjoyed a salary premium of more than 10 per cent.

Some premium is to be expected – you are likely to be bright and highly motivated if you are prepared to uproot yourself to take a degree. And, unless they have government scholarships, most students have to be from a relatively wealthy background to afford the fees and other expenses of international study. A higher salary will probably be a necessity to compensate for the cost of the course. But the scale of increase demonstrated in the report suggests that a UK degree remains a good investment. Three years after graduation, 95 per

The top countries for sending international students to the UK

EU countries (top 20)		%	Non-EU Countries (top 20)		%
Cyprus (EU)	7,384	10.1	China	34,987	25.7
France	6,312	8.6	Hong Kong	12,440	9.1
Germany	5,976	8.2	Malaysia	12,036	8.8
Ireland	5,429	7.4	Nigeria	6,411	4.7
Bulgaria	5,404	7.4	India	5,931	4.4
Romania	5,230	7.2	Singapore	5,354	3.9
Greece	4,659	6.4	United States of America	4,640	3.4
Lithuania	4,437	6.1	Norway	3,967	2.9
Italy	4,099	5.6	Saudi Arabia	3,237	2.4
Spain	3,459	4.7	Canada	2,916	2.1
Poland	3,445	4.7	Pakistan	2,817	2.1
Sweden	2,356	3.2	Korea (South)	2,567	1.9
Belgium	1,777	2.4	Bangladesh	2,316	1.7
Latvia	1,546	2.1	Vietnam	2,124	1.6
Finland	1,423	1.9	Russia	2,026	1.5
Netherlands	1,318	1.8	Switzerland	1,777	1.3
Portugal	1,282	1.8	United Arab Emirates	1,761	1.3
Hungary	1,008	1.4	Sri Lanka	1,516	1.1
Slovakia	968	1.3	Brunei	1,471	1.1
Austria	958	1.3	Thailand	1,378	1
All EU students	**73,006**		**All non-EU students**	**136,221**	

Note: First degree non-UK students. Figures from 2013–14.

cent of the international graduates surveyed were in work or further study. More than 90 per cent had been satisfied with their learning experience and almost as many would recommend their university to others.

A popular choice

Nearly all UK universities are cosmopolitan places that welcome international students in large numbers. Recent surveys by i-graduate, the student polling organisation which also produced the BIS report, put the country close behind the USA among the world's most attractive study destinations. Students from outside the EU now make up more than 13 per cent of all students at UK universities and colleges. More full-time postgraduates – the fastest-growing group – come from outside the UK than within it. In many UK universities you can expect to have fellow students from over 100 countries.

More than 90 per cent of international students declare themselves satisfied with their experience of UK universities in i-graduate surveys, although they are less enthusiastic in the National Student Survey and more likely than UK students to make official complaints. Nevertheless, satisfaction increased by 8 percentage points in four years, according to i-graduate, reflecting greater efforts to keep ahead of the global competition. International students are particularly complimentary about students' unions, multiculturalism, teaching standards and places of worship. Their main concerns tend to be financial, with the UK considered the second-most expensive study location in the world (after the USA), partly because of a lack of employment opportunities. In one survey, only 56 per cent were satisfied with the ability to earn money while studying, and statements from ministers in the new UK Government suggest that controls on this, and particularly on the opportunity to work after completing a degree, are likely to become tougher still.

One way round this in a growing number of countries is to take a UK degree through a local institution or a full branch campus of a UK university. Indeed, there are now almost as many international students taking UK degrees at all levels in their own country as there are in Britain – 320,000 of them outside the EU. The numbers grew by 70 per cent in a decade and are likely to rise further if UK Government policies obstruct universities' efforts to increase the number of students coming to Britain.

Where to study in the UK

The vast majority of the UK's universities and other higher education institutions are in England. Of the 132 universities profiled in this *Guide*, 107 are in England, 15 in Scotland, 8 in Wales and 2 in Northern Ireland. Fee limits in higher education for UK and EU students are determined separately in each administrative area, which in some cases has brought benefits for EU students. All undergraduates from other EU countries are charged the same fees as those from the part of the UK where their chosen university is located, so EU students currently pay no tuition fees in Scotland, for example.

Within the UK, the cost of living varies by geographical area. Although London is the most expensive, accommodation costs in particular can also be high in many other major cities. You should certainly find out as much as you can about what living in Britain will be like. Further advice and information is available through the British Council at its offices worldwide, at more than 60 university exhibitions that it holds around the world every year, or at its Education UK website (**www.educationuk.org**). Another useful website for international students is provided by the UK Council for International Student Affairs (UKCISA) at **www.ukcisa.org.uk**.

Universities in all parts of the UK have a worldwide reputation for high quality teaching and research, as evidenced in global rankings such as those shown on pages 52–54. They maintain this standing by investing heavily in the best academic staff, buildings and equipment, and by taking part in rigorous quality assurance monitoring. The main regulatory bodies include the Quality Assurance Agency for Higher Education (QAA), higher education funding councils for each country of the UK, and the Office for Standards in Education, all of which publish reports on their websites. Professional bodies also play an important role, and there is an Independent Adjudicator for Higher Education who handles student complaints that have not been resolved by universities' own internal procedures.

Although many people from outside the UK associate British universities with Oxford and Cambridge, in reality most higher education institutions are nothing like this. Some universities do still maintain a traditional culture, but most are modern institutions that place at least as much emphasis on teaching as on research and offer many vocational programmes, often with close links with business, industry and the professions. The table below shows the universities that are most popular with international students at undergraduate level. Although some of those at the top of the lists are among the most famous names in higher education, others achieved university status only in the last 20 years.

What subjects to study?

One of the reasons for such diversity is that strongly vocational courses are favoured by

The universities most favoured by EU and non-EU students

Institution (top 20)	EU students	Institution (top 20)	Non-EU students
Glasgow	2,189	Manchester	4,960
Edinburgh	1,844	Liverpool	3,889
Aberdeen	1,817	University College London	3,864
University College London	1,461	University of the Arts London	3,482
Essex	1,443	Nottingham	3,245
University of the Arts London	1,425	Edinburgh	3,241
Middlesex	1,422	Coventry	3,023
Manchester	1,406	Sheffield	2,933
King's College London	1,398	Sunderland	2,916
Westminster	1,373	Warwick	2,478
Coventry	1,327	Imperial College	2,425
London Metropolitan	1,240	St Andrews	2,056
Kent	1,225	Portsmouth	1,993
Portsmouth	1,132	Sheffield Hallam	1,993
Imperial College	1,100	Leeds	1,927
Edinburgh Napier	1,081	Exeter	1,889
Warwick	1,015	Leicester	1,862
Kingston	1,014	Southampton	1,846
Lancaster	1,001	City	1,832
Cambridge	983	Hertfordshire	1,816

Note: First degree non-UK students. Figures for 2013–14.

international students. Many of these in professional areas such as architecture, dentistry or medicine take one or two years longer to complete than most other degree courses. Traditional first degrees are mostly awarded at Bachelor level (BA, BEng, BSc, etc.) and last three to four years. There are also some "enhanced" first degrees (MEng, MChem, etc.) that take four years to complete. The relatively new Foundation degree programmes are almost all vocational and take two years to complete as a full-time course, with an option to study for a further year to gain a full degree. The table below shows the most popular subjects studied by international students. Remember, though, that you need to consider the details of any university course that you wish to study and to look at the ranking of that university in our main league table in chapter 4 and in the subject tables in chapter 5.

English language proficiency

The universities maintain high standards partly by setting demanding entry requirements, including proficiency in English. For international students, this usually includes a score of 6 or 7 in the International English Language Testing System (IELTS), which assesses English language ability through listening, speaking, reading and writing tests. Under visa regulations introduced in 2011, universities are able to vouch for a student's ability in English. This proficiency will need to be equivalent to an "upper intermediate" level (level B2) of the CEFR (Common European Framework of Reference for Languages) for studying at an

The most popular subjects for international students

Subject	EU students	Non-EU students	Total students	% of all international students
Business studies	10,586	27,211	37,796	18.1
Accounting	2,418	14,887	17,305	8.3
Law	3,704	9,368	13,073	6.2
Economics	2,620	7,215	9,835	4.7
Art and design	3,534	5,407	8,942	4.3
Computing	4,088	4,710	8,797	4.2
Electrical and electronic engineering	1,336	5,287	6,623	3.2
Mechanical engineering	1,641	4,944	6,585	3.1
Politics	3,315	3,009	6,324	3.0
Biological sciences	2,898	2,980	5,878	2.8
Mathematics	1,356	4,230	5,586	2.7
Psychology	2,950	2,511	5,462	2.6
Communication and media studies	2,664	2,663	5,327	2.5
Civil engineering	1,248	3,331	4,578	2.2
Architecture	1,939	2,388	4,327	2.1
Medicine	945	3,348	4,293	2.1
Hospitality, leisure, recreation and tourism	1,841	2,335	4,175	2.0
Drama, dance and cinematics	2,258	1,631	3,888	1.9
Pharmacology and pharmacy	709	2,532	3,241	1.5
Other subjects allied to medicine	1,315	1,509	2,824	1.3

Note: First degree non-UK students Figures for 2013–14.

undergraduate level (roughly equivalent to a score of 5 to 6.5 in IELTS).

There are many private and publicly funded colleges throughout the UK that run courses designed to bring the English language skills of prospective higher education students up to the required standard. However, not all of these are Government approved. Some private organisations such as INTO (**www.intohigher.com**) have joined with universities to create centres running programmes preparing international students for degree-level study. The British Council also runs English language courses at its centres around the world.

Tougher student visa regulations were introduced in 2012 and have since been refined. Although universities' international students should not be denied entry to the UK, as long as they are found to have followed immigration rules, some lower-level preparatory courses taken by international students have been affected. It is, therefore, doubly important to consult the official UK government list of approved institutions (web address given at the end of this chapter) before lodging an application.

How to apply

You should read the information below in conjunction with that provided in chapter 6, which deals with the application process in some detail.

Some international students apply directly to a UK university for a place on a course, and others make their applications via an agent in their home country. But most applying for a full-time first degree course do so through the Universities and Colleges Admissions Service (UCAS). If you take this route, you will need to fill in an online UCAS application form at home, at school or perhaps at your nearest British Council office. There is lots of advice on the UCAS website about the process of finding a course and the details of the application system (**www.ucas.com/ucas/undergraduate/getting-started/international-and-eu-students**).

Whichever way you apply, the deadlines for getting your application in are the same. For those applying from within an EU country, application forms for most courses starting in 2016 must be received at UCAS by 15 January 2016. Note that applications for Oxford and Cambridge and for all courses in medicine, dentistry and veterinary science have to be received at UCAS by 15 October 2015, while some art and design courses have a later deadline of 24 March 2016.

If you are applying from a non-EU country to study in 2016, you can submit your application to UCAS at any time between 1 September 2015 and 30 June 2016. Most people will apply well before the 30 June deadline to make sure that places are still available and to allow plenty of time for immigration regulations, and to make arrangements for travel and accommodation.

Entry and employment regulations

Visa regulations have been the subject of continuing controversy in the UK and many new rules and regulations have been introduced, often hotly contested by universities. The Government was criticised for increasing visa fees, doubling the cost of visa extensions, and ending the right to appeal against a refusal of a visa.

It also introduced a points system for entry – known as Tier 4 – which came into effect in 2009. Under this scheme, prospective students can check whether they are eligible for entry against published criteria, and so assess their points score. Universities are also required to provide a Confirmation of Acceptance for Studies (CAS) to their international student entrants, who must have secured an unconditional offer, and the institutions must appear as a "Tier 4 Sponsor" on the Home Office's Register of Sponsors. Prospective students have to demonstrate that, as well as the necessary qualifications, they have English language proficiency and enough money for the first year of their specified course. This includes the full fees for the first year and, from November 2015, living costs of £1,265 a month for the duration of the course, up to a maximum of nine months, if studying in London (£1,015 a month in the rest of the UK). Under the new visa requirements, details of financial support are checked in more detail than before.

All students wishing to enter the UK to study are required to obtain entry clearance before arrival. The only exceptions are British nationals living overseas, British overseas territories citizens, British Protected persons, British subjects, and non-visa national short-term students who may enter under a new Student Visitor route. Visa fees have been increased again (to £322 for a Tier 4 visa, plus £150 a year healthcare surcharge) and the details of the regulations are continually reviewed by the Home Office. You can find more about all the latest rules and regulations for entry and visa requirements at **www.gov.uk/browse/visas-immigration/study-visas**.

The rules and regulations governing permission to work vary according to your country of origin and the level of course you undertake. If you are from a European Economic Area (EEA) country (the EU plus Iceland, Liechtenstein and Norway) or Switzerland, you do not need permission to work in the UK, although you will need to be ready to show an employer your passport or identity card to prove you are a national of an EEA country. Students from outside the EEA who are here as Tier 4 students are allowed to work part-time for up to 20 hours a week during term time and full-time during vacations. These arrangements apply to students on degree courses; stricter limits were introduced in 2010 for lower-level courses. If you wish to stay on after you have graduated, you can apply for permission under Tier 2 of the new points-based immigration system, but you will need a sponsor and the work must be considered "graduate level", commanding a salary of at least £20,800. The reforms abolished the Tier 1 two-year post-study period for graduates who do not have such a sponsor. They will be required to apply for a new visa from scratch. Full details are on the Home Office study visas website above.

A new Tier 1 Graduate Entrepreneur Scheme enables up to 1,000 graduates to remain in the UK if they have "genuine and credible business ideas and entrepreneurial skills". Successful applicants, who will be selected by their university, will be allowed to stay in the UK for 12 months, with the possibility of a further 12-month extension.

Bringing your family

Since 2010, international students on courses of six months or less have been forbidden to bring a partner or children into the UK, and the latest reforms extend this prohibition to all undergraduates except those who are government sponsored. Postgraduates studying for 12 months or longer will still be able to bring dependants to the UK, and most universities can help to arrange facilities and accommodation for families as well as for single students. The family members you are allowed to bring with you are your husband or wife, civil partner (a same-sex relationship that has been formally registered in the UK or your home country) or long-term partner and dependent children. You can find out more about getting entry clearance for your family at **www.ukcisa.org.uk**.

Support from British universities

Support for international students is more comprehensive than in many countries, and begins long before you arrive in the UK. Many universities have advisers in other countries.

Some will arrange to put you in touch with current students or graduates who can give you a first-hand account of what life is like at a particular university. Pre-departure receptions for students and their families, as well as meet-and-greet arrangements for newly arrived students, are common. You can also expect an orientation and induction programme in your first week, and many universities now have "buddying" systems where current students are assigned to new arrivals to help them find their way around, adjust to their new surroundings and make new friends. Each university also has a students' union that organises social, cultural and sporting events and clubs, including many specifically for international students. Both the university and the students' union are likely to have full-time staff whose job it is to look after the welfare of students from overseas.

International students also benefit from free medical and subsidised dental and optical care and treatment under the UK National Health Service (non-EU students will have had to pay a healthcare surcharge when paying for their visa to benefit from this), plus access to a professional counselling service and a university careers service.

At university, you will naturally encounter people from a wide range of cultures and walks of life. Getting involved in student societies, sport, voluntary work, and any of the wide range of social activities on offer will help you gain first-hand experience of British culture, and, if you need it, will help improve your command of the English language.

Useful websites

The British Council, with its dedicated Education UK site designed for those wishing to find out more about studying in the UK:
www.educationuk.org

The UK Council for International Student Affairs (UKCISA) provides a wide range of information on all aspects of studying in the UK:
www.ukcisa.org.uk

UCAS, for full details of undergraduate courses available and an explanation of the application process:
www.ucas.com/ucas/undergraduate/getting-started/international-and-eu-students

For the latest information on entry and visa requirements:
www.gov.uk/browse/visas-immigration/student-visas

Register of sponsors for Tier 4 educational establishments:
www.gov.uk/government/publications/register-of-licensed-sponsors-students

For a general guide to Britain, available in many languages:
www.visitbritain.com

13 Applying to Oxbridge

Oxbridge (as Oxford and Cambridge are called collectively) not only dominates UK higher education; the two universities are recognised as among the best in the world, regularly featuring among the top five in global rankings. But that is not why they merit a separate chapter in this *Guide*.

The two ancient universities have different admissions arrangements to the rest of the higher education system. Although part of the UCAS network, they have different deadlines from other universities, you can only apply to one or the other, and selection is in the hands of the colleges rather than the university centrally. Most candidates apply to a specific college, although you can make an open application if you are happy to go anywhere.

There have been reforms to the admissions system at both universities in recent years, in order to make the process more user-friendly to those who do not have school or family experience to draw upon. In particular, the business of choosing a college has been intimidating for many prospective applicants. Candidates are now distributed around colleges more efficiently, regardless of the choices they make initially.

There is little to choose between the two universities in terms of entrance requirements, and a formidable number of successful applicants have the maximum possible grades. However, that does not mean that the talented student should be shy about applying: both have fewer applicants per place than many less prestigious universities, and admissions tutors are always looking to extend the range of schools and colleges from which they recruit. For those with a realistic chance of success, there is little to lose except the possibility of one wasted space out of five on the UCAS application.

Overall, there are about five applicants to every place at Oxford and Cambridge, but there are big differences between subjects and colleges. As the tables in this chapter show, competition is particularly fierce in subjects such as medicine and English, but those qualified to read geology or classics have a much better chance of success. The pattern is similar to that in other universities, although the high degree of selection (and self-selection) that precedes an Oxbridge application means that even in the less popular subjects the field of candidates is certain to be strong.

The two universities' power to intimidate prospective applicants is based partly on myth. Both have done their best to live down the Brideshead Revisited image, but many sixth-formers still fear that they would be out of their depth there, academically and socially.

In fact, the state sector produces about 58 per cent of entrants to Oxford and Cambridge, and the dropout rate is lower than at almost any other university. The "champagne set" is still present and its activities are well publicised, but most students are hard-working high achievers with the same concerns as their counterparts on other campuses. A joint poll by the two universities' student newspapers showed that undergraduates were spending much of their time in the library or worrying about their employment prospects, and relatively little time on the river or even in the college bar.

State school applicants

Both universities and their student organisations have put a great deal of effort into trying to encourage applications from state schools, and many colleges have launched their own campaigns. Such has been the determination to convince state school pupils that they will get a fair crack of the whip that a new concern has grown up of possible bias against independent school pupils. In reality, however, the dispersed nature of Oxbridge admissions rules out any conspiracy. Some colleges set relatively low standard offers to encourage applicants from the state sector, who may reveal their potential at interview. Some admissions tutors may give the edge to well-qualified candidates from comprehensive schools over those from highly academic independent schools because they consider theirs the greater achievement in the circumstances. Others stick with tried and trusted sources of good students. The independent sector still enjoys a degree of success out of proportion to its share of the school population.

Choosing the right college

Simply in terms of winning a place at Oxford or Cambridge, choosing the right college is not quite as important as it used to be. Both universities have got better at assessing candidates' strengths and finding a suitable college for those who either make an open application or are not taken by their first-choice college.

Cambridge: The Tompkins Table 2015

College	2015	2014	College	2015	2014
Trinity	**1**	1	Robinson	**16**	20
Magdalene	**2**	10	Sidney Sussex	**17**	17
Churchill	**3**	6	King's	**18**	14
Emmanuel	**4**	5	Gonville and Caius	**19**	15
Pembroke	**5**	2	Fitzwilliam	**20**	19
Peterhouse	**6**	12	Newnham	**21**	22
Queens'	**7**	7	Corpus Christi	**22**	18
Trinity Hall	**8**	3	Murray Edwards	**23**	26
Downing	**9**	11	Girton	**24**	23
St John's	**10**	16	Hughes Hall	**25**	27
Jesus	**11**	4	Wolfson	**26**	25
Selwyn	**12**	13	Homerton	**27**	24
St Catharine's	**13**	21	St Edmund's	**28**	28
Christ's	**14**	9	Lucy Cavendish	**29**	29
Clare	**15**	8			

At Oxford, subject tutors from around the university put candidates into bands at the start of the selection process, using the results of admissions tests as well as exam results and references. Applicants are spread around the colleges for interview and may not be seen by their preferred college if the tutors think their chances of a place are better elsewhere. Almost a quarter of successful candidates are offered places by a college other than the one they applied to.

Cambridge relies on the "pool", which gives the most promising candidates a second chance if they were not offered a place at the college to which they applied. Those placed in the pool are invited back for a second round of interviews early in the new year. The system lowers the stakes for those who apply to the most selective colleges – in 2013 about 21 per cent of offers came via the pool. Cambridge still interviews more than 80 per cent of applicants, whereas the new system at Oxford has resulted in more immediate rejections in some subjects. In medicine, fewer than a third of Oxford's applicants are interviewed, while in biochemistry almost all were.

However, most Oxbridge applicants still apply direct to a particular college, not only to maximise their chances of getting in, but because that is where they will be living and socialising, as well as learning. Most colleges may look the same to the uninitiated, but there are important differences. Famously sporty colleges, for example, can be trying for those in search of peace and quiet.

Thorough research is needed to find the right place. Even within colleges, different admissions tutors may have different approaches, so personal contact is essential. The tables in this chapter give an idea of the relative academic strengths of the colleges, as well as the varying levels of competition for a place in different subjects. But only individual research will suggest where you will feel most at home. For example, women may favour one of the few remaining single-sex colleges (Murray Edwards, Newnham and Lucy Cavendish at Cambridge). Men have no such option.

Oxford: The Norrington Table 2015

College	2015	2014	College	2015	2014
Magdalen	**1**	9	Harris Manchester	**16**	8
New	**2**	4	St Hilda's	**17**	21
Wadham	**3**	5	Mansfield	**18**	25
Balliol	**4**	20	Trinity	**19**	11
Lincoln	**5**	10	University	**20**	24
St Catherine's	**6**	12	St Hugh's	**21**	17
St John's	**7**	2	Exeter	**22**	15
St Anne's	**8**	13	St Peter's	**23**	22
Keble	**9**	18	Brasenose	**24**	19
Corpus Christi	**10**	14	Queen's	**25**	29
Worcester	**11**	3	Lady Margaret Hall	**26**	26
Oriel	**12**	23	Merton	**27**	1
Jesus	**13**	6	Somerville	**28**	27
Hertford	**14**	7	St Edmund Hall	**29**	28
Christ Church	**15**	16	Pembroke	**30**	30

Oxford applications and acceptances by course

Arts	Applications 2014	Applications 2013	Acceptances 2014	Acceptances 2013	Acceptances to Applications % 2014	Acceptances to Applications % 2013
Ancient and modern history	73	81	18	14	24.7	17.3
Archaeology and anthropology	72	101	24	20	33.3	19.8
Classical archaeology and ancient history	84	67	24	19	28.6	28.4
Classics	291	293	106	123	36.4	42
Classics and English	37	30	12	8	32.4	26.7
Classics and modern languages	30	23	9	8	30	34.8
Computer science and philosophy	50	23	8	9	16	29
Economics and management	1,149	1,192	86	84	7.5	7
English	1,100	1,142	231	240	21	21
English and modern Languages	115	117	18	18	15.7	15.4
European and Middle Eastern languages	37	28	3	8	8.1	28.6
Fine art	193	189	27	28	14	14.8
Geography	322	371	76	77	23.6	20.8
History	1,001	1,029	234	246	23.4	23.9
History and economics	84	99	16	13	19	13.1
History and English	85	89	9	7	10.6	7.9
History and modern languages	106	87	23	16	21.7	18.4
History and politics	288	279	33	39	11.5	14
History of art	122	137	13	12	10.7	8.8
Law	1,262	1,302	185	196	14.7	15.1
Law with law studies in Europe	287	317	34	31	11.8	9.8
Mathematics and philosophy	83	90	15	16	18.1	17.8
Modern languages	515	573	172	189	33.4	33
Modern languages and linguistics	61	72	27	27	44.3	37.5
Music	208	221	66	70	31.7	31.7
Oriental studies	148	168	45	48	30.4	28.6
Philosophy and modern languages	66	51	15	13	22.7	25.5
Philosophy and theology	121	118	25	28	20.7	23.7
Physics and philosophy	135	146	16	16	11.9	11
Philosophy, politics and economics (PPE)	1,651	1,640	240	232	14.5	14.1
Theology	120	91	40	28	33.3	30.8
Theology and oriental studies	4	4	1	1	25	25
Total Arts	**9,778**	**10,178**	**1,851**	**1,884**	**18.9**	**18.5**

The findings in the Tompkins Table (see page 272) are not officially endorsed by Cambridge University itself. However, since 2007 we have been able to publish the "official" Norrington Table from Oxford. Sanctioned or not, both tables give an indication of where the academic powerhouses lie – information which can be as useful to those trying to avoid them as to those seeking the ultimate challenge. Although there can be a great deal of movement year by year, both tables tend to be dominated by the rich, old foundations. Both tables are

Oxford applications and acceptances by course cont

Sciences	Applications 2014	Applications 2013	Acceptances 2014	Acceptances 2013	Acceptances to Applications % 2014	Acceptances to Applications % 2013
Biochemistry	424	399	102	90	24	22.6
Biological sciences	424	428	103	111	24.3	25.9
Biomedical sciences	229	193	36	33	15.7	17.1
Chemistry	684	638	187	180	27.3	28.2
Computer science	238	147	22	23	9.2	15.6
Earth sciences (Geology)	111	116	26	34	23.4	29.3
Engineering sciences	922	720	159	157	17.2	21.8
Engineering, economics and management	-	100	-	10	-	10
Experimental psychology	238	212	46	50	19.3	23.6
Human science	178	155	25	31	14	20
Materials science (including MEM)	118	79	33	33	28	41.8
Mathematics	1,015	917	178	161	17.5	17.6
Mathematics and computer science	153	119	28	28	18.3	23.5
Mathematics and statistics	143	172	13	22	9	12.8
Medicine	1,433	1,471	152	149	10.6	10.1
Physics	1,113	1,011	176	173	15.8	17.1
Psychology and philosophy (PPL)	161	161	24	29	14.9	18
Total Sciences	**7,584**	**7,038**	**1,310**	**1,314**	**17.3**	**18.7**
Total Arts and Sciences	**17,362**	**17,216**	**3,161**	**3,198**	**18.2**	**18.6**

Note: the dates refer to the year in which the acceptances were made.

compiled from the degree results of final-year undergraduates. A first is worth five points; a 2:1, four; a 2:2, three; a third, one point. The total is divided by the number of candidates to produce each college's average.

In both universities, teaching for most students is based in the colleges. In practice, however, in the sciences this arrangement holds good only for the first year. One-to-one tutorials, which are Oxbridge's traditional strength for undergraduates, are by no means universal. Teaching groups remain much smaller than in most universities, and the tutor remains an inspiration for many students.

The applications procedure

Both universities have set a UCAS deadline of 15 October 2015 (at 6pm) for entry in 2016 or deferred entry in 2017. You may also need to take a written test and submit examples of your work – the exact requirements vary depending on the course you select, so check this carefully. See pages 20–21 for details of assessment tests, which are now being used for an increasing number of subjects. In addition, once Cambridge receives your UCAS form, you will be asked to complete an online Supplementary Application Questionnaire (SAQ). The deadline for this will be 22 October 2015 in most cases. For international applications to Cambridge you must also submit a Cambridge Online Preliminary Application (COPA), by

Cambridge applications and acceptances by course

	Applications		Acceptances		Acceptances to Applications %	
Arts, Humanities and Social Sciences	**2014**	**2013**	**2014**	**2013**	**2014**	**2013**
Anglo-Saxon, Norse and Celtic	58	57	25	30	43.1	52.6
Architecture	403	395	43	41	10.7	10.4
Asian and Middle Eastern studies	114	113	49	40	43.0	35.4
Classics	155	155	74	70	47.7	45.2
Classics (4 years)	40	54	13	18	32.5	33.3
Economics	1,105	1,206	152	156	13.8	12.9
Education	113	95	35	36	31.0	37.9
English	767	718	193	199	25.2	27.7
Geography	314	309	101	97	32.2	31.4
History	607	637	198	190	32.6	29.8
History of art	87	77	26	22	29.9	28.6
Human, social and political sciences	898	877	186	198	20.7	22.6
Land economy	206	215	53	50	25.7	23.3
Law	1,047	933	204	212	19.5	22.7
Linguistics	100	109	30	30	30.0	27.5
Modern and medieval languages	383	388	169	168	44.1	43.3
Music	151	146	66	59	43.7	40.4
Philosophy	235	258	42	53	17.9	20.5
Theology and religious studies	89	110	43	50	48.3	45.5
Total Arts, Humanities and Social Sciences	**6,872**	**6,852**	**1,702**	**1,719**	**24.8**	**25.1**
Science and Technology	**2014**	**2013**	**2014**	**2013**	**2014**	**2013**
Computer science	583	521	101	86	17.3	16.5
Engineering	2,161	1,927	326	294	15.1	15.3
Mathematics	1,336	1,360	236	234	17.7	17.2
Medical sciences	1,861	1,867	287	260	15.4	16.9
Natural sciences	3,170	2,860	660	619	20.8	21.6
Psychological and behavioural sciences	422	382	66	64	15.6	16.8
Veterinary medicine	347	416	70	74	20.2	17.8
Total Science and Technology	**9,880**	**9,333**	**1,746**	**1,652**	**17.7**	**17.4**
Total	**16,752**	**16,185**	**3,448**	**3,371**	**20.6**	**20.8**

Note: the dates refer to the year in which the acceptances were made.
Mathematics includes mathematics and mathematics with physics. Medical sciences includes medicine and the graduate course in medicine.
The Tripos courses in chemical engineering, management studies and manufacturing engineering can be taken only after Part 1 in another subject.
Applications and acceptances for these courses are recorded under the first year subjects taken by the applicants involved.

20 September or 15 October 2015; check the Cambridge website for full details. You may apply to either Oxford or Cambridge (but not both) in the same admissions year, unless you are seeking an Organ award at both universities. Interviews take place in December for those short-listed (for international applicants, Cambridge holds some interviews overseas while Oxford holds some interviews over the internet, though medicine interviewees must come to Oxford). Applicants will receive either a conditional offer or a rejection early in the new year.

For more information about the application process and preparation for interviews, visit **www.undergraduate.study.cam.ac.uk/** and **www.ox.ac.uk/admissions/undergraduate**.

Oxford College Profiles

Balliol

Oxford OX1 3BJ	01865 277777	www.balliol.ox.ac.uk
Undergraduates: 377	Postgraduates: 297	undergrad.admissions@balliol.ox.ac.uk

Famous as the alma mater of many prominent post-war politicians, Balliol has maintained a strong presence in university life and is usually well represented in the Union and most other societies. Academic standards are formidably high, as might be expected in the college of Wyclif and Adam Smith, and it usually falls in the top ten of the Norrington Table. Library facilities are good and include the Taylor law library. Balliol began admitting overseas students in the 19th century and has cultivated an attractively cosmopolitan atmosphere. Most undergraduates are offered guaranteed accommodation in college for their first and final years. Graduate students are usually lodged in the Graduate Centre at Holywell Manor, ten minutes' walk from the main site. Balliol is strong in rugby, football and rowing, and has a thriving music and drama scene. It is one of the few colleges to run an annual charity musical. "Bruce's Brunch", organised by the Welfare Officer, bring a steady stream of interesting speakers to Balliol. Hall food is good quality and the JCR has its own cafeteria. The student-run bar is among the most popular in Oxford.

Brasenose

Oxford OX1 4AJ	01865 277510 (admissions)	www.bnc.ox.ac.uk
Undergraduates: 364	Postgraduates: 209	admissions@bnc.ox.ac.uk

Brasenose may not be the most famous Oxford college, but it makes up for its discreet image with an advantageous city-centre position, nestled beside the stunning Radcliffe Camera. The alma mater of David Cameron, Brasenose was one of the first colleges to admit women in the 1970s, and now has a near-even split. BNC, as the college is often known, has a strong rugby reputation, having won the rugby cuppers 14 times over the years. Named after the door knocker on the 13th-century Brasenose Hall, the college has a pleasant, intimate ambience conducive to study. Law, PPE, medicine and modern history are traditional strengths, and competition for places in these subjects is intense. The library is 24-hour and there is a separate law library. Sporting standards are as high as at many much larger colleges and the college puts on a successful annual Arts Week. The annexe at Frewin Court, five minutes from the main site, means nearly all undergraduates can live in, and many postgraduates can also live in the St Cross Building. College rooms vary in quality, but are priced accordingly.

Christ Church

Oxford OX1 1DP | 01865 276181 (admissions) | www.chch.ox.ac.uk
Undergraduates: 417 | Postgraduates: 174 | admissions@chch.ox.ac.uk

The college, founded by Cardinal Wolsey in 1525, boasts the largest quad in Oxford, complete with an ornamental pond full of Japanese koi carp, donated by the Empress of Japan. Around half of offers tend to be made to state school pupils, which leaves Christ Church with among the highest proportion of private school students. The student-run Ambassadors scheme set up in 2013 is helping the college shake its public school image and endeavours to improve access opportunities. The magnificent 18th-century library is one of the best in Oxford and is supplemented by a separate law library. Recent sporting strengths are found in netball and football, and the river is close by for the aspiring oarsman; the men's crew are currently 2nd in the division. Accommodation for all three years is rated by college undergraduates as excellent and includes flats off Iffley Road as well as a number of beautifully panelled shared sets (double rooms) in college. Christ Church food is highly regarded and a three-course dinner (served daily in the "Hogwarts" hall) is exceptionally cheap. The college bar has recently been refurbished. The chapel is also the cathedral of the Diocese of Oxford – England's smallest medieval cathedral. The constant stream of tourists is mildly disruptive to collegiate life.

Corpus Christi

Oxford OX1 4JF | 01865 276693 (admissions) | www.ccc.ox.ac.uk
Undergraduates: 249 | Postgraduates: 95 | admissions.office@ccc.ox.ac.uk

Corpus, one of Oxford's smallest colleges, is naturally overshadowed by its Goliath-like neighbour, Christ Church, but makes the most of its intimate, friendly atmosphere and exquisite beauty. Although the college has only around 350 students including postgraduates, it has an admirable 24-hour library. Academic expectations are high and English, Classics, PPE and medicine are especially well-established. Corpus can offer accommodation to all its undergraduates, one of its many attractions to those seeking a smaller community in Oxford. Rooms in the new, off-site Lampl building are modern and en suite. Many of the older rooms are due to be refurbished. The college is also one of the most generous with bursaries, giving travel, book and vacation grants at an almost unparalleled level across the university. Scholars are particularly well rewarded. The MBI Al-Jaber Auditorium is a large, modern and pleasant space built into a bastion of the medieval city wall and is used for music and drama, as well as for parties, art exhibitions, seminars and lectures. Corpus's drama company, the Owlets, is highly regarded in Oxford. The college sports grounds are shared with University College, but sporting success is relatively limited.

Exeter

Oxford OX1 3DP | 01865 279648 (academic secretary) | www.exeter.ox.ac.uk
Undergraduates: 334 | Postgraduates: 185 | admissions@exeter.ox.ac.uk

Founded in 1314 by Walter de Stapeldon, Bishop of Exeter, Exeter is the fourth oldest college in the university. Alma mater to J.R.R. Tolkien, Alan Bennett and Philip Pullman, Exeter is full of history. Nestling between the High Street and Broad Street, it could hardly be more central. Most undergraduates are guaranteed three years of college accommodation, although many second-year students currently live out. Graduate students are housed off-site on the Exeter House campus. The Cohen Quad, located on Walton Street, is due to open in Autumn 2016 and will provide 90 en-suite bedrooms and a wide range of state-of-the-art facilities. While Rector (2004–14), Frances Cairncross, former managing editor of *The Economist*, created a new dynamic at the college, with regular, high profile speaker events and the only college careers service. Among an array of societies, the John Ford Society exists to fund dramatic ventures; the Fortescue Society to talk about the law; the PPE Society to bring in high-profile speakers. The College puts something back into the local community through its own vacation project, EXVAC, a student-run scheme that raises funds through sponsorship and takes children from disadvantaged backgrounds on holiday during the Easter vacation.

Harris Manchester

Oxford OX1 3TD | 01865 271009 (admissions tutor) | www.hmc.ox.ac.uk
Undergraduates: 76 | Postgraduates: 123 | enquiries@hmc.ox.ac.uk

Founded in Manchester in 1786 to provide education for non-Anglican students, Harris Manchester finally settled in Oxford in 1889 after spells in both York and London. A full university college since 1996, its central location with fine buildings and grounds in Holywell Street is very convenient for the Bodleian, although the college also has an excellent library. Harris Manchester admits mature students only (21 or older) to read for undergraduate and graduate degrees, predominantly in the arts. Most members live in, and the Siew-Sngiem Clock tower, which opened in 2014, provides five hotel-worthy rooms and was featured in *Country Living* magazine. All meals are provided – indeed the college encourages its members to dine regularly in hall. Its food is among the finest in Oxford. The college has few sporting facilities (a croquet lawn and a college punt), but members can use two central Oxford gyms without charge and can play sport for other college or university teams. Other outlets include the college Drama Society and the chapel.

Hertford

Oxford OX1 3BW | 01865 279404 (admissions) | www.hertford.ox.ac.uk
Undergraduates: 405 | Postgraduates: 189 | admissions@hertford.ox.ac.uk

Though tracing its roots to the 13th century, Hertford is determinedly modern. It was one of the first colleges to admit women and celebrated its 40th anniversary of co-education with a portrait display of Hertford women from every generation since 1974. It is popular with state school applicants, thanks to its strong commitment to access. The 2014 student-led sponsored cycle ride from Hertford's Bridge of Sighs to the Bridge of Sighs in Venice raised £300,000 for the college's bursaries and grants fund, enabling Hertford to continue with its financial generosity in the years to come. It is close to the History Faculty library (Hertford's neighbour) and the Bodleian library. Its proximity to the King's Arms and the Turf Tavern, two of Oxford's most popular pubs, bolsters the already vibrant social scene. Accommodation has improved, thanks in part to the Abingdon House and Warnock House complex close to the Thames near Folly Bridge, and the college can now lodge all of its undergraduates, often at subsidised rates (fourth lowest rent in the university), albeit in disparate parts of the city.

Jesus

Oxford OX1 3DW | 01865 279721 (admissions) | www.jesus.ox.ac.uk
Undergraduates: 340 | Postgraduates: 190 | admissions.officer@jesus.ox.ac.uk

Jesus, the only Oxford college to be founded in the reign of Elizabeth I, suffers from something of an unfair reputation for insularity. Alma mater to T.E. Lawrence and Harold Wilson, Jesus was ranked the top Oxford college for overall student satisfaction over the five-year period 2010–14. Close to most of Oxford's main facilities, Jesus has three compact quads, the second of which is especially enticing in the summer. The college's JCR is well-equipped. Sporting success has tailed off in recent years, but the college has a symphony orchestra shared with St Peter's. Accommodation is almost universally excellent and relatively inexpensive. Self-catering flats in north and east Oxford have enabled every graduate to live in throughout his or her Oxford career. The range of accommodation available to undergraduates is similarly good and is available for the full length of any course. The new Ship Street Centre contains 33 en-suite rooms for first-year students and a lecture theatre. The college's Cowley Road development, next to the college's sports ground, was described by the students' union as "some of the plushest student housing in Oxford". A new student hub initiative seeks to increase the number of successful Welsh applicants.

Keble

Oxford OX1 3PG 01865 272711 (admissions) www.keble.ox.ac.uk
Undergraduates: 420 Postgraduates: 232 college.office@keble.ox.ac.uk

Keble is one of Oxford's most distinct colleges, built of brick in unmistakably extravagant Victorian Gothic style. Keble was founded in 1870 with the intention of making Oxford education more accessible, and the college remains proud of "the legacy of a social conscience". With around 450 undergraduates, Keble is one of the biggest colleges in Oxford, and with guaranteed college accommodation for most undergraduates for three years, its vibrant community spirit provides Keble students with a coveted social life. Graduates are housed in the Acland site on Banbury Road, a two-minute walk from the main college. It is strong in the sciences, where it benefits from easy access to the Science Area and the Radcliffe Science Library. The college's sporting record remains exemplary, with rugby, rowing and netball traditional strengths. A high proportion of Keble students also play university-level sport. Sport does not dominate Keble undergraduate life, however, with its thriving music and drama societies, which make use of the modern O'Reilly Theatre. The college hall, where students wishing to dine must wear gowns six nights a week, is one of the most impressive in the university. The annual Keble Ball is one of the best black tie events in Oxford.

Lady Margaret Hall

Oxford OX2 6QA 01865 274310 (admissions) www.lmh.ox.ac.uk
Undergraduates: 390 Postgraduates: 205 admissions@lmh.ox.ac.uk

Lady Margaret Hall, Oxford's first college for women, has been co-educational since 1978 and now enjoys an equal gender balance. For many students, LMH's comparative isolation – the college is three-quarters of a mile north of the city centre – is a real advantage, ensuring a clear distinction between college life and university activities, and a refuge from tourists. For others it means a long journey to central library facilities, and an even longer journey to the university sports facilities on Iffley Road, shared with Trinity College. Although the neo-Georgian architecture is not to everyone's taste, the college's beautiful gardens back onto the Cherwell River, allowing LMH to have its own punt house, tennis courts and 12 acres of land. The construction of a front courtyard, with new teaching facilities and postgraduate accommodation, should be completed in late 2015. Accommodation is guaranteed for first-, second- and third-year students since the opening of the Pipe Partridge Building, which also houses a new JCR, dining hall and lecture theatre. Thanks to the Simpkins Lee Theatre,

LMH has long been one of Oxford's centres for student drama. Former editor-in-chief of *The Guardian*, Alan Rusbridger, became the new college principal in October 2015.

Lincoln

Oxford OX1 3DR 01865 279836 (admissions) www.lincoln.ox.ac.uk
Undergraduates: 294 Postgraduates: 289 admissions@lincoln.ox.ac.uk

Small, central Lincoln cultivates a lower profile than many other colleges with comparable assets. The college's 15th-century buildings and beautiful library – a converted Queen Anne church – combine to produce a delightful environment in which to spend three years. The college's relaxed atmosphere is justly celebrated and city-centre accommodation is provided by the college for all undergraduates throughout their careers. Graduate students are housed a few minutes' walk away in Bear Lane, at the EPA Science Centre close to the university science area and at a new site on Little Clarendon Street. Finalists live in a recently refurbished complex on Museum Road, by Keble and the University Parks. Lincoln's food is outstanding, among the best in the university. The college admires its chef so much that it commissioned a portrait of him for the hall. Sporting achievement is impressive for a college of this size, but tends to fall short of larger colleges that have more players to choose from. Lincoln has one of the largest number of scholarships available for graduate students.

Magdalen

Oxford OX1 4AU 01865 276063 (admissions) www.magd.ox.ac.uk
Undergraduates: 403 Postgraduates: 179 admissions@magd.ox.ac.uk

Perhaps the most beautiful Oxbridge college, Magdalen is known around the world for its tower, its deer park and its May morning celebrations. The college has shaken off its public school image to become a truly cosmopolitan place, with a large intake from overseas and one of the highest proportion of state school pupils. The college is consistently high in the Norrington Table and has won University Challenge a record four times over the years. The library is currently under refurbishment and will provide three times the number of reader spaces when it opens in Spring 2016. First-year students are accommodated in the Waynflete Building and are allocated rooms in subsequent years by ballot. Undergraduates can be housed in college for the full length of their course. Rents are not cheap compared to other colleges, but there is financial help on offer. The college bar is one of the best in Oxford and backs onto a riverside terrace from which the students can go punting. Magdalen is well suited to creative individuals, with a successful film society, drama society and choir. The college has had a lot of success on the river in recent years.

Mansfield

Oxford OX1 3TF 01865 270920 (admissions) www.mansfield.ox.ac.uk
Undergraduates: 220 Postgraduates: 122 admissions@mansfield.ox.ac.uk

Formally becoming an Oxford College in 1995, Mansfield's attractive site is fairly central, close to the libraries and the science faculty. Its proximity to University Parks facilitates collegiate sporting enthusiasm, most notably for croquet and quidditch. With just over 200 undergraduates, the community is close-knit. The less intimidating atmosphere of Mansfield is perhaps helped by its strong representation of state school students; among the highest ratio in the university. First- and third-year students live in college accommodation, either on site or in an annex in east Oxford, while second years currently have to find their own accommodation. Fund-raising efforts are underway for the new Love Lane building that will provide additional accommodation as well as a home for Oxford's Institute of Human Rights. The library is open 24 hours, and the JCR is among the largest of any college. The new café and sun terrace are also popular among students. Mansfield spearheads the Oxford FE Initiative, encouraging applications to the university from further education colleges.

Merton

Oxford OX1 4JD	01865 276299 (admissions)	www.merton.ox.ac.uk
Undergraduates: 294	Postgraduates: 279	admissions@admin.merton.ox.ac.uk

Founded in 1264 by Walter de Merton, Bishop of Rochester and Chancellor of England, Merton is one of Oxford's oldest and most prestigious colleges. Quiet and beautiful, with the oldest quad in the university, Merton has high academic expectations of its undergraduates, reflected in its position usually at or near the top of the Norrington Table. The medieval library is the envy of other colleges. Accommodation is some of the cheapest in the university, of good standard and offered for all three years. Merton's food is well-priced and among the best in the university; formal hall is served six times a week. Merton's many diversions include the Merton Floats, its dramatic society, the Bodley Club for literary speakers, an excellent Christmas Ball every three years and the peculiar Time Ceremony, set up in the 1970s as a spoof tradition to "maintain the integrity of the space-time continuum during the transition from British Summer Time to GMT". Music at Merton has come on impressively in the past few years; following the establishment of its choral foundation, both its choir and the organ have an ever-growing reputation throughout the university and further afield. Sports facilities are excellent, although participation is more important than the final score.

New College

Oxford OX1 3BN	01865 279512 (admissions)	www.new.ox.ac.uk
Undergraduates: 448	Postgraduates: 279	admissions@new.ox.ac.uk

New College is actually rather old (founded in 1379 by William of Wykeham), large and much more relaxed than most expect behind its daunting facade. It is a bustling place, as proud of its excellent music and its bar as of its academic prestige. Musical students flourish here thanks to the choir, orchestra and chamber groups. There is a band room and there are plans to build a new music building on Mansfield Road. Traditionally poor at attracting state school students, the college has been making particular efforts to change this, inviting applications from schools that have never sent candidates to Oxford. All first-, second- and fourth-year students can live in college and almost all of the third years can if they wish. The college's library facilities are impressive. The sports ground is nearby and includes good tennis courts. A sports complex, named after Brian Johnston, opened in 1997, at St Cross Road. The sheer beauty of New College remains one of its principal assets and the college gardens are a memorable sight, especially the other-worldly mound in the heart of the college. The Commemoration Ball, held every three years, is a highlight of Oxford's social calendar. Students benefit from summer access to the college chalet (shared with Balliol and University) near Mont Blanc.

Oriel

Oxford OX1 4EW	01865 276522 (admissions)	www.oriel.ox.ac.uk
Undergraduates: 319	Postgraduates: 186	admissions@oriel.ox.ac.uk

Oriel is a friendly, centrally-located college with a strong sense of identity. The college is traditionally described as having "a strong crew spirit", reflecting its traditions on the river; the Oriel men's crew retained their position as Head of the River in 2015. Academically, it tends to inhabit the middle reaches of the Norrington Table. The well-stocked library is open 24 hours. Oriel has a strong sporting reputation and facilities include a boathouse, impressive sports ground, squash courts and multiple gyms. Accommodation is variable, but includes 55 newly renovated student rooms with some impressive views over Oxford, as well as rooms on the Island Site on Oriel Street. Oriel provides accommodation for the duration of an undergraduate course, be it three or four years, and extensive (mainly graduate) accommodation is provided one mile away off the popular Cowley Road. The college has a lively arts scene which includes a drama society, an a capella group, barbershop quartet and an annual "Arts Week" held in Hilary Term. Eight choral scholarships and two organ scholarships underpin the college's successful chapel choir.

Pembroke

Oxford OX1 1DW	01865 276412 (admissions)	www.pmb.ox.ac.uk
Undergraduates: 364	Postgraduates: 216	admissions@pmb.ox.ac.uk

Tucked away off St Aldate's, Pembroke is a welcoming and inclusive community with an improving state school intake, thanks to its access schemes. The college is historically impoverished, but by no means shy when awarding undergraduate scholarships and prizes. Pembroke is now able to accommodate all undergraduates after a new quad was opened in April 2013, and the Sir Geoffrey Arthur Building on the river, ten minutes' walk away, offers excellent facilities; in addition to 100 student rooms there is a concert room, computer room and a multi-gym. College food is among the most expensive in Oxford and students must pre-pay for a minimum of six dinners a week, which discourages Pembroke students from eating elsewhere; good for maintaining Pembroke's renowned community feel, but poor for establishing inter-college relationships. Rowing is strong, with Pembroke men's crew positioned third on the river and the women's crew second in their division. Squash and tennis courts are available at the nearby sports ground. A bronze memorial to the former college fellow J.R.R. Tolkien is due to be installed during the 2015–16 academic year.

Queen's

Oxford OX1 4AW	01865 279161	www.queens.ox.ac.uk
Undergraduates: 352	Postgraduates: 122	admissions@queens.ox.ac.uk

Despite being one of the most striking sights of the High Street, Queen's is one of Oxford's least dynamic colleges. Its academic record is average, usually occupying the lower end of the Norrington Table. Modern languages, chemistry and mathematics are reckoned among the strongest subjects. The library is as beautiful as it is well stocked. All students are offered accommodation, first years being housed in modernist annexes in east Oxford, and the college has converted a large number of rooms into en-suite facilities. The three-room sets are excellent and choosing to share reduces the termly rent substantially. Queen's can be insular and is largely apolitical, but has a strong college enthusiasm for sport, particularly rugby and netball. The college also has an excellent mixed choir and an orchestra, and stages a summer musical. The college's beer cellar is one of the most popular in the university and the JCR facilities are also better than average; the daily JCR afternoon tea is a must. An annual dinner commemorates a student, said to have fended off a bear by thrusting a volume of Aristotle into its mouth. Postgraduates are accommodated in St Aldate's House, a modern building close to the town centre.

St Anne's

Oxford OX2 6HS | 01865 274840 (admissions) | www.st-annes.ox.ac.uk
Undergraduates: 432 | Postgraduates: 308 | enquiries@st-annes.ox.ac.uk

Architecturally uninspiring (a Victorian row with concrete "stack-a-studies" dropped into their back gardens), St Anne's makes up in community spirit what it lacks in awesome grandeur. One of the largest colleges, it has an above-average proportion of state school students. A women's college until 1979, it has an excellent library, which is now 24-hour and is very well-stocked; it is rich in law, Chinese and medieval history texts. The college has recently had a strong presence in the university journalism scene, and its rugby team tends to do well in the inter-college league. Students also enjoy close proximity to the University Parks. Accommodation is guaranteed to undergraduates for three years, and the college also operates an equalisation scheme, giving grants to students wishing to live out. Graduates are housed in an 82-room hall of residence in Summertown, a five-minute cycle ride away. St Anne's students benefit from exclusive access to a number of internships organised by the college.

St Catherine's

Oxford OX1 3UJ | 01865 271703 (admissions) | www.stcatz.ox.ac.uk
Undergraduates: 479 | Postgraduates: 322 | admissions@stcatz.ox.ac.uk

Arne Jacobsen's modernist design for "Catz", one of Oxford's youngest and largest undergraduate colleges, has attracted much attention as the most striking contrast to the lofty spires of Magdalen and New College. Close to the law, English and social science faculties, the university science area and the pleasantly rural Holywell Great Meadow, St Catherine's is a lot closer to the city centre than it feels. The Wolfson library is open until midnight. Rooms are small but tend to be warmer than in other, more venerable, colleges, and are now available on site for first-, second- and third-year students. There is an excellent theatre, as well as an on-site punt house, gym and squash courts. Like many of the larger colleges, sporting success is high. The college hosts the Cameron Mackintosh Chair of Contemporary Theatre, whose incumbents have included Meera Syal, Kevin Spacey, Arthur Miller and Sir Ian McKellen. St Catherine's has one of the best JCR facilities in Oxford.

St Edmund Hall

Oxford OX1 4AR | 01865 279011 (admissions) | www.seh.ox.ac.uk
Undergraduates: 408 | Postgraduates: 257 | admissions@seh.ox.ac.uk

St Edmund Hall – "Teddy Hall" – has one of Oxford's smallest college sites but one of its most populous. The college offers students the chance to live in its medieval quads right in the heart of the city. With the male/female ratio nearly equal, the college is shedding its image as a home for "hearties". Nonetheless, the sporting culture is still vigorous, St Edmund's winning the mixed lacrosse cuppers in 2015 and coming runner-up to Keble in the rugby cuppers. Academically, Teddy Hall tends to yo-yo between the middle and the bottom of the Norrington Table. It hosts four annual prizes for journalism, including a £500 award for a student from within the college. The unique library is a converted church. College accommodation is reasonable and can be offered for three years, either on the main site or in three annexes, one near the University Parks, and two on Iffley Road, where many of the rooms have private bathrooms.

St Hilda's

Oxford OX4 1DY | 01865 286620 (admissions) | www.st-hildas.ox.ac.uk
Undergraduates: 401 | Postgraduates: 162 | college.office@st-hildas.ox.ac.uk

October 2008 marked a milestone for St Hilda's and the university as a whole, as the college welcomed its first mixed-sex intake. Although the college, founded in 1893, lasted more than 100 years as an all-female institution, the governing body voted in 2006 to admit men. There are now equal numbers of males and females. The college has long languished at the lower end of the Norrington Table. Like the other originally female colleges, St Hilda's boasts an impressive library, which is particularly well stocked for English. The college has beautiful riverside gardens, allowing students to go punting from the college site, and is close to the lively social scene in multi-ethnic east Oxford. Accommodation is guaranteed to first years and finalists, and the common room and student-run bar have been renovated and enlarged with improved disabled access. Many of the rooms offer some of the best river views in Oxford, with the city's spires as a backdrop. The standard of food is high, yet all students living on-site have access to kitchens. St Hilda's commitment to music is particularly strong and its facilities world class. Women's hockey is particularly strong, winning the 2015 cuppers event.

St Hugh's

Oxford OX2 6LE | 01865 274910 (admissions) | www.st-hughs.ox.ac.uk
Undergraduates: 433 | Postgraduates: 296 | admissions@st-hughs.ox.ac.uk

One of the lesser-known colleges, St Hugh's was criticised by students in 1986 when it began admitting men. There is now an equal male/female ratio, a better balance than at most Oxford colleges. Like Lady Margaret Hall, St Hugh's picturesque setting is a bicycle ride from the city centre. It is an ideal college for those seeking a place to live and study away from the madding crowd, and is well liked for its pleasantly bohemian atmosphere and beautiful gardens. Despite having one of the biggest and best college libraries, academic pressure remains comparatively low. St Hugh's guarantees on-site accommodation to undergraduates for the duration of their degree, although the standard of rooms is variable. The quality of food is high and kitchen facilities are among the best in Oxford. The new Dickson Poon Building provides an additional place to work and socialise. Sport, particularly football, is taken quite seriously. As the college enjoys extensive grounds compared to most colleges, there is space for a croquet lawn and tennis courts. It is generous with financial support given that it is one of the poorest colleges.

St John's

Oxford OX1 3JP | 01865 277317 (admissions) | www.sjc.ox.ac.uk
Undergraduates: 398 | Postgraduates: 225 | admissions@sjc.ox.ac.uk

St John's is one of Oxford's powerhouses, excelling in almost every field and boasting arguably the most beautiful gardens in the university. Founded in 1555 by a London merchant, it is Oxford's wealthiest college, and makes the most of its resources by providing guaranteed college accommodation at a subsidised rate for all its undergraduates in addition to generous annual book grants and prizes. Co-educational since 1979, the matriculation of the 2,000th St John's woman was marked by a year of celebratory events in 2015. Academic standards are high, with English, chemistry and history among the traditional strengths, and all students benefit from the impressive library. The college is usually challenging for the top spot in the Norrington Table. However, the emphasis on academia tends to limit the St John's social scene despite its close proximity to some of Oxford's best-known pubs: the Eagle and Child and the Lamb and Flag. St John's has a strong sporting tradition with a particular strength in women's rowing. As befits such an all-round strong college, entry is fiercely competitive.

St Peter's

Oxford OX1 2DL	01865 278863 (admissions)	www.spc.ox.ac.uk
Undergraduates: 343	Postgraduates: 166	admissions@spc.ox.ac.uk

Opened as St Peter's Hall in 1929, St Peter's has been an Oxford college since 1961. Its medieval, Georgian and 19th-century buildings are in the city centre and close to most of Oxford's main facilities. Though still young, St Peter's is well-represented in university life and has pockets of academic excellence, despite being towards the bottom of the Norrington Table. History tutoring is particularly good. St Peters made it to the semi-finals of University Challenge in 2015. Accommodation is offered to students in their first and third years, varying from traditional rooms in college to new purpose-built rooms a few minutes' walk away. The college's facilities are impressive, including one of the university's best JCRs and a popular student bar. The college has a proud sporting heritage, being particularly strong at rugby and rowing. St Peter's is known as one of Oxford's most vibrant colleges socially. It is strong in acting, journalism and music. Thanks to a new partnership with Laura Ashley, a generous bursary scheme will be available for the next five years.

Somerville

Oxford OX2 6HD	01865 270619 (admissions)	www.some.ox.ac.uk
Undergraduates: 390	Postgraduates: 145	secretariat@some.ox.ac.uk

Named after the astronomer Mary Somerville (1780–1872), one of the most celebrated scientific writers of her day, Somerville was one of the first two colleges at Oxford founded to admit women. Since 1994 it has admitted men and women equally, while retaining its pioneering and inclusive ethos. Alma mater to Margaret Thatcher, Indira Gandhi, Shirley Williams, Nobel prizewinner Dorothy Hodgkin, novelist Iris Murdoch and a host of famous writers and scientists, Somerville is one of the most international colleges, and one of the most diverse. Accommodation in college is provided for three years to most undergraduates (with some second years currently living out) and all first-year postgraduates. There are kitchens in all buildings and subsidised food in hall, with 68 new en-suite rooms overlooking the university's developing new centre at the Radcliffe Observatory Quarter. Sport is strong at Somerville with its own gym, and rowing and other facilities shared with other colleges. The library, one of the most beautiful and largest college libraries, is 24-hour. The college has a good choir, active music society and a strong arts and drama presence.

Trinity

Oxford OX1 3BH	01865 279860 (admissions)	www.trinity.ox.ac.uk
Undergraduates: 305	Postgraduates: 132	admissions@trinity.ox.ac.uk

Architecturally impressive and boasting beautiful lawns (which you can actually walk on), Trinity is one of Oxford's least populous colleges, admitting some 80 undergraduates each year. It is ideally located, beside the Bodleian, Blackwell's bookshop and the White Horse pub, a short stroll from the University Parks and the town centre. Trinity has shaken off its reputation for apathy, and whilst members are active in all walks of university life, the college has its own debating and drama societies, as well as sharing a fierce rivalry with neighbouring

Balliol. Usually, all undergraduates are given a room on the main site in their first and second years, with the majority of third and fourth-years living in a purpose-built block a mile and a half north of the main site. Students rate the food highly for both its quality and price. Trinity's Commemoration Ball, held once every three years, has one of the biggest budgets in Oxford and is a popular event.

University

Oxford OX1 4BH   01865 276959 (admissions)   www.univ.ox.ac.uk
Undergraduates: 372   Postgraduates: 187   admissions@univ.ox.ac.uk

University is the first Oxford college to be able to boast a former student in the Oval Office, as the former President Clinton was a Rhodes Scholar at University in the late 1960s. The college is probably Oxford's oldest – a claim fought over with Merton – and tends to be rather insular. Academic expectations are high and the college prospers in most subjects. Thanks to a newly refurbished accommodation block, first- and third-year undergraduates are guaranteed a college room. University is particularly well represented on the river, with both men and women's crews doing well in recent years. Students from the state sector can benefit from a generous bursary scheme, and University's access programme is among the best in Oxford. The college also has access to a chalet in the foothills of Mont Blanc, with student parties welcome in the summer.

Wadham

Oxford OX1 3PN   01865 277545 (admissions)   www.wadham.ox.ac.uk
Undergraduates: 440   Postgraduates: 136   admissions@wadh.ox.ac.uk

Founded by Dorothy Wadham in 1609, Wadham is known in about equal measure for its progressive and liberal atmosphere and its leftist politics. The JCR – or student union (SU) as it has rebranded itself – is famously dynamic and politically active, although the breadth of political opinion is greater than its left-wing stereotype suggests. The college is very strong on admitting students from state schools, owing to its successful Student Ambassador Scheme. Its gardens are beautiful, hosting Shakespearian performances each summer and the somewhat rough-hewn chapel is similarly memorable. The college has a good 24-hour library, with a well-stocked Persian history section. Wadham is the only college with no formal hall and a recent SU motion brought in "veggie Mondays". Accommodation is guaranteed in first year and at least one further year. Fourth years and graduates are either offered accommodation in Merifield, the college's modern development of shared flats in Summertown, or choose to live in private accommodation. Journalism, music and drama play an important part. Highlights in the social calendar are Queer Festival, a riotous celebration of LGBTQ culture, and Wadstock, the college's open-air spring music festival. The women's rowing team have been Head of the River for two years and the men's 1st VIII are in the top division.

Worcester

Oxford OX1 2HB   01865 278391 (admissions)   www.worc.ox.ac.uk
Undergraduates: 411   Postgraduates: 157   admissions@worc.ox.ac.uk

Worcester is to the west of Oxford what Magdalen is to the east: a spacious contrast to the urban rush of the city centre. The college's rather mediocre exterior conceals a delightful environment, including some striking Baroque architecture, extensive gardens (awarded best lawn in Britain) and a lake. The college gardeners even post horticultural updates to their newly founded blog. The dramatic society makes use of the beautiful grounds, with annual summer Shakespeare performances in the gardens. The 24-hour library is strongest in the arts, but the college's strengths lie in chemistry and mathematics. Accommodation, guaranteed for three years, is either within the college grounds or less than 300 metres from it. Rent is among the highest in the university, but pricing bands for graded accommodation provide options. Sport plays an important part in college life, as befits the only college with playing fields on site. Worcester is a noted powerhouse in both men and women's football. Worcester boasts good quality and reasonably priced formal halls, available four nights a week, with a Michelin-star chef every Wednesday. Like Magdalen and New, it is home to the Commemoration Ball once every three years, a highlight of the Oxford social calendar.

Cambridge College Profiles

Christ's

Cambridge CB2 3BU 01223 334983 (admissions) www.christs.cam.ac.uk
Undergraduates: 415 Postgraduates: 161 admissions@christs.cam.ac.uk

It is hard to believe that Christ's occupies the position that is does when you are inside its haven-like courts. It is a medieval world away from the town centre that bustles up and down outside its door. Though it hosted some of Cambridge's most notable alumni including John Milton and Charles Darwin, it is one of the smallest colleges. Accommodation is offered to students for all three years of their degree either within the college walls or just behind them on Jesus Lane and 40 per cent of rooms are en suite. The college is strong in the natural sciences and geography – proximity to the relevant faculties may help – but it also boasts an enviable Visual Arts Centre and is one of the few colleges to have an artist-in-residence. Christ's also has a modern gallery and theatre space in New Court, which is made good use of by the amateur dramatic society and Christ's Films, one of the best-attended student film groups. The ten-minute cycle ride to the sports pitches is a regular commute for Christ's students, who have won the college Cuppers football competition more times than any other college. Christ's is also one of only five Oxbridge colleges to have its own pool, which was recently refurbished.

Churchill

Cambridge CB3 0DS 01223 336202 (admissions) www.chu.cam.ac.uk
Undergraduates: 480 Postgraduates: 244 admissions@chu.cam.ac.uk

As most Churchillians will tell you there are benefits to being situated a little way out of the city centre. The college is in 40 acres of parkland near the maths and engineering faculties and the University Sports Centre and boasts some of the best facilities. A new gym, a theatre/cinema, music room and recording equipment, squash and tennis courts, grass pitches and the largest dining hall in Cambridge are all found on site. Accommodation is available for students for the three years of their undergraduate degree, and a new court is set to open in July 2016. Many rooms are en suite and Churchill does not charge a fixed bill for catering, which lowers the rent. Though it was the first all-male college to welcome female students in 1972, it has one of the lowest male:female ratios with a 71 per cent male undergraduate body. In other aspects, the college is one of the least traditional: students are allowed to walk on the grass (a rarity amid the historic quads of Cambridge) and don't wear academic gowns when dining formally in hall. It also has one of the highest intakes of state school students (over 80 per cent). Its success in this year's Tompkins Table may be thanks to what students have called its "dangerously comfortable" library.

Clare

Cambridge CB2 1TL 01223 333246 (admissions) www.clare.cam.ac.uk
Undergraduates: 484 Postgraduates: 202 admissions@clare.cam.ac.uk

In an enviable location on the Backs under the shadow of King's College Chapel and next door to Trinity Hall, Clare is the second oldest college in Cambridge and also one of the most applied-to. Its elegant quads are beloved by a student body with a strong reputation for music – and not only in the traditional sense, though its choir is world-renowned. Clare Cellars, the student bar, often plays host to DJ and live music nights that draw students from across the university. It also attracts big names for its May Ball, which in recent years have included The Futureheads and Pendulum. The college is popular with arts students for its proximity to the Sidgwick Site faculties, particularly if you manage to secure room in Memorial Court, a stone's throw from the University Library. Many students also enjoy the independence of living in "Clare Colony", a set of converted townhouses a ten-minute cycle from college. The college has an enthusiastically attended boat club and, although the majority of sports facilities are 15 minutes away by bike, there are squash courts on site. Despite the apparent focus on arts, science places are fiercely competitive and Clare counts David Attenborough among its alumni.

Corpus Christi

Cambridge CB2 1RH 01223 338056 (admissions) www.corpus.cam.ac.uk
Undergraduates: 286 Postgraduates: 159 admissions@corpus.cam.ac.uk

Corpus is the only Oxbridge college to have been founded by townspeople and also boasts the oldest court of any Oxbridge college – New Court has been lived in and used for study since the 14th century. It has plenty of new facilities, though, ranging from recently opened accommodation on the Leckhampton site just over a mile away, which is also home to the college's sports pitches and gym, to the Corpus Playroom upon whose boards have trod theatre greats including Emma Thompson, Stephen Fry (the Playroom's patron) and Hugh Bonneville (a college alumnus). Even though it is squeezed amid the buildings on Trumpington Street, the college boasts two libraries – the Taylor Library, where the main collection and study areas are found, and the Parker Library where the college's rare books and manuscripts are kept – and it houses undergraduates for all three years of their degree. Academia is prized and rooms are partly allocated on the basis of the previous year's exam results – a rule not many students like. On the sports front, Corpus tends to join up with King's and Christ's Colleges to form collaborative "CCK" sports teams.

Downing

Cambridge CB2 1DQ 01223 334826 (admissions) www.dow.cam.ac.uk
Undergraduates: 441 Postgraduates: 148 admissions@dow.cam.ac.uk

Beyond a fairly unassuming gate on busy Regent Street, you will find the elegant neo-Classical quadrangle of Downing with a paddock that is in daily use throughout the summer term for revision, picnics and impromptu sports. Founded in 1800 for the study of law and natural sciences, it is generally thought that its academic strength still lies in these areas, and given that it backs on to the science faculties of the Downing Site, it is certainly a favoured choice for natural science students. It is also renowned for its sporting prowess. The inter-college rugby team is strong and the college rowing teams have won the past two years' May "Bumps". A new accommodation block, unveiled in 2014, supplement rooms across the college which are generally of a high standard. Those living out are situated in houses behind the college and next to Parker's Piece, a three-minute walk away. The Howard Theatre, a 120-seater space opened in 2010, hosts regular plays as well as meetings of The Blake Society, a popular arts group named in honour of alumnus Quentin Blake.

Emmanuel

Cambridge CB2 3AP 01223 334290 (admissions) www.emma.cam.ac.uk
Undergraduates: 495 Postgraduates: 153 admissions@emma.cam.ac.uk

Many students don't realise that Emmanuel regularly features around the top of the Tompkins Table, such is the relaxed atmosphere of this centrally located college. It may help that the college puts on an extensive programme of pastoral events during the exam term that ranges from yoga to bouncy castles. "Emma" is also known for having the cheapest student bar, which is a student favourite. Founded in 1584 with a Puritan ethos – one of the earliest alumni was John Harvard, founder of the eponymous American university – Emmanuel is one of the most egalitarian of the older colleges. It has a 50:50 gender split and two-thirds of the student population come from the state sector. It welcomed its first female master, Dame Fiona Reynolds, in 2013. Thanks to its generous endowment it can also afford to provide well-subsidised accommodation, split between older sets in college (some of which involve a short outside walk to the nearest bathroom) and houses around the edge of Parker's Piece, one of Cambridge's largest green spaces, just outside the college. Sports are inclusive and well-attended, even if teams are not always wildly competitive. The football squad does well and there is a strong boat club. It is the only college to provide an in-house students laundry service, which is hugely popular.

Fitzwilliam

Cambridge CB3 0DG   01223 332030 (admissions)   www.fitz.cam.ac.uk
Undergraduates: 449   Postgraduates: 225   admissions@fitz.cam.ac.uk

Thanks to being moved out of the centre of Cambridge in 1963, the purpose-built "Fitz" doesn't delight in the city's most beautiful architecture. That said, its pretty gardens are a well-kept secret and at the top of its most recent building work, a £5-million library designed by award-winning architect Edward Cullinan, you will be standing at the highest point in Cambridge. Founded in the 19th-century in order to open up Cambridge to students from all backgrounds, Fitz has a three-quarters state-educated student body. Community values are high and fostered by all the freshers living together in first year. Students are accommodated throughout their degrees in one of the 400 rooms in college or further 167 in houses minutes from the college gate. In Cambridge terms, the college isn't renowned for academe (coming 20th in this year's Tompkins Table) and enjoys something of a party reputation. The bar is a popular hub and the café is always busy with students enjoying the Wi-Fi and homemade cake. Fitz does well on the sports pitches and has well-kept sports facilities nearby for football, rugby, cricket, hockey and tennis, as well as a gym.

Girton

Cambridge CB3 0JG   01223 338972 (admissions)   www.girton.cam.ac.uk
Undergraduates: 488   Postgraduates: 162   admissions@girton.cam.ac.uk

The joke among Cambridge students is that many have not even heard of Girton as it is "so far away" – in fact a 15-minute cycle up the Huntingdon Road, apparently far enough to discourage many students. However, it also means that Girton's lawns, orchards and majestic brick buildings are something of an oasis. The 50 acres of grounds provide first-class facilities, including a recently refurbished indoor swimming pool, a gym, sports pitches, tennis, squash and basketball courts, as well as a dark room, conference rooms and one of the university's largest college libraries. Accommodation is either in college or in Wolfson Court, a three-acre annexe with its own cafeteria. Rents are renowned to be cheap. Originally founded as a women's college, the college has always had a "Mistress" (not that this title prevents men taking on the job) and was the first women's college to go co-educational in 1976. Nowadays it is just over half male, but still has the highest number of female Fellows of any co-ed college. The college regularly hosts art exhibitions and has its own museum, which is a legacy of Pre-Raphaelite involvement with the college.

Gonville and Caius

Cambridge CB2 1TA | 01223 332440 (admissions) | www.cai.cam.ac.uk
Undergraduates: 571 | Postgraduates: 166 | admissions@cai.cam.ac.uk

Stepping into Gonville and Caius (known as Caius and pronounced "keys") is like stepping into most films you have ever seen about Oxbridge. There are small old-world courts and turrets and a wealth of tradition. Founded in 1348 as Gonville Hall, it is one of the oldest colleges and holds onto some antiquated customs, such as requiring students to wear gowns in hall every night of the week. In the unique matriculation and graduation ceremonies, students pass through the symbolic gates in college. Students have to pay for a certain number of dinners in hall every term, all of which are three-course affairs preceded by a Latin grace. In other respects, though, Caius is a forward-looking place. The £13-million Stephen Hawking Building, named after the world-famous physicist who celebrates 50 years as a Fellow this year, offers well-kept modern accommodation, as does Harvey Court, which was renovated in 2011. The college holds regular events such as the first university "Women in Economics" day, and has a strong rowing team, who came top of the river in this year's inter-college "Bumps" competition. It tends towards the middle of the Tompkins Table, but the college library, formerly the university library, is a treat.

Homerton

Cambridge CB2 8PH | 01223 747252 (admissions) | www.homerton.cam.ac.uk
Undergraduates: 551 | Postgraduates: 417 | admissions@homerton.cam.ac.uk

Homerton is the largest Cambridge college and, although it will celebrate its 250th anniversary in 2018, is also theoretically the newest. It was originally founded in 18th-century London, but moved to Cambridge in 1894 and only received its Royal Charter in 2010. Originally a teacher-training college, it still has the largest number of students studying the education tripos (around a fifth of the college) though it welcomes applicants to all courses. Unusual among Cambridge colleges for having more women than men (around 60:40 ratio), it is a forward-looking college that also has one of the highest percentages of state-educated students (over 80 per cent). Its location near the station, some 15 minutes cycle out of town, is often commented upon, but the modernity of the college and its spacious setting mean that students enjoy an experience more akin to a campus university. Two large halls of residence house undergraduates for all three years of their degrees, so they can make good use of the squash courts, sports pitches and croquet lawn. The large dining hall built in 1889 is a beautiful neo-Gothic structure, regularly used for candlelit formals, and the college has one of only two listed gymnasia in the world. Homerton is particularly strong in the arts, and the college boasts two Poet Laureates among its alumni, Carol Ann Duffy and Andrew Motion.

Hughes Hall

Cambridge CB1 2EW | 01223 334897 (admissions)k | www.hughes.cam.ac.uk
Undergraduates: 105 | Postgraduates: 375 | admissions@hughes.cam.ac.u

The oldest of the graduate colleges, Hughes Hall was founded as a small institution to train women to be teachers in 1885. Nowadays it welcomes both sexes, and mature undergraduates as well as graduate students. The college's main strengths lie towards the science end of the spectrum and include engineering, medicine and economics. Partly as a result of the more mature intake, the college has a strong tradition on the sports field and often provides Blues for rowing, rugby and other university teams. While many of the students tend to gravitate towards their faculty, the college has a relatively new library (completed in 2008) and in

September 2016 will open a new student hall and study space. All the accommodation, which is provided to single undergraduates and affiliated students, is in and around Mill Road, Cambridge's most cosmopolitan area, much loved for its international eateries.

Jesus

Cambridge CB5 8BL 01223 339455 (admissions) www.jesus.cam.ac.uk
Undergraduates: 532 Postgraduates: 249 undergraduate-admissions@jesus.cam.ac.uk

Of all the colleges near the city centre, Jesus enjoys the most spacious setting. As well as on-site football, rugby and cricket pitches, three squash courts and no fewer than ten tennis courts, the college is also a few oars' lengths from the Cam and minutes from the college boat house. No surprise then that the college enjoys something of a sporty reputation. It is also home to a stunning chapel with a classical chart-topping choir, is the closest college to the ADC (home to the Cambridge Footlights) and amid the extensive grounds, biennial sculpture exhibitions are held. The students perform well academically, too, across a range of subjects, and despite the large undergraduate population, it has one of the highest ratios of Fellows to students. Recently refurbishment means that accommodation is largely of a high standard, and despite occasional grumbles about a lack of cooking facilities, this is balanced by the fulsome praise of the college "caff". It is also home to a popular bar and a May Ball that attracts first years in particular from across the university.

King's

Cambridge CB2 1ST 01223 331255 (admissions) www.kings.cam.ac.uk
Undergraduates: 403 Postgraduates: 172 undergraduate.admissions@kings.cam.ac.uk

The college with the most iconic architecture (and bullish porters manning the gates to control the number of tourists), King's occupies prime position on the Backs. People from all over the globe queue to attend services in the world-famous chapel, which is 500 years old this year. Despite this and the fact that it was originally founded in 1441 as a college for boys from Eton, King's is proudly one of the least establishment colleges. Having thrown off the tradition of gowns, it has also done away with the Fellows' "High Table" in the dining hall and hangs a hammer and sickle flag in its bar – though its presence there is hotly debated each year. Four-fifths of the students are state educated and the college actively seeks out applications from those with disadvantaged backgrounds. It was also one of the first all-male colleges to admit women. Students are actively involved in a range of societies, not least the all-important debating group, King's Politics. Accommodation is spread across old rooms with mullioned windows (some of which are a staircase or two from the nearest bathroom) and en-suite rooms in the newer hostels. King's students are also proud of the "King's Affair", an "anti"-May Ball, which attracts long queues for tickets, and sometimes opens up the chapel as a dancefloor.

Lucy Cavendish

Cambridge CB3 0BU 01223 330280 (admissions) www.lucy-cav.cam.ac.uk
Undergraduates: 111 (women only) Postgraduates: 154 lcc-admissions@lists.cam.ac.uk

Unique among Oxbridge colleges, Lucy Cavendish (fondly known as "Lucy" to members) only takes mature female students. As one might expect, the atmosphere is supportive to a tee, though for those after a more stereotypical "student" experience, social life in Lucy is more about pizza and film nights than a rowdy bar. The college, which celebrates 50 years this year, is richly diverse and sticks to its founding remit of being for "smart, inspirational women". Students range from 21 to over 60, and its strengths lie in a range of subjects, partly thanks to its proximity to the maths, engineering and veterinary faculties and the Sidgwick Site for arts. It encourages women's writing through the Lucy Cavendish Fiction Prize for unpublished female writers. Accommodation is provided for all students in college or in nearby houses. A comfortable new complex was opened in Histon Road in 2014, which includes provision for families. There is a well-equipped gym on site and the college shares a boathouse with Hughes Hall. There are also myriad societies ranging from Zumba to craft. The relatively small proportion of undergraduates (around 40 per cent) means that Lucy does not feature highly on the Tompkins Table and funding is such that occasionally students have directors of studies based at other colleges

Magdalene

Cambridge CB3 0AG 01223 332135 (admissions) www.magd.cam.ac.uk
Undergraduates: 377 Postgraduates: 133 admissions@magd.cam.ac.uk

Whether or not his influence is responsible, the arrival of former Archbishop of Canterbury Rowan Williams as Master has coincided with Magdalene making dramatic leaps up the Tompkins Table. The college came second this year, with a third of students achieving firsts. Situated on the edge of the town centre along the River Cam, Magdalene has the longest river frontage of any college. Students are often found revising on "The Beach" during the summer exam term. One of the university's oldest colleges, it is also one of the most traditional. It was the last male college to admit women (in 1988) and is known to students across the university for its triennial white-tie ball, to which some arrive in punts. Its candlelit formal dinner, in the stained glass windowed hall is one of the cheapest in Cambridge. Sport accounts for much of the social life – Magdalene shares a sports ground with the equally sporty St John's, although it has its own Eton Fives court. As well as a stunning chapel (home to a well-respected choir), the college has one of the most famous libraries in town: the Pepys Library, a collection of 3,000 books and manuscripts donated by the famous diarist, who studied at Magdalene. Accommodation varies and is found across the college or in 21 houses and hostels nearby. Students are mixed together, which helps inter-year mingling.

Murray Edwards

Cambridge CB3 0DF 01223 762229 (admissions) www.murrayedwards.cam.ac.uk
Undergraduates: 374 (women) Postgraduates: 99 admissions@murrayedwards.cam.ac.uk

Cantabrigians are finally getting used to calling Murray Edwards by the name it was given in 2008 following a £30-million endowment from alumna Ros Edwards, though its original name "New Hall" still occasionally slips out. One of Cambridge's three female-only colleges, it is possibly the most gregarious of them. It is a friendly, relaxed college whose students spend much time mingling with the other hill colleges, Fitzwilliam, St Edmund's and Girton. It also has a renowned garden party during May Week. Murray Edwards is a hive of activity, both social and academic (though it tends toward the lower end of the Tompkins ratings). The art room regularly hosts life drawing, students and Fellows can have their own allotments to grow herbs and vegetables, and sport is strong. The college often provides Blues players to the university teams and has its own teams in everything from Ultimate Frisbee to croquet. "The Dome", the college's popular dining hall, is a focal point and plays host to a big termly party, "Dome Life". Murray Edwards also houses the largest collection of women's art in Europe, which includes work by Barbara Hepworth, Tracey Emin and Paula Rego.

Newnham

Cambridge CB3 9DF 01223 335783 (admissions) www.newn.cam.ac.uk

Undergraduates: 384 (women) Postgraduates: 210 admissions@newn.cam.ac.uk

Newnham is proud of its feminist heritage. In 1871 it was the first college to be set up for women to enable them to attend lectures at Cambridge (though they would have to wait until 1948 to be admitted as full members of the university) and its alumni include Sylvia Plath, Germaine Greer, Emma Thompson, A.S. Byatt and Mary Beard. It is the largest women-only college and has an all-female fellowship. For arts students it is little further than a roll out of bed to reach the Sidgwick Site and an on-site arts centre known as "The Old Labs" is well-used for events, plays and exhibitions. For those who want male company, Newnham often joins up with neighbouring Selwyn for socials and formals. Because it has no chapel, it also has a combined choir with Selwyn. Newnham students wax lyrical about the gardens that are part of 18-acre grounds, which also include sports pitches and tennis courts. Accommodation is provided in college for all three years and the atmosphere is tight-knit. Despite having one of the largest college libraries, Newnham does tend to languish near the bottom half of the Tompkins Table, perhaps partly due to the extra-curricular activity taking place.

Pembroke

Cambridge CB2 1RF 01223 338154 (admissions) www.pem.cam.ac.uk

Undergraduates: 456 Postgraduates: 170 adm@pem.cam.ac.uk

Once you've found the gate to Pembroke (the college is tucked into the corner of Pembroke and Trumpington Streets), few want to leave. Renowned as one the most beautiful colleges, it has quiet gardens and an elegant Christopher Wren chapel, which is 350 years old this year. Other key anniversaries recently marked 30 years since the arrival of women in the college and the 60th anniversary of the Pembroke Players, the college's drama group, who regularly take productions to the Edinburgh Festival. Pembroke students love the college for the cheap rents (though rooms are not the most salubrious, particularly in second year), a buzzy café and a variety of facilities that include a gym and Europe's oldest bowling green. Pembrokians put in solid performances on and off the sports pitch. This year they were finalists in both male and female inter-college football tournaments, a close second in the "May Bumps" rowing and maintained their place in the top five colleges of the Tompkins Table. In October 2015, Lord Smith of Finsbury, previously Culture Secretary under Tony Blair, became Master.

Peterhouse

Cambridge CB2 1RD 01223 338223 (admissions) www.pet.cam.ac.uk

Undergraduates: 265 Postgraduates: 109 admissions@pet.cam.ac.uk

The smallest and oldest undergraduate college, Peterhouse is often regarded as old in attitudes and home to some quirky traditions. However, it has near parity of men and women and welcomes one of the highest percentages of state sector applicants in the university. The small size means it is a close-knit community, though some do say it also means gossip whistles around the college fast. The central location is much appreciated by students who also enjoy roaming in "The Deer Park" (although it no longer is home to deer) in which the city centre seems far away. Accommodation is provided for all undergraduates, including those studying for four years. Rooms are large, of a reasonable standard and never more than ten minutes from college, though kitchens are not always well-equipped – perhaps all the more reason to enjoy the regular and cheap candlelit formal hall. The college doesn't have its own sports grounds, but does make good use of other colleges' facilities, never more than ten minutes away. It does have a squash court and in 2015 opens a new gym. Peterhouse is particularly strong in arts subjects and has numerous societies. It does less well on the science side and this means its academic performance can vary from year to year. The past year saw a solid performance, with nearly a third of students gaining firsts.

Queens'

Cambridge CB3 9ET 01223 335540 (admissions) www.queens.cam.ac.uk
Undergraduates: 504 Postgraduates: 325 admissions@queens.cam.ac.uk

The third largest of the colleges (in terms of students) and one of the oldest, Queens' is a bustling hub that spans both sides of the River Cam, with Sir Isaac Newton's famous Mathematical Bridge joining the two. Buildings range from the ancient crevices of Cloister Court to the rather less scenic 1970s Cripps Court. As a result, accommodation can range from historic sets (shared with one or two other students) to more basic modern rooms, of which a few are en-suite. A new alumni-funded development called "The Round" has transformed the old Cripps Court car park into pretty gardens and a new porter's lodge. Strong in the sciences, which is reflected in the awards and bursaries available for medicine, engineering and other subjects, Queens' performs well academically. Drama is also popular and the Fitzpatrick Hall is regularly used for performances, as well as for rowdy college "bops" that spill over from the bustling college bar. Sports clubs include everything from volleyball and water polo to badminton and chess, as well as the usual suspects: rugby, rowing and a good hockey side. The students enjoy the use of a recently built multi-gym, three squash courts and a spacious sports ground shared with Robinson, just under a mile away.

Robinson

Cambridge CB3 9AN 01223 339143 (admissions) www.robinson.cam.ac.uk
Undergraduates: 414 Postgraduates: 131 apply@robinson.cam.ac.uk

Robinson has made a virtue of its austere redbrick exterior. The Red Brick Café is eternally popular with students. Brickhouse, the student theatre company, makes full use of the outdoor theatre space, and the chapel is renowned for its fantastic acoustics and organ. Although it is not the most architecturally beautiful college, it has very good facilities. Student rooms are refurbished on a rolling programme over the summer, making them some of the best kept in the university. That said, rents are among the highest. The college canteen is fondly known as "The Garden Restaurant" and is regularly spoken of as one of the finest in Cambridge. Though the college tends to rest in the second half of the Tompkins Table (it was 16th in 2015), it is conveniently situated just behind the University Library and minutes away from the arts faculties on the Sidgwick Site. For those who like sport, Robinson often wields strong teams and the men's rowing team won blades in the Lent "Bumps" rowing competition. The sports grounds are shared with Queens', Selwyn and King's College, but are less than a mile from the main college site.

St Catharine's

Cambridge CB2 1RL 01223 338319 (admissions) www.caths.cam.ac.uk
Undergraduates: 481 Postgraduates: 142 undergraduate.admissions@caths.cam.ac.uk

Despite a prominent place on King's Parade, one of the largest student bodies and an open court that you can see into from the street, St Catharine's maintains an unassuming reputation. Fondly referred to as "Catz", the college has not one but two libraries, thanks to the faith put in the learning to be gained from books by the original benefactor, Robert Woodlark. Academic results have varied, though Catz made a dramatic leap from 21st to 13th place in the latest Tompkins Table and for the first time since 2000 the college is fielding a team in University Challenge. Students live on site in the first year before moving out to the popular St Chad's complex, where accommodation is split into shared flats with octagonal bedrooms. The building has been renovated for the 2015 academic year and a new porter's lodge added. The only oft-voiced complaint is that there are no ovens, which has resulted in some innovative cooking. Sports are enthusiastically played and the women's hockey team won the inter-college competition this year. The college also has a well-attended drama group called The Shirley Society, who make good use of the auditorium that opened in June 2013 along with a new student bar and common room.

St Edmund's

Cambridge CB3 0BN 01223 336086 (admissions) www.st-edmunds.cam.ac.uk
Undergraduates: 111 Postgraduates: 283 admissions@st-edmunds.cam.ac.uk

Set amid the hill colleges in the northwest of the city, St Edmund's has students from over 50 different countries, making it one of the most diverse university communities. Thanks to its mature student base – it celebrates 50 years as a graduate college this year – it often provides experienced sportsmen and women to the Varsity teams. Four "Eddies" students took part in 2015's boat race, for example. It has a well-equipped gym on site and an extended building project has seen the recent opening of three accommodation blocks, including the Brian Heap Building which, with its dining hall, kitchens and en-suite rooms, is a popular choice. Maisonettes and small flats are available for couples and small families. Though gowns are still worn to formal occasions, St Edmund's cultivates a relaxed atmosphere. There is no Fellows' high table in hall and, uniquely among all the Cambridge colleges, there is a Catholic chapel. As with many of the graduate colleges, the social scene is marginally more staid, and it lacks the enormous endowments of some of the larger colleges.

St John's

Cambridge CB2 1TP 01223 338703 (admissions) www.joh.cam.ac.uk
Undergraduates: 578 Postgraduates: 239 admissions@joh.cam.ac.uk

If the stunning architecture of St John's wasn't already recognisable enough – it is home to Cambridge's famous Bridge of Sighs – it will be familiar to fans of the Oscar-winning film, *The Theory of Everything*, in which the college provided the backdrop. St John's is known for fielding fearsome sports teams – the "Red Boys" rugby team once again won the inter-college league this year – and for its May Ball, for which tickets are highly coveted. It is also known for its stunning chapel and a strong musical tradition. As well as the chapel choir, the Gentlemen of St John's singers tour worldwide. The college has something of an "old boys club" reputation and, though this is mostly down to tradition rather than statistics, it does have one of the lowest intakes of students from the state sector. There is a generous endowment and bursaries are readily available for travel and further learning. The laddish social life largely revolves around the rugby team. John's tends towards the middle of the Tompkins Table academically, but this may be set to change. The college climbed to tenth place in the 2015 rankings from 16th the previous year.

Selwyn

Cambridge CB3 9DQ 01223 335896 (admissions) www.sel.cam.ac.uk
Undergraduates: 405 Postgraduates: 124 admissions@sel.cam.ac.uk

Students' major gripe about Selwyn is its distance from facilities like supermarkets and cash machines (in Cambridge terms, a ten-minute cycle ride) but its location has major advantages. Set amid tranquil gardens, it is on the doorstep of the Sidgwick Site, which makes the lecture commute a two-minute walk for arts and humanities students. It was among the first colleges to admit women and was the first to appoint a female head porter, although the gender balance is about 70:30 in favour of men. All students can be accommodated for three years of their course within 400 metres of the central site and the 1960s-built Cripps Court across the road has just re-opened after a £13-million refurbishment. Many rooms are en-suite. Though Selwyn doesn't often top inter-college tournaments, sports are played enthusiastically and are promoted through the Hermes and Sirens Clubs, longstanding male and female sports clubs that fund grants for various teams. Sports pitches are just a mile from the college and are shared with King's and Queens' colleges. The chapel choir is also well-supported and sings services three times a week as well as recording and touring. Selwyn tends towards the middle-ground academically, but the social life, which revolves around the modern bar and the popular Winter Ball, is vibrant.

Sidney Sussex

Cambridge CB2 3HU 01223 338872 (admissions) www.sid.cam.ac.uk
Undergraduates: 369 Postgraduate: 156 admissions@sid.cam.ac.uk

Despite being directly opposite the town centre's main supermarket, Sidney's 16th-century red brick walls hide tranquil private gardens and quiet courts. It's a small college and students are housed either in atmospheric rooms in college or in one of 11 nearby hostels. Sidney is also known for good food – its catering department has taken top prize in the university-wide culinary competition numerous times – and the largely student-run bar, which is notoriously cheap and home to well-attended "bops". Music is strong in the college and the chapel houses a grand piano, harpsichord and two organs, as well as hosting an award-winning chapel choir and, rather more bizarrely, Oliver Cromwell's head in the ante-chapel. The boathouse is a short walk across Jesus Green, and all other sports can be played on grounds shared with Christ's, a ten-minute cycle ride away. Participation is largely valued over performance. Also nearby is the university's renowned ADC theatre, towards which many students gravitate. Plays are also put on in the Front Court gardens in summer. Sidney tends to be stronger in sciences than the arts and usually appears in the middle of the Tompkins rankings.

Trinity

Cambridge CB2 1TQ 01223 338422 (admissions) www.trin.cam.ac.uk
Undergraduates: 710 Postgraduates: 243 admissions@trin.cam.ac.uk

The often re-told (and re-hashed) legend that you can walk all the way to Oxford from Trinity without leaving college land may not be true, but it is indicative of the sheer size and wealth of Oxbridge's largest college. Trinity has the largest endowment, the biggest undergraduate population and the highest number of Nobel prizewinning alumni. It even owns the O2 Arena in London. Unsurprisingly, college facilities are outstanding and with such a large number of students, you should find like-minded types. Heavily subsidised accommodation is among the most atmospheric in town and nearly half have en-suite bathrooms. For the fifth year running, Trinity has topped the Tompkins table with over 40 per cent of undergraduates attaining firsts. Students have access to the inspiring Wren Library (the largest in any college), which is home to 300,000 volumes including early folios of Shakespeare and even the original Winnie-the-Pooh manuscript. Trinity also has impressive gym facilities, as well as squash and badminton courts on site. The sports pitches are a short walk away. A little sport might be necessary to work off the good food of the catering team, which includes its own ice cream chef funded by a kind Trinity alumnus. Given its numerous traditions and historic opulence, it may be of little surprise that Trinity has an historically low number of students from state schools, just over half in the latest intake.

Trinity Hall

Cambridge CB2 1TJ	01223 332535 (admissions)	www.trinhall.cam.ac.uk
Undergraduates: 385	Postgraduates: 140	admissions@trinhall.cam.ac.uk

Although "Tit Hall", Cambridge's fifth oldest college, enjoys river frontage, unlike other colleges found on the Backs it has a tiny, unassuming entrance that many pass by without a second glance. Its small size means that it's a close-knit place which, sandwiched between Trinity and Clare, is ideally placed for short cycle rides to the University Library, Sidgwick Site and the centre of town. While some students have to live a five- to ten-minute cycle away on the Wychfield Site, the standard accommodation is not to be sniffed at. The 90 rooms at Wychfield are en-suite and some were refurbished in 2015. Another accommodation block with more en-suites will be opened in October 2016. The boathouse and dining hall have been refurbished recently and Tit Hall won the coveted top award for cocktail making in the 2015 University Culinary Competition. The college performs well academically, despite a small drop in Tompkins rating in 2015 from third to eighth. Sport is also strong and Tit Hall counts Olympic medal-winning cyclist Emma Pooley among its alumnae.

Wolfson

Cambridge CB3 9BB	01223 335918	www.wolfson.cam.ac.uk
Undergraduates: 162	Postgraduates: 317	ugadministrator@wolfson.cam.ac.uk

Wolfson is marking its 50th anniversary in 2015, having started life as University College. Its name was changed to Wolfson eight years later in recognition of a generous grant from the Wolfson Foundation. As part of the 50th anniversary the college aims to raise £5 million, which will go into improved accommodation and student grants. Although it is primarily a college for graduate students, Wolfson is also home to around 120 mature undergraduates and is one of the few colleges to offer part-time study. It is rare among the Cambridge colleges for other reasons, too. The head of college is referred to as the President, rather than Master, and it does not have a separate table for Fellows in hall. While the 1970s buildings are not among the town's most notable, the gardens are a treat and the college is not far from the path to Grantchester, which runs along the side of the river to the chocolate-box local village. It is a 20-minute walk into town, though facilities in and around the college are good and most of the diverse student body can be accommodated in the "old" 1970s blocks or newer 1990s buildings nearby. As well as a tennis court and gym, Wolfson has a strong boat club, and is renowned for a busy schedule of lectures and seminars from notable guests.

14 University Profiles

This chapter provides profiles of every university that appears in *The Times and Sunday Times* league table. In addition there are profiles for the two major suppliers of part-time degrees, the Open University and Birkbeck College, and also for those institutions which did not release data for use in the table (University College Birmingham, University of Wales Trinity St David and Wolverhampton). However, we do not have separate profiles for specialist colleges, such as the Royal College of Music (**www.rcm.ac.uk**) or institutions that only offer postgraduate degrees, such as Cranfield University (**www.cranfield.ac.uk**). Their omission is no reflection on their quality, simply a function of their particular roles. A number of additional institutions with degree-awarding powers are listed at the end of the book with their contact details.

The federal University of London (**www.london.ac.uk**) is by far Britain's biggest conventional higher education institution, with more than 120,000 students. The majority study at colleges in the capital, but such is the global prestige of the university's degrees that over 54,000 students in 180 different countries take University of London International Programmes. The university, which celebrated its 175th anniversary in 2011, consists of 17 self-governing colleges, the Institute in Paris and the School of Advanced Study, which comprises ten specialist institutes for research and postgraduate education (details at **www.sas.ac.uk**). City University will join the university in 2016. The following colleges have their own entries in this chapter: Birkbeck College, Goldsmiths, King's College London, London School of Economics and Political Science, Queen Mary, Royal Holloway, SOAS and University College London. Contact details for its other constituent colleges are given on page 566.

Guide to the profiles

The profiles contain valuable information about each university. You can find contact details, including postal address, telephone number for admission enquiries, email or web addresses for admissions and prospectus enquiries, web addresses for the university, the students' union and for sports facilities, and any university grouping that the institution is affiliated to (Russell Group, etc.). In addition, each profile provides information under the following headings:

- **The Times and Sunday Times rankings** For the overall ranking, the figure in bold refers to the university's position in 2016 and the figure in brackets to 2015. All the information listed below the heading is taken from the main league table. See chapter 4 for explanations and the sources of the data.
- **Undergraduates** The number of full-time undergraduates is given first followed by part-time undergraduates (in brackets). The figures are for 2013–14, and are the most recent from the Higher Education Statistics Agency (HESA).
- **Postgraduates** The number of full-time postgraduates is given first followed by part-time postgraduates (in brackets). The figures are for 2013–14, and are the most recent from HESA.
- **Mature students** The percentage of undergraduate entrants who were 21 or over at the start of their studies in 2014. The figures are from UCAS.
- **International students** The number of undergraduate overseas students (both EU and non-EU) as a percentage of full-time undergraduates. The figures are for 2013–14, and are from HESA.
- **Applications per place** The number of applicants per place for 2014, from UCAS.
- **From state-school sector** The number of young full-time first-degree entrants from state schools or colleges in 2013–14 as a percentage of total young entrants. The figures are from HESA.
- **From working-class homes** The number of young full-time first-degree entrants in 2013–14 whose parental occupations are skilled, manual, semi-skilled or unskilled (NS-SEC classes 4–7) as a percentage of total young entrants. The figures are from HESA.
- **Accommodation** The information was obtained from university accommodation services, and their help is gratefully acknowledged.

Undergraduate fees and bursaries

Details of tuition fees and financial support for UK students starting in 2016–17 are given wherever possible. Tuition fees for international students are for 2015–16. For Scotland and Northern Ireland the figures are for 2015–16, while for Wales, details of government support for students are for 2015–16, the latest available when this book went to press. It is of the utmost importance that you check university websites for the latest information. In England the Office for Fair Access (**www.offa.org.uk**) publishes "Access Agreements" for every English university on its website. Each agreement outlines the university's plans for fees, financial support and measures being taken to widen access to that university and to encourage students to complete their courses.

In the summary given on the profile pages: *RUK* describes students from the Rest of the UK at Scottish and Northern Irish universities; and *Household income* is the income that comes into a student's home before tax (but after a few allowances have been taken). For a young student, this will tend to be parental income; for married and mature students, it is all the income coming into his or her home.

Universities also offer a variety of scholarships and bursaries. There is not space in this book to give details of such awards and, again, you are advised to check university websites for details.

University of Aberdeen

Aberdeen is to open its first overseas campus in 2016, at Changwon in South Korea, making it the first UK university to have a base in that country. The campus will specialise in the offshore-related disciplines that are among Aberdeen's greatest strengths. The university has been chosen to lead a new MSc programme aimed mainly at people working in the UK oil and gas industry. At its own underwater research facility, Oceanlab, at Newburgh, north of Aberdeen, its engineers lead the world in creating systems capable of operating at depths down to 11,000 metres. The university's expertise is spread much more widely, however: it is close to the top 50 universities in the world for the proportion of research appearing in leading international journals. Three-quarters of the work submitted for the 2014 Research Excellence Framework was rated as world-leading or internationally excellent. The university was placed top in the UK for environmental and soil science and in the top three for psychology and English.

Established in 1495, Aberdeen is the UK's fifth oldest university. It has been enjoying record demand for places since the adoption of "Sixth Century Courses", which include cross-disciplinary degrees such as risk in society, sustainability and the digital society. Even on traditional degree programmes, students can try out three or four subjects before committing themselves at the end of their first or even second year. The modular system is so flexible that the majority of students change their intended degree before graduation. The aim is to give graduates broader knowledge and more intellectual flexibility. The university added 100 academic posts to deliver the new courses and strengthen its research. Assessors were highly complimentary about Aberdeen in the university's latest quality audit, praising the "transformative" effect of curriculum reforms, the quality of online learning resources, personal tutoring and employability initiatives.

The university expects to invest £377 million on capital projects by 2019. The futuristic Sir Duncan Rice Library, named after the Principal who commissioned it, cost £57 million and was chosen as one of the 12 best new buildings in Scotland. A £22-million Aquatic Centre, with 50-metre pool, opened in 2014, completing the Aberdeen Sports Village, which offers some of the best facilities at any university in the UK. Student services had already been transformed, and the redeveloped Butchart Centre gave the Students' Association a social focus on campus. The latest development is the new Rowett Institute, a glass-fronted building spread over five floors, which will open before the end of

King's College
Aberdeen AB24 3FX

01224 272090/91 (admissions)
sras@abdn.ac.uk
www.abdn.ac.uk
www.ausa.org.uk
Affiliation: none

***The Times and Sunday Times* Rankings**

Overall Ranking: **45** (last year: 44)

Teaching quality:	**108**	77.4%
Student experience:	**=68**	83.7%
Research quality:	**43**	29.9%
Entry standards:	**16**	446
Student–staff ratio:	**20**	13.4
Services & facilities/student:	**35**	£2,107
Expected completion rate:	**84**	84.1%
Good honours:	**32**	77.1%
Graduate prospects:	**37**	76.2%

the year. It includes a specialist Human Nutrition Unit which will enable volunteers to take part in rigorous dietary trials and studies in modern and comfortable surroundings. The university established the English-speaking world's first chair in medicine and has produced its share of advances since. The £20-million Suttie Centre has added a modern teaching and learning centre for medical education and clinical skills. Roughly half of the students study medicine, science or engineering, half the arts or social sciences. The student population is almost equally balanced between men and women, a quarter coming from low-income families.

Today's university is a fusion of two ancient institutions which came together in 1860. The original King's College buildings are the focal point of an appealing campus, complete with cobbled main street and attractive Georgian buildings, about a mile from the city centre. It is said to be one of the largest wireless campuses in Europe. Medicine is at Foresterhill, a 20-minute walk away. Buses link the two sites with the Hillhead residential complex. Almost a third of all students come from the north of Scotland, but one in six is from England among a total of 120 nationalities. Although the winters are long, the climate is warmer than the uninitiated might expect and transport links are good. Students find the city lively and welcoming, but expensive: the JobLink service provides a good selection of part-time employment. Aberdeen has been named as Scotland's safest university city, while the region has been rated as the UK's top environment in which to live and work.

The students' centre in The Hub brings together dining and retail outlets with support services, including the accommodation and careers offices. The university's ICT network has over 1,500 computers for student use. All new undergraduates are guaranteed housing – an important benefit in a city with the highest rents in Scotland. Aberdeen is also one of four Scottish universities collaborating in a new initiative to promote spin-out companies.

Undergraduate Fees and Bursaries

- » Fees for Scottish and EU students 2015–16 — No fee
- » Fees for Non-Scottish UK (RUK) students for 2015–16 — £9,000
  capped at £27,000 for 4-year courses and £36,000 for 5-year courses; no cap for medicine and dentistry.
- » Fees for international students 2015–16 — £13,000–£16,200
  Medicine — £28,600
- » Entrance scholarships (£1,000–£3,000), sports, music and other scholarships available for Scottish students.
- » For RUK students (2015–16): household income below £20K, £3,000 for three years; £20K–£30K, £2,000 for three years. Merit scholarships (AAB at A level or equivalent) excluding medicine, £3,000 for four years.
- » Check the university's website for the latest information.

Students

Undergraduates:	**9,545**	**(830)**
Postgraduates:	**2,155**	**(1,295)**
Mature students:	**14.6%**	
International students:	**24.3%**	
Applications per place:	**7.5**	
From state-sector schools:	**80.2%**	
From working-class homes:	**25.1%**	
Satisfaction with students' union	**58%**	

For detailed information about sports facilities:
www.abdn.ac.uk/sportandexercise

Accommodation

Number of places and costs refer to 2015–16
University-provided places: about 3,691
Percentage catered: 12%
Catered costs: £154–£169 a week (39 weeks).
Self-catered costs: £99–£146 a week (39–51 weeks).
First-year students are guaranteed accommodation.
International students: as above.
studentaccomm@abdn.ac.uk
www.abdn.ac.uk/accommodation/

Abertay University

Best known for its courses in computer arts and games design, Abertay is also pioneering accelerated degrees in Scotland. Seven degrees, including those star offers, can now be taken in three years, rather than the norm of four north of the border. The final two years consist of 45 weeks rather than the usual 30. Other subjects available in this format – unique so far in Scotland – include business studies, ethical hacking, sports development, and food and consumer science. The change was part of a curriculum reform encouraging problem- and work-based approaches to learning, focusing on real-world issues and teamwork rather than sitting in conventional lectures. The academic year is divided into two long terms, in each of which undergraduates take one module, followed by a four-week term that is used for assessment and preparation for future study.

American academics surveyed by the *Princeton Review* rated Abertay among the best places in the world to study games design, while Sony chose the university as the site for the largest teaching laboratory in Europe for its PlayStation consoles. The university opened Europe's first research centre dedicated to computer games and digital entertainment, and more recently established a centre for research into systems pathology. It hosts the first Interactive Media Academy in the UK and the national Centre for Excellence in Computer Games Education, and also has the largest number of courses in this area accredited by Skillset, the Government-sponsored training council for the creative industries. The university is upgrading its own IT facilities to match, investing £3 million last year in an extensive programme of software upgrades and hardware replacement across the campus, including a new Wi-Fi network. Abertay provides almost one computer for every five students – one of the highest ratios of PC to student in Britain, and is promising further improvements in the next year.

But the university is not just about computer games. Abertay launched Scotland's first degrees in bioinformatics and biotechnology, and now claims to be a leader for teaching and research in environmental science. A series of specialist research centres has been established in areas as diverse as urban water systems, bioinformatics, earth systems and environmental sciences. The latest are in sustainability assessment, visualisation and enhancement, and food and innovation.

Based in the centre of Dundee, all the university's teaching and learning buildings are within five minutes' walk of each other. They are modern and functional, such as the innovative White Space facility, the

Bell Street
Dundee DD1 1HG

01382 308080
sro@abertay.ac.uk
www.abertay.ac.uk
www.abertaysa.com
Affiliations: million+; GuildHE

***The Times and Sunday Times* Rankings**

Overall Ranking: **97** (last year: 106)

Teaching quality:	**=77**	80%
Student experience:	**78**	83.1%
Research quality:	**=90**	5.1%
Entry standards:	**57**	338
Student–staff ratio:	**119**	21.4
Services & facilities/student:	**83**	£1,563
Expected completion rate:	**119**	75.5%
Good honours:	**=60**	70.4%
Graduate prospects:	**74**	65.6%

university's flagship creative learning and working environment, where students study alongside industry professionals who are working on real commercial or broadcast projects. A new graduate school provides dedicated study space for postgraduates, as well as training and professional development opportunities.

The university doubled in size during the 1990s and has grown to around 5,500 since tuition fees were abolished for Scottish students. Most are based in Dundee, but Abertay's degrees are also taught as far away as Malaysia. The university enjoyed big increases in applications in the early years of this decade, but enrolments have fallen recently, partly because of the planned withdrawal of uneconomic courses. There have been occasional suggestions that Abertay might merge with neighbouring Dundee University – most recently in 2011 – but it is now firmly on an independent path.

Degrees are predominantly vocational, with more subjects being added every year. Food and consumer sciences, creative sound production, and digital forensics are recent examples. All courses can be taken on a part-time basis, and new programmes aim to offer students the chance to spend at least 30 per cent of their time in industry. Entrance requirements have risen consistently over the last five years, even beyond those sought-after computing courses. Law and forensic psychobiology, for example, both demand ABBB in Scottish Highers or BCC at A level. Well-qualified A-level students are eligible for direct entry into second year if they do not opt for an accelerated degree.

The university hosts the Dundee Academy of Sport, launched in partnership with Dundee and Angus College – a venture using sport as a vehicle for learning across the school curriculum and throughout life. The city has seen considerable investment recently, including the development of its waterfront, centred on the £80-million V&A Dundee design museum, which is now under construction. The city has a large student population and the cost of living is modest. A 500-bed student village, which opened in 2010, allows all first-years to be guaranteed accommodation.

Undergraduate Fees and Bursaries

» Fees for Scottish and EU students 2015–16 No fee
» Fees for Non-Scottish UK (RUK) students for 2015–16 £7,250
» Fees for international students 2015–16 £10,700–£12,700
» For RUK students: household income below £17K, annual bursary £1,750; household income £17K–£24K, £1,000; household income £24K–£34K, £500.
» Check the university's website for the latest information.

Students

Undergraduates:	**4,060**	**(285)**
Postgraduates:	**240**	**(175)**
Mature students:	**38.1%**	
International students:	**10.5%**	
Applications per place:	**6**	
From state-sector schools:	**95.8%**	
From working-class homes:	**33.8%**	
Satisfaction with students' union	**68%**	

For detailed information about sports facilities:
www.sport.abertay.ac.uk/

Accommodation

Number of places and costs refer to 2015–16
University-provided places: 668
Percentage catered: 0%
Self-catered costs: £59.00–£115.00 a week (38, 42 or 51 weeks).
All new entrants (home and international) guaranteed accommodation if conditions are met. Pre-payment discount available (some residential restrictions).
Free bus travel for students living in Alloway Halls.
residences@abertay.ac.uk;
http://www.abertay.ac.uk/studentlife/accommodation/

Aberystwyth University

Aberystwyth has begun to move back up our league table after falling to its lowest-ever position last year, but there is a long way to go to reach its target of the top 30 in the UK and the top 250 in the world. The university's strategic plan emphasises the student experience, which has been its Achilles heel in recent rankings. It has done well in the International Student Barometer, which gauges satisfaction levels among international students, but is yet to make the same progress in the National Student Survey. Applications were down 13 per cent in 2014 and there was a fall of nearly 200 students taking up places. Despite the fee concessions offered to Welsh students, who make up about a third of Aber's intake, the demand for places has dropped by almost a third since 2011.

Scores in the 2014 Research Excellence Framework showed improvement on the 2008 assessments, with the departments of international politics, geography and earth science, and the Institute of Biological, Environmental and Rural Sciences (IBERS) doing particularly well. Overall, two-thirds of the research submitted was judged to be world-leading or internationally excellent, with all the submissions in computer science and art judged at this level for their external impact. However, such was the increase in grades throughout the UK that Aber still lost ground in our research ranking. IBERS, which serves 1,500 undergraduate and research students and focuses on sustainable land use, climate change, renewable energy and the security of food and water supplies, has been one of the main growth points. The Institute, which has a link with Bangor University, has 360 staff, making it one of Europe's largest in this field. IBERS has a new building on the main Penglais campus and is also at the centre of a new innovation and research campus, which opened this year at Gogerddan. Aber has the widest range of land-related courses in the UK.

The university has doubled its planned investment in student accommodation and teaching and research facilities, taking total spending to £100 million. The first students have moved into new residences close to the existing student village and within walking distance of the Penglais and Llanbadarn campuses. They provide self-catering accommodation for 1,000 students, with a central hub that includes social and learning facilities. The latest phase of a £3.6-million upgrade of teaching and learning facilities was completed in 2014, and an upland agricultural research centre is being developed near Aberystwyth. The original Old College Building is to be redeveloped as an arts centre, with postgraduate accommodation and study spaces.

The attractive seaside location remains

Penglais
Aberystwyth
Ceredigion SY23 3FL

01970 622021 (admissions)
ug-admissions@aber.ac.uk
www.aber.ac.uk
www.abersu.co.uk
Affiliation: none

***The Times and Sunday Times* Rankings**

Overall Ranking: **=79** (last year: 93)

Teaching quality:	**101**	78.4%
Student experience:	**110**	80.4%
Research quality:	**45**	28.1%
Entry standards:	**=83**	312
Student–staff ratio:	**=78**	17.8
Services & facilities/student:	**104**	£1,386
Expected completion rate:	**48**	89.3%
Good honours:	**88**	65.1%
Graduate prospects:	**91**	62.5%

a draw for applicants. Although the oldest of the Welsh universities, Aberystwyth has long prided itself on a modern outlook: it was among the pioneers of the modular degree system and allowed students flexibility between subjects even before that. Every student is given the opportunity of a year's work experience in commerce, industry or the public sector, either at home or abroad. Those who have taken advantage of the scheme have achieved better than average degrees and enhanced their employment prospects. Welsh-medium teaching is thriving, with more courses available in the language. Well over 90 per cent of the undergraduates are state educated – a higher proportion than the mix of subjects would imply – but the proportion from working-class homes is below the university's benchmark. A Student Welcome Centre continues to offer advice on everything from money problems to learning difficulties long after undergraduates have enrolled, helping to produce one of the lowest dropout rates in Wales, now projected at 7 per cent.

Aber boasts one of higher education's most informative websites and also publishes a special guide for parents. There is 24-hour access to the computer network, and the four university libraries are complemented by the National Library of Wales. Aberystwyth town is compact and travel to other parts of the UK slow, so applicants should be sure that they will be happy to spend three years or more in a tight-knit community. Many are: the university scores well in *Times Higher Education* student experience survey for its facilities and community atmosphere. The students' guild is the largest entertainment venue in the region. There is plenty of out-of-season accommodation to supplement the university's extensive stock. Sports facilities are good and well used, and include a 400-metre running track, 50 acres of playing fields, a 3G pitch, refurbished swimming pool, a climbing wall and specialist outdoor facilities for water sports.

Undergraduate Fees and Bursaries

- Fees for UK/EU students 2016–17 £9,000
- Welsh Assembly non-means-tested grant (2015–16) to pay fees above £3,810 for Welsh students.
- Fees for international students 2015–16 £10,500–£12,000
- For all UK students: household income less than £34K, bursaries on sliding scale £600–£1,000; £400 bursary in Year 1 for all those in university accommodation.
- Students with 320 UCAS points from best 3 A levels, or equivalent, £1,000 a year. Entrance scholarships by examination. Sports, music and subject awards.
- Check the university's website for the latest information.

Students

Undergraduates:	**7,830**	**(1,730)**
Postgraduates:	**1,040**	**(565)**
Mature students:	**11.8%**	
International students:	**13.7%**	
Applications per place:	**4.4**	
From state-sector schools:	**93.7%**	
From working-class homes:	**32.1%**	
Satisfaction with students' union	**59%**	

For detailed information about sports facilities:
www.aber.ac.uk/en/sportscentre/

Accommodation

Number of places and costs refer to 2015–16
University-provided places: 3,750
Percentage catered: 15%
Catered costs: £101.85 (twin) – £116.20 (single) a week (39 weeks).
Self-catered costs: £78.05 (budget) – £136.50 (single) a week (39, 40 or 50 weeks).
First years are guaranteed accommodation if conditions are met.
International: guaranteed for those classed as overseas for fees.
accommodation@aber.ac.uk;
www.aber.ac.uk/en/accommodation/

Anglia Ruskin University

Already one of the biggest universities in Eastern England, Anglia Ruskin is planning to grow by another 20 per cent in the next two years while "driving up" entry qualifications by attracting more applicants. Other targets include exceeding the national average for student retention, achievement, satisfaction and graduate employment, thereby improving the university's position in league tables. It is a demanding agenda, but the growth has already started, and Anglia was named Entrepreneurial University of the Year in 2014.

A prototype regional university, Anglia Ruskin has campuses in Chelmsford, Cambridge and Peterborough, serving more than 35,000 students, studying at a range of levels. There are also university centres in Harlow and King's Lynn. The university has invested £122 million in the last five years, adding facilities such as medical simulation suites, forensic science labs, mock hospital wards and a courtroom, where students can practise their skills in safe but realistic environments. The Cambridge campus has been redeveloped at a cost of £35 million, and two buildings dedicated to Health and Social Care have been added in Chelmsford. There is also a purpose-built music centre and full-size professional theatre on the Chelmsford campus, as well as a sports hall and business centre with a high-tech Bloomberg Financial Markets Lab. The university plans to spend another £98 million over the next four years, beginning with the development of a new site five minutes' walk from the East Road campus in Cambridge. A new science centre will open there in 2017.

Anglia was the last university to retain a polytechnic title, discarding it only in 2005. It took the name of John Ruskin, who founded the Cambridge School of Art, which evolved into one part of Anglia Ruskin. The university has a history of providing innovative courses: the BOptom (Hons) is the only qualification of its kind in the UK and the hearing aid audiology course was among the first to lead directly to registration. Paramedic science is the latest addition. Anglia Ruskin was also the first UK University to sign the Rio + 20 Declaration of Higher Education Institutions. Its Global Sustainability Institute, established in 2011, is building an international reputation for its research, and Anglia Ruskin is aiming to make sustainability an important part of every student's experience.

The university also aims to instil entrepreneurial values among both students and staff. Many courses are recognised by industry and a large number are professionally accredited. Among its latest initiatives is a £7-million business

Chelmsford Campus:
Bishop Hall Lane,
Chelmsford CM1 1SQ
Cambridge Campus:
East Road,
Cambridge CB1 1PT
0845 271 3333 (enquiries)
answers@anglia.ac.uk
www.anglia.ac.uk
www.angliastudent.com
Affiliation: million+

***The Times and Sunday Times* Rankings**

Overall Ranking: **108** (last year: 110)

Teaching quality:	**=39**	82.5%
Student experience:	**=63**	83.9%
Research quality:	**=88**	5.4%
Entry standards:	**124**	254
Student–staff ratio:	**=93**	19
Services & facilities/student:	**102**	£1,419
Expected completion rate:	**113**	79.3%
Good honours:	**116**	58.4%
Graduate prospects:	**76**	65%

innovation centre in Chelmsford, which includes a Startup Lab for students to test and develop their ideas. Nearly all the students attended state schools or colleges and almost 40 per cent are from the four poorest socio-economic groups. The projected dropout rate has been improving, and is now slightly better than the national average for its subjects and entry grades. Each undergraduate has an adviser to help compile a degree package which can look at the chosen subject from different points of view to maximise future job prospects. Three-quarters of the full-time undergraduate leavers who find jobs in the UK stay in East Anglia. The university has an innovative scheme placing graduates with the region's small firms – usually the companies that are least likely to take on those emerging from higher education.

The results of the 2014 Research Excellence Framework showed that at least some world-leading research is undertaken in all five faculties. The best results were in music, drama and the performing arts, where 40 per cent of the research was found to have "outstanding" impact, but there were good results, too, in health subjects, media studies, and geography and environmental science.

The social scene naturally varies between the campuses, all of which are within an hour of London by train. The university offers a range of sporting facilities, from swimming and tennis to climbing and studio classes at all of the sites. Chelmsford has an on-campus sports centre with a well-equipped gym, while Cambridge also has a gym, sports centre and swimming pool. There is limited collaboration with Cambridge University at the Cambridge Centre for Cricketing Excellence, and at the base for Anglia Ruskin's Rowing Club. The university's flourishing programme to encourage sporting participation is particularly successful at elite level in judo. Sports facilities in Cambridge are being improved with the addition of a new pavilion, and both grass and artificial pitches, including one 3G surface. Anglia Ruskin students have access to Vivacity's clubs in Peterborough, where there are also leisure centres and a lido.

Undergraduate Fees and Bursaries

- » Fees for UK/EU students 2016–17 £9,000
  - Foundation degree £7,500
  - Undergraduate courses at associated colleges £7,500–£8,500
- » Fees for international students 2015–16 £10,300–£12,250
- » Household income below £25K, £200 bursary and £400 book and study-related grant each year.
- » Household income above £25K, £400 book and study-related grant each year.
- » Check the university's website for the latest information.

Students

Undergraduates:	**13,395**	**(3,890)**
Postgraduates:	**1,800**	**(1,610)**
Mature students:	**35%**	
International students:	**12.6%**	
Applications per place:	**5.9**	
From state-sector schools:	**96.4%**	
From working-class homes:	**38.7%**	
Satisfaction with students' union	**63%**	

For detailed information about sports facilities:
www.anglia.ac.uk/student-life/sports-and-societies

Accommodation

Number of places and costs refer to 2015–16
University-provided places: Cambridge, 703 plus 1,237 referral rooms; Chelmsford, 511
Percentage catered: 0%
Self-catered costs: Cambridge: £88–£170 a week; Chelmsford: £111–£119 a week.
Most first years are accommodated. Distance restrictions apply.
International students: conditions and deadline apply.
essexaccom@anglia.ac.uk; cambaccom@anglia.ac.uk
www.anglia.ac.uk/student-life/accommodation

Arts University Bournemouth

The Arts University Bournemouth (AUB) has dropped more than 20 places in our table this year after a decline in graduate employment levels. AUB still compares favourably with other arts universities on this measure but, with scores close together in this area of the table, a drop of 5 percentage points in the proportion of graduates going straight into professional jobs or continuing to study has been damaging. With applications growing rapidly since university status arrived in 2012, there are now around 3,000 students based on a single campus, which is being upgraded in several areas at a cost of £17 million. Among the highlights are a new photography building with flexible teaching spaces and IT suites, and a Crab drawing studio, which is the first of its kind to be built in the UK this century. Its curved design produces a softer light for drawing to be taught and practised.

The university has operated as a specialist institution since 1885 and is now one of only 15 higher education institutions in the UK devoted solely to the study of art, design and media, five of which appear in our table. There are degrees in acting, architecture, dance, event management and film production, as well as art and design subjects. The university describes its courses as having a "highly practical streak" designed to give students an edge in a competitive creative world. Only 12 staff were entered for the 2014 Research Excellence Framework, when 43 per cent of their work was rated as world-leading or internationally excellent. Students and staff work together on an innovative programme of professional practice and research, with different disciplines encouraged to work together. The staff includes many with experience in, and continuing engagement with, the creative industries, while the careers service provides students with subject-specific and generic advice on future employment. Industry liaison groups and visiting tutors keep the university abreast of developments in the creative industries, while alumni return regularly as lecturers.

AUB's campus in Wallisdown straddles Bournemouth and Poole. It includes The Gallery, which showcases work by students and other contemporary artists, hosting talks, events and film nights to support the exhibition programme. There is also an Enterprise Pavilion (eP) on campus to develop, attract and retain new creative businesses in the South West. The purpose-built library includes the Museum of Design in Plastics, which holds over 12,000 artefacts of predominantly 20th- and 21st-century mass-produced design and popular culture. The items are selected specifically to support the academic courses taught at the university. Laser cutting machinery and

Wallisdown
Poole
Dorset BH12 5HH

01202 533011
hello@aub.ac.uk (enquiries)
www.aub.ac.uk
www.aubsu.co.uk
Affiliation: GuildHE

***The Times and Sunday Times* Rankings**
Overall Ranking: **81** (last year: 59)

Teaching quality:	**=57**	81.4%
Student experience:	**111**	80%
Research quality:	**116**	2.4%
Entry standards:	**=67**	322
Student–staff ratio:	**=42**	15.3
Services & facilities/student:	**126**	£684
Expected completion rate:	**=28**	92.3%
Good honours:	**83**	66.2%
Graduate prospects:	**94**	61.4%

a 3-D printer feature among the high-tech equipment available to students. AUB has a Skillset Media Academy in partnership with Bournemouth University, offering eight accredited courses in areas from animation to make-up for media and performance. The two universities also bid successfully to become a Screen Academy, through which Skillset recognises excellence in film and the broader screen-based media. The most recent audit of the university by the Quality Assurance Agency resulted in the highest possible grade, commending the academic standards. The MArch programme has recently been validated by the Royal Institute of British Architects, which already validated the BA course, allowing students to qualify entirely through AUB.

More than 30 per cent of the undergraduates are from working-class homes and 95 per cent attended state schools or colleges – both figures close to the national average for AUB's subjects and entry qualifications. The low dropout rate is a point of particular pride – at only 5 per cent, it is half the university's benchmark figure. More than a third of undergraduates have been receiving either scholarships or bursaries. Support for students arriving in 2016 will include bicycle vouchers, support for educational visits and hardship loans.

The university has 560 places in its halls of residence and flats, giving priority in their allocation to overseas students and those with disabilities or other medical conditions. Most of the places are in the newest development, in the centre of Bournemouth, which was completed in 2014. There is plenty of privately rented accommodation in the area. The university keeps a register of approved housing at the **www.aubstudentpad.com** website and runs accommodation days in July and August for current and prospective students to find potential housemates. Bournemouth has a large and cosmopolitan student population and one of the most vibrant club scenes outside London. The capital is less than two hours away and is easily reached by regular train and coach services or via good motorway links.

Undergraduate Fees and Bursaries

» Fees for UK/EU students 2016–17	£9,000
Year abroad	£1,000
» Fees for international students 2015–16	£13,500

» Course material fee waived for all students.
» Household income below £25K, £200 progression scholarship at Level 6 to assist with final year projects.
» Check the university's website for the latest information.

Students

Undergraduates:	**2,840**	**(25)**
Postgraduates:	**55**	**(20)**
Mature students:	**8.3%**	
International students:	**12.5%**	
Applications per place:	**6.4**	
From state-sector schools:	**95.1%**	
From working-class homes:	**31.5%**	
Satisfaction with students' union	**64%**	

For detailed information about sports facilities:
www.aubsu.co.uk/clubsandsocs/clubs/

Accommodation

Number of places and costs refer to 2015–16
University-provided places: 560
Percentage catered: 0%
Self-catered costs: £115 (double, shared); £115–£130 (single en suite); £120 (double en suite); £130–£145 (single studio); £135 (double studio) a week.
First years and students with medical conditions/disabilities have priority.
International students have priority.
http://aub.ac.uk/plan-visit-apply/accommodation/

University of the Arts London

University of the Arts London (UAL) features in the top ten in the world for art and design in the QS subject rankings, and is gradually building an estate to do justice to that billing. Having seen Central Saint Martin's move into the new King's Cross development, new premises for Camberwell College of Arts are seeing an investment of £62 million as part of the regeneration of the Elephant and Castle, and the London College of Fashion is moving onto the Olympic Park in Stratford to form part of an Arts Quarter there. Only an inability, shared by most arts-based institutions, to match the high levels of student satisfaction seen at generalist universities holds UAL back in our league table. Although the university did better in the sections of the National Student Survey focusing on teaching quality, it was last for those relating to the broader student experience.

Already the biggest art and design university in Europe, it will soon have room to capitalise on the renewed demand for places experienced by the six constituent colleges. Arts subjects – and institutions – suffered disproportionately from the introduction of £9,000 fees. But UAL saw a strong recovery in the volume of applications in 2013 and 2014, amounting to a 17 per cent increase over the two years. The university also performed well in the 2014 Research Excellence Framework, when 83 per cent of the work submitted was considered world-leading or internationally excellent. All of it reached one of the top two categories for its external impact. Perhaps more impressively for prospective applicants, all four nominees for the 2015 Turner Prize have studied, taught or carried out research at UAL.

Five of the colleges came together as the London Institute in 1989 before becoming a university 15 years later. The five became six when Wimbledon College of Arts joined in 2006, bringing an international reputation in theatre design and the UK's largest school of theatre. The founding members, which continue to use their own names and enjoy considerable autonomy, were Camberwell College of Arts, Central Saint Martins, Chelsea College of Arts, London College of Fashion and London College of Communication (formerly the London College of Printing). A global reputation attracts more than 5,500 international students and 2,000 from other EU countries among a total of 17,000.

Big changes were already under way before university status arrived: a £70-million development next door to the Tate Gallery produced prestigious new premises for Chelsea College. Another £32

272 High Holborn
London WC1V 7EY

0207 514 6197 (admissions)
admissions@arts.ac.uk
www.arts.ac.uk
www.suarts.org
Affiliation: none

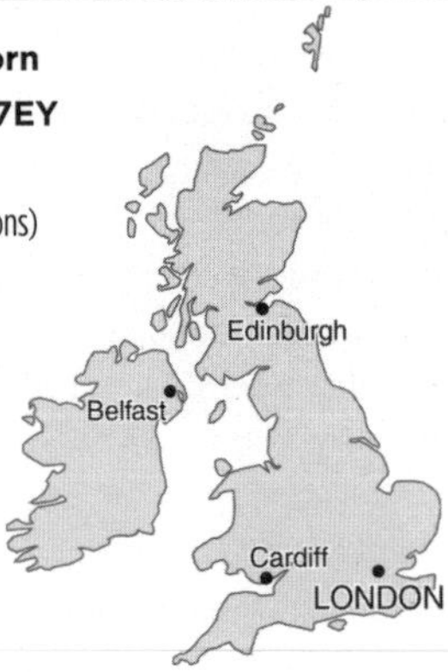

***The Times and Sunday Times* Rankings**

Overall Ranking: **99** (last year: 85)

Teaching quality:	**118**	75.9%
Student experience:	**127**	74.5%
Research quality:	**72**	8%
Entry standards:	**71**	320
Student–staff ratio:	**=40**	15.1
Services & facilities/student:	**68**	£1,711
Expected completion rate:	**74**	85.5%
Good honours:	**=104**	61.8%
Graduate prospects:	**108**	59.2%

million was spent on new headquarters for the College of Communication at the Elephant and Castle. The biggest completed project has brought Central Saint Martins together on one site for the first time. The £200-million campus is based on a Grade II listed former granary near King's Cross station, which accommodates a new School of Performing Arts as well as the college's existing art, fashion and design courses. The new building was voted the world's best higher education building in 2012. The next two developments will bring together London College of Fashion's 6,500 students and staff for the first time in its 100-year history and create a new academic extension and additional student accommodation for Camberwell College of Arts.

All the colleges make good use of visiting lecturers, who keep students abreast of developments in their field. The university has also been running weekend classes and summer schools in an attempt to broaden the intake. More than a third of the undergraduates come from the four poorest socio-economic groups, while 95 per cent attended state schools or colleges. Students have access to the largest art and design specialist careers centre in the country, while the pioneering Emerging Artists Programme continues to support graduates in the early years of their careers. The university holds the only recruitment festival tailored to the needs of creative graduates, providing access to hundreds of industry professionals for networking opportunities and advice.

The colleges vary considerably in character and facilities, although a single students' union serves them all. The university's student hub provides a central place for students to work, socialise and share ideas, as well as being the location for student services such as housing and careers. The university has 15 residences spread around the colleges, following the opening of two more in Elephant and Castle and Finsbury Park. House-hunting workshops help those who have to rely on the expensive private housing market. The university owns no sports facilities, although it has arranged student discounts with a number of providers.

Undergraduate Fees and Bursaries

- » Fees for UK/EU students 2016–17 £9,000
- » Fees for international students 2015–16 £15,950
- » Household income below £25K, minimum of £1,000 each year.
- » Range of scholarships available.
- » Check the university's website for the latest information.

Students

Undergraduates:	**13,695**	**(340)**
Postgraduates:	**2,420**	**(685)**
Mature students:	**23%**	
International students:	**41.7%**	
Applications per place:	**7.6**	
From state-sector schools:	**95.6%**	
From working-class homes:	**32.4%**	
Satisfaction with students' union	**58%**	

For detailed information about sports facilities:
www.suarts.org/arts-active

Accommodation

Number of places and costs refer to 2015–16
University-provided places: 3,051
Percentage catered: 0%
Self-catered costs: £102 – £273 a week.
First-year students are offered accommodation if conditions are met. Priority for disabled and students under 18, and those from outside London.
International students: guaranteed if conditions met.
accommodation@arts.ac.uk;
www.arts.ac.uk/study-at-ual/accommodation/

Aston University

Aston will celebrate its 50th year as a university in 2016 with a newly landscaped campus that is attracting more students than ever. Gone are the last of the 1970s buildings and facilities, replaced by modern and spacious student accommodation, open green spaces and the remodelled Chancellor's Lake. Applications are up by more than a third in two years, enabling Aston to take 40 per cent more undergraduates in 2014 than 2011. More than a third of them come with ABB or better at A level, attracted by a consistently good graduate employment record, which is the university's main selling point. Seven out of ten students have a work placement, often abroad, and the target is 100 per cent by 2020. Many later secure graduate jobs at the scene of their placement.

Set in the heart of Birmingham, the university has remained resolutely specialist in business, science and technology, languages and social science, concentrating on degrees with professional placements even when they were in decline elsewhere. After considerable growth in recent years, there are now nearly 12,000 students – around 9,000 of them undergraduates. With the Government's relaxation of recruitment controls, the aim is to grow to 13,000 by 2017. By then, Aston expects to open its own medical school, which will train much-needed doctors for disadvantaged communities. It will also launch new degrees in subjects such as applied physics and neurosciences.

The university has been concentrating on improving the student experience and boosting research performance, with the eventual aim of becoming a top ten university. The MyAston mobile app, used regularly by 80 per cent of students, gives access course materials and other information remotely and at a time of users' own choosing. The completion of the Aston Student Village has provided 3,000 en-suite rooms on campus, maintaining the guarantee of accommodation for all first-year students. A £215-million programme of improvements includes an impressive library opened in 2010. The Woodcock Sport Centre, which includes a Grade II listed swimming pool, followed in 2011 and has since acquired a new sports hall with indoor courts and team sports facilities. Aston's active students' union is set to be rehoused in purpose-built premises in the middle of the campus. More chemistry and chemical engineering laboratories have been provided and £16.5 million spent on the European Bioenergy Research Institute.

Once a college of advanced technology, Aston remains strong in engineering and the sciences, although the highly rated business school accounts for almost half

Aston Triangle
Birmingham B4 7ET

0121 204 4444 (course enquiries)
ugenquiries@aston.ac.uk
www.aston.ac.uk
www.aston.ac.uk/union
Affiliation: none

***The Times and Sunday Times* Rankings**

Overall Ranking: **30** (last year: =34)

Teaching quality:	**21**	83.3%
Student experience:	**11**	87.9%
Research quality:	**48**	25.8%
Entry standards:	**45**	369
Student–staff ratio:	**=46**	15.5
Services & facilities/student:	**=42**	£1,997
Expected completion rate:	**37**	90.9%
Good honours:	**43**	75.1%
Graduate prospects:	**=26**	78.8%

of the students. The business school will relocate to a new centralised position on campus after a £19-million revamp. New undergraduates are offered 12 online study skills modules before the formal start of their course. Aston has also introduced a free programme of language tuition for all students, covering six languages including Arabic and Mandarin, as part of its efforts to help boost employability further. More than a quarter of first-year students use the service.

At the forefront of employer-led degrees, the university was awarded £1.6 million to set up a Foundation Degree Centre to establish new courses and explore other ways of delivering qualifications. There is a wide range of joint honours programmes for those who prefer not to specialise.

The projected dropout rate has improved considerably in recent years and at 7.6 per cent is ahead of the national average for Aston's subjects. The intake is diverse, with more than 40 per cent of the undergraduates coming from working-class homes, nine out of ten of whom go on to obtain graduate-level jobs. Six out of ten undergraduates come from outside the West Midlands and around a fifth from outside the UK.

Although still relatively small, Aston did well in the 2014 research assessments, doubling the proportion of work in the top two categories to 80 per cent. Life and health sciences led the way, with business and management, politics and engineering also producing good results. New research centres in enterprise, healthy ageing, Europe, and neuroscience and child development proved their worth. The £6-million Aston Brain Centre opened in 2011, combining research and teaching in a single unique facility. Research funding is at record levels, with the new Aston Institute for Photonics Research proving particularly successful.

Recent developments have also helped to place Aston among the top dozen universities in the People and Planet Green League of sustainability for the past five years. It has been given "Platinum Eco Campus" status for demonstrating a lasting commitment to sustainability.

Undergraduate Fees and Bursaries

» Fees for UK/EU students 2016–17	£9,000
Placement year	£1,000
Foundation degree	£6,000
» Fees for international students 2015–16	£13,500–£16,500

- » Household income up to £18K, £1,000 university accommodation discount in year 1.
- » Excellence scholarship (AAB at A level or equivalent), £1,000 fee waiver, accommodation discount or cash in year 1.
- » For all Home/EU students, £1,000 placement year scholarship as cash or fee waiver.
- » Check the university's website for the latest information.

Students

Undergraduates:	**7,575**	**(555)**
Postgraduates:	**1,975**	**(885)**
Mature students:	**8.5%**	
International students:	**18.5%**	
Applications per place:	**7.1**	
From state-sector schools:	**94%**	
From working-class homes:	**43.9%**	
Satisfaction with students' union	**60%**	

For detailed information about sports facilities:
www.aston.ac.uk/prospective-students/sport/

Accommodation

Number of places and costs refer to 2015–16
University-provided places: 3,017
Percentage catered: 0%
Self-catered accommodation: £119–£132; £147–£161 with Aston Meal Plan (42 weeks).
First years are guaranteed accommodation if they fulfil requirements and apply by the deadline.
International fee-paying students: as above.
accom@aston.ac.uk
www.aston.ac.uk/accommodation/

Bangor University

Bangor has the most satisfied students in Wales both for the quality of teaching and the student experience, but has still dropped two places in *The Times and Sunday Times* league table this year. Its clubs and societies, which are free to students, were voted the best in the UK in the Whatuni website's Student Choice Awards. Applications fell in 2014, but the university still filled more places than in any of the previous five years. Bangor finished among the top 50 universities in the 2014 Research Excellence Framework, with half of the schools rated in the top 20 in the UK, leisure and tourism, languages and psychology leading the way.

The small North Wales city is said to be among the cheapest in the UK in which to study, and the standard of university accommodation has been rated in the top ten. A new student village of 600 rooms will open in 2015, close to the city centre, with a range of accommodation from en-suite studio apartments to townhouses. There will also be a café bar, shop, laundrette, common rooms and sports and fitness facilities on site.

Other parts of the university estate have already been redeveloped, with the addition of a £5-million environmental sciences building and a £3.5-million Cancer Research Institute, which is attracting specialists of international repute. A combination of private funds and a £5-million European grant was used to establish a Business Management Centre on a waterfront site. A new £40-million Arts and Innovation Centre forms a bridge between the university's upper campus and the nearby science site. It will be a social hub for students, with a bar and café as well as a theatre, studio, cinema, lecture theatres and exhibition spaces. The main sports centre, Canolfan Brailsford, was refurbished and renamed in 2014. It has a two-storey gym, including 50 cardiovascular machines, a six-platform Olympic lifting area, two sports halls, an aerobics studio, cycling studio, gymnastics hall, climbing wall and squash courts.

The university has a community focus that dates back to a 19th-century campaign which saw local quarrymen putting part of their weekly wages towards the establishment of a college. The School of Lifelong Learning continues the tradition with courses across North Wales, but the university has also built a worldwide reputation in areas such as environmental studies and ocean sciences. The 23 academic schools are all within walking distance of each other, apart from the School of Ocean Sciences, which is two miles away in Menai Bridge.

Bangor is an expanding centre for Welsh-medium teaching. Although a majority of students come from outside Wales – there

College Road
Bangor
Gwynedd LL57 2DG

01248 388484 (admissions)
admissions@bangor.ac.uk
www.bangor.ac.uk
www.undeb.bangor.ac.uk
Affiliation: none

***The Times and Sunday Times* Rankings**

Overall Ranking: **52** (last year: 50)

Teaching quality:	**=6**	85.8%
Student experience:	**=12**	87.8%
Research quality:	**47**	27.2%
Entry standards:	**=69**	321
Student–staff ratio:	**=57**	16.5
Services & facilities/student:	**103**	£1,387
Expected completion rate:	**100**	81.8%
Good honours:	**=92**	64.1%
Graduate prospects:	**63**	67.7%

is a strong link with Ireland, for example – around 20 per cent speak the language and one of the halls of residence is for Welsh-speakers and learners of the language. Bangor also has a flourishing international exchange programme, which gives students the option of studying overseas for one extra year in a wide variety of destinations in Europe, North America, Australia and the Far East. In addition, there is a Peer Guiding scheme, where second- and third-year students mentor new students and arrange social activities for them, which is one of the largest schemes in the UK.

Over 95 per cent of the students come from state schools or colleges, and almost a third are from working-class homes. For 2016 entry, the university is offering scholarships and bursaries worth over £3.7 million, which range from merit awards based on pre-entry examinations, to sports scholarships and awards in number of other subjects. The university's Talent Opportunities Programme, which operates in schools across North Wales, targets potential applicants from lower socio-economic families who have little or no history of going on to university.

There is a strong focus on student support, including a pioneering dyslexia unit, which offers individual and group support throughout students' courses. The Study Skills Centre helps with the transition to university and provides continuing academic support. In addition, the Bangor Employability Award (BEA) has been introduced to enhance students' career prospects by accrediting co-curricular and extracurricular activities, such as volunteering and part-time work, that are valued by employers.

The university is in the top 30 in an international league table for its green credentials. The city is little more than a stone's throw from Snowdonia with its attractions for sports enthusiasts. Social life for most students is concentrated on the students' union, which has around 150 clubs and societies, covering a range of interests, activities and sports.

Undergraduate Fees and Bursaries

- » Fees for UK/EU students 2016–17 £9,000
- » Welsh Assembly non-means-tested grant (2015–16) to pay fees above £3,810 for Welsh students
- » Fees for international students 2015–16 £11,500–£15,000
- » Bangor Bursary: household income below £25K, £1,500 a year; household income £25K–£40K, £750 a year.
- » Merit Scholarships (up to £3,000) and other awards, based on performance in special entrance exam in January 2016.
- » Welsh-medium study bursaries, sports and academic awards.
- » Check the university's website for the latest information.

Students

Undergraduates:	**7,125**	**(905)**
Postgraduates:	**1,580**	**(1,035)**
Mature students:	**21.6%**	
International students:	**12.6%**	
Applications per place:	**4.9**	
From state-sector schools:	**95.5%**	
From working-class homes:	**32.7%**	
Satisfaction with students' union	**73%**	

For detailed information about sports facilities: www.bangor.ac.uk/brailsford

Accommodation

Number of places and costs refer to 2015–16
University-provided places: around 2,900
Percentage catered: 0%
Self-catered costs: £80–106 (standard); £108–£140 (en-suite, large en suite, premium en suite, premium plus en suite and deluxe en suite) a week (40–42 weeks UG contract). Also studios from £144–£175 a week.
All first-year students are guaranteed places.
International undergraduates: as above.
halls@bangor.ac.uk; www.bangor.ac.uk/accommodation

University of Bath

Bath is taking advantage of record applications and the relaxation of recruitment controls to increase the number of places it offers. An additional 300 undergraduates started courses in 2014, following 12 per cent growth in applications, and the demand for places has been even stronger in 2015. With nearly eight applicants for every place, Bath remains among the most selective universities in the country. But those who win places generally do not regret it: Bath could not quite repeat last year's success in the National Student Survey, but it achieved the best score in the *Times Higher Education* student experience survey of 2015. Despite slipping two places in *The Times and Sunday Times* league table, it is still in the top 12.

Although it celebrates its 50th anniversary as a university in 2016, Bath remains relatively small; a third of its 15,000 students are postgraduates. The modern campus on the edge of Bath cannot live up to the magnificence of the city's architecture, but the 200-acre site has pleasant grounds, with academic, recreational and residential facilities in close proximity. The university is rated among the top 15 in the world in the GreenMetric environmental ranking.

The sports facilities are outstanding and were used as a training base in sports as diverse as athletics, judo, swimming and beach volleyball in the run up to London 2012 and the 2014 Commonwealth Games. The university's Sports Training Village was chosen to host the Paralympics GB team ahead of the London Olympics and will do so again before Rio 2016. There is a new 50-metre swimming pool, indoor running track, multipurpose sports hall, eight indoor tennis courts and indoor facilities for athletics, shooting, fencing and judo. There is even a newly revamped skeleton start area, as used by Lizzy Yarnold, the 2014 Olympic gold medallist, and her predecessor Amy Williams. Eleven alumni and athletes who train at the university won medals in London. Over 1,500 students compete regularly at every level from regional leagues to national tournaments. Bath pioneered sports scholarships more than 20 years ago and there will be a range of them available for 2016.

By the start of the academic year in 2016, a four-year, £150-million capital programme will be nearing completion. Additional teaching accommodation for 2,000 students opened in 2013 and is connected to the main campus parade by a "skywalk" bridge. A £43-million student accommodation complex has added 708 en-suite bedrooms in 75 flats, along with a 350-seater restaurant. The Edge, which opened in 2015, has a theatre, performance studio, rehearsal studios, three galleries and a café for use

Claverton Down
Bath BA2 7AY

01225 383019 (admissions)
ask-admissions@bath.ac.uk
www.bath.ac.uk
www.bathstudent.com
Affiliation: none

The Times and Sunday Times **Rankings**

Overall Ranking: **12** (last year: 10)

Teaching quality:	**=31**	82.7%
Student experience:	**=18**	87%
Research quality:	**24**	37.3%
Entry standards:	**11**	479
Student–staff ratio:	**=53**	16.2
Services & facilities/student:	**41**	£2,023
Expected completion rate:	**8**	96.1%
Good honours:	**=9**	84.1%
Graduate prospects:	**7**	85.2%

by staff and the wider community. It is also home to the School of Management's executive education training suite. Two more academic buildings are due to open in 2016, one for engineering and design and the other for psychology. The Claverton campus also features a modern student centre and a dedicated centre for postgraduates.

Research is thriving: nearly a third of Bath's submission to the 2014 Research Excellence Framework was judged to be world-leading, with 87 per cent in the top two categories. The research grants and contracts portfolio is worth £120 million and there are 25 international multidisciplinary strategic partnerships with top-ranked institutions worldwide. Bath is a highly internationalised university, with over 25 per cent of its students coming from outside the UK, representing over 100 nationalities.

Most degree courses have a practical element, and assessors have praised the university for the work placements it offers. Most undergraduates take courses with placements, in the UK or abroad, or a period of overseas study, which helps to produce consistently outstanding graduate employment figures. Student entrepreneurship is actively encouraged through a number of initiatives and projects. Recent additions to the portfolio of courses include integrated undergraduate master's degrees in sport and exercise science and also in psychology, which can be taken over four years, or five with a placement. New programmes in astrophysics, aerospace, physical health and international development are being added in 2015.

A quarter of the undergraduates come from independent schools. Many take advantage of the nightlife of nearby Bristol, which is only a few minutes away by public transport. The popular students' union has a Gold Best Bar None award for the management of its bar and nightclub, and has also been commended for its provision for international students. The university's support services include a new virtual learning environment and centralised provision of advisory services.

Undergraduate Fees and Bursaries

- » Fees for UK/EU students 2016–17 £9,000
  Franchised Foundation degree £7,500
- » Fees for international students 2015–16 £14,300–£18,100
- » Household income £20K or below and other criteria, £3,000 cash each year (including unpaid placement or overseas study year).
- » Range of scholarships and bursaries available.
- » Check the university's website for the latest information.

Students

Undergraduates:	**10,550**	**(255)**
Postgraduates:	**2,150**	**(2,195)**
Mature students:	**2.9%**	
International students:	**21.5%**	
Applications per place:	**7.9**	
From state-sector schools:	**75.8%**	
From working-class homes:	**17.3%**	
Satisfaction with students' union	**83%**	

For detailed information about sports facilities:
www.bathstudent.com/sport

Accommodation

Number of places and costs refer to 2015–16
University-provided places: 4,086
Percentage catered: 23%
Catered cost: £170–£204 a week.
Self-catered cost: £62 (shared) – £155 (en-suite single) a week.
First years guaranteed accommodation if conditions are met, and applications received by 1 July.
International students: as above. Exchange students are housed on a reciprocal basis.
www.bath.ac.uk/accommodation/

Bath Spa University

Bath Spa has forged a series of international partnerships to ensure that its students leave as "global citizens" with insights into the world beyond education. The university focuses on creativity, culture and enterprise, and has helped to found the Global Academy of Liberal Arts (GALA). All students have the opportunity to collect a Global Citizenship award by completing a module that covers a range of cross-cutting issues with relevance to all subjects in the arts, humanities and sciences. The university has also established Bath Spa Global, which helps international students to integrate within the UK education system before they progress to the second year of full degree programmes. They receive language tuition, academic instruction and information on UK history and culture, as well as the opportunity to become involved in local community projects. International students now comprise 15 per cent of Bath Spa's intake.

The university is far from new, although it was awarded the title only in 2005. The history of its predecessor colleges goes back 160 years, and it boasts some famous alumni, including Body Shop founder Anita Roddick and Turner Prize winner Sir Howard Hodgkin. The university's Newton Park headquarters, four miles outside the World Heritage city of Bath, is in grounds landscaped by Capability Brown in the 18th century, with a handsome Georgian manor house owned by the Duchy of Cornwall as its centrepiece. Newton Park is the base for all students except those taking art and design subjects, and provides a study environment where historic buildings blend sympathetically with modern facilities. A £70-million development completed in 2014 provides impressive new study facilities for students, particularly in the field of digital arts. By contrast, the Creative Writing Centre is housed in the 14th-century gatehouse, a scheduled ancient monument.

The university has been expanding gradually as the volume of applications has continued to grow. To accommodate the extra students, a student village of 550 study bedrooms has opened on campus and additional housing for 460 students is being built in the city centre, where the Sion Hill campus is home to the Bath School of Art and Design. A £6-million redevelopment there has produced specialist facilities that are some of the best in the country. There is also a postgraduate centre at Corsham Court, a 16th-century manor house near Chippenham. About a third of Bath Spa's students are postgraduates, including a large cohort training to be teachers who form part of a new Institute for Education at the university.

The latest innovation is the School of

Newton Park
Newton St Loe
Bath BA2 9BN

01225 875875 (enquiries)
enquiries@bathspa.ac.uk
www.bathspa.ac.uk
www.bathspasu.co.uk
Affiliation: million+

***The Times and Sunday Times* Rankings**

Overall Ranking: **58** (last year: 70)

Teaching quality:	=6	85.8%
Student experience:	=31	85.8%
Research quality:	=73	7.9%
Entry standards:	=75	318
Student–staff ratio:	=93	19
Services & facilities/student:	89	£1,517
Expected completion rate:	=43	89.9%
Good honours:	45	74.5%
Graduate prospects:	=120	55.1%

Business and Entrepreneurship, which is offering one of the few degree programmes in Europe to combine design thinking with global business, entrepreneurship and creativity. Other striking developments have included four-year Integrated Masters courses in a number of creative subjects – a relatively unusual model in the arts and humanities, but one that offers advantages to students in terms of funding and progression opportunities. Bath Spa is also building a reputation for expertise in the field of creative computing, with several new courses, ranging from software development to gaming.

Results in the National Student Survey have been good, especially for teaching quality. Students like the "small and friendly" atmosphere. Bath Spa also enjoyed its best-ever research assessments in 2014, when more than half of a relatively small submission was rated as world-leading or internationally excellent. The university will receive an 86 per cent increase in research funding as a result. It had strengthened its research capacity in key areas such as creative writing and art and design through the appointment of high profile professors including Fay Weldon and Gavin Turk.

Despite a setting that would seem to be a magnet for applicants from independent schools, just over 93 per cent of the home intake is state educated, and more than a third are from working-class homes. Two-thirds of the students are female, reflecting the arts and social science bias in the curriculum, and a quarter of all students are over 25. The latest projected dropout rate of less than 7 per cent is much better than the national benchmark for the university's courses and entry grades. The university is also proud of its environmental record and has been successful in the People and Planet Green League. Sports facilities are not extensive, but a new gym in the students' union has improved them, and some of the university's sports teams do well in local competitions.

Undergraduate Fees and Bursaries

» Fees for UK/EU students 2016–17	£9,000
Franchised Foundation and first degrees	£7,500–£9,000
» Fees for international students 2015–16	£11,300

» Household income below £25K, some bursaries with priority criteria: £1,000 cash in years 1 and 2, £1,500 in year 3.

» Check the university's website for the latest information.

Students

Undergraduates:	**5,100**	**(120)**
Postgraduates:	**895**	**(1,095)**
Mature students:	**15.2%**	
International students:	**4.6%**	
Applications per place:	**6.9**	
From state-sector schools:	**93.1%**	
From working-class homes:	**34.6%**	
Satisfaction with students' union	**68%**	

For detailed information about sports facilities: www.bathspasu.co.uk/opps/clubsandsocs/clubs

Accommodation

Number of places and costs refer to 2015–16

University provided places: 1,525 in halls; 13 in Independent Housing

Percentage catered: 0%

Self catered: £99.00 – £170.00 a week (39 – 51 weeks).

First years are housed provided requirements are met. Residential restrictions apply.

International students (first year of study): students with a disability or medical condition have priority.

http://thehub.bathspa.ac.uk/services/housing

University of Bedfordshire

Bedfordshire more than doubled the number of academics it entered for the latest official research assessments, and was rewarded with one of the biggest increases in funding for research at any university. With scores in the National Student Survey also improving in recent years, the university has started to climb back towards the positions it occupied in our league table earlier in the decade. Almost half of the work submitted for the 2014 Research Excellence Framework was placed in the top two categories, with social work and social policy, health subjects and English producing particularly good results. The university received the Queen's Anniversary Prize in 2013 for applied research on child exploitation, which influenced new safeguarding policy and practice.

Applications steadied in 2014 after two years of decline, although the university has met its recruitment targets every year since £9,000 fees were introduced. Bedfordshire has been praised for its successes in widening participation, not only in enrolling students from groups that are under-represented in higher education, but also in helping them to achieve good results. Almost all the undergraduates are state educated and more than half come from the four lowest socio-economic classes. Around a third of undergraduates are 21 or over on entry and nearly one in five students comes from outside the EU, many taking postgraduate courses.

Bedfordshire has spent £180 million on its six campuses since the university changed its identity in 2006, when the former Luton University took over De Montfort's campus in Bedford. Another £120 million has been committed for a range of projects over the next few years. The latest major development was the opening of an attractive new campus in Milton Keynes, the fastest-growing city in the UK, in 2013. University Campus Milton Keynes, which is a partnership with the local authority, opened with 100 students and will expand to around 550 by 2018.

However, the bulk of Bedfordshire's students will still be on the university's town-centre site in Luton, where a new £46-million library is due to open early in 2016. A new campus centre opened there in 2010, with teaching and exhibition space as well as the students' union, information desks and a careers and employment centre. A £40-million student halls complex with en-suite facilities, phone and high-speed internet access, a Postgraduate and Continuing Professional Development Centre and a well-equipped media arts centre have followed.

The Bedford campus, in a leafy setting 20 minutes' walk from the town centre, has

University Square
Luton
Bedfordshire LU1 3JU

01234 400400
admissions@beds.ac.uk
www.beds.ac.uk
www.bedssu.co.uk
Affiliation: million+

***The Times and Sunday Times* Rankings**

Overall Ranking: **110** (last year: 108)

Teaching quality:	**=73**	80.4%
Student experience:	**=82**	82.7%
Research quality:	**=77**	7%
Entry standards:	**127**	229
Student–staff ratio:	**=86**	18.3
Services & facilities/student:	**64**	£1,721
Expected completion rate:	**111**	80.1%
Good honours:	**120**	56.6%
Graduate prospects:	**112**	58.3%

a new campus centre comprising a 280-seat auditorium and a students' union, as well as an accommodation block for 600 students. The Gateway, a new £25-million teaching and learning building, opened in January 2015. The campus is home to the Education and Sport Faculty, with around 2,500 students, making it the UK's largest provider of physical education teacher training, as well as a national centre for other subjects at primary and secondary level. Another 1,000 students take subjects such as performing arts, law and business management.

The Putteridge Bury campus, a neo-Elizabethan mansion on the outskirts of Luton, doubles as a management centre and conference venue, as well as an academic teaching space. It is also home to the Business School's postgraduate programme. Nursing and midwifery students in the growing Faculty of Health and Social Sciences are based at the Butterfield Park campus near Luton, or at the Oxford House development in Aylesbury, Buckinghamshire. Placements are available at a wide range of hospitals, including Stoke Mandeville, Wycombe General, Luton and Dunstable, and Bedford.

Vocational courses include a portfolio of two-year Foundation degrees, which range from software development to media production and sport science. Most are taught at partner colleges across the region. The university pioneered electronic assessment, with more than 10,000 students in disciplines from accountancy to biology tested by computer. Bedfordshire was also awarded a national centre of excellence in personal development planning and employability, aiming to link student learning with life after university.

The dropout rate has improved considerably and the latest projection of 12.5 per cent is better than the national average for Bedfordshire's courses and entry qualifications.

Both Luton and Bedford have their share of pubs, clubs and restaurants, and London is 30–40 minutes away by train. Bedfordshire was named among the top 15 universities for its environmental record in the People and Planet League. It was the first university in England to promise not to invest in the fossil fuel industry, following a national student campaign, and is Fairtrade accredited.

Undergraduate Fees and Bursaries

» Fees for UK/EU students 2016–17	£9,000
Foundation degree	£6,000
» Fees for international students 2015–16	£9,750

» Welcome package of, on average, £350 for university services in year 1; £50 in years 2 and 3.
» Progression fund for students from partner colleges.
» Range of other scholarships and bursaries available.
» Check the university's website for the latest information.

Students

Undergraduates:	**10,740**	**(2,160)**
Postgraduates:	**3,255**	**(1,685)**
Mature students:	**34.2%**	
International students:	**13.7%**	
Applications per place:	**7.3**	
From state-sector schools:	**99.1%**	
From working-class homes:	**50.8%**	
Satisfaction with students' union	**70%**	

For detailed information about sports facilities:
www.beds.ac.uk/sportbeds

Accommodation

Number of places and costs refer to 2015–16
University-provided places: about 2,530
Percentage catered: 0%
Self-catered costs: £97–£172 a week.
First years cannot be guaranteed a place, but help is available to find alternative housing in the private sector.
International students: as above.
www.beds.ac.uk/studentlife/accommodation
Bedford and Luton campuses: info@studentvillagebeds.com

Birkbeck, University of London

Birkbeck has transformed itself since higher fees triggered a nationwide collapse in part-time enrolments. Once known exclusively for part-time education, the college is now offering all its undergraduate degrees on a full-time basis, but taught in the evening. The new format has been an instant hit with students of all ages, not least because they qualify for student loans and maintenance grants. Applications have trebled since the first courses were introduced in 2011, and last year the demand for places grew by another 60 per cent as the number of "three-year, full-time, evening-taught" courses increased again. Like the part-timers who still have a portfolio of courses to choose from, the new students appreciate the opportunity to combine daytime work with evening study and believe it will give them a head start in their chosen career when they graduate.

Birkbeck does not appear in our main league table – although it features in several subject tables – because it cannot be compared fairly with other universities on some of the measures. Its academic reputation is not in doubt, however, and it is ranked among the top 250 universities in the world by *Times Higher Education* magazine. More than 80 per cent of its eligible academics were entered for the 2014 Research Excellence Framework and their results placed the college in the top 30 of all UK institutions. Almost three-quarters of the work submitted was rated world-leading or internationally excellent, with psychology and environmental science in the top six nationally. Birkbeck is part of the University of London and has its own degree-awarding powers if it chose to exercise that right. For the foreseeable future, it will continue to award University of London degrees, which are valued by employers around the world.

Founded in 1823, Birkbeck now has over 18,000 students, most of them based near the University of London's headquarters in Bloomsbury. However, the college expanded beyond central London for the first time in 2013. Since 2005 it had offered courses in Stratford, East London, but it now shares a new five-storey building there with the University of East London. University Square Stratford is the first shared project of its kind in the capital, and Birkbeck's contribution is courses in law, business and a BSc in community development and public policy. Facilities include a 300-seat lecture theatre, learning centre, student support centre and seminar rooms for 3,400 students.

Between the two sites there will be more than 70 three-year degrees available in 2016, in addition to the four-year part-time programmes that have been Birkbeck's

Malet Street
Bloomsbury
London WC1E 7HX

020 7631 6000 (general enquiries)
info@bbk.ac.uk
www.bbk.ac.uk
www.birkbeckunion.org
Affiliation: none

***The Times and Sunday Times* Rankings**

The available data do not match the data used to rank the other full-time universities, so Birkbeck could not be included in the league table this year.

traditional fare. New three-year full-time evening-taught degree programmes available from 2015 include a BSc economics, BA global cinemas and screen arts, and a BA history of art either with film or with curating. Fees vary according to course, but most of the three-year degrees cost £9,000 a year. Generous financial support is available for students with low household incomes.

Courses are tailored to the employment market. For example, a BSc in applied accounting and business is run in collaboration with the Institute of Chartered Accountants in England and Wales, allowing trainee accountants to combine work and study to gain their qualifications at a substantially lower cost and much sooner than if they took a degree before completing their professional qualification. Birkbeck graduates enjoy high average starting salaries – among the best in the sector – partly because many of them are mature students returning to already successful careers. There is a professional in-house recruitment service linking employers with Birkbeck students and graduates.

Birkbeck welcomes applications from people without traditional qualifications and continues to attract non-traditional learners of all ages and backgrounds: four out of ten students are from low socio-economic groups. Students apply for Birkbeck's three-year courses through UCAS, but the college takes direct applications for its four-year programmes. Applicants who have taken A level or an equivalent qualification recently are made offers based on the UCAS tariff, but others are assessed by the college on the basis of interviews and/or short tests. The My Birkbeck Student Centre acts as a front door to all the college's student support services, from help in choosing courses and submitting applications to information about financial support and study skills.

Almost £20 million has been spent improving the college's buildings. Bloomsbury is easily accessible by public transport and cycle routes. Most Birkbeck students live in the capital, but full-time students looking for housing can apply to the University of London Housing Service.

Undergraduate Fees and Bursaries

- » Fees for full-time UK/EU students 2016–17 £9,000
- » Fees for international students 2015–16 £13,000
- » Full-time students with household income below £25K, £800 a year as fee waiver or cash bursary; £600 a year for 4-year part-time students; £400 a year for 6-year part-time students.
- » Part-time students with household income of £25K–£40K, bursary of £600 a year pro-rata, depending on intensity of study.
- » 10% discount on tuition fees for trade union members.
- » Check the university's website for the latest information.

Students

Undergraduates:	**1,660**	**(9,145)**
Postgraduates:	**1,090**	**(3,650)**
Mature students:	**65.7%**	
International students:	**12.3%**	
Applications per place:	**5.8**	
From state-sector schools:	**86%**	
From working-class homes:	**39.7%**	
Satisfaction with students' union	**58%**	

For detailed information about sports facilities: www.student-central.london/activities

Accommodation

Number of places and costs refer to 2015–16

The university has 50 places in the intercollegiate halls of residence, and these are normally reserved for full-time international students. The university also has an agreement with UNITE for self-catered places within their halls of residence.

Catered costs: £132.30 (twin) – £232.40 (en-suite single).

Self-catered: £279 (2-bed flat) – £599 (1-bed flat).

Contact: www.bbk.ac.uk/mybirkbeck/services/facilities/accommodation

University of Birmingham

Birmingham started the trend for unconditional offers, which has gathered pace this year, and appears to have profited handsomely from the move. The number of applications rose by almost 6,000, or 15 per cent, in 2014 and the university took 400 students more than in the previous year. Unconditional offers went to students in 33 subjects who were predicted better than three As at A level – and a third of the recipients took them up. The scheme has since been extended to 54 subjects, from African studies and anthropology, mathematics, modern languages to social work and chemistry, and may be expanded further in 2016. The initiative was a response to the lifting of Government recruitment controls and was one of the factors that brought Birmingham the title of *The Times and Sunday Times* University of the Year for 2013–14.

The university also achieved good results in the 2014 Research Excellence Framework, when over 80 per cent of its submission was rated as world-leading or internationally excellent. Its performance took Birmingham into the top 20 for research quality and has helped to maintain its position in our top 20 overall. The university was ranked in the top five for philosophy, history, classics, theology and religion, area studies, chemical engineering, and sport, exercise and rehabilitation studies. Birmingham has become the first link in a chain of Cancer Research UK Centres, while a £60-million fundraising campaign launched in 2009 is starting to support projects ranging from research into brain injury, ageing and clean energy to scholarships and a centre for heritage and cultural learning. Birmingham also has a partnership with the University of Nottingham on a series of research projects and other activities.

Birmingham was the original "redbrick" university. The 230-acre campus in leafy Edgbaston is dominated by a 300-foot clock tower, one of the city's best-known landmarks, and boasts its own train station. Dentistry is located in the city centre, while part of the School of Education is in Selly Oak, a mile from the Edgbaston campus. Drama is also located there, along with the BBC Drama Village, which is part of a strategic alliance between the university and the corporation. The university is part way through a long-term programme of investment. A new Student Services Hub has seen part of the redbrick Aston Webb Building remodelled to house a number of different services including employability, careers and a 400-seat lecture theatre. Work has started on a new library, due to open in the summer of 2016, and a cultural hub that will embrace new and emerging

Edgbaston
Birmingham B15 2TT

0121 414 3344
admissions@bham.ac.uk
www.birmingham.ac.uk
www.guildofstudents.com
Affiliation: Russell Group

***The Times and Sunday Times* Rankings**

Overall Ranking: **17** (last year: 15)

Teaching quality:	**=64**	80.8%
Student experience:	**=56**	84.2%
Research quality:	**26**	37.1%
Entry standards:	**=23**	426
Student–staff ratio:	**=46**	15.5
Services & facilities/student:	**18**	£2,461
Expected completion rate:	**=12**	94.8%
Good honours:	**8**	84.4%
Graduate prospects:	**5**	86.7%

technologies for an enhanced student experience. A new sports centre, opening early in 2016, will boast Birmingham's first 50-metre swimming pool, a multi-sport hall, a range of activity and fitness studios, an extensive gym, six glass-backed squash courts and various other facilities.

The university's 32,000 students include over 7,000 from outside the UK. The Access to Birmingham (A2B) scheme, which encourages students from the West Midlands whose families have little or no experience of higher education to apply to university, is being extended to students in other parts of England. In 2016, students whose household income is less than £36,000 will qualify for the university's Chamberlain awards of between £1,000 and £2,000 a year. Three-quarters of the undergraduates undertake work experience as part of their course. There has been £3.5-million investment in an employability initiative which will include internships and mentoring by some of the university's most successful alumni. The university also encourages interdisciplinary study, for example allowing undergraduates to combine technology with subjects ranging from Latin or modern Greek to the management of floods and other natural disasters.

Most of the halls and university flats are conveniently located in an attractive parkland setting near the main campus. There are more than 5,000 university-owned beds, and accommodation in the private sector is also plentiful. The campus is less than three miles from the city centre, but the area has plenty of shops, pubs and restaurants. With its own nightclub among the facilities on campus, some students do not even stray that far, but the city is acquiring a growing reputation among the young. The sports facilities are some of the best in the country and other student facilities on campus are also first-rate. They include a medical practice and the university's own station. There is also an outdoor pursuits centre by Coniston Water in the Lake District. The Active Lifestyles Programme attracts 4,000 students to 150 different courses.

Undergraduate Fees and Bursaries

- Fees for UK/EU students 2016–17 £9,000
- Fees for international students 2015–16 £13,195–£17,145
  Medicine £17,145–£31,000
- Household income up to £36K, Chamberlain Awards of £1,000–£2,000 a year, with priority to care leavers and those with lowest household income.
- Scholarships of £1,200 a year through Access to Birmingham scheme.
- Range of other scholarships and bursaries available.
- Check the university's website for the latest information.

Students

Undergraduates:	**18,140**	**(1,045)**
Postgraduates:	**7,845**	**(5,310)**
Mature students:	**7.4%**	
International students:	**11.9%**	
Applications per place:	**7.7**	
From state-sector schools:	**80.7%**	
From working-class homes:	**23.5%**	
Satisfaction with students' union	**72%**	

For detailed information about sports facilities:
www.sport.bham.ac.uk

Accommodation

Number of places and costs refer to 2015–16
University-provided places: 5,005
Percentage catered: 30%
Catered costs: £121–£186 a week.
Self-catered costs: £85–£147 a week.
All first years are guaranteed housing (subject to conditions).
International students: as above.
www.birmingham.ac.uk/undergraduate/accommodation

Birmingham City University

Birmingham City has been showcasing the achievements of graduates who have made their mark in leading companies such as Disney, Aston Martin and Harrods to show potential students how the university's degrees can help them "shape the world". Applicants have been coming forward in record numbers, some attracted by the prospect of unconditional offers for those who achieve BBC at AS level or a DMM profile in BTEC qualifications and make the university their first choice. By 2014, the university was in the top 20 for applications after successive significant increases.

One important selling point has been the City Centre Campus development, the first phase of which opened in 2013 at Millennium Point. The £125-million development will become the university's main base, helping to create a Learning Quarter in Eastside. The first phase houses design-related courses and the whole of Birmingham School of Media. The second phase, the Curzon Building, welcomes its first students in September and will house business, law, social science and English courses, as well as a new library, IT and student support facilities. A third phase of development, set to open in 2017, will create additional teaching space and house Birmingham Conservatoire, one of the university's best-known features.

The university has been remodelling its estate for some time, and now has four sites in and around the city centre, plus one in the north and another in the south of Birmingham. City North, at Perry Barr, until recently the main base, will close in 2017. Computing and engineering, as well as the Birmingham School of Acting, have already transferred to the city centre. Europe's largest school of jewellery is nearby in the famous Jewellery Quarter. The City South campus, in Edgbaston, has been refurbished for the Faculty of Health, with a prize-winning library, IT suites, teaching facilities and recreational space. Meanwhile, the Bournville campus hosts a new college offering preparatory courses for overseas students to support the university's international ambitions.

Birmingham City has thrived since changing its name from the University of Central England in 2007, with the demand for places growing by almost 50 per cent. There are strong links with business and the professions, including pioneering work in green technology, which is attracting support from national and regional partners. There is a strong emphasis on making graduates "job-ready", with support schemes and work placements among a raft of initiatives designed to help develop skills and knowledge for the workplace. Students have access to learning tools such as Shareville

University House
15 Bartholomew Row
Birmingham B5 5JU

0121 331 5595 (enquiries)
enquiries via website
www.bcu.ac.uk
www.bcusu.com
Affiliation: none

The Times and Sunday Times **Rankings**

Overall Ranking: **105** (last year: =91)

Teaching quality:	**=103**	78%
Student experience:	**=115**	79.3%
Research quality:	**=97**	4.3%
Entry standards:	**100**	300
Student–staff ratio:	**111**	20.4
Services & facilities/student:	**71**	£1,693
Expected completion rate:	**=81**	84.4%
Good honours:	**76**	67.3%
Graduate prospects:	**79**	64.8%

– a virtual learning environment where students can engage with real-life scenarios.

The Faculty of Business, Law and Social Sciences has launched a number of three-year Professional Practice courses, where the first two years of a degree are studied on campus, while the final year is completed and assessed in the workplace. Several degrees in the Faculty of Computing, Engineering and the Built Environment are now available as four-year integrated Master's awards, offering seamless progression from a Bachelor's to a Master's degree. The university has launched a range of scholarships and bursaries to encourage undergraduates to stay on for postgraduate study.

The prize-winning Student Academic Partners scheme has spawned a formal agreement between the university and the students' union to improve the student experience. Internal student surveys have led to the introduction of internet tutorials in engineering and new help with research for law and social science undergraduates. Six out of ten students come from the West Midlands, many from ethnic minorities and 45 per cent from the poorest socio-economic groups. The completion rate has been improving and is now better than the national average for the university's courses and entry grades. Birmingham City is working with schools in the region to encourage more young people to go on to higher education. Many students enter through the network of associated further education colleges, which run foundation and access programmes.

The university made a relatively small submission to the 2014 national research assessments, but 60 per cent of the work reached the top two categories and almost 90 per cent was judged to have delivered "outstanding" or "very considerable" external impact. Most research is applied, with an accent on employment in the region.

University accommodation is guaranteed for first years whose homes are outside Birmingham; another 650 rooms for students on the City Centre Campus are planned for 2016–17. The city's student scene is highly rated and has become a draw for many young applicants.

Undergraduate Fees and Bursaries

» Fees for UK/EU students 2016–17	£9,000
Placement year	no fee
Foundation degree	£6,000
» Fees for international students 2015–16	£11,500–£12,600
	£14,900 (Conservatoire and acting)

» 15% of additional fee income to be spent on additional access and student success measures.

» Check the university's website for the latest information.

Students

Undergraduates:	**15,650**	**(3,120)**
Postgraduates:	**1,855**	**(1,915)**
Mature students:	**27.3%**	
International students:	**7.6%**	
Applications per place:	**6.9**	
From state-sector schools:	**97.6%**	
From working-class homes:	**45.2%**	
Satisfaction with students' union	**66%**	

For detailed information about sports facilities:
www.bcusu.com/sports

Accommodation

Number of places and costs refer to 2015–16
University-provided places: 2,485
Percentage catered: 0%
Self-catered costs: £96.50 (standard) – £128.50 (extra large) a week (39, 40, 41, 42, 43, 51 weeks).
Accommodation guaranteed for first years if conditions are met.
International students are guaranteed accommodation.
www.bcu.ac.uk/student-info/accommodation

University College Birmingham (UCB)

University College Birmingham (UCB) is unique among UK universities in having a third of its students taking further education programmes. It believes that would place it at a disadvantage in league tables such as ours, so it has again instructed the Higher Education Statistics Agency not to release its data. Consequently, UCB does not appear in our main league table or any of the subject tables. Nevertheless, it has done well in the National Student Survey and claims to have fewer complaints from students than any university in the Midlands. There was a 15 per cent increase in applications in 2014 and further growth of 20 per cent this year.

UCB chose not to change its name when full university status arrived in 2013, in order to preserve its identity. It was the largest of a dozen colleges to become universities, with more than 5,000 higher education students and nearly 2,500 taking further education courses. The new university traces its history back more than 100 years to the foundation of a Municipal Technical School offering cookery and household science courses. Several different titles followed until it became a university college in 2007 and received degree awarding powers, although some degrees are still accredited by the University of Birmingham. The core subjects are hospitality, tourism, business, sport and education. The most recent Ofsted inspection rated the further education provision as outstanding, while 100 per cent of students in the most recent exit survey rated their postgraduate teacher training as good or better. UCB has an international reputation in hospitality and tourism, with about a third of the students coming from outside the UK.

Based in the city centre, UCB is located close to the International Convention Centre, Symphony Hall and the Library of Birmingham, as well as the main shopping areas. The main campus is at Summer Row, with New Street train station a five-minute walk away. UCB is investing £50 million on new teaching facilities in Birmingham's historic Jewellery Quarter – just a short walk from the main campus. The four-storey first phase of the development, which has been funded from within the university's reserves, opened in 2014. It features dedicated facilities for undergraduate and postgraduate study, a flexible learning centre, three lecture theatres, teaching rooms, IT facilities and a café. Phase Two will see the development of a new campus, which may allow new subjects to be added. Existing specialist teaching facilities include high-quality training kitchens, commercial training restaurants, a full bakery and a new

Summer Row
Birmingham B3 1JB

0121 604 1040 (admissions)
admissions@ucb.ac.uk
www.ucb.ac.uk
www.ucbsu.com
Affiliation: GuildHE

***The Times and Sunday Times* Rankings**

University College Birmingham blocked the release of data from the Higher Education Statistics Agency and so we cannot give any ranking information.

£2-million Food Science and Innovation Suite.

The university focuses on giving students an advantage in the highly competitive graduate job market. Many courses include full- or half-year industrial placements, including overseas opportunities in the USA, Hong Kong, Canada and Europe. As well as arranging placements, the expanded careers and employability team, hired@UCB, provides students with support to develop skills, such as communication, teamwork, problem solving and time management, through work experience, workshops, volunteering, part-time and seasonal work. There are strong relationships with employers, including a job-shop service which is accessible 24 hours a day and Unitemps, which provides employment opportunities to students during their studies.

UCB has one of the most socially diverse student bodies in the country – more than half are from a black or minority ethnic background. Student ambassadors promote further and higher education to young people from a range of backgrounds. Almost all the undergraduates are state educated and 54 per cent come from the four poorest socio-economic groups. There are fee waivers for students from low-income families. Retention rates have been improving and are good for some groups, but the projected dropout rate for all undergraduates remains significantly worse than the national average for UCB's courses and entry qualifications, at nearly 18 per cent.

More than 1,000 students can be accommodated in UCB's halls of residence, and accommodation can be offered to all years and programmes of study. The Maltings halls are ten minutes' walk from UCB and Cambrian Hall is only 150 yards from the main campus. Both offer among the best value in the Midlands. The Spa, at Richmond House on Newhall Street, offers hairdressing salons, beauty therapy suites, a sports therapy clinic, a multi-gym, and a fitness assessment suite. There is also a gym and sports hall at The Maltings site, which are open on weekday evenings and at weekends. Two restaurants staffed by the university's students are open to the public, as well as to students and staff.

Undergraduate Fees and Bursaries

» Fees for UK/EU students 2016–17	£8,830
Placement term or year	no fee
» Fees for international students 2015–16	£9,300

» English students with household income below £16,190, £1,090 fee waiver each year.
» In addition, £1,090 fee waiver each year for students previously on a full-time FE programme at UCB in 2014/15.
» For students from selected colleges a £1,090 fee waiver for year 1.
» Check the university's website for the latest information.

Students

Undergraduates:	**3,530**	**(980)**
Postgraduates:	**375**	**(110)**
From state-sector schools:	**98.2%**	
From working-class homes:	**54.2%**	
Satisfaction with students' union	**68%**	

For detailed information about sports facilities:
www.ucb.ac.uk/facilities/gym-and-sports.aspx

Accommodation

Places and costs refer to 2015–16
University-provided places: 1,074
Percentage catered: 0%
Self-catered costs: £81 (shared); £90 (standard); £100 (en suite); £151 (twin) (42 weeks).
Priority is given to disabled students (new and returning) and new full-time students by application date.
International students: guaranteed housing if conditions are met.
accommodation@ucb.ac.uk;
www.ucb.ac.uk/facilities/accommodation/

Bishop Grosseteste University

Bishop Grosseteste (BGU), currently one of the smallest universities with less than 2,200 students, is planning to almost double in size over the next five years. The expansion will include more mature students taking work-based courses and more from non-traditional backgrounds, as well as increases in the numbers of postgraduates and research students. At the same time, the university is aiming improve already high levels of student retention, satisfaction and graduate employment. BGU already draws nearly 40 per cent of its undergraduates from the four lowest socio-economic groups and is in the top 30 for its completion and student satisfaction.

Based on an attractive, leafy campus in uphill Lincoln, not far from the cathedral and castle, Bishop Grosseteste celebrated 150 years of teacher training in 2012. The former university college used to be too small to become a university, but a change of rules allowed it to take the title in 2013. Named after a theologian and scholar who was bishop of Lincoln in the 13th century, BGU is still proudly associated with the Church of England, although it welcomes students of all faiths and none. It describes itself as a Church university within the Anglican tradition.

The campus is already gearing up for a larger intake. The former college canteen and dining room is being turned into teaching accommodation that will be ready for use in September 2015. Close to the campus, another 37 en-suite bedrooms will also become available then as part of the university's ongoing programme of expansion of student accommodation. A new complex of flats has replaced an older hall of residence, and together with the extensive refurbishment of an existing hall, has brought the number of campus rooms to more than 200. The university also took on a purpose-built accommodation with 76 additional rooms near the campus in 2013.

The university entrance and reception area has been remodelled at a cost of £250,000. Other recent developments have seen the campus theatre equipped with a new digital projection system, surround sound and fully refurbished seating to double as a cinema which can also stage theatrical productions. The Venue is now home to the Lincoln Film Society and is open to staff, students and the public. The library has been extended and given a new name: the Cornerstone Building. It houses the Student Support and Learning Advice teams, as well as Library Services. The students' union building has had a major refit and new restaurant, teaching and learning spaces have been added.

Lincoln LN1 3DY

01522 583658 (admissions)
admissions@bishopg.ac.uk
www.bishopg.ac.uk
www.bgsu.co.uk
Affiliations: GuildHE, Cathedrals Group

***The Times and Sunday Times* Rankings**

Overall Ranking: **=112** (last year: =102)

Teaching quality:	**=62**	80.9%
Student experience:	**=108**	80.6%
Research quality:	**118**	2.1%
Entry standards:	**=112**	284
Student–staff ratio:	**126**	28.6
Services & facilities/student:	**125**	£743
Expected completion rate:	**42**	90%
Good honours:	**=109**	60.4%
Graduate prospects:	**=59**	69.1%

The new strategic plan envisages broadening the range of courses BGU offers. Business (team entrepreneurship), health and social care, sociology, psychology and counselling, and history and archaeology were introduced in September 2015. The portfolio covers a range of arts and social sciences, but teacher training still dominates. Ofsted rates the courses for primary teachers as "Excellent" and those for secondary as "Good". The university has been allocated 50 places to train teachers of children aged up to nine years old on programmes leading to the new Early Years Teacher Status introduced to raise the status and quality of the early years workforce. The new courses will mean that, for the first time, Bishop Grosseteste will train teachers of every age group, including adults.

The university is divided into three schools: Teacher Development, Humanities and Social Sciences. A popular new psychology degree, which attracted twice the target enrolment when it was introduced in 2013, has been awarded accreditation by the British Psychological Society. Only 11 staff entered the 2014 Research Excellence Framework, but some work was classed as "world-leading" in education, English and history, the three subjects in which the university was assessed.

A business start-up centre has opened on campus and is proving popular with new businesses and entrepreneurs. BG Futures differs from other incubation centres by emphasising the university's values of equality and diversity. The university has secured European funding to support 50 paid graduate internships for small- and medium-sized businesses based within the city boundaries.

The Sport and Fitness Centre has a sports hall which can cater for a variety of different sporting activities and fitness classes and a well-appointed fitness suite. Ten acres of sports fields are close by. The city of Lincoln is one of the fastest-growing in the UK, with relatively low living costs. It may not compete with the big conurbations for youth culture, but it has a growing student population and a range of bars and nightclubs to serve it.

Undergraduate Fees and Bursaries

- » Fees for UK/EU students 2016–17 £9,000
  Foundation degree £6,750
- » Fees for international students 2015–16 £10,000
- » Household income below £25K, bursary of £550 (honours), £415 (foundation); household income £25K–£30K, £275 (honours) and £208 (foundation); in addition £100 for mature students, £150 for student parents and students from areas of low participation.
- » BGU Learning Fund awards of up to £2,000 a year, awarded by application after registration.
- » Check the university's website for the latest information.

Students

Undergraduates:	**1,710**	**(20)**
Postgraduates:	**365**	**(300)**
Mature students:	**31.9%**	
International students:	**0%**	
Applications per place:	**3**	
From state-sector schools:	**98.7%**	
From working-class homes:	**37.5%**	
Satisfaction with students' union	**66%**	

For detailed information about sports facilities:
www.bishopg.ac.uk/student/sportscentre/

Accommodation

Places and costs refer to 2015–16
Places Provided: 217 on campus; 76 off campus.
Percentage catered: 0%
Self-catered costs: £97.50–£126.00 a week (34 or 44 weeks).
Priority is given to disabled and new full-time students on a first come, first served basis.
International students: limited accommodation is available.
www.bishopg.ac.uk/student/accommodation/

University of Bolton

Bolton has enjoyed the biggest increase in applications of any university in 2015 – a rise of more than 25 per cent – after a three-year period in which the demand for places had declined. The upturn in its fortunes comes as the university prepares to move its student accommodation, law school and head office into the centre of Bolton, while also investing heavily in its main campus. A £40-million student village on council-owned land will house 850 students, replacing two existing halls with smaller capacity. Another collaboration with the council and local NHS produced the Bolton One development, a £31-million health, leisure and research centre on the main campus. It boasts a multi-sports hall, climbing wall and a sports and spinal injuries clinic, as well as a 25-metre competition swimming pool and a therapeutic hydrotherapy pool, fitness suite and community gym. A £10-million facility for science and engineering is due to be completed in 2016, when a new Health Sciences Faculty to teach biomedical sciences and subjects allied to health and dentistry will also open. A University Technical College for 14–19 year-olds will open at the same time, along with new all-weather sports facilities, and a Creative Industries and Technologies Centre to house the industry-leading special effects courses will follow in 2017.

The university traces its roots back 190 years to one of the country's first three mechanics institutes. The student population is one of the most ethnically diverse in the UK, with around a quarter of British students coming from ethnic minority communities. Just over 40 per cent of the undergraduates are over 21 on entry and a similar proportion study part-time – a significant proportion at a time when part-time numbers have plummeted nationally. Bolton exceeds all the access measures designed to widen participation in higher education: over half of the undergraduates are from working-class homes and the proportion from areas without a tradition of higher education is among the highest in the UK, at almost 25 per cent. The downside is that, despite successive big improvements, the projected dropout rate remains significantly higher than the national average for Bolton's courses and entry qualifications, at more than 20 per cent.

Bolton is the first university in the UK, if not the world, to host a professional motor racing team and next year will see the opening of the new national centre for motorsport engineering. The purpose-built Centre for Advanced Performance Engineering (CAPE), which is run in conjunction with a motorsports company, is the base for the race team and runs

Deane Road
Bolton BL3 5AB

01204 903903 (applications)
admissionss@bolton.ac.uk
www.bolton.ac.uk
www.boltonsu.com
Affiliation: million+

***The Times and Sunday Times* Rankings**

Overall Ranking: **=123** (last year: 120)

Teaching quality:	**=52**	81.6%
Student experience:	**=106**	80.8%
Research quality:	**113**	2.9%
Entry standards:	**110**	287
Student–staff ratio:	**=83**	17.9
Services & facilities/student:	**124**	£959
Expected completion rate:	**124**	71.2%
Good honours:	**123**	54.9%
Graduate prospects:	**102**	60.1%

degree courses in automotive performance engineering and motorsport technology. Students work and learn alongside engineers and mechanics from the team, as well as the university's mechanical engineering lecturers. General engineering was one of two areas to see a majority of their work rated as world-leading or internationally excellent in the 2014 Research Excellence Framework. The best results were in English and almost a third of the university's submission reached the top two categories. About 1,100 of its students are postgraduates, taking qualifications up to and including PhDs.

The university has partner colleges in several Asian countries and a branch campus in the United Arab Emirates. The Ras al-Khaimah campus opened in 2008, offering a range of undergraduate and postgraduate courses identical to those taught at Bolton. The £1-million development near Dubai is designed to take 700 students. Those at Bolton have the opportunity to study in the UAE for part of their degree course. Earlier rationalisation of sites has provided additional and enhanced teaching space, facilities to interact with industry and a new students' union. In 2013, the university launched the Bolton Business School, which hosts business, law and accountancy courses, along with the Centre of Islamic Finance.

The building programme at the Deane campus has included a design studio and three floors of teaching and learning space where students work on actual briefs for companies seeking design solutions. Within the Innovation Factory is a new social learning zone which includes students' union offices, advice centre, bar and social facilities, plus a computer access room. Bolton has partnered with the owners of ten dental practices in the North of England to offer a state-of-the-art practice on campus and new clinical simulation facilities in Bolton One, where the university has launched a range of dental courses with their input and support. There are new degrees in advanced dental nursing and dental hygiene and therapy, and a Diploma of Higher Education for clinical dental technicians.

Undergraduate Fees and Bursaries

» Fees for UK/EU students 2016–17	£9,000
Placement year	£500
Courses at partner colleges	£5,996–£9,000
» Fees for international students 2015–16	£11,250

» For those with at least ABB at A level or equivalent, a bursary of £1,000 a year.

» For students playing sport at county level or above, a bursary of £1,000 a year.

» Vice-Chancellor's Award, up to £15,000, for most outstanding and academically gifted students (max. three awards a year).

» Check the university's website for the latest information.

Students

Undergraduates:	**4,040**	**(1,700)**
Postgraduates:	**425**	**(670)**
Mature students:	**43.3%**	
International students:	**6.8%**	
Applications per place:	**5.5**	
From state-sector schools:	**99.3%**	
From working-class homes:	**53.5%**	
Satisfaction with students' union	**68%**	

For detailed information about sports facilities: http://bolton.ac.uk/Sport/

Accommodation

Number of places and costs refer to 2015–16
University-provided places: 700
Percentage catered: 0%
Self-catered costs: £78.50 a week (39 weeks).
All first years are generally accommodated.
International students: accommodation is secured for these students.
accomm@bolton.ac.uk
www.bolton.ac.uk/accommodation

Bournemouth University

Such is Bournemouth's strength in media subjects that 60 animation graduates worked on the Oscar-winning film *Gravity* and many were involved in producing the visual effects for *Interstellar.* The university was designated as England's only centre for excellence in media practice and hosts the National Centre of Computer Animation, a field in which it was awarded a Queen's Anniversary Prize in 2012. State-of-the-art equipment includes a motion capture facility for real-time animation, which is used in teaching and available for use by outside companies. But there have also been successes in other areas: the decision to invest £1 million a year on academic appointments and the fusion of teaching and research paid off in the 2014 Research Excellence Framework, when 60 per cent of the university's entry was judged to be world-leading or internationally excellent. It was one of the biggest proportions at any post-1992 university and a considerable improvement on previous results, with Bournemouth finishing top in the UK for tourism research. The university appointed 150 academics in three years to "foster the development of an academically led culture". Its Fusion fund is designed to promote "the combination of inspirational teaching, world-class research and the latest thinking in the professions".

The university has also been improving its two campuses. A £10-million student centre opened this year on the Talbot Campus, in Poole, where 80 per cent of the university's 17,000 students are taught. A new £22-million academic building will follow in 2016. The Lansdowne Campus is less than two miles away in the town centre and will be the site of the new Bournemouth International College, which opens this September, providing preparatory courses for overseas students. It also houses the Faculty of Health and Social Sciences and serves as the centre of postgraduate study for the Faculty of Management. The university is expanding postgraduate opportunities, promising up to 100 doctoral places each year until 2018, many of them fully funded.

Every undergraduate is promised a work placement, typically 40 weeks in length. An independent survey published in 2013 showed that Bournemouth had the highest proportion of graduates (almost 90 per cent) with some form of work experience on their CV – a feature that invariably translates into good graduate employment prospects. The retail management degree, for example, notched up eight successive years of full employment. Both applications and enrolments have risen in each of the last two years, although relatively modest scores in the National Student Survey have held

Talbot Campus
Fern Barrow
Poole
Dorset BH12 5BB

01202 961916 (enquiries)
askBUenquiries@bournemouth.ac.uk
www.bournemouth.ac.uk
www.subu.org.uk
Affiliation: none

***The Times and Sunday Times* Rankings**

Overall Ranking: **=82** (last year: 88)

Teaching quality:	**=120**	75.2%
Student experience:	**117**	78.8%
Research quality:	**=64**	9%
Entry standards:	**64**	329
Student–staff ratio:	**=71**	17.4
Services & facilities/student:	**55**	£1,831
Expected completion rate:	**=63**	86%
Good honours:	**=39**	75.5%
Graduate prospects:	**69**	66.4%

the university back in our league table.

Virtually all students take up the offer of personal development planning, both online and with trained staff, while 1,400 first years also take advantage of peer-assisted learning, receiving advice and mentoring from more experienced undergraduates. Bournemouth has been increasing its use of education technology, for example to enable its part-time students to study from home or the workplace and reduce the amount of time they need spend on campus. More than 1,500 scholarships worth £1,244 each were awarded in 2013–14 to recognise academic, sporting and musical excellence. In addition, the Global Horizons Fund helps students and staff to travel overseas for study, research or work or life experience.

A total of 33 different professional bodies accredit Bournemouth's degrees. The university claims a number of firsts in its portfolio of courses, notably in the areas of tourism, media-related programmes and conservation. Degrees in public relations, retail management, scriptwriting and tax law were all ahead of their time. Foundation degrees are delivered in five further education colleges in Dorset and Somerset, as well as on the main campus. They support the needs of business in the creative arts, media and tourism. Top-up courses are available for those who wish to turn their qualification into an Honours degree.

An increasingly fashionable seaside location and the subject mix attract more middle-class students than at most new universities, although 94 per cent attended state schools. The campuses are served by a subsidised bus service and students are discouraged from bringing cars. The students' union's Old Fire Station bar is among many nightlife options. Sports facilities have been improving following a refurbishment of the gym, with the addition of a new multipurpose large studio. There is a wide range of accommodation: students based in halls of residence in Poole enjoy a millionaire's view of the harbour. The university finished in the top ten in the 2014 People and Planet Green League of environmental performance and has an EcoCampus Gold Award, as well as holding Fairtrade status.

Undergraduate Fees and Bursaries

» Fees for UK/EU students 2016–17	£9,000
Foundation degree	£6,000
Placement year	£790
» Fees for international students 2015–16	£9,500–£13,000

» Around 700 bursaries of £2,000 in year 1; priority to those from low-income families or low-participation areas.
» Care leaver's bursary of £6,000 year 1, £5,000 years 2 and 3.
» Check the university's website for the latest information.

Students

Undergraduates:	**11,905**	**(3,005)**
Postgraduates:	**1,560**	**(1,265)**
Mature students:	**19.3%**	
International students:	**8.7%**	
Applications per place:	**5.7**	
From state-sector schools:	**94%**	
From working-class homes:	**30.1%**	
Satisfaction with students' union	**74%**	

For detailed information about sports facilities:
http://microsites.bournemouth.ac.uk/sportbu

Accommodation

Number of places and costs refer to 2015–16
University-provided places: about 3,200
Percentage catered: 2%
Catered costs: from £169 a week
Self-catered costs: £92–£135 (single en suite); £136–£160 (single studio) a week including bus pass.
The university expects to offer all first years a place to live.
Residential restrictions apply.
International students: guaranteed if conditions are met.
www1.bournemouth.ac.uk/discover/accommodation

University of Bradford

Bradford was the leading pioneer of the green policies that have swept UK universities, and its £70-million modernisation plan is keeping the university at the forefront of that movement. The new Bright Building, where the re:centre links the university with local business, has been given the highest ever environmental rating at a higher education institution. Built almost entirely from natural and/or recycled products, it has taken over that title from the university's sustainable student village. The Green, with its 1,000 rooms, was the most visible sign of the "ecoversity" programme, which addressed issues of sustainable development in all the university's practices, including the curriculum. The development won a Green Gown award for sustainability and took the Best Student Housing prize in 2013. Having reduced its carbon footprint by 35 per cent and saved in excess of £7 million, Bradford has been named among the top six universities in the world for carbon reduction.

The university has also begun to climb back up in *The Times and Sunday Times* league table after slipping below a number of post-1992 institutions. The volume of applications rose in 2014 after two years of decline, although there was a small dip in enrolments. Bradford had pulled off something of a coup in the previous year with the appointment of Professor Brian Cantor as vice-chancellor. As vice-chancellor of the University of York, Professor Cantor oversaw major expansion, establishing a new campus and taking the university into the Russell Group, but he faces different challenges at Bradford. Perhaps the major advantage at undergraduate level is the vocational slant of the courses and the accent on work experience and placements, which regularly place Bradford well up the employment tables. Other distinctive features include the world-renowned peace studies department and a highly rated School of Management, whose distance learning MBA is ranked in the top ten in the world by the *Financial Times*.

The university's modernisation plan includes a £7-million investment in new and upgraded teaching facilities. There has been a major refurbishment of the library, which attracted another Green Gown award for its insulation and natural ventilation. Other recent developments include a £1.5-million engineering laboratory containing equipment that can be used across the engineering disciplines. The university is also leading a £12-million programme to create a Digital Health Zone for the city to develop new healthcare products and links with practitioners.

More than half of the undergraduates

Richmond Road
Bradford
BD7 1DP

0800 073 1225; 0300 456 2666
course-enquiries@bradford.ac.uk
www.bradford.ac.uk
www.ubuonline.co.uk
Affiliation: none

***The Times and Sunday Times* Rankings**

Overall Ranking: **75** (last year: 76)

Teaching quality:	**=92**	78.8%
Student experience:	**=53**	84.4%
Research quality:	**=62**	9.2%
Entry standards:	**81**	314
Student–staff ratio:	**=78**	17.8
Services & facilities/student:	**63**	£1,731
Expected completion rate:	**85**	83.8%
Good honours:	**48**	74%
Graduate prospects:	**43**	75.2%

are from working-class homes – the biggest proportion at any of the older universities. Over 15 per cent of the university's students are from overseas, many of them taught in partner institutions in Singapore, Brunei, Malaysia, Pakistan and India. Nearer home, there are alliances with a number of further education colleges to help boost participation in a region where it is well below the national average. The colleges offer Foundation degrees in areas such as public sector administration, community justice, engineering technology and enterprise in IT.

The relatively small, lively campus is close to the city centre, with only the management school on a different site, two miles away in a 14-acre parkland setting. Improvements on the City Campus have included new sports facilities incorporating a gym and climbing wall, and an improved sports hall. There is also a distinctive four-storey Atrium, which has brought together all student support services in a single, open-plan social space, and "Student Central", which houses the students' union.

A separate online portal is available to applicants and new students to smooth their transition to higher education. Computer-assisted learning is increasing in many subjects, making use of unusually extensive IT provision and a new wireless network. Some courses feature online assessment and the use of laptops in lectures. The university entered less than a quarter of eligible academics for the 2014 assessments of research, but their work produced good results. Almost three-quarters of it was rated in the top two categories, with allied health, management and archaeological science producing particularly good grades. There were also high scores for the impact of Bradford's research in archaeology, politics and management.

Places in halls are reasonably priced and all have internet connections. Rents for private housing were among the lowest in any university city in 2014. The university has particularly good provision for disabled students, who account for 6 per cent of the university population. Bradford's senior management group includes the Director of Student Success to ensure that the student voice is heard in future developments.

Undergraduate Fees and Bursaries

» Fees for UK/EU students 2016–17	£9,000
Placement year	£900
» Fees for international students 2015–16	£12,100–£14,410

» Household income below £30K, £500 a year with conditions.

» For those with at least ABB at A level or equivalent, scholarship of £2,000 year 1; £1,500 years 2 and 3 (values 2015–16).

» Check the university's website for the latest information.

Students

Undergraduates:	**8,815**	**(960)**
Postgraduates:	**855**	**(1,875)**
Mature students:	**24.9%**	
International students:	**15.7%**	
Applications per place:	**7.6**	
From state-sector schools:	**96%**	
From working-class homes:	**56.2%**	
Satisfaction with students' union	**78%**	

For detailed information about sports facilities:
www.bradford.ac.uk/unique/

Accommodation

Number of places and costs refer to 2015–16
University-provided places: 1,051
Percentage catered: 0%
Self-catered costs: £102.34.00 (standard) – £110.74 (en suite) a week (42 weeks).
All first-year undergraduate students are guaranteed accommodation (terms and conditions apply).
accommodation@bradford.ac.uk
www.bradford.ac.uk/student/accommodation/

University of Brighton

The demand for places at Brighton has risen by almost 20 per cent this year, ten times more than the national average. Engineering, computing, applied psychology and criminology were among the subjects showing increases in 2014, and their upward trend has accelerated in the current round of applications, keeping the university among the top 30 in terms of overall popularity. More than nine out of ten courses include a placement or the option of a sandwich year. The four-year fashion textiles degree, for example, offers work placements in the USA, France and Italy, as well as Britain.

The university's fashionable seaside location helps to attract students, as do the modern campuses, which have seen more than £100 million of investment in the past decade. Teaching facilities have been updated on the Moulsecoomb campus in Brighton itself, where there is a new building for pharmacy and biosciences. A third academic building and £40 million of student accommodation is planned for the campus. A similar amount has been committed to halls of residence and support facilities in nearby Varley Park. In addition, a new academic building has opened in Hastings and facilities for the College or Arts and Humanities are being expanded on the Grand Parade campus in Brighton, which also hosts the Design Council's national archive. There is more to come: Brighton has become the first post-1992 university to raise money from the bond markets to fund further campus improvements.

Brighton came of age as one of the first new universities to be awarded a medical school. Run jointly with Sussex University, the school is now training almost 140 doctors a year. Its headquarters, on Brighton's Falmer campus, has also provided a new base for applied social sciences, such as criminology and applied psychology. The two universities have been collaborating since Brighton was a polytechnic, and there is a joint research building for science policy and management studies. The university is also engaged in imaginative regional initiatives. Its campus in Hastings, which focuses on digital and broadcast media, runs a number of schemes to draw people from the region into higher education.

There are 21,000 students on five campuses. The School of Education, as well as languages and literature students, moved into a new building on the Falmer campus, which now also boasts a £7.3-million sports centre. The university's wealth of teaching facilities are designed to build real-life skills, and include a radio station and TV studio, a podiatry hospital, a physiotherapy clinic, a flight simulator, rapid prototyping facilities,

Mithras House
Lewes Road
Brighton BN2 4AT

01273 600900 (switchboard)
admissions@brighton.ac.uk
www.brighton.ac.uk
www.bsms.ac.uk
www.brightonsu.com
Affiliation: none

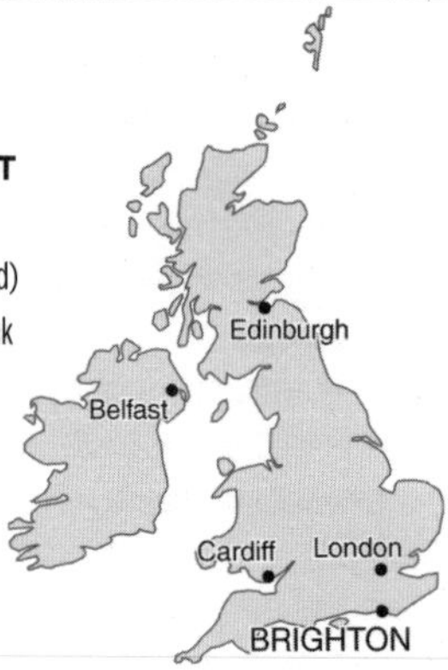

***The Times and Sunday Times* Rankings**

Overall Ranking: **90** (last year: 82)

Teaching quality:	**=97**	78.6%
Student experience:	**=104**	80.9%
Research quality:	**=73**	7.9%
Entry standards:	**=69**	321
Student–staff ratio:	**=65**	17.1
Services & facilities/student:	**105**	£1,357
Expected completion rate:	**=57**	86.9%
Good honours:	**71**	68.2%
Graduate prospects:	**=65**	66.9%

industrial textile rooms, and a clinical skills and simulation suite for nursing students. At Eastbourne there is a new library and extensive leisure and sports facilities, which attracted the Swedish tennis team for its pre-Olympic preparations. Sport science laboratories and 354 en-suite residential places have been added, and improvements made to the learning resources centre, lecture theatres and refectory.

Brighton was in the top quarter of universities for the impact of the research submitted to the 2014 national assessments. Two-thirds of its work was placed in one of the top two categories – a big improvement on 2008, when Brighton was already among the most successful of the post-1992 universities. The university is perhaps best known for its strength in art and design, which was recognised in the award of national teaching centres in design and creativity. But it also has a growing reputation in areas such as sport and hospitality, as well as scoring well in teacher education rankings.

The university has a cosmopolitan air, with more overseas students and a more middle-class UK intake than most post-1992 universities. Among the efforts to widen participation are progression partnerships with 22 primary and over 50 secondary schools and colleges in the South East of England, where eligible students are guaranteed offers for many Brighton courses, as well as financial support from the university. Over 2,000 students applied from Compact partnership schools in 2014, the first full year of operation. The university also holds a Charter Mark for its commitment to care leavers and has a higher-than-average number of disabled students. Students have a personal tutor and there is an award-winning student services department. There are well-established mentoring, entrepreneurship and volunteering schemes for students to develop themselves outside the classroom.

Most students like Brighton's lively social scene, despite the high cost of living for those not in hall. Eastbourne is also popular, and both towns offer plentiful accommodation to supplement the university's stock.

Undergraduate Fees and Bursaries

» Fees for UK/EU students 2016–17	£9,000
Foundation degrees at partner colleges	£7,000–£7,500
Placement year	£1,000
» Fees for international students 2015–16	£11,780–£13,500
Medicine	£27,405

» Household income below £16.1K, £2,000 in year 1; £16.1K–£25K, £1,000 in year 1.

» Eligible students from the Compact Plus outreach programme, £1,000 in years 2 and 3.

» Household income below £25K and studying architecture, pharmacy and teaching, £1,000 in year 4

» Check the university's website for the latest information.

Students

Undergraduates:	**13,855**	**(2,795)**
Postgraduates:	**1,870**	**(2,175)**
Mature students:	**23.6%**	
International students:	**12.5%**	
Applications per place:	**7.2**	
From state-sector schools:	**94%**	
From working-class homes:	**30.3%**	
Satisfaction with students' union	**58%**	

For detailed information about sports facilities: http://sport.brighton.ac.uk

Accommodation

Number of places and costs refer to 2015–16

University-provided places: 2,107; 367 in private sector university-managed houses or flats.

Percentage catered: 55%

Catered costs: £151–£171 a week.

Self-catered costs: from £108 a week.

First years have priority for housing if conditions are met.

International students: guaranteed accommodation if conditions are met.

accommodation@brighton.ac.uk; www.brighton.ac.uk/living-here

University of Bristol

Bristol's place among the leading universities in the UK was triumphantly confirmed in the 2014 Research Excellence Framework, when the university ranked alongside Oxford in the top four. It was rewarded for entering more than 90 per cent of its eligible staff – a higher proportion than Oxford – and still seeing 83 per cent of its research rated as world-leading or internationally excellent. Among the many successes, geography consolidated its position as the leader in its subject, while the entire submissions in clinical medicine, health subjects, economics and sport and exercise sciences were placed in the top categories for their external impact. The results have helped to maintain Bristol's position in our top 20, but improvements are needed in student satisfaction for it to make further progress. It is already in the top 40 in the world, according to the QS rankings.

The university has increased the size of its undergraduate intake by 40 per cent – more than 1,300 places – in three years, taking full advantage of the lifting of restrictions on the numbers it is allowed to recruit. There are now 15,000 undergraduates, although Bristol remains one of the smaller universities in the Russell Group. The university's official strategy is to "stay relatively compact and nurture the collegial atmosphere that makes it a true community as well as an ambitious and challenging place to be."

Popular with applicants from all types of school, Bristol has long been favoured by the independent sector as a natural alternative to Oxbridge. To broaden the intake, departments may make slightly lower offers to the most promising applicants from the bottom 40 per cent of schools and colleges at A level. Over 2,400 such offers were made in 2014, but the proportion from low-income groups remains less than one in seven. The university has spent more than £15 million since 2006 on recruiting and supporting students from disadvantaged backgrounds. Some 600 local students take the Access to Bristol course while at school or college, for example, and receive a substantial bursary and a year's free tuition if they go on to a Bristol degree and their family income is less than £25,000. Nevertheless, 40 per cent of entrants in 2013 came from independent schools, the highest proportion outside Oxbridge.

The university celebrated its centenary in 2009 and has since passed the £100-million target for a fundraising campaign which has helped the university to create new chairs and embark on a number of building projects, including a centre for the highly rated chemistry department. The largest estate investment programme in the university's history is currently underway, with £200 million of projects due to be

Senate House
Tyndall Avenue
Bristol BS8 1TH

0117 394 1644
ug-admissions@bristol.ac.uk
www.bristol.ac.uk
www.bristolsu.org.uk
Affiliation: Russell Group

***The Times and Sunday Times* Rankings**

Overall Ranking: **20** (last year: 19)

Teaching quality:	**119**	75.5%
Student experience:	**=99**	81.5%
Research quality:	**6**	47.3%
Entry standards:	**8**	487
Student–staff ratio:	**=22**	13.7
Services & facilities/student:	**45**	£1,976
Expected completion rate:	**=3**	96.6%
Good honours:	**7**	86.3%
Graduate prospects:	**22**	79.6%

completed by 2016. A £54-million Life Sciences Building was completed in 2014, when new study centres were opened in the university precinct and in the students' union. Bristol is committed to providing extra study spaces to match its growing student population. A new 400-seat lecture theatre has been completed recently and the arts faculty headquarters refurbished.

An extension to one of the halls at Stoke Bishop has added 320 residential places. The university struggled initially to keep pace with the growth in the number of students, but it will continue to guarantee accommodation for all new undergraduates in 2016, as long as they accept an offer by the end of July. An impressive sports complex with a well-equipped gym has been developed at the heart of the university precinct, where the careers centre has also been refurbished. The students' union houses one of the city's biggest live music venues as well as a café, bars, theatre and swimming pool. A £31-million refurbishment and redesign was completed this year, providing more space for community activities, student societies and sports clubs.

Bristol possesses a vibrant youth culture and, as one of the country's most prosperous cities, offers job opportunities to students and graduates alike. The university merges into the centre, its famous gothic tower dominating the skyline from the junction of two of the main shopping streets. Despite its hills, Bristol is England's first Cycling City and was chosen by *The Sunday Times* as the best city in the UK in which to live. It is also European Green Capital for 2015. Most students enjoy life there, although the high cost of living can be a drawback. The dropout rate is among the lowest in Britain, and one student in five stays in the city after graduation. The university won a police-approved Secured Environments award for its crime protection work.

Undergraduate Fees and Bursaries

- » Fees for UK/EU students 2016–17 £9,000
- » Fees for international students 2015–16 £15,200–£18,300
  Dentistry, medicine, veterinary medicine £18,300–£33,900
- » For each year, students with household income below £25K, bursary of £2,000; household income £25K–£42.6K, sliding scale £1,500–£500.
- » For students in the Access to Bristol scheme with household income below £25K, £9,000 fee waiver in year 1 plus eligible for Access to Bristol annual maintenance bursary of £3,750.
- » Range of other scholarships and bursaries available.
- » Check the university's website for the latest information.

Students

Undergraduates:	**14,510**	**(470)**
Postgraduates:	**3,885**	**(1,305)**
Mature students:	**5.9%**	
International students:	**15.3%**	
Applications per place:	**8.1**	
From state-sector schools:	**59.7%**	
From working-class homes:	**13.7%**	
Satisfaction with students' union	**40%**	

For detailed information about sports facilities:
www.bris.ac.uk/sport

Accommodation

Number of places and costs refer to 2015–16
University-provided places: about 5,633
Percentage catered: 32%
Catered costs: £120.52 (shared room) – £179.16 a week.
Self-catered costs: £78.18 (shared room) – £175.00 a week.
First years are guaranteed one offer of accommodation provided conditions are met.
International students: accommodation is guaranteed provided conditions are met.
www.bristol.ac.uk/accommodation/

Brunel University London

Brunel will celebrate its 50th anniversary as the new entrants arrive in 2016, having invested more than £400 million in recent years on its campus in northwest London. The university will also benefit from increased research funding after a good performance in the 2014 Research Excellence Framework. Over 60 per cent of a large submission was rated as world-leading or internationally excellent, with sports sciences achieving the best results and ranking in the top five departments in the UK. Brunel did particularly well in the new assessments of the external impact of research. In public health, art and design, politics, and environmental and earth sciences, 100 per cent of the work achieved three or the maximum four stars for impact.

The university invariably registers higher levels of student satisfaction than others in the capital. In *Times Higher Education*'s (*THE*) latest survey of the student experience, respondents were particularly complimentary about the sports facilities and library, which is open 24 hours a day. The library and Brunel's world-class sports facilities have accounted for much of the investment on campus, which retains its original 1960s architecture, but with the addition of striking new buildings and landscaping. There have been many new and refurbished social, teaching and residential facilities, and more green spaces for students to enjoy. The latest major construction project was the £30-million Eastern Gateway Building, which provided new teaching and research facilities, a large auditorium, a café and an art gallery.

Brunel has also changed academically. The eight schools have been replaced by three colleges (business, arts and social sciences; engineering, design and physical sciences; and health and life sciences). There are also three autonomous interdisciplinary research institutes to encourage academics from different subjects to work together and produce innovative courses and research projects. The highest-profile example has been the establishment of the first Centre for Comedy Studies Research, launched by Brunel alumni Jo Brand and Lee Mack. The new Educational Excellence Centre will encourage innovative teaching and the use of technology in the classroom, while another new unit will nurture students' business skills and exploit the university's research. Brunel tries to enhance graduates' employment prospects through work placements and the inclusion in degree courses of skills modules, such as oral and written communication, business and computer literacy.

The latest strategic plan sets the goal of confirming the university's standing in the top third of UK higher education, making

Kingston Lane
Uxbridge
UB8 3PH

01895 265265 (admissions)
contact via website
www.brunel.ac.uk
http://brunelstudents.com
Affiliation: none

***The Times and Sunday Times* Rankings**

Overall Ranking: **60** (last year: 47)

Teaching quality:	**102**	78.2%
Student experience:	**=66**	83.8%
Research quality:	**49**	25.4%
Entry standards:	**51**	352
Student–staff ratio:	**=55**	16.4
Services & facilities/student:	**52**	£1,904
Expected completion rate:	**51**	87.7%
Good honours:	**=68**	68.8%
Graduate prospects:	**=86**	63.4%

stronger connections between teaching and research, and further improving the quality of students' experience. There has been significant growth in courses focusing on new technologies such as multimedia design and broadcast media, as well as health and social care. The university is training 40 postgraduates to deliver Robo-Code sessions at secondary schools to encourage more girls to go into engineering and computer programming. Other innovations include creative writing, professionally accredited journalism, sonic arts, aviation engineering and pilot studies, motorsport engineering and games design. Benjamin Zephaniah took up his first academic position as Chair of Creative Writing, and Will Self has joined as Professor of Contemporary Thought. Brunel's Institute for the Environment won a Queen's Anniversary Prize for pioneering research revealing the link between chemicals in rivers and reproductive health.

Over 40 per cent of the undergraduates are from low-income families – well ahead of the national average for Brunel's courses and entry qualifications. More than half come from the UK's ethnic minorities and there is also a large contingent of international students. The International Pathways and Language Centre was named as the top-performing British university language centre under the British Council's accreditation framework. A new international strategy promotes study opportunities abroad. Brunel features in the top 25 in THE's latest ranking of the world's leading universities under 50 years old, scoring highly for its international outlook.

A tradition of sporting excellence saw a number of students compete in the London Olympic and Paralympic Games, and in the Commonwealth Games. The level of facilities is such that Brunel hosted the South Korean Olympic and Canadian Paralympic teams. The university has won awards for its provision for disabled students, and for its placement and careers service. Student accommodation has been transformed as part of the campus improvements. With the refurbishment of existing halls of residence and further construction there are now more than 4,500 places for new first-year, full-time students.

Undergraduate Fees and Bursaries

» Fees for UK/EU students 2016–17	£9,000
Placement year	£1,000
» Fees for international students 2015–16	£13,500–£16,500

- » 300 bursaries, with priority criteria, of £1,000 a year.
- » 30 Academic Excellence scholarships of £6,000 a year for those with at least AAA at A level or equivalent.
- » 30 Local Borough scholarships of £6,000 cash or fee waiver each year; 6 Alumni scholarships of £6,000 a year.
- » Other scholarships for care leavers, local students and in some subjects.

Students

Undergraduates:	**9,815**	**(260)**
Postgraduates:	**3,110**	**(1,145)**
Mature students:	**12%**	
International students:	**19.9%**	
Applications per place:	**10.4**	
From state-sector schools:	**94.8%**	
From working-class homes:	**42.1%**	
Satisfaction with students' union	**73%**	

For detailed information about sports facilities:
www.brunel.ac.uk/services/sport

Accommodation

Number of places and costs refer to 2015–16
University-provided places: 4,531
Percentage catered: 0%
Self-catered costs: £104.00 (standard) – £132.50 (en suite); £198.25 (studio flat) a week.
All new full-time first-year students (UG and PG) are eligible for on-campus accommodation.
International students: as above.
www.brunel.ac.uk/life/accommodation
accom-uxb@brunel.ac.uk

University of Buckingham

For many years Britain's only private university, Buckingham is still the only one in our main league table, now well established in the top 50. Buckingham had too few students to be classified in some measures for several years, but has seen dramatic growth in this decade. The latest and most prestigious development has seen the opening of the UK's first private not-for-profit medical school, where the first 64 students arrived in January 2015. The course, which was "massively oversubscribed", is 4.5 years long, modelled on Leicester University's MBChB programme, and its costs are in line with the overseas rate at other medical schools. The university has had a postgraduate medical school for seven years, attracting overseas medical graduates.

Buckingham, which celebrates its 40th anniversary in 2016, has a new vice-chancellor at the start of the 2015 academic year, the political historian and independent school headmaster Sir Anthony Seldon joining from Wellington College. He will find a university that is in the top three for staffing levels and which has some of the most satisfied students in the country. It has boosted spending on student facilities, refurbishing the refectory, introducing Wi-Fi across the whole campus and expanding the library and teaching space. In addition, £3 million has been spent on refurbished buildings for the Medical School, including a new 106-seat lecture theatre and a tablet-style large Anatomage table. There is a rolling programme of refurbishment of student accommodation and the first-ever campus bank has been established. There is even a new Afro-Caribbean hair salon, opened by former students for their successors who would otherwise have to go to London

Even before the arrival of £9,000 fees elsewhere, Buckingham claimed to be no more expensive than other universities because its intensive two-year degrees cut maintenance costs and accelerate entry into employment. Total fees for British and EU undergraduates taking the two-year degree from January 2016 will be £24,888 for home and EU students, and £34,320 for those from other countries. There is a range of scholarships for both home and international candidates. Small group tutorials, which have all but disappeared outside Oxbridge, are common: the average tutorial group contains about six students. Only its absence from the Research Excellent Framework, which was restricted to state-funded institutions, prevented the university from finishing higher in our table. However, the university has a number of research groups and over 170 research students. One high-profile project has involved excavations at Stonehenge, which

Hunter Street
Buckingham MK18 1EG

01280 820313 (admissions)
info@buckingham.ac.uk
www.buckingham.ac.uk
www.buckingham.ac.uk/life/social/su
Affiliation: none

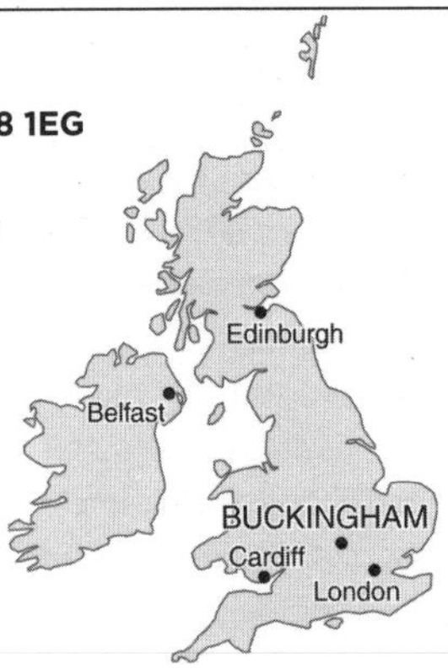

***The Times and Sunday Times* Rankings**

Overall Ranking: **=38** (last year: 48)

Teaching quality:	**1**	88%
Student experience:	**=7**	88.4%
Research quality:	**n/a**	n/a
Entry standards:	**=97**	304
Student–staff ratio:	**2**	10.5
Services & facilities/student:	**46**	£1,972
Expected completion rate:	**=60**	86.3%
Good honours:	**126**	50.7%
Graduate prospects:	**11**	83.4%

have led to Buckingham's first Massive Open Online Course (MOOC) about the site, attracting thousands of students from all over the world.

A Conservative-backed experiment of the 1970s, Buckingham has long been an accepted part of the university system, with no party political ties. Its degrees carry full currency in the academic world and teaching standards are high. The university's culture of responsiveness to students was praised by the Quality Assurance Agency in its last report on the university. Its own statement on its independence declares that Buckingham was founded on the principles of classical liberalism, and teaches the ideals of free-thinking and liberal political thought.

Students can begin courses in January, July or September, most of which run for two 40-week years, minimising disruptive career breaks for mature students. Just over half of the students are from overseas, but the proportion from Britain is growing. They have the option of a three-year degree in the humanities, and other schools are now following suit. New courses in 2015 include a series of joint honours degrees in international relations or politics, four new English degrees and others in accounting, business management, computing and economics. A new Foundation Department provides English language tuition for those with an IELTS score below 6.5. There are also international Foundation programmes and a pre-Master's for business for those whose first degree is not in a business-related subject.

Buckingham's two sites are within walking distance of each other. The main campus includes the refectory, bar and fitness centre, with the Radcliffe Centre, which hosts internal and external events, nearby. The law school is within walking distance of the main campus. Two historic buildings have been refurbished at a cost of almost £2 million, and a new six-acre site has been acquired to make room for future expansion. Buckingham's campus has been judged to be the safest in the country. There is a university cinema, and the town of Buckingham is pretty, with a good selection of pubs and restaurants. Milton Keynes and Oxford are nearby.

Undergraduate Fees and Bursaries

Note: that the degree courses only last two years, except medicine (4.5 years).

- Fees for UK/EU students for degree course starting in January 2016: £12,444; medicine: £35,525.
- Fees for international students for degree course starting in January 2016: £17,160; Medicine: £35,525.
- Household income below £42.6K, bursary of £1,100 a year.
- Scholarship of £2,500 for students (excluding medicine) with at least ABB at A level or equivalent; continued in year 2 based on academic performance.
- Five Counties scholarship of £2,500 a year for students from Buckinghamshire, Bedfordshire, Hertfordshire, Northamptonshire and Oxfordshire.

Students

Undergraduates:	**1,205**	**(55)**
Postgraduates:	**910**	**(70)**
Mature students:	**28.6%**	
International students:	**51.5%**	
Applications per place:	**15.8**	
From state-sector schools:	**77.5%**	
From working-class homes:	**30%**	
Satisfaction with students' union	**72%**	

For detailed information about sports facilities: www.buckingham.ac.uk/life/thingstodo/sport

Accommodation

Number of places and costs refer to 2015–16

University-provided places: 545

Percentage catered: 0%

Self-catered accommodation: £88.00–£205.50 a week (48 weeks).

All first-year students are guaranteed accommodation if they follow the application process.

International students: same as above.

accommodation@buckingham.ac.uk; www.buckingham.ac.uk/life/accommodation

Buckinghamshire New University

Buckinghamshire New University is opening an innovative new campus for higher education and professional development courses in Aylesbury this autumn. University Campus Aylesbury Vale will host programmes taught by the university and Aylesbury College, with employers helping to determine, shape and develop the curriculum, which will include foundation degrees, top-up courses and foundation programmes. It will be equipped with technologies for teaching, learning and research, including an assisted living laboratory and a cyber-security facility. The campus is a new departure for the university, which had been concentrating most of its activities on its headquarters in High Wycombe. Nursing was the exception, having moved into a new building in Uxbridge, on the north-west edge of London. A £200-million development plan has seen the prize-winning Gateway Building transform the town-centre campus with improved teaching, social and administrative space. The complex includes a new sports hall, gym, treatment rooms and sports laboratory, open to the public as well as to students. At the same time, collaboration with two of the world's biggest IT companies is resulting in one of the most advanced student networks in UK higher education. Two new accommodation blocks in High Wycombe added 108 en-suite rooms to the university's residential stock, doubling the size of the student village and bringing the number of places owned by Bucks to 885.

There are now some 9,000 students, two-thirds of them full-time undergraduates. Over 30 per cent of undergraduate first-years are over 21 years old and nearly 60 per cent are female. Applications grew in line with the national average in 2014, but there was only a small increase in enrolments. Bucks has continued to do well against the Government's benchmarks for widening participation in higher education: almost all the entrants are from state schools or colleges, and just over 40 per cent are from working-class homes. The projected dropout rate of little more than 10 per cent for those who entered in 2014 was significantly lower than the national average for its subjects and entry qualifications. The nursing provision is the largest in the London area and has growing links with the Imperial College London Healthcare Trust, including a joint appointment designed to promote innovation. The child nursing courses attract particularly good ratings. New laboratories and teaching rooms are planned on the Uxbridge campus.

Bucks offers an unrivalled package

Queen Alexandra Road
High Wycombe
Buckinghamshire
HP11 2JZ

0330 123 2023 (enquiries)
advice@bucks.ac.uk
www.bucks.ac.uk
www.bucksstudentsunion.org
Affiliations: GuildHE

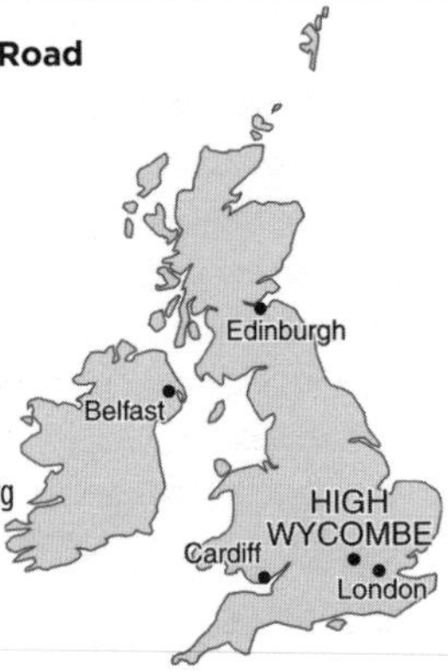

***The Times and Sunday Times* Rankings**

Overall Ranking: **109** (last year: 116)

Teaching quality:	**=55**	81.5%
Student experience:	**103**	81.1%
Research quality:	**121**	1.5%
Entry standards:	**=122**	257
Student–staff ratio:	**122**	21.8
Services & facilities/student:	**=42**	£1,997
Expected completion rate:	**93**	82.5%
Good honours:	**119**	57%
Graduate prospects:	**115**	57.6%

of free activities through its "Big Deal" programme, which has been running since before the introduction of £9,000 fees. The programme entitles all students to free entertainment, recreational activities, events and sport. It was extended in 2014 through the "Big Deal on Course" to cover essential textbooks, equipment and materials, photocopying credits, and a contribution to the cost of field trips, up to a value of £1,000 over three years. There are also means-tested bursaries to cover essential field trip costs above the standard package, a fund to assist with travel costs to attend job interviews, work placements and internships, and the university will pay for gown hire at graduation ceremonies. Nevertheless, satisfaction ratings remain among the lowest in the National Student Survey and continue to hold the university back in our league table. Bucks is also in the bottom three for research quality, having entered only 24 staff for the 2014 Research Excellence Framework. Almost 40 per cent of their work reached one of the top two categories, with art and design producing much the best results.

Sport plays an important part of life at the university, which partners the London Wasps rugby union team in a relationship which trades coaching for Bucks students for courses for Wasps players. But the university's main aim is to contribute to the social and economic life of the region, embracing workplace learning and close ties with local businesses. Employees of the bed company Dreams, which is based in High Wycombe, take a Foundation degree in retail management while at work, for example. The National School of Furniture works with local employers and further education colleges, offering qualifications from certificate level to PhD. Bucks has also won awards for its training of commercial pilots and courses for music industry management. Other Foundation degrees are run at partner colleges and include animation and visual effects, protective security management, and sports coaching and performance. New courses introduced in 2015 include sport development and coaching, business and marketing, political studies, and criminology.

High Wycombe has a range of student pubs and clubs and is within easy reach of London.

Undergraduate Fees and Bursaries

- Fees for UK/EU students 2016–17 — £9,000
  Franchised courses at partner colleges — £6,000–£9,000
- Fees for international students 2015–16 — £9,500, £13,000
- Household income below £25K with additional criteria, 100 bursaries of £1,000 a year; support for additional study and employability activities.
- "Big Deal" package which encourages participation in a range of sporting, recreational and social activities.
- Check the university's website for the latest information.

Students

Undergraduates:	**5,690**	**(2,295)**
Postgraduates:	**365**	**(725)**
Mature students:	**31.1%**	
International students:	**6.1%**	
Applications per place:	**5.7**	
From state-sector schools:	**97.1%**	
From working-class homes:	**42%**	
Satisfaction with students' union	**81%**	

For detailed information about sports facilities:
www.bucksstudentsunion.org/activities/sports/

Accommodation

Number of places and costs refer to 2015–16
University-provided places: 885
Percentage catered: 0%
Self-catered costs: £103.03 (standard) – £171.58 (studio) a week (42 weeks).
First-year students applying before 30 June are guaranteed accommodation.
International students: priority allocation for first years.
accom@bucks.ac.uk;
http://bucks.ac.uk/home_eu_students/accommodation/

University of Cambridge

Cambridge has moved back into a clear lead at the top of our table after sharing first place with Oxford last year. The light blues produced the best results in the 2014 Research Excellence Framework (REF), and are again among the leaders for student satisfaction. The university also tops more than half of the 66 subject tables and is in the top five in all three main world rankings. Cambridge entered 95 per cent of eligible academics for the REF – no university involved a higher proportion – and 87 per cent of their work was rated as world-leading or internationally excellent. It achieved the UK's best results in aeronautical and electronic engineering, business and management, chemistry, classics and clinical medicine.

Cambridge has the highest entry standards of any UK university, demanding at least A*AA at A level in arts subjects and two A*A*A in the sciences, although candidates may be made a lower offer if their school or personal circumstances are thought to disadvantage them. In some subjects, there will be additional tests, such as Cambridge's own Sixth Term Examination Papers in mathematics. With around five applicants for each place – fewer if you choose your subject carefully – the competition for places appears less intense than at the popular civic universities, but the real difference is that nine out of ten entrants have at least three A grades at A level. That competition shows no sign of easing since the university has barely increased the size of its intake with the relaxation of recruitment restrictions. Indeed, there were 640 more applications in 2014 and only 70 additional places.

Research facilities are constantly upgraded. The £26-million Maxwell Centre will open before the end of the year on the West Cambridge site, for example. Research scientists from industry will occupy laboratory and desk space alongside Cambridge research groups. The centre will provide laboratory and meeting spaces for 230 people working on fundamental physics. A new centre for biodiversity and conservation, named after Sir David Attenborough, will follow on the New Museums site. Part of the project will see the Museum of Zoology reopen in 2016. The first phase of the £1-billion North West Cambridge development will open in 2017. The final development will include 100,000 square metres of academic and research space, as well as accommodation for 2,000 postgraduates, 1,500 homes for university staff and another 1,500 private houses. There will also be community facilities including a primary school, shops and sports centre.

More than 60 per cent of undergraduates now come from the state system, but the

The Old Schools
Trinity Lane
Cambridge CB2 1TN

01223 333308 (admissions)
admissions@cam.ac.uk
www.cam.ac.uk
www.cusu.co.uk
Affiliation: Russell Group

***The Times and Sunday Times* Rankings**

Overall Ranking: **1** (last year: =1)

Teaching quality:	=13	83.8%
Student experience:	28	86.3%
Research quality:	1	57.3%
Entry standards:	1	602
Student–staff ratio:	=5	11.3
Services & facilities/student:	2	£3,432
Expected completion rate:	1	98.4%
Good honours:	3	89.3%
Graduate prospects:	3	89.3%

proportion of working-class undergraduates remains low, at only 10 per cent. Summer schools, student visits and, in some colleges, sympathetic selection procedures are helping to attract more applications from comprehensive schools and further education colleges. There are generous bursaries of up to £3,500 a year, according to parental income.

The application system has been simplified slightly, with candidates no longer required to complete an initial Cambridge form, as well as their UCAS form. However, they are sent the Supplementary Application Questionnaire, after they have submitted their UCAS form, covering the applicant's academic experience in more detail. The tripos system was a forerunner of the currently fashionable modular degree, allowing students to change subjects (within limits) midway through their courses. Students receive a classification for each of the two parts of their degree.

Choosing a college is an additional complication for those not familiar with Cambridge. Brief profiles of all the undergraduate colleges appear in Chapter 13. Making the right choice is crucial, both to maximise the chances of winning a place and to ensure an enjoyable three years if you are successful. Applicants can take pot luck with an open application if they prefer not to opt for a particular college. But, though the statistics show that this route is equally successful, only a minority takes it. Most teaching is now university-based, especially in the sciences, and a shift of emphasis towards the centre has been taking place more generally.

A £16-million sports centre opened in 2013, featuring a large sports hall and a strength and conditioning wing. Cambridge is not for everyone, however bright. The amount of high-quality work to be crammed into eight-week terms can prove a strain, although the projected dropout rate of 1.1 per cent is the lowest at any university. Most students relish the experience and reap the rewards in their careers.

Undergraduate Fees and Bursaries

» Fees for UK/EU students 2016–17	£9,000
» Fees for international students 2015–16	£15,063–£22,923
Medicine	£36,459
College fees	£5,400–£7,720

- UK and EU students who are eligible for tuition fee support are not liable for College fees.
- Household income below £25K, bursary of £3,500 a year (£5,600 for some mature students); household income £25K–£42.6K, bursary of up to £3,500 a year.
- Many college scholarships and bursaries.
- Check the university's website for the latest information.

Students

Undergraduates:	**11,865**	**(290)**
Postgraduates:	**6,485**	**(935)**
Mature students:	**4.2%**	
International students:	**19.6%**	
Applications per place:	**5**	
From state-sector schools:	**60.6%**	
From working-class homes:	**10.8%**	
Satisfaction with students' union	**32%**	

For detailed information about sports facilities: www.sport.cam.ac.uk

Accommodation

www.undergraduate.study.cam.ac.uk/why-cambridge/student-life/accommodation

Also see chapter 13 for information about individual colleges.

College websites provide accommodation details.

Canterbury Christ Church University

The purchase of Canterbury Prison, near the university's main campus, should provide residential accommodation for up to 250 students in September 2016, but it will also offer a longer-term opportunity to bring Canterbury Christ Church closer together. The main gate, with its inscription "County Gaol and House of Correction", will have to remain, but the demolition of some of the buildings will allow some departments that are spread around the city to be relocated. The university's estates framework notes a "strong desire among students and staff to create a sense of identity." Over £11 million was invested 2013–14 alone in the university's three main bases in Canterbury, Broadstairs and Chatham, and a fourth centre in Tunbridge Wells. More student accommodation will open in autumn 2015 in the centre of Canterbury, where a new students' union and other facilities opened in 2012.

Canterbury Christ Church has 18,000 students and may expand over the next few years. More than half come from Kent, but 1,000 are from Europe or further afield. Almost all of the undergraduates are state educated and well over a third come from the four poorest socio-economic groups.

The former Church of England college achieved university status in 2005, and is the region's largest provider of courses for the public services, with teacher training courses that are highly rated by Ofsted, and strong programmes in health and social care, nursing and policing. The university remains a Church of England foundation and has the Archbishop of Canterbury as its Chancellor.

Seven out of ten students are female – partly the result of the subject mix, with its emphasis on health subjects and education. Recent developments have included the introduction of special educational needs and inclusion studies, and a counselling, coaching and mentoring degree, helping to meet the fast-growing demand for careers in both areas. Business degrees have been strengthened with new industry placement years and facilities such as the Bloomberg Trading Room, while computing courses have developed a focus on cybercrime – an area of research in which the university is a national leader. Almost half of Canterbury Christ Church's submission to the 2014 research assessments was placed in the top two categories, resulting in one of the biggest percentage increases in funding at any university. New developments include the UK Institute for Migration Research and new health alliances through the England Centre for Practice Development.

The purpose-built campus at Broadstairs offers a range of subjects from commercial

North Holmes Road
Canterbury CT1 1QU

01227 782900 (enquiries)
admissions@canterbury.ac.uk
www.canterbury.ac.uk
www.ccsu.co.uk
Affiliations: Cathedrals Group; million+

***The Times and Sunday Times* Rankings**

Overall Ranking: **107** (last year: 96)

Teaching quality:	**=66**	80.7%
Student experience:	**94**	81.9%
Research quality:	**96**	4.5%
Entry standards:	**116**	279
Student–staff ratio:	**=88**	18.4
Services & facilities/student:	**117**	£1,212
Expected completion rate:	**=96**	82.3%
Good honours:	**=81**	66.5%
Graduate prospects:	**114**	57.8%

music to digital media, photography, and early childhood studies. The Salomons Centre, just outside Tunbridge Wells, caters exclusively for postgraduate courses, while the newly expanded Medway site at Chatham offers a variety of education and health programmes. The Institute of Medical Sciences has been launched there for postgraduate education and research, building on the university's work in stem cell research and minimally invasive surgery. The majority of the students, however, are at the university's main campus at Canterbury, a World Heritage Site and one of the safest university cities in the country. Augustine House, a £35-million library and student services centre, with specialist teaching and IT facilities, was joint winner of the Society of College, National and University Librarians' 2013 award for the best library design. All campuses are interconnected by a high-speed data network, providing access to online teaching and learning materials, the student web portal and email. The student support service – i-zone – can be accessed online or via staff at the i-zone desks.

The university contributes to the cultural life of Canterbury with the Sidney Cooper Gallery, which hosts exhibitions and workshops from visiting artists as well as work by students before the best goes on to be exhibited in London galleries. It has also renovated St Gregory's Centre for Music, a historic concert venue, and opened separate rehearsal, practice and performance spaces in a building named after Sir Peter Maxwell Davies, who is a visiting professor.

Social and sports facilities naturally vary between the campuses, although the students' union is present on all of them. The sports centre in Canterbury includes a large adaptable sports hall and a fitness suite, a sports and exercise studio and performance analysis rooms. The centre hosted the pre-Olympic training camp for the Puerto Rico team in 2012. The university also has facilities at Polo Farm Sports Club close to the city, which includes a premier location for hockey. There are 12 acres of playing fields about a mile from the main campus.

Undergraduate Fees and Bursaries

- » Fees for UK/EU students 2016–17 £9,000
  Degree courses at partner colleges £4,500–£9,000
- » Fees for international students 2015–16 £9,710
- » Household income below £25K, bursaries of up to £1,000 a year, reviewed annually.
- » Sports, music and local student awards available. Up to £300 support for dyslexic students.
- » Check the university's website for the latest information.

Students

Undergraduates:	**10,515**	**(3,430)**
Postgraduates:	**1,350**	**(2,130)**
Mature students:	**26.6%**	
International students:	**6.5%**	
Applications per place:	**5.5**	
From state-sector schools:	**97.9%**	
From working-class homes:	**37.3%**	
Satisfaction with students' union	**60%**	

For detailed information about sports facilities:
www.canterbury.ac.uk/christ-church-sport

Accommodation

Number of places and costs refer to 2015–16
University-provided places: 1,922
Percentage catered: 0%
Self-catered costs: £92.50–£187.00 a week.
Accommodation guaranteed for first years if conditions are met.
International students: as above.
accommodation@canterbury.ac.uk
www.canterbury.ac.uk/study-here/accommodation/

Cardiff University

Cardiff has embarked on a £450-million masterplan that will include a new Innovation Campus and provide much-improved facilities for student services, as well as a new library, on the main Cathays Park site. Although not all of the developments will be completed while 2016 entrants are at the university, they will benefit from the planned Centre for Student Life, which will act as a one-stop shop for students seeking advice and linked to the redesigned Students' Union, where the facilities have already been upgraded. A new multipurpose venue there provides social, learning and meeting space during the day and then becomes a nightclub.

The perennial choice as *The Sunday Times* Best Welsh University, Cardiff is the only member of the Russell Group of research-led universities in Wales and its sole representative in the top 200 of the world rankings. It is also one of the few universities in the UK to boast two Nobel laureates on its staff. Three years of growth, in which the size of the undergraduate intake increased by more than 25 per cent, came to a halt in 2014, although the demand for places continued to rise sharply. The university now has over 28,000 students, including 6,000 from outside the UK. Entry requirements have been rising and more than half of all applicants achieve at least AAB grades at A Level.

A third of Cardiff's students come from Wales, but it is the international dimension that has been the university's main focus recently. A new Global Opportunities Programme provides studying, working and volunteering options across the world to enhance the student experience. The aim is for 17 per cent of undergraduates to undertake at least four weeks study, work or volunteering overseas by 2017. The university has also launched a Languages for All programme, giving students the chance to learn a language alongside their chosen degree for free. Students are also offered the Cardiff Award to boost their employment prospects by recognising the skills acquired from extracurricular activities.

An audit by the Quality Assurance Agency complimented the university on its "powerful academic vision and well-developed and effectively articulated mission to achieve excellence in teaching and research". Student support services, including counselling facilities and the help offered to dyslexics, were among the features singled out for praise. New degree programmes include applied software engineering, Portuguese, environmental geography, modern languages and translation, human and social sciences, and social analytics. One undergraduate in seven comes from an independent school and

Cardiff
CF10 3XQ

029 2087 4455 (enquiries)
contact via website
www.cardiff.ac.uk
www.cardiffstudents.com
Affiliation: Russell Group

***The Times and Sunday Times* Rankings**

Overall Ranking: **33** (last year: 27)

Teaching quality:	**=66**	80.7%
Student experience:	**29**	86%
Research quality:	**34**	35%
Entry standards:	**=23**	426
Student–staff ratio:	**30**	14.2
Services & facilities/student:	**78**	£1,638
Expected completion rate:	**19**	93.4%
Good honours:	**=30**	77.8%
Graduate prospects:	**18**	80.1%

little more than one in five has a working-class background. The 5 per cent projected dropout rate is comfortably the lowest in Wales.

Cardiff would have finished higher in our league table if it had entered more academics for the 2014 Research Excellence Framework: at 62 per cent of eligible staff, the entry was 12 percentage points smaller than any other Russell Group university's. However, the results were stellar, with 87 per cent of the submission rated as world-leading or internationally excellent. Cardiff was in the top three for the impact of its research, and civil and construction engineering was rated top in the UK. The university attracts more than half of the research funding awarded in Wales.

The university occupies a significant part of Cardiff's civic complex around Cathays Park. The five healthcare schools at the Heath Park campus share a 53-acre site with the University Hospital of Wales. The £18-million Cochrane Building provides teaching and learning facilities for all healthcare schools based there. The School of Dentistry has a new Dental Education Clinic offering students some of the UK's most modern training facilities. Other recent projects have included a £30-million science development and a £13.5-million learning and teaching centre for the Business School, which includes a 60-seat trading room and two large lecture theatres.

Library services continue to improve access to resources, increase the range of electronic resources, extend self-service provision and improve the environment for the study of rare collections. The IT working environment gives students online access to information about their studies and social life, from reading lists to social events. The university guarantees a residential place for those applying through the normal admissions cycle. The main residential site at Talybont boasts a "sports training village", and there is also a newly refurbished city-centre fitness suite and a sports ground. A new student residence with 178 beds opened there in 2014. Cardiff is a popular student city, relatively inexpensive and with a good range of nightlife and cultural venues.

Undergraduate Fees and Bursaries

- » Fees for UK/EU students 2016–17 £9,000
- » Welsh Assembly non-means-tested grant (2015–16) to pay fees above £3,810 for Welsh students.
- » Fees for international students 2015–16 £14,000–£26,130
  Medicine and dentistry £17,500–£31,000
- » Household income up to £50K, bursary of £1,000 in year 1.
- » Scholarship of £1,500 (year 1) and £750 (years 2 and 3) to students achieving grades AAA at A-level or equivalent in selected subjects.
- » For Welsh students from Communities First areas either £1,000 university accommodation discount or £500 travel bursary. Welsh medium and other subject scholarships available.
- » Check the university's website for the latest information.

Students

Undergraduates:	**17,550**	**(3,945)**
Postgraduates:	**4,455**	**(4,230)**
Mature students:	**13.8%**	
International students:	**13.9%**	
Applications per place:	**7.3**	
From state-sector schools:	**84.6%**	
From working-class homes:	**20.4%**	
Satisfaction with students' union	**87%**	

For detailed information about sports facilities:
www.cardiff.ac.uk/sport

Accommodation

Number of places and costs refer to 2015–16
University-provided places: 5,353
Percentage catered: 6.4%
Catered costs: £106–£129 a week.
Self-catered costs: £85–£120 a week.
All first years (except Clearing students) are guaranteed accommodation if conditions are met.
Policy for international students: guaranteed accommodation if conditions are met.
www.cardiff.ac.uk/for/prospective/accommodation.html

Cardiff Metropolitan University

International students have voted Cardiff Met the best university in the UK for student support for the past five years. Now the rest of the student body has added their own accolade, with the university winning *Times Higher Education* magazine's 2014 award for the most improved student experience. Applications have risen by almost 20 per cent in two years, which enabled the university to take almost 500 additional undergraduates in 2014. Cardiff Met has been awarded the Government's Charter Mark four times, the judges commenting particularly on the level of student satisfaction.

The university is celebrating the 150th anniversary of the founding of the Cardiff School of Art, which eventually evolved into Cardiff Met. The last incarnation was as the University of Wales Institute, but the present name was adopted in 2011 to stress its location in the Principality's capital. A report for the Welsh government cast doubt on the long-term viability of Cardiff Met as an independent university after it resisted pressure to become part of the new University of South Wales. But the university is showing no lack of confidence in its future, having committed £50 million to improvements on its three campuses. The new purpose-built School of Art and Design is now open on the Llandaff campus and has won an award from the Royal Society of Architects in Wales. A new campus centre, with a shop and catering facilities, had already been added, along with an Information Zone for student services. The Cyncoed campus had also benefited from a new student centre with a nightclub and all the normal catering and leisure facilities.

Cardiff Met is one of Britain's leading centres for university sport, with team performances that do justice to some excellent facilities. In recent years, the university has had British university champions in sports ranging from archery and gymnastics to squash, weightlifting and judo. More than 300 past or present students are internationals in 30 sports. Fifteen of them, including two gold medallists, took part in the London 2012 Olympic and Paralympic Games, where the university also provided three coaches and a physiologist. The £7-million National Indoor Athletics Centre is Cardiff Met's pride and joy, but other facilities are also of high quality. As well as participating in a thriving sports club scene, around 2,000 students pursue sport and dance related courses.

Cardiff Met entered only 35 academics for the 2014 Research Excellence Framework out of 381 who were eligible – only two universities entered a smaller

Llandaff Campus
Western Avenue
Cardiff CF5 2YB

029 2041 6010 (enquiries)
askadmissions@cardiffmet.ac.uk
www.cardiffmet.ac.uk
www.cardiffmetsu.co.uk
Affiliation: University Alliance

***The Times and Sunday Times* Rankings**

Overall Ranking: **103** (last year: 90)

Teaching quality:	**89**	79.1%
Student experience:	**=95**	81.8%
Research quality:	**106**	3.9%
Entry standards:	**=77**	317
Student–staff ratio:	**=93**	19
Services & facilities/student:	**67**	£1,712
Expected completion rate:	**=98**	82.2%
Good honours:	**108**	60.6%
Graduate prospects:	**=104**	59.8%

proportion. But the small submission scored well, with 80 per cent of the work rated in the top two categories. Postgraduates and research students make up nearly a quarter of the student population. All six teacher training courses, including the postgraduate pathways, are rated as excellent by Estyn, the school inspectorate.

Students from Wales account for two-thirds of the 8,000 undergraduates. Half of them are from Cardiff or the Vale of Glamorgan. Nearly 95 per cent of the UK undergraduates attended state schools and more than a third come from working-class homes. However, the dropout rate had worsened in the latest survey and, at almost 14 per cent, is higher than the UK average for the university's subjects and entry grades. Around a quarter are mature students and there are over 1,000 are international students. There are also more than 6,500 students studying for Cardiff Met degrees in Bangladesh, Bulgaria, Egypt, Greece, Hong Kong, India, Lebanon, London, Malaysia, Morocco, Serbia, Singapore, South Korea and Sri Lanka. The international partnerships provide an opportunity for students to spend part of their studies abroad.

The two sites in Cardiff are close to the city centre. The Cyncoed campus, housing education and sport, is the main centre of activity, particularly for first years. As well as the new student centre, the athletics centre is there, together with a multitude of outdoor facilities and also the upgraded Welsh Sports Centre for the Disabled. The IT suite has 250 computers available 24 hours a day. The Llandaff campus hosts the School of Management, design, engineering, food science and health courses. The student centre at Llandaff includes a dyslexia support unit among a number of advice and representation services, and a learning centre with more than 300 computers. During term-time, the Rider bus service links all the campuses with other parts of Cardiff. The halls of residence are a mile from the main campus on the Plas Gwyn Residential Campus, where there are enough hall places to accommodate most first years.

Undergraduate Fees and Bursaries

- » Fees for UK/EU students 2016–17 £9,000
- » Welsh Assembly non-means-tested grant (2015–16) to pay fees above £3,810 for Welsh students.
- » Fees for international students 2015–16 £10,200–£11,400
- » For Welsh students from Community First areas with household income below £42.6K, £1,050 package each year.
- » Academic excellence award, sports and hospitality and tourism scholarships, and bursaries for Cardiff residents.
- » Check the university's website for the latest information.

Students

Undergraduates:	**8,145**	**(585)**
Postgraduates:	**3,660**	**(1,005)**
Mature students:	**24%**	
International students:	**16.8%**	
Applications per place:	**4.3**	
From state-sector schools:	**94.4%**	
From working-class homes:	**33.1%**	
Satisfaction with students' union	**67%**	

For information about sports facilities:
www.cardiffmet.ac.uk/about/sport/

Accommodation

Number of places and costs refer to 2015–16
University-provided places: 947
Percentage catered: 34%
Catered cost: £135.50–£148.50 a week during term.
Self-catered costs: £98.00–£104.50 a week.
First-year students have no guarantee; terms and conditions apply.
International students: accommodation is reserved, subject to availability and if conditions are met.
accomm@cardiffmet.ac.uk
www.cardiffmet.ac.uk/accommodation

University of Central Lancashire (UCLan)

Already one of the country's largest universities, with some 30,000 students, UCLan has increased the size of its undergraduate intake by 25 per cent in the last two years. It already dominates the centre of Preston after investing more than £100 million in buildings and equipment. Now a £200-million campus masterplan will allow the university to expand further and upgrade other facilities. It will incorporate green spaces and improve access for pedestrians and cyclists, as well as adding developments such as the £30-million Engineering Innovation Centre that is due to open in 2018. Recent projects have included the £13-million Sir Tom Finney Sports Centre and a £12.5-million building housing the university's forensic science, chemistry and fire courses. The main campus also boasts Europe's largest 3-D lecture theatre and a 24-hour-access library, as well as forensic crime scene houses, a moot court room, a motorsports workshop and child observation lab.

UCLan has always been one of the most enterprising post-1992 universities, teaching dentistry, pharmacy and astrophysics. Now medicine is being offered to international students, on a five-year MBBS programme costing £35,000 a year, in line with the overseas fees at other medical schools. The Dental School was one of the few to open in 100 years, while the architecture degree was the first for a decade. The university also has a branch campus in Cyprus, and was the UK's first post-1992 institution to appear in the QS World University Rankings. A separate rating of teaching, research and facilities by QS gave the university four out of five stars.

The university's roots stretch back to 1828 and it has built a strong reputation in a variety of fields. Its academics work with NASA on solar dynamics, with the Department of Health on sector-leading stroke research, and with the Bill and Melinda Gates Foundation on nutritional science. There are also collaborations with the Football Association, Professional Golfers' Association and International Olympic Committee on sport and exercise science research. There was some world-leading research in all 16 subject areas that were assessed in the 2014 Research Excellence Framework. The Undergraduate Research Internship Scheme enables students from all disciplines to work on research projects for up to ten weeks.

UCLan has a strong focus on entrepreneurship and has established a range of business incubation facilities for its students and graduates. UCLan is consistently in the UK's top three for

Preston
Lancashire PR1 2HE

01772 892400 (course enquiries)
uadmissions@uclan.ac.uk
www.uclan.ac.uk
www.uclansu.co.uk
Affiliation: none

***The Times and Sunday Times* Rankings**

Overall Ranking: **92** (last year: =77)

Teaching quality:	**=73**	80.4%
Student experience:	**=71**	83.5%
Research quality:	**=85**	5.6%
Entry standards:	**=79**	315
Student–staff ratio:	**=65**	17.1
Services & facilities/student:	**=38**	£2,052
Expected completion rate:	**104**	81.6%
Good honours:	**112**	60%
Graduate prospects:	**92**	62.4%

the number of graduate start-ups, with 77 per cent still trading after two years. The university works with a wide variety of industrial partners and many undergraduate programmes are directly linked to them. All students can take advantage of work placements and other opportunities to enhance their employability. Travel bursaries are available for study or work experience abroad, and there is free tuition is a variety of languages, including Arabic, Chinese, Japanese and Russian. The Confucius Institute, on the Preston campus, supports the development of Chinese culture in the North West. More than 500 students have been helped to visit China.

There are over 500 undergraduate programmes and UCLan has extended its four-year Foundation Entry Honours degrees across the majority of its portfolio, providing a route into university for people without traditional qualifications or those returning to education. Always among the leaders in widening participation, the university has another campus in Burnley, giving local students the opportunity to gain qualifications without leaving home. The campus hosts a collaboration with Cisco Systems for advanced manufacturing, incorporating robotics, computer vision, non-destructive testing and component assembly. Nearly 45 per cent of UCLan's undergraduates come from the four lowest socio-economic classes, a high proportion of them local people in their twenties or thirties. Many take external programmes delivered in further education colleges, which have been praised for their quality by assessors.

The university is in the top 30 for environmental performance in the People and Planet Green League and was the first in the UK to install solar trackers. The sports facilities were used as official training venues for the 2012 Olympics and the 2013 Rugby League World Cup. UCLan has nearly 50 teams in the British Universities and Colleges Sport (BUCS) league. Compared with Manchester or Liverpool, the security risks and cost of living are both low, yet Preston is only 50 minutes away from both cities. The students' union, which was ranked in the top three in the North West in 2014, offers a range of sporting clubs, societies and a Give It A Go programme.

Undergraduate Fees and Bursaries

- Fees for UK/EU students 2016–17 £9,000
  - Burnley campus £7,000
  - Degree courses at partner colleges £6,000–£9,000
  - Placement year £900
- Fees for international students 2015–16 £11,450–£12,450
- For students at Preston campus with household income below £20K, £2,000 bursary in year 1; household income £20K–£25K, £1,000.
- Support packages for care leavers and young adult carers.
- Check the university's website for the latest information.

Students

Undergraduates:	**16,605**	**(5,395)**
Postgraduates:	**1,415**	**(3,175)**
Mature students:	**31.7%**	
International students:	**8.3%**	
Applications per place:	**5.5**	
From state-sector schools:	**98.4%**	
From working-class homes:	**43.9%**	
Satisfaction with students' union	**71%**	

For detailed information about sports facilities:
www.uclansu.co.uk/teamuclan

Accommodation

Number of places and costs refer to 2015–16
University-provided places: around 2,200
Percentage catered: 0%
Self-catered costs: £79.03–£83.02 (non en-suite) – £97.37–£99.54 (en suite) a week (42 weeks); £86.87–£107.80 (self-contained flats).
The Student Accommodation Service will assist all first years find suitable accommodation either in university owned/leased halls of residence, private sector registered halls or shared houses.
International students: as above.
www.uclan.ac.uk/accommodation/

University of Chester

Chester opened the UK's first new engineering faculty for two decades in 2014 when it welcomed the first students to its new Thornton Science Park campus near Ellesmere Port. The former Shell research facility, which boasts world-class laboratories and also hosts small and multinational businesses, became the university's fifth campus. A sixth will open this autumn, with the new self-contained Queen's Park Campus in Handbridge, Chester, housing the Business School. The university also has a campus in Warrington and three others in Chester itself. Enrolments have risen for four years in a row, coinciding with record applications, and the university has been investing in new facilities to cater for them. The main refectory has been refurbished, around £3 million has been spent overhauling the university's learning resources centre, and improved sports facilities have cost another £1 million. The latest addition is the £4.8-million Food Science and Technology Innovation Centre, which supports the food industries in Cheshire and the North West.

The university has been celebrating the 175th anniversary of its parent institution, the first purpose-built college for the training of teachers. William Gladstone was among the founders of the Church of England college, which pre-dated all the English universities apart from Oxford, Cambridge, London and Durham. The link with the Church remains, as does the teacher training provision, which has been rated "outstanding" by Ofsted. But there was already a much broader range of courses by the time university status arrived in 2005. Degrees have been designed to support the practical and vocational demands of the professions, with many including an extended period of work experience. There is also a range of Foundation degrees, mainly in health subjects.

The main campus is only a short walk from the centre of Chester, a 32-acre site boasting manicured gardens and a number of new developments. The adjacent Riverside Innovation Centre provides facilities and support for new and growing businesses, including those run by entrepreneurial students and graduates. A second campus is home to the Faculty of Arts and Media, and a third site was added in 2010, following the purchase of the city's historic County Hall, which now houses the faculties of Health and Social Care and Education and Children's Services. The Warrington campus, which has eight halls of residence, focuses on the creative industries and public services. It has high-quality production facilities and the university has links with the BBC in Salford, which opens up new employment opportunities

Parkgate Road
Chester CH1 4BJ

01244 511000 (enquiries)
enquiries@chester.ac.uk
www.chester.ac.uk
www.chestersu.com
Affiliation: Cathedrals Group

***The Times and Sunday Times* Rankings**

Overall Ranking: **87** (last year: 67)

Teaching quality:	**=31**	82.7%
Student experience:	**=68**	83.7%
Research quality:	**=100**	4.1%
Entry standards:	**=101**	299
Student–staff ratio:	**=55**	16.4
Services & facilities/student:	**66**	£1,714
Expected completion rate:	**109**	80.5%
Good honours:	**=96**	63.4%
Graduate prospects:	**=84**	63.6%

for graduates. The library has been tripled in size, and a business centre opened for students and local firms. There is also a venue which regularly attracts up-and-coming acts.

About a quarter of the undergraduates are over 20 on entry and two-thirds are female. Nearly all are state educated, and almost 40 per cent have working-class roots. Progression agreements guarantee interviews to students at a number of local colleges, subject to certain conditions, but there is no reduction in entry requirements. The projected dropout rate has been improving and, at 11 per cent, now matches the national average for the university's courses and entry standards. The university almost doubled the number of submissions made to the 2014 Research Excellent Framework compared with the 2008 assessments. Some research was judged to be world-leading in all but one of the 15 subject areas, but Chester has fallen 20 places in our table this year.

A student contract of the type that is becoming universal in higher education sets out clear conditions on the offer of a place, as well as detailing the university's responsibilities. Students promise to "study diligently, and to attend promptly and participate appropriately at lectures, courses, classes, seminars, tutorials, work placements and other activities which form part of the programme". The university undertakes to deliver the student's programme, but leaves itself considerable leeway beyond that. There are extensive sports facilities at Warrington and especially on the main campus in Chester, where new tennis courts, a 100-metre sprint track and a floodlit 3G multi-use sports pitch have been added. A new hall of residence on the main campus has added more than 200 rooms and another 160 places have been added through the purchase of a former Travelodge, allowing most first-years to be offered university accommodation. In keeping with the university's Christian foundation, there are chapels on two campuses and a number of other faith spaces. Student union facilities form the basis of the social scene on all campuses, but the picturesque city of Chester also has a lot to offer.

Undergraduate Fees and Bursaries

» Fees for UK/EU students 2016–17	£9,000
Foundation degree	£7,650
Foundation degree at partner colleges	£4,995–£7,650
» Fees for international students 2015–16	£10,800

» Household income below £25K, £1,000 cash, year 1; £500, years 2 and 3, pro-rata for part-time students.
» Local students with at least ABB or equivalent with household income below £42.6K, £1,000, year 1; £500, years 2 and 3.
» Care leaver's and young carers bursaries.
» Check the university's website for the latest information.

Students

Undergraduates:	**8,625**	**(2,100)**
Postgraduates:	**1,550**	**(2,465)**
Mature students:	**19.1%**	
International students:	**4.9%**	
Applications per place:	**8**	
From state-sector schools:	**97.5%**	
From working-class homes:	**36.7%**	
Satisfaction with students' union	**78%**	

For detailed information about sports facilities:
www.chestersu.com/sports-societies

Accommodation

Number of places and costs refer to 2015–16
University-provided places: approx 1,442
Percentage catered: 38% (including semi-catered)
Catered costs: £120.70–£157.50 a week.
Self-catered costs: £63.70–£155.00 a week.
First years cannot be guaranteed accommodation.
International students: guaranteed accommodation if they apply by the advertised date.
www.chester.ac.uk/accommodation
accommodation@chester.ac.uk

University of Chichester

Chichester features regularly among the top 20 universities in the National Student Survey, benefiting from the small scale of its two campuses in seaside towns. Nine out of ten students made the university their first choice, and a dropout rate of only 5.5 per cent is less than half the national average for its courses and entry qualifications. Chichester is aiming to be internationally recognised as a "beacon of good practice for high quality, student-centred higher education" by 2020 and is clearly well on the way to achieving that. The smallest of the nine universities created in 2005, it still has fewer than 6,000 students, although that total will rise as the university expands its provision in science and technology. An £8-million grant will fund a new Engineering and Digital Technology Park on the Bognor Regis Campus, adding 500 undergraduate and postgraduate places a year by 2020.

The current portfolio of some 300 courses ranges from adventure education to humanistic counselling, fine art and the psychology of sport and exercise. The PE teacher training course is one of the largest in the country and is highly rated by Ofsted. Chichester achieved university status as one of a new band of institutions that were expected to focus on teaching rather than research. But it was given the power to award research degrees in 2014 and entered a quarter of its eligible staff for the Research Excellence Framework. There were good results in music, drama and performing arts, English and sport.

The university traces its history back to 1839, when the college that subsequently bore his name was founded in memory of William Otter, the education-minded Bishop of Chichester. It became a teacher training college for women, who still account for two-thirds of the places, and eventually merged with the nearby Bognor Regis College of Education. The Chichester campus – now the larger of two – continues to carry the Bishop Otter name, signifying a continuing link with the Church of England. The chapel was refurbished and its surroundings landscaped in 2013. Both campuses have seen improvements recently, carried out in the summer to minimise the inconvenience to students.

In Bognor Regis, the Dome has been transformed into a business and research centre and a new learning resources centre established. The second phase of the university's investment plan aims to bring facilities on the Bishop Otter campus up to the same standard as those in Bognor Regis. The learning resources centre has been overhauled and a coffee shop added. The Alexandra Theatre in Bognor is used as a base for the musical theatre programme and there are links, too, with the Chichester

College Lane
Chichester
W. Sussex PO19 6PE

01243 816000 (admissions)
admissions@chi.ac.uk
www.chi.ac.uk
www.ucsu.org
Affiliations: GuildHE;
Cathedrals Group;

***The Times and Sunday Times* Rankings**

Overall Ranking: **=69** (last year: 65)

Teaching quality:	**12**	84%
Student experience:	**=40**	85.3%
Research quality:	**81**	6.4%
Entry standards:	**=86**	310
Student–staff ratio:	**=71**	17.4
Services & facilities/student:	**118**	£1,194
Expected completion rate:	**=43**	89.9%
Good honours:	**64**	69.3%
Graduate prospects:	**116**	57.5%

Festival Theatre. The Mathematics Centre, at Bognor, has an international reputation, working with over 30 countries as well as teaching the university's own students. It has become a focal point for curriculum development in Britain and elsewhere.

This summer, the music block on the Chichester Campus is being redeveloped to become a three-storey music centre providing high-quality learning and rehearsal space. The construction of a new academic block on the campus is also under way, with completion expected by January 2017. The building will include a multi-use space that may be used for dance or as a cinema or theatre, as well as additional teaching space, IT facilities and a bigger, more modern student union shop.

Residential places are roughly equally divided between the two campuses, enabling Chichester to guarantee accommodation to anyone making the university a firm choice before the January UCAS deadline. There is a university bus service linking the two and there are students' union bars at each. Sports facilities are good and the university was chosen to provide training facilities before the 2012 Olympic Games. Since then, a sports dome has been added to the existing tennis courts to provide an all-weather, multi-sport facility, and a new running track has been installed. The Tudor Hale Centre for Sport includes state-of-the-art laboratories, a refurbished fitness suite, sport injury clinic and teaching clinic. The university also runs a Gifted Athlete Programme, which has supported a Commonwealth judo champion and a potential 2016 Olympic sailor, among others. The small cathedral city of Chichester is best known as a yachting venue, and Bognor is said to have the longest stretch of coastline in the south where all types of water sports are available. Both offer a good supply of private housing and some student-oriented bars. Much of the surrounding countryside has been designated an area of outstanding natural beauty.

Undergraduate Fees and Bursaries

- Fees for UK/EU students 2016–17 £9,000
  Placement year £1,800
- Fees for international students 2015–16 £10,250–£11,700
- Household income below £42K, £1,000 cash bursary year 1; £500, years 2 and 3.
- Range of other scholarships and bursaries available.
- Check the university's website for the latest information.

Students

Undergraduates:	**4,310**	**(480)**
Postgraduates:	**350**	**(495)**
Mature students:	**14.9%**	
International students:	**2.4%**	
Applications per place:	**5.1**	
From state-sector schools:	**96.9%**	
From working-class homes:	**33.2%**	
Satisfaction with students' union	**75%**	

For detailed information about sports facilities:
www.ucsu.org/sports-societies/susport/

Accommodation

Number of places and costs refer to 2015–16
University-provided places: 751
Percentage catered: 58%
Catered costs: £143.29 (single) – £160.79 (single, en suite) a week.
Self-catered costs: £96.18 (single) – £147.07 (en suite) a week.
All catered and self-catered rooms available either 37 or 40 weeks.
First years applying by deadline and then making Chichester first choice are guaranteed accommodation.
International students: as above.
www.chi.ac.uk/study-us-0/accommodation

City University London

City will be part of the University of London by the time new entrants arrive in 2016. City will continue to set its own entrance requirements and award its own degrees, but will become one of the 18 autonomous colleges within the federal university. Professor Paul Curran, the Vice-Chancellor, said the move would strengthen City's international profile and expand its research and education capabilities. City has been marketing itself as the "international university in the heart of London" and added the name of the capital to its title to make the most of its greatest asset. Once a college of advanced technology, the university now has more than a quarter of its students taking business courses, and nearly as many taking health and community subjects, with the remainder studying law, computing, mathematics, engineering, journalism and the arts. It has declared an intention to "rebalance" its undergraduate intake, focusing on the university's strengths in business and law, largely at the expense of health subjects, and has been increasing its average entry qualifications while doing so.

The university has also been recruiting strongly to improve its research performance, although it entered little more than half of its eligible academics in the 2014 assessments. Three-quarters of its submission to the 2014 Research Excellence Framework was rated as world-leading or internationally excellent, with music and business producing the best results. The Cass Business School is one of City's great strengths, ranking among the top 50 business schools in the world. Based in the heart of the financial district, it has built up an impressive cadre of visiting practitioner lecturers who find it easy and convenient to visit. The City Law School was the first in London to offer a "one-stop shop" for legal training, from undergraduate to professional courses. The School of Journalism, within the School of Arts, is highly regarded and the university has launched the UK's first graduate school of journalism in £12-million premises. There is a flourishing short course programme which ranges from sitcom writing to e-business.

City's Northampton Square campus has been rejuvenated and another £130 million of refurbishment and new developments are planned over the next four years. The library has been renovated at a cost of £2.3 million, giving students more space, upgraded technology and better support. The Student Centre and Careers Centre have been refurbished and a new common room added. The School of Law has been upgraded and the School of Health Sciences has moved to the main campus with new facilities, including a new biomedical and

Northampton Square
London EC1V 0HB

020 7040 5060
enquiries@city.ac.uk
www.city.ac.uk
www.culsu.co.uk
Affiliation: none

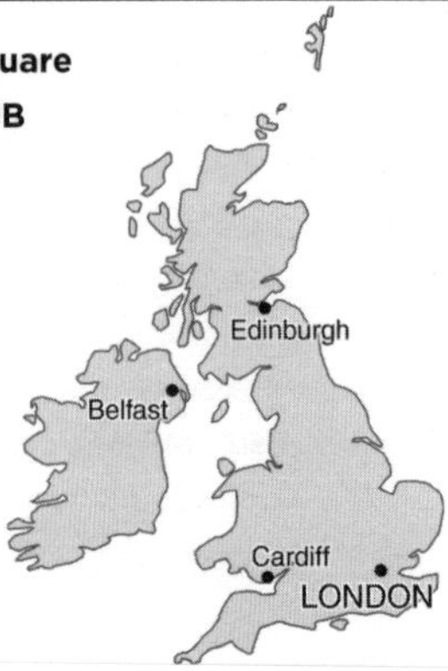

***The Times and Sunday Times* Rankings**

Overall Ranking: **=41** (last year: 46)

Teaching quality:	**=31**	82.7%
Student experience:	**=35**	85.6%
Research quality:	**53**	21.4%
Entry standards:	**41**	379
Student–staff ratio:	**52**	16.1
Services & facilities/student:	**22**	£2,368
Expected completion rate:	**=63**	86%
Good honours:	**49**	73.8%
Graduate prospects:	**25**	78.9%

clinical skills centre. The students' union is popular and the Student Centre, which provides advice on a range of topics, is the only one in the UK to be recognised by the Institute of Customer Service.

Both applications and enrolments have grown in each of the last two years, and City attracts international students from more than 160 countries. City has links with 50 European universities and many more further afield, and many students spend a year of their course abroad. There is a range of scholarships worth up to £3,000 a year for students who achieve exceptional grades at A level, International Baccalaureate or other qualifications. There are over 18,000 students, 46 per cent of them postgraduates – one of the highest proportions in the UK. City also remains among the most popular universities at undergraduate level, with 10.5 applications for each place. The university has also increased its part-time numbers, against the national trend, with many students taking short courses that do not lead to a formal qualification. City has a better record than most of its peer group for widening participation in higher education, with over 46 per cent of its undergraduates coming from low-income groups.

The university has strong links with business and the professions, and reaps the benefits with consistently good graduate employment figures. Courses have a practical edge, and many of the staff hold professional, as well as academic, qualifications. Six interdisciplinary centres have been launched to increase collaborative teaching and research, as well as to build stronger links between industry and academia. The redeveloped sports centre, between the campus and the business school, has seen much-needed improvements. The 3,000 square metres of floor space at CitySport is available to students, staff and the local community. At its heart is the Saddlers Sport Hall, which meets Sport England standards and has seating for up to 400 spectators, and the centre also has a separate fitness area.

Undergraduate Fees and Bursaries

- Fees for UK/EU students 2016–17 £9,000
- Fees for international students 2015–16 £13,000–£16,500
- For English students with household income below £42.6K, annual bursaries of £800–£1,400.
- Mature students with household income under £42.6K, £1,000 a year.
- Limited number of university accommodation bursaries of £2,000 a year.
- Lord Mayor of London Scholarship, from £1,000 a year for ABB at A Level or equivalent to £3,000 a year for at least A*AA (subject dependent).
- Other scholarships and bursaries available.
- Check the university's website for the latest information.

Students

Undergraduates:	**8,100**	**(1,545)**
Postgraduates:	**6,050**	**(2,450)**
Mature students:	**19.8%**	
International students:	**34.3%**	
Applications per place:	**10.5**	
From state-sector schools:	**92.3%**	
From working-class homes:	**46.2%**	
Satisfaction with students' union	**62%**	

For detailed information about sports facilities:
www.city.ac.uk/sport-and-leisure

Accommodation

Number of places and costs refer to 2015–16
University-provided places: 1,345 through private providers
Percentage catered: 0%
Self-catered costs: £140–£190 a week.
Accommodation is guaranteed for first-year undergraduates if conditions are met. Residential restrictions apply.
International students: guaranteed if conditions are met.
accomm@city.ac.uk
www.city.ac.uk/study/undergraduate/accommodation

Coventry University

Last year, Coventry achieved the highest ever position in our league table by a post-1992 university, and it remains ahead of its peer group, as well as ten older foundations. It was *The Times and Sunday Times* "Modern University of the Year" in 2014 and is again in 2015. Coventry's rise has been spectacular: ten years ago it was 41 places lower and only 12 off the bottom of the table. Much of its success is due to student satisfaction ratings that are among the highest in the country, but it has shown ambition in a number of areas. It was among the first provincial universities to offer courses in London and took its rivals by surprise by opening its own no-frills university college when £9,000 fees were introduced in 2012. Now it is developing a campus in Scarborough, which opens in September 2016 as part of a new £45-million sports and education facility.

Not surprisingly, applications rose by 12 per cent in 2014 and the size of its undergraduate intake increased by 580 students as the university entered the top 50. Students like the guaranteed return of marked work within ten days and the opportunity to make their own assessments of academics, who receive awards for excellent teaching. The Centre for Academic Writing offers advice on essays and theses, while the Maths Support Centre includes a statistics advisory service and specialist support service for dyslexics. Coventry halved the number of degree programmes it offers in order to focus on the most popular, successful courses and produce a well-designed and coherent portfolio. It has embraced computer-assisted learning, supported by an expanded computer network, and prioritised employability through the Add+vantage scheme. Its modules cover a wide range of skills and help students gain work-related knowledge and prepare for a career. The Institute for Applied Entrepreneurship (IAE) helps students and small firms to start up and grow a business.

The university traces its origins back to 1843, and is spending £150 million to rejuvenate its 33-acre campus close to the city centre. Much of the ten-year programme involves student facilities such as the showcase turreted library, which cost £20 million. A new £55-million engineering and computing building includes a dedicated ethical hacking lab, an ex-RAF Harrier Jump Jet and a wind-tunnel built by the Mercedes F1 team, all of which are used by undergraduates. The Hub contains the students' union, a music venue, plenty of informal study space, shops and restaurants. There is a £60-million health building, and other recent projects have included more residential accommodation, an arts

Priory Street
Coventry CV1 5FB

024 7765 2222 (admissions)
studentenquiries@coventry.ac.uk
www.coventry.ac.uk
www.cusu.org
Affiliation: University Alliance

***The Times and Sunday Times* Rankings**

Overall Ranking: **47** (last year: 42)

Teaching quality:	**2**	87.6%
Student experience:	**=3**	89.3%
Research quality:	**=107**	3.8%
Entry standards:	**=86**	310
Student–staff ratio:	**31**	14.6
Services & facilities/student:	**62**	£1,732
Expected completion rate:	**=68**	85.8%
Good honours:	**=74**	67.4%
Graduate prospects:	**45**	74.2%

centre and a sports centre. The Institute for Advanced Manufacturing and Engineering has a new bespoke "Faculty on the Factory Floor" unit at Unipart's Coventry manufacturing site. Undergraduate and postgraduate programmes in manufacturing engineering have been designed to provide students with an academic learning environment blended with access to real industry projects.

The university college is on the main campus and caters for students who do not require the full range of services. Its courses lead to Coventry degrees or diplomas, but fees in 2016 will be below £7,000 for engineering degrees and less than £6,000 for classroom-based subjects. The London campus, which opened in 2013, is business-oriented and mainly for international students. A degree in global business management includes a workplace project and a period of study abroad, while one-year top-up programmes give international students entry into the final year of a BA degree. The new Coventry University Scarborough campus is being developed in partnership with the borough council and a number of businesses. The site will include a library, engineering and science laboratories, a mock law court and social space. Coventry is also investing to increase its research capacity, but its results in the 2014 Research Excellence Framework were in sharp contrast to those for student satisfaction.

The university is in the bottom ten for research quality, having entered only 13 per cent of its eligible academics for assessment. Over 60 per cent of their work was considered world-leading or internationally excellent, with health subjects producing 94 per cent at this level.

Over 40 per cent of the undergraduates have working-class backgrounds, and almost all attended state schools. The dropout rate is better than the national average for the university's courses and entry qualifications. Student residences are within easy walking distance of the campus and city centre. Students in Coventry welcome the relatively low cost of living there, and the city is not short of student-oriented nightlife.

Undergraduate Fees and Bursaries

- Fees for UK/EU students 2016–17 — £8,581–£9,000
  Foundation degree — £5,570
  Courses provided by Coventry University College and Scarborough Campus — £5,835–£6,896
- Fees for international students 2015–16 — £10,766–£12,871
- Scholarship of £1,000 a year for students from low participation areas.
- Scholarships for sporting excellence and exceptional academic achievement.
- Check the university's website for the latest information.

Students

Undergraduates:	**17,190**	**(3,120)**
Postgraduates:	**3,220**	**(2,100)**
Mature students:	**17.9%**	
International students:	**24.2%**	
Applications per place:	**7.2**	
From state-sector schools:	**97.4%**	
From working-class homes:	**40.9%**	
Satisfaction with students' union	**79%**	

For detailed information about sports facilities:
www.coventry.ac.uk/life-on-campus/student-life/sport-coventry/

Accommodation

Number of places and costs refer to 2015–16
University-provided places: 3,054 (includes 1,160 beds on Nomination Agreements)
Percentage catered: 14%
Catered costs: £136 (38 weeks).
Self-catered costs: £105–£135 (40–44 weeks).
First years are guaranteed housing provided conditions are met.
International students: as above.
accomm.ss@coventry.ac.uk; www.coventry.ac.uk/study-at-coventry/student-support/accommodation/

University for the Creative Arts (UCA)

Already sizeable by the standards of a specialist university with more than 5,000 students, UCA added a drama school in autumn 2015. A new BA (Hons) acting and performance course is being launched with Farnham Maltings, where students will have access to a network of theatre professionals, as well as performance and rehearsal spaces, and a screening room. Farnham houses one of the four campuses across Kent and Surrey, where two well-established art colleges came together to form the university. The constituent colleges all date back to Victorian times. The location of each is given in the map below: Canterbury (1), Epsom (2), Farnham (3) and Rochester (4).

The largest of the three Kent campuses, at Rochester, offers a full range of art and design, including fashion, photography and specialist design courses. The purpose-built campus is set on a hillside overlooking the city centre and River Medway. Halls of residence with 214 places are close to the campus, which has studio space, library and learning resource centre, and a gallery. Students taking UCA's popular media courses, who use studios in Maidstone at the largest independent studio complex in the UK, also have access the facilities of the Rochester campus. Degrees in interactive media production and media business management were added to the renamed existing degree in television production for 2015.

At Canterbury, the accent is on architecture, but there are also degrees in fine art, interior design and more general art and design. The modern site is close to the city centre and contains purpose-built studios, workshops and lecture theatres. The Canterbury School of Architecture is the only such school to remain within a specialist art and design institution, encouraging collaboration between student architects, designers and fine artists.

By far the largest enrolment is at Farnham, in Surrey, which was declared a Craft Town in 2013, with active support from the university. More than 2,000 students take courses in art, design, cinematics, communications – and now drama there. A purpose-built student village in the centre of town has 350 rooms and there are two galleries, as well as teaching space and a library and learning centre. The campus includes research centres in animation, crafts and sustainable design. Courses range from pre-degree Foundation courses in art and design to degrees in film production, sports journalism and three-dimensional design. A new suite of media and creative writing courses was launched in 2014. Additional facilities have been provided for

UCA Canterbury
New Dover Road
Canterbury
CT1 3AN

01252 892883 (enquiries)
enquiries@ucreative.ac.uk
www.ucreative.ac.uk
http://ucasu.com
Affiliation: GuildHE

***The Times and Sunday Times* Rankings**

Overall Ranking: =**62** (last year: 74)

Teaching quality:	**=31**	82.7%
Student experience:	**=99**	81.5%
Research quality:	**111**	3.4%
Entry standards:	**=61**	332
Student–staff ratio:	**10**	11.7
Services & facilities/student:	**33**	£2,122
Expected completion rate:	**=68**	85.8%
Good honours:	**=109**	60.4%
Graduate prospects:	**125**	52%

the growing computer games arts degree course, which now has a dedicated studio room with specialist computers.

The second base in Surrey, at Epsom, specialises in fashion, graphics and new media, although it offers general art and design courses at further education level. Degrees include music journalism and fashion promotion and imaging. There is a modern library and learning resource centre for more than 1,200 students, a bar and café on campus and three halls of residence. A new £5.9-million teaching block includes learning and resource facilities, a 200-seat auditorium and a digital media centre. Photovoltaic cells on the roof and solar water heating will ensure that at least 20 per cent of the energy it uses is generated on site.

The university offers four-year degrees, incorporating a Foundation year, as well as the three-year format, and two-year Foundation degrees, which can be topped up to produce honours. UCA's courses are also taught in five partner colleges, including one in India. Dr Simon Ofield-Kerr, the Vice-Chancellor, plans to increase international student numbers, while also maintaining UCA's local roots. All the students will be "required" to develop international perspectives, understanding and ambitions so that they are able to practise across the world. Collaboration between courses is encouraged, so that students benefit from exposure to a range of disciplines. Results in the National Student Survey have been poor in all eight years of polling, as they have been for art and design in most universities. But almost two-thirds of the university's small submission to the Research Excellence Framework was rated world-leading or internationally excellent and 90 per cent was placed in the top two categories for its impact.

Many staff are practitioners as well as academics, and the colleges have produced a string of famous graduates, such as Tracey Emin, Karen Millen and Zandra Rhodes, who has now become the university's Chancellor. Other high-profile alumni include the jeweller Stephen Webster, Oscar-winning animators Michael Dudok de Wit and Suzie Templeton, artists Humphrey Ocean and Tacita Dean, and textile designer Roger Oates.

Undergraduate Fees and Bursaries

- » Fees for UK/EU students 2016–17 £9,000
- » Fees for international students 2015–16 £11,870
- » Household income up to £25K, £600 bursary a year.
- » Internal progression bursaries to degree courses and creative scholarships available
- » Check the university's website for the latest information.

Students

Undergraduates:	**4,765**	**(60)**
Postgraduates:	**155**	**(100)**
Mature students:	**15.5%**	
International students:	**10.5%**	
Applications per place:	**5.3**	
From state-sector schools:	**97.6%**	
From working-class homes:	**41.5%**	
Satisfaction with students' union	**57%**	

For detailed information about sports facilities: http://ucasu.com/clubs

Accommodation

Places and costs refer to 2015–16
University-provided places: 969
Percentage catered: 0%
Self catered costs: £66.69 (twin); £117.23–£121.97 (single); £122.35–£133.93 (en suite) a week (39 weeks).
Priority is given to disabled students (new and returning) and new full-time students by distance.
International students: guaranteed housing if application received by mid June.
www.ucreative.ac.uk/uca-accommodation

University of Cumbria

Cumbria's focus since its establishment in 2007 has been on attracting more students from a region of unusually low participation in higher education, as well as on serving the social and economic needs of the county. Almost all the undergraduates are state educated, four in ten are from working-class homes and the proportion from areas without a tradition of higher education is one of the highest in England, at one in five. The university is spending £1.2 million to develop new degrees in science, technology, engineering and mathematics (STEM) subjects and a high-spec laboratory in Carlisle because there is still no provision at this level within Cumbria in mainstream STEM subjects such as biology and chemistry. The first three new courses are being launched in 2015 in biology, zoology and marine and fresh water conservation. For 2016, new courses will be added in chemistry, biomedical science and other related areas. Overall, applications have been rising and are almost back to the record level reached in 2012.

The university now operates on five sites in Cumbria, although the largest single campus is in Lancaster. There are two campuses in Carlisle and one in Workington, as well as a university centre at Furness College, in Barrow. Nearly a third of first years are 21 or over, and only a quarter come from Cumbria itself. There are partnerships with the four further education colleges in the county to provide higher education locally. The university was finally established after a series of false starts, formed by the amalgamation of a former teacher training college and an arts institute, with the addition of two campuses acquired from the University of Central Lancashire. It has reopened one of the UK's most attractive campuses, in the Lake District setting of Ambleside, mainly as the base for the country's largest programme of outdoor education degrees. The former college site had been mothballed as a result of financial difficulties that have now been overcome. The transfer of courses from Newton Rigg, near Penrith, is part of a ten-year estates plan. Another element saw the university's London campus move to a new site on the doorstep of Canary Wharf in 2013. The Education Faculty has been helping schools and training teachers in East London for more than 15 years.

The university's headquarters are in Carlisle, where the larger of the two sites is in a parkland setting close to the River Eden. The second campus, closer to the city centre, boasts a new Learning Gateway, an innovative multimedia learning resource centre, and a sports centre with a four-court sports hall and well-equipped fitness room. The former Cumbria Institute of the Arts

Fusehill Street
Carlisle, Cumbria CA1 2HH

0845 606 1144 (enquiries)
enquirycentre@cumbria.ac.uk
www.cumbria.ac.uk
www.ucsu.me
Affiliations: million+;
Cathedrals Group

***The Times and Sunday Times* Rankings**

Overall Ranking: **119** (last year: 95)

Teaching quality:	**=111**	76.9%
Student experience:	**122**	77.6%
Research quality:	**122**	1.2%
Entry standards:	**=101**	299
Student-staff ratio:	**123**	22.3
Services & facilities/student:	**120**	£1,093
Expected completion rate:	**=71**	85.7%
Good honours:	**90**	64.7%
Graduate prospects:	**=77**	64.9%

can trace its history in Carlisle back to 1822, eventually becoming the only specialist institute of the arts in the North West, and one of only a small number of such institutions in the country. The creative arts are one of the main areas earmarked for development and produced by far the best results in the 2014 Research Excellence Framework (REF), with 90 per cent of the submission judged to have world-leading or internationally excellent impact. Overall, Cumbria is just two places off the bottom of our research ranking, having entered only 27 academics for the REF, 8 per cent of those eligible. Almost 30 per cent of their work was placed in the top two categories.

There are more than 4,500 students in Lancaster, at the former St Martin's College, which was founded by the Church of England in 1964. It is a ten-minute walk from Lancaster town centre. The centrepiece is the Gateway, a £9.2-million development which provides a range of student services. There is also a modern library and excellent sports facilities, including a £2.5-million sports complex, gymnastics centre and fitness centre. The university is one of the largest teacher training providers in England, and has relaunched its business school with an emphasis on programmes in areas of particular strength, such as small- and medium-sized enterprises, ethics and leadership, and sustainability. Business interaction centres in Carlisle and Ambleside support business development and student entrepreneurship.

The Ambleside campus has been refurbished and new amenities provided in conjunction with the Lake District National Park Authority. Research has restarted there and the campus will host more business and enterprise activity, as well as some new courses and outdoor education degrees. The Institute for Leadership and Sustainability (IFLAS), which is part of the business school, is developing a portfolio of activities that make the best use of its unique setting.

Undergraduate Fees and Bursaries

- » Fees for UK/EU students 2016–17 £9,000
  Foundation degree £7,000–£9,000
- » Fees for international students 2015–16 £10,500–£15,500
- » For household income below £25K, up to 240 bursaries of £1,000 a year; up to 50 bursaries of £1,000 a year for students entering at foundation year; up to 21 part-time bursaries of £500 a year.
- » Up to 8 progression scholarships for students from partner colleges of £500 a year.
- » Check the university's website for the latest information.

Students

Undergraduates:	**5,770**	**(1,925)**
Postgraduates:	**905**	**(1,025)**
Mature students:	**29.6%**	
International students:	**1.4%**	
Applications per place:	**5.2**	
From state-sector schools:	**98.3%**	
From working-class homes:	**42.3%**	
Satisfaction with students' union	**54%**	

For detailed information about sports facilities:
www.cumbria.ac.uk/StudentLife/Sport

Accommodation

Number of places and costs refer to 2015–16
University-provided places: 1,000
Percentage catered: 20%
Catered costs: £74.10–£110.00 a week (plus catering plan).
Self-catered costs: £64.65–£110.00 a week.
First year are guaranteed halls accommodation if Cumbria is first choice.
International students: guaranteed halls accommodation if conditions are met.
www.cumbria.ac.uk/StudentLife/Accommodation/

De Montfort University

De Montfort University Leicester (DMU) is aiming to provide the most comprehensive programme of overseas study at any UK university in order to expand its students' cultural horizons and make them employable across the world. From autumn 2015, every undergraduate course will include at least one module that offers an international experience through a network of overseas universities and businesses. The #DMUglobal programme is aiming to give 11,000 students – more than half of the current total – courses, internships or fieldwork overseas by 2020. There are already strong links with business and industry, such as the partnerships with Hewlett-Packard and Deloitte, which support innovative educational programmes, as well as research collaborations.

DMU achieved the biggest rise of any university in last year's table, jumping 32 places. Work has begun on striking new buildings for some of DMU's best-known schools: Fashion and Textiles, Arts, Design, and Architecture. The Fletcher Complex, which should be complete in 2016, will be the latest phase of a £136-million "campus transformation project" which will include an upgraded students' union, improved catering facilities, and a "green lung" at the heart of the campus, producing more outdoor social space. The work has been partly funded through one of the first investment bonds issued to a post-1992 university. The university has already spent more than £140-million concentrating all its activities on its Leicester headquarters, when once it stretched from Bedford to Lincoln via Milton Keynes.

Other campus developments have included the diversion of part of the ring road to allow the university to open up the 15th-century Magazine Gateway building, now a focal point of a university quarter with public open spaces and new links to the city centre. The £35-million Hugh Aston Building catering for around 6,000 students, includes a court room, law library, dedicated law clinic and bookshop, as well as more conventional teaching facilities. Elsewhere, the 24-hour library was remodelled with wireless networks and rooms equipped with audio visual and IT facilities, and new games development studios have been installed to enable students to see their work in 3-D. An £8-million leisure centre includes a 25-metre swimming pool and an eight-court sports hall.

Almost 60 per cent of DMU's research activities were judged to be world-leading or internationally excellent according to the 2014 Research Excellence Framework, the UK-wide initiative to assess the quality of research in UK universities. Home to more than 60 specialist research groups and

The Gateway
Leicester LE1 9BH

0116 250 6070 (enquiries)
contact via website
www.dmu.ac.uk
www.demontfortstudents.com
Affiliation: none

***The Times and Sunday Times* Rankings**

Overall Ranking: **53** (last year: 54)

Teaching quality:	**=41**	82.4%
Student experience:	**=49**	84.6%
Research quality:	**=67**	8.9%
Entry standards:	**=91**	307
Student–staff ratio:	**91**	18.7
Services & facilities/student:	**51**	£1,924
Expected completion rate:	**59**	86.5%
Good honours:	**58**	70.9%
Graduate prospects:	**35**	76.9%

institutes, the university focuses on "real world" research such as solar powered housing, hospital infection control, housing policy research and participation in the £1-billion EU project to simulate a human brain. A multimillion pound investment has enhanced the university's excellent creative technology studios, which feature video, audio and radio production suites, as well as recording studios and laboratories with the latest broadcast and audio analysis technology. A Performance Arts Centre for Excellence allows the university to deliver innovative teaching for students of dance, drama and music technology.

Four further education colleges across the East Midlands are associates. Leicester College, Henley College, North Warwickshire and Hinckley College and Confetti ICT are linked into DMU's network and offer its Foundation degrees and other courses. The university has a proud record for widening access to higher education, with more than 40 per cent of undergraduates coming from working-class homes. It was one of the first to set up an employment agency to help students find part-time work as well as find careers upon graduation. De Montfort also has a strong reputation for the support it gives to disabled students. The university offers students the opportunity to participate in the award-winning Square Mile programme, which uses DMU's academic expertise and a network of student volunteers to offer potentially life-changing services to the local community, as well as national and international projects. These have included free support for primary and secondary schools in the city, a successful diabetes screening programme, a campaign to recruit people to the national stem cell register, and a development project in India. The dropout rate has improved consistently: at less than 10 per cent, it is now significantly lower than the national average for the university's courses and entry grades.

Leicester has become a more vibrant location, and has recently benefited from a £3-billion regeneration project. Rents in the private sector are low and the university has more than 2,300 rooms in halls within walking distance of the city centre.

Undergraduate Fees and Bursaries

» Fees for UK/EU students 2016–17	£9,000
Foundation degree	£6,000
Placement year / year abroad	£650
» Degree courses at partner colleges	£6,000–£7,950
» Fees for international students 2015–16	£11,750–£12,250

- » Vice-Chancellor's Fund: academic scholarships of £1,000 a year and bursaries of £200 a year; bursaries of £1,000 a year for students on access courses.
- » Range of bursaries of £1,000 a year to help vulnerable groups of students.
- » Vice-Chancellor's 2020 scholarship: 50% discount on fees for master's degrees for students graduating with 2:1 or higher undergraduate degree.

Students

Undergraduates:	**14,655**	**(1,755)**
Postgraduates:	**940**	**(2,295)**
Mature students:	**20.8%**	
International students:	**10.5%**	
Applications per place:	**5.5**	
From state-sector schools:	**97.5%**	
From working-class homes:	**42.1%**	
Satisfaction with students' union	**75%**	

For information about sports facilities:
www.demontfortstudents.com/getinvolved/sports/

Accommodation

Number of places and costs refer to 2015–16
University-provided places: around 2,300
Percentage catered: 0%
Self-catered costs: £89 (standard) – £157 (studio) a week (38–43 weeks).
First years cannot be guaranteed accommodation.
International students: new students are guaranteed housing.
accommodation@dmu.ac.uk
www.dmu.ac.uk/study/undergraduate-study/accommodation/

University of Derby

Derby guarantees that 85 per cent of its classes contain fewer than 30 students and that undergraduates can have access to their personal tutor whenever they need it. In an age when contact hours and staff feedback are hot topics, both are significant. The university has student representatives on all its senior management committees – another aspect of its focus on student needs, which has taken it into the top ten for teaching quality in the National Student Survey. The Institute for Learning Enhancement and Innovation works with academic staff to ensure that students receive the best possible learning experience. The university's emphasis on "real world learning" is underlined by facilities that include a simulated hospital and working radiography suite; industry standard kitchens and a fine dining restaurant; computer games suites; a commercial spa and salon; a law court and sports science gym and a 58-acre Outdoor Leadership Centre.

A £75-million programme is creating a University Quarter for the city of Derby. The latest addition is a striking copper office block that has been vacant since it was completed in 2013, but will now house the law school. By 2017, there will also be a £12-million building nearby for science, technology, engineering and maths, financed partly through a funding council grant. The Markeaton Street site currently hosts arts, design, engineering and technology courses, while courses in health and social care are based at Britannia Mill, ten minutes' walk away. The university's main campus is two miles from the city centre, and caters for most of the main subjects including business, computing, science, humanities, education and law. The students' union, multi-faith centre and main sports facilities are on this site, which also houses clinical skills facilities, including a purpose-built iDXA suite, opened in 2014. The three bases are linked by free shuttle buses and the UniBus service, which also connects with the train station and city centre. The university also owns and runs the 550-seat Derby Theatre in the city centre, which houses theatre arts programmes as well as continuing as a producing theatre.

Beyond its home city, the university teaches nursing in Chesterfield and has a campus in Buxton that is based in the former Devonshire Royal Hospital and offers courses in spa, outdoor recreation and hospitality management, as well as further education programmes. The landmark building houses a training restaurant, a beauty salon and a health spa, as well as more conventional teaching facilities. The UK's only degree in ecotourism was launched there in 2013, while a Foundation

Kedleston Road
Derby DE22 1GB

01332 591167 (enquiries)
askadmissions@derby.ac.uk
www.derby.ac.uk
www.udsu.co.uk
Affiliation: none

***The Times and Sunday Times* Rankings**

Overall Ranking: **84** (last year: 81)

Teaching quality:	**=9**	84.4%
Student experience:	**=40**	85.3%
Research quality:	**115**	2.5%
Entry standards:	**107**	290
Student–staff ratio:	**45**	15.4
Services & facilities/student:	**87**	£1,540
Expected completion rate:	**=86**	83.7%
Good honours:	**101**	62.7%
Graduate prospects:	**103**	60%

degree in spa management is also taught in London, at the London School of Beauty and Make-up. A new sports centre opened in Buxton in 2012.

The university entered only 19 per cent of its eligible academics for the 2014 Research Excellence Framework, when almost 30 per cent of its submission reached one of the top two categories. Business engagement is a higher priority. The Institute for Innovation in Sustainable Engineering, for example, supports advanced manufacturing with 3-D printing and advanced testing, and other work with industrial partners such as Rolls Royce. A University Technical College opens in autumn 2015 for students aged between 14 and 19, with a focus on manufacturing, and Rolls Royce again is among the partners. Derby is also working with the Association of Chartered Certified Accountants, the Association of Accounting Technicians and Sage to offer a Higher Apprenticeship Degree as a route to a professional accounting qualification.

Almost 40 per cent of undergraduates are from working-class homes and 20 per cent come from areas of low participation in higher education – well above the national average for the courses and entry qualifications. Derby claims to award more work-based qualifications than any other UK university, while a Foundation programme allows students to start a course at a partner college before transferring to the university. Business and management is much the biggest academic area, but work placements are encouraged in all relevant subjects. The "Skillbuilder" career development programme covers a range of transferable skills to assist graduates in the employment market. Derby is at the forefront of developing a Higher Education Achievement Record that students can make available electronically to prospective employers. Distance learning is a growth area, either online or through Derby's nine regional centres. Prospective students can even sample a virtual open evening.

The university spent £30 million in five years to maintain its guarantee of accommodation for all first years and has improved student facilities. A new £10-million sports centre is due to open on the main campus by the end of 2015.

Undergraduate Fees and Bursaries

- » Fees for UK/EU students 2016–17 £9,000
  Placement year £1,000
- » Fees for international students 2015–16 £10,900–£11,725
- » Household income up to £25K, bursary of £1,000 a year; household income £25K–£36.6K, £600 a year.
- » Bursary for students from Buxton and Leek Colleges.
- » Range of other scholarships and bursaries available.
- » Check the university's website for the latest information.

Students

Undergraduates:	**10,120**	**(3,240)**
Postgraduates:	**815**	**(2,005)**
Mature students:	**22.9%**	
International students:	**8.8%**	
Applications per place:	**6.5**	
From state-sector schools:	**98.1%**	
From working-class homes:	**37.1%**	
Satisfaction with students' union	**64%**	

For detailed information about sports facilities:
www.teamderby.com

Accommodation

Number of places and costs refer to 2015–16
University-provided places: 2,500
Percentage catered: 0%
Self-catered costs: £96.67 (standard) – £117.32 (en suite plus).
First-year students are guaranteed accommodation if they apply by the specified date.
Policy for international students: as above.
studentliving-housingteam@derby.ac.uk
www.derby.ac.uk/campus/accommodation

University of Dundee

Dundee's reputation as a leader in the life sciences has been enhanced with strong results in the 2014 Research Excellence Framework (REF), which placed the university top for biological sciences, and by the opening of the £50-million Discovery Centre to encourage interaction between different disciplines. Dundee had already received a Queen's Anniversary Prize for the achievements of its Centre for Anatomy and Human Identification. But the university's successes are not confined to the life sciences: for the sixth successive year it was the top university in Scotland in *Times Higher Education* (*THE*) magazine's student experience survey, its central facilities voted the best in the UK. *THE* rates it among the top 20 universities in the world founded in the last 50 years.

The university has completed a £200-million campus redevelopment designed by the leading architect, Sir Terry Farrell. Among the buildings added in recent years are those for clinical research, interdisciplinary research and applied computing. There have been extensions to the library and the sports centre, while almost £40 million was spent on wireless-networked student residences. The IT facilities include superfast broadband and are among the best in the UK, allowing the latest technologies to be used to enhance teaching. The university doubled in size over two decades and there are now more than 15,000 students, including a healthy number from overseas. Dundee has been looking outwards to achieve the "critical mass" which experts regard as essential to break into the higher education elite, with the acquisition of education, nursing and art colleges, which have greatly increased its scope. But it resisted ministerial encouragement to amalgamate with Abertay Dundee University in 2012.

Flagship work in the life sciences and medicine is led by research into cancer and diabetes. The new Discovery Centre is an annexe of the College of Life Sciences, which already benefits from the £13-million Wellcome Trust Building and the Sir James Black Centre, which cost £21 million. Its academics were the first in Britain to be invited to take part in Japan's Human Frontier science programme and are now the most-quoted researchers in their field. Set in 20 acres of parkland, the medical school is the one of the few components of the university outside the compact city-centre campus – some of the nursing and midwifery students are 35 miles away in Kirkcaldy.

Other successes in the REF assessments included civil engineering, which came in the top three in the UK, and maths and general engineering, which were both in the

Nethergate
Dundee DD1 4HN

01382 383838 (enquiries)
contact via website
www.dundee.ac.uk
www.dusa.co.uk
Affiliation: none

***The Times and Sunday Times* Rankings**

Overall Ranking: **37** (last year: 45)

Teaching quality:	**=9**	84.4%
Student experience:	**17**	87.1%
Research quality:	**41**	31.2%
Entry standards:	**31**	410
Student–staff ratio:	**=26**	13.9
Services & facilities/student:	**=85**	£1,545
Expected completion rate:	**=63**	86%
Good honours:	**35**	76.1%
Graduate prospects:	**19**	80%

top ten. The university leads one of four "knowledge exchange hubs for the creative economy", tasked with bringing academics together with business and charities, and raising public awareness of the creative industries. The highly rated design courses are taught at the Duncan of Jordanstone College of Art. The university is a key participant in the Dundee-based V&A project to improve design in Scotland.

Vocational degrees predominate, helping to produce consistently strong graduate employment. The university claims to send more graduates into the professions than any other institution in Scotland, and only Oxbridge graduates came out ahead of Dundee's in a national survey of starting salaries. Most degrees include a career planning module and an internship option, and students are now provided with their own personal development website. The Enterprise Gym gives students the chance to improve their self-reliance and employability, and exercise their business creativity through business enterprise skills development training. Students can take the Scottish Internship Graduate Certificate, an eight-month programme combining a six-month internship with career management learning. There is a global equivalent, lasting seven months and with an internship in India or China.

Two-thirds of Dundee's students are from Scotland and nearly one in ten from Northern Ireland. Scholarships and bursaries introduced in 2014 save students from the rest of the UK up to £8,000 in their first year. More than one undergraduate in five comes from an area with little tradition of higher education, although less than 30 per cent are from working-class homes. Applicants have access to MyDundee, an online portal giving further information during the application process and to prepare them for the academic year. The city is profiting from regeneration programmes, and enjoys a cost of living that is among the lowest at any UK university city. Spectacular mountain and coastal scenery is close at hand and the city offers lively city nightlife, but students' social life tends to be concentrated on one of Scotland's most active students' unions.

Undergraduate Fees and Bursaries

- » Fees for Scottish and EU students 2015–16 No fee
- » Fees for Non-Scottish UK (RUK) students 2015–16 £9,000 capped at £27,000, except for architecture, dentistry and medicine.
- » Fees for international students 2015–16 £12,950–£15,950
  Medicine £21,000–£31,500
  Dentistry £28,600–£40,000
- » Widening Access bursaries for some Scottish students.
- » For RUK students, household income below £20K, £3,000 a year; £20K–£42K, £1,000 a year.
- » RUK scholarship (most subjects) of £3,000 a year for those with at least ABB at A level or equivalent; RUK Discover Dundee scholarship of £2,000 in year 1.

Students

Undergraduates:	**8,845**	**(1,465)**
Postgraduates:	**1,705**	**(3,180)**
Mature students:	**25.1%**	
International students:	**13.9%**	
Applications per place:	**8.3**	
From state-sector schools:	**87.3%**	
From working-class homes:	**27.3%**	
Satisfaction with students' union	**88%**	

For detailed information about sports facilities:
www.dundee.ac.uk/ise

Accommodation

Number of places and costs refer to 2015–16
University-provided places: 1,587
Percentage catered: 0%
Self-catered costs: £115.64–£136.64 a week.
First-year students are guaranteed accommodation if conditions are met. No residential restrictions.
International students are guaranteed accommodation if conditions are met.
residences@dundee.ac.uk
www.dundee.ac.uk/accommodation

Durham University

Widely seen as the north of England's nearest equivalent to Oxbridge, Durham has a collegiate structure and high standards that have made it a permanent fixture in our top ten. The demand for places has been even stronger since Durham joined the Russell Group of leading research universities in 2012, and it is rated in the top 100 in the world both by *Times Higher Education* magazine and QS. However, the picturesque setting which is another draw for applicants has become a source of controversy, after three students drowned in the River Wear after nights out in the space of 14 months. The university commissioned a review by the Royal Society for the Prevention of Accidents, which recommended that the university's alcohol policies should be revisited and new safety measures implemented. Students have acted as volunteer wardens since the deaths, and other measures have included the provision of late-night taxis.

Undergraduates apply to one of 15 colleges, all of which are mixed. Colleges range in size from 300 to 1,300 students and are the focal point of social life, although all teaching is undertaken in central academic departments. There are significant differences in atmosphere and student profile, ranging from the historic University College, in Durham Castle, to modern buildings on the city's outskirts and on Queen's Campus, 23 miles away at Stockton-on-Tees. Investment continues on the Mountjoy Site for the sciences, with improved student facilities and an extension of the Bill Bryson Library (named after Durham's former Chancellor). There is a new law school and a £16.6-million extension of the Business School is now complete. A new physics research centre is due to open in 2016. But the main development has been the Palatine Centre, a £50-million student services hub at the heart of the university.

Durham is the third-oldest university in England, and holds on to its academic traditions. Wherever possible, teaching takes place in small groups and most assessment is by written examination. Four-fifths of the work assessed for the 2014 Research Excellence Framework was rated as internationally excellent or world-leading. Areas of particular strength include anthropology, archaeology, chemistry, classics, education, English, law, music, physics and theology. The university's greatest experiment was the establishment of the Stockton campus. Initially a joint venture with Teesside University, Stockton is now home to a wide range of courses including applied psychology, business and business finance, pharmacy and primary education. The campus has also seen the

The Palatine Centre
Stockton Road
Durham DH1 3LE

0191 334 6128 (admissions)
admissions@durham.ac.uk
www.dur.ac.uk
www.durhamsu.com
Affiliation: Russell Group

***The Times and Sunday Times* Rankings**

Overall Ranking: **5** (last year: 6)

Teaching quality:	**48**	81.9%
Student experience:	**23**	86.7%
Research quality:	**16**	39%
Entry standards:	**5**	523
Student–staff ratio:	**=36**	14.9
Services & facilities/student:	**7**	£2,648
Expected completion rate:	**=3**	96.6%
Good honours:	**5**	87.4%
Graduate prospects:	**8**	84.4%

fulfilment of Durham's long-held ambition to restore the medical education it lost when Newcastle University went its own way in 1963. Medics study for two years in Stockton, concentrating on community medicine, before transferring to Newcastle to complete their degree. Social facilities for the 2,000 students in Stockton have been upgraded, and a £5.5-million sports centre has been added to relocate some of the university's elite sports activities from Durham as part of a strategy to increase integration between the two locations. The university's aim is for the campus to be equal in academic status to Durham City, focusing on interdisciplinary research and covering the full range of research, taught postgraduate and undergraduate study.

The university attracts a largely middle-class student body, with more than a third of undergraduates coming from independent schools. But a scheme that targets able pupils from schools in the North East, Cumbria and West Yorkshire has helped to bring in more applicants from non-traditional backgrounds. In addition to the normal open days, all those who receive an offer are invited to a special visit day to see if Durham is the university for them. Around 90 per cent come from outside the northeast of England and many are visiting the region for the first time.

The university dominates the small cathedral city of Durham to an extent which sometimes causes resentment, but adds considerably to the local economy. For those looking for nightlife, or just a change of scene, Newcastle is a short train journey away. Sports facilities are excellent and Durham is among the premier universities in national competitions. The university hosts centres of excellence in cricket, rowing, tennis and fencing, and offers a range of sports scholarships. Nine out of ten students take part in sport on a regular basis, and Durham's College Sport programme is one of the largest intramural competitions in the UK. Some 500 teams compete in 18 sports every week. In 2015 Durham University was named "Sports University of the Year" by *The Times* and *The Sunday Times.*

Undergraduate Fees and Bursaries

- Fees for UK/EU students 2016–17 £9,000
- Fees for international students 2015–16 £14,900–£18,900
- Household income below £25K, £1,800 a year for college living expenses or as cash if living out.
- Students from the Supported Progression Compact Scheme, £5,500 a year (in year 1, as an accommodation subsidy).
- Academic, music, art and sports scholarships based on circumstances or by competition, up to £2,000.
- Scholarships for students from Co. Durham up to £10,000 a year.
- Check the university's website for the latest information.

Students

Undergraduates:	**12,280**	**(260)**
Postgraduates:	**3,205**	**(1,450)**
Mature students:	**5.9%**	
International students:	**16.8%**	
Applications per place:	**6.6**	
From state-sector schools:	**63.3%**	
From working-class homes:	**14.2%**	
Satisfaction with students' union	**42%**	

For detailed information about sports facilities:
www.teamdurham.com

Accommodation

Number of places and costs refer to 2015–16
University-provided places: 4,239
Percentage catered: 69%
Catered costs: £173.74–£229.31 a week (29–38 weeks).
Self-catered costs: £119.89–£138.92 a week (38 weeks).
First-year undergraduates become members of one of the university's colleges or societies and offered university housing.
International students: all first-year undergraduates are offered university accommodation.
www.dur.ac.uk/undergraduate/accommodation/

University of East Anglia

The University of East Anglia (UEA) invariably produces some of the best scores in the National Student Survey. If that is about catering for its 17,000 students' every need, the university will surely have stolen a march on its rivals with its latest facility: the nap nook. Based on a development at James Maddison University in the United States, it offers students a room with comfortable furniture and blackout curtains where they can have 40 minutes' sleep between lectures, eyeshades and anti-microbial pillows provided. The idea is to provide respite after an all-night session in the library, or elsewhere, aiding concentration and promoting good health.

Applications to UEA recovered strongly in 2014 after two years of decline, and the university is planning to increase enrolments over the next few years. It has embarked on a new development of 915 residential places to allow for expansion, the first 500 of which should be ready in September 2016. Other recent developments include the opening of a £19-million medical education and research building named after Bob Champion, the Grand National-winning jockey whose cancer trust was the biggest donor, on the Norwich Research Park. The university has also been engaged in an ambitious building and refurbishment programme on its 320-acre campus on the outskirts of Norwich. The Law School has new premises on the Earlham Hall complex and a Gymnastics Centre has been added to UEA's community Sportspark. There is also a new Enterprise Centre to develop students' entrepreneurial skills in an age when self-employment is increasingly common for new graduates.

The base in the City of London for international students that UEA shared with a private company has closed, as the university streamlines its portfolio of courses and concentrates its activities on Norwich. But the university is not abandoning its international ambitions – it has opened an office in Kuala Lumpur, and overseas students are expected to account for much of the coming expansion. UEA celebrated its 50th anniversary in 2013, still offering some of the highly regarded broad subject combinations that it pioneered in its early days. The university had been moving rapidly up our league table, occupying its highest ever position last year. It has slipped back this year, but is still in the top 20.

Environmental science is traditionally the flagship school – another international ranking placed UEA in the top 30 in the world for the impact of its research in this field. The Climatic Research Unit and the Government-funded Tyndall Centre for Climate Change Research, which has a hub in Shanghai, are among the leaders in the

Norwich Research Park
Norwich NR4 7TJ

01603 591515 (admissions office)
admissions@uea.ac.uk
www.uea.ac.uk
www.ueastudent.com
Affiliation: none

***The Times and Sunday Times* Rankings**

Overall Ranking: **18** (last year: 14)

Teaching quality:	**=22**	83.2%
Student experience:	**6**	88.8%
Research quality:	**32**	35.8%
Entry standards:	**32**	408
Student–staff ratio:	**=22**	13.7
Services & facilities/student:	**21**	£2,378
Expected completion rate:	**32**	91.9%
Good honours:	**26**	78.8%
Graduate prospects:	**=54**	70.3%

investigation of climate change. But social work and pharmacy produced even better results in the 2014 Research Excellence Framework, when 82 per cent of all the work submitted by the university was placed in one of the top two categories.

Art history has the benefit of the Sainsbury Centre for the Visual Arts, perhaps the greatest resource of its type on any British campus. The refurbished and extended centre houses a priceless collection of modern and tribal art in a building designed by Norman Foster. Creative writing is another of UEA's best-known features and the recipient of a Diamond Jubilee Queen's Anniversary Prize, while health studies have been among UEA's fastest-developing areas in recent years. Throughout the university, students can bring any inquiries to four learning and teaching "hubs", one for postgraduates, another for nursing and two for undergraduates in the other 25 schools.

Nine out of ten undergraduates come from state schools or colleges, and more than a quarter have a working-class background. Most undergraduates have the opportunity of work experience as part of their course. An academic adviser guides all students on their options under the modular course system and monitors their progress through to graduation. The university has sharpened its focus on employability with a strategy that promotes the development of the academic and wider skills that employers demand through the curriculum. In addition, a Graduate Intern Programme enables recent graduates to work for between four and twelve weeks at a business in the eastern region.

UEA opened University Campus Suffolk in 2007, in partnership with Essex University, with a main site in Ipswich and smaller bases in Bury St Edmunds, Great Yarmouth, Lowestoft and Otley. The university itself is situated in parkland, with easy access to Norwich, voted one of the best small cities in the world. The Sportspark is impressive, and the university was chosen as the base for the English Institute of Sport in the East.

Undergraduate Fees and Bursaries

» Fees for UK/EU students 2016–17	£9,000
Courses at partner colleges	£6,999–£8,500
» Fees for international students 2015–16	£14,000–£17,500
Medicine	£28,000

» Household income below £16K, £1,800 a year as fee waiver, accommodation discount or cash; £16K–£20K, £1,000 a year.

» Entry scholarships, £1,000 cash for students with at least AAA or equivalent. Subject scholarships and annual Excellence Awards (£1,000).

» Check the university's website for the latest information.

Students

Undergraduates:	**11,170**	**(920)**
Postgraduates:	**3,315**	**(1,740)**
Mature students:	**19.4%**	
International students:	**20.9%**	
Applications per place:	**7.4**	
From state-sector schools:	**90.1%**	
From working-class homes:	**25.7%**	
Satisfaction with students' union	**76%**	

For detailed information about sports facilities:
www.ueasport.co.uk

Accommodation

Number of places and costs refer to 2015–16
University-provided places: 3,841
Percentage catered: 0%
Self-catered costs: £70.68–£188.90 (38 weeks).
First years are guaranteed accommodation if conditions are met.
Distance restrictions.
International students (non EU) cannot be guaranteed accommodation.
accom@uea.ac.uk
www.uea.ac.uk/accommodation; www.twitter.com/uea_accom

University of East London

Every undergraduate at the University of East London (UEL) receives a free Samsung tablet, pre-loaded with core e-textbooks, as part of the university's efforts to cater for a student population where more than half are the first in their family to experience higher education. The initiative costs £2 million and another £3 million has been invested in new centralised "helpdesks" in the Student Support hubs at both Docklands and Stratford campuses. Extending access to higher education has always been at the heart of UEL's mission. Barely more than half of first years arrive with A levels and a similar proportion are 21 or older on entry – many choosing to start courses in February rather than in the autumn. Over half of the undergraduates come from working-class homes, many from the area's large ethnic minority populations. A successful mentoring scheme for black and Asian students has become a model for other institutions, while a guidance unit advises local people considering returning to education.

UEL's new vision prioritises engagement with the local community, encouraging students to use their knowledge and skills to improve the lives of others. The Legal Advice Centre provides pro bono advice, while students and graduates working in the not-for-profit Civic Architecture Office have supported projects ranging from local school expansions to prison rehabilitation initiatives. Staff and students are actively encouraged to undertake short and longer-term projects as part of study, research or volunteering.

Student satisfaction rates had been improving, but they dipped this year and UEL is bottom of our table despite a creditable showing in the 2014 Research Excellence Framework. The amount of world-leading research doubled, compared with the 2008 assessments, and 62 per cent of the work submitted was placed in the top two categories. The university was ranked equal first in England for the impact of its psychology research, all of which reached the top grade. But the highest projected dropout rate in the UK, of over 40 per cent, is one of several indicators holding the university back. The student charter urges undergraduates to adopt the "35-hour attitude", which means studying for at least 35 hours a week, making good use of the Learning Resources Centre and handing work in on time.

The university is building on the legacy of the London 2012 Olympics, when it hosted the United States team at its new £21-million sports and academic centre at the Docklands Campus, called the Sports Dock. The prize-winning waterside campus,

Stratford Campus,
Water Lane
London E15 4LZ
Docklands Campus
University Way
London E16 2RD
020 8223 3333 (admissions)
study@uel.ac.uk
www.uel.ac.uk
www.uelunion.org
Affiliation: million+

***The Times and Sunday Times* Rankings**
Overall Ranking: **127** (last year: 119)

Teaching quality:	**122**	75%
Student experience:	**119**	78.5%
Research quality:	**76**	7.2%
Entry standards:	**115**	281
Student–staff ratio:	**125**	23.6
Services & facilities/student:	**80**	£1,636
Expected completion rate:	**127**	67.5%
Good honours:	**124**	53.9%
Graduate prospects:	**127**	45.6%

in the shadow of Canary Wharf, was the first new campus in London for 50 years. The focus has now shifted to nearby Stratford, the original headquarters in UEL's days as a pioneering polytechnic, where a joint venture with Birkbeck, University of London, opened in 2013. The £33-million University Square development offers a range of subjects including law, performing arts, dance, music and information technology as daytime or evening courses. Elsewhere in Stratford, the Great Hall in University House now boasts a high-tech, 230-seat fully retractable lecture theatre, while the health and bioscience laboratories have been refurbished. The Cass School of Education has opened and a new £14.7-million library houses extensive digital resources and a 24-hour café.

In addition, the Noon Centre for Equality and Diversity in Business gives extra help to black, Asian, and minority ethnic students to prepare for a successful career in business. UEL is also strong on provision for disabled students and houses the Rix Centre for Innovation and Learning Disability. Most degrees are vocational and almost 1,000 businesses are involved in mentoring programmes and/or a work-based learning initiative which offers accredited placements. Centres of excellence include an Islamic Banking and Finance Centre, partly funded by one of Saudi Arabia's biggest banks, which has become a hub for international scholars in this field. The Centre for Clinical Education is London's only provider of clinical facilities and training in podiatry.

University housing is not plentiful, although there are now 1,200 bed spaces and the rents are good value for London. The social mix means that UEL has not been the place to look for the archetypal partying student lifestyle, although the Docklands campus has changed this to some extent and Stratford has been transformed since the Olympics. Sports facilities and new students' union premises have been added at both Stratford and Docklands. With almost 30 student-run sports clubs, UEL's high performing sports programme featuring £2 million in scholarships and bursaries is attracting talented young athletes. UEL students won six medals at the 2014 Commonwealth Games.

Undergraduate Fees and Bursaries

- Fees for UK/EU students 2016–17 £9,000
- Fees for international students 2015–16 £10,700
- Welcome bursary of £140 for first-year English students.
- Sports scholarships, support for vulnerable students and enhanced study skills and employability schemes.
- Check the university's website for the latest information.

Students

Undergraduates:	**11,300**	**(1,600)**
Postgraduates:	**2,060**	**(2,215)**
Mature students:	**44.8%**	
International students:	**8.2%**	
Applications per place:	**7.6**	
From state-sector schools:	**98.1%**	
From working-class homes:	**53.6%**	
Satisfaction with students' union	**61%**	

For detailed information about sports facilities:
www.uel.ac.uk/sport

Accommodation

Number of places and costs refer to 2015–16
University provided places: 1,200
Percentage catered: 0%
Self-catered costs £124.61 (en-suite single) – £164.19 (studio flat) a week (37 weeks).
First years are guaranteed accommodation if conditions are met; priority given to disabled students.
International students: same as above
www.uel.ac.uk/residential
dlres@uel.ac.uk

Edge Hill University

Edge Hill was the 2014 *Times Higher Education* (*THE*) magazine's University of the Year, chosen for its successes in student satisfaction and graduate employment, its financial performance and regional engagement. The university has spent more than £250 million in ten years improving and extending the 160-acre campus at Ormskirk, in West Lancashire. Entrants in 2016 will benefit from a new £30-million sports complex, as well as a 144-bed residential development that will bring the number of students who can be accommodated on campus to more than 2,000. The university's flagship building, Creative Edge, is only a year old and houses industry-standard equipment and resources for students on media, film, animation, advertising and computing degrees. The complex is also home to the Institute for Creative Enterprise, which acts as an interface between academic research and the creative industries, giving students the opportunity to work on live TV and secure work placements without leaving the campus. The Label Recordings, Edge Hill's own record label, also gives students the chance to work in an industry setting on everything from talent spotting and recording, to creating music videos, and PR and marketing campaigns.

New degrees for 2015 will take full advantage of the new facilities, spanning sport, music, the performing arts and web design. Those planned for 2016 focus on criminology and policing, which was one of Edge Hill's successes in the 2014 Research Excellence Framework. Psychology, English, sport and media produced the best results. Scores for all six areas in which the university submitted work showed improvement compared with the last assessments, in 2008. The SOLSTICE e-learning centre is recognised officially as a national centre of excellence in teaching and learning. It has a particular focus on learning in the workplace, but is involved with curriculum development and delivery in all three of the university's faculties. Three-quarters of all graduates leave with professional accreditation. All students have a personal tutor, as well as access to counsellors and financial advice.

Although university status arrived only in 2005, Edge Hill moved to its landscaped campus in the 1930s and has been training teachers since the 19th century. It has long since expanded into other subjects, but remains the UK's largest provider of secondary teacher training and courses for classroom assistants. The university also won the lion's share of funding to deliver further training for qualified secondary school teachers. Beyond Ormskirk, there are seven satellite campuses in Liverpool,

St Helens Road
Ormskirk
Lancashire L39 4QP

01695 657000 (enquiries)
contact via website
www.edgehill.ac.uk
www.edgehillsu.org.uk
Affiliation: none

***The Times and Sunday Times* Rankings**

Overall Ranking: **68** (last year: 72)

Teaching quality:	**=22**	83.2%
Student experience:	**=71**	83.5%
Research quality:	**=92**	4.9%
Entry standards:	**=72**	319
Student–staff ratio:	**51**	15.7
Services & facilities/student:	**57**	£1,809
Expected completion rate:	**62**	86.2%
Good honours:	**84**	65.8%
Graduate prospects:	**83**	63.8%

Manchester and other parts of the North West to facilitate local learning. In addition, a range of further education colleges in the region teach the university's Foundation degrees. Edge Hill has one of the highest proportions of state-educated students in England – almost 99 per cent – and just over 40 per cent of undergraduates have a working-class background. The projected dropout rate has improved markedly and, at less than 9 per cent, is much better than the university's benchmark. An award-winning student finance support package rewards achievement, as well as encouraging students to complete their studies, rather than simply offering incentives for enrolling.

Enrolments have remained steady since £9,000 fees were introduced and showed a healthy increase in 2014. There are now about 17,000 students on full or part-time courses, with more taking distance learning programmes. Female students outnumber the men by 2:1. Large numbers are enrolled on part-time postgraduate courses for the professions. Since 2014, all undergraduates on arts and science programmes have the opportunity to undertake a sandwich year in industry or a year studying abroad to enhance their learning and boost their employability. All students have a personal tutor, as well as access to counsellors and financial advice. Undergraduates were sufficiently satisfied to make Edge Hill the top post-1992 university in *THE*'s 2014 student experience survey, finishing in the top quarter overall.

There are plans for significant expansion following the purchase of land adjoining the campus. The spacious Student Hub building houses the students' union and also contains shopping and dining facilities, open access computers and social space. Other recent developments include a new biosciences building and upgraded accommodation for geosciences. The new sports complex has 3G pitches, a competition-standard athletics track, with a new sports centre, including 25-metre swimming pool, 100-station fitness centre and 8-court sports hall. These facilities have enabled Edge Hill to introduce a range of new undergraduate degree programmes including human biology, ecology, motion graphics, games programming, and networking, security and forensics.

Undergraduate Fees and Bursaries

» Fees for UK/EU students 2016–17	£9,000
Foundation degree	£6,000
Year abroad	£800
» Fees for international students 2015–16	£11,150

- » Scholarship of £1,000 for those with at least 320 UCAS points.
- » Access scholarship of £1,000, year 1; £500, years 2 and 3, particularly for mature students. Entrance and on-course scholarships of £1,000, year 1, £500, years 2 and 3, not linked to subject choice, in sport, performing arts, creative arts and volunteering.
- » Academic achievement awards of £500 for those excelling in years 1 and 2.

Students

Undergraduates:	**9,585**	**(3,050)**
Postgraduates:	**1,085**	**(3,025)**
Mature students:	**24.7%**	
International students:	**1.5%**	
Applications per place:	**6**	
From state-sector schools:	**98.6%**	
From working-class homes:	**40.3%**	
Satisfaction with students' union	**76%**	

For detailed information about sports facilities: www.edgehill.ac.uk/edgehillsport

Accommodation

Number of places and costs refer to 2015–16
University provided places: 1,700
Percentage catered: 17.6%
Catered costs: £101 a week (40 weeks).
Self-catered costs: £65 – £112 a week (40 weeks).
First years cannot be guaranteed housing. Residential restrictions apply.
Students designated overseas for fees are guaranteed accommodation if conditions are met.
www.edgehill.ac.uk/undergraduate/accommodation

University of Edinburgh

Edinburgh produced Scotland's best performance in the 2014 Research Excellence Framework (REF), but continuing problems with student satisfaction leave it well behind St Andrews in our table and outside the top 20 overall. That has not affected its popularity, however. Applications have risen by more than 8,000 in two years and are now higher than at any point in the university's history. With the numbers accepted growing by only 300 over the same period, the competition for places is intense. The university retains a special status north of the border, where it is regarded as the nearest thing to Oxbridge. More than 80 per cent of the research submitted for the REF was judged to be world-leading or internationally excellent. Sociology, earth systems and environmental sciences, including geography, and computer science and informatics were among the leaders in the UK. However, Edinburgh faces cuts in Scottish Government funding of up to £14 million, including an £8-million reduction in research support, which the university has warned will place it at a disadvantage against its counterparts in England and elsewhere.

Edinburgh became the latest UK university to boast a Nobel Laureate on its staff when Professor Peter Higgs was awarded the 2013 physics prize for predicting the existence of the so-called "God particle". The new Higgs Centre for Theoretical Physics will offer masters programmes and enable students to take up PhDs in relevant areas. Professor Higgs' success will boost Edinburgh's performance in at least one of the international rankings that currently give the most positive view of the university: it is rated just outside the top 20 in the world by QS. The fact that more than a quarter of its undergraduates come from outside the UK testifies to its worldwide reputation. Edinburgh is the largest university in Scotland. Its buildings are spread around the city, but most border the historic Old Town. These include the university's main library, which has been redeveloped at a cost of £60 million. The science and engineering campus is two miles to the south.

The university is one of the two most expensive in the UK for British undergraduates from outside Scotland, who pay £9,000 for the full four years of their degree. But there is a range of bursaries, some worth up to £7,000 a year to English, Welsh or Northern Irish students. Other measures to broaden the intake include an eight-week summer school for local teenagers and support for students in the transition to higher education. The university has always attracted a high proportion of middle-class candidates –

Old College
South Bridge
Edinburgh EH8 9YL

0131 650 4360 (admissions)
contact via website
www.ed.ac.uk
www.eusa.ed.ac.uk
Affiliation: Russell Group

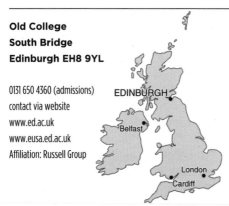

***The Times and Sunday Times* Rankings**

Overall Ranking: **22** (last year: =22)

Teaching quality:	**123**	74.5%
Student experience:	**=87**	82.4%
Research quality:	**10**	43.8%
Entry standards:	**9**	484
Student–staff ratio:	**=13**	12.2
Services & facilities/student:	**=38**	£2,052
Expected completion rate:	**=33**	91.3%
Good honours:	**12**	83%
Graduate prospects:	**29**	78.6%

many from England – and is a favourite in independent schools, whose students take about three places in ten. Selection guidelines aim to look beyond grades to consider candidates' potential, giving particular weight to references and personal statements. The university is also addressing the unusually low scores in the National Student Survey with a new personal tutor system and a peer support scheme, among other measures designed to improve the student experience. New undergraduates generally take three subjects in both their first and second years before choosing a final degree subject.

Recent campus improvements include a new informatics building and the development of a "BioQuarter", a ground-breaking collaboration between the university and a number of public bodies that is intended to consolidate Scotland's reputation as a world leader in biomedical science. A new library opened in 2014 on the science and engineering campus, named after Noreen and Kenneth Murray, the Edinburgh-based husband and wife team who developed the Hepatitis B vaccine. The Business School has relocated to the main campus and a research centre has been established for the study of Islamic civilisation and issues relating to Islam in Britain. Elsewhere, £90 million has been spent on the redevelopment of the Easter Bush site, where a veterinary school building, a research building for the recently incorporated Roslin Institute and a cancer centre opened in 2011. A new Centre for Robotics, a collaboration with Heriot-Watt University, opened in 2015, bringing together dozens of scientists and engineers from both institutions, together with about 40 partners from industry.

The university's Centre for Sport and Exercise was extended in 2010, adding to the already impressive sports facilities. Considerable sums have also been spent making the university more accessible to disabled students. The students' union operates on several sites and there is a regular bus link between the science areas and the main university around George Square. The city is a treasure-trove of cultural and recreational opportunities, and most students thrive on Edinburgh life.

Undergraduate Fees and Bursaries

- » Fees for Scottish and EU students 2015–16 — No fee
- » Fees for Non-Scottish UK (RUK) students 2015–16 — £9,000 a year, for up to 4 years (total £36,000)
- » Fees for international students 2015–16 — £15,850–£20,850
  - Medicine — £24,400–£47,200
  - Veterinary medicine — £29,000
- » Scottish students receiving SAAS bursaries and living outside Edinburgh, accommodation bursary of £500–£2,000 a year.
- » Edinburgh RUK Bursary taken as fee waiver or cash: household income below £16K, £7,000 a year (£3,810 for Welsh students), and then a sliding scale to £42.6K, £5,700–£500 (£3,810–£500 for Welsh students).

Students

Undergraduates:	**18,395**	**(620)**
Postgraduates:	**6,550**	**(2,055)**
Mature students:	**9%**	
International students:	**27.5%**	
Applications per place:	**10.1**	
From state-sector schools:	**69.6%**	
From working-class homes:	**17.5%**	
Satisfaction with students' union	**62%**	

For detailed information about sports facilities:
www.ed.ac.uk/sport-exercise

Accommodation

Number of places and costs refer to 2015–16
University-provided places: about 5,087
Percentage catered: 23%
Catered costs: £131.25–£252.98 a week.
Self-catered costs: £60.48–£139.16.
First years are guaranteed an offer of accommodation providing they fulfil requirements. Residential restrictions apply.
International students: housing guaranteed if conditions are met.
accom.allocations@ed.ac.uk
www.accom.ed.ac.uk

Edinburgh Napier University

The demand for places at Edinburgh Napier has increased for six years in a row, with the volume of applications in 2014 twice what it was at the end of the last decade. Entry qualifications have risen consistently over the same period, as the number of undergraduate places has failed to keep pace, although there was an increase of 450 places last year. Initially, rising demand was fuelled by changes in art and design and nursing qualifications, but it now reflects genuine growth in popularity, both in Scotland and overseas. The 13,000 students on the Edinburgh campuses include almost 4,000 international students, while another 4,000 take courses delivered with partners in China, Hong Kong, India and Singapore.

Once Scotland's first and largest polytechnic, Edinburgh Napier is named after the inventor of logarithms, John Napier. The university is spending more than £100 million on campus improvements, the most recent development being a new student residence in the city centre. The revamped Sighthill campus is home to the schools of Nursing, Midwifery and Social Care, and Life, Sport and Social Sciences. The student-focused campus includes a five-storey learning resource centre, an environmental chamber and biomechanics laboratory, and a large simulation and clinical skills centre with mock hospital wards and a high dependency unit simulator suite. Integrated sports facilities feature a well-equipped fitness centre and a sports hall. The Engineering and the Built Environment, Arts and Creative Industries and Computing faculties have been brought together on the Merchiston campus, where there is a new student hub and reception area, as well as fully soundproofed music studios. Screen Academy Scotland, run in partnership with Edinburgh College of Art (now part of the University of Edinburgh), reflects the university's strong reputation in film education. The Napier Students' Association is also based on the campus, and the library has been refurbished and is now open 24 hours a day during the first two trimesters.

The 500-seat computing centre at Merchiston is also open all hours during trimesters 1 and 2, and students have access to online lecture notes and study aids via Moodle, the university's Virtual Learning Environment. The web-based system supports learning, teaching and assessment via the student portal and is accessible from smart phones and tablet computers. The university has plans for continued development of study spaces to access technology-based learning. There are fully networked libraries on each campus and a multimedia language laboratory and adaptive learning centre for students with

Craiglockhart Campus
Edinburgh EH14 1DJ

0333 900 6040 (admissions)
contact via website
www.napier.ac.uk
www.napierstudents.com
Affiliation: million+

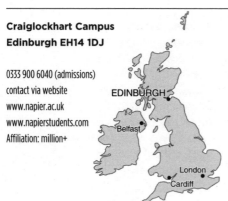

***The Times and Sunday Times* Rankings**

Overall Ranking: **93** (last year: 97)

Teaching quality:	**75**	80.2%
Student experience:	**=68**	83.7%
Research quality:	**=94**	4.6%
Entry standards:	**=53**	347
Student–staff ratio:	**=109**	20.3
Services & facilities/student:	**119**	£1,155
Expected completion rate:	**106**	81.2%
Good honours:	**=54**	71.4%
Graduate prospects:	**=59**	69.1%

special needs. The Craiglockhart campus houses the business school, which features a glass atrium with a cyber café and lecture theatres. Once a hydropathic hotel and then a hospital to treat shell-shocked soldiers during World War I, the architecture blends history and modernity. The campus also houses the War Poets Collection, an exhibition displaying the work of Siegfried Sassoon and Wilfred Owen. The Craiglockhart studio has been refurbished and offers an assortment of fitness classes. Digital screen technology has been installed on all three campuses in 2015 to aid internal communication.

The modular system allows movement between courses at all levels, and the option of starting courses in January, rather than September. A model to other universities trying to reduce non-completion rates, Edinburgh Napier uses its students to mentor newcomers, runs bridging programmes and offers pre-term introductions to staff and information on facilities, as well as running summer top-up courses and teaching employability skills and personal development. The latest projected dropout rate of less than 9 per cent represents continued improvement on previous years and betters the UK average for the subjects on offer. Widening participation is high on the university's list of priorities, and more than 30 per cent of undergraduate places go to students from working-class homes. More than 2,000 students enter through "articulation routes", using their college qualifications to gain direct entry into year two or three of a Napier degree.

Many courses include a work placement, while the Confident Futures programme is said to be unique in higher education, using workshops to improve students' confidence and help them to develop skills, attributes and attitudes that will enhance their chances of being successful both while at university and in their careers. For the growing numbers choosing to start their own businesses, Bright Red Triangle (BRT), the university's student enterprise service, offers free office space and advice to students and alumni. It has helped about 300 companies to launch, more than half of which are still active. BRT also runs a commercial consulting practice, which employs students to work on commercial projects.

Undergraduate Fees and Bursaries

- Fees for Scottish and EU students 2015–16 — No fee
- Fees for Non-Scottish UK (RUK) students 2015–16 — £9,000 capped at £27,000 for 4-year courses and £36,000 for 5-year courses.
- Fees for international students 2015–16 — £11,250–£13,060
- For RUK students, household income below £25K, £2,000 a year; £25K–£42.6K, £1,000 a year. RUK merit award of £1,000 a year for students with at least BBB at A level or equivalent.
- Scholarships and other bursaries available.
- Check the university's website for the latest information.

Students

Undergraduates:	**9,060**	**(1,540)**
Postgraduates:	**980**	**(1,110)**
Mature students:	**40.4%**	
International students:	**17.7%**	
Applications per place:	**7.7**	
From state-sector schools:	**93.7%**	
From working-class homes:	**31%**	
Satisfaction with students' union	**64%**	

For detailed information about sports facilities:
www.napier.ac.uk/about/campuses/engage/

Accommodation

Number of places and costs refer to 2015–16
University-provided places: 1,264 plus 248 in nominations agreements
Percentage catered: 0%
Self-catered costs: £105 (standard); £126 (cluster en-suites); £140 (studios) (38 and 50 weeks).
First years and direct entrant undergraduates are guaranteed a place provided requirements are met.
International students: as above.
www.napier.ac.uk/study/edinburgh/accommodation/

University of Essex

Having spent many years trying to live it down, Essex is now embracing its radical past, telling prospective applicants that it welcomes independent thinkers and "rebels with a cause". The approach appears to be working. Applications are up 15 per cent in 2015 – seven times the national average – good news for a university that plans to increase student numbers by 50 per cent over five years. It has already added 850 undergraduate places since 2012 and is now among the ten fastest growing universities in the UK. To support its expansion while improving staffing levels, Essex announced the largest recruitment of academics in its history, with 57 new posts. The university has also set itself a target of reaching the top 25 in our league table with every subject in the top 20 per cent of its discipline. Although it has dropped three places in this edition, it is in credit over the last two years –and has only ten places to go to achieve its goal.

Essex, which celebrated its 50th anniversary in 2014, is ranked by *Times Higher Education* magazine in the top 100 in the world for social sciences and in the top 200 overall. The university received the only Regius professorship in Political Science in the awards to mark the Queen's Diamond Jubilee. It achieved the best results in the 2014 Research Excellence Framework (REF) in politics and was in the top ten for economics and art history. The REF results as a whole represented a big improvement on an already successful set of assessments in 2008. The university moved into the top 25 in our research ranking, with almost 80 per cent of a large submission rated world-leading or internationally excellent.

The main campus is set in 200 acres of parkland two miles from Colchester. The university has been refurbishing its 1960s buildings while adding new ones. The Albert Sloman Library has expanded by 30 per cent and the new Silberad Student Centre opened in 2015, providing a central point for student services, plus a 24-hour learning hub, new IT facilities, a media centre and 250 study spaces. The new developments, costing more than £200 million, include a £1.4-million gym, renovation of the students' union bar, a café with adjoining learning space and shared IT workspace. Future projects include a £10-million science, technology, engineering and mathematics building and a new teaching centre. Wivenhoe House, the original centrepiece of the campus, has been converted into a four-star hotel, home to and run by the Edge Hotel School. Essex Business School will opened a new £21-million "zero carbon" building in autumn 2015.

The incorporation of the East 15 Acting School, in Loughton, as a department of the university was Essex's first venture beyond

Wivenhoe Park
Colchester
Essex CO4 3SQ

01206 873666 (enquiries)
admit@essex.ac.uk
www.essex.ac.uk
www.essexstudent.com
Affiliation: none

***The Times and Sunday Times* Rankings**

Overall Ranking: **35** (last year: 32)

Teaching quality:	**=15**	83.7%
Student experience:	**=9**	88%
Research quality:	**25**	37.2%
Entry standards:	**82**	313
Student–staff ratio:	**=40**	15.1
Services & facilities/student:	**12**	£2,574
Expected completion rate:	**73**	85.6%
Good honours:	**=66**	68.9%
Graduate prospects:	**81**	64.1%

Colchester. There has since been heavy investment in a third site in the centre of Southend – a modern multi-faculty campus offering courses in business, health and the arts. There is an accommodation complex which also houses a gym and fitness studio, while The Forum comprises a public and academic library, learning facilities, café and gallery. Another regional project has seen Essex collaborate with the University of East Anglia on University Campus Suffolk, which offers courses in Ipswich and at smaller centres across the county.

The student population is unusually diverse for a pre-1992 university, with high proportions of mature and overseas students. More than a third of undergraduates are from working-class homes and 95 per cent went to state schools or colleges. The university's employability initiatives were praised by the Quality Assurance Agency. The award-winning Frontrunners scheme, established by the university and students' union, arranges on-campus, paid work experience for students. There is also an extensive internship programme and many courses offer work placement opportunities. The Big Essex Award recognises students' extracurricular activities, volunteering and work experience, while Essex Abroad supports students studying, working or volunteering overseas. The university does not charge a fee for a full year abroad or a placement year.

Social and sporting facilities are good, with an active students' union and some 40 acres of land on campus devoted to sports facilities. Essex has started offering free access to sports, doubling the number of student sports club members to 4,000; another 2,400 students take part in drop-in sessions. All new first years are guaranteed a place in university accommodation, which has been voted some of the best in the UK. Some ground-floor flats have been adapted for disabled students. A £23-million development opened on campus in 2013 and another 1,000 places are planned. All the campuses are within easy access of London.

Undergraduate Fees and Bursaries

- » Fees for UK/EU students 2016–17 £9,000
  Placement year/ overseas year no fee
- » Fees for international students for 2015–16 £12,500–£14,500
- » Household income below £25K, bursary of £1,000 in years 1 and 2, £500, year 3.
- » Household income up to £25K, bursary of £1,000 in years 1 and 2, £500, year 3.
- » Other bursaries and scholarships available. Enhanced student learning and employability programmes.
- » Check the university's website for the latest information.

Students

Undergraduates:	**9,445**	**(1,395)**
Postgraduates:	**2,180**	**(960)**
Mature students:	**14.6%**	
International students:	**30.5%**	
Applications per place:	**6.8**	
From state-sector schools:	**95.4%**	
From working-class homes:	**36.2%**	
Satisfaction with students' union	**73%**	

For detailed information about sports facilities: www.essex.ac.uk/sport

Accommodation

Number of places and costs refer to 2015–16

University-provided places: 4,677

Percentage catered: 0%

Self-catered costs: Colchester: £75.11 (South Towers) – £137.69 (Meadows ensuite) a week; Southend: £132.09 (ensuite) – £162.89 (studio flat).

New first years are guaranteed accommodation if conditions are met.

International students: new students, as above.

accom@essex.ac.uk; www.essex.ac.uk/accommodation

University of Exeter

Exeter has increased the size of its undergraduate intake by almost a third, adding nearly 1,500 students, since it joined the Russell Group and government recruitment restrictions began to be relaxed in 2012. Firmly established in our top ten, it is aiming to become one of the top 100 universities in the world, with the expectation that further growth will be focused on international students. The university has been restructuring its staff to bring in more academics to achieve its targets without going deeper into debt. It has already invested £380 million on the main Streatham Campus, close to the centre of Exeter, one of the most attractive settings at any university. Now it is the turn of the St Luke's Campus, a mile from the main campus, where the Living Systems Building will open next year, completing a £10.5-million redevelopment and providing research, teaching and student study space.

Always among the leading universities in the National Student Survey, Exeter also recorded much-improved results in the 2014 assessments of research. More than 80 per cent of a large submission to the Research Excellence Framework was rated as world-leading or internationally excellent, with clinical medicine, psychology and education producing particularly good results. The university has also been introducing a raft of new degrees, including several undergraduate Masters courses and five new pathways in the medical sciences. A legal practice course taught by the University of Law for graduates who want to become solicitors will be added in 2016.

Developments on the Streatham Campus have included £130 million for student residences, substantial investment in the Business School, a new Mood Disorders Centre and new facilities for biosciences and the Law School. The jewel in the crown of the new developments is the Forum, a £50-million development which creates a central hub and features an extended library, new student services centre, technology-rich learning spaces, a new auditorium and additional social and retail facilities. Impressive new sports facilities, featuring a well-equipped fitness centre, opened in 2014.

The medical school, at the St Luke's Campus, has been extended, with new teaching and research facilities, complementing a £27.5-million health education and research centre at the Royal Devon and Exeter Hospital. The school grew out of the former Peninsular College of Medicine and Dentistry, which was established in association with Plymouth University in 2006. The partners have gone their separate ways, with Plymouth taking dentistry and Exeter offering a

Northcote House
The Queen's Drive
Exeter EX4 4QJ

0300 555 6060 (UK admissions)
ug-ad@exeter.ac.uk
www.exeter.ac.uk
www.exeterguild.org
www.fxu.org.uk
Affiliation: Russell Group

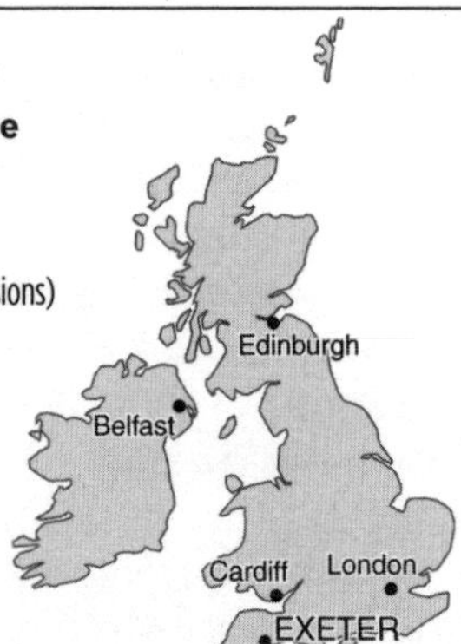

The Times and Sunday Times **Rankings**

Overall Ranking: **7** (last year: 7)

Teaching quality:	**=35**	82.6%
Student experience:	**14**	87.7%
Research quality:	**18**	38%
Entry standards:	**14**	463
Student–staff ratio:	**=49**	15.6
Services & facilities/student:	**15**	£2,559
Expected completion rate:	**9**	95.7%
Good honours:	**=9**	84.1%
Graduate prospects:	**=20**	79.8%

BSc in medical sciences in addition to the established Bachelor of Medicine, Bachelor of Surgery (BMBS). The new pathways, in genetics and genomics, neuroscience, pharmacology, environment and public health, and health research, include the option of a competitive entry Professional Training Year. The highly rated department of sport and health sciences and the graduate school of education are also located at St Luke's.

The university's other base is the £100-million Penryn Campus in Cornwall, which has helped boost applications in recent years. Shared with Falmouth University, the campus offers Exeter degrees in biosciences, geography, geology, clean energy, English, history, politics and mining engineering. A £30-million Environment and Sustainability Institute has opened on the campus and there is a new base there for the Business School. A new sports centre and a £5.5-million Science and Engineering Research Support facility are currently under construction.

Almost a third of Exeter's undergraduates come from independent schools – a much higher proportion than the national average for the university's subjects and entry qualifications, although this figure has been coming down gradually. The share of places taken by students from the four poorest socio-economic groups, at only 16 per cent, is among the lowest in the UK. However, the dropout rate of less than 4 per cent is also among the lowest. Exeter's longstanding international focus is exemplified by a growing range of four-year programmes "with international study". All students are offered tuition in foreign languages and even some three-year degrees include the option of a year abroad. Career management skills are built in and students have a wide range of work experience opportunities. The Career Zone has been expanded to increase career support and internships, while the university's Exeter Award provides official recognition of extracurricular activities. The number of student volunteers is among the highest at any university.

Over £20 million has been invested in first-class sports facilities in the last few years. Exeter, for example, is one of only nine UK universities to have indoor tennis facilities to national competition standards. There is no shortage of student-oriented bars and clubs in the city.

Undergraduate Fees and Bursaries

» Fees for UK/EU students 2016–17	£9,000
Placement year/ Year abroad	no fee
» Fees for international students 2015–16	£15,500–£18,000
Medicine	£27,000

» Household income below £16K, bursary of £2,000, year 1, £1,500 year 2 onwards; household income 16K–£25K, £1,000 bursary each year.

» A range of bursaries and scholarships available.

Students

Undergraduates:	**14,915**	**(135)**
Postgraduates:	**3,345**	**(1,125)**
Mature students:	**7.8%**	
International students:	**21.9%**	
Applications per place:	**6.8**	
From state-sector schools:	**67.4%**	
From working-class homes:	**16.3%**	
Satisfaction with students' union	**77%**	

For detailed information about sports facilities: http://sport.exeter.ac.uk

Accommodation

Number of places and costs refer to 2015–16
University-provided places: 5,471
Percentage catered: 24%
Catered costs: £152.74–£224.98 a week (32 weeks).
Self-catered costs: £102.83–£151.55 a week (40, 42, 44 or 51 weeks).
Unaccompanied first years are guaranteed accommodation provided conditions are met.
International students: as above.
sid@exeter.ac.uk;
www.exeter.ac.uk/accommodation

University of Falmouth

Falmouth is again the top arts university in our league table this year and also enjoyed a 30 per cent increase in applications, the biggest at any university in 2014. This surge in popularity enabled it to increase the size of its undergraduate intake by more than 300 students. Having jumped 26 places last year, in its second year in *The Times and Sunday Times* table, Falmouth remains on the verge of the top 50 and is one of the leading modern universities. There are still fewer than 5,000 students taking a range of subjects including architecture, digital media and creative writing, as well as the art and craft courses that were its exclusive territory for almost a century. The university still regards itself as a specialist institution, but degrees now include acting, business entrepreneurship and marketing.

Founded in 1902 as Falmouth School of Art, the institution merged in 2008 with Dartington College of Arts in south Devon, thereby adding a variety of performance-related courses to its portfolio. The former Dartington courses have relocated to a purpose-built Performance Centre on the Penryn campus, which Falmouth has shared with the University of Exeter since 2002. The unique joint students' union, FXU, serves all Falmouth students and those attending Exeter's Cornish outpost.

Falmouth has invested more than £100 million on its two campuses over the past decade. Among the new facilities are a design centre, art studios, TV studio, 117-seat cinema, motion capture studio, video editing suites, specialist animation software, audio suites, professional-standard photography studios, darkrooms, photography store and the Performance Centre with fully sprung Harlequin dance floors, rehearsal studios, practice rooms and flexible theatre space. The Exchange, which contains teaching and library space as well as study areas, opened in 2012 on the Penryn campus, where an Academy for Innovation and Research focuses particularly on the digital economy and sustainable design. The research programme covers areas such as smart technologies, future transport solutions, pervasive media, eco-town developments and Britain's ageing population, as well as art. A 54-place nursery and a new £4-million Sports Centre will be open before the start of the academic year in 2016.

The original Falmouth campus, near the town centre, boasts subtropical gardens and an outdoor sculpture canopy, as well as studios, library and catering facilities. Most courses demand between 260 and 300 UCAS tariff points, but portfolios or auditions are as important as A levels on many courses. Some degrees hold out the possibility of unconditional offers for promising applicants. About 60 per cent of

Woodlane
Falmouth
Cornwall TR11 4RH

01326 213 730 (admissions)
admissions@falmouth.ac.uk
www.falmouth.ac.uk
www.fxu.org.uk
Affiliation: GuildHE

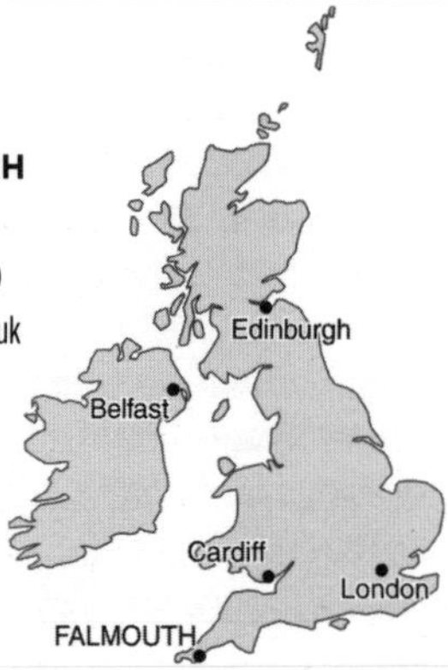

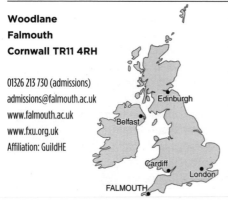

***The Times and Sunday Times* Rankings**

Overall Ranking: **56** (last year: 51)

Teaching quality:	**=15**	83.7%
Student experience:	**=71**	83.5%
Research quality:	**=94**	4.6%
Entry standards:	**90**	309
Student–staff ratio:	**120**	21.5
Services & facilities/student:	**61**	£1,755
Expected completion rate:	**75**	85.4%
Good honours:	**=52**	72%
Graduate prospects:	**44**	74.5%

the undergraduates are female, and almost 96 per cent were state educated, with almost 30 per cent coming from working-class homes. The university has an internal teaching qualification for staff to ensure high standards in teaching, learning and assessment.

Most of the 38 degrees planned for 2016 are single honours. The university has introduced new "externally facing" courses, including programmes that enable students to set up a business while studying. The BA in business entrepreneurship uses the successful Team Academy model for teaching, prioritising practical experience and mentoring. There are new degrees in digital games and computing for games. "Alacrity Falmouth", launched in 2014, is a graduate entrepreneurship programme with a focus on digital games. There is also a focus on the "learning and leisure" market, making use of Cornwall's tourist attractions, businesses and landmarks.

An extended Media Centre on the Penryn Campus, with new computers, a 3-D printer and stereoscopic projector, houses the Photographic Centre. Falmouth has been awarded Skillset Academy status for its media courses. The animation and visual effects department has become part of the Cross Channel Film Lab, which aims to develop innovative visual effects for use in low-budget feature film production, working on films alongside experts within the industry.

The university offers each new arrival a student mentor for a year to support them during their transition to university life. Glasney Student Village, on the Penryn Campus, which is shared with the University of Exeter, was extended in 2012. There are also residential places in Falmouth, enabling the university to guarantee all full-time first years accommodation as long as they apply by the published deadline. The Sports Centre has a gymnasium, exercise studio and multi-use games area. As befits the seaside location, there are many water sports activities. Students make full use of Cornwall's coastline and rugged moors, but there are good transport links to London and Europe. Plenty of tourist-related work is available and there is lively nightlife during the holiday season.

Undergraduate Fees and Bursaries

- » Fees for UK/EU students 2016–17 £9,000
- » Fees for international students 2015–16 £12,000
- » Support for students from households with low incomes and from Cornwall. Details not available in August 2015.
- » Range of scholarships and bursaries by subject, for travel and for care leavers and disabled students.
- » Check the university's website for the latest information.

Students

Undergraduates:	**3,655**	**(55)**
Postgraduates:	**120**	**(180)**
Mature students:	**12.1%**	
International students:	**5.6%**	
Applications per place:	**3.9**	
From state-sector schools:	**95.8%**	
From working-class homes:	**28.8%**	
Satisfaction with students' union	**80%**	

For detailed information about sports facilities:
www.fxplus.ac.uk/enjoy/sports-recreation

Accommodation

Places and costs refer to 2015–16
University-provided places: approx. 1,500
Percentage catered: 0%
Self-catered costs: £75.74 (shared en suite) – £126.28 (single en suite) for 42 weeks.
First year full-time students are guaranteed housing if conditions are met.
International students: non EU students, as above.
accommodation@fxplus.ac.uk;
www.fxplus.ac.uk/live

University of Glasgow

Glasgow has moved into the top dozen universities in the UK for research after a much-improved performance in the latest assessments, although the university remains behind Edinburgh and St Andrews in our table. It ranked in the UK top ten in 18 subject areas, the best results coming in architecture, agriculture, veterinary science and chemistry. Glasgow has also led the university sector in responding to the refugee crisis, offering fee waivers and extending eligibility for scholarships, as well as taking in two Syrian academics to study for PhDs. The political awareness of its students had already been highlighted when Mhairi Black won a seat in the general election when still a Glasgow undergraduate.

Following this year's closure of the Western Infirmary site, Glasgow plans to invest £80 million in new buildings and equipment and £55 million on refurbishing facilities over the next five years. The addition of the 15-acre site will allow the university to expand, reshaping its estate in a way that it describes as the third major staging point in its 560-year history. It also plans to extend its global reach and is already on the verge of the top 50 in the QS World University Rankings. Glasgow opened its first overseas branch in 2011, as part of an agreement with the Singapore Institute of Technology (SIT) to deliver joint engineering and mechatronics degree programmes. Students will complete three years at one of SIT's partner polytechnics before finishing their studies at the University of Glasgow Singapore. Nearly 15 per cent of the undergraduates in Glasgow are from outside the UK. They seem to enjoy the experience, having voted Glasgow fourth in the UK and top among Russell Group universities in i–graduate's independent International Student Barometer.

However, almost two-thirds of the students come from Scotland – many from Glasgow and the surrounding area – the university benefits more than some of its rivals from the policy of free tuition for Scottish students. Glasgow enjoys the rare distinction of having been established by Papal Bull, and began its existence in the chapterhouse of Glasgow Cathedral in 1451. Since 1871 it has been based on the Gilmorehill campus in the city's fashionable West End. The Veterinary School and outdoor sports facilities are located at Garscube, four miles away, and there is also a campus at Dumfries, which is taking liberal arts and teacher education degrees to southwest Scotland. The university has spent £7.5 million improving teaching and learning facilities and plans to spend a further £3.5 million by 2017. In addition, more than £13 million has been invested in

University Avenue
Glasgow G12 8QQ

0141 330 2000 (switchboard)
student.recruitment@glasgow.ac.uk
www.gla.ac.uk
www.guu.co.uk
www.qmunion.org.uk
Affiliation: Russell Group

***The Times and Sunday Times* Rankings**

Overall Ranking: **26** (last year: 26)

Teaching quality:	**=77**	80%
Student experience:	**20**	86.9%
Research quality:	**12**	39.9%
Entry standards:	**13**	470
Student–staff ratio:	**=32**	14.7
Services & facilities/student:	**31**	£2,142
Expected completion rate:	**50**	88.4%
Good honours:	**=30**	77.8%
Graduate prospects:	**23**	79.3%

improved sporting and social facilities.

Glasgow is no stranger to innovation: it was the first university in Britain to have a school of engineering, and the first in Scotland to have a computer. It has now appointed Scotland's first Gaelic language officer and the country's first chair of Gaelic. The latest development is the £20-million Stratified Medicine Scotland Innovation Centre at the new Queen Elizabeth University Hospital Campus, which involves a consortium of universities, NHS Scotland and industry partners. Glasgow's position as a leading centre for the development of precision medicine has been bolstered by the award of £3.4 million to create the largest molecular pathology node in the UK. A new learning and teaching hub is planned to enhance student experience and support growth. It will contain more than 1,200 formal and informal learning spaces and a new lecture theatre.

Almost half of the university's applications are for arts or sciences degrees, rather than specific subjects, reflecting the popularity of a flexible system that allows students to delay choosing a specialism until the end of their second year. The university operates a number of access initiatives, including the Top Up programme, which has been working with schools in the West of Scotland since 1999, and the Talent Scholarships, which are worth £1,000 a year to 60 academically able entrants who could face financial difficulties in taking up a place at Glasgow. Nevertheless, little more than 20 per cent of the undergraduates are from working-class homes. The Club 21 programme provides students with paid work experience placements in the UK and overseas.

Most students like the combination of campus and city life, with the added bonus that Glasgow has been rated among the most cost-effective cities in which to study. Undergraduates have the choice of two students' unions, plus a sports union supporting more than 40 clubs and activities. New union facilities, including a nightclub and four café-bars, are due to open in autumn 2015.

Undergraduate Fees and Bursaries

- Fees for Scottish and EU students 2015–16 — No fee
- Fees for Non-Scottish UK (RUK) students 2015–16 — £9,000 a year, capped at £27,000 for most courses; no cap for dentistry, medicine and veterinary medicine.
- Fees for international students 2015–16 — £14,500–£18,200
  Medicine, dentistry and veterinary medicine — £33,000
- Talent Scholarships of £1,000 a year for students facing financial difficulties in taking up a place.
- For RUK students, household income below £25K, £3,000 cash year 1, £2,000, subsequent years; £25K–£42.6K, £2,000 year 1, £1,000 subsequent years. Scholarship of £1,000 a year for most students with at least AAA at A level or equivalent.
- Check the university's website for the latest information.

Students

Undergraduates:	**16,810**	**(3,040)**
Postgraduates:	**5,750**	**(1,790)**
Mature students:	**16.9%**	
International students:	**19.2%**	
Applications per place:	**7.4**	
From state-sector schools:	**86.5%**	
From working-class homes:	**21%**	
Satisfaction with students' union	**75%**	

For detailed information about sports facilities:
www.gla.ac.uk/services/sport

Accommodation

Number of places and costs refer to 2015–16
University-provided places: 3,457
Percentage catered: 7%
Catered costs: £158.13 – 174.86 a week.
Self-catered costs: £88.62 (twin) – £144.55 (large single en suite) a week.
First years are guaranteed accommodation if conditions are met. .
International students: first years are guaranteed accommodation if conditions are met. 10% of returners are also housed.
www.gla.ac.uk/undergraduate/accommodation/

Glasgow Caledonian University

With Alex Salmond performing the 2014 opening and Nicola Sturgeon, his successor as First Minister, choosing it as the venue for her first public appearance in the United States, Glasgow Caledonian's new campus in New York has become a potent symbol of Scottish dynamism as well as a bold statement by the university. GCU was the first Scottish university to open a campus in London and it is the first in the UK to venture across the Atlantic. The university's international approach was already well established through the co-founding of the Grameen Caledonian College of Nursing in Bangladesh, an affiliation with an engineering college in Oman, and partnerships in China, India and South America. GCU describes itself as a University for the Common Good and has become the first in Scotland to be named as one of 24 Ashoka U Changemaker Campuses committed to social enterprise and innovation. The Chancellor is the Nobel Laureate and anti-poverty campaigner, Professor Muhammad Yunus.

Fashion is at the heart of the New York and London campuses. The university's British School of Fashion has partnerships with firms such as House of Fraser and Marks and Spencer, which has a design studio in GCU London and funds a £50,000 scholarship programme. There are also courses in fashion business creation, luxury brand marketing and management, luxury retail management and international fashion marketing. Across the university, almost two-thirds of the undergraduate programmes are accredited by professional bodies and more than half include work placement opportunities. GCU is one of the largest providers of graduates to the NHS in Scotland. As the only Scottish university delivering optometry degrees, it trains 90 per cent of the country's eye care specialists. The School of Engineering and Built Environment teaches three-quarters of Scotland's part-time construction students, while Glasgow School for Business and Society pioneered subjects such as entrepreneurial studies and risk management and offers highly specialist degrees, such as tourism management and consumer protection.

In Glasgow, more than £70 million has been invested to create a single campus that does justice to a thriving institution of 17,000 students, where applications rose by almost 10 per cent in 2014. The centrepiece will be the £30-million Heart of the Campus development, which is due to open in 2016. It will feature a striking new glass reception area and atrium, a 500-seat teaching and conference facility, and a new eating mall.

Cowcaddens Road
Glasgow G4 0BA

0141 331 8630 (enquiries)
studentenquiries@gcu.ac.uk
www.gcu.ac.uk
www.gcustudents.co.uk
Affiliation: none

***The Times and Sunday Times* Rankings**

Overall Ranking: **94** (last year: 84)

Teaching quality:	**=109**	77%
Student experience:	**=85**	82.5%
Research quality:	**=77**	7%
Entry standards:	**44**	372
Student–staff ratio:	**=117**	21.2
Services & facilities/student:	**=85**	£1,545
Expected completion rate:	**89**	83.2%
Good honours:	**62**	70.1%
Graduate prospects:	**56**	70.2%

The £1.2-million Doble Innovation Centre for On-line Systems will create new research and student placement opportunities in the engineering sector. The campus includes the only INTO centre in Scotland, running preparatory courses for international students. The health building brings together teaching and research facilities, including a virtual hospital. Health was one of the university's strengths in the 2014 Research Excellence Framework, which placed half of GCU's submission in the top two categories. It was in the top 20 in the UK for allied health research and did well in social work and social policy, and the built environment.

Other learning resources include multi-media studios, a Fashion Factory and an eye clinic equipped with latest technologies for teaching and research. Student facilities include the Arc sports centre, 24-hour computer labs, an employability centre and Students' Association building. GCU was among the top ten universities in the 2015 People and Planet Green League of environmental and ethical performance. It was also the first university in Scotland to achieve EcoCampus Platinum status for sustainability.

Widening participation in higher education has always been one of the university's main aims. The Caledonian Club works with children as young as three years old and their families in Glasgow and London. More than a third of the undergraduates are from working-class homes and about three-quarters are the first in their family to attend university. The Advanced Higher Hub offers students in their final year at schools across Glasgow specialist teaching, access to GCU's facilities and preparation for university life. The university has introduced a series of measures – such as better academic, social and financial support – for those at risk of dropping out. The projected dropout rate of less than 9 per cent is now the lowest among Scotland's post-1992 universities and better than the UK average for GCU's courses and entry qualifications.

Student satisfaction levels have failed to keep pace with rises elsewhere, although there have been some good results in the barometer of international student opinion. Glasgow is a lively city with a large student population, where the cost of living is reasonable.

Undergraduate Fees and Bursaries

- » Fees for Scottish and EU students 2015–16 No fee
- » Fees for Non-Scottish UK (RUK) students 2015–16 £7,000 a year, capped at £25,000 for 4-year courses.
- » Fees for international students 2015–16 £10,200–£11,000
- » For RUK students, household income below £25K, £2,000 fee waiver for 3 years. £1,000 fee waiver for 3 years for students with at least ABB at A level or equivalent. Principal's Common Good Scholarship: 5 full course fee waivers for first-generation, talented students from low income households.
- » Check the university's website for the latest information.

Students

Undergraduates:	**11,320**	**(2,505)**
Postgraduates:	**1,745**	**(1,185)**
Mature students:	**37.1%**	
International students:	**7.8%**	
Applications per place:	**6.6**	
From state-sector schools:	**96.7%**	
From working-class homes:	**35.1%**	
Satisfaction with students' union	**70%**	

For detailed information about sports facilities:
www.gcu.ac.uk/arc/

Accommodation

Number of places and costs refer to 2015–16
University-provided places: 660
Percentage catered: 0%
Self-catered costs: £98.32 (standard) or £111.42 (en suite) a week (39 weeks).
All students are entitled to apply, but priority will be based on age, distance from the university and, if international students, residence in a country outside the EU.
accommodation@gcu.ac.uk
www.gcu.ac.uk/study/undergraduate/accommodation

University of Gloucestershire

Gloucestershire has been experiencing a boom year after the demand for places slipped in 2014. Applications have risen by 6 per cent – three times the national average – and the numbers confirming offers of places had shot up by 18 per cent when the official UCAS deadline passed. With only 8,000 students, the university is planning gradual growth to ensure financial stability without sacrificing a community feel that is popular with students. A third of them stay in the county after graduating, many of them taking up jobs in local schools after training to be teachers. The university hopes to open an 800-place student village in 2017 to accommodate the additional students, subject to planning permission. It has invested more than £16 million in new buildings and facilities over the past six years and now has much bigger plans. A performing arts centre is set for the Oxstalls Campus, in Gloucester, where the business school will also be relocated from its current base in Cheltenham.

Gloucestershire was the first university for more than a century to have formal links with the Church of England when it achieved full university status in 2001. The three campuses are only seven miles apart, so students are not as isolated as they are in some split-site institutions. The main Park Campus is on the attractive site of the former College of St Mary, a mile from the centre of Cheltenham, and houses the Faculty of Business, Education and Professional Studies. Art and design, and the Institute of Education and Public Services are closer to the town centre, at Francis Close Hall. The Oxstalls Campus was purpose-built a year after university status arrived and caters for sport and exercise sciences, leisure, tourism, hospitality and event management. Oxstalls also houses the Countryside and Community Research Institute, the largest rural research centre in the UK, which produced much the best results in the 2014 Research Excellence Framework. Overall, 44 per cent of Gloucestershire's submission was rated as world-leading or internationally excellent, but fewer than 20 per cent of the eligible staff took part.

The university claims to offer undergraduates more time with academics than almost any other in the UK. In most subjects, students are said to spend at least a quarter of their time in lectures, seminars or other supervised activities. Most teaching groups are relatively small and 14 of the staff have been recognised as National Teaching Fellows by the Higher Education Academy. Originally a teacher training college founded in 1847, the

The Park Campus
The Park
Cheltenham GL50 2RH

0844 801 1100 (admissions)
admissions@glos.ac.uk
www.glos.ac.uk
www.yourstudentsunion.com
Affiliation: Cathedrals Group

***The Times and Sunday Times* Rankings**

Overall Ranking: **88** (last year: 83)

Teaching quality:	**=81**	79.8%
Student experience:	**84**	82.6%
Research quality:	**=107**	3.8%
Entry standards:	**=77**	317
Student–staff ratio:	**107**	19.7
Services & facilities/student:	**65**	£1,720
Expected completion rate:	**=60**	86.3%
Good honours:	**51**	72.4%
Graduate prospects:	**119**	55.7%

university's primary training courses are still rated as outstanding by Ofsted. There is a good range of work placements for other students, which are undertaken by a third of all undergraduates. The Degreeplus initiative combines internships with additional training to improve students' employment prospects after graduating. There are dedicated "helpzones" on each campus providing advice on academic or personal issues.

Gloucestershire has a longstanding focus on green issues, and finished once again in the top six in the People and Planet Green League of universities' environmental performance for 2015. There are allotments for students, diplomas in environmentalism and an International Research Institute in Sustainability that brings together researchers from around the world, undertaking work for agencies such as UNESCO. The university has also launched a Gloucestershire Growth Hub, in association with the Local Enterprise Partnership, to help local businesses and give students more opportunities to work on "real life" business projects.

The university's intake is diverse, with nearly all the undergraduates coming from state schools and a third from working-class homes. About a third are recruited from Gloucestershire, and a quarter from elsewhere in the South West of England. There is also a joint venture with INTO providing preparatory programmes for international students. The projected dropout rate has improved dramatically over recent years, and the latest projection of 5 per cent is well below the national average for the university's subjects and entry qualifications. In addition to its conventional degrees, the university is offering a range of two-year "fast track" degrees, in subjects such as biology, events management and law.

Gloucestershire has a strong sporting tradition and is the only university to have a professional rugby league team. It hosted the Malawi Olympics team for the London 2012 games, and the facilities include a sports hall, gym and tennis courts. All first-year applicants are guaranteed housing in university halls or managed accommodation if they make Gloucestershire their first choice and apply by the required deadline.

Undergraduate Fees and Bursaries

- » Fees for UK/EU students 2016–17 £9,000
  Foundation degrees at partner colleges £6,000–£7,500
  Placement year £1,000
- » Fees for international students 2015–16 £11,500
- » Students from Compact schools and Strategic Alliance partners with at least ABB at A level or equivalent, £1,000 scholarship; other students from these institutions, £500.
- » Care leaver's package includes 50% fee waiver and up to £4,500 a year for living and studying costs.
- » Enhanced hardship fund.

Students

Undergraduates:	**6,060**	**(650)**
Postgraduates:	**540**	**(715)**
Mature students:	**20.9%**	
International students:	**3.6%**	
Applications per place:	**4.4**	
From state-sector schools:	**97.4%**	
From working-class homes:	**33.6%**	
Satisfaction with students' union	**65%**	

For detailed information about sports facilities:
www.glos.ac.uk/life/societies

Accommodation

Number of places and costs refer to 2015–16
University-provided places: about 1,403
Percentage catered: 0%
Self-catered costs: £96–£146 a week (40 weeks).
First-year undergraduates have priority for halls.
International students: first-year undergraduates are guaranteed accommodation if conditions are met.
accommodation@glos.ac.uk
www.glos.ac.uk/life/accommodation

Glyndŵr University

Glyndŵr is moving out of its London campus, where 2,000 students – nearly a quarter of the total enrolment – were educated, in order to regain its licence to bring students into the UK. The university's "Highly Trusted" status was suspended when more than 200 students were judged by UK Visas and Immigration to have invalid English language qualifications. With international student fees providing more than 20 per cent of its income, the five-month suspension threatened the future of the university. Ceasing recruitment to the London campus was a condition of the reinstatement of the licence, although Glyndŵr is now seeking an alternative site in the capital. The row came as enrolments were recovering strongly after three years of decline. They were down again in 2014, despite a small increase in applications.

The former North East Wales Institute of Higher Education took the name of the 15th-century Welsh prince Owain Glyndŵr (who championed the establishment of universities throughout Wales) when it was awarded university status in 2008. The university has two campuses in Wrexham and one at Northop, in Flintshire, on the site of the former Welsh College of Horticulture. The Flintshire campus is the first university presence in the county, and £1.7 million has been invested to make it a centre of excellence for land- and animal-based studies.

Glyndŵr has over 8,000 students, but fewer than half are full-time undergraduates. Over half are 21 or more on entry. Nearly all the undergraduates are state-educated, approaching half of them coming from the four poorest socio-economic groups – far more than average for the university's subjects and entry grades. Glyndŵr also has the largest proportion of disabled students in Wales and was nominated for an award for its provision for them. There is a dedicated centre for students with disabilities that assesses students' needs before they embark on a course.

The two campuses in Wrexham are within five minutes' walk of each other. The university's art school is based at the Regent Street Campus, nearer the town centre.

In 2011, Glyndŵr became the only university to own an international football stadium – the oldest in the world – when it bought the Racecourse Ground to safeguard the future of Wrexham FC and provide more facilities for its students. The Glyndŵr Wrexham Football Academy, a partnership between the university and the club, allows professional footballers to take degrees without interrupting their careers – the only initiative of its kind in the UK. The university already had a partnership with the club, whose land, next door to the

Mold Road
Wrexham
LL11 2AW

01978 293439 (enquiries)
enquiries@glyndwr.ac.uk
www.glyndwr.ac.uk
www.studentsguild.glyndwr.ac.uk
Affiliation: none

***The Times and Sunday Times* Rankings**

Overall Ranking: **122** (last year: 113)

Teaching quality:	**=69**	80.5%
Student experience:	**=115**	79.3%
Research quality:	**117**	2.3%
Entry standards:	**=122**	257
Student–staff ratio:	**124**	23.3
Services & facilities/student:	**60**	£1,757
Expected completion rate:	**118**	75.8%
Good honours:	**125**	53.6%
Graduate prospects:	**=70**	66.3%

university's Plas Coch site, hosts the 200-bed student village. Part of the Plas Coch Hostel was transformed in 2013 into a library featuring more than 13,000 books collected by a New York scholar. The campus also contains a modern sports centre that includes two floodlit artificial pitches, an international standard hockey pitch, a human performance laboratory and indoor facilities that contain a sports hall with a 1,000 square-metre sprung floor.

Glyndŵr has embarked on a series of academic developments, including two-year fast-track degrees and the four-year Master's degrees in art and design, engineering and computing. The £2-million Centre for the Child, Family and Society, based on a Scandinavian concept, allows those working in the field of child development to hone their skills in both an academic and practical manner. The Advanced Composite Training and Development Centre, at Broughton, is a partnership with Airbus, which has a large plant nearby. Research carried out there will help to improve the efficiency of aircraft and feed into the university's undergraduate engineering courses, which are also developed in association with Airbus. The Centre for the Creative Industries has up-to-date TV, radio and online production studios, which are the regional home of BBC Cymru Wales as well as playing a key role in the university's television degree.

At St Asaph, the university has a centre for the research and development of cutting-edge opto-electronics technology and the headquarters of its commercial arm, Glyndŵr Innovations, which was named among the top businesses in Wales for growth. The university entered only 34 academics for the 2014 Research Excellence Framework, but a third of their work was judged to internationally excellent, with some world-leading.

Two-thirds of the students are local, many living at home, which inevitably affects the social scene, but eases the pressure on residential accommodation. Wrexham is not without nightlife, and there has been a £90,000 upgrade of the students' union, where the Centenary Club has become a popular venue.

Undergraduate Fees and Bursaries

- Fees for UK/EU students 2016–17 £9,000
- Welsh Assembly non-means-tested grant (2015–16) to pay fees above £3,810 for Welsh students.
- Fees for international students 2015–16 £10,250
- On a selection of courses, £1,000 cash in year 1 for applicant with highest UCAS tariff and for highest achieving applicant without UCAS tariff.
- Care leaver's and sports scholarships.
- Check the university's website for the latest information.

Students

Undergraduates:	**4,185**	**(2,910)**
Postgraduates:	**795**	**(510)**
Mature students:	**57.1%**	
International students:	**38.7%**	
Applications per place:	**3.8**	
From state-sector schools:	**99%**	
From working-class homes:	**47%**	
Satisfaction with students' union	**64%**	

For detailed information about sports facilities:
www.sport.glyndwr.ac.uk

Accommodation

Number of places and costs refer to 2015–16
University-provided places: 230
Percentage catered: 0%
Self-catered costs: £80 (single, shared kitchen and bathroom) – £95.00 (en suite) a week (37 weeks).
First-year full-time undergraduates are given priority in accordance with the university's allocation policy.
International students: guaranteed housing if conditions are met.
www.glyndwr.ac.uk/en/Accommodation/
accommodation@glyndwr.ac.uk

Goldsmiths, University of London

The demand for places at Goldsmiths has shot up by more than a quarter in two years, as its strengths in the creative arts have been supplemented by new courses in subjects such as clinical psychology, management and entrepreneurship, and politics, philosophy and economics (PPE). The intake of undergraduates has increased for four years in a row and hit a record high in 2014, as more applicants made Goldsmiths their first choice. But, with little more than 8,000 students, it remains small for a multi-faculty university and intends to grow further in the next few years. New courses for 2015 in economics, arts management and criminology should help it achieve that objective. It is just outside the top ten in the world for art and design in the QS subject rankings, although it has dropped 11 places in our table after a decline in student satisfaction.

Goldsmiths is based on a single site campus that has a mixture of traditional and modern buildings. The Professor Stuart Hall Building contains purpose-built media facilities such as radio and TV studios, the Ben Pimlott Building boasts state-of-the-art research facilities and studio space for art students, while the flagship Richard Hoggart Building has been refurbished and re-landscaped to create a space for outdoor arts and events. This refurbishment is part of a £6-million programme of investment in the campus that also includes a new recording studio – giving music students the chance to record in a professional setting – and a new Fairtrade coffee shop and social learning space in the Library building. A 19th-century church on campus has been transformed into a space for teaching, exhibitions, performances and studios, and there are plans to create an art gallery elsewhere on campus.

Alumni such as Damien Hirst and Antony Gormley are at the top of their fields. In recent years, director Steve McQueen won the Best Picture Oscar for *12 Years A Slave*, James Blake won the Mercury Prize for his album *Overgrown*, and Laure Prouvost was named winner of the Turner Prize, making her the seventh former Goldsmiths student to receive the award. The £10,000 Goldsmiths Prize, launched in 2013, has cemented Goldsmiths' position in the field of creative writing, a subject offered at both undergraduate and postgraduate level, and former students have won awards including *The Sunday Times* Young Writer of the Year Award and the Dylan Thomas Award, while two MA creative and life writing graduates were named in *Granta*'s 2013 Best of Young British Novelists list.

New Cross
London SE14 6NW

020 7078 5300 (enquiries)
course-info@gold.ac.uk
www.gold.ac.uk
www.goldsmithssu.org
Affiliation: none

***The Times and Sunday Times* Rankings**

Overall Ranking: **66** (last year: 55)

Teaching quality:	**113**	76.6%
Student experience:	**126**	76.3%
Research quality:	**36**	33.4%
Entry standards:	**48**	360
Student–staff ratio:	**35**	14.8
Services & facilities/student:	**110**	£1,319
Expected completion rate:	**=94**	82.4%
Good honours:	**18**	81.4%
Graduate prospects:	**=117**	56%

Of the work submitted for the 2014 Research Excellence Framework, 70 per cent was considered world-leading or internationally excellent, placing Goldsmiths just outside the top 20 universities on this measure. The best results came in communication and media studies, and the college did particularly well in the new assessments of research impact. The entire submission in music was considered world-leading in this respect.

Already well integrated into its southeast London locality, Goldsmiths is committed to increasing recruitment from the surrounding boroughs. It offers bursaries of up to £9,000 to Lewisham students from low-income families and other awards for those living nearby. Around a third of new undergraduates are 21 or over on entry with a strong representation from the area's ethnic minorities, and there is a growing cohort of international students. Nine out of ten UK undergraduates are state educated, and one in three comes from the four poorest socio-economic groups.

The portfolio of courses spans the humanities, social sciences, cultural studies, computing, and entrepreneurial business and management. There are integrated work placements on many degrees and workshops help students to develop entrepreneurial skills. Goldsmiths also places great emphasis on equipping students with creative thinking skills. The Gold Award encourages students to develop the skills and experience that employers are looking for, while the Higher Education Academic Achievement Report recognises students' co-curricular achievements.

There is a thriving music scene; a varied events programme includes music recitals, exhibitions, public lectures and readings. The students' union has a strong tradition in volunteering and in recent years it has won several awards for its campaigning on ethical and environmental issues. There are around 1,400 rooms available in halls of residence, many of which are in New Cross, and all are within a 30-minute commute of the campus. Priority for places is given to international students and new undergraduates from outside the London area. There is a well-equipped and affordable gym on campus, but the sports pitches are 30 minutes away.

Undergraduate Fees and Bursaries

» Fees for UK/EU students 2016–17 £9,000
Placement year £1,000
» Fees for international students 2015–16 £12,700–£18,850
» Ten £9,000 a year awards for best students from Lewisham and five £4,500 a year awards for students from other local boroughs.
» Range of scholarships and bursaries for local students, mature students, care leavers, disabled students, refugees, travel costs, computer, music and education students.
» Check the university's website for the latest information.

Students

Undergraduates:	**4,890**	**(140)**
Postgraduates:	**2,040**	**(1,040)**
Mature students:	**24.5%**	
International students:	**20.1%**	
Applications per place:	**6.6**	
From state-sector schools:	**90.5%**	
From working-class homes:	**32.9%**	
Satisfaction with students' union	**57%**	

For detailed information about sports facilities:
www.gold.ac.uk/sports/

Accommodation

Number of places and costs refer to 2015–16
University-provided places: over 1,400 (on- and off-campus halls of residence managed by Goldsmiths or private providers).
Percentage catered: 0%
Self-catered costs: £109–£195 a week (includes heating, lighting and internet costs).
Priority is given to new full-time students that meet the conditions of their offer; distance restrictions apply.
International students will be given priority.
www.gold.ac.uk/accommodation

University of Greenwich

Average entry grades at Greenwich have increased by over 125 UCAS points in five years, the equivalent of more than five grades at A level. The rise is reflected in the university's highest-ever proportion of students achieving good honours degrees. But applicants have not been deterred – the demand for places was up by nearly 10 per cent in 2014. There are now 22,000 students on the university's campuses in south-east London and Kent, while another 16,000 are taking Greenwich courses at 48 institutions as far afield as Malaysia, Trinidad and Egypt. The university has a longstanding commitment to extend access to higher education: over half the undergraduates come from the four poorest socio-economic groups – one of the biggest proportions in the UK.

The university accurately describes its main campus as "one of the grandest university settings in the world". The former Royal Naval College buildings designed by Sir Christopher Wren conjure up images of history and science in equal measure. The main campus, which is part of a World Heritage Site, serves over half the university's students. A £25-million project is under way to redevelop the Dreadnought Building as a student centre. As well as revamped learning and teaching spaces, it will feature a large campus café and a variety of new social spaces, as well as the students' union, a gym and the university's key student services.

There are plans, too, for a new "student hub" at the university's shared Medway Campus, in Chatham, where facilities are being upgraded in partnership with the University of Kent. A listed building is being transformed into a student centre, with entertainment and social spaces, in consultation with the students. The campus houses the schools of pharmacy, science and engineering, the Natural Resources Institute, nursing and some business courses. True to the university's commitment to cut carbon emissions, a combined heat and power plant is being built to provide the campus's electricity and hot water. The scheme is part of a €6-million international project, led by the university's Faculty of Engineering and Science, to investigate sustainable sources of energy for the future. Greenwich is in the top 20 in the People and Planet Green League of universities' environmental performance.

Other schools are situated at Avery Hill, a Victorian mansion on the outskirts of southeast London, which boasts a £14-million sports and teaching centre with a café, sports hall and 220-seat lecture theatre. There are also laboratories for health courses that replicate NHS wards. The campus contains a student

Old Royal Naval College
Park Row
Greenwich
London SE10 9LS

020 8331 9000 (course enquiries)
courseinfo@gre.ac.uk
www.gre.ac.uk
www.suug.co.uk
Affiliation: University Alliance

***The Times and Sunday Times* Rankings**
Overall Ranking: **106** (last year: 98)

Teaching quality:	**88**	79.2%
Student experience:	**=87**	82.4%
Research quality:	**=92**	4.9%
Entry standards:	**=79**	315
Student–staff ratio:	**=103**	19.6
Services & facilities/student:	**96**	£1,479
Expected completion rate:	**80**	84.7%
Good honours:	**100**	62.9%
Graduate prospects:	**113**	58.2%

village of 1,300 rooms, alongside teaching accommodation for the social sciences. The large education faculty is one of the few to offer both primary and secondary teacher training courses.

In Greenwich, the new Stockwell Street development is the centrepiece of a £150-million investment programme. The university's own specialists in architecture contributed to a building dedicated to research and teaching that includes 14 landscaped roof terraces. There is a large architecture studio, a model-making workshop, TV and sound studios, while students from across the campus will use the building's large library and other facilities. The investment programme includes a new hall of residence nearby, which opened in 2014, providing 356 en-suite rooms, as well as a café and gym.

More than half of Greenwich's students take professionally accredited degree programmes. The university is spending £450,000 on Greenwich Connect, a programme designed to bring innovation to its teaching and learning in order to produce graduates who not only have good academic knowledge but also the skills sought by employers, such as a high level of digital literacy, familiarity with new technology and expertise in social media. Greenwich is also the only university in the country to have an on-campus strategic relationship with a recruitment firm. It has invested more than £1 million in the service, launched in 2013, which aims to place final-year students or recent graduates in full-time, graduate-level jobs that are suited to their skills, as well as finding them high-quality internships and other opportunities along the way.

The university is also increasing the number of research-active staff as part of an ambitious programme of investment in research. The £17-million annual income from research and consultancy is among the largest proportion at any former polytechnic. Many of the 5,000 international students are postgrads or research students.

More than 200 academics entered the 2014 Research Excellence Framework – a considerable increase on 2008 – and 42 per cent of their work was placed in the top two categories.

Undergraduate Fees and Bursaries

» Fees for UK/EU students 2016–17	£9,000
Partner colleges degree	£8,400–£9,000
Foundation degree	£6,000
Placement year	£1,000
» Fees for international students 2015–16	£10,850

» Greenwich Scholarship Programme (GSP) for those with household income below £25K, £1,000 fee waiver, £200 voucher and £800 in-kind support in year 1; conditions apply.

» Access Scholarship for students with household income below £25K and not receiving a GSP award, £500 for university services in year 1.

» For all other Home/EU students, £200 university services in year 1.

Students

Undergraduates:	**13,790**	**(3,230)**
Postgraduates:	**2,290**	**(2,645)**
Mature students:	**32.7%**	
International students:	**14.7%**	
Applications per place:	**8.8**	
From state-sector schools:	**98.1%**	
From working-class homes:	**55.8%**	
Satisfaction with students' union	**62%**	

For detailed information about sports facilities:
www2.gre.ac.uk/about/campus/facilities/sport

Accommodation

Number of places and costs refer to 2015–16
University-provided places: 2,500
Percentage catered: 0%
Self-catered costs: £119.93–£187.53 a week.
First years are guaranteed a place. Conditions apply.
International students: new students get priority.
ah.accommodation@gre.ac.uk (Avery Hill Campus)
gr.accommodation@gre.ac.uk (Greenwich Campus)
me.accommodation@gre.ac.uk (Medway Campus)
www2.gre.ac.uk/study/accommodation

Harper Adams University

Harper Adams is the higher-placed of two specialist agricultural universities in this year's table, as well as holding down a place in the top ten for agriculture and forestry. Even before university status arrived in 2012, it had established a regular place near the top of the National Student Survey and was achieving good employment rates for its graduates. There are now more than 4,500 students, but little more than half are on campus at any one time. The rest are on placement years or accredited part-time programmes in industry. They include a growing number of international students; the university won *Times Higher Education* magazine's 2015 award for the best international strategy, partly for its links with four agricultural universities in China.

Based in a single campus in the Shropshire countryside, the university offers degrees in business, veterinary nursing and physiotherapy, land and property management, engineering and food studies, as well as agriculture. There is also a range of Foundation degrees that can be converted into Honours. New degrees in food science, automotive and mechanical engineering, and environmental management are planned for 2016.

The university has been upgrading its teaching and research facilities, and also investing in new academic appointments. A new teaching block opened last year, adding a 260-seat lecture theatre, IT classrooms, accessible computers and seminar rooms. The Agricultural Engineering Innovation Centre also opened in 2014, and a Veterinary Services Centre followed in 2015 as a response to rising demand for courses in veterinary nursing, clinical animal behaviour and veterinary physiotherapy. The students' union, careers service and café are all under one roof at the heart of the campus, where open access computers allow students to work and socialise in the same area.

The Main Building, which dates from the opening of the institution in 1901, was once the centre of all campus activities with bedrooms, teaching rooms and even a shooting gallery. The Bamford Library is one of the largest specialist land-based collections in the UK, with 41,000 books and 3,000 journals. But the new university's most prized feature is its 640-hectare commercial farm, which has been undergoing a multimillion-pound development, including expanded dairy, pig and poultry units. At its heart, Ancellor Yard is a redevelopment of the original farm courtyard, the former home of Thomas Harper Adams after whom the university is named. It houses the Frank Parkinson Farm Education Centre and the Frontier Crops Centre. The £2-million dairy unit serves 400 cows. A new Food Innovation Centre is being built on the

Newport
Shropshire TF10 8NB

01952 815000 (admissions)
admissions@harper-adams.ac.uk
www.harper-adams.ac.uk
www.harpersu.com
Affiliation: GuildHE

***The Times and Sunday Times* Rankings**

Overall Ranking: **49** (last year: 63)

Teaching quality:	**=35**	82.6%
Student experience:	**=3**	89.3%
Research quality:	**84**	5.7%
Entry standards:	**63**	331
Student–staff ratio:	**=83**	17.9
Services & facilities/student:	**36**	£2,077
Expected completion rate:	**40**	90.6%
Good honours:	**117**	58.3%
Graduate prospects:	**=47**	73.3%

main campus by Dairy Crest, as part of a unique collaboration that will enhance the company's product development through regular interaction with staff and students, as well as giving it access to leading research.

Not surprisingly, given its agricultural specialisms, the university is one of a shrinking band where male students marginally outnumber female. Nearly one undergraduate in five went to an independent school, but still almost half have a working-class background. Almost every course includes work placements, provided by a network of 500 employers, some of whom also endow student scholarships. The projected dropout rate of only 4 per cent is among the lowest in the country and less than half the national average for the university's courses and entry qualifications.

Harper Adams has become a new centre of excellence for entomology teaching and research in the UK, and has launched the Soil and Water Management Centre, an industry-led initiative to help UK farming make the most of its two most precious assets. It has also established the Centre for Integrated Pest Management and the National Centre for Precision Farming, which promotes and evaluates the use of technology in the industry, building on the university's reputation as an innovator in specialist engineering. Harper Adams entered only 17 staff for the 2014 Research Excellence Franwork – two fewer than in 2008 – but more than half of their work was considered to be internationally excellent or world-leading.

There will be more than 800 residential places on campus in 2016, following the addition of two new halls this year. First years take priority in the allocation of places. A shuttle bus runs three times a day for students living in nearby Newport to get to the campus and there is free parking for students. Sports facilities include a gymnasium, heated outdoor swimming pool, rugby, cricket, football and hockey pitches, tennis courts and an all-weather sports pitch. There is a dance/fitness studio and even a 4x4 club.

Undergraduate Fees and Bursaries

» Fees for UK/EU students for 2016–17	£9,000
Placement year	£1,800
» Fees for international students 2015–16	£10,200

» Range of scholarships and sponsorships available.

» Check the university's website for the latest information.

Students

Undergraduates:	**2,245**	**(2,170)**
Postgraduates:	**80**	**(305)**
Mature students:	**4.5%**	
International students:	**4.7%**	
Applications per place:	**4.8**	
From state-sector schools:	**82.4%**	
From working-class homes:	**47.6%**	
Satisfaction with students' union	**71%**	

For detailed information about sports facilities:
www.harper-adams.ac.uk/facilities/sports.cfm

Accommodation

Places and costs refer to 2015–16

University-provided places: 830

Percentage catered: 52%

Catered costs: £111.00 – £161.50 a week (36 weeks).

Self-catered costs: £100.00 – £127.75 a week (36 weeks).

Priority is given to new full-time students on a first come, first served basis. Provision for students with disabilities.

International students: entitled to housing for first year of study.

www.harper-adams.ac.uk/accommodation/

Heriot-Watt University

For nearly two centuries Heriot-Watt has followed the values of George Heriot and James Watt – two giants of industry and commerce who gave the university its name – focusing on practical, applied learning. The Edinburgh-based university's strengths lie mainly in the physical sciences, mathematics, business and management, engineering, and the built environment. It has fostered interdisciplinary teaching and research, with a battery of employment-related degrees which invariably produce a good rating for graduate prospects. The formula has international appeal: more than a third of the students on its three Scottish campuses are from outside the UK – one of the biggest proportions at any university – and Heriot-Watt also delivers courses to over 22,000 students in 140 countries, either through distance learning or at one of the 50 partner institutions overseas. It is Scotland's most international university, responsible for almost half of all the country's degrees awarded to people studying overseas.

The main campus, in an attractive parkland setting in the Edinburgh suburb of Riccarton, still has a modern feel more than 40 years after it opened. There are two smaller Scottish bases in Orkney and Galashiels, as well as a striking new campus in Malaysia and another in Dubai. A £34-million project has seen the opening of new residences at both Heriot-Watt's Edinburgh and Scottish Borders campuses. Additional accommodation is under construction at the Edinburgh campus, which will also be the location for the purpose-built Oriam National Performance Centre for Sport. The £33-million facility will feature a Hampden Park replica pitch, outdoor synthetic and grass pitches for football and rugby, a nine-court sports hall, a 3G indoor pitch and a fitness suite, as well as world-class facilities for sports science and medicine. The £20-million Lyell Centre, which is scheduled to open in early 2016, will be a major research centre for geological, petroleum and marine sciences, staffed by the university and the British Geological Survey, which will have its Scottish headquarters there.

The university's Scottish Borders campus in Galashiels, 35 miles south of Edinburgh, specialises in textiles, fashion and design. It offers one of the few degrees in the world in menswear and the only course in Scotland in fashion communication. Heriot-Watt and Borders College share the merged campus to deliver higher and further education in a region that has been historically under provided. The campus at Stromness in Orkney is for postgraduates, and specialises in renewable energy. There is also an "associate campus" in London, at the independent West London College,

Edinburgh Campus
Edinburgh EH14 4AS

0131 451 3376 (admissions)
ugadmissions@hw.ac.uk
www.hw.ac.uk
www.hwunion.com
Affiliation: none

***The Times and Sunday Times* Rankings**

Overall Ranking: =**38** (last year: 41)

Teaching quality:	**=64**	80.8%
Student experience:	**=56**	84.2%
Research quality:	**28**	36.7%
Entry standards:	**28**	413
Student–staff ratio:	**=61**	16.9
Services & facilities/student:	**34**	£2,120
Expected completion rate:	**56**	87.4%
Good honours:	**=52**	72%
Graduate prospects:	**=33**	78.1%

where students take Heriot-Watt degrees in business, accountancy, finance, hospitality and tourism, information technology, and fashion. The 3,800 students in Dubai take business, engineering, science and technology, or textiles and design courses. Numbers in the Gulf state are expected to rise further. The new Malaysian campus is now open, with space for up to 4,000 students to take a range of degree programmes in science, engineering, business, mathematics and design. Heriot-Watt won an award from the Scottish Council of Development and Industry, partly for its support for international students.

More than half of the UK-based students are from Scotland and 15 per cent from other parts of Britain. Nine out of ten are from state schools and colleges, while nearly a quarter come from working-class homes. The projected dropout rate of less than 7 per cent is better than the UK average for the university's courses and entry qualifications. More than 80 per cent of the work submitted for the 2014 Research Excellence Framework was rated as world-leading or internationally excellent, and Heriot-Watt was among the leaders in the UK in mathematics, general engineering and architecture, planning and the built environment, where it made joint submissions with Edinburgh. The university did particularly well in the new assessments of the impact of research and has gone up three places overall in *The Times and Sunday Times* league table.

The students' union was named Scottish Student Union of the Year by NUS Scotland. The halls of residence are conveniently placed and house some 1,750 students. Built in the grounds of a former country house, the landscaped campus boasts a loch and a sunken garden. Regular bus services link the campus to the city centre and its wide range of nightlife and cultural events. The university has a programme of sports scholarships, and representative teams do well. Music also thrives: there is a professional Director of Music and a number of music scholarships, as well as a varied programme of musical events.

Undergraduate Fees and Bursaries

- » Fees for Scottish and EU students 2015–16 — No fee
- » Fees for Non-Scottish UK (RUK) students for 2015–16 — £9,000
- » Fees for international students 2015–16 — £13,020–£16,420
- » Range of scholarships and bursaries for Scottish students, of up to £1,000 a year.
- » For RUK students entering at year 1, £2,250 fee waiver each year plus £1,500 bursary in year 1. From year 2, and for students entering at year 2, with household income below £25K, £3,000 bursary each year; household income £25K–£42.6K, £2,000 a year. RUK academic scholarship of £1,000 a year for students who achieve specified grades at A level, or equivalent.
- » Check the university's website for the latest information.

Students

Undergraduates:	**6,675**	**(645)**
Postgraduates:	**2,075**	**(1,500)**
Mature students:	**16.9%**	
International students:	**25.4%**	
Applications per place:	**8.5**	
From state-sector schools:	**90.1%**	
From working-class homes:	**24.5%**	
Satisfaction with students' union	**63%**	

For detailed information about sports facilities:
www.hw.ac.uk/sports.htm

Accommodation

Number of places and costs refer to 2015–16
University places provided: 1,753
Percentage catered: 0%
Self-catered costs: £86.52 (standard) – £155.05 (en suite) a week.
All new first years are guaranteed accommodation provided conditions are met and applications in place by noon on 21 August.
International students: as above.
halls@hw.ac.uk
www.hw.ac.uk/student-life/campus-life.htm

University of Hertfordshire

Hertfordshire has built a reputation in the UK as perhaps the leading "business-facing university" and has now set out to make the same mark internationally. Developing a global perspective in its curriculum and establishing more international partnerships are among the priorities in a new strategic plan, partly in order to recruit more overseas students. There has been a significant increase in overall applications in 2015; enrolments had already returned to the numbers seen before £9,000 fees were introduced in 2012. The university plays an important role in the regional economy and even runs the local bus service, as well as offering work placements and study abroad on many courses.

The university has two main sites, including a purpose-built £120-million campus, close to the original Hatfield headquarters, which boasts some outstanding facilities. The two sites are linked by cycle ways, footpaths and shuttle buses. The de Havilland Campus, named after the aircraft manufacturer which once occupied the site, has a learning resources centre, £15-million sports complex and 1,600 networked, en-suite residential places. The £10-million Law School includes a fully functioning court room with a public gallery, mediation centre and law clinic. New for 2015 on the College Lane Campus, Hutton Hub brings together a counselling centre, students' union, pharmacy, bank and a juice bar. The campus will have 2,500 new residential places by 2016, as well as sports pitches, a campus gym and social spaces. The development will be a true zero-carbon project, built to the highest environmental standards. Already in place, the Forum is a £38-million entertainment venue with three entertainment spaces, a restaurant, a café and multiple bars, which attracts young people from all over the county, as well as the university's students. In addition, a new science building, opening at the end of 2015, will bring all science teaching areas under one roof, with high-tech laboratories and areas for informal learning and socialising.

Health subjects account for the largest share of places. An innovative degree in paramedic science was Britain's first, its students using the UK's largest medical simulation centre to learn how to treat patients in emergency situations. This year sees the launch of a new four-year undergraduate Master of Optometry programme. The opening of a School of Pharmacy and a postgraduate medical school strengthened its position in the health sector. The creative arts have also been growing, with the addition of a £10-million media centre on the College Lane Campus boasting the latest technology for the teaching of music, animation, film,

College Lane
Hatfield
Hertfordshire AL10 9AB

01707 284800 (admissions)
ask@herts.ac.uk
www.herts.ac.uk
http://hertfordshire.su
Affiliation: University Alliance

***The Times and Sunday Times* Rankings**

Overall Ranking: **76** (last year: 79)

Teaching quality:	**=97**	78.6%
Student experience:	**=80**	82.8%
Research quality:	**=85**	5.6%
Entry standards:	**=75**	318
Student–staff ratio:	**=75**	17.7
Services & facilities/student:	**47**	£1,964
Expected completion rate:	**=63**	86%
Good honours:	**=78**	67%
Graduate prospects:	**42**	75.3%

television and multimedia. It includes one of the region's largest art galleries. An Automotive Centre has upgraded the teaching facilities for that branch of engineering, as well as boosting interaction with industry – every British Formula One team has at least one Hertfordshire graduate.

The student intake is more diverse than might be expected, given the location and subject mix: more than four undergraduates in ten come from working-class homes and 98 per cent are state-educated. The 11 per cent projected dropout rate is an improvement on previous years and is now better than the national average for the university's subjects and entry grades. The Careers and Employment Service offers students support for two years after they graduate as well as during their time at university. The Enterprise Team helps to turn business or social enterprise ideas into successful ventures.

In the 2014 Research Excellence Framework, more than half of Hertfordshire's work was placed in one of the top two categories. The best results were in history, where 45 per cent of the submission was judged to be world-leading and all of it was given the top grade for its external impact. Nursing, philosophy and astronomy also performed well. The university claims that 10 per cent of all known planets were discovered by Hertfordshire's astronomers.

The award-winning learning and resource centre at College Lane is among Britain's biggest. It and the learning resource centre on the de Havilland Campus are open 24 hours a day and seven days a week, providing 3,000 study places, 1,200 computer workstations and Wi-Fi. The StudyNet information system has been a leader in its field, giving staff and students their own storage space. Students can use it for study, revision or communication, as well as to access university information. The £15-million Hertfordshire Sports Village includes a 110-station health and fitness centre, a 25-metre pool, physiotherapy and sports injury clinic and a large, multipurpose sports hall. Principally for student use, it is also open to local residents.

Undergraduate Fees and Bursaries

» Fees for UK/EU students 2016–17	£9,000
Foundation degrees at partner colleges	£6,000
» Fees for international students 2015–16	£11,000–£11,500

» Household income up to £25K, Herts Success programme for student welcome, retention and employability.

» Scholarships for local students, sports and engineering.

» Check the university's website for the latest information.

Students

Undergraduates:	**15,805**	**(3,960)**
Postgraduates:	**1,995**	**(3,540)**
Mature students:	**19.1%**	
International students:	**14.7%**	
Applications per place:	**7.6**	
From state-sector schools:	**97.8%**	
From working-class homes:	**41.9%**	
Satisfaction with students' union	**74%**	

For detailed information about sports facilities:
www.uhsport.co.uk

Accommodation

Number of places and costs refer to 2015–16.
University provided places: 3,849
Percentage Catered: 0%
Self-catered costs: £84.00 (twin); £128.24–£145.74 (single en suite); £168.07 (studio) a week.
First years are guaranteed accommodation if applications are made before given deadlines.
International students: as above.
accommodation@herts.ac.uk
www.herts.ac.uk/university-life/student-accommodation

University of the Highlands and Islands

The University of the Highlands and Islands is developing rapidly, almost doubling the number of applications it received in two years up to 2014. It has been increasing its enrolments, but a new campus at Inverness and further developments at its Shetland College and at its West Highland College, at Portree on the Isle of Skye, as well as the opening of the £6.5-million Alexander Graham Bell Life Science Centre at its Moray College, will enable it to do more justice to the surge in popularity.

The students are predominantly mature and part-time, drawn largely from the Highlands and Islands, but the university has begun to recruit more young entrants, as well as attracting greater numbers from the rest of Scotland, other parts of the UK and overseas. Students take a broad range of qualifications, from higher national certificates and diplomas to degrees and professional development awards. Teaching is increasingly through "blended" learning, combining online and face-to-face teaching, with small class sizes and extensive use of video conferencing. The university is offering its first accelerated degree this year, with geography available at Inverness or at Lews Castle College UHI, on Lewis, over three years rather than the usual four.

A federation of 13 colleges and research institutions spread across hundreds of miles in the Highlands and Islands of Scotland, the university is unlike any other in the UK. As such, it fits uneasily into our league table – it proved impossible to calculate a meaningful staff/student ratio last year, for example, from the unique mix of part-time and full-time staff and students. UHI's colleges spread from Dunoon in the southwest to the village of Scalloway, the ancient capital of the Shetland Islands, in the north. The university's network of campuses is much wider, however. Argyll College, for example, has 13 sites on the mainland and on islands such as Arran, Islay and Mull. UHI courses are also taught at more than 50 learning centres located throughout the Highlands and Islands, Moray and Perthshire. Some colleges are relatively large and located in the urban centres such as Perth, Elgin and Inverness. Others are smaller institutions, including some whose primary focus is research. The university insists, however, that all have a student-centred culture and an individual approach.

Several of the colleges are in spectacular locations. Lews Castle College UHI in Stornoway in the Outer Hebrides, for example, is set in 600 acres of parkland. It claims "possibly the UK's most attractive location to study art" for its harbour-side Lochmaddy campus in North Uist. Sabhal

126 Ness Walk
Inverness IV3 5QS

0845 272 3600 (course enquiries)
contact via website
www.uhi.ac.uk
www.uhisa.org.uk
Affiliation: million+

***The Times and Sunday Times* Rankings**

Overall Ranking: **126** (last year: 121)

Teaching quality:	**=92**	78.8%
Student experience:	**125**	76.5%
Research quality:	**n/a**	n/a
Entry standards:	**119**	272
Student–staff ratio:	**n/a**	n/a
Services & facilities/student:	**127**	£558
Expected completion rate:	**126**	68.6%
Good honours:	**118**	57.9%
Graduate prospects:	**=117**	56%

Mòr Ostaig UHI is the only Gaelic-medium college in the world, set in breath-taking scenery on the Isle of Skye, while the Highland Theological College UHI is in Dingwall. West Highland College UHI does not even have a central campus, although its degree in adventure tourism management is taught in Fort William, close to Ben Nevis. North Highland College UHI has opened a new equestrian centre in Caithness, six miles from the main campus in Thurso, with international-sized outdoor and indoor arenas.

A report to the Highland Regional Council recommended the establishment of UHI in 1990 and envisaged that the process might take four years. The region had already waited a lot longer than that for a university: Perth was first identified as a suitable location for a university in 1425. The UHI Millennium Institute was finally established as a higher education institute in 2001 and university status arrived ten years later. There are now 7,500 students taking more than 100 undergraduate courses at 70 learning centres across the region, or entirely online. UHI was the first higher education institution to publish a Gaelic language plan, promising students more opportunities to learn Gaelic, improve existing skills, or study for qualifications entirely through the language on a growing number of courses.

The university's priority is to give people living in the region local access to learning and research relevant to their needs and to those of local employers. UHI is widely acknowledged as a major asset to the regional economy, helping to create and sustain businesses, as well as championing local culture and the environment. There are a dozen research centres specialising in everything from agronomy and marine science to Nordic studies, diabetes and rural childhood. They helped to produce some extremely good results in the 2014 Research Excellence Framework. Almost 70 per cent of the research submitted for review was classified as world leading or internationally excellent, but the large proportion of part-time staff made it impossible to compile an accurate score for research quality in our table.

Undergraduate Fees and Bursaries

Fees for Scottish and EU students 2015–16	No fee
Online courses	£4,800–£5,880

Fees for Non-Scottish UK (RUK) students for 2015–16
£7,920–£9,000, capped at £23,760–£27,000 for 4-year courses.

Fees for international students 2015–16	£8,800–£10,560

For RUK students , household income below £20K, £1,620 bursary; £20K–£22.5K, £1,080; £22.5–£25K, £540, all for three years.

Other bursaries and special funds are available, including 30 entrance bursaries of £500 for two years for Scottish students on selected online courses.

Check the university's website for the latest information.

Students

Undergraduates:	**4,570**	**(2,430)**
Postgraduates:	**105**	**(365)**
Mature students:	**33.3%**	
International students:	**4.2%**	
Applications per place:	**3.7**	
From state-sector schools:	**95.6%**	
From working-class homes:	**39.5%**	
Satisfaction with students' union	**45%**	

For detailed information about sports facilities: Sports provision for each campus is through local community facilities.

Accommodation

On-site halls of residence are available at four of the partner colleges. The other colleges provide lists of local lodgings or private rented accommodation. Some international students prefer to stay with host families.

Perth College UHI: pc.enquiries@perth.uhi.ac.uk
Sabhal Mòr Ostaig UHI: trusadh@smo.uhi.ac.uk
Lews Castle College UHI: enquiries@lews.uhi.ac.uk
www.uhi.ac.uk/en/studying-at-uhi/first-steps/accommodation

University of Huddersfield

Recent research suggested that students wanted all their lecturers and tutors to have a teaching qualification. Huddersfield is ahead of the game since every academic is a member of the Higher Education Academy, the professional body devoted to raising teaching standards. Members of the university's staff have won nine National Teaching Fellowships in the last seven years. It is also focusing on graduate employment, students' other great concern. Every undergraduate does some work experience as part of their degree course and a third take extended placements in business or industry, putting the university in the top ten on this measure. Many students now develop their own businesses for the work placement component of their course, taking advantage of the advice and facilities available at the university's Duke of York Young Entrepreneur Centre. With 70 per cent of graduates emerging with a professional qualification, Huddersfield has maintained strong employment rates and attracted a string of awards for entrepreneurship and its overall performance. There is a BA in enterprise development and all degree courses embed entrepreneurship into the curriculum.

The university has long been a leader in widening participation in higher education. Over 46 per cent of full-time undergraduates are from working-class homes – far more than the national average for the university's courses and entry qualifications – and many come from areas without a tradition of higher education. The university has opened satellite centres in Barnsley and Oldham to widen participation further. The dropout rate has improved, and the latest projection of 12 per cent is better than the national benchmark. The university takes its local responsibilities seriously. Its Graduate Opportunities Programme provides careers advice and guidance to all unemployed graduates – whatever their former university – who live in the areas of Calderdale and Kirklees. The newly opened £1.5 million Heritage Quay archive centre serves both students and public, and will soon include a Holocaust Heritage and Learning Centre, intended to be a major resource for the region.

Huddersfield is investing £58 million on teaching and research facilities, and has brought the university together on one town-centre campus with a combination of new builds and imaginative conversions. The 19th-century Ramsden Building, the historical heart of the university, has been refurbished and there are ultra-modern facilities behind its carefully preserved exterior. Canalside, a refurbished mill complex, provided extra space for mathematics and computing, and

Queensgate
Huddersfield
HD1 3DH

01484 473 969 (admissions)
aro@hud.ac.uk
www.hud.ac.uk
www.huddersfield.su
Affiliation: University Alliance

***The Times and Sunday Times* Rankings**

Overall Ranking: **=69** (last year: =77)

Teaching quality:	**46**	82.2%
Student experience:	**62**	84%
Research quality:	**61**	9.4%
Entry standards:	**60**	333
Student–staff ratio:	**=78**	17.8
Services & facilities/student:	**84**	£1,551
Expected completion rate:	**90**	83%
Good honours:	**=92**	64.1%
Graduate prospects:	**46**	74.1%

education occupies another mill site. The university has created "pocket parks" and a landscaped area along the reopened Narrow Canal to provide additional green space. It spent £4 million on a new students' union, which includes alcohol-free social areas to encourage participation by those overseas students and ethnic minorities who would otherwise avoid the facilities. Recent developments include a striking creative arts building and a new business school. A £22.5-million Learning and Leisure Centre opened in 2014, bringing together library, computing, sport, leisure, catering, social and meeting facilities. The next big project is a £27.5-million building for the Law School and the School of Music, Humanities and Media.

A tradition of vocational education dates back to 1841, and the university has a long-established reputation in areas such as textile design and engineering. Even many arts and social science courses have a vocational slant – for example, politics features a six-week placement, which often takes students to the House of Commons. Some of the most successful areas in the 2014 Research Excellence Framework were in the arts and social sciences. Huddersfield did well overall, entering almost a third of its academics for assessment and still seeing nearly 60 per cent of its work rated world-leading or internationally excellent. But there were particularly good results in music, drama and performing arts, as well as in English, social work and social policy.

Recent research initiatives include the establishment of a Centre for Evolutionary Genomics, an £8-million Centre for Innovative Manufacturing in Advanced Metrology, a Turbocharger Research Institute and new facilities for the Institute of Railway Research, which is set to conduct research on HS2. The Medium Energy Ion Scattering Accelerator, relocated from Daresbury Laboratories, is one of only ten of its type in the world, and the university's materials research will be bolstered by a new £3.5-million, EPSRC-backed electron microscope.

Most residential accommodation is now concentrated in the Storthes Hall Park student village, but additional housing is available at Ashenhurst, just over a mile from the campus. Town–gown relations are good, although students tend to base their social life around the students' union. There is easy public transport access to Leeds.

Undergraduate Fees and Bursaries

- Fees for UK/EU students 2016–17 £9,000
  Placement year £750
- Fees for international students 2015–16 £12,500–£13,500
- 1,000 bursaries of £1,000 in year 1 to students with household income below £25K and either a minimum of 280 UCAS points or joining Foundation programmes in science and engineering.
- Enhanced retention and career development programme.

Students

Undergraduates:	**13,095**	**(1,870)**
Postgraduates:	**1,785**	**(2,425)**
Mature students:	**22.1%**	
International students:	**12.8%**	
Applications per place:	**5.6**	
From state-sector schools:	**98.5%**	
From working-class homes:	**46.6%**	
Satisfaction with students' union	**67%**	

For detailed information about sports facilities:
www.hud.ac.uk/sport-fitness-health/

Accommodation

Number of places and costs refer to 2015–16
University-provided places: 1,666 in privately owned halls
Percentage catered: 0%
Self-catered costs: £69–£99 a week.
First years are housed on a first come, first served basis provided conditions are met.
International students: as above.
huddersfield@digstudent.co.uk; hudlets@hud.ac.uk
www.hud.ac.uk/uni-life/accommodation

University of Hull

Hull has transferred the degree courses from its Scarborough campus to concentrate all its undergraduate provision on its original base in its home city so that teaching can be better aligned with research. In 2016, however, it will be validating new degrees on the campus, which is now being operated by Hull College, in a strategic partnership with the university. Among the areas planned for 2016 at the new University Campus Scarborough, a stone's throw from Coventry University's new venture in the town, are health, education and early years, and coastal and environmental studies. Applications to Hull have risen for the past two years, but the numbers actually enrolling were down in 2014. The university went up five places last year after falling into the bottom half of our league table for the first time, but it is back there this year after a drop of nine places.

Hull has been focusing on improvements to the student experience after traditionally high levels of satisfaction have slipped a little in recent years. The Brynmor Jones Library, redeveloped at a cost of £27.4 million, has a striking new atrium and revamped exterior that will be the centrepiece of the campus. Another £2 million has been spent remodelling University House, which accommodates student services and a refurbished students' union. Impressive new music facilities, including ambisonic studio, ensemble practice room and recording space, are being developed in the run-up to the City of Culture celebrations in 2017, following the refurbishment of the Middleton Hall concert venue. The £2.5-million refurbishment of The Lawns at Cottingham, where seven hall of residence house 1,000 students, has brought improved student dining and social spaces as well as a gym and lecture facilities. Another 560 rooms will open on campus in 2016.

The 94-acre main campus, less than three miles from the centre of Hull, has seen new buildings for languages and chemistry, a Graduate Research Institute and a state-of-the-art sport, health and exercise science laboratory in recent years. The adjoining West Campus contains the Business School, a new Enterprise Centre to support local firms and the medical school, which is run jointly with the University of York. The university and the city have always commanded loyalty among students, who appreciate the modest cost of living and ready availability of accommodation, as well as the quality of courses. The council is spending £25 million to transform the city centre to celebrate its award as the City of Culture.

A longstanding focus on Europe shows in the wide range of languages available

Cottingham Road
Hull HU6 7RX

01482 466100 (admissions)
admissions@hull.ac.uk
www.hull.ac.uk
www.hyms.ac.uk
www.hullstudent.com
Affiliation: none

***The Times and Sunday Times* Rankings**

Overall Ranking **67** (last year: 58)

Teaching quality:	**=77**	80%
Student experience:	**=66**	83.8%
Research quality:	**54**	16.7%
Entry standards:	**=61**	332
Student–staff ratio:	**=69**	17.3
Services & facilities/student:	**70**	£1,698
Expected completion rate:	**=63**	86%
Good honours:	**56**	71.2%
Graduate prospects:	**=67**	66.7%

at degree level, with the purpose-built Language Institute heavily used by students regardless of subject. Strength in politics is reflected in a steady flow of graduates into the House of Commons. The Westminster Hull Internship Programme (WHIP) offers a year-long placement and month-long internships for British politics and legislative studies students. The Legal Advice Centre, staffed by law students, provides guidance and advice to the public. There is also a focus on employability, which includes the option of a 20-credit module on career management skills. The careers service approaches undergraduates early in their time at Hull and sets up meetings with potential employers.

More than 60 per cent of the work entered for the 2014 Research Excellence Framework was rated as world-leading or internationally excellent, although Hull made a relatively small submission for a pre-1992 university. The best results were in the allied health category, where 87 per cent of the research was awarded three or four stars, while geography and computer science also did well. A new biomedical research building, funded partly through a gift from a local businessman, will focus on cancer and cardiovascular and metabolic diseases – both areas in which the university has an international reputation. By bringing together both academics and health professionals, it aims to quickly translate research into tangible benefits for patients. An Institute for Learning encourages academics to put research findings into practice, developing training courses and developing the university's interest in lifelong learning.

Over 90 per cent of Hull's undergraduates are state-educated and three in ten are from low-income families. Nearly one undergraduate in five is from an area with little tradition of participation in higher education, far higher than the national average for the university's courses and entry qualifications. The popular and active students' union was one in only eight universities to achieve a Gold at the Best Bar None Awards in 2014. New football pitches have been added recently on campus and the Sports and Fitness Centre has been attracting praise.

Undergraduate Fees and Bursaries

» Fees for UK/EU students 2016–17	£9,000
Foundation degree	£7,000
» Fees for international students 2015–16	£12,300–£14,700
Medicine	£25,930

- » Scholarship for those with at least AAB at A Level or equivalent and household income below £42.6K, £2,100 a year. If not eligible for this scholarship and household income below £25K, bursary of £2,100 in year 1.
- » HYMS has its own bursary scheme (£2,400 a year bursary for 5 years when household income below £25K).
- » Check the university's website for the latest information.

Students

Undergraduates:	**11,950**	**(2,335)**
Postgraduates:	**2,375**	**(1,355)**
Mature students:	**28.3%**	
International students:	**11.3%**	
Applications per place:	**6.1**	
From state-sector schools:	**92%**	
From working-class homes:	**34.2%**	
Satisfaction with students' union	**78%**	

For detailed information about sports facilities:
www2.hull.ac.uk/student/sportscentre1.aspx

Accommodation

Number of places and costs refer to 2015–16
University-provided places: 2,601 (owned stock); 150 (leased/associated stock)
Percentage catered: 49%
Catered costs: £91.53–£149.10 (34–37 weeks).
Self-catered costs: £71.23–£118.02 (37–50 weeks).
New first years are guaranteed housing if conditions are met.
International students: as above.
rooms@hull.ac.uk
www2.hull.ac.uk/student/accommodation-new.aspx

Imperial College of Science, Technology and Medicine

Imperial's research was found to have greater impact on the economy and society than any other university's when this was assessed for the first time in the 2014 Research Excellence Framework. Imperial had the best results in the country in 8 of the 14 areas in which it submitted work and 90 per cent of its research was rated as world-leading or internationally excellent. The results, which placed Imperial second only to Cambridge in our research ranking, were by far the best it has produced. Never out of the top five in our overall league table, Imperial also features in the top ten of both the QS and *Times Higher Education* world rankings.

A new School of Design Engineering, funded through a £12-million donation from the James Dyson Foundation, should improve its performance still further. The School, the first new engineering department to be established at Imperial in two decades, will be housed in the former Post Office building near the main campus, which the college purchased recently from the Science Museum. An even bigger donation – £40 million from Michael Uren, an industrialist and Imperial graduate – is helping Imperial to develop a 25-acre site near the former BBC Television Centre in West London. The gift will fund a biomedical engineering centre at the heart of the Imperial West campus. The full development will cost a total of £3 billion and will also feature a Research and Translation Hub, bringing together the academic and business communities. Imperial now has nine sites in London, due mainly to the expansion of its activities in medicine in the 1990s, but undergraduates in most other subjects will continue to be based at the original South Kensington campus.

Entrance requirements are high. Even in subjects that struggle for candidates elsewhere, entrants average better than A*AA at A level and there are almost seven applications per place. More than a third of the undergraduates are from independent schools – one of the highest proportions at any university and considerably more than the benchmark calculated by the Higher Education Statistics Agency. About a third of the undergraduates are female – a proportion that has risen steadily over recent years – and roughly the same proportion of total student population are from outside the EU. The projected dropout rate of less than 4 per cent is among the lowest in the UK.

The Faculty of Medicine is one of Europe's largest in terms of its staff and student numbers, as well as its research

South Kensington Campus
London SW7 2AZ

020 7589 5111 (switchboard)
contact via website
www.imperial.ac.uk
www.imperialcollege union.org
Affiliation: Russell Group

***The Times and Sunday Times* Rankings**

Overall Ranking: **3** (last year: 4)

Teaching quality:	**=81**	79.8%
Student experience:	**=12**	87.8%
Research quality:	**2**	56.2%
Entry standards:	**3**	568
Student-staff ratio:	**=5**	11.3
Services & facilities/student:	**4**	£2,974
Expected completion rate:	**5**	96.5%
Good honours:	**6**	87.3%
Graduate prospects:	**2**	91.1%

income. There are teaching bases attached to a number of hospitals in central and west London, while the UK's first Academic Health Science Centre (AHSC), run in partnership with Imperial College Healthcare NHS Trust, aims to translate research advances into patient care. The centre is one of only five in the country, denoting international excellence in biomedical research, education and patient care. In its first overseas venture, Imperial is also a partner in a new medical school in Singapore, run jointly with Nanyang Technological University.

Engineering degrees last four years and lead to an MEng. Imperial is unique in the UK for providing teaching and research in the full range of engineering disciplines. The growing business school is Imperial's main venture beyond the world of science and technology. It is highly rated and is accredited by the three largest and most influential business school accreditation associations worldwide. There is also an environmental research campus at Silwood Park, 25 miles west of London.

The Imperial Horizons programme, designed to give students an edge in their future career, provides opportunities to debate global challenges such as climate change, drawing on expertise from across the university. Many degrees offer a work placement or year abroad, and students are actively encouraged to seek summer internships. The Undergraduate Research Opportunities Programme offers "hands-on" research experience. Imperial's graduates have the second-highest average starting salaries in the UK.

A university in its own right since leaving the University of London in 2007, Imperial continues to upgrade and expand its facilities on its campus close to the South Kensington museums. A second residential complex and refurbishments to the central library were followed by improvements to the students' union bar and nightclub. Further improvements to the library are being phased in over several years to minimise disruption. The students' union claims to have the largest selection of clubs and societies in the country. Outdoor sports facilities are remote, but a new and well-equipped sports centre on the South Kensington campus offers students free gym and swimming facilities.

Undergraduate Fees and Bursaries

» Fees for UK/EU students 2016–17	£9,000
Placement year	£900–£1,800
Year overseas	£900–£1,350
» Fees for international students 2015–16	£23,500–£26,500
Medicine	£36,400

- Household income up to £16K, £5,000 cash; £16K–£42.6K, £4,000 cash.
- Range of subject scholarships and Rector's Scholarships
- Check the university's website for the latest information.

Students

Undergraduates:	**8,885**	**(0)**
Postgraduates:	**5,895**	**(1,445)**
Mature students:	**4.2%**	
International students:	**39.7%**	
Applications per place:	**6.6**	
From state-sector schools:	**64.8%**	
From working-class homes:	**16.3%**	
Satisfaction with students' union	**78%**	

For detailed information about sports facilities:
www3.imperial.ac.uk/sports

Accommodation

Number of places and costs refer to 2015–16
University-provided places: 2,577
Percentage catered: 0%
Self-catered costs: £96–£262 a week.
First-year undergraduates are guaranteed accommodation if application received by 31 July.
International students: as above.
accommodation@imperial.ac.uk
www.imperial.ac.uk/study/campus-life/accommodation

Keele University

Keele was in the top three universities both for teaching quality and the broader student experience in the 2015 National Student Survey. The university's response to student feedback on the library service was a perfect example of what produces such results. Improvements included a new group study area, more silent study places, longer opening hours and extra investment in online journals and e-books. The 10,000 students share the largest campus in the country, 600 acres of parkland near Stoke. Gradual expansion is under way, with the university taking an additional 200 undergraduates in 2014, as it aims to grow by up to a third over the next five years. Much of the growth will be at postgraduate level.

More than £115 million has been spent on the campus since the turn of the century. The latest phase has transformed the heart of the campus, reconfiguring the Union Square plaza and providing a social hub for both informal and formal events. A third of all undergraduates, as well as many postgraduates and even some staff, live on a campus which includes an arboretum and has won a clutch of environmental awards. The university's commitment to green issues was underlined by the choice of environmental campaigner Jonathan Porritt as Chancellor. Keele won two Green Gown awards for sustainability in 2014, including one for continuous improvement. Students can grow their own fruit and vegetables on campus, and all undergraduates can take a module in sustainability or environmental studies.

Keele has gone further than most universities to help its graduates in the employment market by formally recognising their achievements both in and out of the classroom. The distinctive Keele Curriculum, introduced as the university celebrated its 50th anniversary in 2012, covers voluntary and sporting activities as well as the academic core. It is the only one in the UK that can lead to accreditation by the Institute of Leadership and Management. The student charter identifies ten "graduate attributes" that include independent thinking, synthesising information, creative problem solving, communicating clearly, and appreciating the social, environmental and global implications of all studies and activities. The university has been at the forefront of moves to record in more detail what graduates have achieved through a Higher Education Annual Report.

The academic year divided into two 15-week semesters, with breaks at Christmas and Easter. Nearly all undergraduates have the option of spending a semester abroad at one of the university's partner universities. Nine out of ten undergraduates are state

Keele
Staffordshire ST5 5BG

01782 734010 (admissions)
admissions.ukeu@keele.ac.uk
www.keele.ac.uk
http://.keelesu.com
Affiliation: none

***The Times and Sunday Times* Rankings**

Overall Ranking: **43** (last year: 40)

Teaching quality:	**3**	87%
Student experience:	**2**	90.2%
Research quality:	**52**	22.1%
Entry standards:	**49**	358
Student–staff ratio:	**=26**	13.9
Services & facilities/student:	**113**	£1,273
Expected completion rate:	**38**	90.8%
Good honours:	**70**	68.4%
Graduate prospects:	**=38**	76.1%

educated and approaching 30 per cent come from working-class homes. The university has been trying to broaden its intake further by offering special projects and masterclasses in local schools and hosting a summer school. The projected dropout rate of less than 7 per cent is well below the national average for the university's subjects and entry qualifications.

Health subjects have been the main focus of development in recent years. First degrees in physiotherapy and nursing and midwifery were added to the well-established postgraduate medical school. Keele also offers a five-year undergraduate medical course taught in new facilities on the Keele campus, at the University Hospital of North Staffordshire NHS Trust, three miles away, and at the Associate Teaching Hospital at the Shrewsbury and Telford Hospitals NHS Trust. Students take the distinctive Keele undergraduate degree programme. Facilities for pharmacy and the natural sciences have also been improved. The latest development is a £2.8-million extension of the Anatomy Skills Facility. Keele's results in the 2014 Research Excellence Framework showed considerable improvement on the 2008 assessments. Over 70 per cent of the work submitted was placed in the top two categories, with researchers in primary care and health sciences, pharmacy, chemistry, science and technology, the life sciences, and history scoring particularly well.

The university is within an hour's drive of Manchester and Birmingham. Crime statistics suggest that Keele is the safest university campus in the West Midlands. For those who live off campus, the cost of living in the Potteries and the surrounding area is relatively low. The highly rated students' union, which has undergone a £2.7-million renovation, offers entertainment on campus every night of the week. It has won the Best Bar None Gold Award, for responsible drinking and a safe environment, for five years in a row. The sports facilities have benefited from a new all-weather pitch, and the leisure centre has a refurbished fitness suite. A new £2.9-million nursery caters for more than 100 children from three months to school age.

Undergraduate Fees and Bursaries

» Fees for UK/EU students 2016–17	£9,000
Placement year	£500
Year abroad	£1,350
» Fees for international students 2015–16	£12,500–£15,100
Medicine	£25,100

» English students with household income below £25K, bursary of £1,000 a year.

» Scholarships for those with excellent pre-entry qualifications of up to £2,000 a year.

» Study abroad bursary of £1,000 for those with household income below £25K.

» Check the university's website for the latest information.

Students

Undergraduates:	**6,925**	**(630)**
Postgraduates:	**965**	**(1,460)**
Mature students:	**16.3%**	
International students:	**16.6%**	
Applications per place:	**9.2**	
From state-sector schools:	**92.4%**	
From working-class homes:	**28.3%**	
Satisfaction with students' union	**86%**	

For detailed information about sports facilities:
www.keele.ac.uk/sport

Accommodation

Number of places and costs refer to 2015–16
University-provided places: 3,200
Percentage catered: 5%
Catered costs: £139.32–£158.40 a week (37 weeks).
Self-catered costs: £59.99–£177.20 a week (34–51 weeks).
First years are guaranteed accommodation on campus if Keele is first or firm choice university.
International students: guaranteed accommodation for the duration of their course. Deadlines apply.
www.keele.ac.uk/studyatkeele/accommodation

University of Kent

Kent has been celebrating its 50th anniversary after achieving outstanding results in the latest official assessments of university research and gaining a nomination as our University of the Year. Almost three-quarters of the work submitted for the Research Excellence Framework was judged world-leading or internationally excellent. The successes, led by social work and social policy, music and drama, and modern languages, have helped Kent to its highest-ever position in our league table. The university was already a perennial high-performer in the National Student Survey and is also in the top 20 for staffing levels.

The university has opened its first new college for undergraduates in 45 years in 2015. Turing College has 800 study bedrooms and a hub building with social and study areas, catering facilities and a launderette. The development maintains Kent's position as one of the best-provided universities for accommodation, with nearly 5,500 places in Canterbury alone for 15,000 full-time students there. Every student is attached to college, although they do not select it themselves. The colleges act as the focus of social life – especially in the first year – and include academic as well as residential facilities.

Kent's original low-rise campus is set in 300 acres of tidy parkland overlooking Canterbury. Recent developments include the prize-winning Colyer-Fergusson Music Building and Kent School of Architecture's new Crit Building. Among several other major projects is an ongoing redevelopment of the library, while a media centre opened in 2014. The student centre has a nightclub large enough to attract big-name bands, as well as a theatre, cinema and bars. Two further developments are due to open in 2016: a new law clinic, with a dedicated mooting chamber, and a new building for Kent Business School and the School of Mathematics, Statistics and Actuarial Science, allowing two of the university's most successful departments to expand.

The university also has a Medway campus, at the old Chatham naval base, which is shared with Greenwich and Canterbury Christ Church universities. The School of Pharmacy, is the main feature of a £50-million development which now has more than 2,000 students from the university. The School of Arts opened there in 2012, with flexible work spaces for painting, sculpture, printmaking, film, photography, music and performance projects. There is also a £1-million sculpture workshop and recording studios, as well as more than 1,000 residential places. Grade 2 listed former swimming baths are being converted into a student hub, incorporating

The Registry
Canterbury
Kent CT2 7NZ

01227 827272 (admissions)
information@kent.ac.uk
www.kent.ac.uk
www.kentunion.co.uk
Affiliation: none

***The Times and Sunday Times* Rankings**

Overall Ranking: **=23** (last year: 30)

Teaching quality:	**=55**	81.5%
Student experience:	**=38**	85.4%
Research quality:	**33**	35.2%
Entry standards:	**=46**	363
Student–staff ratio:	**=17**	12.9
Services & facilities/student:	**91**	£1,513
Expected completion rate:	**39**	90.7%
Good honours:	**21**	80%
Graduate prospects:	**36**	76.7%

facilities for the students' union, bar and other social spaces, for occupation in September 2016. The university also has a base in Tonbridge serving 3,000 part-time students, who are mainly taught in associate colleges.

Capitalising on its location, Kent has become probably the UK's most active in Europe, both in terms of its participation in EU programmes and in its continental ventures. Styling itself "the UK's European university", Kent now has postgraduate sites in Brussels, Paris, Athens and Rome, as well as giving many undergraduates the option of a year abroad. There are partnerships with over 100 European universities.

Kent encourages all its academics to take a Postgraduate Certificate in Higher Education. Its staff have been awarded National Teaching Fellowships in five of the last six years. The student population is more diverse than many in the south of England: over nine out of ten undergraduates are state educated and 30 per cent come from working-class homes. Entry grades have been rising in most subjects. Offers are pitched according to the UCAS points tariff, although those taking A levels are expected to pass at least three subjects (one of which may be general studies). In 2015 Kent offered scholarships of £2,000 a year (renewable annually) to candidates who achieved at least three As at A level, or the equivalent. Where one subject is maths or a modern foreign language, the threshold was AAB. The 2016 scholarships have yet to be announced. Graduates of all disciplines fare well in the employment market – the university regularly features among the top 20 for graduate starting salaries.

Campus security is good, although some complain that Canterbury itself is expensive and limited socially. Residential accommodation was upgraded and extended with the £25-million redevelopment of Keynes College and completion of the Park Wood student village. Sports facilities have improved considerably following an investment of £4.8 million in a fitness suite that includes an extensive range of free weights, as well as four Olympic power-lifting platforms. A multipurpose fitness and dance studio has also been built, and a new indoor tennis centre has been added alongside the sports centre.

Undergraduate Fees and Bursaries

» Fees for UK/EU students 2016–17	£9,000
Partner colleges	£5,640–£9,000
Placement year / year abroad	£865 / £1,350
» Fees for international students 2015–16	£12,890–£15,380

» Household income below £42.6K and meeting various conditions with priority to those from areas of low participation in higher education, a bursary of £2,000 years 1 and 3, £1,500 year 2.

» Partner school and college scholarships of £1,000 a year; subject and academic achievement scholarships.

Students

Undergraduates:	**14,675**	**(525)**
Postgraduates:	**2,595**	**(1,210)**
Mature students:	**10.8%**	
International students:	**19.9%**	
Applications per place:	**6.7**	
From state-sector schools:	**92.7%**	
From working-class homes:	**30%**	
Satisfaction with students' union	**71%**	

For detailed information about sports facilities:
www.kent.ac.uk/sports

Accommodation

Number of places and costs refer to 2015–16
University-provided places: 5,417
Percentage catered: 12%
Catered costs: £106–£226 a week.
Self-catered costs: £106–£157 a week.
First years are guaranteed accommodation provided applications received before 31 July.
International students: as above.
hospitality-enquiry@kent.ac.uk
www.kent.ac.uk/accommodation

King's College London

King's is to rent the iconic Bush House, the former headquarters of the BBC World Service, opposite its Strand campus, in order to upgrade its teaching facilities and make room for a fast-growing student population. King's has been one of the Russell Group institutions to take greatest advantage of the relaxation of recruitment restrictions: the intake of undergraduates has grown by 30 per cent – more than 1,000 students – in three years. With applications continuing to rise, there is scope to continue. The college was going to make further changes to its campus with the demolition of Georgian and Victorian buildings on the Strand, but withdrew its application after protests from conservationists. King's had already expanded into the East Wing of Somerset House, providing impressive new premises for the School of Law, and earmarked £140 million of further campus developments. But, with more than 28,000 students and growing numbers of researchers, conditions were becoming cramped. King's will begin to occupy Bush House and its four neighbouring buildings in September 2016.

Once known primarily for science, King's now has a distinguished reputation across nine schools, including humanities, law and social sciences, which includes war studies. The college's research strength has established it in the top 20 of the QS World University Rankings, although poor student satisfaction keeps it out of the top 20 in our league table. In the 2014 Research Excellence Framework, 85 per cent of the college's submission was judged to be world-leading or internationally excellent, placing it in the top 15 on this measure. Law, education, clinical medicine and philosophy all ranked in the top three in the country and there were good results in general engineering, history, psychology and communication and media studies. The results produced the biggest increase in research funding of any university. Today's researchers follow in a tradition that has seen King's play a part in many of the advances that shape modern life, including the discovery of DNA and the development of radar. Twelve alumni or academics have won Nobel Prizes. It is Europe's largest centre for the education of doctors, dentists and other healthcare professionals, and home to six Medical Research Council centres. King's Health Partners Academic Health Sciences Centre represents a pioneering collaboration between the college and three NHS foundation trusts.

King's is one of the oldest and largest of the University of London's colleges, and describes itself as "the most central university in London" because four of its five campuses are within a single square

Strand
London WC2R 2LS

020 7848 7000 (enquiries)
contact via website
www.kcl.ac.uk
www.kclsu.org
Affiliation: Russell Group

***The Times and Sunday Times* Rankings**

Overall Ranking: **27** (last year: 29)

Teaching quality:	**125**	73.9%
Student experience:	**114**	79.7%
Research quality:	**9**	44%
Entry standards:	**15**	455
Student–staff ratio:	**=5**	11.3
Services & facilities/student:	**29**	£2,198
Expected completion rate:	**24**	92.8%
Good honours:	**11**	83.2%
Graduate prospects:	**6**	85.7%

mile around the banks of the Thames. The fifth is not far away at Denmark Hill in south London. The original Strand site and the Waterloo campus, which includes the largest university building in London, house most of the non-medical departments. Nursing and midwifery and some biomedical subjects are also based at Waterloo, while medicine and dentistry are mainly at Guy's Hospital, near London Bridge, and in the St Thomas' Hospital campus, across the river from the Houses of Parliament. The Denmark Hill campus houses the Institute of Psychiatry, as well as more medicine and dentistry. Libraries on all the main campuses have been upgraded recently – part of a £60-million programme of improvements to student facilities.

About one student in five is from outside the European Union, many of them among the 6,500 postgraduates. An institutional audit by the Quality Assurance Agency gave King's the highest mark, stressing the excellence of the student support services. Graduates enjoy among the best employment rates in the UK and typically also earn some of the highest starting salaries. The college's location means King's students are in an enviable position for accessing opportunities for work experience. More than a quarter of the undergraduates come from independent schools, but a similar proportion are from low-income families – significantly better than average for the courses and entry qualifications. The college's Access to Medicine course, which attracts talented students from generally low-performing schools into medical degrees, has now been replicated for dentistry, with the Enhanced Support Dentistry Programme.

Accommodation at King's is plentiful and spread over a variety of residences, from busy central locations to quieter, residential areas. As well as nearly 700 intercollegiate places run by the University of London available to King's undergraduates, there are more than 4,000 places in university-owned provision. Some of the outdoor sports facilities are a long train ride from the college, but there are facilities for all the main sports, as well as rifle ranges, two gyms and a swimming pool.

Undergraduate Fees and Bursaries

» Fees for UK/EU students 2016–17	£9,000
Year abroad	£1,350
» Fees for international students 2015–16	£15,600–£20,700
Medicine and dentistry	£36,050

» King's Living Bursary of £1,500 (household income below £25K) or £1,000 (£25K–£42.6K), payable for all years.
» Bursaries and merit scholarships, including 50 Access to Professions scholarships of £3,000 for years 1–3 for certain courses in medicine and dentistry; 25 Dickson Poon law scholarships of £9,000 a year and 50 of £6,000 a year.
» Enhanced student hardship fund.
» Check the university's website for the latest information.

Undergraduates:	**13,505**	**(2,905)**
Postgraduates:	**6,350**	**(4,885)**
Mature students:	**17%**	
International students:	**25.2%**	
Applications per place:	**8.7**	
From state-sector schools:	**72.4%**	
From working-class homes:	**25.9%**	
Satisfaction with students' union	**66%**	

For detailed information about sports facilities:
www.kcl.ac.uk/campuslife/sport

Accommodation

Number of places and costs refer to 2015–16
University-provided places: 4,803; 700 intercollegiate.
Percentage catered: 100% of intercollegiate
Catered costs: £137.90 (standard single) – £455.00 (studio) a week.
Self-catered costs: £140 (standard single) – £282 (studio) a week (40 weeks).
New full-time undergraduate students are guaranteed the offer of one year in accommodation if specific conditions are met.
International students: priority for new students.
www.kcl.ac.uk/study/ug/residences/

Kingston University

Kingston focused on helping its students to start their own companies long before most universities saw the need. The Enterprise Department was established more than a decade ago, giving advice to would-be entrepreneurs in any subject and the possibility of financial support with start-ups. Kingston has now been among the top two universities for graduate start-ups for six years in succession and is also among the leading institutions for turnover from those companies. There were 319 start-ups in 2013–14, an increase of almost 50 per cent on the previous year, and the combined turnover of all the university's start-ups came close to £30 million. A career focus runs through all Kingston's courses. The university has the third largest engineering faculty in London, for example, with its own Learjet and a flight simulator to support its highly regarded aeronautical engineering courses.

The university markets itself as in "lively, leafy London", making a virtue of its suburban, riverside location southwest of central London as well as its proximity to the bright lights. Two of its four campuses are close to Kingston town centre; another, two miles away, is at Kingston Hill; the fourth is in Roehampton Vale, where a site once used as an aerospace factory now contains a new technology block. Kingston has opened three impressive new buildings as part of a £123-million programme to revitalise its entire estate.

The university has already spent £20 million on the John Galsworthy Building on the main campus, which incorporates lecture theatres, flexible teaching space and information technology suites as well as a "Knowledge Centre" for students to do coursework. The Business School acquired a new £26-million home in 2012, and a new learning resources centre is part of an £11-million improvement programme at the University's Knights Park campus, which includes the refurbishment of studio space, an upgraded reception and gallery area and external landscaping. Library facilities on each campus have been upgraded, bringing together library, computing and multimedia facilities to encourage interactive and group learning. The learning resources centres have received government recognition for excellent customer service. The main centres are open 24 hours a day during term-time weekdays, while a high-tech self-issue system has speeded up borrowing.

The School of Art, which is rated in the top 100 in the world by QS, is celebrating its 140th anniversary with a grant from the Heritage Lottery Fund to make a film capturing its evolution, and exploring the stories and personalities connected with it. Arts and design achieved among the best

River House
53–57 High Street
Kingston upon Thames
KT1 1LQ

0844 855 2177 (enquiries)
aps@kingston.ac.uk
www.kingston.ac.uk
www.kusu.co.uk
Affiliation: University Alliance

***The Times and Sunday Times* Rankings**

Overall Ranking: **111** (last year: 117)

Teaching quality:	**116**	76.1%
Student experience:	**=112**	79.9%
Research quality:	**=90**	5.1%
Entry standards:	**=101**	299
Student–staff ratio:	**=98**	19.3
Services & facilities/student:	**79**	£1,637
Expected completion rate:	**=98**	82.2%
Good honours:	**=74**	67.4%
Graduate prospects:	**=96**	60.7%

results in the 2014 Research Excellence Framework (REF), together with history and English, where the whole submission was given the top grade for its external impact. The university entered relatively few academics for the REF – only 16 per cent of the eligible staff – but 60 per cent of the submission reached the top two categories and there was some world-leading research in each of the nine areas in which it was assessed. Kingston is to head the largest project in a new Government-funded programme to boost postgraduate study. Its aim is to encourage students who might not normally become postgraduates to continue on to Master's courses in science, technology, engineering and mathematics and then track how they progress.

The Faculty of Health, Social Care and Education (run jointly with St George's, University of London) now has more than 7,000 students and has won two major NHS London contracts, which will increase numbers in nursing and physiotherapy. There is a link with the Royal Marsden School of Cancer Nursing and Rehabilitation, enabling some students to spend up to half of their course on clinical placements working in hospital, primary care and community settings.

Kingston has one of the most ethnically mixed student populations of any UK university, and many undergraduates are also the first in their family to experience higher education. More than a quarter of Kingston's places go to mature students and 42 per cent to those from working-class families. Most students like the university's location, although they complain about the high cost of living. A "one-stop shop" deals with student issues ranging from careers and accommodation to complaints and financial advice. A unit, thought to be unique in the UK, offers free mediation of disputes involving local people under the supervision of accredited staff from the university law school. More than £20 million has been spent on halls of residence and Kingston's sports facilities have improved with the addition of a £2.65-million sports pavilion and upgraded sports ground.

Undergraduate Fees and Bursaries

- Fees for UK/EU students 2016–17 £9,000
  Foundation degree £4,950–£6,000
- Fees for international students 2015–16 £11,300–£13,700
- Household income below £25K and meeting various conditions, at least 250 bursaries of £2,000 in year 1.
- Progression awards (£500–£1,500) to years 2 and 3 with conditions. Assistance from Study Support and Retention Fund.
- Range of other scholarships and bursaries available.
- Check the university's website for the latest information.

Students

Undergraduates:	**16,290**	**(1,495)**
Postgraduates:	**2,325**	**(2,940)**
Mature students:	**30.6%**	
International students:	**14.9%**	
Applications per place:	**8.6**	
From state-sector schools:	**95.2%**	
From working-class homes:	**42%**	
Satisfaction with students' union	**61%**	

For detailed information about sports facilities:
www.kingston.ac.uk/sport

Accommodation

Number of places and costs refer to 2015–16
University-provided places: 2,365; private hall: 214
Percentage catered: 0%
Self-catered costs: £111.25–£280 a week (university provided; 40 weeks); £186.00 and £266.00 (private hall; 50 weeks).
Self-catering accommodation is offered to most first years who make Kingston their firm choice through UCAS.
International students: as above, offered places if conditions met, subject to availability.
www.kingston.ac.uk/accommodation/

Lancaster University

Lancaster is aiming to be among the top ten universities in the UK and the top 100 in the world by 2020. Both are realistic ambitions, although the university's last appearance our top ten was four years ago. A big improvement in grades from the 2014 Research Excellence Framework, when 83 per cent of its work was considered world-leading or internationally excellent, might have sparked a return. But other leading universities improved even more or submitted more academics for assessment. Nevertheless, there were particularly good results in maths, computing and health subjects, and a strong performance across the board. Lancaster remains comfortably the highest-placed university in the northwest of England.

The university's strategic plan commits it to becoming a "global player" in both teaching and research. It is already the only UK university with a presence in sub-Saharan Africa, having opened a branch campus in Ghana. There are also partnerships with universities in India, Pakistan, Malaysia and China that mean more students are taking a Lancaster degree overseas than in the UK. Hundreds of Lancaster students also spend part of their courses in America, Asia, Australia or Europe. The university has always championed a flexible degree structure, in which most undergraduates can broaden their first-year studies by taking a second or third subject. The final choice of degree comes only at the end of that year.

Still a relatively small university, Lancaster has 13,000 students on a 360-acre parkland campus. Undergraduates join one of eight residential colleges on campus, which become the centre of most students' social life. Most house between 800 and 900 students in self-catering accommodation, and each has its own bar and social facilities. The historic city of Lancaster is a ten-minute bus ride away. Both the campus and city have been rated among the safest in the UK.

The campus has had a £500-million makeover, with much of the money going on eco-friendly student residences. Lancaster has held the title of Best University Halls since 2010 in the National Student Housing Survey, and is one of only three UK universities to be awarded an International Accommodation Quality Mark, indicating over 90 per cent positive feedback from international students. The university is set to spend millions more on refreshing the campus walkways and completely renovating its library. A 24-hour student learning space provides flexible learning environments and social space with up-to-date technology. Other recent developments include a leadership centre for the highly rated Management School, which has helped

Bailrigg
Lancaster LA1 4YW

01524 592028 (admissions)
ugadmissions@lancaster.ac.uk
www.lancaster.ac.uk
http://lusu.co.uk
Affiliation: none

***The Times and Sunday Times* Rankings**

Overall Ranking: **11** (last year: 12)

Teaching quality:	**=43**	82.3%
Student experience:	**=38**	85.4%
Research quality:	**15**	39.1%
Entry standards:	**18**	436
Student–staff ratio:	**=22**	13.7
Services & facilities/student:	**14**	£2,566
Expected completion rate:	**=17**	93.5%
Good honours:	**33**	76.9%
Graduate prospects:	**15**	82.5%

4,700 students to find work placements in the micro-business and start-up sector. Lancaster was awarded the Small Business Charter Gold Award – one of only three – in recognition of the role it has played in helping to kick-start British enterprise.

An award-winning building for engineering has seen undergraduate numbers double in the last five years. The university has also brought together art, design and theatre studies with the university's public art gallery, concerts and theatre, invested heavily in design and established a Confucius Institute as a hub for Chinese language teaching and culture. Lancaster has been the most successful university at reducing carbon emissions, winning particular praise for its innovative wind turbine project, which generates approximately 15 per cent of its annual electricity consumption. The university has won a string of environmental awards for its residences and other facilities.

Lancaster is more successful than most research universities in widening participation among under-represented groups. Nine out of ten undergraduates are state educated and a quarter come from the four lowest socio-economic classes. Outreach activity includes summer schools for 600 sixth-formers and college students, masterclasses for 2,000 and mentoring for 250 students. The projected dropout rate of 6 per cent matches the national average for the subjects on offer. Combined degree programmes, with 200 courses to choose from, are especially popular. The degree portfolio now includes medicine. The university has established a new department of chemistry, which offers an undergraduate degree in the subject. Other recent developments have included a research centre specialising in bipolar disorder and a new Centre for Organisational Health and Wellbeing.

Some of England's most unspoilt countryside is on the university's doorstep, including the Lake District and the Forest of Bowland. The university hosts a thriving live arts scene for the campus, the city and the region, with professional theatre, dance, exhibitions and concerts. Sports facilities are good and conveniently placed, with £20-million sports centre on campus. Road and rail communications are good, but Lancaster is inevitably more limited for off-campus nightlife.

Undergraduate Fees and Bursaries

- » Fees for UK/EU students 2016–17 £9,000
- » Fees for international students 2015–16 £13,930–£17,470
  Medicine £27,500
- » Household income below £42.6K, £1,000 a year cash bursary.
- » Scholarship of £2,000 in year 1 for those with A*A*A at A Level or equivalent. Scholarship of £1,000 a year for those with A*AA at A Level or equivalent and with household income below £42.6K.
- » Check the university's website for the latest information.

Students

Undergraduates:	**9,265**	**(150)**
Postgraduates:	**2,215**	**(1,450)**
Mature students:	**6%**	
International students:	**28.3%**	
Applications per place:	**7.1**	
From state-sector schools:	**90.1%**	
From working-class homes:	**25.2%**	
Satisfaction with students' union	**69%**	

For detailed information about sports facilities:
www.lancaster.ac.uk/sport

Accommodation

Number of places and costs refer to 2015–16
University-provided places: 6,600 (plus about 900 places in university-managed houses)
Percentage catered: 5%
Catered costs: £129.08 (standard) – £166.88 (en suite) a week.
Self-catered costs: £88.20 (standard) – £150.15 (studio) a week.
All first years are normally accommodated; no formal guarantee for Insurance, Clearing and late applicants.
International students: as above.
www.lancaster.ac.uk/sbs/accommodation/

University of Leeds

Always among the most popular universities in the country, Leeds has reached its highest-ever position in our league table after climbing 15 places in two years. Now 14th, it is also the runner-up for our University of the Year award, as it was in the 2015 *Guide*. Leeds attracted an additional 5,000 applications in 2014, increasing its intake of undergraduates again. The university has been investing heavily in more academics, as well as campus improvements. There are more than 560 undergraduate programmes, with students encouraged to take courses outside their main subject. The distinctive new Leeds Curriculum requires undergraduates to undertake a research project in their final year, which is intended to be seen as the "pinnacle of their academic achievement" and is weighted accordingly. Leeds was commended by the Quality Assurance Agency for its enhancement of the student learning experience. The Student Education Service provides support from the point of application to beyond graduation, and the university is establishing a new Institute for Teaching Excellence and Innovation. Leeds has been awarded more National Teaching Fellowships (20) than any other university in England.

A member of the Russell Group of research-led universities, Leeds occupies a 98-acre site within walking distance of the city centre. A £500-million capital programme for the next five years has begun with the opening of a new undergraduate library, with 1,000 seats, flexible facilities and on-site academic skills support. There is also a new £42-million Enterprise and Innovation Centre, which will assist students with start-up plans and accelerate business creation and growth across the city. Another major development will link the engineering buildings with those for physical sciences. Previous improvements have included a new home for the Institute of Communications Studies with 41 edit suites, TV and radio studios, newsroom and 60-seat cinema, a £12.5-million Energy Research building and the refurbishment of the Leeds Dental Institute. The already large students' union, famous for its long bar and big-name rock concerts, has been extended and will be refurbished in 2016. The union is the only one in the country to have won two gold standard awards in the Students' Union Evaluation Initiative.

Leeds features among the top 100 in the QS World University Rankings, and in the top 50 for English, education, communication and media studies, geography, and earth sciences. More than 80 per cent of the research assessed in the 2014 Research Excellence Framework was considered world-leading or internationally

Leeds
LS2 9JT

0113 343 2336 (enquiries)
study@leeds.ac.uk
www.leeds.ac.uk
www.luu.org.uk
Affiliation: Russell Group

***The Times and Sunday Times* Rankings**

Overall Ranking: **14** (last year: 17)

Teaching quality:	**=15**	83.7%
Student experience:	**=9**	88%
Research quality:	**27**	36.8%
Entry standards:	**20**	431
Student–staff ratio:	**21**	13.6
Services & facilities/student:	**19**	£2,418
Expected completion rate:	**=17**	93.5%
Good honours:	**15**	82.2%
Graduate prospects:	**32**	78.4%

excellent, placing the university in the top ten in the UK in 30 per cent of its subject areas. The university is truly cosmopolitan, with 5,000 international students from 141 countries among a total of more than 31,000. Leeds has one of the largest Study Abroad programmes in the country, with nearly 200 options ranging from Spain to Singapore. It is part of the Worldwide Universities Network, which brings together 18 research-led universities to collaborate on research and postgraduate programmes.

The LeedsforLife service provides students with academic and careers advice, as well as help to identify work placements and volunteering opportunities. It is available for five years after graduation. The award-winning Careers Centre hosts some of the world's biggest employers at the university, as well as advising those who choose to set up on their own. Leeds does better than many big city universities in the National Student Survey. Just over a fifth of the undergraduates attended independent schools and a similar proportion come from the four poorest socio-economic groups – both missing the university's benchmark for widening participation in higher education. The university has devoted one of the largest amounts of any institution to student support, and will continue to do so in 2016, when up to a third of UK and EU undergraduates are expected to benefit.

The rise of Leeds as a shopping and clubbing centre has added to the attractions of the university. Over 2,500 students volunteer in the local community and 400 students are trained as mentors and tutors supporting schools in the region. Leeds guarantees accommodation for all first-year undergraduates, international and exchange students and students with disabilities. In recent years there has been an increase in students living in purpose-built student accommodation close to campus and the city centre. Sports and social facilities are first rate, and Leeds teams regularly excel in competition. The university hosts one of six centres of cricketing excellence. It has more playing field space than any other, while The Edge sports centre includes a 25-metre swimming pool and a huge fitness suite.

Undergraduate Fees and Bursaries

» Fees for UK/EU students 2016–17	£9,000
» Fees for international students 2015–16	£13,500–£17,500
Medicine	£28,000
Dentistry	£30,750

» Leeds Financial Support as cash, accommodation contribution or fee waiver, household income below £10K, £3,000, Foundation year (year 0), £2,500 other years; £10K–£25K, £3,000 year 0, £2,000 other years; £25K–£30K, £1,500 all years; £30K–£36K, £1,000 all years; £36K–£42.6K, £500 all years.

» Foundation year fee waiver of £3,000 (household income below £25K) and £1,500 (household income £25K–£42.6K).

» A range of scholarships and bursaries are available.

» Check the university's website for the latest information.

Students

Undergraduates:	**22,320**	**(945)**
Postgraduates:	**4,950**	**(2,760)**
Mature students:	**9.3%**	
International students:	**11.4%**	
Applications per place:	**8.4**	
From state-sector schools:	**79.1%**	
From working-class homes:	**21%**	
Satisfaction with students' union	**92%**	

For detailed information about sports facilities:
http://sport.leeds.ac.uk

Accommodation

Number of places and costs refer to 2015–16
University-provided places: 7,900
Percentage catered: 23%
Catered costs £141–£191 a week (39 weeks).
Self-catered costs: £86–£162 a week (41–51 weeks).
Single first years are guaranteed a place if conditions are met.
International students: guaranteed to full free-paying undergraduates if conditions are met.
www.accommodation.leeds.ac.uk
accom@leeds.ac.uk

Leeds Beckett University

The demand for places had already started to recover from two disastrous years in which applications dropped by almost 30 per cent when the former Leeds Metropolitan University changed its name to Leeds Beckett. The university announced that it had "outgrown" its old identity and adopted the name of its campus at Beckett Park amid protests from students and alumni. Having implemented the change and led the university from a perilous financial position to regular surpluses, Professor Susan Price has passed the leadership baton to Professor Peter Slee, who has moved from Huddersfield University with the aim of capitalising on the city's central position in the Government's Northern Powerhouse plans. The university has achieved Customer Service Excellence accreditation for the entire university, one of only two in the UK to do so. It also holds the Gold Investors in People standard, and is the only university to achieve both of these independent standards. Students are included on the committees that design and manage courses.

Little more than half of all undergraduates are taking conventional full-time degrees, such is the popularity of sandwich and part-time courses. It is intended that all Leeds Beckett students should leave the university with three graduate attributes: to be enterprising, digitally literate and have a global outlook. All undergraduate courses have been redesigned with these qualities in mind and all include at least two weeks work-related learning a year. The university has a longstanding reputation for widening participation in higher education: well over 90 per cent of undergraduates are state-educated and more than a third come from low-income families. The university runs a wide range of summer schools, which benefit more than 24,000 young people a year. A Regional University Network of further education colleges enables students to take Leeds Beckett courses locally. However, the university's projected drop-out rate of 20 per cent is among the highest in the country.

There are two bases in Leeds: the City Campus, in the heart of the city centre, and the Headingley Campus, three miles away in 100 acres of park and woodland at Beckett Park. The latter boasts outstanding sports facilities, including a new sports arena and multi-use sports pitches. The sports centre offers a variety of options for performance and participation sport, alongside the £2-million Carnegie Regional Tennis Centre and teaching accommodation for education,

City Campus
Leeds
LS1 3HE

0113 812 3113 (enquiries)
admissionsenquiries@leedsbeckett.ac.uk
www.leedsbeckett.ac.uk
www.leedsbeckettsu.co.uk
Affiliation: none

***The Times and Sunday Times* Rankings**

Overall Ranking: **114** (last year: 111)

Teaching quality:	**100**	78.5%
Student experience:	**=82**	82.7%
Research quality:	**=100**	4.1%
Entry standards:	**109**	288
Student–staff ratio:	**114**	20.7
Services & facilities/student:	**106**	£1,341
Expected completion rate:	**114**	78.8%
Good honours:	**=104**	61.8%
Graduate prospects:	**110**	58.5%

informatics, law and business. Over 7,000 students take part in some form of sporting activity, and there is a range of sports scholarships. The Athletic Union hosts 48 clubs and the 50 university teams are among the most successful in national competition. An annual pass for both the Headingley and City campus facilities currently costs £125. In the first developments of their kind, a new stand was built at the Headingley rugby ground, with classrooms, coaching facilities and social space for use by the university and the two professional clubs, and a new pavilion at the adjacent Test and County Cricket ground has similar multi-use facilities.

The City Campus has seen a £100-million transformation and is still being improved. The futuristic Rose Bowl lecture theatre complex next to Leeds Civic Hall houses the business school, while Broadcasting Place is home to the Faculty of Arts and Society. The former BBC building next door has reopened as Old Broadcasting House and hosts the Enterprise Office, which helps identify opportunities to generate commercial income and support bids for funding and contracts. Recent campus developments include a £1-million clinical skills suite and cutting-edge biomedical sciences laboratories, and the library has been refurbished. A growing emphasis on educational technology is enhanced by 24-hour libraries, which have achieved the Customer Service Excellence standard for ten years in a row. They contain more than 800 computers and over 2,000 study spaces.

The university almost doubled the number of academics it entered for the 2014 Research Excellence Framework compared with the 2008 assessments. Just over a third of their work was rated as world-leading or internationally excellent, with architecture and sports studies producing much the best results. Leeds Beckett's reputation is mainly for applied research: three interdisciplinary research institutes focus on health, sport and sustainability, and there are ten centres in more specialist fields such as retail excellence, active lifestyles and diversity and equity.

Leeds Beckett is benefiting from the city's growing reputation for nightlife, but it is making its own contribution with a famously lively entertainments scene. With 4,500 bed spaces, those who accept places before Clearing are guaranteed university accommodation.

Undergraduate Fees and Bursaries

» Fees for UK/EU students 2016–17	£9,000
Placement year	no fee
» Fees for international students 2015–16	£9,500

» Students with at least ABB at A level or equivalent, £1,000 fee waiver in year 1.
» Associated schools and colleges bursary of £300 in year 1.
» Enhanced student hardship fund.
» Check the university's website for the latest information.

Students

Undergraduates:	**17,610**	**(3,320)**
Postgraduates:	**1,395**	**(2,575)**
Mature students:	**15.7%**	
International students:	**5.2%**	
Applications per place:	**6.1**	
From state-sector schools:	**94.3%**	
From working-class homes:	**35.7%**	
Satisfaction with students' union	**63%**	

For detailed information about sports facilities:
www.leedsbeckett.ac.uk/sport

Accommodation

Number of places and costs refer to 2015–16
University-provided places: 4,500
Percentage catered: 0%
Self-catered costs: £87.50–£170.00 a week (40–45 weeks).
First years with Conditional Firm or Unconditional Firm offers guaranteed accommodation.
International students: guaranteed accommodation of conditions are met.
accommodation@leedsbeckett.ac.uk
www.leedsbeckett.ac.uk/accommodation

Leeds Trinity University

Leeds Trinity has invested £15 million in campus improvements and is planning to spend another £25 million to cater for 1,000 more students over the next five years. Meeting the target will require expansion of almost 30 per cent, although undergraduate enrolments fell slightly in 2014 despite a healthy increase in applications. The university has been increasing the variety of degrees available to applicants and is planning seven more in 2016. They will range from marketing and sport to criminology, creative and professional writing, and a two-year course in mathematics education. The university already offers accelerated two-year degrees in education and sport, and tourism and leisure management. Like all the university's undergraduate programmes, they include full-time professional work placements.

Leeds Trinity is one of two institutions given university status in 2012 that are Catholic foundations. It "promotes dialogue and teaching of the Catholic Church", but is not controlled by the Church and welcomes students of all faiths and none. The university grew out of two Catholic teacher training colleges established in the 1960s. Education is still the biggest subject – a new Institute for Childhood and Education will pool the expertise of its acclaimed departments of Primary Education, Secondary Education and Children, Young People and Families – but there are also departments of media, film and culture; journalism; business, management and marketing; psychology and sport, health and nutrition.

The university's campus is 20 minutes northwest of Leeds city centre, in Horsforth. The latest big development was the upgrading of the Media Centre, which is now fully digital for video and audio operations, and students are able to shoot in HD following the purchase of broadcast-quality portable cameras. A new range of computers and studio cameras have been installed to meet the demands of journalism and media production courses. The Centre for Journalism has developed two additional multimedia newsrooms with easy access to studios, equipment and edit suites. A new residential block with 228 bedrooms and an additional learning and teaching building are due to open before the start of the academic year in 2016.

The three-year Digital Campus project involves the investment of £1.2 million to provide a seamless, resilient and flexible ICT environment, accessible from off campus. The launch of a self-service system for borrowers at the library has already doubled usage figures. The Students' Union was re-launched in 2013, when it relocated to the main campus building and

Brownberrie Lane
Horsforth
Leeds LS18 5HD

0113 283 7123 (admissions)
admissions@leedstrinity.ac.uk
www.leedstrinity.ac.uk
www.ltsu.co.uk
Affiliations: GuildHE, Cathedrals Group

***The Times and Sunday Times* Rankings**

Overall Ranking: **91** (last year: =91)

Teaching quality:	**19**	83.5%
Student experience:	**=89**	82.3%
Research quality:	**119**	2%
Entry standards:	**=112**	284
Student–staff ratio:	**121**	21.7
Services & facilities/student:	**97**	£1,470
Expected completion rate:	**=101**	81.7%
Good honours:	**=66**	68.9%
Graduate prospects:	**72**	65.8%

restructured itself to have a greater focus on academic representation and meeting the needs of a diverse range of students. Extra social space for students and staff has been developed at the same time. The student bar and venue has been revamped and given a new location. A new Student Achievement Team offers one-to-one tutorials, group tutorials and seminars and workshops to promote academic skills. In 2015 the university opened the Trinity Enterprise Centre to help students launch their own businesses. Its advice and facilities are available to local businesses as well as students.

Leeds Trinity's stated aim is to be an "autonomous teaching-led research-informed institution providing higher education characterised by vocational excellence". Only 20 academics were entered for the 2014 Research Excellence Framework, but there were good results in communication, cultural and media studies, and library and information management. The flagship research centre, the Leeds Centre for Victorian Studies, celebrated its 20th anniversary in 2014.

Nearly two-thirds of the students are female and almost as many are the first in their family to attend university. Leeds Trinity exceeds all its national benchmarks for widening participation in higher education: just over 40 per cent of undergraduates come from working-class homes, while nearly a quarter are from areas with little tradition of sending students to university – one of the highest proportions in the country. The projected dropout rate has improved considerably and is now lower than the national average for Leeds Trinity's courses and entry qualifications. There are still little more than 3,000 students, despite recent growth. The new university was displaying high levels of student satisfaction well before its new status was conferred, and does particularly well on feedback, a bone of contention in many universities.

Among the outreach activities is a new Children's University, based on the campus, which offers high quality, exciting and innovative learning activities outside normal school hours to children aged seven to 14.

Sports facilities are good and include a 3G pitch and new changing facilities. The city is one of the most popular with students, although the campus is not central.

Undergraduate Fees and Bursaries

- Fees for UK/EU students 2016–17 £9,000
  Foundation degree £5,000
- Fees for international students 2015–16 £10,000–£11,500
- Household income below £25K, a bursary of £1,000 paid in year 2 only.
- Enhanced student hardship fund.
- Check the university's website for the latest information.

Students

Undergraduates:	**2,675**	**(70)**
Postgraduates:	**185**	**(390)**
Mature students:	**12.1%**	
International students:	**1.3%**	
Applications per place:	**8.3**	
From state-sector schools:	**98.9%**	
From working-class homes:	**41.4%**	
Satisfaction with students' union	**68%**	

For detailed information about sports facilities:
www.leedstrinity.ac.uk/student-life/trinity-sport

Accommodation

Places and costs refer to 2015-16
University-provided places: 575
Percentage catered: 35%
Catered costs: £111–£120 a week (41 weeks).
Self-catered costs: £90–£119 a week (41 weeks).
Priority is given to first-year students.
International students: same as above.
accommodation@leedstrinity.ac.uk
www.leedstrinity.ac.uk/student-life/accommodation

University of Leicester

The discovery of the body of Richard III by the university's archaeologists brought global attention to Leicester and continued to benefit it in the 2014 Research Excellence Framework, when almost three-quarters of its work in the subject was rated as world-leading in impact. Across all subjects, the same proportion of Leicester's research was either at this level or classified as internationally excellent overall, with the School of Museum Studies producing the best results, as it did in 2008. The results, which were also good in clinical medicine, biology, earth science and general engineering, brought a substantial increase in research funding. The raised profile of the university, which won a string of awards, has also helped to increase applications, which were up 5 per cent in 2014. It fell out of our top 20 this year as a result of declining student satisfaction, although it maintained its high spending on student facilities and has among the best staffing levels.

New degree options will be available to students entering in 2016, with the aim of providing the most flexible curriculum in the UK. Undergraduates will be able to choose single, joint or major/minor courses. The move follows research by the university which revealed strong demand among current students and prospective applicants for more flexibility in degree options. Those choosing a major/minor programme will have the flexibility to combine a wide range of subjects, including new areas such as global studies. They will be able to spend 75 per cent of their time studying their principal subject and 25 per cent on the minor element. Many existing subjects will be available as majors and minors, with more coming on stream in later years. The university has also introduced a number of employability initiatives, including a new undergraduate internship programme which promises to make up to 500 paid internships available each year.

Leicester's period in the limelight has coincided with the implementation of a £1-billion development plan. A new £42-million Centre for Medicine is taking shape and a £12.5-million cardiovascular research centre is already open. Clinical medicine is taught at the city's three hospitals, but all other teaching and much of the residential accommodation is concentrated in a leafy suburb a mile from the city centre. The £32-million library has doubled the available space and brought the total number of workspaces to 1,500. The university has a long-established reputation in space science, with Europe's largest university-based space research facility, including the £52-million National Space Centre. The Department of Genetics, where DNA fingerprinting was discovered, is

University Road
Leicester LE1 7RH

0116 252 5281 (admissions)
admissions@le.ac.uk
www.le.ac.uk
www.leicesterunion.com
Affiliation: none

***The Times and Sunday Times* Rankings**

Overall Ranking: **=28** (last year: 20)

Teaching quality:	**=106**	77.5%
Student experience:	**=53**	84.4%
Research quality:	**=37**	31.8%
Entry standards:	**=37**	386
Student–staff ratio:	**=13**	12.2
Services & facilities/student:	**10**	£2,600
Expected completion rate:	**=26**	92.5%
Good honours:	**28**	78.3%
Graduate prospects:	**50**	72.1%

another star feature. The university believes in blending teaching and research: it was the only institution to see three of its academics awarded National Teaching Fellowships in 2014, adding to an already impressive total.

The university was founded as a memorial to the fallen of the First World War and it has been playing a full part in the commemoration of the war's centenary. Little more than 10,000 full-time undergraduates are based on the main campus, but substantial postgraduate and distance learning programmes bring Leicester close to the size of other big city universities. The undergraduate population is among the most socially diverse of any university in our top 30. Nearly nine out of ten undergraduates come from state schools and 28 per cent are from low-income families. Leicester has over 4,200 student bed spaces, so first years are guaranteed a residential place. New facilities at Oadby Student Village include group study areas, social spaces, cinema room and a refurbished bar. Many second- and third-year students also live in hall, although the majority choose to live in the reasonably priced private accommodation available nearby. The main sports facilities are conveniently located: currently, students will pay a basic membership fee of £133 a year to use them.

As a city, Leicester is not one of the most fashionable student destinations, but its ethnic diversity makes for a rich cultural experience, and in term time 12 per cent of the population are students. It is big enough to provide all the normal sports and entertainment opportunities, but also offers events such as the biggest Diwali celebrations outside India. The Demos Bohemian index rated Leicester the second most creative city in Britain behind London, and Birmingham is also easily accessible via public transport. The award-winning students' union has been refurbished and is the only union in the country to contain an O_2 Academy.

Undergraduate Fees and Bursaries

» Fees for UK/EU students 2016–17	£9,000
Placement year	£1,000
» Fees for international students 2015–16	£14,000–£17,270
Medicine	£17,270–£35,170

- » Household income below £25K or completed approved Compact Scheme, a bursary of £1,000 a year.
- » Academic scholarship of £1,000 for university services, books and stationery for those with at least AAB at A level or equivalent (excluding medical students).
- » Enhanced student hardship fund.
- » Check the university's website for the latest information.

Students

Undergraduates:	**10,050**	**(855)**
Postgraduates:	**3,520**	**(2,325)**
Mature students:	**12.7%**	
International students:	**22.9%**	
Applications per place:	**8.2**	
From state-sector schools:	**88.7%**	
From working-class homes:	**27.6%**	
Satisfaction with students' union	**72%**	

For detailed information about sports facilities:
www2.le.ac.uk/offices/sports

Accommodation

Number of places and costs refer to 2015–16
University-provided places: 4,205
Percentage catered: 25%
Catered costs: £130.90–£228.90 a week (30 weeks).
Self-catered costs: £81.20–£179.20 (39–42 weeks).
First-year students are guaranteed accommodation if conditions are met.
International students: as above.
accommodation@le.ac.uk
www2.le.ac.uk/offices/accommodation

University of Lincoln

Lincoln's move to a purpose-built campus next to a marina in the centre of the city brought about the most dramatic transformation of a university in modern times, following its move from Hull. Now the university has announced a further upgrading that will cost £130 million, the equivalent of its annual income. The funding includes a £48-million loan from the European Investment Bank, and will provide new teaching and research facilities, as well as on-campus accommodation for another 500 students. The accent will be on science and health subjects, with major new developments in both areas by 2017. Lincoln is already among the top 15 post-1992 universities in our table and close to the top 60 overall.

The university markets itself as "the modern university in a historic setting", referring to the impressive campus that has been developed since its opening in 1996. The most recent addition is the new £14-million Science and Innovation Park, launched in collaboration with Lincolnshire Co-operative. Its first major building, the Joseph Banks Laboratories, opened in 2014 as the new base for the university's schools of chemistry, life sciences and pharmacy. The £7-million Engineering Hub, built in collaboration with Siemens and emda, was the UK's first purpose-built engineering school in 25 years, and won an award for collaboration with business and industry. A library in a converted warehouse and a students' union and entertainment venue in a former railway engine shed were among the imaginative campus developments. There have also been an £11-million Art and Design Building, new science laboratories, sports facilities and a School of Architecture. A £6-million performing arts centre contains a 450-seat theatre and three large studio spaces, while the Human Performance Centre is a regional facility for excellence in sport, coaching and exercise science.

Lincoln has won national recognition for its collaboration with local business and industry, for example with the National Centre for Food Manufacturing, based in Holbeach, which specialises in the production of chilled foods. The Lincoln Business School has a thriving business incubation unit and the university delivers work-based learning for companies and for the armed forces. A one-stop-shop provides students with careers advice, enhances their CVs, helps them to gain work experience and find jobs, as well as supporting graduates who are setting up their own businesses. The university has expanded its graduate internship scheme and runs a popular summer placement programme. It is also working to increase its international profile, launching a Foundation programme

Brayford Pool
Lincoln LN6 7TS

01522 886644 (enquiries)
contact via website
www.lincoln.ac.uk
http://lincolnsu.com
Affiliation: University Alliance

***The Times and Sunday Times* Rankings**

Overall Ranking: **=62** (last year: 60)

Teaching quality:	**60**	81.1%
Student experience:	**=49**	84.6%
Research quality:	**58**	10.3%
Entry standards:	**58**	335
Student–staff ratio:	**85**	18
Services & facilities/student:	**=74**	£1,665
Expected completion rate:	**=52**	87.6%
Good honours:	**89**	65%
Graduate prospects:	**53**	70.7%

to prepare overseas students before joining the first year of an undergraduate degree.

Lincoln initially concentrated on social sciences and now has a much wider range of courses for its 14,000 students. Science provision has expanded considerably, with pharmacy, chemistry and zoology recent additions and the School of Architecture now has over 400 students. The new School of Mathematics and Physics welcomes its first students this autumn. There was a good performance in the 2014 Research Excellence Framework, when more than half of a large submission was rated as internationally excellent or world leading, and the university was placed in the top ten nationally for agriculture and health subjects. The university is committed to research-engaged teaching across its curriculum, and encourages undergraduates to work with postgraduates and academic staff on research projects. Several degrees can be taken as work-based programmes, with credit awarded for relevant aspects of the jobs. Lincoln was the first university to win a Charter Mark for exceptional service. In its most recent Quality Assurance Agency review, the university was commended for the innovative ways in which it gives its students a voice.

More than a third of the undergraduates come from the four poorest socio-economic groups and the improved dropout rate of less than 10 per cent is below the average for the subjects on offer, given the entry standards. Lincoln leads the *Magna Carta – Education for Liberty* network, which encourages and supports more young people from local schools and colleges to access higher education. The university has generally done well in the National Student Survey, with good results recently in journalism, psychology, drama, English, and sport and exercise science.

The city is adapting to its student population with new bars and clubs, while the Students' Union was named Union of the Year by the National Union of Students, in recognition of its successes in influencing university policy and increasing student participation. The campus already has more than 1,600 beds, and along with private developments close to the university now provide well over 4,000 residential places.

Undergraduate Fees and Bursaries

- Fees for UK/EU students 2016–17 £9,000
  Placement year / year abroad no fee
- Fees for international students 2015–16 £12,084–£14,522
- Household income below £40K, bursary of £500 a year (except for repeat years).
- Scholarships and bursaries for local students, sports, engineering and care leavers.
- Enhanced student hardship fund.
- Check the university's website for the latest information.

Students

Undergraduates:	**9,545**	**(1,665)**
Postgraduates:	**980**	**(1,210)**
Mature students:	**14.5%**	
International students:	**8.9%**	
Applications per place:	**5.2**	
From state-sector schools:	**97.5%**	
From working-class homes:	**35.7%**	
Satisfaction with students' union	**73%**	

For detailed information about sports facilities:
www.lincoln.ac.uk/home/campuslife/sportatlincoln

Accommodation

Number of places and costs refer to 2015–16
University-provided places: 1,600
Percentage catered: 0%
Self-catered costs: £102–£134 a week.
Student accommodation prioritised by distance within application date.
International students are given detailed information and assistance.
accommodation@lincoln.ac.uk
www.lincoln.ac.uk/home/accommodation/

University of Liverpool

Liverpool is experiencing unprecedented levels of demand for its places, with two years of rising applications followed by further growth of more than 20 per cent in 2015. The university has increased its intake of undergraduates by almost 1,000 students as a result. Most entrants in 2016 will have the opportunity to spend a year studying in China, where Liverpool has a campus in the historic city of Suzhou, run in partnership with Xi'an Jiaotong University. Undergraduates in electrical engineering and electronics, computer science and maths already have that option, while Chinese students can complete the latter part of their studies in Liverpool. The university, which featured in the latest QS ranking of higher education in the five BRICS countries, is expected to have 10,000 students by the end of this year.

At home, Liverpool is investing £600 million in its city-centre campus, as well as adding a postgraduate site in the City of London for professional courses. The 10-year development plan for the main campus has already provided new and upgraded teaching and research facilities, as well as improved leisure facilities and more student accommodation. New teaching laboratories for the sciences are said to be Europe's most advanced. The university is also spending £70 million on interdisciplinary research facilities for the health and life sciences that will bring together more than 600 scientists to focus on the major health challenges of the 21st century. The management school is being extended, and the Guild of Students building has been refurbished. Other new developments include the award-winning £28.6-million Central Teaching Hub, which provides world-class facilities for the teaching of physical sciences, additional student social space and a £4-million investment in sports facilities. The library now offers 24-hour access following a £17-million redevelopment.

The university is committing nearly 30 per cent of its additional fee income to support for students from lower-income backgrounds and enhanced measures to prevent students from dropping out. More than a quarter of new undergraduates qualify for a support package totalling £2,000 a year for the duration of their course. The 5 per cent projected dropout rate is better than average for Liverpool's subjects and entry grades. The proportion of undergraduates from working-class homes is among the highest in the Russell Group of leading research-based universities, although still slightly less than the national average for the courses and entry qualifications. Liverpool entered a relatively low proportion of its eligible academics for a Russell Group university in the 2014

Liverpool L69 3BX

0151 794 5927 (enquiries)
irro@liv.ac.uk
www.liv.ac.uk
www.liverpoolguild.org
Affiliation: Russell Group

***The Times and Sunday Times* Rankings**

Overall Ranking: **=38** (last year: 36)

Teaching quality:	**105**	77.9%
Student experience:	**76**	83.4%
Research quality:	**40**	31.5%
Entry standards:	**34**	404
Student–staff ratio:	**11**	11.8
Services & facilities/student:	**26**	£2,217
Expected completion rate:	**=33**	91.3%
Good honours:	**41**	75.4%
Graduate prospects:	**=38**	76.1%

Research Excellence Framework, which held it back in our research ranking even though 70 per cent of the work was judged to be world-leading or internationally excellent. Chemistry produced spectacular results, with more than half of its research considered world-leading and only 1 per cent not in the top two categories. Computer science and general engineering also scored particularly well.

Liverpool is involved in collaborations with universities in Chile, Mexico and Spain that will allow students to complete part of their degree at one or more of these institutions via a range of options such as projects or placements. The university intends not only to increase the number of students who study abroad, but also to expand the availability of courses for those who may not be able to travel. It is already the largest provider of online postgraduate courses in Europe, with some 10,000 students taking Liverpool degrees all around the world. Liverpool also has one of Europe's largest facilities for training dentists and there has been substantial investment in new educational technology. But by far the biggest spending programme, totalling some £250 million, is devoted to student accommodation. More than 2,000 study bedrooms were added on the campus in two years and the university's off-campus accommodation is being refurbished. New residences will also be built at the Greenbank site, at suburban Mossley Hill, to provide a self-contained student village.

The Guild of Students is the centre of campus social activity. The university's indoor and outdoor sports facilities have been refurbished at a cost of £4.5 million and a new gym has opened at the Greenbank Halls site. A 25-metre swimming pool is open to the public as well as students. The university has one of the largest careers resources centres in the UK and has introduced an innovative programme of "boot camps" giving new graduates opportunities for networking with employers while developing employability skills. More than £2 million is being invested in student and graduate internships, most of them paid and lasting for substantial periods.

Undergraduate Fees and Bursaries

» Fees for UK/EU students 2016–17	£9,000
Foundation year at partner colleges	£5,000
» Fees for international students 2016–17	£13,400–£16,800
Medicine, dentistry and veterinary medicine	£29,950

» Household income below £25K, a bursary of £2,000 a year; household income £25K–£42.6K, £1,000 a year.

» Other scholarships and bursaries are available.

» Check the university's website for the latest information.

Students

Undergraduates:	**16,370**	**(485)**
Postgraduates:	**3,030**	**(1,460)**
Mature students:	**11.8%**	
International students:	**25.2%**	
Applications per place:	**8.2**	
From state-sector schools:	**87.7%**	
From working-class homes:	**23.8%**	
Satisfaction with students' union	**66%**	

For detailed information about sports facilities:
www.liv.ac.uk/sports

Accommodation

Number of places and costs refer to 2015–16
University-provided places: 4,404
Percentage catered: 42%
Catered costs: £137.20–£189.70 a week.
Self-catered costs: £121.10–£149.80 a week.
First-year students are guaranteed accommodation if Liverpool is their first choice, application is received by 31 August and requirements are met.
International students: as above and must apply by 31 July.
accommodation@liv.ac.uk; www.liv.ac.uk/accommodation

Liverpool Hope University

Liverpool Hope is back in our league tables this year after a long period in which it declined to release data because it believed such exercises were biased in favour of wealthier institutions with a longer history. Its council decided that league table methodologies had become more reliable and the university might place itself at a disadvantage by continuing to boycott them. Hope is certainly more successful on its return: it finished bottom on its one previous appearance, but is now almost 50 places up the table and in the top five for student satisfaction with the quality of teaching, feedback and academic support. The university's top priorities are student satisfaction and employability although, as a unique ecumenical university, it includes "taking faith seriously" among its five key values.

Hope was formed from the merger of two Catholic and one Church of England teacher training colleges in 1980, and now sponsors an academy with the same dual-faith character. A university since 2005, it describes itself as "teaching led, research informed and mission focused". It is in the top 20 of all universities for the percentage of academic staff with doctorates. More than half of the eligible staff were entered for the 2014 Research Excellence Framework – far more than at most post-1992 universities – and there were good results in education and theology. Undergraduates are introduced to a research culture and the final year of degree courses includes research-led seminars in which the students to choose specialisms that particularly interest them.

The university has moved away from modular degrees to an integrated curriculum, with a "disciplinary core" in each subject to ensure that all students, whether taking single or combined honours, have a similar experience and get a more rounded view of their subject. Most opt for combined subject degrees, choosing after the first year whether to give them equal weight or to go for a major/minor arrangement. The university has increased its national recruitment profile, with nearly 60 per cent of students now coming from beyond Merseyside. Undergraduates can register for the Service and Leadership Award, which is credit rated and runs alongside their degree work. Students can volunteer locally, within the region or internationally as part of Global Hope, the university's award winning overseas charity. The university has links with a number of overseas institutions which share its mission and values.

Hope saw a 24 per cent increase in applications in 2014 and increased its enrolment by more than 100 students. Nearly 20 per cent of the undergraduates

Hope Park
Liverpool L16 9JD

0151 291 3111 (enquiries)
enquiry@hope.ac.uk
www.hope.ac.uk
www.hopesu.com
Affiliation: Cathedrals Group

***The Times and Sunday Times* Rankings**

Overall Ranking: =**79** (last year: n/a)

Teaching quality:	**5**	86.8%
Student experience:	**27**	86.4%
Research quality:	**=62**	9.2%
Entry standards:	**=97**	304
Student–staff ratio:	**=100**	19.4
Services & facilities/student:	**73**	£1,667
Expected completion rate:	**91**	82.8%
Good honours:	**=96**	63.4%
Graduate prospects:	**124**	53.9%

are over 20 on entry and female students outnumber their male counterparts by more than two to one. Hope comfortably exceeds all the official benchmarks for widening participation in higher education. Almost all the undergraduates are state educated, over 40 per cent are from working-class families and more than one in five is from an area with little tradition of higher education – one of the highest proportions in England. The Network of Hope brings university courses to sixth-form colleges across the northwest of England, in areas where there is limited higher education.

The university is concentrated on two sites in Liverpool, and there is a residential outdoor education centre in Snowdonia, North Wales. The main campus – Hope Park – is three miles from the city centre in the suburb of Childwall, while the creative and performing arts are based at the more central Creative Campus in Everton, where a performance centre houses one of only three Steinway Schools in England, as well as practice rooms, recording spaces and a theatre. The £5-million main library, on the Hope campus, has 270,000 items and 700 study spaces, with electronic access from other sites. Recent campus developments have included a Centre for Education and Enterprise, which supports local business and hosts the Faculty of Education. There is a new food court and a library and reading room on the Creative Campus, with a Renaissance-style garden which includes an outdoor performance area. An £8.5-million Science building is under construction and will house specialist laboratories for nutrition, genomics, cell biology and psychology, as well as facilities for sport and exercise science which will include a 25-metre biomechanics sprint track.

Sports facilities have been improving, and there is enough residential accommodation to guarantee places for new entrants who apply before Clearing. Liverpool is a popular student city and the university has partnerships with the Royal Liverpool Philharmonic Orchestra, Liverpool Tate, the National Museums Liverpool and Liverpool Sound City to develop cultural programmes.

Undergraduate Fees and Bursaries

- Fees for UK/EU students 2016–17 £9,000
- Fees for international students 2015–16 £10,800
- In 2015/16for students with AAA at A level or equivalent, £5,000 over three years.
- Enhanced student hardship fund.
- Range of other scholarships and bursaries available.
- Check the university's website for the latest information.

Students

Undergraduates:	**4,120**	**(195)**
Postgraduates:	**820**	**(1,105)**
Mature students:	**18.2%**	
International students:	**2.8%**	
Applications per place:	**6.9**	
From state-sector schools:	**98.8%**	
From working-class homes:	**41.8%**	
Satisfaction with students' union	**68%**	

For detailed information about sports facilities:
www.hope.ac.uk/hopeparksports

Accommodation

Number of places and costs refer to 2015–16
University-provided places: 1,153
Percentage catered: 0% (catering packages an optional extra)
Self-catered costs: £77–£87 (shared); £100–£123 (en suite) a week.
First years are guaranteed accommodation if Liverpool Hope is their first choice and they apply before Clearing.
International students: rooms are available at specific locations, depending on course.
accommodation@hope.ac.uk
www.hope.ac.uk/halls/

Liverpool John Moores University (LJMU)

Liverpool John Moores (LJMU) is hoping to create a "connected university village" that will locate all students and staff in the city centre. Subject to planning permission, work will begin on site early in 2016 and parts of the development should be operational for the academic year beginning in 2017. The university currently has three campuses, one of which is four miles outside the city, but the new development is due for completion in 2018. Investments totalling £180 million over the last ten years have transformed the existing facilities. Developments include the award-winning John Lennon Art and Design Building and the £25.5-million life sciences building, where the world-class facilities include an indoor 70-metre running track and labs for testing cardiovascular ability, motor skills and biomechanics functions. The £37.6-million Redmonds Building houses Liverpool Screen School, with its industry-standard TV and radio studios, the Liverpool Business School and the School of Law. A £5-million grant will see teaching accommodation for science, technology, engineering and maths upgraded for the start of the 2016–17 academic year.

Naming itself after a football pools millionaire set a pattern of innovation for LJMU. Early examples included the original student charter and the first degrees in sports science and criminal justice, as well as the first distance learning degree in astronomy. A new Teaching and Learning Academy has been launched in 2015 to enhance all aspects of the student experience at LJMU, from the transition from school, through university and into the workplace. There is a library on each of the three campuses, two of which are open 24 hours a day, seven days a week during semesters. The university's virtual learning environment, Blackboard, enables students to access most teaching materials and a range of other support features online.

Liverpool John Moores attracted near-record applications in 2014, taking its intake of undergraduates back to the levels experienced before the fees went up to £9,000. Perhaps the biggest draw for prospective students is the prizewinning World of Work (WoW) initiative, which is the best-known feature of the university's focus on employability. The programme, which has been shaped and steered by leading companies and business organisations, encourages all undergraduates to become expert in eight transferable skills, applicable to a wide range of careers. All students are offered extensive work-related learning opportunities, both paid and voluntary

Kingsway House
Hatton Garden
Liverpool L3 2AJ

0151 231 5090 (course enquiries)
courses@ljmu.ac.uk (enquiries)
www.ljmu.ac.uk
www.liverpoolsu.com
Affiliation: University Alliance

The Times and Sunday Times **Rankings**

Overall Ranking: **74** (last year: 71)

Teaching quality:	**=52**	81.6%
Student experience:	**=43**	85%
Research quality:	**=67**	8.9%
Entry standards:	**55**	344
Student–staff ratio:	**=88**	18.4
Services & facilities/student:	**109**	£1,332
Expected completion rate:	**83**	84.2%
Good honours:	**44**	74.9%
Graduate prospects:	**88**	63.3%

and some located overseas. The Centre for Entrepreneurship supports students and graduates who want to start up in business, become self-employed or work freelance, as well as helping to embed enterprise education in the curriculum.

The university has more than 21,000 students in its home city and another 4,500 taking LJMU courses overseas. Most are based in an area between Liverpool's two cathedrals, while the IM Marsh Campus specialises in education and community studies. More than 40 per cent of the students are drawn from the Merseyside area. The university's efforts to extend access to higher education are successful: almost all the undergraduates are state-educated and 42 per cent come from the four poorest socio-economic groups. A wide range of scholarships and bursaries include the John Lennon Imagine Awards, match-funded through a gift of £260,000 from Yoko Ono, which help students who have either been in local authority care or who are estranged from their parents. The university has a number of disability support services, and an improved dropout rate is now much better than the national average for the university's courses and entry grades.

A growing research reputation is a source of particular pride. More than 60 per cent of the work submitted for the Research Excellence Framework was rated world-leading or internationally excellent, with the proportion topping 80 per cent in physics. The university was ranked second in the UK for sports science and fourth among post-1992 universities for law and education. The physics results covered astronomy, in which researchers and students use the university's own robotic telescope in the Canary Islands.

Liverpool was ranked in the ten best cities in the world to visit in 2014 by Rough Guides and is one of the most affordable student cities in the UK. Student facilities have been improving and there are discounts on theatre tickets and free access to art exhibitions and orchestral performances. Sports facilities include an Olympic-sized swimming pool, two golf courses, fitness suites and weights rooms and all-weather football pitches. Students also have free off-peak access to 11 Lifestyles Fitness Centres across the city.

Undergraduate Fees and Bursaries

» Fees for UK/EU students 2016–17	£9,000
STEM Foundation year	£6,000
Placement year	£975
Year abroad	no fee
» Fees for international students 2015–16	£11,000–£12,000

» Household income below £25K, a bursary of £500 a year (excluding Foundation year).

» Further academic, sports and care leaver's awards including 100 Academic Excellence scholarships of £1,000 a year and six Vice-Chancellor's Scholarships of £10,000 a year.

» Check the university's website for the latest information.

Students

Undergraduates:	**17,085**	**(1,365)**
Postgraduates:	**1,130**	**(1,735)**
Mature students:	**18.3%**	
International students:	**7.9%**	
Applications per place:	**6.1**	
From state-sector schools:	**97.5%**	
From working-class homes:	**41.8%**	
Satisfaction with students' union	**55%**	

For detailed information about sports facilities:
www.ljmu.ac.uk/sport

Accommodation

Number of places and costs refer to 2015–16

University-provided places: 3,800 plus 15,000 through Liverpool Student Homes.

Percentage catered: 0%

Self-catered costs: £88–£130 a week.

All new students are guaranteed a place in university approved housing, even if applying through Clearing.

International students: as above.

accommodation@ljmu.ac.uk

www.ljmu.ac.uk/accommodation

London Metropolitan University

London Met's new strategic plan describes the next five years as perhaps the most challenging in its history. This is due mainly to the instability surrounding higher education as a whole, but Professor John Rafferty, the Vice-Chancellor, acknowledges that the university has found the new environment particularly difficult. London Met is about half the size it was at its peak and, with applications dropping for four years in a row, it expects to become smaller still before it is able to begin growing again. It is reviewing its courses and buildings to maximise the quality it provides at its reduced scale. The new offer includes a guarantee of an accredited, work-related learning opportunity for all students to provide real-world experience in preparation for the graduate jobs market. There will also be £1,000 bursaries for all students who qualify for a full maintenance loan, and every course will have a presence on the university's virtual learning environment, with more opportunities for students to learn remotely, at times and in locations that suit them.

London Met was the product of the 2002 merger of London Guildhall and North London universities, although its origins date back to the mid 19th century. The university's sites are centred on the City of London and the capital's Holloway Road, where there is a Graduate Centre designed by Daniel Libeskind. The university has strong business links, especially in London's "Tech City", where the university has a business accelerator which has been named in the top five in Europe. It provides regular workshops, bootcamps and an incubator programme for students thinking of setting up their own businesses. It now also offers 40 new graduates internships and additional training in a variety of different areas.

The university has always catered particularly for groups who are under-represented at traditional universities. More than a third of the students are Afro-Caribbean, and the proportion of mature students is among the highest in England. More than half of the UK undergraduates come from low-income families – far above the average for the courses and entry qualifications. The projected dropout rate improved in the latest survey, but is still among the four highest in the UK, at more than 21 per cent. Student support services have been remodelled and a new Peer Assisted Student Support (PASS) scheme sees successful second- and third-year students coach first years on their course. This extra support has been known to improve progression and attainment by up to 10 per cent.

166–220 Holloway Road
London N7 8DB

020 7133 4200 (enquiries)
admissions@londonmet.ac.uk
www.londonmet.ac.uk
www.londonmetsu.org.uk
Affiliation: million+

***The Times and Sunday Times* Rankings**

Overall Ranking: **125** (last year: 123)

Teaching quality:	**117**	76%
Student experience:	**118**	78.6%
Research quality:	**110**	3.5%
Entry standards:	**126**	239
Student-staff ratio:	**=103**	19.6
Services & facilities/student:	**123**	£1,000
Expected completion rate:	**120**	75.3%
Good honours:	**122**	55.1%
Graduate prospects:	**126**	47.7%

Undergraduates take year-long modules consisting of 30 weeks of timetabled teaching. Over a year, students will typically study four modules and receive a minimum of 60 teaching hours per module. The university is in the top ten for the amount of supervised teaching time and expects first-year students to have 12 hours of teaching a week, giving the maximum possible opportunity for development and guidance. Overall satisfaction has improved by 7 percentage points in two years, helping the university to move away from the bottom of the National Student Survey as a whole.

There has been increased investment in the campus, with more study zones, as well as major improvements to the Guildhall Faculty of Business and Law building at Moorgate and in the Cass Faculty of Art, Architecture and Design, at Aldgate. A newsroom for journalism students was opened in 2012, and the refurbished library on the Holloway Road site has more computers and informal learning spaces, as well as a café. The £30-million Science Centre features one of the largest teaching laboratories in Europe, with 280 workstations, specialist laboratories and a nuclear magnetic resonance room. However, London Met entered far fewer academics for the 2014 Research Excellence Framework than it did in the 2008 assessments, only 15 per cent of those eligible. As a result, it has slipped down our research ranking, even though half of its submission was rated as world-leading or internationally excellent and there were particularly good scores in English and health subjects.

There is a new headquarters for the students' union on the Aldgate site to add to the well-used building on Holloway Road. The university has also been working hard to reduce its carbon footprint and is among the top five universities on this measure. Residential accommodation is limited, but many of London Met's students live at home. There are nine fitness centres, as well as other sports facilities. The competitive teams are successful and the social scene is lively, particularly in north London.

Undergraduate Fees and Bursaries

» Fees for UK/EU students 2016–17	£9,000
Foundation degree at partner colleges	£5,999–£9,000
» Fees for international students 2015–16	£10,500

» Household income below £25K, a bursary of £1,000 a year.
» Progression bursary of £1,000 for students on Extended degree / year 0 courses who progress to year 1.
» Range of other scholarships and bursaries available.
» Check the university's website for the latest information.

Students

Undergraduates:	**11,465**	**(1,640)**
Postgraduates:	**1,495**	**(1,660)**
Mature students:	**56.4%**	
International students:	**12.7%**	
Applications per place:	**8.9**	
From state-sector schools:	**98%**	
From working-class homes:	**53.2%**	
Satisfaction with students' union	**60%**	

For detailed information about sports facilities:
www.londonmet.ac.uk/services/sport-and-recreation/

Accommodation

Number of places and costs refer to 2015–16
University-provided places: Students have access to accommodation in a wide range of halls of residences provided by specialist student accommodation providers.
Percentage catered: 0%
Self-catered costs: Single rooms from £133–£389 a week.
The university cannot guarantee a place in halls.
International students: as above.
www.londonmet.ac.uk/services/studentservices/advice-and-well-being/accommodation/

London School of Economics and Political Science (LSE)

The LSE is one of the top universities in the world for the social sciences, a reputation that attracts the highest proportion of international students at any publicly funded university and has seen it jump 36 places in the latest QS World University Rankings. But it is bottom of our new measure of teaching quality, taken from the National Student Survey, and this shock outcome has contributed to a drop of four places in our table. The LSE took more undergraduates in 2014 than at any time in its recent history, but there were still more than 10 applicants for every place. The School is planning to "grow steadily over time" and to refine its admissions system so that those with the greatest potential (and not just the highest grades) gain entry. But it is likely to remain the most selective institution in our table in terms of applications per place.

The LSE has been hemmed in by its cramped estate around London's Aldwych, which is being developed as the School also expands into nearby buildings. It opened its first new building for more than 40 years in 2014, the Saw Swee Hock Student Centre (SAW), which houses the students' union, the careers and accommodation services and a multi-faith prayer centre. Now the school is spending £120-million on its centre buildings redevelopment, which will replace a number of existing buildings. It had already improved and extended the teaching space considerably and added converted Government buildings near the campus.

Areas of study range more broadly than the School's name suggests: the 250 undergraduate courses range as far as management, mathematics and environmental policy. A new degree planned for 2016 is a three-year BSc in finance. The LSE was again among the leading universities in the latest assessments of research, with more "world-leading" research than any university in our table. It was the clear leader in the social sciences, with particularly good results in social work and social policy, where only 4 per cent of the submission did not reach the top two categories, an achievement that was almost matched in communication and media studies.

The School has a long history of political involvement, from its foundation by Beatrice and Sidney Webb, pioneers of the Fabian movement, to the 31 alumni and former staff who are MPs and 42 current members of the House of Lords. The tradition lives on, not only among the academics, but in a students' union which claims to be the only one in Britain to hold weekly general meetings at which every

Houghton Street
London WC2A 2AE

020 7955 7125 (admissions)
contact via website
www.lse.ac.uk
www.lsesu.com
Affiliation: Russell Group

***The Times and Sunday Times* Rankings**

Overall Ranking: **9** (last year: 5)

Teaching quality:	**127**	72.1%
Student experience:	**120**	78.4%
Research quality:	**4**	52.8%
Entry standards:	**4**	533
Student–staff ratio:	**=8**	11.4
Services & facilities/student:	**11**	£2,584
Expected completion rate:	**=12**	94.8%
Good honours:	**16**	82.1%
Graduate prospects:	**=30**	78.5%

student may attend and vote. More than 30 past or present heads of state have either been LSE students or academics, as have 16 Nobel prizewinners in economics, literature and peace – including George Bernard Shaw, Bertrand Russell, Friedrich von Hayek and Amartya Sen. The latest of them was Professor Christopher Pissarides, who shared the prize for economics in 2010.

Its international character not only gives the LSE global prestige, but also an unusual degree of financial independence: only a small proportion of its funding comes from Government sources. Almost 30 per cent of the British undergraduates are from independent schools, one of the highest proportions in England. Substantial efforts are being made to attract a broader intake: the school is spending half of its additional fee income on student support and other activities to widen participation – a bigger proportion than any other university. The LSE's projected dropout rate of 5 per cent is among the lowest at any university.

The Norman Foster-designed redevelopment of the Lionel Robbins Building houses a much-improved library. The move was a welcome one since the number of books borrowed by LSE students is more than four times the national average, according to one survey. Routes between many of the buildings have been pedestrianised, in keeping with a commitment to green issues that has seen the School in the top echelons of the People and Planet Green League of universities' environmental performance for six years in a row.

Partying is not the prime attraction of the LSE for most applicants, who tend to be serious about their subject, but London's top nightspots are on the doorstep for those who can afford them. The 4,000 residential places for fewer than 10,000 full-time students offer a good chance of avoiding central London's notoriously high private sector rents; there are spaces in hall for all first-year undergraduates who want them.

Undergraduate Fees and Bursaries

- Fees for UK/EU students 2016–17 £9,000
  Year abroad £1,350
- Fees for international students 2015–16 £17,040
- For UK students, annual bursary of £4,000 for those with household income below £18K, decreasing in five bands to £750 for household income £40K–£42.6K.
- Range of specific scholarships available.
- Two awards for asylum seekers of £9,000 fee waiver and up to £11,000 bursary of each year.
- Check the university's website for the latest information.

Students

Undergraduates:	**3,965**	**(70)**
Postgraduates:	**5,510**	**(605)**
Mature students:	**2.7%**	
International students:	**45.5%**	
Applications per place:	**10.3**	
From state-sector schools:	**71.4%**	
From working-class homes:	**17.9%**	
Satisfaction with students' union	**58%**	

For detailed information about sports facilities:
www.lsesu.com/activities/sports/

Accommodation

Number of places and costs refer to 2015–16
University-provided places: 3,740; 240 intercollegiate
Percentage catered: about 38%
Catered costs: £100.80–£266.00 a week (30, 38 or 40 weeks).
Self-catered costs: £124.25–£339.00 a week (38, 40 or 50 weeks).
New first years are guaranteed an offer of accommodation.
International students: new undergraduates are guaranteed an offer. New graduate students enter a lottery.
accommodation@lse.ac.uk
www.lse.ac.uk/lifeAtLSE/accommodation/

London South Bank University

London South Bank often appears near the top of comparisons of graduate salaries, partly because so many of its students are established in their careers before trying higher education and return to well-paid jobs. The latest cohort has done even better than usual, with average salaries of £28,900 – nearly £8,000 above the national average. Three-quarters of those completing degrees in 2013 had professional or managerial jobs within six months of graduating, or were continuing their studies, a jump of 27 percentage points compared with the previous year. About half of the students are at least 21 on entry and more than a quarter are part time. Many of the 15,000 undergraduates take sandwich courses and most of the conventional degrees are focused on the jobs market.

The university hopes to benefit from the £3-billion regeneration of the Elephant and Castle area on its doorstep. But Vice-Chancellor Professor David Phoenix is not waiting for that to make changes that he hopes will make the university more attractive to students and more successful with business and industry. He wants more students to spend part of their course in industry, and he plans to create more of a campus feel by knitting together the university's various buildings with more green spaces. LSBU has already invested over £50 million in modern teaching facilities, and developments costing another £38 million are planned. A £4-million media centre will open in late 2015 with recording studios, a newsroom and cinema. Applications have risen for three years in a row and enrolments were up in 2014.

Three-quarters of the students are from the capital and more than half are drawn from ethnic minorities. The diversity of the intake is encouraged by initiatives such as the summer school for local people to upgrade their qualifications. The courses start at the end of June and are limited to 15 hours a week so as not to affect students' benefit entitlement. South Bank has always given a high priority to widening participation in higher education and takes far more students from the lowest socio-economic groups than other universities with similar courses and entry qualifications. However, the projected dropout rate is among the highest in the country and the university struggles in the National Student Survey.

LSBU is targeting much of its fee income on measures to ensure that more students complete their courses in the expected time. A new system tracks grades and offers targeted support to students who might be in difficulties. LSBU degrees are also

103 Borough Road
London SE1 0AA

0800 923 8888 (course enquiries)
course.enquiry@lsbu.ac.uk
www.lsbu.ac.uk
www.lsbsu.org
Affiliation: million+

***The Times and Sunday Times* Rankings**

Overall Ranking: **120** (last year: 122)

Teaching quality:	**=109**	77%
Student experience:	**=101**	81.3%
Research quality:	**=64**	9%
Entry standards:	**125**	248
Student–staff ratio:	**68**	17.2
Services & facilities/student:	**88**	£1,523
Expected completion rate:	**121**	74.6%
Good honours:	**107**	61%
Graduate prospects:	**62**	67.9%

taught at a network of overseas colleges that stretches from China to the Caribbean.

The main campus is in Southwark, not far from the South Bank arts complex. It includes the Centre for Efficient and Renewable Energy in Buildings, a unique teaching, research and demonstration resource for low-carbon technologies, and the UK's first inner-city green technology research centre. The £10-million Clarence Centre for Enterprise and Innovation opened in 2014 to support students' start-up businesses and provide a gateway for the local community to access the university's expertise. LSBU is one of the top universities for "knowledge transfer partnerships" with outside organisations and trains staff in some 900 companies. The university entered more academics for the 2014 Research Excellence Framework than for previous assessments and scored well on the external impact of its research, with almost three-quarters of the submission placed in the top two categories on this measure.

Some health students are based on the other side of London, in hospitals in Romford and Leytonstone, where there is a smaller satellite campus in Havering to supplement that in Southwark. The university now trains 40 per cent of London's nurses and has well-regarded courses in occupational therapy and radiography. New courses include a suite of extended MEng courses in engineering for undergraduate entry, which are the most direct route to Chartered Engineer status.

A new student centre opened in 2012, bringing the students' union and many support services together to make them more convenient and accessible. LSBU is one of the few universities in central London to have its halls of residence close by: all halls are less than a ten-minute walk away. The university's new-look sports centre opened in July 2014 after a million-pound makeover, with a multipurpose sports hall, therapy services and facilities that include a 40-station fitness suite and a sports injury clinic. Southwark Council contributed £300,000 to improve the facilities and guarantee public access. The university provides a comprehensive sports scholarship scheme.

Undergraduate Fees and Bursaries

- » Fees for UK/EU students 2016–17 £9,000
  Foundation degree £5,950–£9,000
- » Fees for international students 2015–16 £10,500–£11,500
- » Up to 300 scholarships of £2,000 in year 1, based on need. See website for criteria.
- » Support schemes to improve progression beyond year 1.
- » Additional support to extend academic experience for students with at least ABB at A level or equivalent.
- » Check the university's website for the latest information.

Students

Undergraduates:	**9,460**	**(4,545)**
Postgraduates:	**1,760**	**(2,455)**
Mature students:	**50.3%**	
International students:	**7.7%**	
Applications per place:	**10.1**	
From state-sector schools:	**97.2%**	
From working-class homes:	**51%**	
Satisfaction with students' union	**65%**	

For detailed information about sports facilities:
www.lsbu.ac.uk/academy-of-sport

Accommodation

Number of places and costs refer to 2015–16
University-provided places: 1,300
Percentage catered: 0%
Self-catered costs: £114–£117.25 (standard) – £141.70 (en suite) a week.
First-year UK students are not guaranteed accommodation, but high priority is given to those living outside Greater London.
International students: first years are guaranteed accommodation if conditions are met.
www.lsbu.ac.uk/student-life/accommodation

Loughborough University

Loughborough is best known for its illustrious sporting pedigree, but its academic reputation has been growing rapidly in recent years. The university shot into our top 20 last year after a rise of six places and has retained its position after an impressive showing in the 2014 Research Excellence Framework (REF). Only eight universities entered such a high proportion of their eligible staff – 88 per cent – for the REF. Almost three-quarters of their research was judged to be world-leading or internationally excellent, sport and exercise sciences producing the best results in the UK and six other subject areas featuring in the top ten. The university consistently registers among the best scores in the National Student Survey and has been awarded five stars in the QS global rating of its facilities and performance in teaching, research, employability and internationalisation.

Loughborough has opened a London campus in the Queen Elizabeth Olympic Park, moving into the former press and broadcast centres for the Games, initially to run postgraduate and executive courses and conduct research. Undergraduates will continue to be taught on the popular campus in the East Midlands, where applications rose by 10 per cent in 2014. The 216-acre site has seen a new business school, upgraded art facilities and large student union extension, as well as new and refurbished residential accommodation. The first phase of a £68-million accommodation development has more than 5,000 rooms, with another 1,300 bedrooms to come in four new halls.

Most subjects are available either as three-year full-time or longer sandwich degrees, which include a year in industry. This has helped to give graduates a strong employment record, as well a dropout rate of less than 5 per cent, which is particularly low for the subjects Loughborough offers. The university is a leader in the use of computer-assisted assessment, offering students the chance to gauge their own progress online. However, despite high spending on student support and outreach activities, Loughborough misses all its access benchmarks: fewer than a quarter of the undergraduates are from working-class homes and only 6 per cent are from areas of low participation in higher education. The Office for Standards in Education rates Loughborough in its top category for teacher training in physical education, design and science. Loughborough is also a leader in art and design and remains a major centre of engineering, with more than 2,800 students in a £20-million integrated engineering complex. Civil, aeronautical and automotive engineering are particularly strong.

The adjacent Science and Enterprise Park includes the £59-million BAE-sponsored Systems Engineering Innovation Centre.

Loughborough
Leicestershire LE11 3TU

01509 223522 (admissions)
admissions@lboro.ac.uk
www.lboro.ac.uk
www.lsu.co.uk
Affiliation: none

***The Times and Sunday Times* Rankings**

Overall Ranking: **13** (last year: 13)

Teaching quality:	**8**	84.5%
Student experience:	**=3**	89.3%
Research quality:	**=30**	36.3%
Entry standards:	**36**	397
Student–staff ratio:	**=32**	14.7
Services & facilities/student:	**24**	£2,339
Expected completion rate:	**=20**	93.2%
Good honours:	**22**	79.8%
Graduate prospects:	**10**	83.7%

Close relationships with industry have helped to amass a record haul of seven Queen's Anniversary Prizes. A £5-million grant will see the opening in 2016 of STEMLab, a suite of science and engineering laboratories, workshops, computer-aided design and rapid prototyping facilities, a design studio and informal learning spaces. The development will enable the university to develop a range of programmes in bio-science and bio-engineering.

Sports facilities that were already among the best in the country have improved still further with the opening of a £5.6-million health and fitness centre. The complex contains cardio-vascular equipment, fixed and free weight stations, fitness studios, and a new sports hall providing space for badminton, basketball, netball and volleyball. Loughborough was chosen as the official preparation camp headquarters for Team GB prior to the London 2012 Olympics, and has since been named as the official Innovation Partner of the International Hockey Federation and will be one of two national centres for British swimming as it prepares for the Rio 2016 and Tokyo 2020 Olympic Games. The university will also host a £10-million National Sport and Exercise Medicine Centre of Excellence, one of three in the UK. The campus boasts a 50-metre swimming pool, national academies for cricket and tennis, a gymnastics centre and a high-performance training centre for athletics. The university also hosts the UK's only centre for disability sport and has spent £15-million on its Sports Technology Institute. The programme of sports scholarships is the largest at any university. At the 2014 Commonwealth Games, the university's athletes claimed 35 medals in 7 different sports and would have finished 11th on the medal table if Loughborough was a country.

Social activity is concentrated on a students' union which is among the most popular in the country with its members. The relatively small town of Loughborough, a mile away, is never going to be a clubber's paradise, but both Leicester and Nottingham are within easy reach.

Undergraduate Fees and Bursaries

- Fees for UK/EU students 2016–17 £9,000
- Fees for international students 2015–16 £14,300–£17,950
- For UK (excluding Welsh) students, household income below £18K, a bursary of £2,000, years 1–3; £1,000 fee waiver for placement year; £2,000 bursary and £5,000 fee waiver, year 4 Integrated Masters;
  £18K–£22K, £2,000, years 1–3; £2,000 and £4,000 fee waiver, year 4;
  £22K–£25K, £1,000, years 1–3; £1,000 and £3,000 fee waiver, year 4;
  enhanced terms for mature students.
- Scholarships of £3,000 a year for high achievers from low HE participation areas; subject, music and sports scholarships.
- Check the university's website for the latest information.

Students

Undergraduates:	**11,775**	**(230)**
Postgraduates:	**2,420**	**(1,540)**
Mature students:	**3.4%**	
International students:	**10.2%**	
Applications per place:	**7.4**	
From state-sector schools:	**83%**	
From working-class homes:	**21.9%**	
Satisfaction with students' union	**91%**	

For detailed information about sports facilities:
http://loughboroughsport.com

Accommodation

Number of places and costs refer to 2015–16
University-provided places: 5,662
Percentage catered: 42.5%
Catered costs: £134 – £180 (39-week contract)
Self-catered costs: £85 – £151 (39-week contract)
Undergraduate first-year first-choice students are guaranteed accommodation if they apply prior to 1 August.
International students: guaranteed housing in same residence for two years.
www.lboro.ac.uk/services/campus-living/accommodation/

University of Manchester

Manchester has maintained its position in our top 30 this year, while its international reputation is higher still. Its excellence in research has taken it to just outside the top 30 in the QS World University Rankings and close to the top 50 in *Times Higher Education* magazine's equivalent. More than 80 per cent the work submitted to the 2014 Research Excellence Framework was considered world-leading or internationally excellent, although the university entered a lower proportion of its academics than many of its peers in the Russell Group. Manchester remains the most popular university in the country in terms of total applications, and its student satisfaction ratings, which have held it back in domestic rankings, have begun to improve in the last two years. Manchester has more international students than any other UK university, drawn from 154 countries, and has 129 nationalities among its workforce.

The university has embarked on a £1-billion, ten-year plan to create a single world-class campus with new student facilities and buildings for teaching and research, as well as major improvements to its public spaces. The first phase is now underway and will include a new Manchester Engineering Campus development, new centres for the School of Law and the Alliance Manchester Business School – renamed this year after a £15-million donation – as well as a major refurbishment of the university library, and a bigger and better students' union. The university is also spending several million pounds to bring benefits to the local area, capitalising on improvements due to be made to Oxford Road. The Manchester Cancer Research Centre and the National Graphene Institute have already opened and the Whitworth Art Gallery has been refurbished. The overriding aims are to improve the student experience and reduce carbon emissions.

But outstanding teaching is one of the three goals in the university's strategy to be among the top 25 in the world by 2020. The Learning Through Research Initiative funds undergraduates to work with researchers and £20 million has been set aside to attract top academics. The new recruits will join three Nobel prizewinners on the staff. Sir John Sulston, who chairs the Institute of Science, Ethics and Innovation, won the prize for physiology and medicine in 2002. Professors Andre Geim and Professor Konstantin Novoselov brought the all-time complement of laureates to 25 when they took the physics prize in 2010 for the discovery of graphene. In addition to the National Graphene Institute, a £60-million Graphene Engineering Innovation Centre is planned, as is the Sir Henry

Oxford Road
Manchester M13 9PL

0161 275 2077 (admissions)
ug-admissions@manchester.ac.uk
www.manchester.ac.uk
http://manchesterstudents
union.com
Affiliation: Russell Group

***The Times and Sunday Times* Rankings**

Overall Ranking: **=28** (last year: 28)

Teaching quality:	**90**	79%
Student experience:	**48**	84.7%
Research quality:	**13**	39.8%
Entry standards:	**19**	435
Student–staff ratio:	**19**	13.2
Services & facilities/student:	**50**	£1,926
Expected completion rate:	**=22**	92.9%
Good honours:	**38**	75.7%
Graduate prospects:	**=30**	78.5%

Royce Institute for Materials Research, a £235-million project that is a major part of the Government's 'Northern Powerhouse' initiative.

The 2004 merger with the neighbouring University of Manchester Institute of Science and Technology (UMIST) created the biggest conventional university in the UK outside the federal University of London. One result was the largest engineering school in the UK, with a £20-million budget and 1,200 students. The first phase of a new chemical engineering facility, with a sophisticated industrial pilot plant as well as teaching laboratories, opened in 2011. The £24-million "Learning Commons" building opened in 2012, the first phase providing more than 1,000 flexible learning spaces, high-quality IT facilities, and a hub for student-centred activities and learning support services. A new teaching block helps to cater for 2,000 undergraduates following a problem-based curriculum in the medical school, and a £60-million development will create a new hotel, conference venue and executive education centre for the business school.

The university has been trying to broaden its intake, with a particular focus on increasing recruitment from the city and its surrounding area. It admits more low-income students than most of the other universities in the Russell Group and is now close to the national benchmarks for widening participation. The Manchester Leadership Programme and the University College for Interdisciplinary Learning encourage students to think beyond academia and towards their impact as citizens. Employers in *The Times*' top 100 companies named Manchester as their favourite recruiting ground in 2015 – an important accolade when some firms limit their recruiting visits – and they also rate the careers service highly.

Manchester's famed youth culture and the university's position at the heart of a huge student precinct help to ensure keen competition for places, and hence high entry standards, in most subjects. There are first-rate sports facilities and the university's teams frequently rank near the top of the BUCS league. A 3,000-room student village is being built on the Fallowfield Campus, adding to the university's large stock of accommodation.

Undergraduate Fees and Bursaries

- » Fees for UK/EU students 2016–17 £9,000
- » Fees for international students 2015–16 £14,500–£19,000
  Medicine £19,000–£33,000
- » Household income below £25K, £2,500 a year; £25K–£35K, £1,000 a year.
- » Foundation year bursary of £5,000–£2,000 for household income up to £35K.
- » Household income up to £35K, bursaries of £675–£2,500 for year abroad or placement year.
- » Manchester Access Programme scholarships of £1,000 a year.

Students

Undergraduates:	**25,795**	**(685)**
Postgraduates:	**7,975**	**(3,465)**
Mature students:	**10%**	
International students:	**24.7%**	
Applications per place:	**7.8**	
From state-sector schools:	**82.3%**	
From working-class homes:	**23.8%**	
Satisfaction with students' union	**75%**	

For detailed information about sports facilities:
www.sport.manchester.ac.uk

Accommodation

Number of places and costs refer to 2015–16
University-owned/managed places: 8,030
Percentage catered: approx 28%
Catered costs: £91.58 – £175.40 a week (40 weeks).
Self-catered costs: £70.00 – £157.10 a week (40 weeks).
First years are guaranteed housing provided conditions are met.
International non-EU students are guaranteed accommodation for the duration of their stay if conditions met.
accommodation@manchester.ac.uk
www.accommodation.manchester.ac.uk

Manchester Metropolitan University

Manchester Metropolitan (MMU) has more undergraduates than any university in our table – and is still growing. Applications were up by more than 6,000 in 2014, increasing the competition for places as the numbers accepted were similar to the previous year. Entry standards were already higher than at most post-1992 universities. More than 1,000 courses are offered in over 70 subjects, more of them professionally accredited than at any other university and many involving work placements.

The five sites in Manchester have now been reduced to two linked campuses as part of a £350-million investment programme, much of which has been devoted to learning resources rather than buildings. The prize-winning EQAL programme, for example, recast undergraduate courses in line with student feedback and integrated them with the Moodle virtual learning environment. The new buildings have been winning prizes, however. The Brooks Building, which hosts the education and health faculties, won an award for regeneration, while the new Manchester School of Art and the £10-million students' union building were honoured in the RIBA national awards.

The university is also proud of its record on green issues, finishing in the top three of the People and Planet Green League of environmental performance for the second time in a row in 2015.

The Birley Fields Campus, which includes the Brooks Building, is one of the most environmentally sustainable in the UK. It is close to the original All Saints Campus, on the university's border with Hulme and Moss Side. New science and engineering buildings at All Saints cost £42 million, while an impressive new £75-million business school headquarters next to the Mancunian Way opened in 2012. The School of Art opened there the following year. A third campus at Crewe, 40 miles south of Manchester, serves 800 trainee teachers and 3,000 other students taking contemporary arts and sports science. The Cheshire Campus occupies an area now known as the University Quadrant, which features a £6-million drama, music and dance centre, and a £30-million student village, business school and £10-million Sport Science Centre. Future developments costing more than £200 million to improve existing buildings and public spaces across the university are under discussion.

More than a sixth of the students are 21 or over on entry, the group which has seen the biggest decline under the new fees regime. There is a longstanding commitment to extending access to higher education:

All Saints Building
All Saints
Manchester M15 6BH

0161 247 6969 (general enquiries)
contact via website
www.mmu.ac.uk
www.theunionmmu.org
Affiliation: University Alliance

***The Times and Sunday Times* Rankings**

Overall Ranking: **77** (last year: 89)

Teaching quality:	**61**	81%
Student experience:	**92**	82.2%
Research quality:	**75**	7.5%
Entry standards:	**=53**	347
Student–staff ratio:	**=75**	17.7
Services & facilities/student:	**90**	£1,516
Expected completion rate:	**=81**	84.4%
Good honours:	**63**	69.8%
Graduate prospects:	**89**	63%

almost 40 per cent of the undergraduates come from working-class homes, many from areas of low participation in higher education. The projected dropout rate has improved considerably and is now better than the national average for the university's subjects and entry qualifications. The university's overseas links have expanded rapidly in recent years, with MMU offering exchange opportunities in Europe and further afield, as well as establishing teaching bases abroad. There are new partnerships in China and additional locations for exchanges through the EU's Erasmus programme.

Academics are encouraged to take a three-year MA in teaching, but less than a quarter were entered for the 2014 Research Excellence Framework. Almost two-thirds of the work submitted was rated world-leading or internationally excellent, with health, art and design, and English producing the best results. The Poet Laureate, Professor Carol Ann Duffy, is Creative Director of the Writing School in the English department. The university trains more teachers than any other and its courses are rated as outstanding by Ofsted. A Centre for Urban Education has been launched to develop MMU's expertise further.

More than half of the students come from the Manchester area, easing the pressure on accommodation in a city of nearly 90,000 university students. MMU plays an important role in the region's economy, not least because almost two-thirds of graduates stay and work in the North West. The university employs 50 of its own graduates on paid internships for up to 12 months. All first years who request accommodation can be housed, with priority going to disabled students and those who live furthest from Manchester. The university's sports facilities are good and there is an innovative partnership with Manchester City Women's Football Club, promising bespoke education programmes and matchday access for events management students.

The city's attractions do no harm to recruitment levels, but much depends on where the course is based. Those at Crewe can feel isolated, although there is an active students' union on campus. Some potential applicants are daunted by the sheer size of the university, but individual courses and sites usually provide a social circle.

Undergraduate Fees and Bursaries

» Fees for UK/EU students 2016–17	£9,000
Foundation year	£6,000
Placement year / year abroad	£680
» Fees for international students 2015–16	£11,150–£19,000

» For all UK students with household income below £25K, £1,000 a year as university services or accommodation discount; 200 placement year fee waivers.

» Check the university's website for the latest information.

Students

Undergraduates:	**24,640**	**(1,995)**
Postgraduates:	**2,345**	**(3,185)**
Mature students:	**17%**	
International students:	**5.9%**	
Applications per place:	**7.4**	
From state-sector schools:	**96.6%**	
From working-class homes:	**39.2%**	
Satisfaction with students' union	**72%**	

For detailed information about sports facilities:
www2.mmu.ac.uk/sport

Accommodation

Number of places and costs refer to 2015–16
University provided places: 5,094
Percentage catered: 0%
Self-catered costs: Manchester: £92-£140; Cheshire: £93 a week.
All new full-time students will be housed if applications are received by 15 August and requirements are met.
International students: as above.
accommodation@mmu.ac.uk
www.mmu.ac.uk/accommodation

Middlesex University

Middlesex has become a truly international university, with almost twice as many students (42,500) taking its courses outside the UK as there are on its London campus. There are outposts in Mauritius, Dubai and Malta, and the university educates students from 130 countries. Middlesex is the first overseas university in Malta, where it expects to attract students from North Africa and the Middle East, as well as from the island itself. The university has a longstanding focus on Europe and has over 1,800 undergraduates from other EU countries. Across all campuses, more than a quarter of Middlesex's students are from outside the UK. But three-quarters of the full-time students on the main campus are from London, many of them returning to education after a period at work.

The university is under new leadership, following the longest tenure of any vice-chancellor in recent years – Professor Mike Driscoll was at the helm for 20 years. Professor Tim Blackman, who has arrived from the Open University, wants Middlesex to be "the most creative, enterprising and global university". He arrives just as Middlesex has completed a long-running reorganisation programme, which has reduced the seven campuses which used to straggle around north London to one impressive base at Hendon. The university has invested more than £200 million bringing about the transformation and attracting 150 new academics.

The last phase of the programme saw nursing and the other health subjects move to Hendon, where The Grove, the £80-million centre for art, design and media, has won a string of accolades. It includes Sony-designed, equipped and built TV studios and newsroom, and flexible performance and exhibition spaces centred around an atrium. Earlier developments Hendon saw the construction of a new library and the roofing over of the main quadrangle to provide social space. This was followed by a new building for science subjects and the opening of the Forum for student services and facilities that include the students' union, catering and event space. The campus even boasts one of the country's few Real Tennis courts.

Only one institution outside the top three in our table reports higher spending than Middlesex. It is £1,000 per student ahead of many of its peers. ICT facilities have been updated with wireless access throughout the campus and students are sent a free e-book at the start of every module, which the university says will save students £450. The highly flexible course system allows students to start some courses in January if they prefer not to wait until autumn, and offers the option of an extra

The Burroughs
Hendon
London NW4 4BT

020 8411 5555 (enquiries)
enquiries@mdx.ac.uk
www.mdx.ac.uk
www.mdxsu.com
Affiliation: million+

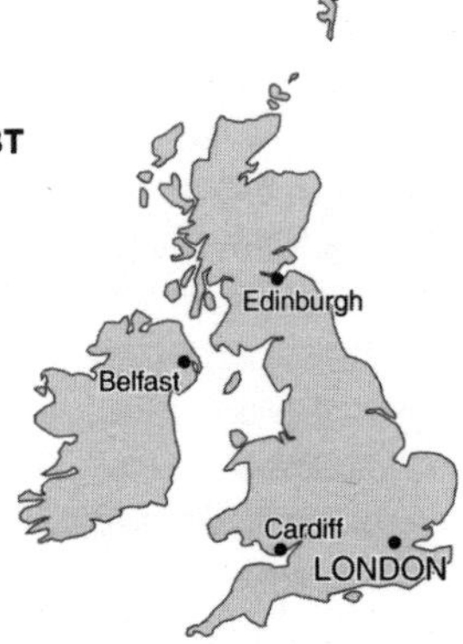

***The Times and Sunday Times* Rankings**

Overall Ranking: **=85** (last year: 75)

Teaching quality:	**=94**	78.7%
Student experience:	**=95**	81.8%
Research quality:	**60**	9.7%
Entry standards:	**120**	270
Student–staff ratio:	**90**	18.5
Services & facilities/student:	**5**	£2,967
Expected completion rate:	**116**	77.8%
Good honours:	**106**	61.3%
Graduate prospects:	**=77**	64.9%

five-week session in the summer to try out new subjects or add to their credits. There is a range of work-based courses that allow participants to gain recognition and academic credit for learning that occurs in the workplace. The conventional degrees are also focused on future employment, many including work placements or the option of a sandwich year.

The university has reorganised into six schools to focus on its strengths in business, computing and the arts. More than a third of the eligible staff were entered for the 2014 Research Excellence Framework, and 58 per cent of their work was placed in one of the top two categories. Art and design produced the best results, with three-quarters of the research assessed as world-leading or internationally excellent.

Applications increased in 2014, reversing a decline in the previous year. More than a third of the full-time undergraduates are 21 or older on entry. Almost all of the British students are state educated, more than half of them coming from the four poorest socio-economic groups. Middlesex is one of seven universities not offering any bursaries in 2015, believing that outreach and retention activities are more effective means of broadening the intake and improving completion rates. The projected dropout rate has improved in recent years, but more than a quarter of degree students are not expected to graduate in the expected time.

There are 940 residential places, with more to come in the next few years. Priority in their allocation is given to international students and other first years whose first choice is Middlesex and who live outside London.

Sports facilities have been improving and now include a well-equipped "fitness pod" at Hendon with a gym and multipurpose outdoor courts. The Sports Development Team at Middlesex is the largest provider of coaching courses in North London.

Beyond Hendon, the West End and London's other attractions are only a tube ride away.

Undergraduate Fees and Bursaries

» Fees for UK/EU students 2016–17 £9,000
» Fees for international students 2015–16 £11,200
» Support to be targeted at widening participation in HE and enhancing students' performance and course completion.
» Academic, sports and other scholarships available.
» Check the university's website for the latest information.

Students

Undergraduates:	**13,455**	**(2,190)**
Postgraduates:	**2,145**	**(2,090)**
Mature students:	**33.5%**	
International students:	**21.1%**	
Applications per place:	**9.7**	
From state-sector schools:	**98.9%**	
From working-class homes:	**55.9%**	
Satisfaction with students' union	**64%**	

For detailed information about sports facilities:
www.mdx.ac.uk/life-at-middlesex/sport

Accommodation

Number of places and costs refer to 2015–16
University-provided places: 940
Percentage catered: 0%
Self-catered costs: £119.70–£259.00 a week (40 weeks).
Full-year students have priority; residential restrictions apply.
International students are guaranteed a room provided they apply by the deadline.
accomm@mdx.ac.uk
www.mdx.ac.uk/life-at-middlesex/accommodation

Newcastle University

Newcastle's aim is to be a "world-class civic university", combining local engagement with growing international activity. It was the first UK university to open an overseas medical school – the first cohort in Johor, Malaysia, graduated in 2014 – and there is a joint venture with Singapore Institute of Technology. Now the focus is on its home city, with the opening in 2015 of the first phase of the £250-million Science Central project, run in partnership with the city council. The university's share of one of the UK's biggest regeneration projects will cost nearly £70 million and has already seen the opening of the Core Building, which houses the Cloud Innovation Centre – part of the School of Computing Science – and the Centre for Professional and Executive Development. The 24-acre city-centre site will bring together academia, the public sector, business and industry to create a centre for urban innovation.

The university's main campus is even closer to the city centre, opening on to the busy Haymarket area. Recent developments include the glass-fronted King's Gate building for student services, which created a new "front door" to the university. New buildings have opened for music and medical sciences, science and engineering laboratories have been upgraded, and disabled access improved. The refurbished library, which is open 24 hours a day during term time, is the only one in the UK to have been awarded five Charter Marks in a row for excellent customer service. A new £2-million physics laboratory supports the introduction of the pure physics degree with first intake in 2015.

A third campus, on the site of the former Newcastle General Hospital, focuses on research into ageing and is another element of the university's lead role in turning Newcastle into one of the six officially designated science cities. The university will spend £200 million in the next three years on student facilities and information technology. The Digital Campus scheme has already produced mobile apps used by around 90 per cent of students each week and a lecture recording service that amassed 29,000 recordings in 2013–14 and received more than 300,000 viewings by students.

The university has opened a campus in London in partnership with INTO, the company which also runs a teaching and accommodation complex on the Newcastle campus to prepare international students for undergraduate and graduate courses. Newcastle University London offers courses from the triple-accredited business school for the international market. There are also strategic partnerships with institutions in Australia, China, Brazil, Angola and Indonesia.

King's Gate
Newcastle upon Tyne
NE1 7RU

0191 208 6000 (enquiries)
contact via website
www.ncl.ac.uk
www.nusu.co.uk
Affiliation: Russell Group

***The Times and Sunday Times* Rankings**

Overall Ranking: **=23** (last year: =22)

Teaching quality:	**47**	82%
Student experience:	**=7**	88.4%
Research quality:	**=21**	37.7%
Entry standards:	**=25**	424
Student–staff ratio:	**=49**	15.6
Services & facilities/student:	**58**	£1,807
Expected completion rate:	**11**	95.1%
Good honours:	**24**	79.2%
Graduate prospects:	**24**	79.1%

The medical school has a partnership with Durham, once Newcastle's parent university, with about a third of trainees spending their first two years at Durham's Stockton campus.

Newcastle is popular with students from independent schools, who took more than a quarter of the places in 2013, but the university was among the first in its peer group to mount substantial programmes to attract more students from non-traditional backgrounds. It leads a national scheme to promote fair access to higher education and its well-established PARTNERS programme, which helps eligible students in the region to gain entry, is being opened up to all schools and colleges in England.

Newcastle has a number of unusual features for a traditional university, such as a fine art degree with intense competition for places, and a longstanding reputation for agriculture, which benefits from two farms in Northumberland. The award-winning ncl+ initiative encourages all students to develop employability skills through extra-curricular activities. Students commit to at least 70 hours of activity, and the award will appear on their Higher Education Achievement Report. The university is in the top 25 for graduate prospects and is one of those most targeted by leading graduate employers. It also registers high levels of satisfaction among both British and international students. Almost 80 per cent of the research entered for the 2014 Research Excellence Framework was judged to be world-leading or internationally excellent. Neuroscience, English and computing science rated as leading departments in the UK.

Newcastle was rated among the top ten universities in *Times Higher Education* magazine's latest student experience survey. The students' union has been refurbished and a Student Forum created alongside it as a central outdoor social space. The campus also hosts an independent theatre, museum and art gallery. The already extensive stock of accommodation was extended in 2014, with more in 2015, and rents elsewhere are reasonable. Sport is a particular strength: a £5.5-million sports centre supplements two older venues, which have been extensively refurbished.

Undergraduate Fees and Bursaries

- Fees for UK/EU students 2016–17 £9,000
- Fees for international students 2016–17 £13,315–£15,490
  Medicine and dentistry £17,080–£31,610
- Household income below £25K, bursary of £2,000 a year; £25K–£35K, £1,000 a year.
- Access scholarships, with conditions, of £500 a year.
- 20 Promise Scholarships of £4,500 fee waiver, £4,500 cash a year for high-achieving students with household income up to £15K. Other widening participation and subject scholarships available.
- Check the university's website for the latest information.

Students

Undergraduates:	**16,250**	**(40)**
Postgraduates:	**4,565**	**(1,555)**
Mature students:	**7.6%**	
International students:	**18.8%**	
Applications per place:	**7**	
From state-sector schools:	**74%**	
From working-class homes:	**21.8%**	
Satisfaction with students' union	**81%**	

For detailed information about sports facilities: www.ncl.ac.uk/sport

Accommodation

Number of places and costs refer to 2015–16
University-provided places: 4,254
Percentage catered: 16%
Catered costs: £131.74 a week.
Self-catered costs: £81.27–£143 a week.
All single undergraduates are guaranteed a room in university-managed accommodation provided requirements are met.
International students: as above.
www.ncl.ac.uk/enquiries/; www.ncl.ac.uk/accommodation/

Newman University

In 2015/16, Newman is offering some of the most generous scholarships at any university: £10,000 over three years for British degree students in subjects other than teacher training who make the university their first choice and achieve at least BBB or ABC at A level. There is no need to make an application – the university will contact eligible students in August – but the recipients will need to pass all their modules first time and average at least 60 per cent to qualify for the following year's payment. The awards are part of a range of scholarships and bursaries, which include others of £2,000 for teacher training students and £12,000 awards for students from the Newman University Catholic Higher Education Network of schools.

The university is one of three Catholic foundations among the crop of institutions that were upgraded in 2012. It takes its name from John Henry Newman, the author of *The Idea of the University* and a Catholic cardinal in the 19th century. His vision of a community of scholars guides the university, which was established in 1968 as a teacher training college, but now has a wider portfolio of degrees, mainly in the social sciences and humanities. The influence of John Henry Newman is evident in the small class sizes and interactive teaching style adopted by the university. The university stresses its Catholic affiliation, but also its commitment to be inclusive in its recruitment and subsequent activities. It says it is proud to welcome staff and students of all religions and backgrounds, adding that, "In line with Newman's view of a university, we focus on a formative education, developing the whole student into independent thinkers who have the ability to question, evaluate and develop creative solutions to problems rather than just retain knowledge about their subject."

Newman has increased its undergraduate intake each year since the award of full university status. It dropped more than 30 places in its second year in the *Guide*, largely because of a decline in student satisfaction, and has fallen further this year, with lower scores on most measures.

A review of courses has resulted in a cut in the number of subject combinations, but added more traditional academic subjects, including maths and economics. Vocational subjects, accounting and finance, and health and social care were also added to the portfolio. All full-time degrees include work placements, some of which are abroad, and undergraduates can opt to study at a partner university in Europe or further afield to broaden their horizons and boost their CVs. There is also a range of part-time courses and Foundation degrees, most of which are taught at Newman, rather than partner

Genners Lane
Bartley Green
Birmingham B32 3NT

0121 476 1181 (admissions)
admissions@newman.ac.uk
www.newman.ac.uk
www.newmansu.org
Affiliation: GuildHE,
Cathedrals Group

***The Times and Sunday Times* Rankings**

Overall Ranking: **=115** (last year: 104)

Teaching quality:	**=26**	83.1%
Student experience:	**=49**	84.6%
Research quality:	**114**	2.8%
Entry standards:	**105**	293
Student-staff ratio:	**92**	18.9
Services & facilities/student:	**98**	£1,458
Expected completion rate:	**123**	73.3%
Good honours:	**121**	56%
Graduate prospects:	**=122**	54.6%

colleges.

The university received one of eight national awards to effect change in the strategic approach to technology in learning and teaching. The successful bid drew on a project designed to improve the university's own students' digital literacy, part of a larger initiative called "Newman in the Digital Age".

Based in Bartley Green, eight miles southwest of Birmingham city centre, the campus is in a quiet residential area with views over the Bartley Reservoir and the Worcestershire countryside beyond. The modern buildings are arranged around a series of inner quadrangles of lawns and trees. A £20-million development programme is now complete and includes an impressive new library and entrance building. The project has also added more lecture theatres, a research centre and a state-of-the-art sport performance suite.

Only 23 academics were entered for the latest research assessments, but that was twice as many as in 2008. Education and history produced the best results, but less than a third of the university's research was placed in the top two categories. Newman does not employ staff for research alone in order to ensure that students have regular contact with active researchers in their area. The university has done well over a number of years in the National Student Survey, scoring particularly highly on personal development. Three-quarters of the undergraduates are female, almost all of them state-educated, and more than half come from working-class homes.

Halls of residence provide single study-bedrooms for 217 students, close to the teaching areas and library. First-year students take priority in their allocation, but those entering through Clearing may have to live off campus. The refurbished fitness suite and performance room have improved sports facilities that already included an artificial sports pitch, sports hall, gymnasium and squash courts. Birmingham city centre, with its abundance of cultural venues and student-oriented nightlife, is about 20 minutes away.

Undergraduate Fees and Bursaries

- Fees for UK/EU students 2016–17 £9,000
- Fees for international students 2015–16 £10,500
- Academic achievement and progression scholarships from £2,000 to £12,000 over three years, subject to conditions. Full details for 2016–17 not confirmed in August 2015.
- Other scholarships and bursaries available.
- Check the university's website for the latest information.

Students

Undergraduates:	**1,685**	**(605)**
Postgraduates:	**370**	**(240)**
Mature students:	**24.8%**	
International students:	**0.6%**	
Applications per place:	**5.6**	
From state-sector schools:	**98.8%**	
From working-class homes:	**55.8%**	
Satisfaction with students' union	**64%**	

For detailed information about sports facilities:
www.newman.ac.uk/sport

Accommodation

Places and costs refer to 2015–16
University-provided places: 217
Percentage catered: 0%
Self-catered costs: around £3,800 (standard) – £5,000 (en suite) for academic year.
Priority, but no guarantee, is given to new first-year students.
International students: guaranteed housing.
www.newman.ac.uk/accommodation/

University of Northampton

Northampton is planning the greatest transformation at any UK university in the last two decades when it moves to a new waterside campus in the town in 2018. The university will take on £300 million of debt – nearly three times its annual income – most of it funded through a bond, which will be the first to be issued by a university using a Treasury guarantee. Undergraduates entering in 2016 may move from the two existing sites in their final year, but will face none of the disruption associated with such major developments elsewhere. The new campus will give the university scope to expand, as well as providing improved facilities.

The project typifies the ambitious nature of a university which, even after a big drop this year, is still ten places higher in our table than it was four years ago. Every student has the opportunity to work in a social enterprise as part of their course, developing new entrepreneurial skills to make them more employable. This may involve a work placement, volunteering or building sustainable social and economic partnerships which would, in turn, be supported by the university. The Ashoka global network of social entrepreneurs named Northampton as the first "Changemaker Campus" in the UK in 2013, and the university has since been ranked as number one in the country for social enterprise.

Although it was awarded university status only in 2005, Northampton can trace its history back to the 13th century. Henry III dissolved the original institution, allegedly because his bishops thought it posed a threat to Oxford. The modern university originated in an amalgamation of the town's colleges of education, nursing, technology and art. It has a particular focus on training for public services in the region, with students combining their studies with work placements in the community. The police and criminal justice studies Foundation degree, for example, is delivered for the Police and Crime Commissioner to prepare students for a career in policing or the criminal justice system.

Overall student numbers have topped 13,000, more than 1,000 of them coming from outside the EU. Business is the university's most popular area, but teacher training and health subjects are not far behind – the university is the region's largest provider of teachers and healthcare professionals. Northampton takes its mission to widen participation in higher education seriously: almost all the undergraduates are state educated and four out of ten come from working class homes – more than the national average for the university's courses and entry qualifications. The university

Park Campus
Boughton Green Road
Northampton NN2 7AL

0800 358 2232 (courses freephone)
study@northampton.ac.uk
www.northampton.ac.uk
www.northamptonunion.com
Affiliation: none

***The Times and Sunday Times* Rankings**

Overall Ranking: **=82** (last year: 56)

Teaching quality:	**=43**	82.3%
Student experience:	**=59**	84.1%
Research quality:	**112**	3.2%
Entry standards:	**114**	283
Student–staff ratio:	**=109**	20.3
Services & facilities/student:	**20**	£2,387
Expected completion rate:	**77**	85%
Good honours:	**91**	64.5%
Graduate prospects:	**=96**	60.7%

entered a quarter of its eligible staff for the 2014 Research Excellence Framework. Only 30 per cent of its research was placed in the top two categories, but there was an outstanding result in history, where two-thirds of the work was considered world-leading or internationally excellent. There are now 11 research centres, focusing on everything from contemporary fiction to anomalous psychological processes and transitional economics in China.

Of the two existing sites, Park Campus is on the edge of Northampton, while the smaller Avenue Campus occupies a more central position. They are linked by a regular and free weekday bus service, as well as by "Boris bikes". Park Campus is set in 80 acres of open green parkland, with accommodation, a sports hall, students' union centre and nightclub. Two of the main buildings have been refurbished and expanded as part of an £80-million programme of improvements, which included an extension to the business school.

Avenue Campus, the centre for art, design, science and technology, and the performing arts, hosts frequent theatre performances and exhibitions in its own art gallery. A £13-million investment saw the conversion of a former school into a technology and research centre with NVision and a 3-D immersive technology and visualisation facility. Another university-backed development is the iCon building in Daventry, which provides a base for a range of green businesses. The university also sponsors a University Technical College in the town, as it does at the nearby Silverstone motor racing circuit.

There are more than 2,100 residential places, including a choice of mixed and single-sex halls. The latest development added 475 rooms in the centre of Northampton. Sports enthusiasts are well catered for, with rugby union, football, first-class cricket and Silverstone on the doorstep. The sports facilities include a modern gym, a sports hall and outdoor pitches on the Park Campus. The town has a number of student-oriented bars, but the two campuses' union bars remain the hub of the social scene. Both London and Birmingham are about an hour away by train.

Undergraduate Fees and Bursaries

» Fees for UK/EU students 2016–17	£9,000
Placement year	£850
Foundation degree	£8,500
» Fees for international students 2015–16	£10,700–£11,700

» Household income below £25K, a bursary of £500 a year.
» Enhanced access and retention support.
» Other scholarships and bursaries available.
» Check the university's website for the latest information.

Students

Undergraduates:	**8,905**	**(2,070)**
Postgraduates:	**795**	**(1,515)**
Mature students:	**29%**	
International students:	**9.8%**	
Applications per place:	**6.4**	
From state-sector schools:	**97.2%**	
From working-class homes:	**40.6%**	
Satisfaction with students' union	**69%**	

For information about sports facilities:
www.northamptonunion.com/activities/sports

Accommodation

Number of places and costs refer to 2015–16
University-provided places: 2,114
Percentage catered: 0%
Self-catered costs: £61.50 (small twin) – £125.50 (en-suite single) a week (42-week contract).
New first years have priority, on first come, first served basis, provided requirements are met.
International students: as above.
accommodation@northampton.ac.uk
www.northampton.ac.uk/study/student-life/accommodation

Northumbria University

Northumbria is the biggest university in the North East of England, with 33,000 students, but has still been raising entry standards in line with its ambitions to win a place among the top 30 in the UK. It considers itself a "new type of excellent university" with a focus on business and the professions, as well as academic excellence. An £18-million staffing plan brought in more academics and enhanced the university's research capability. Northumbria more than doubled the numbers entered for the 2014 Research Excellence Framework compared with the 2008 assessments while improving the results. Sixty per cent of the work was judged to be world-leading or internationally excellent, attracting one of the biggest increases in research funding at any university.

Northumbria has invested £200 million over ten years in its impressive city centre campus and opened another in the City of London in 2014, with an initial focus on business courses. Most subjects are based on the main campus, with health, education and community programmes located at the Coach Lane campus less than two miles away, where £20 million has been spent upgrading facilities. The award-winning City Campus East development is linked to the original main campus by an iconic footbridge spanning Newcastle's central motorway. An expansion of the university library added 100 IT spaces, more social learning and informal space, a zone fitted with Smart boards and a dedicated Language Zone, attracting the second-highest score in *Times Higher Education* magazine's 2015 student experience survey. Coach Lane also has a learning resources centre, as well as new sports facilities and a clinical skills centre, where students can learn in simulated hospital environments. Northumbria's pre-registration nursing programmes were the first in the country to receive accreditation from the Royal College of Nursing.

Around half of the students are from the North East, but numbers drawn from other parts of the UK have been rising year on year. There are more than 3,000 international students on campus and another 4,500 taking Northumbria courses overseas. A school of design is being established in Jakarta, Indonesia, jointly with BINUS International University.

More than a third of the British undergraduates are from the four lowest socio-economic classes. Free one-day taster courses run throughout the year to give prospective students an idea of what university life would be like. While other universities have cut back on their bursaries, Northumbria continues to offer awards worth up to £3,000 to applicants from the

Ellison Place
Newcastle upon Tyne
NE1 8ST

0191 349 5600 (course enquiries)
er.admissions@northumbria.ac.uk
www.northumbria.ac.uk
www.mynsu.co.uk
Affiliation: none

***The Times and Sunday Times* Rankings**

Overall Ranking: =**64** (last year: 66)

Teaching quality:	**=28**	82.9%
Student experience:	**42**	85.1%
Research quality:	**=64**	9%
Entry standards:	**=46**	363
Student–staff ratio:	**=78**	17.8
Services & facilities/student:	**=93**	£1,484
Expected completion rate:	**=52**	87.6%
Good honours:	**73**	67.6%
Graduate prospects:	**=70**	66.3%

poorest homes. There are also 100 Master's bursaries, worth a total of £1 million, to encourage those graduating to continue their studies at Northumbria.

More than 550 employers sponsor undergraduate programmes – one of the highest rates in the UK – and accreditation comes from almost 50 professional bodies. Only three universities had established more start-up companies in a 2013 review of universities' contribution to economic growth. Business and accounting programmes are both accredited by The Association to Advance Collegiate Schools of Business, making Newcastle Business School the only institution in Europe to achieve double accreditation. Teacher education is another strength – all Northumbria's programmes have been rated as outstanding by Ofsted for 13 years in a row – and its post-registration nursing provision was voted the best in Britain for three successive years. The Student Law Office, which offers legal advice under professional supervision as part of a degree, won a Queen's Anniversary Prize in 2014.

Northumbria has been rated as one of the leading universities for sports facilities and has been in the top ten of the British Universities and Colleges Sport (BUCS) league table since 2013–14. A £30-million sports centre includes a swimming pool with an adjustable floor, multiple laboratories, a climbing wall and a 3,000-seat indoor arena for professional sport and other events. There is also a generous sport scholarship scheme that supports talented student athletes throughout their degree programme.

Most first years are offered places in university accommodation that was placed in the top three in the 2014 Student Housing Survey. There are now more than 5,000 residential places, since almost 1,000 new bedrooms became available in 2014 with the opening of new student accommodation in nearby Gateshead. The development is a core element of the regeneration of the town centre and boasts landscaped walkways, fitness facilities and a multi-use games area, as well as offering stunning views across the Tyneside skyline. There is a plentiful supply of privately rented flats and houses in Newcastle, a location that frequently wins awards as the best student city in the UK.

Undergraduate Fees and Bursaries

» Fees for UK/EU students 2016–17	£9,000
Placement year	£1,000
» Fees for international students 2016–17	£12,000–£14,000

- » Household income below £16K, a bursary of £1,000 a year.
- » Academic scholarships for entrants with over 400 UCAS points, £4,000; 360–399 UCAS points, £3,000; 320–359 UCAS points, £2,000.
- » Progression scholarships for those with grades of 70% or above, £1,000; 60%–69.9%, £500.
- » Check the university's website for the latest information.

Students

Undergraduates:	**19,195**	**(3,865)**
Postgraduates:	**2,200**	**(2,300)**
Mature students:	**16.2%**	
International students:	**10.7%**	
Applications per place:	**5.3**	
From state-sector schools:	**93.4%**	
From working-class homes:	**33.8%**	
Satisfaction with students' union	**75%**	

For detailed information about sports facilities:
www.nusportcentral.com

Accommodation

Number of places and costs refer to 2015–16
University-provided places: 5,000
Percentage catered: 5%
Catered costs: £110.25 a week.
Self-catered costs: £70.00 (single) – £126.00 (en suite); £170.10 (studio) a week.
First years who need accommodation can be offered rooms.
International students: first years are guaranteed accommodation if requirements met.
www.northumbria.ac.uk/study-at-northumbria/accommodation/

Norwich University of the Arts (NUA)

NUA makes its first appearance in *The Times and Sunday Times* league table this year, after the relaxation of restrictions on specialist institutions which excluded it when full university status was awarded in 2012. Norwich has long enjoyed a powerful reputation in its field and plans to double in size over the next few years. The process will be gradual so as not to place too much strain on the specialist facilities that its students value highly, but developments such as the opening of a new building for the School of Architecture in 2015 will allow for a larger intake. The school is moving to the Grade II-listed Boardman House, in the city centre, which includes new studios for media students and was purchased as the first stage of a £10-million development plan. The university is already expanding: enrolments have risen for three years in a row and, with the volume of applications rising by 7 per cent in 2015, following a much bigger increase in the previous year, there appears to be plenty of scope for further growth.

Unlike the other arts universities, NUA makes a virtue of focusing entirely on the arts, design and media, rather than venturing into business or the humanities and social sciences. There are only 15 BA degrees and fewer than 2,000 students, 57 per cent of whom are female. New degrees for 2015 include interior architecture and fashion communication and promotion. More than 40 per cent of the undergraduates come from working-class homes and the projected dropout rate is much better the national average for its courses and entry qualifications. There are much higher levels of overall satisfaction than at the other specialist arts universities in the National Student Survey; indeed NUA was in the top 30 of all universities in 2014.

NUA traces its history back to 1845, when the Norwich School of Design was established by the artists and followers of the Norwich School of Painters, the only provincial British group with an international reputation for landscape painting. Former tutors include Lucian Freud, Michael Andrews and Lesley Davenport. The campus is concentrated on the pedestrianised centre of Norwich, from the 13th-century Garth, which is now the photography centre, to the Monastery Media Lab and St Georges, where the traditional high ceilings and huge windows make it an ideal setting for Fine Art. The university's public art gallery enables students to showcase their work and gain experience curating and organising exhibitions, while the library houses the largest specialist art, design and media collection in the eastern region. An Ideas

Francis House
3-7 Redwell Street
Norwich
NR2 4SN

01603 610561 (enquiries)
studentrecruitment@nua.ac.uk
www.nua.ac.uk
www.nuasu.org
Affiliation: GuildHE

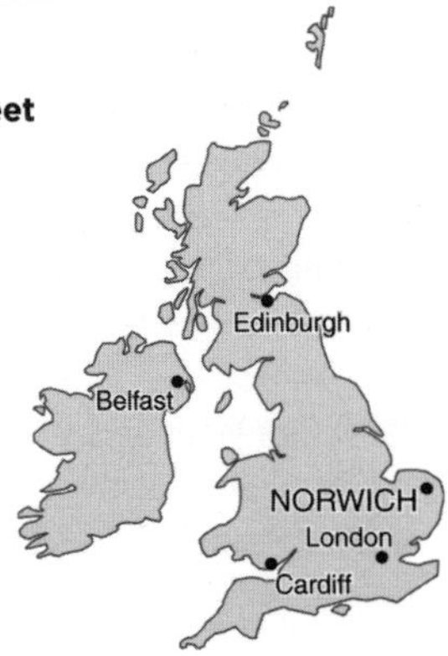

***The Times and Sunday Times* Rankings**

Overall Ranking: **61** (last year: n/a)

Teaching quality:	**=13**	83.8%
Student experience:	**=71**	83.5%
Research quality:	**=85**	5.6%
Entry standards:	**50**	357
Student–staff ratio:	**=78**	17.8
Services & facilities/student:	**115**	£1,236
Expected completion rate:	**49**	88.7%
Good honours:	**59**	70.5%
Graduate prospects:	**=86**	63.4%

Factory building, incorporating a digital start-up incubation hub, and a Digital User Research Lab are additions in 2015.

NUA has invested significantly in hardware and software that is professionally relevant and suitable for its diverse range of academic requirements. IT resources can be accessed in the workshops, library, computer-teaching rooms, seminar rooms, and at numerous terminals available throughout the campus. NUA has its own art materials shop, open daily, which sells basic and specialist art supplies at discounted prices. Individual studio space is provided for all full-time students in the faculties of art and design, while students in the media faculty have access to digital media workstations. Workshops for everything from digital video editing to laser cutting provide specialised resources and are staffed by experienced professionals, including graduates and practising artists.

Most courses include units of self-managed learning and exploration that allow students to concentrate on areas of particular interest. Agreements with tutors focus on personal study and help students negotiate individual pathways through their courses. More than half of the work submitted to the 2014 Research Excellence Framework was judged to be world leading or internationally excellent, with 90 per cent placed in the top two categories for its impact on the broader cultural and economic landscape.

A new residential development in the city centre, opened in autumn 2015, more than doubled the number of rooms managed by the university. The new cluster flats will bring the total to almost 350 rooms, with priority going to international students and first years living furthest away from the university. NUA does not have its own sports facilities, but its students have access to the University of East Anglia's Sportspark, which boasts some of the best facilities in the higher education system, including an Olympic-sized swimming pool. The city is attractive and popular with students, as well as being safer than most university centres.

Undergraduate Fees and Bursaries

- Fees for UK/EU students 2016–17 £9,000
- Fees for international students 2015–16 £12,500
- Household income below £25K, £1,000 bursary a year; household income £25K–£42.6K, £500 a year.
- Other scholarships and bursaries available.
- Check the university's website for the latest information.

Students

Undergraduates:	**1,705**	**(0)**
Postgraduates:	**20**	**(40)**
Mature students:	**13.8%**	
International students:	**4.1%**	
Applications per place:	**3.9**	
From state-sector schools:	**97.8%**	
From working-class homes:	**41.7%**	
Satisfaction with students' union	**59%**	

For detailed information about sports facilities:
www.nua.ac.uk/norwich/sport

Accommodation

Number of places and costs refer to 2015–16
University-provided places: 345
Percentage catered: 0%
Self-catered costs: £99–£150 a week (46 weeks).
First years cannot be guaranteed housing. Distance restrictions apply.
International students: as above
accommodation@nua.ac.uk
www.nua.ac.uk/study/accommodation

University of Nottingham

Nottingham promises an outstanding student experience and a "distinct" approach to internationalisation, which rests on full-scale campuses in China and Malaysia, as well as in its home city. The university was in the top ten in *Times Higher Education*'s latest student experience survey, although this is yet to be repeated in the national assessment of student satisfaction. A member of the Russell Group, Nottingham is in the top 70 in the QS World University Rankings, and now has two bases in China in addition to its original branch campus outside Kuala Lumpur in Malaysia. With 8,000 international students in Nottingham and as many again in Asia, it is the nearest Britain has to a truly global university. The university's stock is high in the UK, too: it is in the top five for the volume of applications and is one of the two universities most targeted by recruiters from *The Times* Top 100 graduate employers.

The main University Park campus in Nottingham is one of the most attractive in the UK, the winner of 12 consecutive Green Flag awards for its 330 acres of parkland and named as the most sustainable campus in the world for the last three years. Now the university is adding a £40-million sports complex and impressive new facilities for synthetic biology and sustainable chemistry. The building programme also includes the extension and refurbishment of the specialist library for engineering and science, which will double in size. A mile away is the 30-acre Jubilee Campus, which houses the schools of management and finance, computer science and education, as well as 750 residential places. New sports facilities, research laboratories, teaching space and student accommodation have all been added in recent years. The newly reorganised Medical School is also close to University Park, with a £4.5-million outpost for nursing at Derby Hospital. The biosciences and the veterinary school are at Sutton Bonington, 12 miles south of the city in a rural setting. The latest development there is a £9-million Amenities Building, which includes a 500-seat dining hall, student common rooms and staff lounge, as well as a graduate centre, faith room and Student Guild service.

Nottingham has shown its strength in research with two Nobel prizes since the millennium for work carried out at the university. Professor Sir Peter Mansfield, who won the medicine prize for research leading to the development of the MRI scanner, has spent almost his entire academic career there. Sir Clive Granger, who won the economics prize, spent 22 years at Nottingham before moving to the USA. More than 80 per cent of the work entered for the 2014 Research Excellence

University Park
Nottingham NG7 2RD

0115 951 5559 (enquiries)
undergraduate-enquiries@nottingham.ac.uk
www.nottingham.ac.uk
www.su.nottingham.ac.uk
Affiliation: Russell Group

***The Times and Sunday Times* Rankings**

Overall Ranking: **25** (last year: =22)

Teaching quality:	**=84**	79.5%
Student experience:	**=63**	83.9%
Research quality:	**20**	37.8%
Entry standards:	**=21**	428
Student–staff ratio:	**28**	14
Services & facilities/student:	**37**	£2,055
Expected completion rate:	**=20**	93.2%
Good honours:	**23**	79.3%
Graduate prospects:	**17**	81.3%

Framework was rated as world-leading or internationally excellent. The university was in the UK's top ten in half of the 32 subject areas in which it made submissions, with pharmacy, chemistry and physics producing particularly good results.

Nottingham had well-established links in Asia long before it established its branch campuses in Malaysia and at Ningbo, in China. The purpose-built campuses both have echoes of Nottingham's distinctive clock tower. All students can move between the three countries. The latest venture is collaboration with the East China University of Science and Technology, where the Shanghai Nottingham Advanced Academy will be based. It will deliver joint courses that include periods of study in Nottingham UK, with teaching and research at undergraduate, postgraduate and doctoral levels.

The university has succeeded in broadening its UK intake, but still has more independent school students and fewer from working-class homes than the national average for the subjects it offers. Summer schools and master classes provide support for teenagers from backgrounds without a history of progressing to selective universities and the university has joined the Sutton Trust's Pathways to Law access programme. Once in, students tend to stay the course – the dropout rate of just over 5 per cent is among the best in the country. The Nottingham Advantage Award offers extra-curricular modules, as well as providing scores of internships for graduates, who enjoy lifetime access to the careers service, which has teams in each faculty.

The two main campuses in Nottingham are within three miles of the city centre, which has a good selection of student-friendly clubs. However, halls of residence and the students' union tend to be the centre of social life for students, especially in the first year. New bars, café facilities and a nightclub were included in a £1-million makeover of union facilities. Sports provision is excellent. Almost £5 million is being spent on two new sports pavilions and the university's playing fields adjoin the main campus in addition to the new complex.

Undergraduate Fees and Bursaries

» Fees for UK/EU students 2016–17	£9,000
» Fees for international students 2015–16	£14,140–£18,210
Veterinary medicine	£18,210–£26,970
Medicine	£19,180–£33,340

» Household income below £15K, a bursary of £2,000 a year; £15K–£25K, £1,500 a year; £25K–£35K, £1,000 a year. Additional £1,000 a year if certain conditions met.

» Range of subject scholarships available.

» Check the university's website for the latest information.

Students

Undergraduates:	**23,155**	**(1,730)**
Postgraduates:	**5,740**	**(2,645)**
Mature students:	**11.6%**	
International students:	**18.4%**	
Applications per place:	**7.6**	
From state-sector schools:	**77.8%**	
From working-class homes:	**19.7%**	
Satisfaction with students' union	**71%**	

For detailed information about sports facilities:
www.nottingham.ac.uk/sport

Accommodation

Number of places and costs refer to 2015–16
University-provided places: 7,500
Percentage catered: 33.3%
Catered costs: £102.55–£202.87 a week (31–51 weeks).
Self-catered costs: £96.45–£159.93 a week (44 or 51 weeks).
First years are guaranteed accommodation if conditions are met.
International undergraduates: as above.
accommodation@nottingham.ac.uk
www.nottingham.ac.uk/accommodation/

Nottingham Trent University

Nottingham Trent was among the top four universities for the number of undergraduates recruited through UCAS in 2014, when it took almost 1,000 more students than in the previous year. There are now 31,000 students at all levels, from over 100 different countries.

The university has spent £350 million in ten years recruiting new staff and upgrading its three campuses. The latest project has seen the redevelopment of the Clifton Campus, five miles from the centre of Nottingham, with a new central pavilion building and teaching suite plus a newly modernised and upgraded refectory and library. The development, which includes a "superlab" for 200 science students, opens in autumn 2015, and the university is to invest £10 million more on its facilities for science, technology, engineering and mathematics (STEM) disciplines. It had already opened a new students' union and 500 student bedrooms, bars and other social space on the main city campus in 2014. Other projects on the campus have included the upgrading of art and design facilities and the Boots Library, as well as new lecture theatres, laboratories, student services areas and restaurants. In addition, £20 million has been spent on a new animal unit and veterinary nursing centre at the Brackenhurst campus, where an eco-friendly library opened in 2013.

Art and design, architecture, law, business and the social sciences are taught on the main campus, while science and technology, education, and the humanities are based at Clifton, which has seen the addition of six new blocks of high-quality student accommodation that will form part of a student village. The Brackenhurst Campus, 14 miles outside Nottingham, is devoted to animal, rural and environmental studies. It includes one of the region's best-equipped equestrian centres, with a purpose-built indoor riding area, as well as 340 residential places.

Best known for fashion and other creative arts, the university also boasts one of the UK's biggest law schools, offering legal practice courses both for solicitors and barristers, as well as degrees. A three-year LLB(Hons) Law and Legal Practice course integrates an LLB law degree with the solicitors' Legal Practice Course. Other recent academic developments include a number of sponsored degrees at the business school, where students work full-time for a company whilst studying. Students have their fees paid by the sponsoring company and also receive a salary. A new management and finance degree gives students a degree and CIMA qualification in four years instead of the usual seven, also with fees and salary paid

Burton Street
Nottingham NG1 4BU

0115 848 4200 (admissions)
contact via website
www.ntu.ac.uk
www.trentstudents.org
Affiliation: University Alliance

***The Times and Sunday Times* Rankings**

Overall Ranking: **54** (last year: 52)

Teaching quality:	**18**	83.6%
Student experience:	**=31**	85.8%
Research quality:	**80**	6.5%
Entry standards:	**=86**	310
Student–staff ratio:	**=63**	17
Services & facilities/student:	**56**	£1,812
Expected completion rate:	**46**	89.6%
Good honours:	**65**	69.2%
Graduate prospects:	**64**	67.6%

by a company. Nottingham Trent is now the fourth in the UK for the number of students on year-long work placements.

The university has been increasing its international profile: as well as hosting more than 2,500 foreign students in Nottingham, it has several thousand more taking its degrees in partner colleges overseas. NTU is aiming to offer all its students an "international learning experience", which may involve a study or work placement abroad, learning a foreign language or studying another culture or country. A third of the undergraduates come from working-class homes and more than nine out of ten attended state schools or colleges. The projected dropout rate continues to improve and is now lower than the national average for the university's courses and entry grades.

An extensive research programme attracted an £8-million donation – thought to be the largest to a post-1992 university – to advance the university's work in cancer diagnosis and therapy. Researchers at the purpose-built facility on the Clifton Campus work with leading cancer research institutions in the USA, Europe and Asia. More than half of the research submitted to the 2014 Research Excellence Framework was considered world-leading or internationally excellent, but NTU still slipped down our research ranking. The best results were in health subjects and general engineering, where more than 80 per cent of the work was placed in the top two categories.

NTU has a strong sporting reputation and generally does well in the BUCS leagues. The Lee Westwood Sports Centre, opened by the golfer himself, is on the Clifton Campus and includes sports halls, studios, fitness suites and a nutrition training centre. NTU alumni include England rugby player Nick Easter and Great Britain hockey players Crista Cullen, Alistair Wilson and Adam Dixon, who was one of three current or former NTU students participating at the 2014 Commonwealth Games. Social life varies between campuses, but all have access to the city's lively cultural and clubbing scene. A bus service links the main campuses and the city's new tram system serves the university.

Undergraduate Fees and Bursaries

- » Fees for UK/EU students 2016–17 £9,000
  - Foundation degree up to £9,000
  - Placement year / year abroad £1,350
- » Fees for international students 2015–16 £11,800–£12,300
- » Household income below £30K, a bursary of £1,000 a year.
- » Additional bursaries for students from particular backgrounds or circumstances.
- » Check the university's website for the latest information.

Students

Undergraduates:	**20,530**	**(1,140)**
Postgraduates:	**2,320**	**(2,855)**
Mature students:	**10%**	
International students:	**7.2%**	
Applications per place:	**5.2**	
From state-sector schools:	**94.2%**	
From working-class homes:	**34.1%**	
Satisfaction with students' union	**83%**	

For detailed information about sports facilities:
www.ntu.ac.uk/sport

Accommodation

Number of places and costs refer to 2015–16
University-provided places: 4,800
Percentage catered: 0%
Self-catered costs: £83.13–£159.88 (44–51 weeks).
First years and new students are guaranteed accommodation if conditions are met.
International students: guaranteed accommodation if conditions are met.
accommodation@ntu.ac.uk
www.ntu.ac.uk/study_with_us/accommodation

The Open University (OU)

The national collapse in part-time higher education has hit the Open University hard: it has lost 28 per cent of its students in five years and gone from healthy surpluses to a £17-million deficit in 2013–14. Peter Horrocks, the new Vice-Chancellor who arrived from the BBC World Service in May 2015, is proposing to reduce the seven faculties to three and shedding some posts, while calling for the OU to become more agile and innovative. He has said the university will have to change for the benefit of its students and be as radical and tough with itself as it was in its early days in the 1970s. Although still much the largest university in the UK and the choice of 60 per cent of all part-time students, the OU now has fewer than 187,000 students, compared with 260,000 at the start of the decade. However, Mr Horrocks has promised "unprecedented" investment in research and continued substantial spending on massive open online courses (MOOCs) that are free to students. The university is hosting FutureLearn, a consortium of leading universities and cultural organisations such as the British Museum and the British Council, offering MOOCs of varying lengths in a growing range of subjects.

The OU remains one of the world's most highly regarded distance learning institutions, a model for universities on every continent. It does not appear in our league table because the absence of on-campus undergraduates makes the OU unsuitable for comparison with conventional universities on some of the measures used. It offers curriculum resources free via its OpenLearn website and was the first UK university to extend free learning to the social media site Bibblio. Its size has not prevented it ranking in the top ten of the National Student Survey every year since 2005. Undergraduate fees are £5,400 for the equivalent of full-time study in 2015 – the cheapest at any university. The OU provides financial support for students from poor backgrounds through its Access to Success programme. Three in ten students are under 25 years old and three-quarters work either full or part-time while studying. Over 60 per cent of undergraduates are female and most live in the UK, but there are now 15,000 students in other countries. The OU offers special support for disabled students and currently has more than 20,000 students with disabilities.

The university's headquarters are at Milton Keynes, Buckinghamshire, but it has 350 study centres and regional centres in each of its 13 regions around the UK, as well as offices and exam centres abroad. The open access principle that was a cornerstone of its foundation remains in place: no formal

Walton Hall
Milton Keynes MK7 6AA

0300 303 5303 (enquiries)
contact via website
www.open.ac.uk
www.open.ac.uk/ousa
Affiliation: none

The Times and Sunday Times Rankings

The available data do not match the data used to rank the other full-time universities, so the Open University could not be included in the league table this year.

qualifications are required to study on most undergraduate programmes. Almost 6,000 part-time associate lecturers (tutors) guide students through degrees. The OU's "Supported Open Learning" system allows students to work where they choose – at home, in the workplace or at a library or study centre. They have contact with fellow students at tutorials, day schools or through online conferencing and electronic forums, social networks and informal study groups. An increasing amount of material is delivered online, and can be accessed on mobile devices as well as computers. The university has been awarded £2.7 million to create online laboratories for science and engineering that are available 24 hours a day for students worldwide to set up and participate in remote-controlled experiments.

The late-night BBC television programmes that were the mainstay of teaching until 2006 are now a thing of the past. Instead, the OU produces mainstream television and radio programming aimed at bringing learning to a wider audience. The university also leads the universities placing material on the iTunes U site and was one of the first in the world to make e-books available there. The 1,100 full-time academics have a proud research record: 72 per cent of the OU's submission for the 2014 Research Excellence Framework was assessed as world-leading or internationally excellent. There was an outstanding result in music, where 94 per cent reached these levels, and good performances in art and design and electronic engineering.

The university covers all the main academic disciplines in its 374 undergraduate modules. In addition to degrees in a named subject, the OU also awards "Open" Bachelor degrees, where the syllabus is designed by the students combining a number of modules. Assessment is by both continual assessment and examination or, for some modules, a major assignment. Except in fast-moving areas such as computing, there is no limit on the time taken to complete a degree.

Undergraduate Fees and Bursaries

- Fees vary depending upon the type of course, on where you live and the number of credits you plan to study. In 2015–16, in England a course of 120 credits of study (a year's full-time study) is £5,400, which can be covered by a tuition fee loan. Access Curriculum year 0 30-credit course reduced to £675.
- In Scotland, Wales and Northern Ireland, a course of 120 credits is £1,666–£2,152, and there may be government assistance in paying the fee.
- For international students, a course of 120 credits is £5,400.
- The costs of all courses are given in the course descriptions: **www.open.ac.uk/courses**
- Various forms of financial help are available. Details are given at: **www.open.ac.uk/courses/fees-and-funding**

Students

Undergraduates:	**0**	**(138,605)**
Postgraduates:	**215**	**(12,015)**
Satisfaction with students' union	**62%**	

Accommodation

As the courses provided are part time, the university does not provide accommodation.

University of Oxford

Oxford has appointed its first female vice-chancellor in more than 900 years of existence. Professor Louise Richardson, a leading scholar on global terrorism, will arrive in January 2015 from St Andrews University, where she has been principal since 2009. She will take over a university that is among the top six in the world, according to the QS and *Times Higher Education* global rankings. However, it has slipped off the top of our table after dropping in the research ranking, largely because it entered a smaller proportion of its academics than its main rivals in the 2014 Research Excellence Framework. It achieved the best results in the UK in nine subject areas and 87 per cent of its submission was rated as world-leading or internationally excellent, but it entered 87 per cent of eligible staff, compared with 95 per cent at Cambridge.

Oxford is the oldest and probably the most famous university in the English-speaking world. Applications rose in 2014, but there was no increase in the numbers accepted. There are fewer than six applicants to each place overall – a much more favourable ratio than at some other leading universities – but 99 per cent of successful candidates achieve at least three As at A level, or their equivalent. Some subjects now demand two A* grades and another A at A level. The university never ceases to remind sixth-formers that Oxford is open to all who can meet the exacting entrance requirements, but it still admits the lowest proportion of undergraduates from the bottom four socio-economic groups – just over one in ten – and the most from independent schools. There have been numerous initiatives to broaden the intake, including summer schools, recruitment fairs and student visits to comprehensive schools. Oxford also offers the most generous financial support in UK higher education for students from poor backgrounds. A £75-million donation helps to provide bursaries and fee waivers worth up to £7,500 a year for those whose family income is less than £16,000.

Applications must be made by mid October – a month earlier if you wish to be interviewed overseas – and it is not possible to apply to both Oxford and Cambridge. There are written tests for some subjects and you may be asked to submit samples of work. Selection is in the hands of the 30 undergraduate colleges, which vary considerably in their approach to this issue and others. Sound advice on colleges' academic strengths and social factors is essential for applicants to give themselves the best chance of winning a place and finding a setting in which they can thrive. A minority of candidates opt to go

University Offices
Wellington Square
Oxford OX1 2JD

01865 288000 (admissions)
contact via website
www.ox.ac.uk
http://ousu.org
Affiliation: Russell Group

***The Times and Sunday Times* Rankings**

Overall Ranking: **2** (last year: =1)

Teaching quality:	**=26**	83.1%
Student experience:	**=21**	86.8%
Research quality:	**3**	53.1%
Entry standards:	**2**	573
Student–staff ratio:	**3**	10.6
Services & facilities/student:	**3**	£3,229
Expected completion rate:	**=6**	96.3%
Good honours:	**1**	92.1%
Graduate prospects:	**4**	87.1%

straight into the admissions pool without expressing a preference for a particular college. The choice is particularly important for arts and social science students, whose tuition is based in college. The university has been lobbying for a rise in the £9,000 undergraduate fees because it claims that the true cost of its world-famous individual or small group tuition is at least £16,000. Although fees will now rise in line with inflation, Oxford is losing £4 million of funding that was designed to help support the tutorial system. Science and technology are taught mainly in central facilities. All subjects operate on eight-week terms and assess students entirely on final examinations – a system some find too pressurised. Nevertheless, Oxford remains just inside the top 20 for student satisfaction.

The development of a new campus on the site of the Radcliffe Infirmary represents the first fruit of the Oxford Thinking fundraising campaign, which passed its £1.25-billion target in 2012 and has been extended to £3 billion. Oxford's biggest capital development for more than a century has provided more student accommodation for neighbouring Somerville College, a new Mathematical Institute building and a new building for the humanities. The £75-million Blavatnik School of Government opens there in autumn 2015. Elsewhere, an £11-million building commissioned by St Antony's College to provide much-needed space for its Middle East Centre opened in May. A £110-million cancer research institute, supported by a £35-million Government grant, is perhaps the most ambitious single project currently planned. Its overriding aim will to make cancer treatments less invasive and more personalised.

In the Science Area, existing buildings are being refurbished and modernised. Among the many recent projects was the opening of a new building at the Botnar Research Centre for research on arthritis, osteoporosis and other bone and joint diseases. The university has identified the digital infrastructure as the next big area of investment.

Undergraduate Fees and Bursaries

- » Fees for UK/EU students 2016–17 £9,000
- » Fees for international students 2015–16 £14,845–£21,855
  Medicine £17,040–£30,100
  College fees £6,925 (£2,848 for clinical medicine years)
- » UK and EU students who are eligible for tuition fee support are not liable for College fees.
- » UK/EU students with household income up to £16K, a bursary of £4,500 a year; £16K–£42.6K, bursary on sliding scale £3,500–£500 a year.
- » In addition Moritz–Heyman scholarships for students with household income below £16K and other conditions, £3,000 a year fee waiver.
- » Wide range of departmental and College awards.
- » Check the university's website for the latest information.

Students

Undergraduates:	**11,380**	**(5,275)**
Postgraduates:	**7,515**	**(1,735)**
Mature students:	**3.1%**	
International students:	**16%**	
Applications per place:	**5.7**	
From state-sector schools:	**57.2%**	
From working-class homes:	**10.6%**	
Satisfaction with students' union	**36%**	

For detailed information about sports facilities: www.sport.ox.ac.uk

Accommodation

www.ox.ac.uk/students/life/accommodation
www.ox.ac.uk/admissions/undergraduate/colleges/college-listing
Also see chapter 13 for information about individual colleges.

Oxford Brookes University

For the first time in 20 years, Oxford Brookes is not among the top five post-1992 universities in our table, although its quality was reconfirmed in the 2014 Research Excellence Framework, when it entered more academics than most of its peer group and still saw almost 60 per cent of its work rated as world-leading or internationally excellent. There were particularly good results in architecture, English and history. The overall performance produced a 41 per cent rise in research funding, among the top ten increases in England. Although other factors have cost the university six places in the table, it remains close to the top 50.

The university has a tradition of innovation that dates back to its time as a polytechnic, when it pioneered the modular degree system that has swept British higher education. The latest example is the Grade Point Average (GPA) system that it introduced to give its students a more accurate assessment of their work on graduation. Students still receive the traditional British honours degree classification as well, but all their marks from the first year onwards now count towards their GPA, which has strong recognition overseas.

Brookes has been celebrating the 150th anniversary of its parent institution, the Oxford School of Art, but its main campus at Headington is almost unrecognisable even from five years ago. The award-winning Abercrombie Building opened in 2013, providing first-class facilities for architecture students with design studios and collaborative learning spaces. The £132-million John Henry Brookes Building followed a year later and was rated among the top 15 new buildings in the UK. It brings together the library and teaching space with the students' union and support services.

The university is spending £13 million a year on refurbishment and some additional building on its Headington and Harcourt Hill campuses. The Faculty of Business is due to move from the Wheatley Campus into modernised facilities in Headington in 2016/17. Wheatley, seven miles from the city centre, will continue to be the base for engineering and technology students. A new engineering building supports the university's status as a Government-designated regional centre for motorsport and high performance engineering: graduates now work in all F1 teams. The Harcourt Hill Campus, at Botley, is the home of the School of Education. There is also a small site in Swindon, which focuses mainly on nursing and has its own osteopathic training clinic. Brookes sponsors a university technical college for 14–19 year-olds in the town.

The university's Oxford location is

Headington Campus
Gypsy Lane
Oxford OX3 0BP

01865 484848 (enquiries)
query@brookes.ac.uk
www.brookes.ac.uk
www.brookesunion.org.uk
Affiliation: University Alliance

***The Times and Sunday Times* Rankings**

Overall Ranking: **55** (last year: 49)

Teaching quality:	**=22**	83.2%
Student experience:	**34**	85.7%
Research quality:	**57**	11.4%
Entry standards:	**52**	348
Student–staff ratio:	**74**	17.6
Services & facilities/student:	**99**	£1,429
Expected completion rate:	**47**	89.4%
Good honours:	**57**	71.1%
Graduate prospects:	**58**	69.2%

an advantage in student recruitment, but the quality of provision is the real draw. Ofsted rates the primary teacher training as outstanding, for example, and Brookes now has eight National Teaching Fellowships, a prestigious award given to academics for excellence in higher education teaching and support for learning. The university is particularly popular with independent schools, which provide just over a quarter of the undergraduates – by far the highest proportion among the new non-specialist universities and twice the national average for the university's subjects and entry grades. However, the proportion from working-class homes, at 45 per cent, is also considerably ahead of the official benchmark. Brookes has been trying to attract more students from state schools and has targeted areas in Oxfordshire and the wider region. An integrated e-learning network is designed to give students greater flexibility over when, where and how they learn.

Students are encouraged to take advantage of a range of placement and exchange opportunities and to take subjects outside their main area of study. The university also has a strong international profile, notably through a global partnership with the Association of Chartered Certified Accountants, which gives Brookes far more students than any other UK university – over 200,000 – taking its qualifications in other countries. At home, Oxford Brookes was one of 11 universities to win a Green Flag award in 2014 and the only one to be given three, one for each campus.

A 25-metre swimming pool and 9-hole golf course have been added to the already impressive sports facilities. Brookes is home to the top university squad for young rowers aiming to get into Team GB and hoping to match the successes of previous alumni who won medals at three consecutive Olympic games. Katherine Grainger, the Olympic 2012 rowing gold-medallist, became Chancellor of the university in 2015. A new £600,000 boathouse opened in 2013. Their cricketers combine with Oxford University to take on county teams. The students' union runs one of the biggest entertainment venues in Oxford, a city that can be expensive, but which offers enough to satisfy most students.

Undergraduate Fees and Bursaries

» Fees for UK/EU students 2016–17	£9,000
Foundation degrees at partner colleges	£7,000
Bachelor degrees at partner colleges	£7,000
Placement year / Year abroad	£1,350
» Fees for international students 2016–17	£12,640–£14,500

» Household income below £10K: a bursary of £2,000 in year 1, £3,000 in years 2 and 3;
£10K–£15K, £1,500 in year 1, £2,500 in years 2 and 3;
£15K–£25K, £1,000 in year 1, £1,750 in years 2 and 3.

» Community scholarships of £1,000 in year 1 for local students.

Students

Undergraduates:	**11,475**	**(2,240)**
Postgraduates:	**2,005**	**(2,180)**
Mature students:	**27.2%**	
International students:	**15.1%**	
Applications per place:	**7.8**	
From state-sector schools:	**74.9%**	
From working-class homes:	**44%**	
Satisfaction with students' union	**49%**	

For detailed information about sports facilities:
www.brookes.ac.uk/brookes-sport

Accommodation

Number of places and costs refer to 2015-16
University-provided places: 4,700
Percentage catered: 3%
Catered cost: £145.21 a week (38 weeks).
Self-catered cost: £105.48–£191.95 (from 38 weeks).
Accommodation is preferentially allocated to first year students who select Oxford Brookes as Firm choice through UCAS and meet all deadlines for application.
International students: as above.
www.brookes.ac.uk/students/accommodation

Plymouth University

Only two post-1992 universities produced better results in the 2014 Research Excellence Framework than Plymouth, which entered a far larger proportion of its academics for assessment than most of its peer group and still saw nearly two-thirds of its research judged world-leading or internationally excellent. The results were welcome good news at the end of a turbulent year, in which Professor Wendy Purcell, the Vice-Chancellor, was suspended and later replaced without explanation from the university. She now has the title of President, but no longer runs the university. Further good news has come in 2015 as the university has topped the People and Planet Green League of environmental performance and featured again in the top 50 of *Times Higher Education* magazine's ranking of the leading universities in the world that are under 50 years old.

Plymouth is the only post-1992 university with its own medical school since ending its partnership with Exeter University in the management of the former Peninsula College of Medicine and Dentistry. The new school is small, with an annual entry of only 75 students taking medicine, but Plymouth has kept all 50 of Peninsula's places in dentistry. As part of the plans, Plymouth spent £25 million on new buildings for the medical and dental school, and is now investing a further £15 million on research facilities. The university is the largest provider of nursing, midwifery and health professional education and training in the region.

Over £200 million has been spent on the main city campus. The library has been extended and upgraded and the students' union refurbished. There have been new buildings for the Faculty of Health and Human Sciences and the Plymouth Institute of Education, as well as a £35-million arts complex. The £1-million Immersive Vision Theatre is thought to be the first of its kind at a UK university, giving the feeling of being "in", rather than just observing, different types of image. The £19-million Marine Building contains the country's most advanced wave tanks, a navigation centre with ship simulator and business incubation space for companies in the marine renewables sector. A new Marine Station opened in 2014, with facilities for scientific diver training, as did a £7-million centre for the performing arts, which has teaching and research facilities, a 250-seat venue and unparalleled disabled access for students.

Plymouth is the region's largest university, around 27,000 students, and is aiming to be the country's top "enterprise university". It was awarded a Queen's Anniversary Prize for Higher and Further Education in 2012 and was the first university to be

Drake Circus
Plymouth
PL4 8AA
01752 585858 (enquiries)
admissions@plymouth.ac.uk
www.plymouth.ac.uk
www.upsu.com
Affiliation: University Alliance

***The Times and Sunday Times* Rankings**

Overall Ranking: **=85** (last year: 80)

Teaching quality:	**=43**	82.3%
Student experience:	**=59**	84.1%
Research quality:	**56**	15.9%
Entry standards:	**=83**	312
Student–staff ratio:	**73**	17.5
Services & facilities/student:	**101**	£1,424
Expected completion rate:	**79**	84.8%
Good honours:	**=78**	67%
Graduate prospects:	**101**	60.2%

awarded Regional Growth Fund money to promote economic development. The university has one of the country's top ten business incubation facilities – part of its managed portfolio of £100 million worth of incubation and innovation assets. In 2013, it became the first university in the world to be awarded the Social Enterprise Mark, the only independent accreditation of social enterprise. Plymouth was awarded national teaching centres in health and social care, experiential learning in environmental and natural sciences, institutional partnerships, and education for sustainable development – all of which have now been brought into the university's core activities. Its academics have won 18 National Teaching Fellowships, one of the best performances of any university.

Plymouth is a partner in the Combined Universities in Cornwall, which is boosting further and higher education in the county. The university has a unique relationship with its 18 partner colleges, which have become a faculty of the university, sharing £3.5 million in capital investment. They spread from Cornwall to Somerset, taking in Jersey, and have 10,000 students studying university courses. The intake reflects Plymouth's position as the working-class hub of the South West, with just over 93 per cent of students state-educated and nearly a third from the poorest social classes. Some 12,000 students undertake work-based learning or placements with employability skills embedded throughout the curriculum, while the Plymouth Award recognises extra-curricular achievements.

Student facilities include a new £3-million Health and Wellbeing Centre and a 1,300-bed student village costing £15 million. Upgraded facilities for water sports and an £850,000 fitness centre have added to the sports facilities, while a range of sports scholarships and bursaries support high-fliers. The university has a partnership with Plymouth Albion Rugby Club to promote and support sport in the city and it invested £2.5 million in the new £45-million Plymouth Life Centre. There are sessions exclusively for students at the international-standard swimming and fitness facility. Plymouth is the only university in the UK to have its own diving and water sports centre.

Undergraduate Fees and Bursaries

» Fees for UK/EU students 2016–17	£9,000
Placement year	£900
» Fees for international students 2015–16	£12,250–£12,500
Medicine	£17,800–£33,000

- » Details of bursaries and scholarships in 2016–17 were not available in August 2015. Consult university website for details.
- » Care leaver's and sports bursaries.

Students

Undergraduates:	**19,735**	**(3,850)**
Postgraduates:	**1,520**	**(1,825)**
Mature students:	**23.8%**	
International students:	**8.0%**	
Applications per place:	**4.9**	
From state-sector schools:	**93.3%**	
From working-class homes:	**30%**	
Satisfaction with students' union	**77%**	

For detailed information about sports facilities:
www.upsu.com/sports/

Accommodation

Number of places and costs refer to 2015–16
University-provided places: 3,000
Percentage catered: 0%
Self-catered costs: £91–£160 a week (40–51 weeks).
First years are guaranteed university provided accommodation if they apply by 31 July, and Plymouth is their firm first choice.
International students: Apply in the same way as UK students.
residencelife@plymouth.ac.uk
www.plymouth.ac.uk/student-life/services/accommodation

University of Portsmouth

Portsmouth is planning to expand its provision in engineering and science after securing a funding council grant that will enable it to open an £11-million Future Technology Centre early in 2017. The centre will provide leading-edge simulation, visualisation, modelling and prototyping facilities, particularly to encourage more female students to take science and technology courses. Already there are 8,500 undergraduates taking STEM (science, technology, engineering and maths) subjects, as Portsmouth's intake has hit record levels. Applications were up by almost 15 per cent in 2014 and have declined only marginally in the current year.

The university has a growing reputation in health subjects. The £9-million Dental Academy trains student dentists in their final year at King's College London in a team-based setting with dental therapists and hygienists. More than 600 radiographers, paramedics, medical technologists, pharmacists, clinicians and social workers graduate each year. Health subjects led the way to a good performance in the 2014 Research Excellence Framework. Almost two-thirds of the work submitted was rated as world-leading or internationally excellent. The best results were in dentistry, nursing and pharmacy, and in physics, with around 90 per cent of the submission reaching the top two categories.

Portsmouth is among the leading post-1992 institutions in our league table, benefiting particularly from strong student satisfaction ratings and good completion rates. It has one of the largest language departments in the country, teaching six languages to degree level and offering free language courses to all students. About 1,000 Portsmouth students go abroad for part of their course, and at least as many come from the continent. The university is an official centre of teaching and research about the EU, and also has 3,000 international students from further afield.

Teaching in all subjects is concentrated on the Guildhall campus in the centre of Portsmouth, with most residential accommodation nearby. The campus has undergone extensive redevelopment. A new £14-million wing on the Eldon Building created an additional 3,000 square metres of space and provided the Faculty of Creative and Cultural Industries with purpose-built facilities, including a 200-seat screening room, exhibition space and a range of studios and seminar rooms. Students in the faculty will also benefit from a partnership with the New Theatre Royal, which will allows them to use the facilities in an £8-million building that adjoins the original theatre.

Responding to feedback from students,

University House
Winston Churchill Avenue
Portsmouth
Hampshire PO1 2UP

023 9284 5566
admissions@port.ac.uk
www.port.ac.uk
www.upsu.net
Affiliation: University Alliance

The Times and Sunday Times **Rankings**

Overall Ranking: **59** (last year: 57)

Teaching quality:	**20**	83.4%
Student experience:	**30**	85.9%
Research quality:	**70**	8.6%
Entry standards:	**=86**	310
Student–staff ratio:	**=57**	16.5
Services & facilities/student:	**82**	£1,617
Expected completion rate:	**=52**	87.6%
Good honours:	**50**	72.7%
Graduate prospects:	**=65**	66.9%

the university has transformed the ground floor of the library into a new social learning space with over 200 more study spaces and 24-hour opening in key periods. The £9-million refurbishment of the Portland Building was completed in 2014, creating new accommodation for the School of Engineering and Portsmouth Business School. Employability skills and training are embedded throughout 450 degree programmes. A significant number are accredited by professional bodies and, wherever possible, students are given opportunities for hands-on practice in their chosen career. High quality simulated learning environments, such as a mock courtroom, pharmacy, journalism newsroom, forensic suite and dental wards provide real-life professional skills.

Almost a third of undergraduates come from the four lowest socio-economic groups, although this is below the national average for the university's subjects and entry qualifications. Much of the extra income from £9,000 fees is being spent on initiatives to broaden the intake, such as summer schools and an award-winning scheme which introduces 11–16 year olds to higher education through workshops, holiday courses and access to university facilities. Unlike many other universities, Portsmouth is also maintaining its spending on bursaries, believing that most of the recipients would have struggled to stay on their courses without financial support. There is a threshold of £25,000 family income to qualify for full bursaries. The 10 per cent projected dropout rate is slightly lower than the university's benchmark.

A £6.5-million student centre caters for the multicultural population of the university and includes alcohol-free areas. Modernised sport, exercise and fitness facilities include gyms, dance studios and a sports hall. The university has invested nearly £1 million in a new all-weather 3G pitch, suitable for football, rugby, lacrosse and American football. Many students live in Southsea, which has a vibrant social scene and quirky shops. Portsmouth has seen considerable regeneration and the cost of living is not as high as at many southern universities, and the sea is close at hand. University-allocated accommodation is offered to around two-thirds of first years who apply, and others are helped to find accommodation in the private rented sector through house-hunting events, online resources and drop-in advice sessions.

Undergraduate Fees and Bursaries

» Fees for UK/EU students 2016–17	£9,000
Courses at partner colleges	£6,000
Placement year / Year abroad	£900
» Fees for international students 2016–17	£12,000–£13,700

» English students (excluding those at partner colleges) with household income below £25K, a bursary of £1,500 in year 1, £1,000 all other years; £25K–£32K, £500 a year.

Students

Undergraduates:	**16,420**	**(1,960)**
Postgraduates:	**1,570**	**(1,950)**
Mature students:	**13.1%**	
International students:	**16.5%**	
Applications per place:	**6.2**	
From state-sector schools:	**96.1%**	
From working-class homes:	**32.7%**	
Satisfaction with students' union	**79%**	

For detailed information about sports facilities:
www.port.ac.uk/students/sport-and-recreation

Accommodation

Number of places and costs refer to 2015–16
University-provided places: almost 3,000
Percentage catered: 25%
Catered costs: £103– £135 a week (38 weeks).
Self-catered costs: £86–£140 (38 weeks).
Majority of first years offered university accommodation.
International, Channel Island and Isle of Man students guaranteed university accommodation subject to terms and conditions.
student.housing@port.ac.uk
www.port.ac.uk/why-portsmouth/accommodation/

Queen Margaret University

Queen Margaret (QMU) is aiming to occupy the ground between "research-intensive" universities and those that are focused mainly on teaching. Much-improved results in the latest assessments of research have convinced the university that it can progress in both activities at the same time. Although only 22 per cent of the eligible staff were entered for the 2014 Research Excellence Framework, almost 60 per cent of their work was considered world-leading or internationally excellent. Renowned for its research in speech and language sciences, QMU saw 92 per cent of its work in this area rated in the top two categories, placing the university second in the UK and first in Scotland. The university has established three flagship areas as a focus for future investment and development: health and rehabilitation, sustainable business, and culture and creativity. It promises "inter-professional" teaching and research to encourage the professions to work better together.

Named after Saint Margaret, the 11th-century Queen of Scotland, the institution dates back to 1875 and was originally a school of cookery for women. True to its roots, the university is investing heavily in research and knowledge exchange facilities in the area of food, launching the Scottish Centre for Food Development and Innovation in 2014. It also has a partnership with the Edinburgh New Town Cookery School, run by a former graduate of QMU, to hone the practical skills of students on the international hospitality management degree. There are now more than 5,000 students, three-quarters of them female, divided between two schools: Arts, Social Sciences and Management, and Health Sciences.

Health is an area of particular strength: QMU has the broadest range of allied health courses in Scotland, from dietetics, podiatry and audiology, to art therapy, music therapy and health psychology. Courses in international health attract students from all over the world. The interdisciplinary drama and performance degree draws together the university's recognised strengths in acting, screen work, community theatre, contemporary performance and playwriting to reflect the current needs of a changing profession. QMU also offers a degree in costume design and construction.

The university moved into an impressive, modern campus designed in consultation with the students in the seaside town of Musselburgh, to the southeast of Edinburgh, when it was awarded university status in 2007. The campus, which has won a string of awards, is one of the most environmentally sustainable in the UK, exceeding current standards. QMU has made sustainability a

Queen Margaret University Drive
Musselburgh EH21 6UU

0131 474 0000 (enquiries)
admissions@qmu.ac.uk
www.qmu.ac.uk
www.qmusu.org.uk
Affiliation: none

***The Times and Sunday Times* Rankings**

Overall Ranking: **96** (last year: 86)

Teaching quality:	**91**	78.9%
Student experience:	**=89**	82.3%
Research quality:	**79**	6.6%
Entry standards:	**56**	341
Student–staff ratio:	**97**	19.1
Services & facilities/student:	**107**	£1,336
Expected completion rate:	**=94**	82.4%
Good honours:	**47**	74.2%
Graduate prospects:	**106**	59.6%

top priority in the curriculum as well as in the way it operates. Specialist laboratories and clinics are well equipped. The nursing simulation lab, for example, is set out like a hospital ward, helping to instil students with the confidence to move on easily to a work placement or career in the NHS or private practice. An impressive learning resource centre, parts of which are open 24 hours a day, offers a variety of study spaces. There are a number of sponsored awards, including five worth £1,000 each from Ryder Cup Europe to fund tourism, hospitality and event students.

QMU is prioritising graduate employment through up-to-date course design that is relevant to the world of work. A growing Employer Mentoring programme offers third and fourth year students the opportunity to meet with an experienced professional with relevant industry experience, while the Careers and Employability Service now offers QMU students and graduates free help and advice for life. An innovative Associate Student Scheme in events management or international tourism and hospitality management operates with Edinburgh College, where students enrol for an Associate BA. It has now been extended to Newbattle Abbey College, in Dalkeith, for degrees in psychology and sociology. Students are taught in college for the first two years of their course, making regular visits to the campus, where some even choose to live, before transferring to QMU. Other institutional partnerships include a joint venture with the East Asia Institute of Management, in Singapore, and there are international programmes in Nepal, Egypt, Saudi Arabia, Greece and Switzerland.

The campus is located next to Musselburgh train station, from where Edinburgh city centre is only a six-minute journey. There is also a frequent bus service from the campus to the city centre. There are 800 residential places on the campus, about 300 of them larger, premier rooms with double beds and more space. Other features include a students' union building, indoor and outdoor sports facilities, a variety of catering outlets and landscaped gardens with a range of environmental features.

Undergraduate Fees and Bursaries

- » Fees for Scottish and EU students 2015–16 No fee
- » Fees for Non-Scottish UK (RUK) students 2015–16 £7,000
- » Fees for international students 2015–16 £10,700–£12,400
- » For RUK students, annual bursaries: household income up to £20K, £2,000 cash; sliding scale to £42.6K, £1,500–£500.
- » Range of other scholarships and bursaries available.
- » Check the university's website for the latest information.

Students

Undergraduates:	**2,905**	**(615)**
Postgraduates:	**565**	**(1,130)**
Mature students:	**32.7%**	
International students:	**17.6%**	
Applications per place:	**8.3**	
From state-sector schools:	**97%**	
From working-class homes:	**31.8%**	
Satisfaction with students' union	**48%**	

For detailed information about sports facilities: www.qmu.ac.uk/sports

Accommodation

Number of places and costs refer to 2015–16

University-provided places: 800

Percentage catered: 0%

Self-catered costs: £99–£116 a week (40 or 50 week contract).

First years are guaranteed accommodation. Residential and age restrictions apply.

International students: guaranteed housing.

accommodation@qmu.ac.uk

www.qmu.ac.uk/accommodation/

Queen Mary, University of London

Applications to Queen Mary (QMUL) have leapt by more than a third since the college joined the Russell Group of leading research universities in 2012. Enrolments, too, are at record levels, having risen by 16 per cent over the last two years, although QMUL is still much smaller than some of its peers in the University of London. Most of the 15,000 students occupy a self-contained campus in the increasingly fashionable East End of London. Even the large medical school, Barts and the London School of Medicine and Dentistry, is based in nearby Whitechapel. However, QMUL's latest venture breaks the mould since it is opening a new medical school in Malta. The new Bachelor of Medicine, Bachelor of Surgery (MBBS) Malta programme will be taught and delivered by QMUL staff on the island of Gozo. It will closely match the London programme, with first students arriving in September 2016.

Back in London's Mile End Road, campus improvements that have cost £250 million over 15 years are continuing. The latest development is a new Graduate Centre, opening early in 2016, for the QMUL's growing population of postgraduates, which will also provide new premises for the School of Economics and Finance. The physics laboratories have been upgraded and refurbishment of the engineering and mathematics buildings will be complete before that start of the academic year in 2016. The historic People's Palace, which brought education to the Victorian masses, is still Queen Mary's most recognisable feature, and has been restored to host cultural events for the institution and the local community. The campus includes an impressive learning resource centre with 24-hour access and an award-winning student village with 2,000 en-suite rooms. The £20-million Arts2 building features a drama studio and lecture theatre. There is even room on campus for the second-oldest Jewish cemetery in England, dating from the 18th century.

The medical school, which is rated in the top 100 in the world by QS, is based the £44-million Blizard Building. Its Institute of Dentistry moved into the first new dental school to be built in the UK for 40 years, when it occupied its new facilities costing £78 million in the Royal London Hospital in 2014. Also on the Whitechapel campus are the new BioEnterprise Innovation Centre for science companies and the Centre of the Cell, the first interactive facility to be based within a working medical school research laboratory to give young people a glimpse of how scientists operate. QMUL has launched a life sciences initiative, bringing together

Mile End Road
London E1 4NS

020 7882 5511 (admissions)
admissions@qmul.ac.uk
www.qmul.ac.uk
www.qmsu.org
Affiliation: Russell Group

The Times and Sunday Times **Rankings**
Overall Ranking: **34** (last year: 37)

Teaching quality:	**=69**	80.5%
Student experience:	**77**	83.3%
Research quality:	**19**	37.9%
Entry standards:	**=29**	411
Student–staff ratio:	**=13**	12.2
Services & facilities/student:	**23**	£2,347
Expected completion rate:	**35**	91.2%
Good honours:	**42**	75.3%
Graduate prospects:	**=47**	73.3%

the Faculties of Science and Engineering, Humanities and Social Sciences, and Barts and the London School of Medicine and Dentistry to work together on personalised healthcare and to address major public health issues both locally and worldwide.

Medicine and the other health subjects did well in the 2014 Research Excellence Framework, but the best results came in the humanities, where QMUL boasts a clutch of high-profile academics. Around 95 per cent of the research in linguistics and in music, drama and the performing arts was rated as world-leading or internationally excellent. Over 85 per cent of QMUL's entire submission reached the top two categories. The college does less well in the National Student Survey, but still outperforms most London institutions. Most lectures are filmed and made available through the Virtual Learning Environment to allow students to go back over parts that they may not have understood. Interdisciplinary study is encouraged: the majority of undergraduates take at least one course in departments other than their own.

Queen Mary has by far the highest proportion of undergraduates from working-class homes in the Russell Group – more than a third. Many come from London's ethnic minority groups and QMUL also attracts 20 per cent of its students from 150 countries outside the UK. There is a flourishing exchange programme, which includes universities in the USA and Japan, as well as Europe, while more than 2,000 students are in Beijing taking joint degrees from QMUL and the Beijing University of Posts and Telecommunications.

Social life centres on the campus, which features a refurbished students' union with a new bar. A subsidised health and fitness centre has helped improve the sports facilities. Students welcome the relatively low prices (for the capital) in east London, and their proximity to the lively youth culture of Spitalfields, Shoreditch and Brick Lane. Queen Mary students can use the sports facilities at the Queen Elizabeth Olympic Park, including the Copper Box indoor arena and the Aquatic Centre's swimming pool.

Undergraduate Fees and Bursaries

- » Fees for UK/EU students 2016–17 £9,000
- » Fees for international students 2015–16 £13,650–£16,950
  Medicine and dentistry £30,000–£30,860
- » Household income below £25K; a bursary of £1,571 a year; £25K–£42.6K, £1,256 a year.
- » Other academic and targeted scholarships available.
- » Check the university's website for the latest information.

Students

Undergraduates:	**11,190**	**(10)**
Postgraduates:	**3,225**	**(995)**
Mature students:	**12.2%**	
International students:	**23%**	
Applications per place:	**9.9**	
From state-sector schools:	**86.6%**	
From working-class homes:	**34.7%**	
Satisfaction with students' union	**74%**	

For detailed information about sports facilities:
www.qmsu.org/sportandfitness/

Accommodation

Number of places and costs refer to 2015–16
University-provided places: 2,277
Percentage catered: 1%
Catered costs: £175 upwards a week for a single room.
Self-catered costs: £125–£165 a week for a single room.
First years giving Queen Mary as first choice get priority, if terms and deadline conditions are met.
International students: All new applicants meeting the criteria are judged equally with home students living outside Greater London.
www.residences.qmul.ac.uk

Queen's University, Belfast

No university entered a higher proportion of its academics than Queen's for the 2014 Research Excellence Framework. Like Cambridge, it submitted work by 95 per cent of its eligible staff for assessment, and 77 per cent was considered world-leading or internationally excellent. The results propelled the university into our top 15 on this measure for the first time, with 14 subject areas ranked in the UK's top 20. Its performance has helped to reverse a decline in the last edition of our league table, and pull it back towards the position in the top 30 that it occupied two years ago.

A member of the Russell Group, Queen's is recognised as Northern Ireland's premier university, with graduates in senior leadership positions in 80 of the province's top 100 companies. Strictly non-denominational teaching is enshrined in a charter which has guaranteed student representation and equal rights for women since 1908. The university is one of only five in the UK to hold a silver Athena Swan Award for tackling the unequal representation of women in science, engineering and technology. Queen's was one of four university colleges for the whole of Ireland in the nineteenth century, and still draws students from all over the island. However, the majority come from Northern Ireland, and Queen's suffers in the comparison of entry grades because relatively few sixth-formers in the Province take four A levels.

The university is based in an attractive part of South Belfast, incorporating a significant part of the Victorian suburb which grew up around the iconic Lanyon building. Queen's has invested £350 million over the last decade enhancing the campus and the surrounding conservation areas – of the university's 250 buildings, 97 are listed – while providing cutting-edge facilities for education and research, and it plans to spend as much again over the next 10 years. The most recent developments have seen the opening of the Centre for Experimental Medicine, the refurbishment of the Ashby Building to create an engineering complex, and the opening of a new graduate school in the historic Lynn Building, which includes a central open-plan, double height, vaulted space with masonry gothic arches. New homes for the schools of law and computer science are due to open for the start of the 2016–17 academic year. Completed projects include the £50-million McClay Library, the award-winning Elms Student Village, a student guidance centre and a £9-million refurbishment of the students' union.

All the university's courses are designed with employability in mind and the Degree Plus programme provides official recognition of extracurricular activities and

University Road
Belfast BT7 1NN

028 9097 3838 (admissions)
admissions@qub.ac.uk
www.qub.ac.uk
www.qubsu.org
Affiliation: Russell Group

***The Times and Sunday Times* Rankings**

Overall Ranking: **31** (last year: 38)

Teaching quality:	**=52**	81.6%
Student experience:	**15**	87.3%
Research quality:	**14**	39.7%
Entry standards:	**=39**	385
Student–staff ratio:	**=36**	14.9
Services & facilities/student:	**44**	£1,996
Expected completion rate:	**36**	91%
Good honours:	**37**	75.8%
Graduate prospects:	**28**	78.7%

achievements to help graduates in the job market. Queen's opened a First Derivatives Trading Room in the Management School, as well as the UK's first combined Graduate and Executive Education Centre, which has become a hub for business in Northern Ireland. Undergraduates are encouraged to take language programmes from a "virtual" language laboratory, which provides online tuition from any computer in the university. IT facilities are good: Queen's was the first institution to meet the national target of providing at least one computer workstation for every five undergraduate students. A new £2-million wireless service will be rolled out to all areas of the campus by January 2016.

Fees for Northern Irish applicants are £3,805 for 2015–16, while those from the rest of the UK pay £9,000. Applications have been growing, but the undergraduate intake will be reduced by 1,000 over the next three years to cope with an £8-million cut in its Government grant. The university has more than 2,000 international students and is a favourite destination for American Fulbright Scholars. It is also among the top ten universities in Europe for the number of students who go on work placements abroad as part of the Erasmus scheme.

Queen's boasts the only full-time university cinema in the UK, as well as an art gallery and theatre, all of which are open to students and the wider community alike. The much-improved city centre is not short of nightlife, but the social scene is still concentrated on the students' union and the surrounding area. Sports facilities, which include a university cottage in the Mourne mountains, have seen a £20-million programme of investment. The new facility at Upper Malone features an arena pitch which can host football, rugby or Gaelic sport, another 14 pitches, a 3-km recreational trail and conference facilities. The Physical Education Centre provides physiotherapy, sports massage and podiatry, while a new Elite Athlete programme offers up to £8,000 of support for leading performers.

Undergraduate Fees and Bursaries

» Fees for NI/EU students 2015–16	£3,805
» Fees for English, Scottish, Welsh (RUK) students	£9,000
» Fees for international students 2015–16	£13,280–£17,035
Medicine	£17,590–£33,170
Dentistry	£26,938

» Household income up to £19.2K, bursary of £380 a year. The top 50 NI students on STEM course, year 1 scholarship of £1,000. 5 Queen's Scholars for NI students giving full fee scholarship for duration of course.

» RUK students (excluding medicine & dentistry) with at least AAB at A Level or equivalent, annual fee waiver of £2,500 or £1,750 plus benefits package; with ABB or equivalent, annual fee waiver of £1,750 or £1,000 plus benefits package; with offer grades, annual fee waiver of £1,250 or £500 plus benefits package.

» Check the university's website for the latest information.

Students

Undergraduates:	**14,400**	**(3,970)**
Postgraduates:	**2,615**	**(2,330)**
Mature students:	**17.5%**	
International students:	**7.4%**	
Applications per place:	**6.7**	
From state-sector schools:	**98.6%**	
From working-class homes:	**32.5%**	
Satisfaction with students' union	**81%**	

For detailed information about sports facilities: www.queenssport.com

Accommodation

Number of places and costs refer to 2015–16

University-provided places: around 2,000

Percentage catered: 0%

Self-catered costs: £69–£119 a week.

First-year students are guaranteed accommodation if conditions are met.

International students: as above.

accommodation@qub.ac.uk

www.stayatqueens.com

University of Reading

Reading has expanded its intake of undergraduates by 13 per cent in the last two years, and will be in a position to grow further in 2016 when it opens a new School of Architecture to capitalise on a strong reputation in the built environment. Real estate, planning and construction management were among the leading players in a highly successful submission for the 2014 Research Assessment Framework. The university entered more academics for assessment than most of its peers and still saw almost 80 per cent of its research rated as world-leading or internationally excellent.

It will be the second successive year in which Reading has launched a new venture, having opened a campus in Malaysia in 2015. Students will take degrees in business, law, the built environment, psychology and pharmacy at the Iksandar Education City, on the southern tip of Malaysia.

The attractive main campus, which won four Green Gown environmental awards in a row, is set in 320 acres of parkland on the outskirts of Reading. The university has spent more than £400 million on improvements. The most recent projects have included a £1.2-million extension to the students' union, two new sports pavilions and a £4.4-million renovation of the library, which is now open 24 hours a day during term time in response to student demand. Other recent building improvements include a new student services centre and business school, £100 million on new and redeveloped halls of residence, a refurbished sports centre, and new catering facilities. The £17-million Hopkins Building added laboratories and teaching space for pharmacy and cardiovascular research, and there is a now a world-class Chemical Analysis Facility and an Enterprise Centre which brings together academic expertise with local and international technology-based businesses.

Originally Oxford University's extension college, Reading was one of only two universities established between the two world wars. As well as its two sites in Reading, the university also owns 2,000 acres of farmland at nearby Sonning and Shinfield, where the renowned Centre for Dairy Research (CEDAR) is located. To these has been added the former Henley Management College, which became the university's business school in 2008. The college's attractive site, on the banks of the river at Henley-on-Thames, houses postgraduate and executive programmes, while undergraduates are taught on the main Whiteknights campus. However, the one-day Henley Future Leaders programme is available to all Reading's students, giving them an opportunity to develop an understanding of leadership,

Whiteknights
PO Box 217
Reading RG6 6AH

0118 378 8372
ugadmissions@reading.ac.uk
www.reading.ac.uk
www.rusu.co.uk
Affiliation: none

***The Times and Sunday Times* Rankings**

Overall Ranking: **32** (last year: 33)

Teaching quality:	**=69**	80.5%
Student experience:	**=31**	85.8%
Research quality:	**29**	36.5%
Entry standards:	**43**	373
Student–staff ratio:	**29**	14.1
Services & facilities/student:	**53**	£1,900
Expected completion rate:	**=28**	92.3%
Good honours:	**34**	76.2%
Graduate prospects:	**=54**	70.3%

change, entrepreneurship and personal development through a series of lectures and seminars. All undergraduates also have the opportunity to take work placements as part of their course, as well as taking career management skills modules that contribute five credits towards their degree classification. The online system, which has 200 web pages of advice, exercises and information, has been bought by 30 other universities and colleges. Sessions are delivered jointly by academics and careers advisors, with input from alumni and leading employers.

Reading is one of the medium-sized campus universities that have demonstrated their appeal through the National Student Survey, often appearing in or near the top 30 on this measure, although this year it suffered from poor student assessment of its teaching quality (=69th in our ranking). About one undergraduate in seven is from an independent school and only a quarter come from working-class homes – below average for the university's subjects and entry qualifications. The university is devoting more than a quarter of the extra income from £9,000 fees to attempts to broaden the intake. It expects to provide cash bursaries for about 2,500 students in 2015–16. Around a fifth of undergraduates now come from outside the UK, many of them attracted by Reading's global reputation for courses and research in agriculture and development.

Sports facilities have been extended. Water sports are a strong focus, with off-campus boathouses on the Thames and a sailing and canoeing club nearby. Representative teams have a good record in inter-university competitions and the campus was chosen as a pre-Olympics training camp for basketball and fencing. The town may not be the most fashionable, but Reading has plenty of nightlife and an award-winning shopping centre. London is easily accessible by train, but the cost of living is on a par with the capital.

The halls of residence are either on or within easy walking distance of campus and the large students' union has been voted among the best in Britain. Students who live off campus can make use of the free bus service to take them back into the town centre.

Undergraduate Fees and Bursaries

- Fees for UK/EU students 2016–17 £9,000
  Placement year / year abroad £1,350
- Fees for international students 2015–16 £14,350–£17,350
- Household income below £25K, a bursary of £1,000 a year; household income below £35K, placement bursaries of £200–£1,000.
- Foundation degree fee waivers of 50% for selected courses.
- Other academic and targeted scholarships available.
- Check the university's website for the latest information.

Students

Undergraduates:	**9,235**	**(85)**
Postgraduates:	**2,690**	**(1,585)**
Mature students:	**9.6%**	
International students:	**16.7%**	
Applications per place:	**6.4**	
From state-sector schools:	**86.1%**	
From working-class homes:	**25.2%**	
Satisfaction with students' union	**85%**	

For detailed information about sports facilities:
www.sport.reading.ac.uk

Accommodation

Number of places and costs refer to 2015–16
University-provided places: about 5,000.
Percentage catered: 18% Catered costs: £137.39–£175.75 (40 weeks, catering during terms).
Self-catered costs: £99.89–£159.60 (40–51 weeks).
First-year undergraduate students are guaranteed a place if conditions are met.
International students: guaranteed if conditions are met.
accommodationonline@reading.ac.uk
www.reading.ac.uk/life/life-accommodation.aspx

Robert Gordon University

A £170-million programme that is bringing Robert Gordon (RGU) together on one site for the first time will be complete well before new entrants arrive in 2016. All teaching already takes place on the Garthdee campus, on the south side of Aberdeen, overlooking the River Dee. A new building for the Scott Sutherland School of Architecture will be the last piece of the jigsaw, although there will be further improvements following the sale of part of the university's historic city centre site. The schools of engineering, computing science and digital media, pharmacy and life sciences moved from the Schoolhill site in the city centre in 2013. A striking green glass library tower with spectacular views over the river and city has become a landmark at the heart of the campus, which is full of graceful curves. Previous developments at Garthdee included additional specialist facilities for the Faculty of Health and Social Care. The Aberdeen Business School, designed by Norman Foster, has being upgraded with new teaching and student learning spaces and an open plan area with IT access, group study areas, exhibition and seminar space.

The university has slipped surprisingly in our table over the last two years, but remains among the leaders for graduate employment – indeed, without distinguishing between different types of jobs, as we do in our table, it had the highest employment rate in the UK in 2014. Close links with the North Sea oil and gas industries help in this respect – among the new facilities is a DART (Drilling and Advanced Rig Training) simulator that provides a full-scale reproduction of an offshore platform or land rig within the Energy Centre. Work placements lasting up to a year have become the norm on all the university's courses. With nursing and health sciences now accounting for 40 per cent of the places, RGU gives itself the soubriquet of the Professional University. The creative industries are a growth area and there is a full portfolio of courses in business, design and engineering.

Named after an 18th-century philanthropist, RGU has a pedigree in education that goes back 250 years. The university now offers about 300 courses and there is also a partnership with North East Scotland College, which allows students to progress from a college-based Higher National Diploma to the third year of an RGU degree course. The university has invested heavily in research, with priority areas that include oil and gas, remote healthcare, big data, and culture and design. But the university is reviewing its research strategy after making a relatively small submission to the 2014 Research Excellence

Garthdee House
Garthdee Road
Aberdeen AB10 7QB

01224 262728 (enquiries)
ugoffice@rgu.ac.uk
www.rgu.ac.uk
www.rguunion.co.uk
Affiliation: none

***The Times and Sunday Times* Rankings**

Overall Ranking: **=69** (last year: 64)

Teaching quality:	**68**	80.6%
Student experience:	**=71**	83.5%
Research quality:	**=103**	4%
Entry standards:	**=39**	385
Student–staff ratio:	**=100**	19.4
Services & facilities/student:	**108**	£1,335
Expected completion rate:	**88**	83.4%
Good honours:	**=78**	67%
Graduate prospects:	**=13**	83.1%

Framework and slipping down our ranking on this measure. More than 40 per cent of the work assessed was placed in the top two categories, with the best results coming in health subjects and communication and media studies.

Like many modern universities, Robert Gordon recruits most of its students locally, with large numbers taking part-time courses. However, overseas student numbers have been growing and the overall demand for places has been more consistent than at most universities north of the border. Efforts to extend access beyond the normal higher education catchment have produced a diverse student population, with three in ten undergraduates coming from working-class homes and nearly 94 per cent from state schools or colleges.

The university has a strong focus on new technology. An award-winning virtual campus was launched with an online course in e-business for postgraduates. It also enables management undergraduates to receive course materials via an intranet, and other degree and short courses are available. The Moodle system is used across Robert Gordon courses for both on-campus and distance learning students, providing teaching, notes, online forums for discussion and electronic submission options.

Aberdeen is a long way to go for students from other parts of the UK, but train and air links are excellent, and the city regularly features in the top ten for quality of life. There is a £12-million sports and leisure centre, which includes a centre of excellence for the region in hockey, as well as a 25-metre swimming pool, three gyms, a climbing wall and bouldering room, a café bar, three exercise studios and a large sports hall. Sports scholarships are available to budding athletes, with Olympic and Commonwealth Games medal-winning swimmer Hannah Miley among the recipients. Although accommodation can be expensive in the private sector, there are enough residential places to guarantee housing to first years from outside the local area.

Undergraduate Fees and Bursaries

» Fees for Scottish and EU students 2015–16	No fee
» Fees for Non-Scottish UK (RUK) students 2015–16	£5,000–£6,750
Pharmacy	£8,500
» Fees for international students 2015–16	£11,000–£14,300

» Academic and targeted scholarships available.
» Check the university's website for the latest information.

Students

Undergraduates:	**7,490**	**(1,870)**
Postgraduates:	**1,715**	**(2,335)**
Mature students:	**27.4%**	
International students:	**14.4%**	
Applications per place:	**5.7**	
From state-sector schools:	**93.6%**	
From working-class homes:	**30.4%**	
Satisfaction with students' union	**55%**	

For detailed information about sports facilities:
www.rgu.ac.uk/student-life/campus-life/rgu-sport

Accommodation

Number of places and costs refer to 2015-16
University-provided places: 1,759
Percentage catered: 0%
Self-catered costs: £100 (single) – £200.00 (flat) a week.
All first-year students are eligible to apply for student accommodation. Residential restrictions apply.
International students: as above.
accommodation@rgu.ac.uk
www.rgu.ac.uk/student-life/accommodation

Roehampton University

Roehampton outperformed all post-1992 universities in last year's Research Excellence Framework, entering two-thirds of its eligible academics for assessment and still seeing 66 per cent of its work rated as world-leading or internationally excellent. The university had the most highly rated dance department in the UK, with 94 per cent of research placed in the top two categories, while the results in education and English were among the best in London. Its successes will produce a 40 per cent increase in funding for research.

Roehampton has become the last university in London to increase its fees for degree courses to £9,000 in 2015. The university does not offer bursaries to students from poor backgrounds, so only those winning scholarships will receive financial support on entry. Roehampton is investing £80 million on new facilities, mainly on its attractive 54-acre main campus in south-west London. Much of the money is going on student accommodation, and a new library will open in 2017. The Grade II-listed Downshire House is being refurbished and three new buildings built in its grounds to create 210 new student bedrooms. Another 390 new bedrooms are being added on the Digby Stuart site, while a recent residential development, 20 minutes from the main campus by public transport, at Vauxhall, includes a swimming pool and other facilities.

Although an independent university only since 2004, Roehampton has a distinguished history dating back to the 1840s, with Whitelands College claiming to be the first in the country to open higher education to women. The university is a collegiate institution with four distinctive colleges, which still maintain some of the traditional ethos of their religious foundations: the Anglican Whitelands, the Roman Catholic Digby Stuart, the Methodist Southlands, and the Froebel, which follows the humanist teachings of Frederick Froebel. Students need not follow any of these denominations to enrol in the colleges, whose leisure facilities and bars are open to all members of the university. Roehampton also has a Jewish resource centre and Muslim prayer rooms. All four colleges are based on a single campus, with stunning parkland and lakes, on or adjacent to Roehampton Lane. It is the first Living Landscape University in London, having joined the Beverley Brook Living Landscape, which neighbours and extends onto the campus. The Growhampton scheme provides opportunities for students to learn practical conservation, as well as teamwork and leadership skills.

The modern university has diversified into business, the arts and humanities,

Erasmus House
Roehampton Lane
London SW15 5PU

020 8392 3232 (enquiries)
enquiries@roehampton.ac.uk
www.roehampton.ac.uk
www.roehamptonstudent.com
Affiliation: Cathedrals Group

***The Times and Sunday Times* Rankings**

Overall Ranking: **78** (last year: 73)

Teaching quality:	**=103**	78%
Student experience:	**=112**	79.9%
Research quality:	**50**	24.5%
Entry standards:	**111**	286
Student-staff ratio:	**=59**	16.8
Services & facilities/student:	**28**	£2,207
Expected completion rate:	**=101**	81.7%
Good honours:	**77**	67.2%
Graduate prospects:	**95**	60.9%

social sciences and the human and life sciences, while maintaining its historic strength in education, which still accounts for a quarter of the students. The new School of Law welcomes its first students in September 2015 and already operates a legal advice clinic for the local community. The university has also embraced the School Direct system of teacher training, operating in partnership with schools as well as running its own postgraduate and undergraduate training programmes. An additional attraction on the main campus is the Glion Institute of Higher Education, a Swiss hospitality management college offering undergraduate and postgraduate programmes in its first overseas venture. The university is in partnership with Laureate, Glion's owners, to offer courses online. Numbers are expanding rapidly in business, information systems, education and public health, and the university already has 3,000 online students.

The Quality Assurance Agency complimented Roehampton on the accessibility of academic staff to students and the positive ways in which they responded to student needs. New schemes to support students into future employment include graduate mentoring from alumni in professional roles and internships in a number of departments, as well as a Santander Internship Scheme providing paid placements for students in local businesses and the chance to study abroad with no additional tuition fees. International partnerships include a new agreement with EU Business School to offer Roehampton-accredited degrees to students across the continent.

Almost 95 per cent of undergraduates were state educated, 44 per cent coming from working-class homes. Most first years who want a hall place are offered one, with priority going to those living furthest away. While rents are not cheap for those who prefer the private sector, students like the proximity of central London and the lively and attractive suburbs around Roehampton. The sports facilities on campus have been enhanced, with a new gym, two football pitches, running track and a multi-use games area. The sport performance and rehabilitation centre provides state-of-the-art laboratory facilities and performance coaching. The university is a high-performance centre for British fencing and sitting volleyball.

Undergraduate Fees and Bursaries

- » Fees for UK/EU students 2016–17 £9,000
  Foundation degree £7,800
- » Fees for international students 2015–16 £12,000
- » Selection of targeted scholarships, including 4 Roehampton scholarships of £27,000 fee waiver for residents of Wandsworth, music and sports scholarships, and £1,000 a year for male primary education students with household income below £25K.

Students

Undergraduates:	**5,890**	**(225)**
Postgraduates:	**1,085**	**(1,335)**
Mature students:	**20%**	
International students:	**9.9%**	
Applications per place:	**4.8**	
From state-sector schools:	**94.7%**	
From working-class homes:	**44.3%**	
Satisfaction with students' union	**70%**	

For detailed information about sports facilities:
www.roehampton.ac.uk/Sport-Roehampton

Accommodation

Number of places and costs refer to 2015–16
University-provided places: 1,710
Percentage catered: 0%
Self-catered costs: £109.20–£125.65 (standard); £143.15–£164.85 (en suite) a week.
First years are given priority if conditions met. Local restrictions apply.
International students: guaranteed for first year
accommodation@roehampton.ac.uk
www.roehampton.ac.uk/Accommodation/

Royal Agricultural University

The Royal Agricultural University (RAU) makes its first appearance in our main table this year, following the relaxation of restrictions on the inclusion of specialist institutions. With one of the highest levels of spending on student facilities and among the best completion rates, it was assured of a respectable debut, and is our University of the Year for Student Retention. However, it has one of the lowest scores for research. Only 12 staff were entered for the 2014 Research Excellence Framework and just 7 per cent of their work was placed in the top two categories. Nevertheless, the RAU has a global reputation in its field, and every monarch since Queen Victoria has visited the attractive campus near Cirencester, in the Cotswolds.

The university has doubled its intake of undergraduates in less than a decade, but still had fewer than 1,200 students in 2014, making it the smallest publicly funded university in the UK. Its size prevented it from attaining university status until 2013, when the Government's rules changed. There are only six degrees and a range of Foundation degrees, as well as a growing portfolio of Master's courses. A new School of Equine Management and Science was established in 2014, joining those focused on agriculture, food and the environment; business and entrepreneurship; and real estate and land management.

The RAU was the first agricultural college in the English-speaking world when it was established in 1845 on the initiative of the Fairford and Cirencester Farmers' Club, which was concerned at the lack of government support for education, particularly in relation to agriculture. As the Royal Agricultural College, it launched its first degree in 1984 and was fully independent until 2001, when it began to receive state funding. It now has students up to PhD level and also delivers degree courses in Hong Kong and China. The number of female students has been rising and has almost reached parity with the men. Almost nine out of ten undergraduates are school or college leavers, rather than mature students, and 15 per cent are from outside the UK.

The institution embarked on its biggest-ever campus development programme in the run-up to university status. A new teaching block opened with seven well-equipped teaching rooms; a biomass heating system has been installed as part of the university's green agenda, but also as a teaching resource; a postgraduate study centre has been added; and a new accommodation block has opened with 50 en-suite rooms. The two university farms, both close to the campus, cover a total of 1,200 acres. Coates Manor Farm focuses

Stroud Road
Cirencester
Gloucestershire
GL7 6JS
01285 889912 (admissions)
admissions@rau.ac.uk
www.rau.ac.uk
www.rau.ac.uk/student-life/leisure/student-union
Affiliation: GuildHE

***The Times and Sunday Times* Rankings**

Overall Ranking: **51** (last year: n/a)

Teaching quality:	**=86**	79.3%
Student experience:	**=35**	85.6%
Research quality:	**123**	1.1%
Entry standards:	**=91**	307
Student–staff ratio:	**115**	20.9
Services & facilities/student:	**6**	£2,887
Expected completion rate:	**=6**	96.3%
Good honours:	**102**	62.6%
Graduate prospects:	**57**	69.7%

on arable farming, while Harnhill Farm is an example of an integrated livestock and cropping system. In addition, there is an equestrian centre providing stabling and livery facilities, and students also have access to a large dairy complex. All are run as commercial enterprises. In 2014, the RAU added a Rural Innovation Centre, which will allow the university to develop its work within the areas of research translation, innovation and agri-technologies.

The institution has always had a reputation for attracting well-heeled students: more than half of the undergraduates come from independent schools – a higher proportion than at Oxford or Cambridge. But 35 per cent come from the four poorest socio-economic groups – also one of the largest proportions in the UK – contributing to a unique student population, in which perhaps only one in seven does not fall into either category. All business, equine and agriculture courses include a 20-week work placement. There is an extensive network of student placement sponsors in the UK and overseas, and part-time work is available both in the university and in nearby Cirencester. The university has been rated within the top ten UK universities and colleges for its Enterprise activities. On campus, there is a well-stocked library and computer suites, as well as specialist laboratories. The virtual learning environment ensures that all teaching materials are available online 24 hours a day.

The small campus in the countryside provides a collegiate atmosphere and is the centre of social activities, including four balls each year. There are eight halls of residence on campus for undergraduates with 350 rooms – enough for most first-years to be offered a place. Private rentals are available in Cirencester and the surrounding area. Sport plays an important part in student life and, in addition to the normal range, there are clubs for polo, clay pigeon shooting, beagling and team chasing (a cross-country equestrian sport). There are ample opportunities to explore the Cotswold countryside and London is only 90 minutes away by train.

Undergraduate Fees and Bursaries

- » Fees for UK/EU students 2016–17 £9,000
- » Fees for international students 2015–16 £10,000
- » Disadvantaged students with household income below £25K, fee waiver or accommodation discount of £1,000–£3,000 a year.
- » Household income £25K–£42.6K and in financial need, fee waiver or accommodation discount of £1,500 in year 1.
- » Skills bursary of £250 in years 1 and 2 to enhance development of personal and professional skills.
- » Academic scholarships, internships and bursaries up to £1,000 for student-led projects.
- » Check the university's website for the latest information.

Students

Undergraduates:	**900**	**(55)**
Postgraduates:	**180**	**(20)**
Mature students:	**15.8%**	
International students:	**8.3%**	
Applications per place:	**3.5**	
From state-sector schools:	**47.6%**	
From working-class homes:	**35%**	
Satisfaction with students' union	**70%**	

For detailed information about sports facilities:
www.rau.ac.uk/student-life/leisure/sports-clubs

Accommodation

Number of places and costs refer to 2015–16
University-provided places: 320
Percentage catered: 20%
Catered costs: £4,824–£7,848 (fully catered); £3,852–£6,876 (dinner, bed and breakfast) for academic year (39 weeks).
Self-catered costs: £5,031 for academic year (39 weeks).
First years cannot be guaranteed accommodation.
International students: as above.
accommodation@rau.ac.uk
www.rau.ac.uk/student-life/living/accommodation/

Royal Holloway, University of London

Royal Holloway has unveiled a £150-million estate plan that is its most ambitious since the completion of its iconic Founder's Building in 1886. The aim is to modernise the facilities with new study, teaching and residential spaces while maintaining the character of one of the UK's most attractive and historic campuses. The centrepiece will be a new library and student centre in the heart of campus, which will open in the spring of 2017. Open 24 hours a day, the new building will also house the careers centre and other student services, shops and cafés. Extensive use of glass will frame and reflect the Founder's Building, which was modelled on a French chateau and opened by Queen Victoria. Other elements in the estates plan include 600 new study bedrooms and the refurbishment of many more, additional teaching and performance space for media and arts students, and a new science building designed particularly to attract more female students into the subjects.

The University of London's "Campus in the Country", as Royal Holloway likes to be known, has already seen investment of around £100 million during this decade. The programme included refurbishment of the 450 student rooms in the Founder's Building, which dominates the 135-acre woodland campus between Windsor Castle and Heathrow. Other recent projects have included extensions to the School of Management and the main library, as well as more student residences. The students' union was upgraded and a new studio theatre added within the listed building that houses the Drama and Theatre Department. The university also redeveloped an old Victorian boilerhouse, turning it into a multifunctional space for lectures with retractable seating for performances and events.

Both Bedford College and Royal Holloway, which amalgamated to form the existing college in 1985, were founded for women only, their legacy commemorated in the Bedford Centre for the History of Women. However, the gender balance in the student population is now roughly equal. Although still best known for the arts, Royal Holloway has a broad portfolio of subjects, including a science Foundation year for those wishing to change academic direction. Applications hit record levels in 2014 after an 11 per cent increase but, despite gradual increases in enrolments, there are still fewer than 10,000 students. This mark will be passed as the new buildings open. Student support includes £1 million for postgraduates so that students who graduate with large debts are not deterred from continuing their studies.

Egham
Surrey TW20 0EX

01784 414944 (admissions)
study@royalholloway.ac.uk
www.royalholloway.ac.uk
www.su.rhul.ac.uk
Affiliation: none

***The Times and Sunday Times* Rankings**

Overall Ranking: **36** (last year: =34)

Teaching quality:	**=35**	82.6%
Student experience:	**=59**	84.1%
Research quality:	**=30**	36.3%
Entry standards:	**35**	398
Student–staff ratio:	**=42**	15.3
Services & facilities/student:	**=74**	£1,665
Expected completion rate:	**=28**	92.3%
Good honours:	**36**	75.9%
Graduate prospects:	**90**	62.7%

More than 80 per cent of the work assessed in the 2014 Research Excellence Framework was judged to be world-leading or internationally excellent, but Royal Holloway still slipped a little on this measure, partly because other leading universities entered a higher proportion of their academics. Geography achieved the best results in England, while earth sciences, psychology, mathematics, music, media arts and drama and theatre were all in their respective top tens. Royal Holloway was chosen as an Academic Centre of Excellence in Cyber Security Research by the UK Government – one of only eight such awards nationwide.

Almost a fifth of the undergraduates come from independent schools, but the proportion coming from working-class homes has been rising. The ethnic mix is above average and the projected dropout rate of less than 6 per cent is below the official benchmark. The Royal Holloway Passport, which is intended to enhance graduates' employability, recognises the additional skills that students gain from many extracurricular activities. An Advanced Skills Programme, covering information technology, communication skills and foreign languages, further encourages breadth of study. The university offers a number of e-degrees and promotes numerous opportunities to study abroad, building on the international flavour of the campus and its links with institutions such as New York, Sydney and Yale universities.

The college's green belt location at Egham, Surrey, ensures that social life is concentrated on the active students' union. However, the centre of London is only 35 minutes away by rail for those determined to seek the high life. Sports facilities are good and a new 3G football and rugby pitch has been installed. Royal Holloway claims to be "the University of London's best sporting college". It has had considerable success with its "student talented athlete award scheme" (STARS). Students enjoy an active cultural scene, and a thriving Community Action programme involves over 1,000 students volunteering with various local organisations and charities. Many students come from London and the Home Counties, and go home at the weekend, but the lively students' union puts on entertainment and activities seven days a week.

Undergraduate Fees and Bursaries

- Fees for UK/EU students 2016–17 £9,000
- Fees for international students 2015–16 £13,200–£14,900
- For all English students with household income below £25K, £1,500 a year; £25K–£42.6K, £500 a year.
- For mature students with household income below £25K with conditions, bursary of £1,000 a year.
- Check the university's website for the latest information.

Students

Undergraduates:	**6,710**	**(450)**
Postgraduates:	**1,840**	**(675)**
Mature students:	**8.1%**	
International students:	**27.6%**	
Applications per place:	**6.9**	
From state-sector schools:	**81.8%**	
From working-class homes:	**26.3%**	
Satisfaction with students' union	**66%**	

For detailed information about sports facilities:
www.royalholloway.ac.uk/sports

Accommodation

Number of places and costs refer to 2015–16.
University-provided places: 2,952
Percentage catered: 37%
Catered costs: £87–£146 a week (30–38 weeks).
Self-catered costs: £125–£165 a week (30–38 weeks).
First years are guaranteed accommodation provided conditions are met.
International students: as above.
studentaccommodation@rhul.ac.uk
www.royalholloway.ac.uk/studyhere/accommodation/home.aspx

University of St Andrews

St Andrews remains Scotland's only representative in our top 20, despite losing its accustomed place as the home of the country's most satisfied students. The university, which is fourth in the table this year, celebrated its 600th anniversary in 2013 and is Scotland's oldest higher education institution and the third oldest in the English-speaking world. Now it has acquired a more unexpected distinction, having been named as the leading university with the cheapest living costs. MoneySuperMarket took account of insurance premiums, crime figures, rents and beer prices in reaching its conclusion. Fees were not part of the calculations: along with Edinburgh, St Andrews has the highest fees in the UK for undergraduates from England, Wales or Northern Ireland. It charges them £9,000 a year for the full four years of a degree, although there are bursaries for students from low-income families. Scots and other EU students continue to pay nothing. With almost 30 per cent of St Andrews students coming from south of the border, the new fees might have been expected to hit recruitment, but enrolments continued to rise in 2014.

International students make up over 40 per cent of the intake and give the university a cosmopolitan feel. St Andrews is particularly popular in the United States, which alone provides nearly a fifth of the first-year students, many on Study Abroad programmes. More than 40 per cent of the UK undergraduates come from independent schools. The university is in the middle of a £100-million fundraising campaign, £13 million of which is to support bright students who would otherwise be unable to attend St Andrews. A hefty contribution came from a gala dinner in New York, attended by the university's highest-profile graduates, the Duke and Duchess of Cambridge, where guests paid $100,000 a table.

Although the university has fewer than 10,000 students, it offers a wide range of courses. Its reputation has always rested mainly on the humanities: St Andrews boasts Europe's first Centre for Syrian Studies, an Institute of Iranian Studies and a Centre for Peace and Conflict Studies. It has the UK's largest mediaeval history department and has now added film studies and sustainable development. It has also taken over the running of the town's Byre Theatre, which is used as teaching space by day while continuing to offer productions in the evenings and at weekends.

The university has been investing heavily in the sciences, which produced some of the best results in the 2014 Research Excellence Framework (REF). More than 90 per cent of two joint submissions with Edinburgh

College Gate
St Andrews
Fife KY16 9AJ

01334 462150 (admissions)
student.recruitment@
st-andrews.ac.uk
www.st-andrews.ac.uk
www.yourunion.net
Affiliation: none

***The Times and Sunday Times* Rankings**

Overall Ranking: **4** (last year: 3)

Teaching quality:	**=22**	83.2%
Student experience:	**=21**	86.8%
Research quality:	**11**	40.4%
Entry standards:	**6**	517
Student–staff ratio:	**=8**	11.4
Services & facilities/student:	**13**	£2,572
Expected completion rate:	**10**	95.3%
Good honours:	**2**	89.6%
Graduate prospects:	**12**	83.3%

in chemistry and physics was rated world-leading or internationally excellent. A £3.7-million physics facility which opened in 2015 will put St Andrews at the forefront of research into superconductors and light-emitting materials, with an ultra-low vibration laboratory that is the most advanced in the UK and one of a handful worldwide. The £45-million Medical and Biological Sciences Building was one of the first in the UK to integrate research facilities for the medical school with the other sciences. The university has the largest optical telescope in Britain and is planning a Green Energy Centre. Overall, more than 70 per cent of the work assessed in the REF reached the top two categories, with classics and history of art scoring particularly well.

The town of St Andrews is steeped in history, as well as being the centre of the golfing world. The university accounts for half of its 18,000 inhabitants. Many of the main buildings date from the 15th and 16th centuries, but sciences are taught at the modern North Haugh site a few streets away. Everything is within walking distance, but bicycles are common. Among the many traditions are academic families, in which third- or fourth-year students help new undergraduates ("bejants" and "bejantines") adjust to university life. Undergraduates also wear a distinctive academic dress – the famous red gown signifies the artists and scientists of the United College and the black gown with its purple cross identifies the divinity students of St Mary's College. Nearly half of students live in university owned accommodation, with first-year undergraduates guaranteed a hall place provided they apply by the end of June.

Students do not come to St Andrews for the nightclubs, but there are no shortage of parties in a tight-knit community. A £12-million extension and redevelopment of the Students' Association building will be complete by the end of 2015. The university is also planning a £14-million transformation of its sports facilities, with a new sports hall, larger and better-equipped fitness suite, and an indoor tennis centre.

Undergraduate Fees and Bursaries

» Fees for Scottish and EU students 2015–16	No fee
» Fees for Non-Scottish UK (RUK) students 2015–16	£9,000
» Fees for international students 2015–16	£17,040
Pre-clinical medicine	£24,500

» For Scottish students with household income up to £34K, bursaries of £1,500 a year.
» For all students on the basis of need, around 90 university accommodation discounts of £3,000 for years 1 and 2.
» For RUK students starting in 2015 with household income below £42.6K, bursary to top up student's official grant and/or loan to £7,500 a year. 2016 RUK scheme not yet announced.
» Other scholarships and bursaries are available.
» Check the university's website for the latest information.

Students

Undergraduates:	**6,580**	**(1,030)**
Postgraduates:	**1,730**	**(395)**
Mature students:	**4.1%**	
International students:	**41.3%**	
Applications per place:	**7.3**	
From state-sector schools:	**59%**	
From working-class homes:	**14.9%**	
Satisfaction with students' union	**75%**	

For detailed information about sports facilities:
www.st-andrews.ac.uk/sport

Accommodation

Number of places and costs refer to 2015–16
University-provided places: 3,909
Percentage catered: 53%
Catered costs: £142–£219 (33 weeks).
Self-catered costs: £90–£201 a week (38 weeks).
Single first-year undergraduates are guaranteed accommodation if they apply by 30 June in year of entry.
Policy for international students: as above.
accommodation@st-andrews.ac.uk
www.st-andrews.ac.uk/accommodation/ug/

St George's, University of London

St George's is the only free-standing medical school in the University of London and the only one in our table. It appears for the first time this year because it qualifies for five of the subject tables, not just medicine. With more than 5,500 students, it is one of the biggest in the country and will soon be larger still: the intake grew by 130 places in 2014 – a 20 per cent increase on the previous year and much the largest recruitment in its 250-year history. The growth has come mainly in areas other than medicine, where numbers are centrally controlled. There is a joint provision with Kingston University in nursing, physiotherapy and radiology, as well as degrees in biomedical sciences and anatomy.

The school was founded in central London, on Hyde Park Corner, where Edward Jenner was a student before performing the first smallpox vaccination. The hide of the cow he used in the original experiment remains at St George's, which moved to Tooting, in south London, in the 1970s. The medical school shares a clinical environment with St George's Hospital, one of the busiest in London. It also works closely with healthcare providers throughout south London to ensure that its courses reflect latest clinical practices and that the students have diverse placement opportunities. The wealth of clinical experience on offer contributes to its popularity with students: applications are near record levels and there was a sharp increase in student satisfaction in 2014.

St George's has a strong research record, which includes the invention of the first endocardial cardiac pacemaker and pioneering work on in vitro fertilisation. It currently has important studies into dementia, malaria and antibiotic resistance. Only Imperial College London scored more highly for the external impact of its work in the 2014 Research Excellence Framework (REF). Overall, 70 per cent of the work submitted for the REF was considered world-leading or internationally excellent. Three research institutes focus on biomedical and scientific discovery, advancing the prevention and treatment of disease in the fields of population health, heart disease and infection – three of the greatest challenges to global health in the 21st century.

The Tooting campus includes a preparatory centre for international students that is run jointly by St George's and the INTO foundation. Most students are taking English language courses or developing other necessary skills through the International foundation programme before joining medical degrees. St George's

Cranmer Terrace
Tooting
London SW17 0RE

020 8725 2333 (enquiries)
study@sgul.ac.uk
www.sgul.ac.uk
www.sgsu.org.uk
Affiliation: none

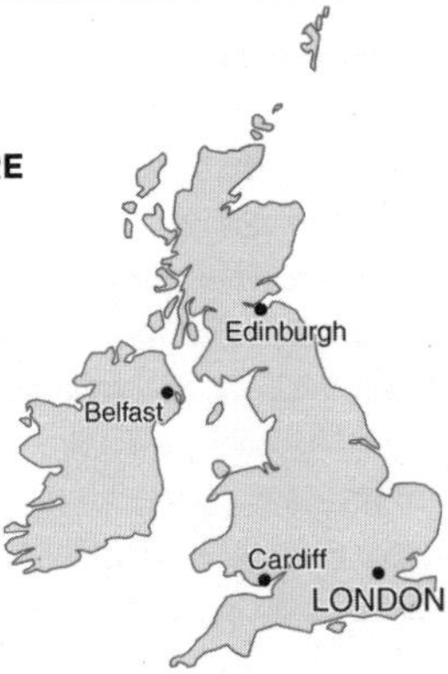

***The Times and Sunday Times* Rankings**

Overall Ranking: **48** (last year: n/a)

Teaching quality:	**=94**	78.7%
Student experience:	**98**	81.6%
Research quality:	**51**	22.2%
Entry standards:	**27**	418
Student–staff ratio:	**=17**	12.9
Services & facilities/student:	**1**	£4,034
Expected completion rate:	**25**	92.7%
Good honours:	**=60**	70.4%
Graduate prospects:	**1**	93.4%

also offers a four-year graduate entry Bachelor of Surgery degree in Cyprus, at the University of Nicosia, where the first students graduated in 2015. St George's was the first UK institution to launch the MBBS Graduate Entry Programme (GEP), a four-year fast-track medical degree course open to graduates in any discipline and which has become an increasingly popular route into the medical profession.

St George's has done more than many medical schools to widen the intake into the profession. There is a shadowing scheme which offers sixth-formers from Wandsworth and Merton state schools the opportunity to accompany a doctor or other healthcare professional at St George's or Queen Mary's Hospital. The school also runs taster days and both spring and summer schools for aspiring doctors, as well as providing a package of financial support worth £2,000 for students with a household income of less than £25,000. St George's almost meets the benchmark of 29 per cent admissions from low-income households, based on the national average for its courses and entry qualifications, although it does not yet meet its target for state-educated entrants.

A £1-million refurbishment of the library took place in 2012 and three laboratories have been upgraded since then. There are 250 workstations in five IT suites, two of which are available 24 hours a day. Other new investments include a virtual reality facility to give lifelike scenarios in an interactive environment to train paramedics about situations they might face in the real world.

New self-catered halls of residence with 150 single en-suite study bedrooms have been built within a 15-minute walk of the campus, bringing the total residential stock to almost 500 rooms. There is a sports centre on campus and competitive teams play in regional and national competitions, but the sports facilities received one of the lowest ratings in Times Higher Education magazine's most recent student experience survey. Tooting Lido, the biggest open-air pool in the country, is not far away and the West End is less than half an hour by tube for shopping and nightlife excursions.

Undergraduate Fees and Bursaries

» Fees for UK/EU students 2016–17	£9,000
Foundation degree	£9,000
» Fees for international students 2015–16	£14,300–£15,970
Medicine	£18,630–£32,663

» English students with household income up to £25K, £2,000 cash year 1, £1,000 following years; household income £25K–£42.6K, sliding scale £1,000–£300 cash in year 1 only. NHS funded students ineligible.

» Academic scholarships and sports bursaries available.

» Check the university's website for the latest information.

Students

Undergraduates:	**2,545**	**(2,045)**
Postgraduates:	**175**	**(740)**
Mature students:	**32.5%**	
International students:	**7.3%**	
Applications per place:	**11.6**	
From state-sector schools:	**81.9%**	
From working-class homes:	**28.4%**	
Satisfaction with students' union	**71%**	

For detailed information about sports facilities:
www.sgsu.org.uk/club-soc/sports-clubs

Accommodation

Places and costs refer to 2015–16
University-provided places: 486
Percentage catered: 0%
Self-catered costs: £152 (standard) – £162 (premium) for 42 weeks.
Undergraduates are prioritised for housing in their first year.
International students: as above.
accommodation@sgul.ac.uk
www.sgul.ac.uk/study/accommodation

University of St Mark and St John

St Mark and St John was the only university in the UK not to take part in the 2014 Research Excellence Framework (REF) – indeed, the only one for more than 20 years to submit no work for the official assessments of research. Professor Cara Aitchison, the Vice-Chancellor, chaired one of the REF panels, but the academic board decided that a small submission and poor results would produce little extra funding and might damage the university's league table position. In fact, the decision ensured that the university would finish bottom of our rankings for research, and contributed to a further 21-place slump in its overall ranking on top of last year's 31-place decline. Only three universities now rank lower.

However, Marjon, as the university is commonly known, was placed top of an index of social mobility produced by a former vice-chancellor for the graduate-level jobs secured by students recruited from poorer backgrounds. Nearly all the undergraduates are state educated and more than 40 per cent come from the four lowest socio-economic groups.

The Plymouth-based university plans to double in size over the next decade, but will still have only about 5,000 students when the programme is complete. The priorities for new courses and research include human biosciences, sport medicine, exercise physiology, psychology, sociology, business and management, accounting, computing, tourism and languages. The aim is to develop a "credible and critical mass" in each area, to make economies of scale and invest in development. The cost will be relatively modest because the spacious greenfield campus has spare capacity following investment in buildings and sports facilities totalling £20 million in recent years. But the university has promised to increase staffing levels in line with student numbers to maintain the small class sizes that are one of its selling points. There will be more students from overseas, but most will still come from Devon and Cornwall.

Established in 1840 as a Church of England teacher training college in London, with the son of poet Samuel Taylor Coleridge as its first principal, the university describes itself as "arguably the third oldest Higher Education Institution in England". The College of St Mark and St John only moved to Plymouth in 1973. Still officially a Church of England Voluntary Institution, it was one of several religious foundations among the universities awarded that status in 2013. The attractive modern Chaplaincy Centre is at the heart of the campus, but there is less emphasis on religion in the new

Derriford Road
Plymouth
Devon PL6 8BH

01752 636890 (admissions)
admissions@marjon.ac.uk
www.marjon.ac.uk
www.marjonsu.com
Affiliations: GuildHE;
Cathedrals Group

***The Times and Sunday Times* Rankings**

Overall Ranking: **=123** (last year: =102)

Teaching quality:	**114**	76.3%
Student experience:	**124**	77.3%
Research quality:		
Entry standards:	**=72**	319
Student–staff ratio:	**=117**	21.2
Services & facilities/student:	**114**	£1,250
Expected completion rate:	**92**	82.6%
Good honours:	**=114**	58.8%
Graduate prospects:	**100**	60.4%

university's promotional material than at some of its counterparts.

The university lists sport at the top of its list of specialisms, followed by education, languages, journalism and the creative arts. The Elite Sport Scholarship programme produced a gold medallist at the Commonwealth Games in swimmer Ben Proud. Recent campus developments have included extensive refurbishment of the library to provide a new social learning space. There has also been a new sports centre, refurbished student housing and a new entrance and student centre. The Journalism and Media Centre opened in 2013, conceived and designed by the lecturers. It includes an iPad teaching room, full iMac classroom, four iMac media editing suites, two of which act as a radio studio, and an editorial meeting room. The two BA programmes – journalism, and sports journalism – are strongly vocational, and the new centre is made available to commercial businesses. Teacher training remains strong, with Ofsted giving an outstanding rating for the leadership and management of courses that run in six counties, as well as in Cyprus and Germany.

The university is located on the outskirts of the city, close to the Dartmoor National Park and within easy reach of the sea. The green agenda extends to an on-campus duck pond and nature trail. An orchard planted with local varieties of apple tree celebrates the biodiversity of the campus. Sports facilities are extremely good: there is a floodlit 3G pitch, climbing wall, 25-metre indoor swimming pool and well-equipped gym, as well as a rehabilitation clinic and sports science lab. The Namibian team used the campus as its base for the 2015 Rugby World Cup.

There are residential places on campus for 456 students in seven halls of residence and 38 village houses; rents compare favourably with most universities. First-year students are guaranteed places and encouraged to take one up while they make the transition to higher education. Those living on campus may only bring a car in exceptional circumstances, but the city centre is a short bus ride from the campus. Plymouth is a lively city that students tend to enjoy.

Undergraduate Fees and Bursaries

» Fees for UK/EU students 2016–17	£9,000
Foundation degree	£6,000–£9,000
» Fees for international students 2015–16	£10,500–£11,250

» Fee waivers for high academic achievement and sports scholarships. Details not available in August 2015.
» Travel and accommodation bursaries for students on placement; enhanced hardship fund.
» Academic scholarships and targeted bursaries available.
» Check the university's website for the latest information.

Students

Undergraduates:	2,075	(140)
Postgraduates:	260	(275)
Mature students:	32.9%	
International students:	3.4%	
Applications per place:	4.3	
From state-sector schools:	97.9%	
From working-class homes:	39.8%	
Satisfaction with students' union	65%	

For detailed information about sports facilities:
www.marjon.ac.uk/marjon-sport/

Accommodation

Places and costs refer to 2015–16
University-provided places: 456
Percentage catered: 65%
Catered costs: £115–£130 (inclusive of dining-in scheme).
Self-catered costs: £85 (small single) – £90 (standard single).
First years are guaranteed accommodation which is allocated on a first-to-go unconditional offer, first served basis.
International students: guaranteed campus or homestay housing.
www.marjon.ac.uk/student-life/university-approved-accommodation/

St Mary's University, Twickenham

St Mary's has appointed a trio of high-profile visiting professors as it goes into its third year as a full university. Dr Mary McAleese, the former President of Ireland, will lecture and research in Irish studies; Cherie Blair in law; and Sir Clive Woodward, who coached England to the 2003 Rugby World Cup, in sport and business. They have joined the largest Catholic university in the UK – one of three created in recent years – with almost 6,000 students, including 1,200 postgraduates. It has resisted the temptation to become even larger by establishing a partnership with Heythrop College, a part of the University of London and the capital's other Catholic higher education institution. A year of negotiations ended with St Mary's deciding to proceed on its own.

Founded in Hammersmith in 1850 by the Catholic Poor Schools Committee to meet the need for teachers for the growing numbers of poor Catholic children, St Mary's moved along the river to Twickenham in 1925. The spectacular Strawberry Hill House has been its centrepiece ever since. The house was designed as a Gothic fantasy between 1747 and 1792 by Horace Walpole, the son of Britain's first Prime Minister. Leased from the university by a trust, the building has now been restored and is open to the public. The campus occupies 35 acres of gardens and parkland close to the Thames, with a variety of modern teaching and residential accommodation. Additional sports facilities are located in neighbouring Teddington, where an £8.5-million sports centre has attracted the New Zealand and South Africa teams for the 2015 Rugby World Cup, which will use the university as a base. A new library, costing £6 million, is now fully open, as is the upgraded student television studio. There is also a new computer suite with the latest Apple MacPro workstations, offering students 24-hour access to professional-grade creative technologies.

Only a third of today's students are training to be teachers and there are growing numbers taking sport, drama, theology and business related degrees. Sixty per cent of the students are female and about 5 per cent of undergraduates come from outside the UK. There are nearly 500 undergraduate degree combinations, including a range of Foundation degrees, across four academic schools covering sport, health and applied science; education, theology and leadership; management and social sciences; and the arts and humanities. Tuition fees are now £9,000 fees, but in 2016 entrants to Foundation degrees will pay no more than £4,500 a year. Over 35 per cent of

Waldegrave Road
Strawberry Hill
Twickenham
London TW1 4SX

020 8240 2314 (admissions)
recruit@stmarys.ac.uk
www.stmarys.ac.uk
www.stmaryssu.co.uk
Affiliations: GuildHE; Cathedrals Group

***The Times and Sunday Times* Rankings**

Overall Ranking: **=100** (last year: 100)

Teaching quality:	**=69**	80.5%
Student experience:	**47**	84.8%
Research quality:	**=103**	4%
Entry standards:	**108**	289
Student–staff ratio:	**=112**	20.6
Services & facilities/student:	**121**	£1,069
Expected completion rate:	**=86**	83.7%
Good honours:	**94**	63.8%
Graduate prospects:	**=67**	66.7%

the UK undergraduates are from working-class homes and the university has a number of outreach schemes designed to broaden the intake further. The E-Mentoring scheme, launched in 2013, in which current students help selected groups of school pupils throughout the academic year, has received excellent feedback from participants. Other initiatives provide academic support and monitor the progress of under-represented groups once they begin courses.

St Mary's missed out on university status when a dozen other colleges were promoted in 2012, but made up for lost time with a respectable position on its debut in our league table. The university appointed Francis Campbell, a career diplomat and one-time private secretary to Tony Blair, as its first vice-chancellor. A former ambassador to the Vatican, he helped to secure a Papal visit to St Mary's in 2010. St Mary's has a continued commitment to training teachers for Catholic and other Christian schools, although it admits students of all faiths and none. Its first stated objective is "To be a distinctive institution within UK higher education, providing a unique experience for our students and staff by virtue of our values and identity as a Catholic university." Cardinal Vincent Nichols, President of the Catholic Bishops' Conference of England and Wales, became the university's chancellor in 2015.

Students like the combination of an attractive setting in southwest London that is only half an hour from Waterloo station by train. The excellent sports facilities attract elite performers. As well as European Games gold medals for alumni Mo Farah and Jo Pavey, 2014 saw two undergraduates win gold medals as part of the victorious Great Britain Rugby Sevens team at the World University Championships. Paralympian David Weir regularly trains at the university. Its strong tradition in sport enabled St Mary's to attract the first Mo Farah Academy to develop outstanding young athletes. The academy, established by St Mary's graduate Farah and his wife, Tania, will support training programmes at St Mary's and at Brunel University, as well as providing scholarships for eight top students a year.

Undergraduate Fees and Bursaries

- Fees for UK/EU students 2016–17 £9,000
  Foundation degree up to £4,500
- Fees for international students 2015–16 £10,130
- Up to 70 St Mary's Scholarships: household income below £25K with conditions, £3,000 cash, fee waiver or accommodation discount, year 1; £2,000 , year 2; £1,000, year 3.
- For others with household income below £25K, bursary of £500, year 1, £300, year2; £200, year 3.
- For students with AAB at A level or equivalent and household income below £42.6K, 30 scholarships of £1,000 cash in year 1.
- Awards for students from Catholic schools and for care leavers; sports scholarships.

Students

Undergraduates:	**3,500**	**(395)**
Postgraduates:	**435**	**(835)**
Mature students:	**16%**	
International students:	**4.1%**	
Applications per place:	**4.6**	
From state-sector schools:	**93.6%**	
From working-class homes:	**37.5%**	
Satisfaction with students' union	**70%**	

For detailed information about sports facilities:
www.stmarys.ac.uk/sport/

Accommodation

Number of places and costs refer to 2015–16
University-provided places: approx 700
Percentage catered: 100%
Catered costs: £115.09 (small twin) – £187.09 (single en suite) inclusive of meal plan (37 weeks).
The university endeavours to provide accommodation to all new applicants who require it and apply by the deadline.
International students: some rooms reserved for new students.
accommodation@stmarys.ac.uk
www.stmarys.ac.uk/student-life/accommodation/

University of Salford

Applications and enrolments have recovered spectacularly since Salford reshaped its portfolio of degrees to concentrate on a more limited range of subjects in media, business, technology, science, engineering and health. In 2014, both were back to the levels seen before £9,000 fees were introduced. But the university continues to struggle in our league table, where it is held back particularly by low levels of degree completion by students and unimpressive graduate prospects. It is the lowest ranked pre-1992 institution, just inside the top 100. There will be significant improvements to the main campus by the time new entrants arrive in 2016, however. The new £81-million Peel Park Quarter, with 1,367 residential places and impressive student facilities, opens in autumn 2015. It will be followed in 2016 by the New Adelphi, a flagship building at the gateway to the campus, which will be the main social hub and also the teaching centre for art, performance, and design and technology students. It will include a 350-seat theatre, industry-standard TV, radio and music studios, as well as exhibition space and café and bar areas. The university also has a £30-million development in MediaCityUK, in Salford Quays, where there are exceptional opportunities to work with BBC staff and other media professionals using the latest equipment, studios and laboratories.

There are three campuses, all of them, apart from Salford Quays, clustered around the River Irwell and within walking distance of Manchester city centre. The landscaped main campus is a haven of lawns and shrubberies. University House, where students go for advice and support, has seen a £3-millon upgrade, while a 1960s teaching building has been remodelled and extended to accommodate six lecture theatres equipped with large screen displays, a series of learning and breakout spaces, plus a café. A £22-million headquarters for the Faculty of Health and Social Care is on the third site, with practice clinics, hospital ward facilities and a human performance laboratory. In addition, the University of Salford Abu Dhabi offers courses, mainly online, in the Gulf state.

Salford, which has around 19,000 students, does well on the Government's access measures: 44 per cent of the undergraduates come from working-class homes and there is a high proportion from areas sending few students to higher education. The dropout rate has fluctuated: the latest projection is an improvement on last year but, at 16 per cent, is still higher than the national average for the subjects and students' qualifications.

The university's growing involvement

The Crescent
Salford
M5 4WT

0161 295 4545 (enquiries)
contact via website
www.salford.ac.uk
www.salfordstudents.com
Affiliation: University Alliance

***The Times and Sunday Times* Rankings**

Overall Ranking: **98** (last year: 105)

Teaching quality:	**76**	80.1%
Student experience:	**=104**	80.9%
Research quality:	**71**	8.3%
Entry standards:	**59**	334
Student–staff ratio:	**=63**	17
Services & facilities/student:	**77**	£1,646
Expected completion rate:	**112**	79.5%
Good honours:	**87**	65.2%
Graduate prospects:	**107**	59.5%

in health has seen the establishment of a national centre for prosthetics and orthotics, and Salford has a high reputation for the treatment of sports injuries. The School of Nursing, Midwifery, Social Work and Social Sciences received outstanding ratings from its regulatory body. The school's component parts work together on projects such as the Salford Institute for Dementia, which carries out research and practice to improve the lives of people living with dementia and their carers.

Engineering is the university's traditional strength, attracting many of the 3,000 overseas students. The university opened the world's first Energy House – a full-size traditional terraced house built in a laboratory for students, researchers and industry to study domestic energy consumption. However, Salford Business School is the main point of growth, with applications up by 27 per cent on last year. It has won multiple awards for innovation and the delivery of its courses via a mix of traditional teaching and business innovation projects. There is also a partnership with the Class of '92, former Manchester United footballers, on a range of business ventures and community engagement projects.

Two-thirds of Salford's courses – and all of them in the business school – offer work placements, some of which are abroad and almost all counting towards degree classifications. The university has partnerships which provide research and work experience with the BBC, Adobe, international research institutions and the Salford China partnership programme among others. The Enterprise Academy scheme was commended by the EU for the success of student start-up businesses. Salford led the way in formally recognising interaction with business and industry as of equal importance to teaching and research. The university entered only a third of its eligible academics for the 2014 Research Excellence Framework, but more than half of their work was found to be world-leading or internationally excellent.

Salford's location is one of its main selling points, with Manchester a prime draw for students. By 2016 there will be more than 3,700 residential places within ten minutes' walk of the main campus, owned either by the university or a partner organisation.

Undergraduate Fees and Bursaries

- Fees for UK/EU students 2016–17 £9,000
  Placement year no fee
- Fees for international students 2015–16 £11,090–£13,050
- For students with at least ABB at A Level or equivalent, £2,000 cash scholarship in year 1.
- For students with household income below £25K and from Greater Manchester, £1,000 cash a year.
- 3 asylum seeker awards of full fee waiver and £500 cash a year.
- Check the university's website for the latest information.

Students

Undergraduates:	**13,580**	**(1,325)**
Postgraduates:	**2,010**	**(1,565)**
Mature students:	**30.2%**	
International students:	**11.6%**	
Applications per place:	**6.3**	
From state-sector schools:	**98.5%**	
From working-class homes:	**43.9%**	
Satisfaction with students' union	**69%**	

For detailed information about sports facilities:
www.salfordstudents.com/activities/sports

Accommodation

Number of places and costs refer to 2015–16
University-provided places: over 2,400
Percentage catered: 0%
Self-catered costs: £79 (standard) – £92 (en suite); £79 – £99.50 (flat) for 42 or 52 weeks.
First years are guaranteed accommodation (terms and conditions apply).
International students: as above.
salford@clvuk.com (Salford Student Village)
www.salford.ac.uk/study/life-at-salford/accommodation

University of Sheffield

Sheffield has taken almost 1,000 additional undergraduates in the last two years, bringing the intake to record levels. The university's growing popularity may be due partly to consistently good ratings from its own students. It was again in the top three in *Times Higher Education* magazine's 2015 student experience survey, when the university was voted the best in the UK for social life and accommodation, as well as for its students' union, which has been the most popular in the National Student Survey (NSS) in every year that unions have been assessed. However, lower levels of satisfaction in other parts of the NSS and a middling performance in the Research Excellence Framework (REF) have prevented Sheffield from regaining a position in the top 20 of our league table.

The university remains in the top 80 in the world, according to the QS rankings, and attracts more than 6,000 international students. Eighty-five per cent of the research submitted to the REF was considered world-leading or internationally excellent, with biomedical sciences, control and systems engineering, history and politics all in the top three in the UK. But the university entered a smaller proportion of its academics than most of its peers in the Russell Group. Former Home Secretary David Blunkett, an alumnus, is a visiting professor in politics, helping to establish the Crick Centre for the public understanding of politics.

The main university precinct now stretches into an almost unbroken mile-long "campus" that ends not far from the city centre. The most striking recent addition – and Sheffield's biggest single investment – is the £81-million Diamond, which opens in September 2015 with a range of specialist engineering features to encourage interdisciplinary teaching and learning. The highly rated Faculty of Engineering, which has 4,000 students, had already opened the £21-million Pam Liversidge Building, named after one of UK's leading female engineers. Sheffield is the lead institution for systems engineering, smart materials and stem-cell technology in a research network of European, American and Chinese universities. There is a separate technology park centred on an advanced manufacturing research centre, in which Boeing is the senior partner. Plans have been submitted for 1.3 million square feet of new buildings at the former airport site.

Previous developments have seen the conversion of the former Jessop Hospital into a new centre for the arts and humanities and the renovation of the original University Library and the Arts Tower, which is still the tallest university building in the country after more than

Western Bank
Sheffield S10 2TN

0114 222 8030 (enquiries)
shefapply@sheffield.ac.uk
www.sheffield.ac.uk
http://su.sheffield.ac.uk
Affiliation: Russell Group

***The Times and Sunday Times* Rankings**

Overall Ranking: **21** (last year: 21)

Teaching quality:	**59**	81.3%
Student experience:	**16**	87.2%
Research quality:	**23**	37.6%
Entry standards:	**=21**	428
Student–staff ratio:	**=36**	14.9
Services & facilities/student:	**40**	£2,031
Expected completion rate:	**15**	94.4%
Good honours:	**=19**	80.4%
Graduate prospects:	**41**	75.7%

40 years. The £23-million Information Commons operates 24 hours a day throughout the year, providing 1,300 study spaces and 500 computers linked to the campus network, as well as more than 100,000 books and periodicals. The university has spent £1.5 million refurbishing a purpose-built student skills centre, which offers support in a number of areas. A new employability strategy includes two internship schemes offering 75 placements within the university.

The student population is more diverse than those in most other Russell Group universities: more than 85 per cent of the undergraduates come from state schools or colleges, although little more than 20 per cent are from working-class homes.

Most university flats and halls of residence are within walking distance, in the suburbs on the affluent west side of Sheffield. Residential accommodation is plentiful and first-years from outside Sheffield are guaranteed a room. Private housing is reasonably priced in student areas close to the university. The Endcliffe student village caters for 3,500 students in a mix of refurbished Victorian houses and new flats, while the Ranmoor Village houses over 1,000 students in self-catering apartments, which include some family apartments and studios.

The excellent sports facilities close to the main university precinct include five floodlit synthetic pitches, a large fitness centre with more than 150 pieces of equipment, swimming pool with sauna and steam rooms, sports hall, fitness studio, multipurpose activity room, four squash courts and a bouldering wall. The 45 acres of grass pitches for rugby, football and cricket are a bus ride away. Sheffield has one of the biggest programmes of internal leagues at any university. The famously lively social scene is based on the students' union, which was extended for the second time in three years in 2013, creating more facilities for students and staff. The city has plenty of student-oriented bars and clubs, and town–gown relations are much better than in most major university centres. Crime statistics identify Sheffield as the safest big city in England.

Undergraduate Fees and Bursaries

» Fees for UK/EU students 2016–17	£9,000
» Fees for international students 2015–16	£14,500–£18,750
Medicine	£18,750–£34,000

» Cash bursaries on sliding scale of £1,500–£750 for UK students with household income up to £42.6K.
» In addition, £1,000 a year bursary for those from disadvantaged areas with household income below £25K.
» £500 a year award for local students achieving ABB at A level (or equivalent).
» Other scholarships and bursaries available.
» Check the university's website for the latest information.

Students

Undergraduates:	**17,530**	**(1,055)**
Postgraduates:	**6,075**	**(1,940)**
Mature students:	**8.5%**	
International students:	**20.3%**	
Applications per place:	**7.4**	
From state-sector schools:	**85.8%**	
From working-class homes:	**20.7%**	
Satisfaction with students' union	**95%**	

For detailed information about sports facilities:
www.sport-sheffield.com

Accommodation

Number of places and costs refer to 2015–16
University-provided places: 5,955
Percentage catered: 8%
Catered costs: £5,650.68 – £6,667.92 (42 weeks; 31 weeks of catering).
Self-catered costs: £4,036.62 – £7,936.11 (42–51 weeks).
First years are guaranteed accommodation if conditions are met.
International students: as above.
accommodationoffice@sheffield.ac.uk
www.sheffield.ac.uk/accommodation

Sheffield Hallam University

Students at Sheffield Hallam are about to reap the final benefits of a £110-million development plan, with new buildings on both the main campuses and the addition of one of the most prominent locations in the city centre as a new home for the Sheffield Institute of Arts. All art and design courses, including fine art, fashion, product design, metalwork and jewellery, will be taught in the former Sheffield Head Post Office when the listed building has been fully refurbished at the end of 2015.

A £30-million development at the City Campus will house the Sheffield Institute of Education from this autumn, training the majority of the region's new teachers, and the Heart of the Campus building at Collegiate Crescent campus opened its doors to students in 2014 and has since won an award from the Royal Institute of British Architects.

The university is also upgrading its science and technology facilities after winning a £10-million grant from the funding council and is a partner in the development of the new Advanced Wellbeing Research Centre, which received £14-million Government funding early in 2015 and will be a key part of Sheffield's Olympic Legacy Park. The Centre for Sport and Exercise Science, with its £6-million research facility, is one of the largest of its kind in Europe, with more than 2,000 students. The faculty is the biggest provider of health and social care training in the UK and offers the widest range of sports courses.

Previous developments focused mainly on the City Campus, near the railway station and Sheffield's central shopping area. The main learning centre was refurbished and all the departments in the arts, computing, engineering and sciences were brought together for the first time, placing them in the heart of Sheffield's cultural industries quarter.

The Sheffield Business School brought together business, finance, management and languages, with several of the university's other specialisms. Business and management courses, which account for easily the biggest share of places, have their own city-centre headquarters, as does the students' union, which took over the spectacular, but ill-fated, National Centre for Popular Music.

The university has been expanding its intake, taking an additional 600 undergraduates in 2014, when it was among the top ten universities in the UK in terms of the volume of applications. It is now one of the growing number of universities to make unconditional offers to the most promising students. Achievement Awards will be offered in an unspecified range of full-time courses starting in 2016.

City Campus
Howard Street
Sheffield S1 1WB

0114 225 5555 (enquiries)
enquiries@shu.ac.uk
www.shu.ac.uk
www.hallamstudentsunion.com
Affiliation: University Alliance

***The Times and Sunday Times* Rankings**

Overall Ranking: **72** (last year: 62)

Teaching quality:	**=62**	80.9%
Student experience:	**=63**	83.9%
Research quality:	**=88**	5.4%
Entry standards:	**=72**	319
Student–staff ratio:	**=65**	17.1
Services & facilities/student:	**48**	£1,932
Expected completion rate:	**=57**	86.9%
Good honours:	**85**	65.7%
Graduate prospects:	**80**	64.7%

The university exceeds all of its access benchmarks and the projected dropout rate of only 8 per cent is lower than average for its courses and entry qualifications. The university has a growing international dimension, with large cohorts taught in partner institutions in Malaysia and other Asian countries, as well as almost 4,000 who come to Sheffield from outside the EU.

The university traces its origins in art and design back to the 1840s and celebrated the centenary of education and teacher training in 2005. It now has 33,000 students, including more than 1,000 taught on franchised courses in further education colleges. Business and industry are closely involved in the development of courses and more than half of the undergraduates take work placements. The university gives a full fee waiver for those who take a complete year out. More than 200 "specialist flexible courses" mix part-time study, distance learning and work-based learning. A "virtual campus" enables all students to access the growing volume of online teaching, assignments and discussion groups even when they are at home or on work placements.

Unlike many big post-1992 universities, Hallam now guarantees accommodation for first years, although the large local intake means that many live at home. Transport in the city is excellent, with both well-run bus and tram services. Sports facilities are supplemented by those provided by the city for the World Student Games. The impressive swimming complex, for example, is on the university's doorstep. The university has taken over the management of Sheffield's only athletics stadium. The redeveloped facility will be available to community groups, schools and local clubs, as well as students. The university partnered with the Tour de France to offer volunteering opportunities for students when the 2014 race started in Yorkshire, continuing the tradition of working with major sporting event organisers.

Undergraduate Fees and Bursaries

- Fees for UK/EU students 2016–17 £9,000
  Placement year £1,800
- Fees for international students 2015–16 £11,500–£12,400
- Details of Sheffield Hallam bursary scheme for 2016 not available in August 2015. Check university website for details.
- Fee waivers of £1,800 for those on placement years. Enhanced hardship fund.
- 6 Vice-Chancellor's Unite Scholarships for care leavers: £3,000 cash bursary and free 52-week Unite student accommodation each year.
- Scholarships and bursaries are available.
- Check the university's website for the latest information.

Students

Undergraduates:	**21,425**	**(4,560)**
Postgraduates:	**2,550**	**(4,565)**
Mature students:	**19.9%**	
International students:	**5.3%**	
Applications per place:	**5.9**	
From state-sector schools:	**96.3%**	
From working-class homes:	**38.7%**	
Satisfaction with students' union	**56%**	

For detailed information about sports facilities:
www.shu.ac.uk/sport/active/

Accommodation

Number of places and costs refer to 2015–16
University-provided places: 5,600
Percentage catered: 0%
Self-catered costs: £83.00–£161.00 a week (43 or 44 weeks).
All first years offered university allocated accommodation if they apply by 1 August deadline date. Unsuccessful applicants supported in finding private housing.
International students: as above, providing conditions are met.
accommodation@shu.ac.uk
www.shu.ac.uk/accommodation

SOAS, University of London

Valerie Amos, the first black woman Cabinet minister and later Leader of the House of Lords, has now become the first black woman to lead a British university. Baroness Amos, who has also been Emergency Relief Coordinator at the United Nations, takes over as director of SOAS as the School prepares to come together on a single campus for the first time for several years. It will move into the North Block of Senate House, the headquarters of the University of London, in 2016, as it celebrates its centenary. Senate House is situated at the western end of the SOAS precinct, and will provide space for a new student hub including accommodation, course registration, student finance, careers and enterprise services, as well as additional teaching facilities.

The only higher education institution in the UK specialising in the study of Africa, Asia and the Middle East has dropped its full title (School of Oriental and African Studies) and promotes itself as SOAS, University of London. The school has a global reputation in subjects relating to two-thirds of the world's population and that excellence will be enhanced by a £20-million gift from a graduate with a passion for South-East Asian art. The donation was worth more than a quarter of SOAS's annual income and will fund new posts, building development and scholarships for Asian students to come to London.

There are 5,400 students on campus, plus over 3,000 studying distance learning programmes. The numbers taking distance learning courses, mainly outside the UK, have grown considerably. The transfer of University of London postgraduate programmes previously taught by Imperial College has made SOAS one of the world's largest providers of distance learning at this level. The students in London come from more than 130 countries, but two-thirds are from Britain and the rest of the EU. Independent school candidates account for almost a fifth of the British entrants to degree courses, while 30 per cent come from the four poorest socio-economic groups. The school has almost doubled its investment in student support with the switch to higher fees, as well as increasing its outreach activities. Applications were up by 12 per cent in 2014, bucking the downward trend in the study of non-European languages across the UK.

The centrepiece of the Bloomsbury precinct is an airy, modern building with gallery space as well as teaching accommodation, a gift from the Sultan of Brunei. The library is one of just five National Research Libraries in the country, holding 1.5 million volumes, periodicals and audio-visual materials in 400 languages,

Thornhaugh Street
Russell Square
London WC1H 0XG

020 7898 4700 (student recruitment)
undergradadmissions@soas.ac.uk
www.soas.ac.uk
http://soasunion.org
Affiliation: none

***The Times and Sunday Times* Rankings**

Overall Ranking: **44** (last year: 31)

Teaching quality:	**=120**	75.2%
Student experience:	**=106**	80.8%
Research quality:	**46**	27.9%
Entry standards:	**33**	407
Student–staff ratio:	**4**	10.9
Services & facilities/student:	**32**	£2,135
Expected completion rate:	**108**	80.7%
Good honours:	**13**	82.9%
Graduate prospects:	**61**	68.3%

and attracts scholars from around the world. More than 40 per cent of degree programmes offer the opportunity to spend a year at one of the school's many partner universities in Africa or Asia.

The school has a much wider portfolio of courses than its name would suggest, offering more than 400 degree combinations and 100 postgraduate programmes. Degrees are available in familiar subjects such as law, music, history and the social sciences, but with a different emphasis. There is also a more limited portfolio of Foundation programmes and language courses. Approximately 45 per cent of undergraduates take a language as part of their degree and the school has now introduced a Language Entitlement programme which offers one term of a non-accredited SOAS Language Centre course free of charge. The £6.5-million Library Transformation Project has added more language laboratories, music studios, discussion and research rooms, gallery space and other facilities. SOAS is in the top 80 in the QS World Rankings for the arts and humanities, which led the way in the 2014 Research Excellence Framework (REF). Music drama and the performing arts produced the best results in a submission in which two-thirds of the work was rated as world-leading or internationally excellent.

There is no separate students' union building, although the students do have their own recently refurbished bar, social space and catering facilities. The former University of London Union – now a student centre – is close at hand, with swimming pool, gym and bars. The West End is also on the doorstep. Nearly 900 residential places are available within 20 minutes' walk of the school. However, the school has few of its own sports facilities and the outdoor pitches are remote, with no time set aside from lectures. Students tend to be highly committed and often politically active – not surprising since many will return to positions of influence in developing countries – and the variety of cultures makes for lively debate.

Undergraduate Fees and Bursaries

- » Fees for UK/EU students 2016–17 £9,000
  Year abroad up to £1,725
- » Fees for international students 2015–16 £16,090
- » For students with household income below £25K, from low participation neighbourhoods, or first generation in HE, 152 Excellence awards of £2,500 a year; study support awards of up to £1,000 in year 1.
- » Other scholarships and bursaries available.
- » Check the university's website for the latest information.

Students

Undergraduates:	**2,940**	**(35)**
Postgraduates:	**1,815**	**(620)**
Mature students:	**22.1%**	
International students:	**39.5%**	
Applications per place:	**6.2**	
From state-sector schools:	**81.6%**	
From working-class homes:	**30.6%**	
Satisfaction with students' union	**71%**	

For detailed information about sports facilities:
http://soasunion.org/activities/sports/

Accommodation

Number of places and costs refer to 2015–16
University-provided places: 770 (Sanctuary Students) 100 (Intercollegiate Halls)
Percentage catered: 14%
Catered costs: £136.50–£347.55 a week.
Self-catered costs: £132.30 – £332.30 a week.
Priority is given to new students on a first come, first served basis.
Residential restrictions apply.
International students: as above, although they are a high priority.
www.soas.ac.uk/students/accommodation

University of South Wales

Two years after its formation through a merger between Glamorgan and Newport universities, South Wales (USW) is rationalising its activities in pursuit of its aim to be the university of choice for vocationally focused education and applied research. That has meant closing one of the five campuses, in Caerleon, near Newport, to new entrants, while investing in the remaining centres. The university is already one of Wales's two largest, with almost 30,000 students, and the University of South Wales Group spreads its net much more widely. The group includes the Royal Welsh College of Music and Drama and Merthyr Tydfil College, while a strategic alliance brings in further education colleges throughout South East Wales. The alliance covers 38 campuses, providing 98,000 learners with advice and structured progression routes from further education to university.

Glamorgan and Newport came together after several years of on/off negotiations and no little political intervention. The two universities had collaborated on the Universities Heads of the Valleys Institute, developing adults' skills in the former mining area. About half of USW's students are full-time undergraduates and of these, a quarter of first years are at least 21 years old. Three-quarters are from Wales and receive grants to reduce the cost of tuition; undergraduates from other parts of the UK will pay fees of £9,000 for courses starting in 2016. The degrees include the full range of science and engineering subjects, from aircraft engineering and mathematics to computing and surveying, at the Pontypridd campus. USW is also a significant player in the arts at its Cardiff campus, notably through its internationally acclaimed film school, whose graduates include double-BAFTA winner Asif Kapadia, and Justin Kerrigan, director of the cult movie *Human Traffic*. There are industry-standard animation facilities, one of the UK's oldest photography schools and a strong reputation for theatre design.

A variety of simulated learning facilities, including the university's own aircraft, moot court room, TV studios, stock exchange trading room, hospital wards, and scenes-of-crime house underline a focus on employability. Sport students train and play on facilities used by Olympic athletes and the All Blacks. There are partnerships with industry leaders and major employers, from British Airways to the National Health Service. The main research strengths are in applied projects, and it is a member of the St David's Day Group, which brings together all Wales's universities to focus on research and innovation. There was a relatively small submission for the 2014

Pontypridd CF37 1DL

08456 76 77 78 (enquiries)
contact via website
www.southwales.ac.uk
www.uswsu.com
Affiliation: University Alliance

***The Times and Sunday Times* Rankings**

Overall Ranking: **=112** (last year: 114)

Teaching quality:	**=106**	77.5%
Student experience:	**121**	78.3%
Research quality:	**=103**	4%
Entry standards:	**=67**	322
Student–staff ratio:	**=103**	19.6
Services & facilities/student:	**100**	£1,425
Expected completion rate:	**=101**	81.7%
Good honours:	**95**	63.6%
Graduate prospects:	**109**	59%

Research Excellence Framework, but half of the work was considered world-leading or internationally excellent. The best results came in a joint submission with Cardiff Metropolitan and Trinity St David universities in art and design, and in sport and exercise science, and social work and social policy.

The Pontypridd campus, 10 miles outside Cardiff, has seen a new home for the Law School and upgraded laboratories, as well as £6-million Learning Resource Centre. Amenities have been improving, with a modern recreation centre and a new students' union. At the university's campus in the heart of Cardiff, the £35-million ATRiuM building, next to the new BBC headquarters, houses the Cardiff School of Creative and Cultural Industries, as well as new premises for law and accounting and finance courses. Other recent developments include a £15-million expansion of facilities for health, science and sport, as well as new halls of residence. The high-quality sports facilities have continued to improve: the university also hosts one of six centres of excellence in cricket. USW has been successful in student competitions, especially in rugby, football and golf. Sports scholarships are available.

The award-winning £35-million Newport City Campus opened in 2011, and a further multi-million pound investment is under way there. Newport is becoming the USW's. home for professional and executive courses, including teacher training, early years, counselling and associated therapies, and part-time business and accounting courses. It is at the heart of Newport's new Cultural Quarter, designed to attract inward investment and strengthen the local economy. Newport was rated the top university in Wales for enterprise education by the Knowledge Exploitation Fund for three years in a row, helping more than 70 new start-up businesses. The city of Newport is undergoing a £2-billion regeneration programme and has plenty of clubs and entertainment venues, including the new multi-million pound Friars Walk entertainment and retail complex, but students in search of serious cultural or clubbing activity gravitate to nearby Cardiff.

Undergraduate Fees and Bursaries

- Fees for UK/EU students 2016–17 £9,000
  Foundation degree £7,500–£8,000
- Welsh Assembly non-means-tested grant (2015–16) to pay fees above £3,810 for Welsh students.
- Fees for international students 2015–16 £11,600
- Excellence Scholarship of £2,000 for those accepting an Unconditional Offer in 2016 and gaining at least ABB at A level or equivalent.
- Flying Start scholarship of £750 and an iPad in year 1 for students with at least 320 UCAS points.
- £1,500 university accommodation discount (Treforest, Newport and Cardiff) for those paying full fees. Not available to those receiving Welsh Government tuition fee grant.

Students

Undergraduates:	**15,610**	**(8,280)**
Postgraduates:	**2,155**	**(3,155)**
Mature students:	**25.5%**	
International students:	**11.4%**	
Applications per place:	**4.3**	
From state-sector schools:	**98.1%**	
From working-class homes:	**37.8%**	
Satisfaction with students' union	**59%**	

For detailed information about sports facilities:
http://sport.southwales.ac.uk

Accommodation

Number of places and costs refer to 2015–16
University-provided places: 1,867
Percentage catered: 0% but catering package available.
Self-catered accommodation: £82–£162 a week (40–51 weeks).
First-year students are offered accommodation. Local restrictions apply.
International students are guaranteed housing.
accom@southwales.ac.uk (Cardiff, Glyntaff & Treforest)
accommodation@southwales.ac.uk (Newport)
http://accommodation.southwales.ac.uk/

Southampton University

Southampton is moving up our top 20 after a stellar performance in the 2014 Research Excellence Framework. It was rewarded for entering nine out of ten eligible academics for assessment when more than 80 per cent of their research was rated as world-leading or internationally excellent, placing Southampton seventh on this measure. The best results came in health subjects, environmental science, psychology, physics, chemistry, electronic engineering and music, drama and performing arts. Relatively modest levels of student satisfaction prevent Southampton from challenging for a place in the overall top ten, but the university has been investing heavily in facilities. The university is in the final phase of a £250-million programme to upgrade its sites in Southampton and Winchester, having also opened a campus in Malaysia dedicated to engineering. The latest developments have added almost 1,500 rooms to the already substantial residential stock in two new accommodation complexes.

The main Highfield Campus is in an attractive green location two miles from the city centre. The students' union has been refurbished and a purpose-built student services centre added to bring together learning support and other advisory facilities. The library has been greatly extended and includes social learning space designed by students. The striking £55-million Mountbatten Building for electronics and computer science and the Optoelectronics Research Centre and the £50-million Life Sciences Building have been added in recent years. Other sites in the city include the National Oceanography Centre Southampton, based in the revitalised dock area. The new £116-million Boldrewood Innovation Campus has been developed with Lloyd's Register and is one of the largest university/business partnerships in the world. The campus is home to the Southampton Marine and Maritime Institute, which combines the university's expertise in ship science with other disciplines such as ocean science, law and business. The Avenue Campus, near the main site, is home to most of the humanities departments, while clinical medicine is based at Southampton General Hospital, where a research centre focuses on respiratory diseases, and the university hopes to open a £25-million cancer immunology centre in 2017. Winchester School of Art, which has been part of the university since 1996, has also enjoyed significant investment in new facilities.

The branch campus, which opened in 2012, is on the southern tip of Malaysia, at the Iksandar Education City development. Here undergraduates can study astronautics and aeronautics, mechanical engineering,

University Road
Southampton SO17 1BJ

023 8059 4732 (admissions)
admissions@southampton.ac.uk
www.southampton.ac.uk
www.susu.org
Affiliation: Russell Group

The Times and Sunday Times **Rankings**

Overall Ranking: **16** (last year: 18)

Teaching quality:	**=86**	79.3%
Student experience:	**=25**	86.5%
Research quality:	**7**	44.9%
Entry standards:	**=29**	411
Student–staff ratio:	**12**	12
Services & facilities/student:	**25**	£2,221
Expected completion rate:	**=26**	92.5%
Good honours:	**=19**	80.4%
Graduate prospects:	**=33**	78.1%

or electronics and electrical engineering for two years before finishing their degree in Southampton. The university has 7,000 international students and a growing number of those from the UK spend time at one of the 322 overseas partner institutions in 54 countries. Medical students can take part of their course in Europe and other students can spend up to a year abroad, paying only 15 per cent of tuition fees for that year.

Southampton is well inside the top 100 in the QS global rankings and the proportion of income derived from research is among the highest in Britain. It has received more than £200 million from the Engineering and Physical Sciences Research Council alone in 2015. There are particular strengths in computer science, where Sir Tim Berners-Lee, inventor of the Worldwide Web, is a professor and Nick Jennings was awarded the only Regius professorship in the subject as part of the Queen's Diamond Jubilee. Southampton was a natural choice as one of the Government's eight academic centres of excellence in cyber security research.

The university has introduced a more flexible curriculum at undergraduate level, with some subjects offering a "major/minor" structure that allows students to spend 25 per cent of their time on a subject other than their original degree choice. There are also new interdisciplinary modules, such as communication in a global world, or sustainability in local and global environments, that are designed to give students a broader perspective. Every undergraduate has an academic adviser to guide their independent learning and progress. Over 86 per cent of the students went to state schools – more than the national average for the courses and entry qualifications and one of the highest proportions in the Russell Group. Students act as ambassadors, associates and mentors in local schools and colleges, as part of the university's efforts to broaden its intake further.

Sports facilities are first class, with an indoor sports complex next to the students' union. The outdoor sports complex has grass and synthetic pitches. Over 1,000 elite athletes, including Sir Chris Hoy, were helped in their Olympic preparation by the university's aerodynamics research and wind tunnel complex.

Undergraduate Fees and Bursaries

- » Fees for UK/EU students 2016–17 £9,000
- » Fees for international students 2015–16 £14,660–£18,010
  Medicine £18,010–£38,315
- » Household income below £16K, £3,000 cash or fee waiver a year; household income £16K–£25K, £1,500 a year.
- » Around 150 bursaries of £1,000 a year for students from the Access to Southampton programme. Enhanced hardship fund
- » Other scholarships and bursaries available.
- » Check the university's website for the latest information.

Students

Undergraduates:	**15,780**	**(415)**
Postgraduates:	**6,055**	**(1,785)**
Mature students:	**14%**	
International students:	**17.2%**	
Applications per place:	**8.3**	
From state-sector schools:	**86.1%**	
From working-class homes:	**22.5%**	
Satisfaction with students' union	**72%**	

For detailed information about sports facilities:
www.southampton.ac.uk/sportandwellbeing/

Accommodation

Number of places and costs refer to 2015–16
University-provided places: more than 6,500
Percentage catered: 8%
Catered costs: £136.22–£187.33 a week.
Self-catered costs: £89.32–£254.80 (family flat) a week.
All full-time first years are guaranteed an offer of accommodation. Conditions apply.
International students: All non-EU students are guaranteed accommodation. Conditions apply.
www.southampton.ac.uk/accommodation

Southampton Solent University

Southampton Solent enjoyed a 7 per cent rise in applications in 2014, as it continued to add new facilities as part of a £100-million development programme. New entrants in 2016 will benefit from a £30-million teaching and learning building that will expand the city-centre campus. The Solent Business School will be relocated to refurbished premises at the heart of the campus in 2017. Other recent developments include a ship-handling centre, a media academy, a new site for the Southampton School of Art and Design and FA-accredited football facilities costing £4 million that are used by the city's Premier League team. The campus is largely functional, but well maintained and conveniently based in the centre of Southampton.

Still the largest of the institutions to be awarded university status in the last 11 years, Solent also offers the widest range of programmes, stretching from further education courses to doctorates. It has an extensive range of "top-up" and extended degrees; and multiple start dates for its courses. The Solent Curriculum plays to the university's strengths in "industry-focused" courses. About 12,000 higher education students embrace a broad-based portfolio that covers business, technology, the creative industries, sport and maritime studies. Students have the opportunity to work on projects for external clients and there is a strong representation of "non-traditional" disciplines, such as yacht and powercraft design, computer and video games, and music journalism and performance. The subject mix may be one reason that the former Southampton Institute is now one of the few universities with a majority of male students.

Solent recruits mainly in London and the south of England, a quarter of the HE students coming from Hampshire, but about 1,500 come from outside the UK. More than a third of the undergraduates come from working-class homes, although this is still below the national average for the university's subjects and entry qualifications. Its support for students was identified as an example of best practice by the Quality Assurance Agency. A Graduate Enterprise Centre provides advice and rent-free offices for those hoping to launch their own businesses, while a Graduate Associate scheme provides employment places for about 100 recent graduates.

A new Research and Innovation Office has been established, but the university finished bottom of those that entered the 2014 Research Excellence Framework. It entered the lowest proportion of eligible academics, at only 7 per cent, and none

East Park Terrace
Southampton SO14 0YN

023 8201 5066 (admissions)
admissions@solent.ac.uk
www.solent.ac.uk
www.solentsu.co.uk
Affiliations: GuildHE; million+

***The Times and Sunday Times* Rankings**

Overall Ranking: =**115** (last year: 115)

Teaching quality:	=84	79.5%
Student experience:	93	82.1%
Research quality:	124	0.5%
Entry standards:	117	276
Student–staff ratio:	=86	18.3
Services & facilities/student:	95	£1,480
Expected completion rate:	117	76.8%
Good honours:	111	60.2%
Graduate prospects:	=122	54.6%

of its research was placed in the top two categories for its external impact. Solent is also held back in our overall league table by amongst the lowest scores for graduate employment prospects.

Creative Arts and Society courses now attract almost as many students as the consistently popular business school. There are new music studios with an industry-standard recording complex, as well as a performance space and dance studio. The Centre for Professional Development in Broadcasting and Multimedia Production includes an online editing suite, digital television studio and gallery, for use by undergraduates as well as community groups and professionals. The university is a Skillset-accredited centre of excellence in television production, broadcast journalism, screenwriting and performance, with expertise in live event broadcast, studio and post-production. Students are part of the official Glastonbury festival filming team, and regularly work on BBC events.

There is particularly strong demand for places in marine and maritime-based courses, which benefit from a world-renowned training and research facility for the superyacht, shipping and offshore oil industries. The university is higher education's premier yachting institution, with a world champion student team that has won the national championships four times in six years and alumni that have gone on to win Olympic and Paralympic gold medals. Three new boats support courses at the purpose-built Watersports Centre, where some activities are targeted towards disadvantaged young people. The Lawrie McMenemy Centre for Football Research is helping to cement the university's reputation for academic study of the sport and, having assumed responsibility for sport development in the city, Solent has also become the country's largest provider of coaching education. A new School of Health, Exercise and Social Science was launched in 2013 to encourage collaboration in health and exercise science, social work and psychology.

Students like the university's location, close to the city centre's shopping area and growing complement of bars and nightclubs. There are more than 2,300 hall places, most of which are allocated to first years. Sports facilities include a sports hall and fitness suite on campus and outdoor pitches, tennis and netball courts four miles away.

Undergraduate Fees and Bursaries

- » Fees for UK/EU students 2016–17 £9,000
  Placement year / Year abroad £1,350
- » Fees for international students 2015–16 £10,380–£10,930
- » Household income below £25K, a £500 bursary each year.
- » 60 Foundation year awards of fee waiver and £1,000 cash for local students from low participation areas.
- » Check the university's website for the latest information.

Students

Undergraduates:	**10,020**	**(1,265)**
Postgraduates:	**115**	**(325)**
Mature students:	**18.7%**	
International students:	**12.1%**	
Applications per place:	**4.9**	
From state-sector schools:	**96.3%**	
From working-class homes:	**36.8%**	
Satisfaction with students' union	**63%**	

For detailed information about sports facilities:
www.solent.ac.uk/sport/

Accommodation

Number of places and costs refer to 2015–16
University-provided places: 2,340
Percentage catered: 0%
Self-catered costs: £85.12–£138.60 a week (41 weeks).
First years are allocated 90% of rooms.
International students: some accommodation is set aside.
accommodation@solent.ac.uk
www.solent.ac.uk/studying/accommodation/accommodation.aspx

Staffordshire University

All Staffordshire's courses, apart from health subjects and some education programmes, will be taught at the university's main campus on the edge of Stoke-on-Trent when new entrants arrive in 2016. A £40-million investment programme will upgrade a number of buildings on the campus, expand the university library, extend student accommodation and improve the public spaces as computing and entertainment technology courses move from Stafford. The university is selling its principal campus in Stafford, but has committed a further £4 million to create a "centre of excellence" in the town for its highly rated nursing and midwifery degrees and other health-related programmes. Staffordshire's engineering provision had already moved to Stoke as the first stage in a plan to create an award-winning, teaching-led university by 2017, with a focus on employability, enterprise and entrepreneurialism. Professor Michael Gunn, the Vice-Chancellor, said concentration made economic sense and would offer the best possible student experience.

Some improvements have already been made on the Stoke campus. A £30-million science block opened in 2012, with the aim of creating a focal point to help drive up the numbers of young people in the region opting to study science, maths and engineering subjects, where career prospects are good. Another £12-million has gone on dedicated student spaces, exhibition areas, cafés and landscaping to create a more attractive study environment. There are modern halls of residence, a sports centre and lively students' union, as well as a 25-acre nature reserve – part of the university's sustained green commitment – which will also be enhanced towards the end of the four-year plan for the campus. The university has been celebrating its centenary on the College Road site, initially as the Central School of Science and Technology. It is now at the heart of Stoke's University Quarter project, which is designed to transform the South Shelton area, as well as encouraging greater participation in higher education. The university has made a commitment to students and employers through the Staffordshire Graduate Programme to ensure that, alongside their academic learning, all students are equipped with employability skills.

Two satellite campuses will survive the reorganisation. Primary teacher training programmes are based at Lichfield, where there is an integrated further and higher education centre, developed in partnership with South Staffordshire College, as well as business start-up units. The other site is in Shrewsbury, where nursing and midwifery

College Road
Stoke-on-Trent ST4 2DE

01782 294400 (admissions)
enquiries@staffs.ac.uk
www.staffs.ac.uk
www.staffsunion.com
Affiliation: million+

***The Times and Sunday Times* Rankings**

Overall Ranking: **95** (last year: 101)

Teaching quality:	**=49**	81.8%
Student experience:	**=80**	82.8%
Research quality:	**55**	16.5%
Entry standards:	**118**	274
Student–staff ratio:	**=59**	16.8
Services & facilities/student:	**81**	£1,620
Expected completion rate:	**115**	78.4%
Good honours:	**=98**	63.2%
Graduate prospects:	**111**	58.4%

students are based in the Royal Shrewsbury Hospital. There are also 15,000 students taking Staffordshire courses outside the UK, almost half of them located around the Pacific Rim. They now make up more than a third of the university's intake, adding to a growing cohort of international students on the university's UK campuses.

Staffordshire is a pioneer of two-year fast-track degrees, which are available in accounting and finance, business management, English and law. There is also an extensive portfolio of two-year Foundation degrees, largely taught by the university's UK partners, which include the National Design Academy. With almost all of its undergraduates state-educated and 42 per cent coming from working-class homes Staffordshire exceeds all the benchmarks for the breadth of its intake. There is good provision for students with disabilities and more than one undergraduate in five comes from areas with little participation in higher education, one of the biggest proportions in the country. The downside is the dropout rate, which was projected at more than 20 per cent in the latest survey – well above the national average for the university's courses and entry qualifications.

Staffordshire increased the size and scope of its submission to the 2014 Research Excellence Framework, compared with previous research assessments, but still entered only 91 academics. The best results were in sport and exercise sciences, although all of the university's research in psychology was placed in the top two categories for its external impact. Applied research is Staffordshire's strong suit: its research has led to the development of new products in markets as diverse as medical technology and recycling.

Stoke is not the liveliest city of its size, but the University Quarter is attracting more social and leisure facilities. The campus is within easy reach of the city centre and has a lively and active students' union. Sports facilities are good and will see more investment as numbers on the Stoke campus rise. Good coaching has helped attract some outstanding athletes, who have access to a sports performance centre to help with training schedules, psychological support and dietary assessments. This year has seen the launch of Team Staffs Sports Elite scholarships worth £6,000.

Undergraduate Fees and Bursaries

» Fees for UK/EU students 2016–17	£9,000
Placement year	£1,200
Courses at partner colleges	£5,270–£9,000
» Fees for international students 2015–16	£10,500

» Students from deprived areas and with lowest household incomes, 500 bursaries of £200 cash and £800 accommodation discount, support for travel costs or institutional services in year 1; £100 and £400 in years 2 and 3.
» Other scholarships and bursaries available.
» Check the university's website for the latest information.

Students

Undergraduates:	**10,065**	**(6,425)**
Postgraduates:	**1,210**	**(2,445)**
Mature students:	**31.4%**	
International students:	**4.8%**	
Applications per place:	**5.9**	
From state-sector schools:	**98.8%**	
From working-class homes:	**41.9%**	
Satisfaction with students' union	**69%**	

For detailed information about sports facilities:
www.staffs.ac.uk/teamstaffs

Accommodation

Number of places and costs refer to 2015–16
University-provided places: 1,041 (Stoke); 605 (Stafford)
Percentage catered: 0%
Self-catered accommodation: £80–£108 a week (38 weeks).
First years have priority, if conditions are met.
International students: have priority, if conditions are met.
accommodation_stoke@staffs.ac.uk
accommodation_stafford@staffs.ac.uk
www.staffs.ac.uk/support_depts/accommodation/

University of Stirling

Stirling continues to grow in popularity, with another 1,000 applications in 2014 taking the university to record levels. Still relatively small, with only 11,000 students, it has one of the most beautiful campuses in the UK, 330 acres of parkland around a loch at the foot of the Ochil Hills. Without Scottish government restrictions, it might be expanding more rapidly, but students appear to like the community feel and easy access to improved facilities. Stirling is particularly well provided with sports facilities, having been designated Scotland's University for Sporting Excellence. The campus is home to national swimming and tennis centres, as well as a golf course and a football academy. The sports centre was recently refurbished and now comprises of a central gym, two strength and conditioning areas with weightlifting platforms and a cycle studio. A new High Performance Sports Science and Sports Medicine Facility opened in 2012. The university runs an international sports scholarship programme and manages Winning Students, the national sport scholarship programme for students in colleges and universities across Scotland.

The university was awarded the maximum five stars in the QS global rating system, which covers teaching, graduate employability, internationalisation and inclusiveness. Academic facilities include a modernised library, a dedicated study zone and more than 700 computers for student use, many available 24 hours a day. The university also has a purpose-built faith centre/chaplaincy which is open to students and staff of all faiths. A joint venture with INTO University Partnerships has resulted in the establishment of teaching centres on the campus and in London to provide preparatory courses for international students. There are two other campuses: one for nurses and midwives in the modern Centre for Health Science, in Inverness, and a Western Isles campus, located in Stornoway, where the teaching accommodation is an integral part of the Western Isles Hospital.

Stirling was the British pioneer of the semester system, which has now become so popular throughout higher education. The academic year is divided into two blocks of 15 weeks with short mid-semester breaks. Students have the option of starting courses in February, rather than September, and can choose subjects from across all seven Schools. Degrees are built up of credits accumulated through modules taken and awarded each semester, rather than at the end of the academic year. Undergraduates can switch the whole direction of their studies, in consultation with their academic adviser, as their interests develop. They can also speed up their progress on a Summer

Stirling Campus
Stirling FK9 4LA

01786 467044 (admissions)
admissions@stir.ac.uk
www.stir.ac.uk
www.stirlingstudentsunion.com
Affiliation: none

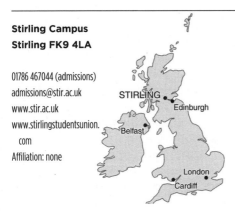

***The Times and Sunday Times* Rankings**

Overall Ranking: **50** (last year: 53)

Teaching quality:	**=94**	78.7%
Student experience:	**=89**	82.3%
Research quality:	**42**	30.5%
Entry standards:	**42**	375
Student–staff ratio:	**39**	15
Services & facilities/student:	**=74**	£1,665
Expected completion rate:	**=71**	85.7%
Good honours:	**72**	67.9%
Graduate prospects:	**=47**	73.3%

Academic Programme, which squeezes a full semester's teaching into July and August. Full-time students are not allowed to use the programme to reduce the length of their course, but part-timers can use it to make rapid progress.

The intake is surprisingly diverse, with nearly 95 per cent of undergraduates state-educated, with almost 30 per cent coming from the four poorest socio-economic groups. Two-thirds of the students are from Scotland, but the remainder come from more than 100 different countries. International exchanges are common, with many of Stirling's students going to American, Asian and European universities each year, while 175 Study Abroad or exchange students come in the opposite direction.

The university has nominated five "core areas" for teaching and research: health and well-being, culture and society, environment, enterprise and economy, and sport. Almost three-quarters of the work submitted to the 2014 Research Excellence Framework was judged to be world-leading or internationally excellent. The best results were in agriculture, veterinary and food science, where Stirling was ranked fourth in the UK. It was also top in Scotland for health sciences and third for psychology.

The first two phases of a £38-million expansion of student accommodation were completed in 2014, with the third phase due to be ready by the end of 2015. Students appreciate the individual attention that a small campus university can offer, although some find the atmosphere claustrophobic. Stirling is not the top choice of night-clubbers, but the students' union won "Best Bar None" status for three years in a row and there is a lively social scene. The MacRobert Arts Centre offers a full programme of cultural activities, while the surrounding countryside offers its own attractions for walkers and climbers. The campus has been described by police as one of the safest in Britain and last year launched the Safe Taxi Scheme. A counselling and wellbeing service offers support for mental and emotional health, while the disability service supports a full range of student needs.

Undergraduate Fees and Bursaries

- » Fees for Scottish and EU students 2015–16 No fee
- » Fees for Non-Scottish UK (RUK) students 2015–16 £6,750
- » Fees for international students 2015–16 £11,275–£13,425
- » For RUK students with at least ABB in one sitting at A Level or equivalent, 'Merit' bursary of £1,000–£2,000 a year.
- » A range of sports scholarships for all students.
- » Check the university's website for the latest information.

Students

Undergraduates:	**6,890**	**(785)**
Postgraduates:	**2,170**	**(1,245)**
Mature students:	**27.7%**	
International students:	**11.1%**	
Applications per place:	**7.5**	
From state-sector schools:	**94.6%**	
From working-class homes:	**29.3%**	
Satisfaction with students' union	**59%**	

For detailed information about sports facilities:
www.stir.ac.uk/sport-at-stirling/

Accommodation

Number of places and costs refer to 2015–16
University-provided places: 2,800
Percentage catered: 0%
Self-catered costs: £85–£137 a week; £155 (studio flat) for 37–50 weeks.
All first years are guaranteed suitable housing arranged by the university.
International students: as above.
accommodation@stir.ac.uk
www.stir.ac.uk/campus-life/accommodation/

University of Strathclyde

At 25,000 square metres – the equivalent of 100 tennis courts – Strathclyde's new £89-million Technology and Innovation Centre is the largest in the UK and the embodiment of the mission the university has had since 1796: to be a "place of useful learning". More specifically, it is aiming to be one of the world's leading technological universities. Professor Sir Jim McDonald, the Vice-Chancellor, has been seeking improvements in research to achieve this goal, and spectacular results in the 2014 Research Excellence Framework (REF) showed that he had got them. Strathclyde is close to the top 20 in our research ranking, with almost 80 per cent of an exceptionally large submission rated world-leading or internationally excellent. The university was top in the UK for physics and top in Scotland for business, among a clutch of eye-catching performances which are sure to attract more leading companies to the new centre, where academic and industrial researchers mix. Strathclyde, which attracted external research funding of more than £50-million in 2013–14, has also been chosen as the European partner for South Korea's global research and commercialisation programme and as the UK headquarters of Fraunhofer Gesellschaft, Europe's largest contract research organisation.

The university is the third largest in Scotland with more than 20,000 students, and has seen 17 per cent growth in the volume of applications in the last two years. They are attracted by the university's promise of courses that are both innovative and relevant to employers' needs – hence product design and innovation, energy systems or international business with modern languages. The approach pays dividends in terms of graduate prospects. Mature students account for one sixth of the undergraduate population. The university has endorsed an international movement to establish "Age-Friendly" universities; its Learning in Later Life programme has established itself as one of Scotland's most successful routes to education for older people. Strathclyde actively promotes wider access, comfortably exceeding the UK average for state-educated students. The projected dropout rate of 6 per cent is lower than average for the university's subjects and entry qualifications.

The business school, which is rated among the top 40 in Europe by *The Financial Times*, is normally considered Strathclyde's greatest strength. It is among the largest in Europe and one of only 55 in the world to be "triple accredited" by the main international bodies. The school has opened its own Indian branch campus near Delhi, while the university's research partners include Stanford, the

16 Richmond Street
Glasgow G1 1XQ

0141 548 2913
ugenquiries@strath.ac.uk
www.strath.ac.uk
www.strathstudents.com
Affiliation: none

***The Times and Sunday Times* Rankings**

Overall Ranking: **46** (last year: 39)

Teaching quality:	**115**	76.2%
Student experience:	**=35**	85.6%
Research quality:	**=21**	37.7%
Entry standards:	**12**	476
Student–staff ratio:	**=98**	19.3
Services & facilities/student:	**54**	£1,872
Expected completion rate:	**=52**	87.6%
Good honours:	**29**	77.9%
Graduate prospects:	**51**	72%

Massachusetts Institute of Technology and Tsinghua University in Beijing. The engineering faculty is the largest in Scotland, and home to the biggest university electrical power engineering and energy research grouping in Europe. Strathclyde Enterprise Pathway allows students to develop, enhance and test their transferable skills, while alumni and businesses in the Strathclyde 100 network support the university's emerging entrepreneurs. Spin-out companies established at the university employ more than 800 people, making annual sales of £800-million. Only four universities in the UK have launched more spin-outs in the last ten years.

Strathclyde, which now adds Glasgow to its name, has been carrying out an ambitious £350-million development programme. All courses are taught on the city-centre John Anderson campus, with the Faculty of Humanities and Social Sciences at its heart, enabling staff to work more closely with colleagues in research and teaching. The developments feature new and improved teaching areas, study space and facilities for students tailored to their specific subjects. A Confucius Institute, which opened in 2012, supports the teaching of Chinese language in Scotland. Away from the campus, the Advanced Forming Research Centre, a research partnership with international engineering firms, has opened near Glasgow Airport.

There is a student village on the main campus with 1,400 rooms and around 500 residential places are nearby in the Merchant City. The ten-floor union building attracts students from all over Glasgow. There are numerous cultural and political clubs and societies, plus over 40 sporting clubs and university teams. Proximity to Glasgow's vibrant and celebrated music scene is a plus, and for those with more sophisticated tastes, there are numerous theatres and arts organisations, as well as standout museums such as the Kelvingrove Gallery, one of Scotland's top attractions. On the sporting side, Strathclyde was the only training venue in Scotland for the London 2012 Olympics, and the university's students and alumni made up 5 per cent of Team Scotland in the Commonwealth Games, when the campus formed part of the cycling road race route.

Undergraduate Fees and Bursaries

- Fees for Scottish and EU students 2015–16 — No fee
- Fees for Non-Scottish UK (RUK) students 2015–16 — £9,000 a year capped at £27,000 for most courses.
- Fees for international students 2015–16 — £12,200–£17,700
- For RUK students, annual bursaries for household income below £20K, £4,250; household income to £42.6K, sliding scale, £2,500–£1,000; year 1 bursary of £1,000 for those in university accommodation; those with at least AAB at A level or equivalent, bursary of £1,000 a year.

Students

Undergraduates:	**11,765**	**(2,275)**
Postgraduates:	**3,465**	**(2,455)**
Mature students:	**15.6%**	
International students:	**12.8%**	
Applications per place:	**6.4**	
From state-sector schools:	**91.6%**	
From working-class homes:	**25.2%**	
Satisfaction with students' union	**75%**	

For detailed information about sports facilities: www.strath.ac.uk/sport

Accommodation

Number of places and costs refer to 2015–16
University-provided places: 1,840
Percentage catered: 0%
Self-catered costs: £97–£129 a week (39 weeks).
First years are offered accommodation if they live further than 25 miles from the university.
International students: as above.
student.accommodation@strath.ac.uk
www.strath.ac.uk/accommodation/

University of Sunderland

Sunderland will have the lowest average fees at any university in England in 2016–17, once all forms of financial support are taken into account. But even it is having to charge the maximum £9,000 for laboratory-based science degrees for the first time. Other degrees will cost £8,750, with foundation degrees priced at £7,500.

The university believes that its students are particularly price-sensitive since almost two-thirds of them have a household income of less than £25,000 a year. Surveys of first-year students found that 38 per cent of them had been influenced in their choice of university by Sunderland's generous package of support, which includes £600 towards public transport costs or university rents, as well as a Sunderland Scholarship of £1,000 in their first two years if they are among the 86 per cent whose household income is less than £42,000. Sunderland sees transport costs as a key barrier to study, especially in its local communities, which are the lifeblood of the university. More than 27 per cent of the undergraduates come from areas of low participation – the highest proportion at any university – while 45 per cent are from working-class homes. A pioneering access scheme offers places to mature students without A levels, as long as they reach the required levels of literacy, numeracy and other basic skills. There are also 89 postgraduate scholarships of £10,000 each for people from under-represented groups.

The university now has three campuses, two in Sunderland and one in London, near Canary Wharf, which offers business, tourism and nursing degrees, as well as postgraduate programmes. Within Sunderland, the university has spent £130 million on its original campus in the city centre and an award-winning 24-acre site on the banks of the River Wear. The Sir Tom Cowie Campus, at St Peter's, is built around a 7th-century abbey described as one of Britain's first universities and incorporates the National Glass Centre, a heritage centre for the glass industry and exhibition space. It houses the business school and the faculties of applied sciences, law, and arts, design and media. A glass and ceramics design degree maintains a Sunderland tradition, while teaching and research in automotive design and manufacture serve the region's modern industrial base. The large pharmacy department is another strength and the well-equipped Faculty of Applied Sciences is one of the largest in the UK, with over 4,000 students.

The £12-million CitySpace has improved the sports and social facilities on the original City Campus and there is a new Sciences Complex and Quad, as well as the Northern Centre for Photography. There

City Campus
Chester Road
Sunderland SR1 3SD

0191 515 3000 (course helpline)
student.helpline@sunderland.ac.uk
www.sunderland.ac.uk
www.sunderlandsu.co.uk
Affiliation: million+

The Times and Sunday Times **Rankings**

Overall Ranking: **104** (last year: 99)

Teaching quality:	**=39**	82.5%
Student experience:	**=56**	84.2%
Research quality:	**=82**	5.8%
Entry standards:	**104**	294
Student–staff ratio:	**=103**	19.6
Services & facilities/student:	**=93**	£1,484
Expected completion rate:	**105**	81.4%
Good honours:	**127**	49.5%
Graduate prospects:	**93**	62.3%

is a £12-million student village and a one-stop-shop for student services, an outdoor performance area and a design centre. Provision for disabled students is excellent, with award-winning information issued to those with disabilities, trained support staff in the libraries and in every academic school, and special modules to help dyslexics. The main campus also houses the North East Regional Assessment Centre, which assesses the requirements of students with disabilities and specific learning difficulties. There is special provision at the five halls of residence.

Sunderland now has more than 16,000 students, including 2,000 from outside the European Union. Many take work placements with the multinational companies that have been attracted to the North East and now have links with the university. The Institute for Automotive and Manufacturing Advanced Practice has a team of 40 researchers and consultants working with local businesses, while nearby Nissan played an important role in designing a course in automotive product development. The media centre provides students with excellent television and video production facilities. The popular media courses now include magazine, fashion and sports journalism. The LLB degree includes space law, the first module of its kind in the UK. Less than a third of the work submitted for the 2014 Research Excellence Framework reached the top two categories, but the university entered almost 40 per cent of the eligible academics, a much higher proportion than most of its peers. There was some world-leading research in 10 of the 13 subjects in which it submitted work.

Sunderland itself is fiercely proud of its identity and has the advantage of a riverside and coastal location. The leisure facilities are better than one might imagine: the city has the North East's only 50-metre swimming pool and dry ski slope, as well as Europe's biggest climbing wall and a theatre showing West End productions. The attractions of Newcastle are less than half an hour away by Metro.

Undergraduate Fees and Bursaries

- Fees for UK/EU students 2016–17 £8,750–£9,000
  Foundation degree at partner colleges £7,500
- Fees for international students 2015–16 £10,000
- For all first-year students, £600 towards local transport costs or campus accommodation.
- Household income below £42.6K, 750 scholarships of £1,000 in years 1 and 2.
- Fee waiver of £1,200 a year for students on Foundation degrees at partner colleges; £500 fee waiver for those who progress to honours degree.
- Enhanced retention and employability schemes.
- Check the university's website for the latest information.

Students

Undergraduates:	**10,560**	**(1,695)**
Postgraduates:	**2,945**	**(820)**
Mature students:	**24.8%**	
International students:	**31.3%**	
Applications per place:	**5.1**	
From state-sector schools:	**97.7%**	
From working-class homes:	**44.8%**	
Satisfaction with students' union	**63%**	

For detailed information about sports facilities:
www.unisportsunderland.com

Number of places and costs refer to 2015–16
University provided places: 1,547 beds in Halls, 548 (The Forge).
Percentage catered: 0%
Self-catered costs: £75.48 (standard room) a week for 40 weeks – £93.84 a week (en suite) for 50 weeks. Option to purchase catering vouchers.
New first years are guaranteed accommodation in accordance with the university's allocation policy.
International students: as above.
http://services.sunderland.ac.uk/facilities/residentialservices/

University of Surrey

Surrey has reached our top ten for the first time, and has been chosen as University of the Year, following two years in which both applications and enrolments have practically doubled while entry standards have continued to rise. The university has been among the most innovative in the UK in recent years, reducing its dependence on state funding even before the introduction of £9,000 fees, developing and extending the campus in Guildford, and launching a joint venture in China. Student satisfaction rates have improved by leaps and bounds, while Surrey's long record of success in graduate employment has also continued. Only its performance in the 2014 Research Excellence Framework (REF) prevented the university from making more progress. Although almost 80 per cent of its work was rated as world-leading or internationally excellent, Surrey slipped slightly on this measure. The best results were in nursing and other health subjects.

The new £45-million veterinary school opens in autumn 2015. Only the second to be established in half a century, it has world-class clinical skills centres, a pathology facility and teaching, research and diagnostic laboratories. It is the latest development in a £400-million programme of campus improvements since 2000. Many of the buildings date from the late 1960s, but the refurbished and extended library and learning centre, and the gleaming Duke of Kent Building, which houses the growing health and medical provision, offer a striking contrast. The campus, ten minutes' walk from the centre of Guildford, includes two lakes, playing fields and enough residential accommodation to enable all first years to live in.

Surrey received the maximum five stars in the QS global rating of universities, which covers facilities, teaching, research, inclusiveness and internationalisation. All students are encouraged to take a free course in a European language alongside their degree, in a programme known as the Global Graduate Award. The university has one of the largest proportions of overseas students at any institution – more than a fifth – and over half of its research publications have an international partner. It is a founding member of the University Global Partnership Network (UGPN), involving North Carolina State University and the Universidad de Sao Paulo in Brazil. There are over 100 strategic partnerships across the globe, but the biggest development has seen the opening of a campus in Dalian, China with the Dongbei University of Finance and Economics.

Surrey has remained true to its roots as a former College of Advanced Technology, with large numbers taking engineering

Guildford
Surrey GU2 7XH

0800 980 3200 (course enquiries)
ug-enquiries@surrey.ac.uk
www.surrey.ac.uk
www.ussu.co.uk
Affiliation: none

The Times and Sunday Times **Rankings**

Overall Ranking: **8** (last year: 11)

Teaching quality:	**4**	86.9%
Student experience:	**1**	90.3%
Research quality:	**44**	29.7%
Entry standards:	**=25**	424
Student-staff ratio:	**=22**	13.7
Services & facilities/student:	**17**	£2,487
Expected completion rate:	**31**	92.2%
Good honours:	**25**	78.9%
Graduate prospects:	**=26**	78.8%

and science subjects. An international consortium has pledged £58-million to support a 5G Innovation Centre that will be home to over 150 researchers and 100 doctoral students. The proportion of research income coming from private business and industry has grown to about 70 per cent. BP sponsored the new Centre for Petroleum and Surface Chemistry, for example. The Surrey Research Park is one of the largest in the UK still to be owned, funded and managed by its host university. Electronic engineering was one of 12 university departments in any subject to be awarded a Regius professorship as part of the Queen's Diamond Jubilee. But the university has other strengths, notably in business and the sector-leading School of Hospitality and Tourism Management. It has also incorporated the Guildford School of Acting and opened the £4.5-million Ivy Arts Centre, with a 200-seat theatre and workshops.

SurreyLearn, the virtual learning environment, allows students to work with others on their courses online and to take part in discussions and blogs, as well as allowing lecturers to set coursework and interact with students. Undergraduates in most subjects undertake work placements of one year, or several shorter periods, often abroad. As a result, most degrees last four years. The dropout rate of less than 6 per cent is better than expected for a university with Surrey's subject and student mix, as is the 31 per cent share of places going to undergraduates from the four poorest socio-economic groups.

The Manor Park Campus, which is effectively an extension of the university's Stag Hill headquarters, provides over 1,800 residential places for students and staff, as well as a reception building with café, bar and lounge areas. The £36-million Surrey Sports Park has extensive indoor and outdoor facilities. The main campus is the centre of social life, and has new leisure facilities, including upgraded dining and social areas. Guildford has plenty of retail, cultural and recreational facilities and the proximity of London (35 minutes by train) is an attraction to many students, although it also helps account for the high cost of living.

Undergraduate Fees and Bursaries

- Fees for UK/EU students 2016–17 — £9,000
- Fees for international students 2015–16 — £13,300–£17,100
  Veterinary medicine — £24,500
- Household income below £25K and from disadvantaged area, £3,000 as campus accommodation discount (or cash if living off campus) in year 1; £3,000 cash in other years.
- Scholarship of £2,000 cash in year 1 on specified courses for those with A*AA at A level or equivalent.
- Sports and other scholarships available.
- Check the university's website for the latest information.

Students

Undergraduates:	**8,985**	**(1,050)**
Postgraduates:	**2,540**	**(1,490)**
Mature students:	**12%**	
International students:	**23.1%**	
Applications per place:	**10**	
From state-sector schools:	**92.7%**	
From working-class homes:	**31.3%**	
Satisfaction with students' union	**79%**	

For detailed information about sports facilities:
www.surreysportspark.co.uk

Accommodation

Number of places and costs refer to 2015–16
University-provided places: 5,063
Percentage catered: 0%
Self-catered costs: £69–£160 a week.
All first years are guaranteed a place if they apply by the deadline. International non-EU students are guaranteed accommodation for the standard duration of their course. Remaining places are allocated to final year students.
www.surrey.ac.uk/accommodation

University of Sussex

There will be more places available at Sussex in 2016 than at any time in its history. The university is planning to increase its undergraduate intake by 50 per cent by 2018, but added only 50 places last year. The aim is to provide opportunities for a more diverse range of students and achieve the "critical mass" that Sussex considers necessary to develop the interdisciplinary approach that has been its hallmark since the 1960s, engage with partners and be internationally competitive in research. Three quarters of the work submitted to the 2014 was judged to be world-leading or internationally excellent, but this was not enough to maintain the university's position in the top 20 on this measure. Nevertheless, it was among the leaders in history, English, psychology and geography.

The campus, four miles from the centre of Brighton in the suburb of Falmer, is already serving a record number of students: 13,800 students, of whom 10,000 are undergraduates. The university has completed a £100-million campus development plan, refurbishing Sir Basil Spence's original buildings and adding new ones. The most recent addition is a £29-million academic building offering a mix of lecture theatres, study and teaching space, and a social centre. The former Gardner Arts Centre will be brought back to life during the coming academic year as an interdisciplinary arts hub for the university and the wider community, and has been renamed after the university's former Chancellor, the former actor and film director Richard Attenborough. The library, which has undergone a £6-million redevelopment and introduced 24-hour opening during term time, has seen a 50 per cent increase in use. An investment of £1.5 million in IT developments has doubled the number of computers available to students and installed Wi-Fi in all the student residences.

Arts and social science students take the biggest share of places, but the physical and life sciences are not far behind. Undergraduates are encouraged to study outside their core area. Sussex reviewed its courses since the switch to higher fees and converted to the semester system. The university believes that two 12-week teaching periods with a mid-year assessment period improves the way students learn and are assessed. Student support includes a work-study programme to help students earn money, funded work placements and three years' aftercare for graduates to help them into a career. The Sussex Plus programme documents and credits students' extra-curricular skills, while a new initiative, Startup Sussex, supports students' creative business ideas and social projects.

Sussex House
Brighton BN1 9RH

01273 876787 (enquiries)
ug.enquiries@sussex.ac.uk
www.sussex.ac.uk
www.bsms.ac.uk
www.sussexstudent.com
Affiliation: none

***The Times and Sunday Times* Rankings**

Overall Ranking: **19** (last year: 25)

Teaching quality:	**=97**	78.6%
Student experience:	**=43**	85%
Research quality:	**=37**	31.8%
Entry standards:	**=37**	386
Student–staff ratio:	**=46**	15.5
Services & facilities/student:	**8**	£2,618
Expected completion rate:	**=22**	92.9%
Good honours:	**27**	78.6%
Graduate prospects:	**9**	84.1%

Although little more than 50 years old, the university can count three Nobel prize winners amongst its alumni. The first fruits of a £50-million fundraising campaign have seen the opening of major research centres on adoption, corruption, Middle East studies and consciousness science. Dedicated student social space is being created in each of the university's 12 schools to encourage staff and students to engage both academically and socially. Relations with neighbouring Brighton University are good. The two institutions operate a joint medical school, which is split between the Royal Sussex County Hospital and the two universities' Falmer campuses.

Sussex is committed to taking candidates with no family tradition of higher education and has a dedicated scheme to support them. The proportion of entrants from state schools is higher than the national average for the university's subjects and entry qualifications, but the share of places going to students from the four poorest socio-economic groups is still lower than expected. Sussex has always attracted overseas students in large numbers and has seen big increases recently. The university has performed consistently well in the International Student Barometer, which gauges overseas students' satisfaction. Together with other first years, they are guaranteed a place in university-managed accommodation that has been expanded and upgraded in recent years. There are now more than 5,000 residential places, and Sussex's plans for the future include a major housing development to replace old accommodation, as well as the construction of a new biomedical sciences building to complement the highly rated Genome Research Centre.

The campus is located within the newly created South Downs National Park, with excellent transport links into town. There is no shortage of social events on campus and Brighton has plenty to offer. Sports facilities were good enough to house pre-Olympic training. Sports scholarships are available to outstanding athletes, including four reserved for basketball and hockey players. Sussex has also opened a purpose-built childcare facility for 100 pre-school children of students and staff.

Undergraduate Fees and Bursaries

- Fees for UK/EU students 2016–17 £9,000
- Fees for international students 2015–16 £14,450–£17,850
  Medicine £27,450
- Students with household income below £42.6K, a £2,000 university accommodation discount (or £2,000 fee waiver) and £1,000 cash in year 1 and Foundation year; £1,000 cash subsequent years (£3,000 cash in study year abroad); enhanced study skills and employability schemes for award recipients.
- Sports and other scholarships available.
- Check the university's website for the latest information.

Students

Undergraduates:	**10,135**	**(10)**
Postgraduates:	**2,660**	**(830)**
Mature students:	**14.2%**	
International students:	**25.7%**	
Applications per place:	**5.7**	
From state-sector schools:	**87%**	
From working-class homes:	**24.2%**	
Satisfaction with students' union	**73%**	

For detailed information about sports facilities:
www.sussex.ac.uk/sport/

Accommodation

Number of places and costs refer to 2015–16
University-provided places: 5,004
Percentage catered: 0%
Self-catered costs: £83.20–£147.00 (single) a week. Some shared rooms available.
First-year students are guaranteed accommodation if conditions are met.
International students: first-year students as above.
housing@sussex.ac.uk
www.sussex.ac.uk/residentialservices

Swansea University

The UK's only university campus with direct access to a beach opens in autumn 2015. The £450-million, 65-acre Bay Campus will be home to the College of Engineering and School of Management, and house 1,445 students in new halls of residence, relieving the pressure on the smallest main site at any pre-1992 university. Its focus will be on applied research with industry – the new Engineering Quarter will house two research institutes, where there will be collaborations with Rolls Royce, Tata Steel and BP in materials testing and energy safety. But the project will also free up space on the original Singleton Park Campus – itself not far from the sea. Applications have risen by more than 50 per cent in two years and the university has added 1,300 to its intake of undergraduates, reaching record levels, so the extra space will be welcome.

Swansea was the UK's first campus university when it opened in 1920, enjoying a prime position at the gateway to the Gower peninsula, which was subsequently declared the UK's first Area of Outstanding Natural Beauty. Some £72 million has been invested in the 47-acre main campus since 2010 and a programme of refurbishment is planned over the next few years. Recent developments have seen the opening of a £1.2-million facility in the university library for the Richard Burton archives. Other additions have included the £4.3-million Digital Technium Building for engineering and a second Institute of Life Science building with a Centre for NanoHealth based within it. The Institute of Life Science is home to Blue C, one of the few supercomputers in the world dedicated to life science research. The medical school celebrated its tenth anniversary in 2014 and is one of the fastest-growing in the UK.

The university is now well established in our top 50, scoring highly on graduate prospects. The Employability Academy provides paid internships and coordinates a variety of career support activities. Four-fifths of the work submitted for the 2014 Research Excellence Framework was assessed as world-leading or internationally excellent, with health subjects, English and general engineering doing particularly well. Undergraduates are encouraged to stray outside their specialist area in their first year. There is good provision for disabled students, whose needs are addressed through a £250,000 assessment and training centre. The student services team was judged the best in the UK in 2013, with those in admissions winning a similar accolade in 2014. Nine out of ten undergraduates come from state schools and colleges, but the 27 per cent share of places going to students from working-class homes is less that the UK average for the university's subjects and

Singleton Park
Swansea SA2 8PP

01792 295111 (enquiries)
admissions@swansea.ac.uk
www.swansea.ac.uk
www.swansea-union.co.uk
Affiliation: none

***The Times and Sunday Times* Rankings**

Overall Ranking: =**41** (last year: 43)

Teaching quality:	**=35**	82.6%
Student experience:	**=25**	86.5%
Research quality:	**35**	33.7%
Entry standards:	**65**	326
Student–staff ratio:	**=42**	15.3
Services & facilities/student:	**59**	£1,787
Expected completion rate:	**45**	89.7%
Good honours:	**46**	74.4%
Graduate prospects:	**16**	81.4%

entry grades. The projected dropout rate of nearly 7 per cent, by contrast, is significantly better than Swansea's benchmark figure.

Swansea has links to more than 100 partner institutions worldwide and offers many degrees that include opportunities to study abroad. The university's medium-term target is to be recognised among the top 200 universities in the world. Although it is still some way off that objective, it has been awarded the maximum five stars in QS's global rating system, which covers facilities, teaching, research and employability, as well as inclusiveness and internationalisation. The department of adult and continuing education teaches mature students throughout the Valleys and elsewhere in South Wales, while the South West Wales Reaching Wider Partnership encourages students who would not usually aspire to attend university, to consider higher education.

Even before the opening of the new campus, the 1,900 computers available for student use represented one of the best ratios at any university. The opening of two new halls of residence has taken the total number of residential places to about 3,500. The £20-million International Sports Village hosted the IPC Athletics European Championships in 2014. Facilities include an athletics track, grass and all-weather pitches, squash and tennis courts plus the indoor athletics training centre and 80-station gym. The adjacent Wales National Pool has a 50-metre and a 25-metre pool and is the Welsh National Performance Centre. The 360 Beach and Water Sports Centre is the only University-operated centre of its kind. At Fairwood, five miles away, the university also has grass and 3G pitches, built in partnership with Swansea City Football Club.

The Bay Campus has a sports hall plus two smaller gyms, but the Singleton Park Campus will remain the focal point of most students' leisure activities. The city has a good range of leisure facilities and Cardiff is less than an hour away by train for those looking for a change of scene.

Undergraduate Fees and Bursaries

- » Fees for UK/EU students 2016–17 £9,000
- » Welsh Assembly non-means-tested grant (2015–16) to pay fees above £3,810 for Welsh students.
- » Fees for international students 2015–16 £12,500–£15,500
- » For those with household income below £15K, a bursary of £500 year 1, £1,250 years 2 and 3; £15K–£25K, £500 year 1, £750 years 2 and 3; £25K–£30K, £500 years 1 and 2 only.
- » Award of £1,000 a year for those with AAA at A level or equivalent; £670 a year for AAB or equivalent.
- » Sports scholarships and care leaver's bursaries available.
- » Check the university's website for the latest information.

Students

Undergraduates:	**10,595**	**(1,810)**
Postgraduates:	**1,655**	**(760)**
Mature students:	**16.2%**	
International students:	**13.9%**	
Applications per place:	**5.7**	
From state-sector schools:	**90.7%**	
From working-class homes:	**26.9%**	
Satisfaction with students' union	**75%**	

For detailed information about sports facilities:
www.swansea.ac.uk/sport/

Accommodation

Number of places and costs refer to 2015–16
University-provided places: about 3,500
Percentage catered: 5%
Catered costs: £90.50 a week (40 weeks).
Self-catered costs: £82–£177 a week (40–51 weeks).
First-year students holding a firm offer are guaranteed accommodation if conditions are met.
International students: offered up to 3 years.
accommodation@swansea.ac.uk
www.swansea.ac.uk/accommodation

Teesside University

Teesside has launched more than 60 new courses for the 2015 academic year in niche areas such as contemporary fashion, aerospace engineering and digital storytelling. The expansion is part of an academic strategy that commits the university to delivering innovative curricula and "transformative educational experiences". Teesside was the first former polytechnic to win *Times Higher Education* magazine's University of the Year award and also has a Queen's Anniversary Prize for its services to business and enterprise. The university is equally well known for its commitment to widening access to higher education, however. The 2015 academic year is the first in which it has charged £9,000 for degree courses, and even in 2016 the fees for Foundation degrees will be held at £6,000 and there will be no fees for students on work placement or years abroad.

Teesside is in the top ten for the proportion of UK undergraduates coming from working-class homes – over 48 per cent – and the 28 per cent share of places going to students from areas of low participation in higher education is twice the national average for Teesside's courses and entry qualifications. The 2015 "Kickstart awards" give new students £500 towards their accommodation costs, travel or other living expenses. The projected dropout rate continues to improve and is now well ahead of the university's benchmark, at less than 10 per cent.

Some £250 million has been invested in the university in recent years. The new Campus Heart features a £20-million teaching building which opened in summer 2015, providing a mix of flexible modern teaching space and offices, freeing up space to further develop the recently refurbished library. There will be a new £2.5-million health and fitness centre, science and engineering facilities are being upgraded and there will be extensive landscaping. Other recent developments include a centre for creative technologies for computing, media and design, where specialist facilities include a new digital sound and TV studio. But the biggest project has been DigitalCity Innovation, the university's centre for digital excellence and entrepreneurship. Some 260 new businesses have been created by the new centre and by graduate enterprise.

Almost two-thirds of the 16,000 undergraduates are from the North East and around a third are 21 or over on entry. Enrolments have risen for three years in a row and scores in the National Student Survey has been improving. The students' union is rated among the top ten in the country and has a new-look bar, social learning space, a shop and postgraduate lounge. Five further education colleges in

Middlesbrough TS1 3BA

01642 218121 (switchboard)
enquiries@tees.ac.uk
www.tees.ac.uk
www.tees-su.org.uk
Affiliation: University Alliance

***The Times and Sunday Times* Rankings**

Overall Ranking: **102** (last year: 94)

Teaching quality:	**=28**	82.9%
Student experience:	**55**	84.3%
Research quality:	**109**	3.6%
Entry standards:	**=94**	306
Student–staff ratio:	**=75**	17.7
Services & facilities/student:	**72**	£1,676
Expected completion rate:	**107**	80.8%
Good honours:	**113**	59.3%
Graduate prospects:	**=104**	59.8%

the Tees Valley each have a centre offering the university's Foundation degrees and other courses, and the university has a £13-million campus in Darlington with a focus on business services, professional education and training support. The Forge, the university's new business engagement hub, is based there.

Only 14 per cent of Teesside's eligible academics were entered for the 2014 Research Excellence Framework, but almost 60 per cent of their work was considered world-leading or internationally excellent – twice as much as in the previous research assessments. Social work and social policy, history and health subjects produced the best results. Five research-led institutes focus on digital innovation, health, culture, social science and technology. The 11,000 health students are by far the largest group in the university. Design and computer animation and gaming are general regarded as the other main strengths. The university supports the career development of its graduates for a minimum of two years after graduation and is expanding paid work placements as part of a student's course. The Get Ahead scheme provides three-month paid internships and training for graduates, as well as helping to provide summer placements for second-year students.

Teesside's main campus is at the heart of Middlesbrough town centre, with shops, bars, cafés and restaurants on the doorstep. The internationally renowned contemporary art gallery and member of the Plus Tate Network, mima, is now part of the university, which has also purchased the former Teesside Central Building, near the campus, to add to its stock of student accommodation. Beyond Middlesbrough there is a beautiful coastal fringe and the North York Moors are nearby. The cost of living is another attraction: both university rents and those in the private sector are amongst the cheapest in the UK. Sports facilities include a newly refurbished gym on campus and a water sports centre on the River Tees. The university supports elite athletes with scholarships, coaching and access to the latest sport science techniques. A £17-million sport and health sciences building has a hydrotherapy pool among its facilities.

Undergraduate Fees and Bursaries

» Fees for UK/EU students 2016–17	£9,000
Year 4 of MEng degree	£4,500
Foundation degree	£6,000
Placement year / Year abroad	no fee
» Fees for international students 2015–16	£10,750

» Enhanced retention, employability and targeted support schemes.

» Range of scholarships available.

» Check the university's website for the latest information.

Students

Undergraduates:	9,285	(6,790)
Postgraduates:	700	(1,290)
Mature students:	35.8%	
International students:	6.4%	
Applications per place:	4.8	
From state-sector schools:	98.8%	
From working-class homes:	48.1%	
Satisfaction with students' union	84%	

For detailed information about sports facilities:
www.tees.ac.uk/sport

Accommodation

Number of places and costs refer to 2015–16
University-provided places: 1,193
Percentage catered: 0%
Self-catered costs: £57.45–£98.40 a week (40 weeks).
First years are guaranteed a place if conditions are met.
International students: guaranteed accommodation if conditions met.
accommodation@tees.ac.uk
www.tees.ac.uk/accommodation

Trinity Saint David, University of Wales

The University of Wales Trinity Saint David (UWTSD) is finalising plans for a £100-million campus on Swansea's waterfront that will be the centrepiece of the merged institution. Purpose-built teaching, learning, research and leisure facilities will be built around the Prince of Wales Dock, if planning permission is granted in autumn 2015. Core student services, including a students' union, a library, sports and leisure facilities should be ready for the final year of most undergraduates entering in 2016, and will sit alongside community and commercial amenities. The 19-acre campus will complement the university's existing £30-million investment in a Cultural Quarter for the city between the Dynevor Centre for Art, Design and Media and the soon-to-be-opened ALEX Design Exchange campus in the former Swansea Central Library.

Two mergers in three years created UWTSD, the second adding the former Swansea Metropolitan University. UWTSD does not appear in any of our league tables, having chosen not to release data, but it expects to return soon. Swansea Met boycotted league tables throughout its brief existence as an independent university, and the new institution felt that a partial assessment might mislead prospective students. The old Trinity Saint David finished just outside the bottom ten on its last appearance in the table and the new version was in the bottom ten for overall satisfaction in the 2015 National Student Survey. It would have been in the bottom five of our research ranking after the Research Excellence Framework, where only 12 per cent of the eligible academics were entered for assessment. The best results were in theology, where 65 per cent of the submission was rated as world-leading or internationally excellent, compared to 46 per cent for the university as a whole.

The university offers students the choice of a rural or urban experience – from the green campuses of Lampeter and Carmarthen to the urban surroundings of Swansea. UWTSD markets itself as both old and new since in the whole of England and Wales, only Oxford and Cambridge were awarding degrees before St David's College, Lampeter. The college went on to become the smallest publicly funded university in Europe before merging with Trinity University College, 23 miles away in Carmarthen, in 2010. The university also has a London campus, near the Oval cricket ground, for international students taking business, management and IT degrees. A group structure connects UWTSD with two large further education colleges in

UWTSD

Carmarthen SA31 3EP
01267 676767
Lampeter SA48 7ED
01570 422351
Swansea SA1 6ED
01792 481000
admissions@uwtsd.ac.uk
www.uwtsd.ac.uk
www.tsdsu.co.uk
Affiliation: Cathedrals Group

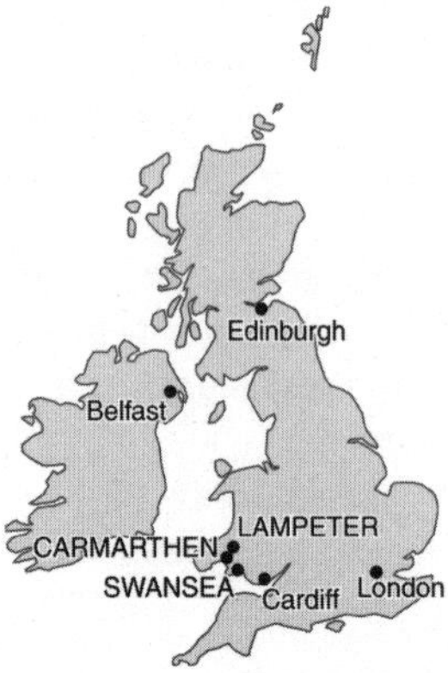

The Times and Sunday Times **Rankings**

University of Wales Trinity Saint David blocked the release of data from the Higher Education Statistics Agency and so we cannot give any ranking information.

southwest Wales, Coleg Ceredigion and Coleg Sir Gâr, in Carmarthenshire.

The UWTSD Lampeter Campus (formerly University of Wales, Lampeter) continues to make a virtue of its size by stressing its friendly atmosphere and intimate teaching style. It remains a small, rural community that suits students who seek a close-knit campus experience. Based on an ancient castle and modelled on an Oxbridge college, St David's College was established to provide a liberal arts education. The original quadrangle remains, but there have been significant changes in recent years, notably the introduction of such subjects as anthropology, archaeology, Chinese, classics and philosophy. A hub has opened for student services and the sports facilities have been extended, while Carmarthen has seen refurbishment of student accommodation and the opening of a new Centre for Learning and Teaching. The Carmarthen Campus was established in 1848. It has a long history of teacher training and has developed a reputation for education-related programmes including early childhood, social inclusion, and youth and community work. In addition, the university offers a range of programmes in the creative and performing arts, as well a growing portfolio within the School of Sport, Health and Outdoor Education, which makes use of the natural resources of west Wales.

The Swansea Campus began life as a college of art in 1853, subsequently joined by education and technical colleges. Based in the centre of Wales's second city, Swansea Met became a university only in 2008 and had expanded to about 6,000 students before becoming part of UWTSD in 2013. Its automotive engineering courses – especially those focused on motorsport – are its best-known feature, but there has been strong demand for places on a variety of vocationally oriented courses. The university surpasses all its benchmarks for widening participation in higher education, although the dropout rate is higher than average for its courses and entry qualifications. The university provides employability support that runs alongside academic programmes, with work placement schemes and internships to provide opportunities for students to build core skills to improve their career prospects.

Undergraduate Fees and Bursaries

- » Fees for UK/EU students 2016–17 £9,000
- » Welsh Assembly non-means-tested grant (2015–16) to pay fees above £3,810 for Welsh students.
- » Fees for international students 2015–16 £10,000
- » Household income below £18K and not receiving Welsh Tuition Fee Grant, bursary up to £1,000.
- » Scholarships and bursaries available, including residential bursaries of up to £400 and Welsh-medium scholarships up to £600.

Students

Undergraduates:	**6,590**	**(2,690)**
Postgraduates:	**1,270**	**(765)**
Satisfaction with students' union	**59%**	

For detailed information about sports facilities:
www.uwtsd.ac.uk/student-life/sport

Accommodation

Number of places and cost refer to 2015–16
L refers to Lampeter, CM to Carmarthen, S to Swansea
University-provided places: 623 (L), 631 (CM), 300 (S)
Percentage catered: 0% (L), 75% (CM); 0% (S)
Catered costs: £84.37–£105.37 (CM) a week (38 weeks).
Self-catered costs: £63.00–£87.92 (S & L) a week (38 weeks).
First years can normally be placed in university accommodation.
International students: guaranteed housing for first year.
www.uwtsd.ac.uk/accommodation

Ulster University

Ulster is having to cut 1,200 places over three years to cope with reductions in its Government grant. About 950 places will go in 2016 and 2017, and the university has already withdrawn some courses in film studies, history, computing and engineering from the 2015 prospectus. Although none of the four campuses is at risk, an internal review will select other courses for closure in 2016 on the basis of the demand for places, student satisfaction and their graduate employment record. The £8.6 million cut in funding has come at a time when the university was expanding: it had increased its intake of undergraduates by almost 1,000 in three years and applications were up again in 2014.

Only this April, Stephen Farry, the Employment and Learning Minister, approved an £11-million teaching block for the Magee campus in Derry-Londonderry to cater for the increased numbers there. Construction is due to start later this year and to take two years. The first phase of Ulster's £250-million campus in Belfast's Cathedral Quarter is scheduled to open this autumn, with two more blocks opposite the main campus building due to be completed by 2018. The development will allow the 12,450 students on the Jordanstown site – historically the main teaching centre – to transfer into the city. The High Performance Sports Centre, which houses the Sports Institute for Northern Ireland, will remain in Jordanstown. Some £20 million has been invested in the sports facilities there, including outdoor and indoor sprint tracks, sports science and sports medicine facilities, which will remain available to students.

The university, which features in *Times Higher Education* magazine's top 100 universities in the world that are under 50 years old, is the largest in Northern Ireland. Most students are from the Province and will pay £3,805 in 2015–16, when fees for students from other parts of the UK were £6,000. Fee levels for 2016–17 are likely to be hotly contested, given the cuts in grant.

Each campus has well-equipped library and computer facilities. Belfast concentrates on art and design, architecture and hospitality. Jordanstown, seven miles out of Belfast, will remain the location for courses starting in 2016 in business and management, the built environment, computing and engineering, health and sport sciences, and social sciences. The university's specialist engineering facilities will also stay on the campus, much of which will eventually be given over to housing shared between students and the local community.

The third campus, at Coleraine on Northern Ireland's north coast, focuses on environmental and life sciences, humanities, modern languages and tourism management.

Cromore Road
Coleraine
BT52 1SA
028 7012 3456
registryjn@ulster.ac.uk
(Jordanstown and Belfast)
registrycm@ulster.ac.uk
(Coleraine and Magee)
www.ulster.ac.uk
http://uusu.org
Affiliation: none

***The Times and Sunday Times* Rankings**

Overall Ranking: **57** (last year: 69)

Teaching quality:	**=28**	82.9%
Student experience:	**=18**	87%
Research quality:	**=37**	31.8%
Entry standards:	**=94**	306
Student–staff ratio:	**=53**	16.2
Services & facilities/student:	**69**	£1,710
Expected completion rate:	**=96**	82.3%
Good honours:	**=81**	66.5%
Graduate prospects:	**=84**	63.6%

The university has spent £15 million on new students' union and catering facilities, and a new teaching block. A Confucius Institute fosters academic, cultural, economic and social ties between the university and China. Coleraine is home to the £1.1-million Centre for Biosciences, whose academics produced the most highly rated work in the 2014 Research Excellence Framework. More than 70 per cent of the university's whole submission was considered world-leading or internationally excellent, with law and nursing and health science also producing outstanding results.

Magee has a focus on the creative and performing arts, nursing and social work, computing, business and management, and social sciences. The university has signed an agreement with the City Council to almost double its footprint in the city with growth in computer science, engineering and creative technologies. A £12-million Centre for Stratified Medicine has opened near the campus, at Altnagelvin Hospital. Ulster also has branch campuses in London and Birmingham, where it offers courses in business, computing and engineering in partnership with the QA Business School.

The university has a growing number of international students – about 1,800 from 80 different countries. The eLearning at Ulster programme provides an alternative mode of study, offering courses online to students all over the world. The university has committed itself to becoming the leading provider of "professional education for professional life". The majority of courses now include the option of a year-long work placement. The National Student Survey has been showing increased levels of satisfaction.

Nearly 100 per cent of undergraduates are from state schools and over 45 per cent come from working-class backgrounds. The university runs workshops in primary schools, as well as organising a range of activities to encourage secondary pupils to try a degree. Its award-winning sports outreach programme has been particularly successful. Accommodation is guaranteed for all first-years students on all four campuses and the students' union is also active at every location. The social life inevitably varies depending on location.

Undergraduate Fees and Bursaries

- Fees for NI/EU students 2015–16 £3,805
- Fees for English, Scottish and Welsh students £6,000
- Fees for international students 2015–16 £12,495
- For NI students with household income below £19.2K, bursary of £380.
- Range of scholarships available.
- Check the university's website for the latest information.

Students

Undergraduates:	**16,315**	**(4,020)**
Postgraduates:	**2,335**	**(3,530)**
Mature students:	**26%**	
International students:	**10.8%**	
Applications per place:	**6.3**	
From state-sector schools:	**99.9%**	
From working-class homes:	**45.8%**	
Satisfaction with students' union	**56%**	

For detailed information about sports facilities:
www.ulster.ac.uk/ulster-life/sport

Accommodation

Number of places and costs refer to 2015–16
University-provided places: 2,366 over three campuses.
Percentage catered: 0%
Self-catered costs: average £73.50 (standard) – £101 (en suite) a week (37 weeks).
First-year students are guaranteed accommodation if conditions are met.
International students: same as above.
accommodation@ulster.ac.uk
www.ulster.ac.uk/accommodation

University College London

UCL has the best staffing levels in the UK and is in our top five for research quality, yet it almost dropped out of the top ten this year. The reason is that, in common with many universities in the capital, it struggles in the National Student Survey. Indeed, only three institutions – all of them in London – have lower levels of satisfaction with the quality of teaching, feedback and support provided by academics. This certainly has not deterred applicants, however, as UCL has taken advantage of the relaxation of recruitment controls to take more undergraduates. Applications rose by more than 6 per cent in 2014, as UCL expanded for the third year in a row. The undergraduate intake was nearly 40 per cent bigger than in 2011. Already comfortably the largest of the University of London's colleges, it now has more than 36,000 students since the incorporation of the Institute of Education in December 2014.

Such was the quality and quantity of UCL's submission to the 2014 Research Excellence Framework that only Oxford will receive a higher research grant for the coming academic year. More than 90 per cent of the eligible academics were entered for assessment and over 80 per cent of their work was rated as world-leading or internationally excellent. UCL had the most world-leading research in medicine and the biological sciences, the largest volume of research in science, technology, engineering and maths, and the biggest share of top grades in the social sciences. It is among the top seven universities in the world in the QS rankings, which place more emphasis on research. Professor John O'Keefe's 2014 Nobel Prize in Physiology or Medicine brought the number of laureates associated with UCL to 29.

UCL has a history of pioneering subjects that have become commonplace in higher education: modern languages, geography and fine arts among them. Students are required to have a foreign language GCSE at grade C or above, although they are allowed to reach this standard during their degree if they have not taken a language at school. UCL is pioneering the idea of education for global citizenship, encouraging students to explore academic ideas from different cultural perspectives and to work on problems of international importance, as well as contributing to their local community and the university's social and cultural life. A quarter of all undergraduates spend part of their course at one of the 300 partner universities overseas.

All first-year students are helped to make the academic and social adjustment to university life through the Transition Programme, which includes peer mentoring and workshops. There is a commitment to

Gower Street
London WC1E 6BT

020 7679 3000 (enquiries)
study@ucl.ac.uk
www.ucl.ac.uk
http://uclu.org
Affiliation: Russell Group

***The Times and Sunday Times* Rankings**

Overall Ranking: **10** (last year: 9)

Teaching quality:	**124**	74.2%
Student experience:	**=101**	81.3%
Research quality:	**5**	51%
Entry standards:	**7**	502
Student–staff ratio:	**1**	10.3
Services & facilities/student:	**9**	£2,608
Expected completion rate:	**14**	94.6%
Good honours:	**4**	87.9%
Graduate prospects:	**=13**	83.1%

teaching in small groups, especially in the second and subsequent years of degree courses. UCL is conscious of its traditions as a college founded to expand access to higher education, and the share of places going to independent school students has been going down but, at almost 30 per cent, it remains among the highest in Britain. About one undergraduate in five is from a low-income family. Concerted attempts are being made to broaden the intake with summer schools, outreach activities and campus-based programmes.

The medical school, with 11 associated teaching hospitals, is a large and formidable unit. UCL will be a founding partner in the new Francis Crick Institute that will open early next year and undertake leading-edge research to advance understanding of health and disease. There is also an archaeology and conservation campus in Qatar. Nearer home, a new School of Management was established in summer 2015. It will open in Canary Wharf in 2016, expanding UCL's research and teaching in business and management, with a focus on innovation, technology management, analytics and entrepreneurship. The next major development will be the opening of a new campus in Stratford on the Queen Elizabeth Olympic Park in 2018. UCL East is envisaged as a radical new model of how a top university campus can be embedded in the local community.

The academic pace can be frantic but, close to the West End and with its own theatre and recreational facilities, there is no shortage of leisure options. Students also have access to the facilities (including rooftop swimming pool) of the student centre in the former University of London Union building in Bloomsbury. Residential accommodation is plentiful and of a good standard. Indoor sports and fitness facilities are close at hand, but the main outdoor pitches, though good enough to attract professional football clubs, are a (free) coach ride away in Hertfordshire.

Undergraduate Fees and Bursaries

- Fees for UK/EU students 2016–17 £9,000
- Fees for international students 2015–16 £15,660–£20,700
  Medicine £30,800
- For all UK/EU students with household income below £12K, a bursary of £2,000 a year; household income £12K–£25K, £1,500 a year; £25K–£37K, £1,000 a year; £37K–£42.6K, £500 a year.
- High-achieving students at London state schools, 20 awards of £4,000 a year.
- Range of departmental and academic scholarships.
- Check the university's website for the latest information.

Students

Undergraduates:	**14,625**	**(790)**
Postgraduates:	**9,750**	**(3,260)**
Mature students:	**6.2%**	
International students:	**36.5%**	
Applications per place:	**7.8**	
From state-sector schools:	**70.3%**	
From working-class homes:	**18.9%**	
Satisfaction with students' union	**62%**	

For detailed information about sports facilities:
http://uclu.org/services/sport

Accommodation

Number of places and costs refer to 2015–16
University provided spaces: 5,201 (including 542 intercollegiate places)
Percentage catered: 30%
Catered costs: £141.33–£209.79 a week (40 weeks).
Self-catered costs: £135.59 (single) – £217.77 (en-suite single) a week (40 weeks).
First years are guaranteed accommodation if conditions are met.
International students: as above.
www.ucl.ac.uk/prospective-students/accommodation

University of Warwick

Warwick, which was our University of the Year in 2014, may become the first UK university to open a campus in California. The university is considering an invitation from Placer County, in the north of the state, to establish a campus for up to 6,000 students in partnership with a non-profit-making trust. Warwick already has a base in Venice and a close partnership with Australia's Monash University. The business school opened a London base in the Shard in 2015, and the university has also agreed to establish a Centre for Urban Science and Progress in the capital in collaboration with New York University and King's College London. The most successful of the "plate glass" universities of the 1960s, Warwick has never been out of the top ten in our league table and is in the top 50 in the QS World University Rankings.

On the main campus, three miles south of Coventry, a £250-million investment programme is under way. A £20-million teaching and learning building, with 500- and 250-seat lecture theatres and innovative social learning spaces, should be completed in 2016. The first phase of a £30-million extension to Warwick Business School will open this year, making it one of the largest business schools in the UK. The university is also planning new interdisciplinary research labs, a humanities building, and improved facilities for a number of other subjects. In addition, Warwick is building the £150-million National Automotive Innovation Centre (NAIC) on its campus, where research engineers from car manufacturers will work closely with Warwick Manufacturing Group. NAIC is part-funded by Government as well as by Jaguar Land Rover and Tata Motors. The Centre will include the world's most adaptable driving simulator for research on driverless cars.

The university has reconfigured its research around its "Global Research Priorities" programme, which focuses on key areas of international significance. Current themes include energy, connecting cultures, food security, global governance, individual behaviour and innovative manufacturing. Almost 90 per cent of the work submitted for the 2014 Research Excellence Framework was rated as world-leading or internationally excellent, confirming Warwick's place among the top ten universities for research. English and computer science produced the best results, but Warwick ranked in the UK's top ten in 14 different subject areas. A new Cancer Research Unit is bringing together experts in maths, physics and engineering to research new treatments using digital technologies. The university has been awarded £14.5-million to establish an

Coventry CV4 7AL

024 7652 3723 (admissions)
ugadmissions@warwick.ac.uk
www.warwick.ac.uk
www.warwicksu.com
Affiliation: Russell Group

***The Times and Sunday Times* Rankings**

Overall Ranking: **6** (last year: 8)

Teaching quality:	**83**	79.6%
Student experience:	**=43**	85%
Research quality:	**8**	44.6%
Entry standards:	**10**	482
Student–staff ratio:	**16**	12.6
Services & facilities/student:	**16**	£2,505
Expected completion rate:	**2**	96.7%
Good honours:	**14**	82.3%
Graduate prospects:	**=20**	79.8%

Advanced Steel Research Centre and is one of six Midlands universities sharing £60 million for new energy research.

The university's mission statement also stresses community links and the extension of access to higher and continuing education. There is a smaller proportion of independent school students than at most Russell Group universities – less than a quarter – although this does not translate into large numbers of working-class undergraduates. The demand for places rose in 2014, but there was a small drop in the number of undergraduates enrolling. The dropout rate is among the lowest in Britain, at little more than 3 per cent. The university will spend £2.4 million in 2016–17 on a "student lifecycle" approach to widening participation, helping non-traditional students from before the application stage through to employment or postgraduate study. The scheme will include bursaries of up to £3,000 a year for those from families with a combined income of less than £35,000.

Warwick is also one of the few leading universities to embrace 2+2 Foundation degrees, running courses in social studies and health and social policy, along with three-year Foundation degrees in early years and person-centred counselling and psychotherapy. Among the new offers in 2015 is a double degree in global politics in association with the University of Waterloo, Canada. There is now a thriving graduate entry medical school, with over 2,000 students.

Warwick added further study spaces in its Rootes Grid in 2013 and created a dedicated off-campus study facility for students living in nearby Leamington Spa. The 750-acre campus has a wide range of on-campus accommodation. The sports facilities are both extensive and conveniently placed, and include a high-quality running track, an indoor climbing centre and an indoor tennis centre. The main sports centre and gym were upgraded in 2013 and further investment is planned in its sports facilities and the already extensive Warwick Arts Centre. Coventry has a growing range of student-oriented facilities and good travel links to London and other parts of the country.

Undergraduate Fees and Bursaries

» Fees for UK/EU students 2016–17	£9,000
2+2 degree	£6,750
Foundation degree	£6,000
» Fees for international students 2015–16	£15,820–£20,180
Medicine (graduate entry)	£18,480–£32,200

- » English students from state schools, household income up to £16K, £2,000 cash a year; £16K–£25K, £1,500 a year; £25K–£35K, £1,000 a year. Additional awards of £1,000 a year subject to criteria.
- » Benefactors Scholarships of £2,000 a year, with priority to those with low incomes and from areas of low participation in HE.
- » Check the university's website for the latest information.

Students

Undergraduates:	**12,675**	**(2,050)**
Postgraduates:	**5,080**	**(5,440)**
Mature students:	**7.1%**	
International students:	**27.7%**	
Applications per place:	**7.8**	
From state-sector schools:	**76.1%**	
From working-class homes:	**18.8%**	
Satisfaction with students' union	**77%**	

For detailed information about sports facilities:
www2.warwick.ac.uk/services/sport

Accommodation

Number of places and costs refer to 2014–15
University-provided places: 6,382 (on campus); 2,000 (head leasing)
Percentage catered: 0%
Self-catered costs: £81–£160 a week (30, 39, 40 and 51 week contracts).
Warwick Accommodation plans to accommodate all first years in campus accommodation (terms and conditions apply).
International students: as above.
www2.warwick.ac.uk/services/accommodation

University of West London

The first phase of West London's £50-million Future Campus project opened in January 2015. Named the Heartspace because of its central location on the university's Ealing campus, it is a vibrant social area for staff and students. The next phase will see the opening of a new library in autumn 2015. Some of the old library space will be transformed into a new student social learning area with a variety of study spaces, over 40 PC desks and a new PC lab. The campus had already seen significant investment, as the university opted for the narrower geographical focus implied when it dropped the title of Thames Valley University. The Slough campus closed and most activities were concentrated on the institution's original base, as UWL set about becoming the country's leading university for employer engagement, with an accent on the creative industries and entrepreneurship. A refurbished students' union with a modern bar area, café and gym opened in 2013, alongside a new performance centre.

The university is offering students guaranteed work placements, in-study financial support and good employment prospects, but applications and enrolments were down marginally in 2014. Undergraduates have access to an award-winning student portal, which combines academic study with social networking. New Honours degrees have been launched in areas such as video production, 3-D design, entrepreneurship, and computing and information systems. The portfolio of two-year Foundation degrees is growing, with employers such as Compaq, Ealing Studios and the Savoy Hotel Group helping to provide courses. Some are run in partner institutions. New degrees launched this year include policing, building surveying, psychology with substance use and misuse studies, film music composition and operating department practice.

Reorganisation of the university has seen the pre-registration nursing courses that dominated the Slough campus move to Reading, leaving just part-time business courses and some post-registration nursing at a different site in Slough. The Reading campus, known as the Berkshire hub, is within walking distance of the station and focuses entirely on nursing and midwifery. The landmark Paragon Building in Brentford, not far from the Ealing campus, remains the headquarters of one of the largest healthcare faculties in Britain, with top-quality ratings for nursing and midwifery. The site contains residential places, as well as teaching facilities.

Approaching half of the students are 21 or over, and about 60 per cent are female. Approaching half of the undergraduates come from low-income families, but

St Mary's Road
Ealing
London W5 5RF

0800 036 8888 (admissions)
courses@uwl.ac.uk
www.uwl.ac.uk
www.uwlsu.com
Affiliation: million+

***The Times and Sunday Times* Rankings**

Overall Ranking: **121** (last year: 109)

Teaching quality:	**=111**	76.9%
Student experience:	**123**	77.5%
Research quality:	**120**	1.6%
Entry standards:	**121**	259
Student–staff ratio:	**=69**	17.3
Services & facilities/student:	**27**	£2,214
Expected completion rate:	**122**	73.9%
Good honours:	**=114**	58.8%
Graduate prospects:	**99**	60.5%

UWL's projected dropout rate of nearly 19 per cent is significantly worse than the national average for its courses and entry qualifications. The university is ethnically diverse, with only 45 per cent of the undergraduates of white, UK origin. Student satisfaction ratings have been improving, but UWL still finds itself towards the bottom of the National Student Survey. There will be means-tested scholarships and bursaries in 2016 to support full-time undergraduates whose household income is below £25,000, and fee waivers for part-time students where income is £42,620 or less. The university has specialist scholarships and bursaries for each of the academic schools, funded through the alumni programme. These are available for students with high academic entry grades and those demonstrating outstanding applied skills.

Among UWL's strengths is the School of Hospitality and Tourism, which is recognised by the Académie Culinaire de France for its culinary arts programmes, while the London College of Music, which is part of the university, has some of the longest-established music technology courses in the country. However, the university is in the bottom five of our research ranking after entering only 13 per cent of eligible academics for the 2014 Research Excellence Framework. A quarter of its submission was judged to be world-leading or internationally excellent, the best results coming in communication and media studies.

The town-centre sites in Ealing and Brentford are linked by a free bus service. The busy Ealing base is within easy reach of central London without the metropolitan hassle that students encounter at some institutions in the capital. Almost half of UWL's students are from London or Berkshire. Residential accommodation is growing, and the Paragon building in Brentford won *Building* magazine's Major Housing Project of the Year award in 2007. The Student Village in Ealing can accommodate up to 440 students and the Paragon 839. However, students who rely on private housing find the cost of living high. The new gym is reserved for student use, and the students' union has also established links with local sports teams, ensuring that all the university's sports clubs have access to good facilities in the vicinity.

Undergraduate Fees and Bursaries

- Fees for UK/EU students 2016–17 £9,000
  Placement year £1,000
- Fees for international students 2015–16 £10,650
- Household income below £25K, 550 awards of £1,000 a year as university accommodation discount or for transport costs.
- £100 credit for learning materials for all new students.
- For students from targeted schools, 50 fee waivers of £9,000 in year 1. Fee waiver of £1,500 a year for part-time students with household income below £42.6K.
- Check the university's website for the latest information.

Students

Undergraduates:	**7,430**	**(2,360)**
Postgraduates:	**725**	**(795)**
Mature students:	**47.1%**	
International students:	**21.1%**	
Applications per place:	**7.8**	
From state-sector schools:	**96.6%**	
From working-class homes:	**47.5%**	
Satisfaction with students' union	**63%**	

For detailed information about sports facilities:
www.uwlsu.com/groups

Accommodation

Number of places and costs refer to 2015–16
University-provided places: 1,279
Percentage catered: 0%
Self-catered costs: £142.99 (en suite); £193.82 (studio) – £508.00 (4-bed house) a week (44 or 52 weeks).
First years are allocated housing on a first come, first served basis.
International students: same as above.
studentservices@uwl.ac.uk
www.uwl.ac.uk/students/undergraduate/accommodation

University of the West of England, Bristol (UWE)

Average entry scores have risen by the equivalent of more than three A-level grades in four years at the University of the West of England, Bristol (UWE). Already the biggest higher education institution in the region, it has not followed the expansion route favoured by many universities. A £250-million campus masterplan is intended to ensure that UWE is competitive in teaching, research and student facilities, but will give it the option of taking more students in future. A new students' union will be open on the main Frenchay Campus for the start of the 2015 academic year, and a £55-million building for the Faculty of Business and Law will be ready in January 2017. At the same time, £35 million is being invested in the Bower Ashton Campus, adding to its commercial broadcast studios with moving image and lens media studios.

There has been investment, too, at the Glenside Campus with upgraded suites for radiotherapy and hospital wards. Eventually, there may even be a 20,000-seat stadium shared with Bristol Rovers on land bought by the university to extend the main campus. The three sites in Bristol are mainly in the north of the city, with regional centres near hospitals in Gloucester and Bath that concentrate on nursing and allied health professions. The main campus, four miles from the city centre, has already doubled in size and seen a number of improvements, including the opening of the UK's largest robotic laboratory and the biggest exhibition and conference centre in the region. The main library is open around the clock during term time. The university has also signed a partnership with Arnolfini, the centre for the contemporary arts, to place 300 creative arts students in its harbourside location.

More than half of the students come from the West Country and there are close links with business and industry. These provide guest lecturers and professors involved in practice, as well as a wide range of work placements, including one of the largest internship schemes at any university. UWE's careers and employment service was rated the best in the country in 2014, partly for an innovative web-based jobs and placement service it runs with the local chamber of commerce. Almost 8,000 organisations advertise vacancies on the UWE's InfoHub portal. The university also runs the UWE Bristol Futures Award to certificate extra-curricular activities and encourage students to acquire leadership qualities and other skills that will help in the employment market.

Law received a commendation from the Legal Practice Board and UWE is one

Frenchay Campus
Coldharbour Lane
Bristol BS16 1QY

0117 328 3333 (admissions)
admissions@uwe.ac.uk
www.uwe.ac.uk
www.thestudentsunion.co.uk
Affiliation: University Alliance

***The Times and Sunday Times* Rankings**

Overall Ranking: **73** (last year: 68)

Teaching quality:	**=77**	80%
Student experience:	**=85**	82.5%
Research quality:	**69**	8.8%
Entry standards:	**66**	324
Student–staff ratio:	**102**	19.5
Services & facilities/student:	**49**	£1,931
Expected completion rate:	**78**	84.9%
Good honours:	**=54**	71.4%
Graduate prospects:	**52**	70.8%

of just four universities recognised by the Forensic Science Society for the quality of courses in the subject. There are some 85 undergraduate and postgraduate courses with professional accreditation and the team entrepreneurship degree has a ground-breaking course structure where students learn through the day-to-day management of their own business. More than 60 per cent of the work submitted for assessment in the 2014 Research Excellent Framework. Health subjects and communication and media studies produced the best results.

UWE has broadened its intake considerably in recent years. The proportion of independent school entrants has dropped to less than 8 per cent, while the share of places going to students from working-class homes is almost 30 per cent. The dropout rate had been coming down, but the latest projection is still above the national average for the university's subjects and entry qualifications.

A network of 15 colleges stretches into Somerset and Wiltshire, offering UWE programmes. Hartpury College, near Gloucester, is an associate faculty of the university, specialising in agriculture, equine studies and other land-based courses. There is also an expanding international network, with institutions in a number of countries offering UWE degrees. The university's own international college, run in partnership with the Kaplan group, provides preparatory courses for a growing number of students from outside the UK coming to Bristol.

Bristol is a hugely popular student centre: an attractive and lively city, but not cheap. University accommodation has become more plentiful in recent years, with another 400 places added to the £80-million student village on the Frenchay campus in 2014. There are now more than 4,500 places across the university and more to come in UWE's masterplan. This includes accommodation for nearly 300 students on the Glenside campus. A £5.5-million sports complex at Frenchay has a 70-station fitness suite, while the separate Wallscourt Farm gym is designed for elite athletes. The university was chosen as a pre-Olympics training site for badminton, fencing, table tennis, indoor volleyball and wrestling.

Undergraduate Fees and Bursaries

- » Fees for UK/EU students 2016–17 £9,000
  Courses at partner colleges £6,000–£9,000
- » Fees for international students 2015–16 £11,250
- » Household income below £25K, 1,300 bursaries of £500 a year.
- » 80 enhanced bursaries of £3,000, year 1 and £1,000 in subsequent years for care leavers, young carers and estranged students.
- » Enhanced hardship fund.
- » Check the university's website for the latest information.

Students

Undergraduates:	**18,855**	**(2,650)**
Postgraduates:	**2,060**	**(3,485)**
Mature students:	**24.6%**	
International students:	**9.8%**	
Applications per place:	**5.1**	
From state-sector schools:	**92.7%**	
From working-class homes:	**29.6%**	
Satisfaction with students' union	**68%**	

For detailed information about sports facilities:
www.thestudentsunion.co.uk/opportunities/sports

Accommodation

Number of places and costs refer to 2015–16
University-provided places: about 4,616
Percentage catered: 0%
Self-catered costs: £3,674–£7,752 (40 to 45 weeks).
First-year students are guaranteed housing in university-approved accommodation provided requirements are met.
International students: as above, and are offered accommodation where possible if they apply outside the deadline date.
accommodation@uwe.ac.uk
www1.uwe.ac.uk/students/accommodation

University of the West of Scotland (UWS)

The University of the West of Scotland (UWS) has invested heavily in two of its four campuses since its formation through the merger of Paisley University and Bell College, in Hamilton. Now it is the turn of a third: a £53-million programme to upgrade the teaching and social spaces on the Hamilton campus will underline the university's commitment to Lanarkshire and provide a focal point for the town. UWS is now among the largest modern universities in Scotland, and has already been adapting to its increased size with a new £81-million campus in Ayr for 3,500 students. More than £30 million has been spent in Paisley, the university's largest base, expanding student accommodation and improving student facilities. The fourth campus in Dumfries is operated in partnership with the University of Glasgow, where a £5.5-million library and student services centre was added soon after the merger.

Applications have risen for three years in a row – by more than 10 per cent in 2014 – but they have not translated into increased enrolments. The university is based in an area of low participation in higher education, although it is within reach of nearly 40 per cent of the population of Scotland. UWS has continued its parent institutions' strong records in attracting under-represented groups onto courses. Hundreds of youngsters aged 14 and 15 attend the "University Experience" to sample a week of student life. Almost all UWS's students are state educated and 40 per cent are from working-class homes, but the projected dropout rate of almost 30 per cent is the highest in the UK, despite an improvement in the latest survey. That is more than twice the benchmark set according to the subject mix and entry qualifications. The university has set itself a series of challenging targets to achieve by 2020, including big increases in student satisfaction, completion rates and the proportion progressing to Honours degrees. The overall intention is to become Scotland's most "student-focused" university.

There are more than 1,000 international students, mainly from other EU countries. The School of Health, Nursing and Midwifery is the largest north of the border – but degrees in subjects such as computer animation, commercial music, computer games technology, sports studies and music technology have all been popular. Teacher training courses feature regularly in the top ten of our Education table. Paisley pioneered credit transfer in Scotland, including credit for non-academic achievement, and the modular course system covers day, evening and weekend

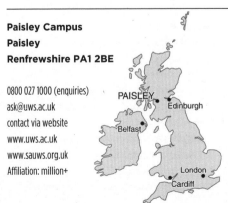

Paisley Campus
Paisley
Renfrewshire PA1 2BE

0800 027 1000 (enquiries)
ask@uws.ac.uk
contact via website
www.uws.ac.uk
www.sauws.org.uk
Affiliation: million+

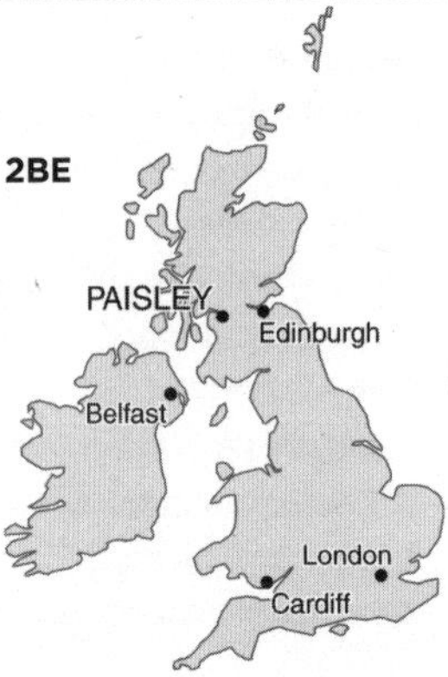

***The Times and Sunday Times* Rankings**

Overall Ranking: **118** (last year: 118)

Teaching quality:	**=49**	81.8%
Student experience:	**=95**	81.8%
Research quality:	**=97**	4.3%
Entry standards:	**96**	305
Student–staff ratio:	**116**	21.1
Services & facilities/student:	**111**	£1,291
Expected completion rate:	**125**	70%
Good honours:	**=98**	63.2%
Graduate prospects:	**73**	65.7%

classes. Most students either take sandwich degrees or have work placements built into their courses, earning an average of £10,000 in the process, but limited employment opportunities in the region means that the impact on graduate employment has not been as great as in some universities. There are close links with business and industry and all students are offered hands-on computer training. Paisley was the first UK university to be approved by Microsoft, Macromedia and Cisco, and has the status of Microsoft Academic Professional Development Centre. A games development laboratory, supported by Sony, is part of a £300,000 package of investment in multimedia and games facilities. Health subjects produced much the best results in the 2014 Research Excellence Framework, when 44 per cent of its submission reached one of the top two categories. UWS also ranks as Scotland's second most active university for knowledge transfer.

The university's main campus, 20 acres in the centre of Paisley, has a modern library and learning resource centre, a £5-million students' union building and upgraded indoor and outdoor sports facilities. UWS is bringing more students into the town centre with the completion of a £17.6-million student accommodation development. The investment includes the refurbishment of some 160 university-owned flats, as well as the construction of a new £13.2-million student residence with 336 bed spaces divided into flats for six students. The attractive Dumfries campus has more than 1,000 UWS students, while the Hamilton campus includes a students' union, an upgraded leisure centre and some accommodation. The Ayr campus is shared with SRUC (Scotland's Rural College) and has a prize-winning library with flexible space for individual or group study, presentation and seminar areas. A £12-million investment in Information Services across all campuses is being phased over three years. A new International Centre and a Research, Enterprise and Engagement hub are being added on the main campus. Paisley is Scotland's largest town, while Hamilton ranks fifth. In both places, the university draws a high proportion of the students from the local area, many on part-time courses.

Undergraduate Fees and Bursaries

- Fees for Scottish and EU students 2015–16 — No fee
- Fees for Non-Scottish UK-domiciled (RUK) students 2015–16 — £7,000
- Fees for international students 2015–16 — £11,000
- Details of RUK bursary for 2016 not available in August 2015. Check university website for details.
- Scholarships and bursaries available.
- Check the university's website for the latest information.

Students

Undergraduates:	**10,180**	**(3,450)**
Postgraduates:	**810**	**(840)**
Mature students:	**53.5%**	
International students:	**4.8%**	
Applications per place:	**5.6**	
From state-sector schools:	**98.9%**	
From working-class homes:	**39.8%**	
Satisfaction with students' union	**61%**	

For detailed information about sports facilities: www.uws.ac.uk/study-at-uws/life-at-uws/sports-and-social/

Accommodation

Number of places and costs refer to 2015–16

University-provided places: 856 (496 at Paisley; 200 at Ayr; 156 at Hamilton; 4 at Dumfries)

Percentage catered: 0%

Self-catered costs: £85 (Hamilton); £109.50–£142.00 (other campuses) a week.

Undergraduates have priority (conditions apply).

International students: single students guaranteed accommodation if conditions are met and applications received by 27 July.

accommodation@uws.ac.uk; www.uws.ac.uk/accommodation

University of Westminster

Applications to Westminster have shot up by almost 30 per cent in two years and the university has increased its intake of undergraduates by 1,000 as a result. The university promises a "dynamic synergy" between the creative arts and design, architecture and the built environment, science and technology, business, law, and the social sciences and humanities. Its ultimate aim is to be the leading "practice-informed" university. Undergraduates are given opportunities to take part in credit-bearing work placements, internships, study abroad, summer schools, voluntary work and entrepreneurial activities. The university changed its undergraduate structure to promote deeper learning through year-long modules and weaves work-related skills into degree programmes.

Westminster makes the most of its metropolitan base. Almost a third of the students are part-timers, for example, when part-time numbers have been dropping sharply elsewhere. There are more than 5,000 students from outside the UK – among the most at any post-1992 institution – and the largest numbers at any UK university from ethnic minorities. Westminster's courses are also taught in nine overseas countries, from Sri Lanka to Uzbekistan, a characteristic which won the university a Queen's Award for Enterprise.

Almost two-thirds of the work submitted for the 2014 Research Excellence Framework was judged to be world leading or university excellent, albeit with less than 30 per cent of the eligible staff entered. Westminster was again among the leading universities for communication and media studies, and there were even better results in art and design, as well as a good performance in English.

The university has continued to invest heavily in its buildings and facilities, with major refurbishment taking place at three of its campuses. The £20-million project at the Marylebone Campus was completed in the autumn of 2012, providing a new social and learning hub for the Faculty of Architecture and the Built Environment and Westminster Business School. A new fabrication laboratory provides excellent faculties for students and will reinforce the faculty's position as one of the UK's leading centres in its field. The Architecture Department is rated joint second in the UK by architects in practice in the *Architects' Journal*: students and staff collected more than 20 RIBA and professional prizes in a year. The Business School has been selected as a Centre of Excellence by the Chartered Institute for Securities and Investment – one of only twelve centres worldwide.

Significant progress has been made on the £38-million redevelopment of the

309 Regent Street
London W1B 2HW

020 7915 5511 (enquiries)
course-enquiries@westminster.ac.uk
www.westminster.ac.uk
www.uwsu.com
Affiliation: none

***The Times and Sunday Times* Rankings**

Overall Ranking: **=115** (last year: 112)

Teaching quality:	**126**	72.9%
Student experience:	**=108**	80.6%
Research quality:	**59**	9.8%
Entry standards:	**85**	311
Student–staff ratio:	**108**	19.9
Services & facilities/student:	**92**	£1,491
Expected completion rate:	**110**	80.4%
Good honours:	**=68**	68.8%
Graduate prospects:	**=120**	55.1%

Harrow site, home to the highly rated Faculty of Media, Arts and Design. Students there are already benefiting from new library and resource centres, and bigger open spaces and better natural light for the fashion and fine art learning areas. There will be spaces for a gallery and catwalk, flexible performance areas, a café, reception and multimedia newsroom. Major refurbishment work at the Regent Campus and Little Titchfield site was completed in 2013, while the School of Life Sciences has recently invested £2-million in modernising its laboratories. In May 2015, the university launched the newly restored Regent Street Cinema, which is considered to be the birthplace of British cinema. The headquarters building, near the BBC's Broadcasting House, houses social sciences, humanities and languages. Westminster offers one of the widest ranges of language teaching of any British university and partners SOAS, University of London, in leading the "Routes into Languages" programme to encourage more people to learn a language.

More than half of the UK undergraduates are from the four poorest socio-economic groups – one of the highest proportions in the UK – and the university also exceeds its benchmark for the admission of students from state schools and colleges. The projected dropout rate has been improving and is now lower than at many similar institutions.

Westminster has added considerably to its stock of residential accommodation in recent years. The latest development saw the opening of a student village for first-years close to Wembley Stadium and Wembley Park tube station, with speedy links to all the university's campuses. The university had already added a £6-million block of halls in Harrow and refurbished its Marylebone halls, but there is no way round the capital's inflated housing market at some stage. The Harrow Campus is lively socially, but those based on the other campuses tend to be spread around the capital. Sports facilities are also dispersed, with playing fields and a boathouse in Chiswick, west London and a fully-equipped gym at the central Regent Campus. Smoke Radio, Westminster's student radio station, has won several awards and has now spawned Smoke Television.

Undergraduate Fees and Bursaries

- Fees for UK/EU students 2016–17 £9,000
- Fees for international students 2015–16 £12,000
- Fee waivers given on a course-by-course basis to local students.
- Details of scholarships and bursaries for 2016–17 not available in August 2015.
- Check the university's website for the latest information.

Students

Undergraduates:	**12,580**	**(3,160)**
Postgraduates:	**2,365**	**(2,095)**
Mature students:	**19.6%**	
International students:	**18.8%**	
Applications per place:	**7.2**	
From state-sector schools:	**96%**	
From working-class homes:	**50.4%**	
Satisfaction with students' union	**51%**	

For detailed information about sports facilities: www.uwsu.com/sports

Accommodation

Number of places and costs refer to 2015–16
University-provided places: 2,061
Percentage catered: 0%
Self-catered costs: £123.90–£209.30 (38–51 week contracts).
First-year students have priority for 1,200 rooms. Residential restrictions apply.
International students: as above.
studentaccommodation@westminster.ac.uk
www.westminster.ac.uk/study/prospective-students/student-accommodation

University of Winchester

Only two universities saw a higher proportion of final-year undergraduates express overall satisfaction with their course than Winchester in this year's National Student Survey (NSS). The university also did particularly well in the questions on the quality of teaching and feedback provided by academics. Our new analysis shows Winchester ranking just outside the top ten for teaching quality in the eyes of its students – by a distance its strongest performance in any of the nine performance indicators in our institutional league table. It is one the few institutions to have appointed its own ombudsman to handle complaints. Its successes were reflected in a 12 per cent increase in applications in 2014, as the undergraduate intake grew for the fourth year in a row. Winchester now has almost 7,000 students – twice as many as when university status was awarded ten years ago. It is involved in a national initiative to promote social entrepreneurship and offers support to graduates who wish to start their own businesses.

Winchester has also been investing in research and held its own in the latest assessments. Almost 45 per cent of the work entered for the 2014 Research Excellence Framework was considered world-leading or internationally excellent, with communications and history producing the best results. A new Sport and Exercise Research Centre opened this year, and the university announced nine fully-funded research studentships to celebrate the 175th anniversary of the original institution's foundation. It was then a Church of England foundation for teacher training and was known as King Alfred College until 2004. The university is still best known for its education courses, which Ofsted rates as outstanding, although they no longer dominate in terms of student numbers. Other degrees span business, arts, humanities, health and social care, and social science. Undergraduates can take advantage of exchange schemes with a number of American universities, as well as some in Japan. The numbers recruited from outside the UK have trebled since 2010. Almost a third of the British students are from low-income families and 96 per cent are state educated.

The main King Alfred Campus has been occupied since 1862. The compact site is on a wooded hillside overlooking the cathedral city, a ten-minute walk away, with views of the surrounding countryside. The campus is well equipped, with theatrical performance spaces, sports hall and fitness suite supplemented by the £3.5-million Winchester Sports Stadium. Open to local people as well as students, the stadium has an Olympic-standard, 400-metre, eight-lane

Sparkford Road
Winchester
Hampshire SO22 4NR

01962 827234 (enquiries)
course.enquiries@winchester.ac.uk
www.winchester.ac.uk
www.winchester
students.co.uk
Affiliations: GuildHE;
Cathedrals Group

***The Times and Sunday Times* Rankings**

Overall Ranking: **=64** (last year: 61)

Teaching quality:	**11**	84.2%
Student experience:	**=43**	85%
Research quality:	**=82**	5.8%
Entry standards:	**=91**	307
Student–staff ratio:	**=61**	16.9
Services & facilities/student:	**116**	£1,226
Expected completion rate:	**76**	85.2%
Good honours:	**=39**	75.5%
Graduate prospects:	**=96**	60.7%

athletics track with supporting facilities for field events and also a floodlit all-weather pitch. Six performing arts studios offer the latest technology for student productions. An award-winning extension to the library provided 450 new study spaces and additional computers, while a modern Learning and Teaching Building significantly improved the facilities for lectures and independent study.

The University Centre also attracted awards, transforming the students' union by adding a nightclub, cinema, catering facilities, a bookshop and a supermarket. A "learning café" creates an informal working space with networked PCs and wireless internet access. Building on the success of this development, the university has developed a second social learning space, with PC access, a café, informal seating areas and outside terracing. The students' union has achieved consistently good ratings in the NSS.

The West Downs Campus, which is only a short walk away, is the base for the business school and the location for a £12-million student village providing more than 700 residential places. There is also a gallery that is open to the public and a centre for research and knowledge exchange. Two other complexes adjacent to the King Alfred Campus provide self-catering accommodation for almost 900 students, while there are three catered halls of residence on the campus itself. Winchester guarantees campus accommodation to first year full-time undergraduates, international students and students with medical needs as long they apply by the deadline.

The newest student village, which opened in 2013, includes a large gym, available to local residents as well as students and staff. The new gym is part of a major investment by the university to enhance its sports facilities. Students value the close-knit atmosphere and find the city is livelier than its staid image might suggest, with a number of bars catering to their tastes. Winchester scored well on security and the campus environment in *Times Higher Education* magazine's student experience survey. Southampton is not far for those who hanker after the attractions of a bigger city, and London is only an hour away by train.

Undergraduate Fees and Bursaries

- Fees for UK/EU students 2016–17 £9,000
  Foundation degree in childhood studies £4,200
- Fees for international students 2015–16 £11,300
- Household income below £25K, a bursary of £1,000 a year; £25K–£42.6K, £600 a year.
- Academic, sport, music, care leavers and young carers scholarships available.
- Check the university's website for the latest information.

Students

Undergraduates:	**5,125**	**(495)**
Postgraduates:	**245**	**(1,015)**
Mature students:	**13.6%**	
International students:	**5%**	
Applications per place:	**4.6**	
From state-sector schools:	**95.9%**	
From working-class homes:	**31.8%**	
Satisfaction with students' union	**83%**	

For detailed information about sports facilities:
www.winchester.ac.uk/campuscitylife/Sportsfacilities

Accommodation

Number of places and costs refer to 2015–16
University-provided places: 1,687 on campus; 225 off campus
Percentage catered: 5%
Catered costs: £4,299 (term-time only).
Self-catered costs: £3,075 – £5,225 (37–41 weeks).
First years are guaranteed accommodation if conditions are met.
International students: non EU, as above.
housing@winchester.ac.uk
www.winchester.ac.uk/startinghere/

University of Wolverhampton

Wolverhampton has declined to release any data for use in league tables since 2009, when it finished just outside the top 100. Its intake of undergraduates has dropped by more than 600 since then, although there was an increase in 2014. The university is one of only three to maintain a boycott this year. A statement on its website says that tables such as ours disadvantage universities like Wolverhampton and do not represent a fair picture of their strengths. As a result, it is missing from both the main ranking and all the subject tables. The statement advises applicants to use publicly available data, such as results from the 2014 Research Excellence, which it claims recognise the university's research as world-leading. In fact, 8 per cent of the Wolverhampton submission was awarded the 4* rating that signified world-leading research. A 2013 figure is quoted for student satisfaction, when the 2014 equivalent was 3 percentage points lower, leaving Wolverhampton in the bottom dozen universities on this measure. In 2015 it was still in the bottom 20 in England.

Wolverhampton has announced a £250-million programme that promises the biggest investment in its history. The five-year project will include new buildings and facilities, as well as investment in teaching, research and skills training. An £18-million building for the business school opens in October 2015 and impressive new engineering facilities are being provided in Telford and Wolverhampton. New courses are being offered in automotive and motorsport engineering, chemical engineering and electronic and telecommunications engineering, followed by the introduction of food engineering and aerospace engineering in 2016–17.

A new science centre. the Rosalind Franklin Building, opened fully in 2015. A bigger project will see the £65-million redevelopment of the derelict Springfield Brewery site in the city, to create a new campus for construction and the built environment. It will house the new West Midlands Construction University Technical College (UTC) and the university's School of Architecture and the Built Environment, eventually providing skills and education from the age of 14, right through to undergraduate and postgraduate courses and executive education. A second UTC will open in West Bromwich in September, specialising in health sciences.

The university has three bases in the West Midlands: the original site in the centre of Wolverhampton, a campus in Walsall dedicated to sport and performance, as well as education and part of the School of Health

Wulfruna Street
Wolverhampton WV1 1LY

01902 321032 (course enquiries)
gateway@wlv.ac.uk
www.wlv.ac.uk
www.wolvesunion.org
Affiliation: none

***The Times and Sunday Times* Rankings**

Wolverhampton blocked the release of data from the Higher Education Statistics Agency and so we cannot give any ranking information.

and Wellbeing, and a purpose-built campus at Telford, in Shropshire, which focuses on business and engineering. In June, the university launched the Wolverhampton School of Art, a new vision for art and design in the city. This year has also seen the opening of University Centre Telford, a partnership with Telford College of Arts and Technology, offering short courses and professional development programmes in a prominent town centre location. The university also offers part-time courses at Stafford and has a branch campus in Mauritius, offering law degrees and an MA in education. Teacher training courses are rated highly by Ofsted, and Wolverhampton academics have been awarded six National Teaching Fellowships. Research mainly serves the needs of business and industry, as well as underpinning teaching. By far the best REF results were in information science, where almost 90 per cent of the research submitted was considered world-leading or internationally excellent.

Wolverhampton's success in widening participation in higher education is such that only six universities have a higher proportion of undergraduates coming from working-class homes. Almost all the students are from state schools and one in five comes from an area of low participation. The university draws two-thirds of its 19,000 students from the West Midlands. A third of the places are filled by mature students and about the same proportion come from the region's ethnic minorities. Big outreach programmes take courses into the workplace; the university is leading a regional scheme to encourage young people to consider higher education.

Student facilities have been improved with the redevelopment of the students' union on the City Campus and the opening of a new union bar on the Walsall Campus. There is a 350-bed student village and sports facilities, including a Sports Science and Medicine Centre which was used to train Olympic contenders. The Performance Hub, the university's centre for performing arts, has exceptional facilities for music, dance and drama. The city of Wolverhampton has a growing nightlife, and the university has been voted the friendliest in the West Midlands. The cost of living is reasonable, and Birmingham is only a metro tram ride away.

Undergraduate Fees and Bursaries

» Fees for UK/EU students 2016–17	£9,000
Foundation degree	up to £7,570
Foundation degree at partner colleges	up to £6,000
Placement year / Year abroad	no fee
» Fees for international students 2015–16	£11,050

» For students with at least ABB at A level or equivalent, a bursary of £2,000 in year 1.

» Fixed number of scholarships for sport and for students from partnership schools, £2,000 in year 1.

» Access bursaries of £2,000 in year 1 for disabled students with hearing loss and care leavers

---

Students

Undergraduates:	**12,635**	**(3,530)**
Postgraduates:	**1,370**	**(1,570)**
From state-sector schools:	**98.9%**	
From working-class homes:	**53.1%**	
Satisfaction with students' union	**66%**	

For detailed information about sports facilities:
www.wlv.ac.uk/study-here/student-life/sport-and-fitness

Accommodation

Number of places and costs refer to 2015–16
University-provided places: 1,646
Percentage catered: 0%
Self-catered costs: £75 – £99 a week (37 weeks).
First-year students are offered accommodation provided requirements are met. Residential restrictions apply.
International students: same as above.
accommodationservices@wlv.ac.uk
www.wlv.ac.uk/study-here/accommodation/

University of Worcester

Worcester has twice the number of students there were when it became a university ten years ago. Applications have been rising much faster than the national average, although progress stalled in 2014. Sport, education and business courses have been particularly popular, and there have been increases, too, in biochemistry, journalism, illustration, nursing and several other health subjects. This year the university is introducing its first mathematics degree, and in 2016 will add law to its course list. Worcester was also one of the most improved in the 2014 Research Excellence Framework compared with previous assessments: it has gone up 20 places in our research ranking, partly because it entered five times as many academics as in 2008. A third of the work was considered world leading or internationally excellent, with history and art and design achieving the best scores. The performance has produced a big increase in research funding.

The university has three campuses less than a mile from each other and all close to the city centre. The main St John's Campus occupies a parkland site 15 minutes' walk from the city centre. It includes science facilities, the National Pollen and Aerobiology Research Unit, the digital arts centre and drama studio, and a modern AstroTurf pitch. The City Campus, opened in 2010, largely occupies the historic buildings of the former Worcester Royal Infirmary in the heart of the City. It includes teaching, residential and conference facilities and is the site of Worcester Business School. Further developments are taking place at the City Campus over the next two years following the acquisition of further adjacent city centre buildings. Almost next door is the university's spectacular library and history centre, The Hive, which brings together many services from Worcestershire County Council, including archaeology and history, with those of the university. The Hive is the first joint public and university library in Britain, and has been shortlisted for or won numerous awards in 2012 and 2013, including Best Civic Building, Best University Contribution to the Community and Best University Library Team.

The other star facility is a 2,000-seat indoor sporting arena, opened in 2013, which is one of only two specialist sports venues in the UK designed specifically for wheelchair athletes as well as the able-bodied. In 2015 the University of Worcester Arena won a national award for Buildings that Inspire, and, as the home of GB Wheelchair Basketball, hosted the 2015 European Wheelchair Basketball Championships. The Arena has also hosted the first ever British Universities

Henwick Grove
Worcester WR2 6AJ

01905 855111 (admissions)
admissions@worc.ac.uk
www.worcester.ac.uk
www.worcsu.com
Affiliation: GuildHE

The Times Rankings

Overall Ranking: **=100** (last year: 107)

Teaching quality:	**=57**	81.4%
Student experience:	**52**	84.5%
Research quality:	**=97**	4.3%
Entry standards:	**99**	301
Student–staff ratio:	**=93**	19
Services & facilities/student:	**122**	£1,062
Expected completion rate:	**=68**	85.8%
Good honours:	**103**	61.9%
Graduate prospects:	**82**	63.9%

and Colleges Wheelchair Basketball championships as well as top-flight netball, basketball and martial arts events. The Arena is on the Riverside Campus, which is mostly for performance sport. A mobile 3-D motion analysis laboratory has been used by the England and Wales Cricket Board. Sports scholarships are offered in partnership with Worcestershire County Cricket Club, Worcester Wolves Basketball Club and Worcester Hockey Club. The university's commitment to disability sports extends to the UK's first disability sport degree. Plans for a fourth campus, to house a science, health and enterprise park, have been "paused".

First as a post-war emergency teacher training college and later as a university college, the institution has always been the only provider of higher education in Herefordshire and Worcestershire. The university remains strong in education and also in nursing and midwifery. Worcester received the best possible inspection report from the Nursing and Midwifery Council and is the partner university for the National Childbirth Trust, delivering all of the trust's antenatal training. The six academic departments also cover applied sciences, geography and archaeology, a business school and arts, humanities and social sciences. An emphasis on employability was commended in an audit by the Quality Assurance Agency.

More than a third of the undergraduates come from working-class homes and the projected dropout rate is better than average for Worcester's subjects and entry standards. The university has long-established projects working with primary schools to try to broaden the intake further. There are excellent links with local businesses and students have access to an extensive "earn-as-you-learn" programme. A number of local partner colleges offer Worcester courses, as well as less conventional study centres such as hospices and specialist national organisations.

The cathedral city is not large, but is safer than many university locations, and has its share of pubs and clubs that cater for a growing student clientele. An active students' union acts as a social hub and the university has almost 1,000 residential places on the St John's and City campuses.

Undergraduate Fees and Bursaries

- Fees for UK/EU students 2015–16 £9,000
  Foundation degree £6,700–£9,000
- Fees for international students 2015–16 £10,920
- Award of £1,000 in year 1 for those with AAB at A level or equivalent. Award of £1,000 for academic achievement after year 1 and year 2.
- Enhanced retention and achievement awards and student hardship fund.
- Check the university's website for the latest information.

Students

Undergraduates:	**7,400**	**(1,485)**
Postgraduates:	**595**	**(815)**
Mature students:	**37.8%**	
International students:	**6.3%**	
Applications per place:	**5.9**	
From state-sector schools:	**97%**	
From working-class homes:	**35.8%**	
Satisfaction with students' union	**66%**	

For information about sports facilities: www.worcester.ac.uk/your-home/sport-at-worcester.html

Accommodation

Number of places and costs refer to 2015–16

University-provided places: 974 university-owned; 360 university-managed.

Percentage catered: 0%

Self-catered costs: £89–£145 a week.

First-year students are guaranteed accommodation, on a first come, first served basis, if conditions are met.

International students are accommodated if conditions are met.

accommodation@worc.ac.uk

www.worcester.ac.uk/your-home/accommodation.html

University of York

York has moved one place back towards the top ten in our table this year, despite losing ground to some of its competitors on research. Although more than 80 per cent of the work submitted for the 2014 Research Excellence Framework was considered world leading or internationally excellent, York submitted a lower proportion of its academics for assessment than most of the leading universities. Nevertheless, eight departments were ranked in the top five for their subject and the university was placed in the top ten for the external impact of its research.

York has invested £750 million on its Heslington East campus since deciding that the university was too small to maximise its research capability and satisfy the growing demand for its places. At the same time, 20 new buildings have opened on the original 200-acre campus nearby, as the university set about increasing its student population by 50 per cent. That has been achieved with entry standards that are still in the top 20 for the UK, and the university has joined the Russell Group. The latest developments, opening in autumn 2015, are a £7 million inter-disciplinary teaching facility which houses new biomedicine programmes and a spectacular new building for the Environment Department. A new teaching block and an extension to the biology department are scheduled to follow in 2016.

The university is situated a mile outside York's historic city centre and roughly a quarter of its students are postgraduates. All students join one of the nine colleges, which combine academic and social roles. Three are on the Heslington East site. Most departments have their headquarters in one of the colleges, but the student community is a mixture of disciplines, years and sexes. Nursing apart, only archaeology and medieval studies are located off campus, sharing a medieval building in the centre of the city. The medical school is a joint venture with Hull University, but York runs its own nursing and midwifery programmes.

York has launched a series of initiatives to boost its students' transferable skills and networking opportunities to enhance their employment prospects. Every student has an online tutorial to identify their strengths and career development needs. York is the first UK university to host a crowd-funding website, and over 2,000 students attend workshops, seminars and networking events with alumni working in senior positions in a range of industries, who advise on securing internships, volunteering experience and graduate employment. The university has established a Winter Interns programme to provide employment for recent graduates and provide them with graduate level training. It is also expanding the

Heslington
York YO10 5DD

01904 324000 (admissions)
ug-admissions@york.ac.uk
www.york.ac.uk
www.hyms.ac.uk
www.yusu.org
Affiliation: Russell Group

***The Times and Sunday Times* Rankings**

Overall Ranking: **15** (last year: 16)

Teaching quality:	**51**	81.7%
Student experience:	**24**	86.6%
Research quality:	**17**	38.3%
Entry standards:	**17**	437
Student–staff ratio:	**=32**	14.7
Services & facilities/student:	**30**	£2,163
Expected completion rate:	**16**	94.3%
Good honours:	**17**	81.6%
Graduate prospects:	**40**	76%

international opportunities open to students, many of whom expect their careers to take them beyond the UK and Europe. There are "international study centres", or themed summer schools, at partner universities and the Centre for Global Programmes is helping to increase the range of exchanges and Study Abroad schemes available to students. Participation in some form of international mobility has increased in three years from less than 4 per cent to almost 10 per cent.

The university has been getting closer to meeting its targets for broadening its undergraduate intake, although the proportion of state-educated entrants, those from working-class homes and areas of low participation in higher education are all marginally lower than the national averages for York's subjects and entry qualifications. Every student has a supervisor responsible for their academic and personal welfare, and undergraduates are entitled to free language tuition and have access to a Mathematics Study Skills Centre. Students can also take the York Award, comprising a range of courses, work placements and voluntary activities which aim to prepare students for employment. Over 600 students work as volunteer teaching assistants in local schools.

Social life on campus is lively. There are television and radio stations, as well as several student newspapers and magazines. Sports facilities are good, and include four sports halls and a dance studio. The £12-million York Sports Village features a 25-metre pool, learner pool, 100-station gym, full-size 3G pitch and three further five-a-side pitches. The university has the only velodrome in Yorkshire, a 1-km cycling track and a new athletics track. Tennis and squash facilities have been refurbished and £30,000 invested in bespoke team coaching. Cultural events abound on campus and in the city, which is also famous for a high concentration of pubs and its music scene. The free Festival of Ideas is the largest of its type in the UK and brings world-class speakers to the campus, as well as including a lively student fringe festival.

Undergraduate Fees and Bursaries

» Fees for UK/EU students 2016–17	£9,000
Placement year / Year abroad	£1,350
» Fees for international students 2015–16	£15,150–£19,500
Medicine	£25,930

» Household income below £25K, accommodation bursary of £2,400, year 1, £1,800 subsequent years; £25K–£35K, £1,000 a year.

» Foundation year fee waiver: household income below £25K, £5,600; above £25K, £3,000.

» Awards for care leavers, Foyer students and those who have completed Realising Opportunities or Next Step York schemes. Other scholarships available.

» Separate scheme for Hull York Medical School.

» Check the university's website for the latest information.

Students

Undergraduates:	**11,565**	**(1,130)**
Postgraduates:	**3,215**	**(770)**
Mature students:	**11.1%**	
International students:	**15%**	
Applications per place:	**7.3**	
From state-sector schools:	**80.7%**	
From working-class homes:	**20.1%**	
Satisfaction with students' union	**61%**	

For detailed information about sports facilities:
www.york.ac.uk/study/student-life/sport/

Accommodation

Number of places and costs refer to 2015–16
University-provided places: 5,668
Percentage catered: 16%
Catered costs: £109.77–£167.65 a week.
Self-catered costs: £103.11–£139.23 a week.
First-year undergraduates are guaranteed accommodation if terms and conditions are met.
International students: as above.
accommodation@york.ac.uk
www.york.ac.uk/study/accommodation/

York St John University

York St John will charge the lowest fees in England in 2016–17 – only £3,500 – on its Foundation degrees in education and theology. But the courses are for a limited range of mature students without traditional qualifications; the fees for all Honours degrees will remain at £9,000. The university is a Church of England foundation that dates back to 1841, when the Diocesan Training School opened with just one pupil on the register, in whose honour the students' union is named. Although it has had full university status since 2006, the power to award research degrees arrived only in 2015, marking its final rite of passage.

Divided between York and Ripon for most of its existence, the university now concentrates all its activities on York. The 11-acre campus faces York Minster across the city walls and is a five-minute walk from the city centre. Now serving 6,400 students, the campus has seen £91 million of development in recent years and more is planned. The Fountains Learning Centre, which provides a striking entrance to the university, has been refurbished. It now has 530 computer workstations, multimedia group-work facilities, 24-hour access to enhanced self-service facilities and an enlarged book stock, as well an internet café and lecture theatre. Nearby, the prize-winning De Grey Court, which cost £15.5 million and serves the health and life sciences, links the university quarter with the city centre.

The university's mission statement says its provision is "shaped" by the York St John's church foundation, although it welcomes students of all beliefs. The Business School is the biggest faculty, having overtaken Education and Theology, as well as Health and Life Sciences. Almost two-thirds of the students are female and there is a growing cohort of international students. The university has launched a number of successful enterprise initiatives. Its latest venture, the Phoenix Centre, a business incubation facility, supports both the university's graduates and new local businesses. More than 97 per cent of the UK undergraduates attended state schools or colleges, and about two in five come from one of the four poorest socio-economic groups. The projected dropout rate of 5 per cent is little more than half the national average for the university's courses and entry qualifications. York St John was also one of only six universities to score full marks for its support of gay and lesbian in an annual guide published by equality charity Stonewall.

The volume of applications has grown by almost 60 per cent since university status arrived, but four years of increases

New Mayor's Walk
York YO31 7EX

01904 876598 (information hotline)
admissions@yorksj.ac.uk
www.yorksj.ac.uk
www.ysjsu.com
Affiliations: Cathedrals Group, GuildHE

***The Times and Sunday Times* Rankings**

Overall Ranking: **89** (last year: 87)

Teaching quality:	**=41**	82.4%
Student experience:	**79**	83%
Research quality:	**=100**	4.1%
Entry standards:	**106**	292
Student–staff ratio:	**=112**	20.6
Services & facilities/student:	**112**	£1,284
Expected completion rate:	**41**	90.4%
Good honours:	**86**	65.4%
Graduate prospects:	**75**	65.3%

came to an end in 2014. The Faculty of Arts has been one of the main points of expansion, especially in degree programmes such as film and television, media and American studies. The university was awarded a national centre for excellence in creativity, based on its work in English and theatre studies, although funding for such programmes has now ceased. Another music technology suite has been added and performance spaces include two dedicated TV studios, digital non-linear edit suites, digital imaging equipment and equipment for sound manipulation. Psychology produced the best results in the 2014 Research Excellence Framework, when the 30 per cent of research regarded as world-leading or internationally excellent represented a big improvement on the 2008 assessments.

Relatively high numbers of local mature students ease the pressure on residential accommodation. As a result, first years who want to live in university-owned accommodation are now guaranteed places. The university offers a choice of catered, semi-catered and private accommodation. Another private development of shared flats and studio apartments opens in autumn 2015. On campus, there is a sports hall, climbing wall, basketball, netball, indoor football and cricket nets. The university's new sports facility, Nestlé Rowntree Park, was officially opened in April 2015. Just under a mile from the campus, the 57-acre site includes a 3G pitch for rugby and football, a synthetic pitch for hockey and small-sided games, three netball courts and three tennis courts, as well as grass pitches, a sprint track and a bowling green. A new sports centre is due to open on the site in September 2016, with sports courts, changing rooms, gym facilities and conference and teaching space. The students' union won the NUS award for Small and Specialist Union of the Year in 2014, having doubled its number of societies and society members. York is popular as a student city with a growing range of clubs as well as, supposedly, a pub for every day of the year.

Undergraduate Fees and Bursaries

- Fees for UK/EU students 2016–17 £9,000
  Foundation degrees in education and theology £3,500
- Fees for international students 2015–16 £10,000–£11,500
- Household income: below £25K, a bursary of £500 a year.
- Enhanced student support programmes.
- Check the university's website for the latest information.

Students

Undergraduates:	**4,810**	**(725)**
Postgraduates:	**415**	**(465)**
Mature students:	**11.3%**	
International students:	**5.5%**	
Applications per place:	**5.7**	
From state-sector schools:	**96.9%**	
From working-class homes:	**37.4%**	
Satisfaction with students' union	**77%**	

For detailed information about sports facilities:
www.yorksj.ac.uk/ysjactive

Accommodation

Number of places and costs refer to 2015–16
University-provided places: 1,750
Percentage catered: 9%
Catered costs: £122–£148 a week (34 weeks).
Self-catered costs: £80–£158 a week (44–48 weeks).
First years choosing university as first choice are guaranteed accommodation.
International students: guaranteed housing.
www.yorksj.ac.uk/campus-residential-services/campus-residential-services/accommodation.aspx

Specialist Institutions of Higher Education

1 Specialist colleges of the University of London

This listing gives contact details for specialist degree-awarding colleges within the University of London not listed elsewhere within the book. Those marked * are members of GuildHE (**www.guildhe.ac.uk**). Fees are given for UK/EU undergraduates for a single year of study.

Courtauld Institute of Art
Somerset House
Strand
London WC2R 0RN
020 7848 2645 **www.courtauld.ac.uk**
Fees 2016–17: £9,000

Heythrop College
Kensington Square
London W8 5HN
020 7795 6600 **www.heythrop.ac.uk**
Fees 2016–17: £9,000

London Business School
Regent's Park
London NW1 4SA
020 7000 7000 **www.london.edu**
Postgraduate only

London School of Hygiene and Tropical Medicine
Keppel Street
London WC1E 7HT
020 7299 4646 **www.lshtm.ac.uk**
Postgraduate medical courses

Royal Academy of Music
Marylebone Road
London NW1 5HT
020 7873 7393 **www.ram.ac.uk**
Fees 2016–17: £9,000

Royal Central School of Speech and Drama*
Eton Avenue
London NW3 3HY
020 7722 8183 **www.cssd.ac.uk**
Fees 2016–17: £9,000

Royal Veterinary College
Royal College Street
London NW1 0TU
020 7468 5147 **www. rvc.ac.uk**
Fees 2016–17: £9,000

University of London Institute in Paris
9–11 rue de Constantine
75340 Paris Cedex 07, France
(+33) 1 44 11 73 83 **www.ulip.lon.ac.uk**
Degrees offered in conjunction with Queen Mary and Royal Holloway colleges

2 Specialist colleges and private institutions

This listing gives contact details for other degree-awarding higher education institutions not mentioned elsewhere within the book. All the institutions listed below offer degree courses, some providing a wide range of courses while others are specialist colleges with a small intake. Those marked * are members of GuildHE (**www.guildhe.ac.uk**). Fees are given for UK/EU undergraduates for a single year of study.

BPP University
6th floor, Boulton House
Chorlton Street, Manchester M1 3HY
Campuses in Abingdon, Birmingham, Bristol, Cambridge, Leeds, Liverpool, London, Manchester.
03331 224 359 **www.bpp.com/bpp-university**
Fees 2015–16: £9,000 (two-year course); £6,000 (three-year course)

Conservatoire for Dance and Drama
Comprised of
Bristol Old Vic Theatre School
Central School of Ballet
London Academy of Music and Dramatic Art (LAMDA)
London Contemporary Dance School
National Centre for Circus Arts
Northern School of Contemporary Dance
Rambert School of Ballet and Contemporary Dance
Royal Academy of Dramatic Art (RADA)
Tavistock House, Tavistock Square
London WC1H 9JJ
020 7387 5101 **www.cdd.ac.uk**
Fees 2016–17: £9,000

Glasgow School of Art
167 Renfrew Street, Glasgow G3 6RQ
0141 353 4500 **www.gsa.ac.uk**
Fees 2015–16: Scotland/EU, no fee
RUK £9,000

Guildhall School of Music and Drama
Silk Street, Barbican, London EC2Y 8DT
020 7628 2571 **www.gsmd.ac.uk**
Fees 2016–17: £9,000

ifs University College
ifs House, 4–9 Burgate Lane
Canterbury, Kent CT1 2XJ
01227 818609
Student campus:
25 Lovat Lane, London EC3R 8EB
020 7337 6293 **www.ifslearning.ac.uk**
Fees 2015–16: £6,000

The University of Law
Birmingham, Bristol, Chester, Exeter, Guildford, Leeds, London (Bloomsbury and Moorgate), Manchester
0800 289997 **www.law.ac.uk**
Fees 2016–17: £9,000 (two-year course)
£6,000 (three-year course)

Leeds College of Art*
Blenheim Walk, Leeds LS2 9AQ
0113 202 8000 **www.leeds-art.ac.uk**
Fees 2016–17: £9,000

Liverpool Institute for Performing Arts*
Mount Street, Liverpool L1 9HF
0151 330 3000 **www.lipa.ac.uk**
Fees 2016–17: £9,000

New College of the Humanities
19 Bedford Square, London WC1B 3HH
020 7637 4550 **www.nchum.org**
Fees 2016–17: £17,992

Pearson College
80 Strand, London WC2R 0RL
0203 441 1301
www.pearsoncollegelondon.ac.uk
Fees 2016: £9,000

Plymouth College of Art*
Tavistock Place, Plymouth PL4 8AT
01752 203434 **www.plymouthart.ac.uk**
Fees 2016–17: £9,000

Ravensbourne*
6 Penrose Way, Greenwich Peninsula,
London SE10 0EW
020 3040 3040 **www.ravensbourne.ac.uk**
Fees 2016–17: £9,000

Regent's University London*
Inner Circle, Regent's Park,
London NW1 4NS
020 7487 7505 **www.regents.ac.uk**
Fees Autumn 2015: £15,350

Rose Bruford College of Theatre and Performance*
Lamorbey Park, Burnt Oak Lane,
Sidcup, Kent DA15 9DF
020 8308 2600 **www.bruford.ac.uk**
Fees 2016–17: £9,000

Royal College of Music
Prince Consort Road, London SW7 2BS
020 7591 4300 **www.rcm.ac.uk**
Fees 2016–17: £9,000

Royal Conservatoire of Scotland
100 Renfrew Street, Glasgow G2 3DB
0141 332 4101 **www.rcs.ac.uk**
Fees 2015–16: Scotland/EU, no fee;
RUK £9,000

Royal Northern College of Music
124 Oxford Road, Manchester M13 9RD
0161 907 5200 **www.rncm.ac.uk**
Fees 2016–17: £9,000

Royal Welsh College of Music and Drama
Castle Grounds, Cathays Park,
Cardiff CF10 3ER
029 2034 2854 **www.rwcmd.ac.uk**
Fees 2016–17: £9,000

St Mary's University College*
191 Falls Road, Belfast BT12 6FE
028 9032 7678 **www.stmarys-belfast.ac.uk**
Fees 2015–16: £3,805; RUK £9,000

Scotland's Rural College
Campuses at Aberdeen, Ayr,
Cupar, Dumfries, Ecclesmachan, near
Broxburn, Edinburgh
0800 269453 **www.sruc.ac.uk**
Fees 2015–16: Scotland/EU, no fee;
RUK £5,600

Stranmillis University College
Stranmillis Road, Belfast BT9 5DY
028 9038 1271 **www.stran.ac.uk**
Fees 2014–15: £3,805; RUK £9,000

Trinity Laban Conservatoire of Music and Dance
Music Faculty: King Charles Court
Old Royal Naval College,
Greenwich, London SE10 9JF
020 8305 4444
Dance Faculty: Laban Building, Creekside
London SE8 3DZ
020 8305 9400 **www.trinitylaban.ac.uk**
Fees 2016–17: £9,000

University Campus Suffolk
Waterfront Building, Neptune Quay
Ipswich IP4 1QJ
Other campuses at Bury St Edmunds,
Lowestoft, Otley, Great Yarmouth
01473 338000 **www.ucs.ac.uk**
Fees 2016–17: £9,000

Writtle College*
Lordship Lane, Writtle, Chelmsford, Essex
CM1 3RR
01245 424200 **www.writtle.ac.uk**
Fees 2016–17: £9,000

Index